BUSINESS DRIVEN DATA COMMUNICATIONS

Michael S. Gendron

Pearson Education International

Boston   Columbus   Indianapolis   New York   San Francisco   Upper Saddle River
Amsterdam   Cape Town   Dubai   London   Madrid   Milan   Munich   Paris   Montreal   Toronto
Delhi   Mexico City   Sao Paulo   Sydney   Hong Kong   Seoul   Singapore   Taipei   Tokyo

If you purchased this book within the United States or Canada you should be aware that it has been imported without the approval of the Publisher or the Author.

Editorial Director: Sally Yagan
Executive Editor: Bob Horan
Director of Editorial Services: Ashley Santora
Editorial Project Manager: Kelly Loftus
Editorial Assistant: Ashlee Bradbury
Director of Marketing: Maggie Moylan
Executive Marketing Manager: Anne Fahlgren
Senior Managing Editor: Judy Leale
Sr. Production Project Manager/Supervisor: Lynn Savino Wendel
Senior Operations Supervisor: Arnold Vila
Operations Specialist: Maura Zaldivar
Creative Director: Jayne Conte
Cover Designer: Bernadette Travis

Full-Service Project Management: Sharon Anderson/Bookmasters, Inc.
Composition: Integra Software Services, Inc.
Printer/Binder: Edward Brothers Malloy

Text Font: Palatino

Credits and acknowledgments borrowed from other sources and reproduced, with permission, in this textbook appear on the appropriate page within text.

Copyright © 2013 by Pearson Education, Inc., publishing as Prentice Hall. All rights reserved. Manufactured in the United States of America. This publication is protected by Copyright, and permission should be obtained from the publisher prior to any prohibited reproduction, storage in a retrieval system, or transmission in any form or by any means, electronic, mechanical, photocopying, recording, or likewise. To obtain permission(s) to use material from this work, please submit a written request to Pearson Education, Inc., Permissions Department, One Lake Street, Upper Saddle River, New Jersey 07458, or you may fax your request to 201-236-3290.

10 9 8 7 6 5 4 3 2 1

ISBN 10:   0-13-305584-1
ISBN 13: 978-0-13-305584-9

Dedication

*This work is dedicated to my son, Christopher,
who stood by and waited . . .*

BRIEF CONTENTS

UNIT 1 ICT Infrastructure Components: A Technical Overview 1

    Chapter 1   ICT Introductory Concepts 5
    Chapter 2   Building the Local Area Network Using Ethernet 41
    Chapter 3   Extending the LAN through WAN Connections 78
    Chapter 4   Wrapping Up Service, User, and Enterprise Components 104

UNIT 1 Summary 131

UNIT 2 Additional ICT Concepts 133

    Chapter 5   Obtaining Services Through Cloud Computing 135
    Chapter 6   Security 160

UNIT 2 Summary 183

UNIT 3 Understanding the Business of Infrastructure Design 185

    Chapter 7   Infrastructure and the Enterprise 186
    Chapter 8   Business Processes 208
    Chapter 9   Assessing the Business Value of ICT Resource Investments 240

UNIT 3 Summary 266

UNIT 4 Steps to the Strategic Alignment of ICT 269

    Chapter 10   Analyzing the Organization and Its Environment 275
    Chapter 11   Designing ICT: Documenting Process and Technology Recommendations 314
    Chapter 12   Summarizing the Business-Driven Infrastructure Design Cycle: Analysis, Design, Implementation, and *Post-Implementation* 363

UNIT 4 Summary 382

Glossary 383
Index 391

CONTENTS

Preface xv
Acknowledgement xx

Unit 1 ICT Infrastructure Components: A Technical Overview 1

Chapter 1 ICT INTRODUCTORY CONCEPTS 5
Introduction 5
  Data Representation and Signal Propagation 6
  Data Communications Techniques 11
  Computer Network and Carrier Concepts 17
  Introduction to Layering and TCP/IP 19
  Regulations, Standards, and TCP/IP 19
Wired Media and Network Typologies 24
  Wired Media 24
  Typologies 25
Switching Hierarchies 27
  Phone System and Circuit Switching 27
  Data Networks and Packet Switching 28
  Addressing 30
TCP/IP Layers, Protocols, and Communication 30
  Layer 5 (Application Layer) 30
  Layer 4 (Transport Layer) 31
  Layer 3 (Internet Layer) 32
  Layer 2 (Data Link Layer) 32
  Layer 1 (Physical Layer) 32
TCP/IP–OSI Architecture and How It Works 34
  Indirect Communication 35
Chapter Summary 38
Vignette Wrap Up 38
End of Chapter Questions/Assurance of Learning 39
Case Exercises 39
Key Words and Concepts 39
References 40

Chapter 2 BUILDING THE LOCAL AREA NETWORK USING ETHERNET 41
Introduction 41
Types of Ethernet Equipment and Media 42
  Media 43
  Adapter Cards: Motherboard Interfaces 43
  Hubs, Repeaters, and Bridges 43
  Bridges and Switches 44
  Switch Characteristics 44

Ethernet: The Technical Details of Its Evolution 48
   Multiple Users and the Network 50
   Physical Layer and Propagation 51
   The Data Link Layer and Frames 52
   Ethernet Summary 53
   Wireless Technologies 54
   Frequency Spectrum 54
   Large-Scale Wireless Technologies 55
   LAN-Based Wireless 56
   802.11 and Ethernet 57
   IEEE 802.11 Wireless Access: The Technical Details 58
   Personal Area Network: Short-Range Wireless 63
Building a LAN 64
   LAN Wiring 64
   Joe Smith's Home LAN 74
Chapter Summary 75
Vignette Wrap Up 76
End of Chapter Questions/Assurance of Learning 76
Case Exercises 77
Key Words and Concepts 77
References 77

Chapter 3 EXTENDING THE LAN THROUGH WAN CONNECTIONS 78
Introduction 78
   LAN vs. WAN Pricing 78
   Types of Connections 79
   Points of Presence 79
   PSDN 80
   PCV and SVC 81
   Pricing WAN and PSDN Connections 82
WAN Technologies 84
   Frame Relay 84
   ATM 88
   General Packet Radio Service (GPRS) 92
   WiMAX 93
   Multiprotocol Label Switching (MPLS) 96
   Metro Ethernet 97
Virtual Private Networks 98
   VPN Types 98
   VPNs IPsec and TLS/SSL 100
Chapter Summary 102
Vignette Wrap Up 102
End of Chapter Questions/Assurance of Learning 102
Case Exercises 102
Key Words and Concepts 103
References 103

Contents **ix**

Chapter 4 WRAPPING UP SERVICE, USER, AND ENTERPRISE COMPONENTS 104
    Introduction 105
    PC Hardware 105
        Factor Form 105
        PC Options 105
        Processor Speed 106
        Summary of PC Selection 107
        Thin Clients 107
    Service Components 107
        Printing Services 108
        Inter/Intra-Office Communications 109
        SAN and NAS 111
        Web Server 112
        E-Mail Server 113
        Application Servers 114
        Database Servers 115
        Application and Desktop Virtualization 116
        Benefits 116
        Security and Policy Services 118
        Summary of Service Components 119
    User Components 119
        The Desktop 119
        PC 120
        Thin Client 120
        Desktop Optical Devices 121
        Printers 121
        Image Scanners 124
        Multifunction Devices 125
        Desktop Productivity Software 125
        Specialized Applications 125
    Enterprise-Wide Components 125
        Benefits of an Enterprise-Wide Component 127
    Chapter Summary 127
    Vignette Wrap Up 128
    End of Chapter Questions/Assurance of Learning 129
    Case Exercises 129
    Key Words and Concepts 130

Unit 1 Summary 131

Unit 2 Additional ICT Concepts 133

  Chapter 5 OBTAINING SERVICES THROUGH CLOUD COMPUTING 135
    Introduction 136
        What Is Cloud Computing? 136
        Attributes of Cloud Computing 139
        Examples of Cloud-Computing Vendors 141

Developing in the Cloud 144
    Private vs. Public Cloud 144
    Service Types in the Cloud 146
    Cloud Development: Microsoft Azure and Sopima 148
Business Considerations of Cloud-Based Applications and Services 152
    On-Premises or the Cloud? 153
    Capital vs. Operational Expenditures and the Cloud 154
    Cloud Computing and Its Impact on the Organization 154
    Making a Business Case for Cloud Computing 157
Chapter Summary 158
Vignette Wrap Up 158
End of Chapter Questions/Assurance of Learning 158
Case Exercises 158
Key Words and Concepts 159
References 159

Chapter 6 SECURITY 160
Introduction 161
Types of Attacks and Threats 162
    System-Fault-Risk Framework 162
    Types of Attacks 163
    Methods of Delivery 169
Stopping Cyber Attacks 170
    Planning and Policies 170
    Access Control 170
    Encryption 171
    SSL/TLS 172
    Client Host Solutions 174
    Network Solutions 175
    Educating the User 179
Chapter Summary 180
Vignette Wrap Up 181
End of Chapter Questions/Assurance of Learning 181
Case Exercises 181
Key Words and Concepts 181
References 182

Unit 2 Summary 183

Unit 3 Understanding the Business of Infrastructure Design 185

Chapter 7 INFRASTRUCTURE AND THE ENTERPRISE 186
Definition of Technology Infrastructure 186
Information Technology Infrastructure and Strategy 188
    Strategic Management and Infrastructure Decisions 189

Introduction to Business and Technology Strategy 189
Two Approaches to Strategic Initiatives: Industry-Wide and Focused 191
Cost Leadership and Differentiation 192

Technology Infrastructure, Information Systems, and Planning 195
Organizational Views 195
The Effect of External Forces on Infrastructure 200
Technology Infrastructure Project Planning 201
Value-Driven Business Modeling 202

An Overview of the Business-Driven Infrastructure Design (BDID) Methodology 202

Chapter Summary 205
Vignette Wrap Up 206
End of Chapter Questions/Assurance of Learning 206
Case Exercises 206
Key Words and Concepts 206
References 207

Chapter 8 BUSINESS PROCESSES 208

Introduction 208
Why Is ICT Implemented? 209
Process Change 209
Process View of the Organization 211
ICT Impact on Economic Outcomes 212
Information and Communication Technology Use 213

Processes in an Organizational Context 214
Existing Infrastructure versus New Infrastructure 214
Organizational Types and Their Processes 215
Defining a Business Process 221
Process Objectives and Attributes 227
Infrastructure Implementation and the Value Chain 228
Always Keep the Customer in Mind 229
What Is a Process? A Summary 229

Enablers of Process Change 230
Innovation vs. Improvement 230
Organizational Enablers 231
ICT as an Enabler 233
Summary of Major Organizational Enablers 236

Chapter Summary 236
Vignette Wrap Up 237
End of Chapter Questions/Assurance of Learning 238
Case Exercises 238
Key Words and Concepts 238
References 238

Chapter 9 ASSESSING THE BUSINESS VALUE OF ICT RESOURCE INVESTMENTS 240

Introduction 240
   Types of IT Project Measurement 241

Defining Payoff 242
   Introductory Theories 242
   Technology Justification Models 247
   Balanced Scorecard (BSC) 258
   An Overview of the BSC Process 258

Chapter Summary 262
Vignette Wrap Up 263
End of Chapter Questions/Assurance of Learning 264
Case Exercises 264
Key Words and Concepts 264
References 265

Unit 3 Summary 266

Unit 4 Steps to the Strategic Alignment of ICT 269

Chapter 10 ANALYZING THE ORGANIZATION AND ITS ENVIRONMENT 275

Strategic Alignment of IT (SAIT) 275
   SAIT: Whose Job Is It? 275
   SAIT: What Is It Really? 277
   Achieving SAIT 278

Value Search Models: Analyzing the Organization 278
   Organizational Value Propositions 278
   Low Cost, Internal Efficiency, and Enhancing Quality Strategies 279
   Product Differentiation Strategies 295

Gap Analysis 301
Val IT Framework 304
Chapter Summary 311
Vignette Wrap Up 311
End of Chapter Questions/Assurance of Learning 311
Case Exercises 312
Key Words and Concepts 312
References 312

Chapter 11 DESIGNING ICT: DOCUMENTING PROCESS AND TECHNOLOGY RECOMMENDATIONS 314

The Total Diagram Set 314
Business Process Modeling 315
   Business Process Modeling Notation and Diagrams 318
   Using TSI to Introduce Modeling 329
   Systems Analysis and the Use of Data Flow Diagrams 337

ICT Technical Frameworks and Models 338
  Functionality List 339
  ICT Hierarchy 340
  Estimating Bandwidth Needs 344
  Creating High-Level ICT Design Documents 350
Chapter Summary 360
Vignette Wrap Up 361
End of Chapter Questions/Assurance of Learning 361
Case Exercises 361
Key Words and Concepts 361
References 362
Additional Readings 313

Chapter 12 SUMMARIZING THE BUSINESS-DRIVEN INFRASTRUCTURE DESIGN CYCLE: ANALYSIS, DESIGN, IMPLEMENTATION, AND POST-IMPLEMENTATION 363

The Business-Driven Infrastructure Design Cycle 363
  The Business-Driven Infrastructure Design Team 365
  Analysis Phase 366
  Design Phase 370
  Implementation Phase 374
  Post-Implementation Phase 377
Chapter Summary 380
Vignette Wrap Up 380
End of Chapter Questions/Assurance of Learning 381
Case Exercises 381
Key Words and Concepts 381
References 381

Unit 4 Summary 382

Glossary 383
Index 391

PREFACE

Business Driven Data Communications is designed to address the needs of business students within an information systems program where they need to learn how to motivate management in their quest for competitive advantage through technology. Many networking and telecommunications books and courses teach the technical side of these topics. However, a paradigm shift is occurring which necessitates that students not only have a technical understanding of telecommunications, but also possess business skills that allow them to convert business imperatives into technologically sound recommendations that enhance both the operational and competitive positioning of the enterprise.

This textbook uses a technology infrastructure/recommendation/build paradigm that we call *business-driven infrastructure design*. Technology infrastructure includes the panoply of software, hardware, media, appliances, services, and cloud-based resources that support the business processes of an enterprise. ***The key assumption underpinning this book is that all technology infrastructures must support the enterprise's drive to achieve competitive advantage.***

PREREQUISITE KNOWLEDGE AND LEVEL

The material has been rigorously class tested (used over ten years, in more than 20 sections of a networking/telecommunications class) with outstanding results. The work students produce in these sections has become the basis for a case competition at the author's university and elsewhere, and has been used successfully by students in their job interview portfolio. Interviewers have been impressed by the content and breadth of material that students posses. Many students attribute their success in the job market and in their own organization to skills and knowledge gained in this course.

The material in this text is easier for students to assimilate if they have the following background courses:

- **Introductory Information Systems:** An introductory understanding of information systems is necessary so students have a basic familiarity with managerial, social-technical, and behavioral views of information systems, as well as its technical components.
- **E-Business:** An e-business course affords students the background that enables them to incorporate e-business innovation into infrastructure building. The world is changing and soon we will drop the "E" and we will no longer have e-business courses, but rather just business courses.
- **Systems Analysis and Design Course**: This course provides a basis for conceptual modeling and assists with students' ability to understand infrastructure design at an appropriate level.
- **Foundational Business Courses:** The more foundational business courses that students have already taken, the greater their capacity to apply business principles to technology infrastructure in support of business processes throughout the course supported by this textbook.

The textbook is designed to serve the needs of junior/senior undergraduate information systems students as well as MBA students. It supports the networking and telecommunications course, as well as a higher-level course in business-driven infrastructure design. It takes a business-driven infrastructure design approach, rather than just a technical networking one. The text presents a revolutionary way to teach essential networking and telecommunications design concepts, within an infrastructure and communication technology building paradigm. Even though this textbook presents a great deal of technical material, it does so with the focus on business process support and infrastructure design.

OUTSTANDING FEATURES

- Rather than a purely technical approach found in many textbooks, or an approach in which cases are just interwoven with technical material, this book takes a business-driven approach. It will present the technical material necessary for students to understand infrastructure building, but not so much technical detail that students become lost in technology. Technology often seems to cause students to lose site of the business problem at hand.
- A running case is included within each unit that reinforces the concepts in each chapter. For each chapter, the end-of-chapter questions will allow students to incorporate their knowledge from other business courses and develop solutions to real-world business problems, providing an assurance of learning.
- Included in each chapter are examples, suggested solutions, and questions for further thought. These examples illustrate the chapter concepts and allow students to understand the material better.

PEDAGOGICAL FEATURES

This book includes a number of pedagogical features that will enhance learning.

- **Business Problem-Solving Focus:** The unit vignettes and in-chapter examples explicate the concepts and allow students to build on previous business and information systems knowledge.
- **Learning Objectives:** Each chapter begins with learning objectives, which are tied to the content of the chapter, end-of-chapter questions, and the case exercises.
- **Unit Vignette:** Each unit has an opening vignette. It is used to teach the concepts in the chapters and to expand on chapter concepts throughout the chapter or in the vignette wrap up.
- **Extensive Graphics:** Each chapter has extensive graphics that will assist the student's comprehension of the essential concepts.
- **Chapter Summaries:** Each chapter ends with a summary of its contents. These summaries capsulate the core chapter concepts, but they were not created so that students can read them in lieu of the chapter content.
- **Key Concepts and Terms**: Also at the end of each chapter is a list of important terms and concepts to assist the student in checking his or her understanding.
- **Vignette Wrap up and Questions:** The unit opening vignette will be used throughout the chapters to explicate and demonstrate the concepts in the chapter. At the end of the chapters, a summary of the vignette and case questions are given to expand on the topics of the chapter and give students the ability to expand their learning.
- **Glossary:** At the end of the text an extensive glossary of terms is included which defines the most difficult terms in this textbook.

ORGANIZATION AND CONTENTS

This textbook is organized into four units based on the core topics of business-driven infrastructure design.

Unit 1. ICT Infrastructure Components: A Technical Overview

- **Introduction to the ICT Infrastructure Architecture** This introduction sets the context for the rest of the textbook by reviewing the information technology infrastructure architecture (see Figure P-1) and explaining the importance of technology infrastructure to any enterprise. A high-level view of information technology offers students a chance to understand what components make up the business information systems architecture of all enterprises.

- **Chapter 1. ICT Introductory Concepts:** Topics include network architecture, standards, OSI, TCP/IP, network typology, and the Internet. Encapsulation and addressing are presented in this chapter. The topics of LANs and WANs and what they mean for network design are introduced. Similarities between telecommunications infrastructure and network implementation are discussed. Switching, routing, and VPNs are introduced, along with examples of small networks based on the opening vignette. Students are challenged to understand these implementations of various network typologies and to apply them.
- **Chapter 2. Building the Local Area Network Using Ethernet:** The previous chapter introduced a number of topics that are essential to understanding this chapter. The previous chapter provided foundational information, while this chapter builds on that foundation. In the current chapter, the topic of LANs, how they are implemented, and what they mean for network design is expanded. Specifics about telecommunications infrastructure and network implementation are introduced. The concepts of switching and routing are discussed further, with examples of networks based on the opening vignette being used to illustrate concepts. Students are challenged to understand the implementations of various network typologies and to apply them to the running case in the text. This chapter discusses the specifics of Ethernet as a network component. This chapter also extends the wired LAN by introducing wireless networking, specifically the IEEE 802.11 standards.
- **Chapter 3. Extending the LAN through WAN Connections:** In the last chapter, LANs were covered extensively, as were structured cabling and other network concepts from the network core to the demarcation point where the LAN connects to a WAN. In this chapter, the WAN is covered, including the topics of ATM, Frame Relay, wide-area Ethernet, and other typologies. The goal is to inform the student (i.e., future business systems analyst/strategist) about the WAN technologies that the network engineer builds.
- **Chapter 4. Wrapping Up Service, User, and Enterprise Components:** Some final concepts of service components are reviewed; then we move to user components. An overview of the PC architecture, desktop applications, and productivity tools is given. The chapter then moves into enterprise-wide software applications and gives an introduction of off-the-shelf application versus home-grown application. Application service providers are covered as well as applications that reside in the organization.

ENTERPRISE-WIDE SOFTWARE COMPONENTS Enterprise-wide software, including ERP, e-commerce/e-business, document management, knowledge management, and other specialized applications.	**User Components**	Items that directly interface with the user, including work-stations, printers, scanners, associated software (especially desktop applications), and specialized applications
	Service Components	Network parts that facilitate network operations with direct user interface, including printing services, inter/intra office communications (i.e., telephone or fax), network attached storage, database/application servers, security servers and appliances, and VPN technology
	Network Components	Items/concepts traditionally thought of as networking and telecommunications equipment, including network switching and routing hardware, media, outside vendor interconnects, and associated items

This figure lists and describes the components of ICT infrastructure architecture from the standpoint of the information technology user.

FIGURE P-1 Information Technology Infrastructure Architecture Framework

Unit 2. Additional ICT Concepts

- **Chapter 5. Obtaining Services Through Cloud Computing:** Cloud computing allows organizations to share information, software, and hardware resources over the Internet. Cloud computing is the next logical step following the client-server computing as a by-product of the evolution of the Internet. Cloud computing allows the user/organization to be unconcerned about the technical details inside the "cloud" but rather with how the services offered from the cloud can be incorporated into the business processes of the organization.
- **Chapter 6. Security:** Security must be understood at several levels. At the physical level, the security of laptops and other devices that can be easily stolen or damaged must be considered. Security at the LAN level must be considered, and ways to control LAN access often needs to be implemented. LAN security must be enhanced through the implementation of firewalls when LANS are interconnected through carrier circuits. Security between partners sharing information and other resources must also be implemented as we move to greater reliance on things like digital transaction and cloud based-computing.

Unit 3. Understanding the Business of Infrastructure Design

- **Chapter 7. Infrastructure and the Enterprise**: Business process and functional views of the enterprise are discussed in this chapter. The text explains how infrastructure and technology strategy are concerned with more than just networking and telecommunications and are actually key aspects of overall business strategy. ICT infrastructure can be viewed as a multilayered architecture, driven by the business imperatives of the enterprise and the technology that must support them. Understanding the competition, knowing the internal business processes of your enterprise, and turning that knowledge into technology infrastructure recommendations are tantamount to creating competitive advantage. Within this chapter, the various conceptual frameworks that underpin business-driven infrastructure design are specifically addressed.
- **Chapter 8. Business Processes:** This chapter covers business process improvement and innovation through the aligning of business strategy with technology infrastructure changes. The emphasis is on bringing about positive changes to business processes that can create and sustain competitive positioning. Existing processes and new processes within a business must add value to a product and must be competitively positioned. In order to understand how to change processes to maximize value, the business systems analyst must understand what a business process is and how to make it a value-creating process.
- **Chapter 9. Assessing the Business Value of ICT Resource Investments:** Once an organization decides on processes for improvement or innovation through information technology infrastructure implementation, it must decide how to measure the success of those process changes. Measurement must be included as unit of the project planning so success of the implementation can be gauged, and so that mid-project changes can be made if necessary. This chapter discusses methods for measurement and gives suggestions to the business systems analyst for creating measurement plans. It is essential that measurements be taken to justify ICT infrastructure investment, to monitor the impact of infrastructure-mediated changes during implementation, and to assess the impact of ICT infrastructure investment. These measurement methods must be defined before a process change project begins.

Unit 4. Steps to the Strategic Alignment of ICT

- **Chapter 10. Analyzing the Organization and Its Environment:** In this chapter students will be presented with a methodology for understanding the organization, its industry, and its competitive environment in relation to technology. This process is predicated on the business concepts from earlier units in this textbook, and at a

minimum requires the technology background of Unit One. Using the ICT value propositions described for the organization, information technology recommendations are made within the layers of the technology infrastructure architecture.
- **Chapter 11. Designing ICT: Documenting Process and Technology Recommendations:** Methods for documenting processes and associated technology are discussed, with an emphasis on using modeling tools. This discussion includes documenting process implementation/innovation/improvement supported by ICT infrastructure, creating final "user appropriate" design documents that graphically describe the infrastructure being proposed, and documenting technology to be designed/implemented by engineers.
- **Chapter 12. Summarizing the Business-Driven Infrastructure Design Cycle: Analysis, Design, Implementation, and Post-Implementation:** Models for costing an infrastructure design are discussed, and implementation planning is reviewed. Measurement of infrastructure success is again discussed and expanded on. The need for post-infrastructure implementation review is discussed along with ways for the design team to stay in touch with the user.

SUPPLEMENTS

- **Websites:** Three websites serve as resources to the instructor and students:
  a. A textbook adopter's website (http://bddc.gendron.info) provides a forum for sharing ideas about teaching infrastructure design classes. On the site are updates and ideas we receive from others. This website also contains animations useful to the student and the instructor.
  b. A LinkedIn group called Business-driven IT Strategy is moderated by the author to create a forum for those that want to discuss this subject further.
  c. The publisher's website (www.pearsonhighered.com/irc) has the following resources available to instructors:
- **PowerPoint Slides:** The PowerPoints highlight text learning objectives and key topics and serve as an excellent aid for classroom presentations and lectures.
- **Instructor's Manual:** An instructor's manual presents the solutions to exercises as well as suggested strategies for teaching the course.
- **Test Item File:** This Test Item File contains over 900 questions, including multiple-choice, true/false, and essay questions. Each question is followed by the correct answer, page reference, and difficulty rating.
- **TestGen:** Pearson Education's test-generating software is available from www.pearsonhighered.com/irc. The software is PC/MAC compatible and preloaded with all of the Test Item File questions. You can manually or randomly view test questions and drag and drop to create a test. You can add or modify test-bank questions as needed.
- **E-Mail the Author:** We encourage e-mail from faculty using this textbook. Send questions, suggestions for improving the text, and ideas about teaching the class to *gendronm@ccsu.edu*.
- **Syllabi**: Textbook adopters' syllabi used in teaching this course are included as they become available.
- **Updates:** Information about changes or corrections to the text is provided as it becomes available.

ACKNOWLEDGMENTS

I would like to acknowledge Dean Siamack Shojai who provided countless hours of support during the creation of this work. Without the mentoring of Dr. William K. Holstein, I would never have learned about creating information systems to achieve competitive advantage . . . my thanks goes to him. I would also like to acknowledge the support staff at my university for their tireless help with many details; without them, I would never have completed this work. Joanne Carroll and Rosa Colón—thanks! Lastly, I would like to acknowledge the countless hours of emotional support I received from Dr. Carol Austad; without her, I would have given up on the completion of this textbook long ago.

UNIT 1

ICT Infrastructure Components: A Technical Overview

Introduction to the ICT Architecture Framework

This introduction sets the context for the rest of this textbook by reviewing the information and communication technology infrastructure architecture used through the textbook. The architecture helps to explain how infrastructure and technology strategy are concerned with more than just networking and telecommunications; that is, ICT strategy takes into account the business intelligence and concomitant applications needed to make an organization competitive. To that end, **information and communication technology (ICT) infrastructure** can be viewed as a multilayered architecture, driven by the business imperatives of the enterprise and the technology that must support them. Understanding the competition, knowing the internal business processes of the enterprise, and turning that knowledge into technology infrastructure recommendations contribute to creating competitive advantage. The objective of this introduction is to define ICT infrastructure, and for the student to learn that computer networks are just one part of the ICT infrastructure, as we cover all the necessary components of ICT that aid in the achievement of competitive advantage.

Definition of Technology Infrastructure

It is easy to say that "businesses need a technology infrastructure to operate," but it is also important to know what is included in that infrastructure. Management Information Systems students often take a course in **networking and telecommunications** to learn technical concepts, but that course usually does not offer a business-driven focus. The technical information taught in those courses is essential to students, especially since the Internet has emerged as the primary global communications medium. Still, a greater business-driven focus is needed, one that takes an all-encompassing view of the organization. Networking and telecommunications classes leave students with a thorough understanding of *how* to implement technology infrastructure, but little about *when* to implement that technology and exactly what technology to implement to achieve efficiency and sustain competitive advantage. Students in traditional networking and telecommunication classes learn about protocols, standards, hardware, and software, but the business focus is often lacking in those classes.

This textbook supplements the technology knowledge necessary for the person in the organization who is responsible for keeping technology in synch with business strategy. That person could be a manager, business systems analyst, chief information officer (CIO), chief technology officer (CTO), or a chief knowledge officer (CKO). (Note: **Business systems analyst** is used throughout this book to indicate the person responsible for those tasks.) The textbook goes beyond technical knowledge and incorporates how technology can enhance the competitive positioning of the enterprise. Linking technical knowledge with competitive positioning is essential to understanding how technology infrastructure and business strategy can and should complement each other. Once that linkage is fully understood, the business systems analyst must stay abreast of technology changes while still keeping informed about business strategy within the organization. In this textbook the technologies that support business strategy are grouped together as information and communication technology (ICT) infrastructure; the architecture found in Figure 1 describes the components contained within that infrastructure.

Networking and telecommunications have traditionally been thought of as protocols; standards; hardware and software; and all the associated media, cabinetry, and ancillary components. However, ICT Infrastructure includes everything from components directly accessed by the user to the back office components that provide network services and network connectivity (see Figure 1). This architecture takes the "30,000-foot view" and includes everything within the networking and telecommunications system, as well as the actual software, hardware, and services necessary to sustain the business. In today's global technology/Internet-enabled era, ICT infrastructure is often the centerpiece of the competitive position for the enterprise. ICT infrastructure and its various components can be discussed in terms of how the user interacts with them. Specifically, ICT includes the following elements:

Enterprise-Wide Software Components. Users often interact with **enterprise applications**, such as an enterprise resource planning (ERP) system. These applications are a complicated set of ubiquitous software

1

ENTERPRISE-WIDE SOFTWARE COMPONENTS Enterprise-wide software, including ERP, e-commerce/e-business, document management, knowledge management, and other specialized applications	User Components	Items that directly interface with the user, including workstations, printers, scanners, associated software (especially desktop applications), and specialized applications
	Service Components	Those network parts that facilitate network operations with direct user interface, including printing services, inter/intra office communications (i.e., telephone or fax), network attached storage, database/application servers, security servers and appliances, and VPN technology
	Network Components	Those items/concepts traditionally thought of as networking and telecommunications equipment, including network switching and routing hardware, media, outside vendor interconnects, and associated items

This figure lists and describes the components of ICT infrastructure architecture from the standpoint of the information technology user.

FIGURE 1 Information and Communication Technology Infrastructure Architecture

that support business processes and cut across the enterprise. Although the user usually only interacts with a small part of each application (i.e., the front-end), these systems are grouped into a category of components called enterprise-wide application components. The enterprise-wide software components cut across organizational departments, include front-end and back office services, and operate together as one system or application. The majority of the application is often transparent to the user (e.g., database and application servers) while the user interacts with a small-footprint front-end. Grouping organizationally ubiquitous applications/systems into enterprise-wide components makes understanding and implementation of ICT technologies easier for the business systems analyst. It is easier to think about these components across the enterprise, rather than as their constituent parts (e.g., servers, front-end software, printers, etc.).

User Components. User components include all the components with which the user directly interacts, such as desktops and other user-accessed hardware and software. All user-accessed components—workstations, printers, scanners, desktop productivity software, and other specialized applications—are included in this category. User components are defined as any hardware or software that the user directly interacts with.

Service Components. Network hardware and software that the user directly interacts with are included in the service components category. These items come under the control of the networking staff, but the user accesses the items directly. For example, the network staff will configure the virtual private network (VPN), but the user will use it and understand that the VPN is necessary to access the enterprise network securely from offsite. There are many types of network services, including printing services; inter/intra-office communications via fax or IP telephony; network accessible storage; and network shared printers, faxes, and storage devices.

Network Components. Those components traditionally thought of as related to networking and telecommunications are grouped in the network components category. Network hardware and software, including switching and routing hardware, cabling/media, and any associated outsourcing for installation, servers, outside vendor interconnects (e.g., **DSL**, leased lines, third-party value-added networks), security, and other appliances are included here.

Each component grouping of ICT is interrelated and must support business processes and enhance the company's operations. Technology infrastructure affects both internal operations and external interactions with suppliers, distributors, and customers. Internal impact on operations should yield increased efficiency within the enterprise and must have payback that occurs within an acceptable period to the organization. The same thing is true of all ICT infrastructures: They must sustain or enhance the competitive positioning of the enterprise through maintaining or increasing the efficiency of internal operations or providing enhanced services to customers.

It is essential that today's information systems graduate be prepared to take a high-level view of ICT and the organization, its business processes, its products, and the technologies needed to support these things. These graduates do not necessarily need to understand all the subtle nuances of hardware and software, but they must understand the linkage between business strategy, ICT infrastructure, and organizational success in order to be a positive part of the team that drives strategic discussions within an enterprise. Frequently, hardware engineers are making the decisions today about which specific technologies to use, whereas the business systems analyst is ensuring that all the technologies fit together to support the business processes and products of the organization. That said, the business systems analyst needs to have an understanding of the technologies and their capabilities although the subtleties of individual technologies often remain the purview of the engineer. The business systems analyst specifies what needs to be done at a macro level and determines how it is to be done, while the engineer handles the specifics of doing the tasks.

Unit Purpose

The ICT architecture, as just described, provides a convenient way to view information infrastructure and to understand how the various technologies interface. We will use that framework to facilitate the discussion of the various technologies that come together to create information/business technology-based infrastructure. The four components of the ICT architecture will be reviewed in this unit: network components, service components, enterprise-wide components, and user components. These components are the basis for all ICT infrastructures. In Unit One, these components are introduced.

The network components of the information technology architecture are the backbone to building infrastructure. To understand the network component of ICT infrastructure, it is necessary to understand various standards and theories including TCP/IP, encapsulation, and addressing. This unit covers network topologies and their similarities to telecom technologies, giving the student the advantage of comparing the two. A thorough review of local, metropolitan, and wide area networks is given along with virtual private networks so the student understands these technologies and how and when to implement them. Lastly, this unit covers other **network technologies** like ATM and Frame Relay, giving the student an understanding of the value of these technologies.

Unit Objectives

Understanding network architectures like OSI and TCP/IP and how they influence networks, including the Internet.

Defining encapsulation, physical/network addressing, and network masks.

Covering network topologies and their implications for network design.

Developing an understanding of the similarities between information and telecom networks.

Introducing switch, hubs, routers, and dial-up technologies, and showing how they come together to create ICT infrastructure.

Incorporating information from this unit helps the students to understand the challenges of local, metropolitan, and wide area networks and the implementation of these various network technologies.

Bringing together the knowledge gained throughout Unit One, the topics of ATM, Frame Relay, and other technologies are discussed.

Understanding all of the components of ICT and how they interrelate to create unified infrastructure that can be use to support the enterprise.

Vignette

For this unit we will use two vignettes, both of which are fictional. One vignette is for Joe Smith, someone who wants to connect to the Internet at home and use that connection to access his office virtual private network. The other vignette is for HealthyWay Health Maintenance Organization, the company for which Joe Smith works. (Any similarities between these vignette's and real life are purely coincidental.)

- HealthyWay HMO has 125 employees. Its chief executive officer, chief financial officer, chief information officer, chief operating officer, and director of marketing each has a private office, with a secretary, arranged in one suite. In addition to executive suite members, HealthyWay has

eight operational managers/assistant managers who are responsible for the various units of the organization. There is one secretary for every two operational managers. The managers report to the various executive suite members. The organizational units include the following staff:
- Finance: 6
- Marketing: 4
- Operations: 75
- Information Systems: 12
- Human Resources: 3

- HealthyWay leases 150,000 square feet in an executive park building.
- Joe Smith is the chief operating officer of HealthyWay and lives in a residential area outside of the city where HealthyWay is located. At his home he has two PCs for which he needs Internet access. Joe also bring a laptop computer home from work, which needs Internet access. All computers in Joe's home will share a printer located in his home office. Joe is fortunate because he has dial-up, DSL, and cable Internet available to him. He has to weigh the options and choose the correct type of Internet connection.

1 ICT INTRODUCTORY CONCEPTS

> **Learning Objectives**
>
> - Know what *analog* and *digital* communications are, and how they differ.
> - Understand *standards* and *protocols* and why they are important.
> - Review the TCP/IP communications model and apply it to encapsulated layered communications.
> - Introduce *addressing* and what it takes to communicate over the Internet.

This chapter introduces many network concepts and the *network components* of the *ICT infrastructure architecture*, which were discussed in the introduction to Unit 1. In the current chapter we are specifically looking at those items/concepts traditionally thought of as networking and telecommunications equipment, including network switching and routing hardware, media, servers, outside vendor interconnects, and associated items (see Figure 1-1). Network architecture, standards, OSI, TCP/IP, and the Internet, as well as encapsulation and addressing, are introduced in this chapter. Examples are provided using the opening vignette. *This chapter attempts to strike a balance between providing enough technical material, so the business systems analyst can make informed recommendations, and an appropriate business focus.*

INTRODUCTION

Business systems analysts need to understand how information and communication technology (ICT) works, and when to implement it. They need to be able to conceptualize ICT infrastructure so they can make informed recommendations. This chapter sets the groundwork for this conceptualization and provides background on the networking and telecommunication portion of ICT infrastructure. This introduction is not exhaustive, but it provides a summary of many concepts that are fundamental to understanding ICT. It specifically focuses on introductory network concepts of ICT architecture. Network components are those technologies that make up what is traditionally thought of as a computer network. The network can be as simple as two computers that communicate with each other over a cable, or as complicated as a large number of computers that are interconnected to create a corporate communications environment. In our opening vignette, we discuss such a network comprised of 125 employees, and we highlight Joe Smith's need to connect back to the office network using the Internet.

    A number of introductory concepts and associated terminologies must be introduced before moving to business concepts. It may seem that this chapter "gets into the weeds" and does not introduce business strategy concepts; however, the goal of this chapter is to build vocabulary and foundational knowledge so the business system analyst can communicate with the network engineer, which sometimes means reviewing or learning basic concepts. The introductory concepts in this chapter set the background necessary to understand how network components work. Some of these concepts will be review for the more technical students, while the more business-oriented student may be new to many of these concepts. The concepts and theories included below are not

ENTERPRISE-WIDE SOFTWARE COMPONENTS — Enterprise-wide software, including ERP, e-commerce/e-business, document management, knowledge management, and other specialized applications	User Components	Items that directly interface with the user, including workstations, printers, scanners, associated software (esp. desktop applications), and specialized applications
	Service Components	Those network parts that facilitate network operations with direct user interface, including printing services, inter/intra office communications (i.e., telephone or fax), network attached storage, database/application servers, security servers and appliances, and VPN technology
	Network Components	Those items/concepts traditionally thought of as networking and telecommunications equipment, including network switching and routing hardware, media, outside vendor interconnects, and associated items

This figure lists and describes the components of ICT infrastructure architecture from the standpoint of the information technology user. The areas highlighted in blue are covered in this chapter.

FIGURE 1-1 **Information Technology Infrastructure Architecture**

exhaustive, but rather give a base from which other theories can be extrapolated. These theories are broken into several sections that include:

- Data representation and signal propagation
- Data communication techniques
- Computer network and carrier concepts
- Introduction to TCP/IP and layering

Data Representation and Signal Propagation

In this section the differences between analog and digital data are discussed. Once those differences are understood, digital signals propagation is explained. By understanding these concepts, the reader will become familiar with how digital signals move through a network.

DATA REPRESENTATION: ANALOG AND DIGITAL

Data are either analog or digital. **Analog** data are things such as sound, temperature, time, and weight. Analog data are continuous; in other words they exist along a continuum. For example, using the metric system of weights, an object might weight 28 grams (1 ounce in the U.S. system of measure), or 28 kilograms, but it could also weight 28.4323 grams. It is possible to get a weight anywhere between 0 and an infinite number of grams, including whole numbers as well as fractional numbers. The same is true for temperature: It could be –15 degrees or +98.6 degrees or anywhere in between and beyond. These are seen in Figure 1-2. **Digital** data are different.

FIGURE 1-2 **Representations of Continuous Data**

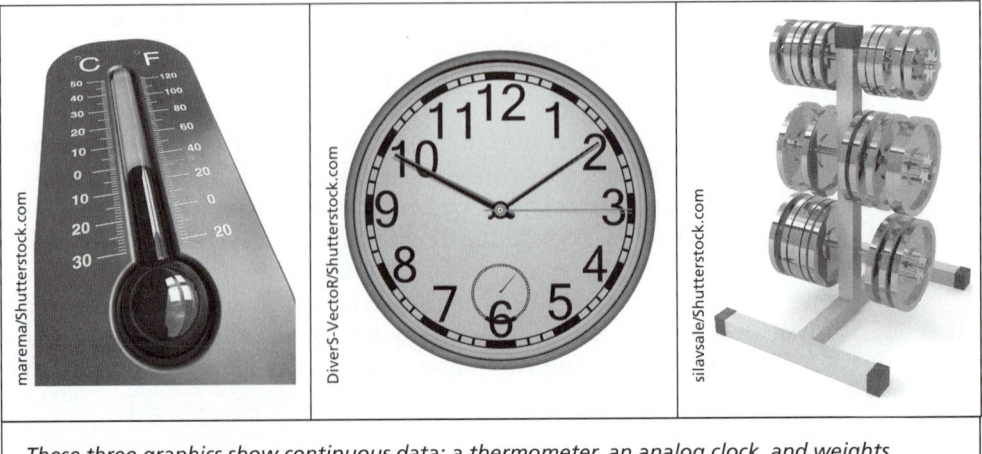

These three graphics show continuous data: a thermometer, an analog clock, and weights.

Chapter 1 • ICT Introductory Concepts   7

FIGURE 1-3 **Bits and Octets**

Bits are represented as 1 or 0	Octets are groupings of 8 bits
1 0	00100111

Digital representation is used by computers to represent real world information such as weight, sound, temperature, or pictures. The question is how to get analog data (numbers and characters as well) in a form that is useful to a computer. The answer is digital data. Digital data are a coded representation of "real life" information. Computers need "real life" information coded in some way so they can manipulate, store, and transmit it. That coding is done using "1" and "0" in a predefined sequence to represent things. These data are coded as a number of bits (Figure 1-3). Bits are commonly grouped in to sets of 8 bites, called octets. These octets are then used as the basis of character representation.

Bits are internal computer representation, but in order to transmit them they need to be converted into electrical signals. Let us assume that we want to represent the binary number 00100111 in electrical voltages for transmission. We might use a scheme where +15 volts represents a 0, and −15 volts represents a 1. That would mean that our sample binary number would be represented as +15+15−15+15+15−15−15−15, or graphically you could see this as shown in Figure 1-4.

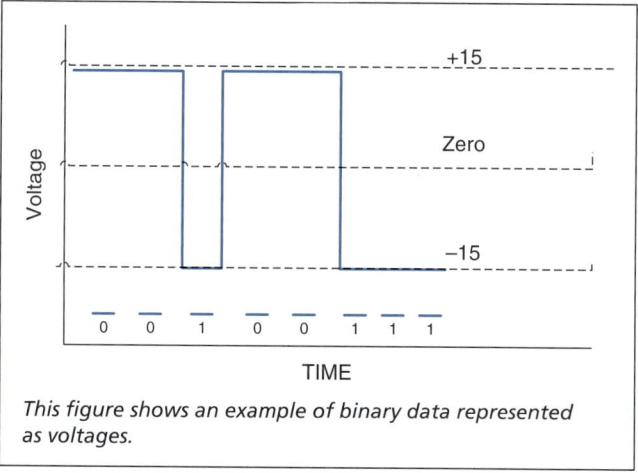

FIGURE 1-4 **Binary Data as Electrical Signals**

This figure shows an example of binary data represented as voltages.

The 1s and 0s used for internal computer coding represent letters, numbers, and special characters just like Morse code. In Morse code "dots" and "dashes" are used to represent characters, while computers use electric signals to represent letters, numbers, and special characters. The dominant scheme for internal representation (encoding) data by a computer is Unicode, which is coordinated by the Unicode Consortium. Unicode and its standard Unicode Transformation Format (UTF) schemes hope to replace many of the existing character coding schemes in use today. Existing character coding schemes are limited in size and scope, and many are incompatible with multi-lingual environments. UTF solved many of those problems.

ISO 8858-1 is one of those existing limited character coding schemes. Unicode is composed of code points (or binary numbers) that represent characters, and the first 256 code points are made identical to the ISO 8858-1 standard to make conversion of existing western text seamless. The binary representation for the 26 characters in the western alphabet can be seen in Table 1-1.

SIGNAL PROPAGATION AND PROPAGATION EFFECTS

Morse code (Figure 1-5) is a familiar way to create signals. Morse code uses a series of "dots" and "dashes" to represent the letter, numerals, and special characters of a message and is a binary signaling mechanism because it has just two states, "on" and "off." The "dots" are considered short elements, and the "dashes" are considered long elements that can be transmitted through some media (e.g., flashes of light or taps of telegraph equipment).

TABLE 1-1 Character to Binary Conversion

Upper Case Characters	Binary	Lower Case Characters	Binary
A	01000001	a	01100001
B	01000010	b	01100010
C	01000011	c	01100011
D	01000100	d	01100100
E	01000101	e	01100101
F	01000110	f	01100110
G	01000111	g	01100111
H	01001000	h	01101000
I	01001001	i	01101001
J	01001010	j	01101010
K	01001011	k	01101011
L	01001100	l	01101100
M	01001101	m	01101101
N	01001110	n	01101110
O	01001111	o	01101111
P	01010000	p	01110000
Q	01010001	q	01110001
R	01010010	r	01110010
S	01010011	s	01110011
T	01010100	t	01110100
U	01010101	u	01110101
V	01010110	v	01110110
W	01010111	w	01110111
X	01011000	x	01111000
Y	01011001	y	01111001
Z	01011010	z	01111010

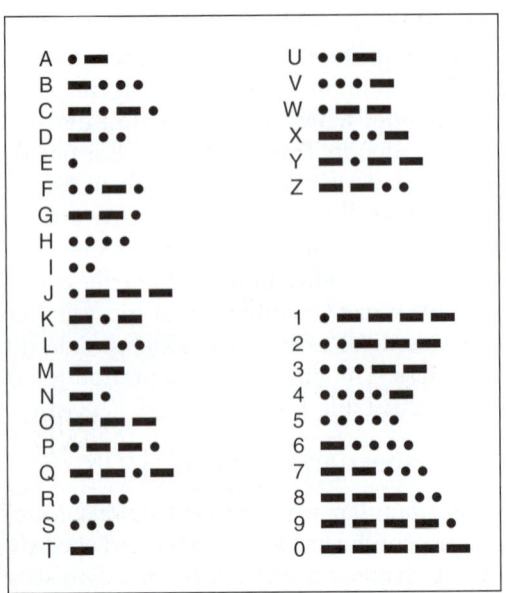

FIGURE 1-5 International Morse Code

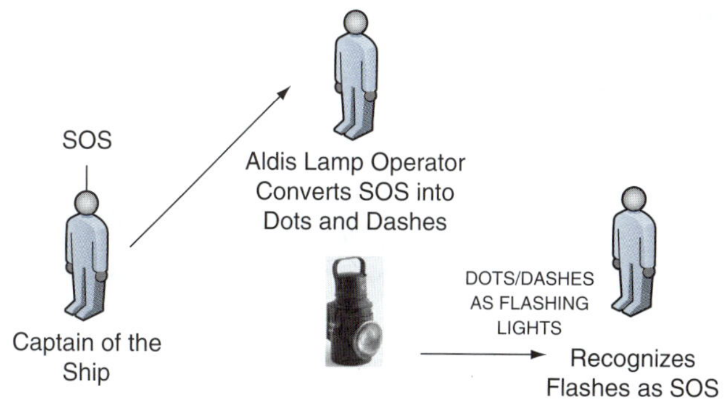

FIGURE 1-6 Morse Code and the Aldis Lamp Operator

The captain wants to send the SOS message; the captain gives this message to the Aldis lamp operator, who encodes "SOS" into dots and dashes. Someone on another ship who knows Morse code recognizes the "SOS" message.

Converting the international distress code SOS, into Morse code would give us DOT DOT DOT DASH DASH DASH DOT DOT DOT. So, how is Morse code signaled? In other words, how do we get the SOS message coded into Morse code from the sender to the recipient? Let's take, for example, the captain of a ship who wants to send out a distress signal using Morse code. The captain instructs the ship's signaling lamp operator (also called an Aldis lamp operator) to propagate that message (Figure 1-6). The lamp operator opens and closes shutters in the front of the lamp, creating a series of flashing dots and dashes that represent "SOS." Because Morse code is recognized by many people, someone may see the signaling and recognize SOS, then respond by sending help. This simple example illustrates the creation of a message, the conversion of the message into Morse code, and the signaling of this message from a sender to a receiver.

As discussed, computers use binary numbers to represent characters. The binary numbers of Unicode (just like any other coding scheme) need to be converted into signals for transmission over a medium such as unshielded twisted pair (UTP) or fiber optic cable. For the sake of describing digital signal propagation we will assume that the encoding scheme UTF-8 is being used. So when we convert the SOS message into binary we would get 01010011 01001111 01010011.

An internal computer's 1s and 0s need to be encoded into electrical, sound, light, or some other scheme to send the data from one computer to another. Assume that a computer has the word "HELLO" in its memory and wants to communicate that to another computer. The word "HELLO" could be represented in five octets (one for each character H E L L O) internal to the computer. In order to transmit those octets over a cable, called media, the octets need to be converted to signals—which, for this discussion, we will assume to be electrical signals but could also be radio waves, light, or some other type of signaling. The electrical signals are propagated over a cable (media) from the sender to the receiver. An example of this can be seen in Figure 1-7.

As signals are propagated, they are subject to what are known as propagation effects. **Propagation effects** are things that affect a signal as it travels across media. Three major propagation effects must be considered in this process: electromagnetic interference (EMI), cross talk, and attenuation.

Electromagnetic Interference. Electromagnetic interference (EMI) is radio interference that all electrical devices create. This interference results from the operations of the components in a device or piece of equipment. For example, when an air conditioner operates it produces a small amount of radio waves as a consequence of its mechanical and electrical component. The same is true for all electrical devices and equipment including computers and network equipment—they all produce EMI. EMI becomes a problem in data communications when the strength of the EMI reaches a level that interferes with data signals being transmitted. EMI is produced by florescent lights, refrigerators, microwave ovens, AC/DC power wiring,

FIGURE 1-7 Propagate Data

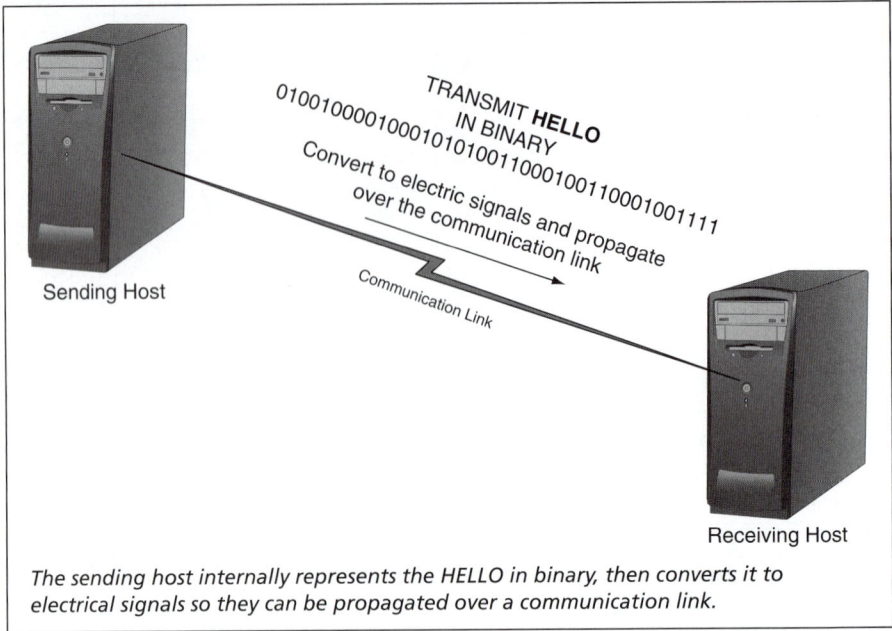

The sending host internally represents the HELLO in binary, then converts it to electrical signals so they can be propagated over a communication link.

and even computers and telecommunication equipment themselves (Figure 1-8). The amount of EMI that a device can legally produce is regulated by government agencies. In the United States, the Federal Communications Commission promulgates regulations which state how much EMI a device may emit. Similar government agencies exist in other countries. EMI becomes a problem in data communications when the EMI is so strong that it enters the media being used to transmit. EMI can destroy the signal being propagated, and make communications difficult or impossible.

Cross Talk. Cross talk is a special case of EMI in which conductors in a cable (which also produce EMI) interfere with each other. Data communication cables often use twisted conductors to reduce cross talk in a bundle of cables. This is described in Figure 1-9.

Attenuation. As signals propagate they become weaker in a process known as attenuation. Once a signal attenuates (weakens) too much it can no longer be understood by the receiver. It is important to note that the more a signal attenuates, the more susceptible it is to EMI. EMI can cause what is referred to as noise errors, and the signal-to-noise is how the ratio between signal strength and EMI noise is represented. A good way to think of signal-to-noise ratio (SNR) and noise errors would be to envision sitting in a room watching TV as someone comes into

FIGURE 1-8 EMI

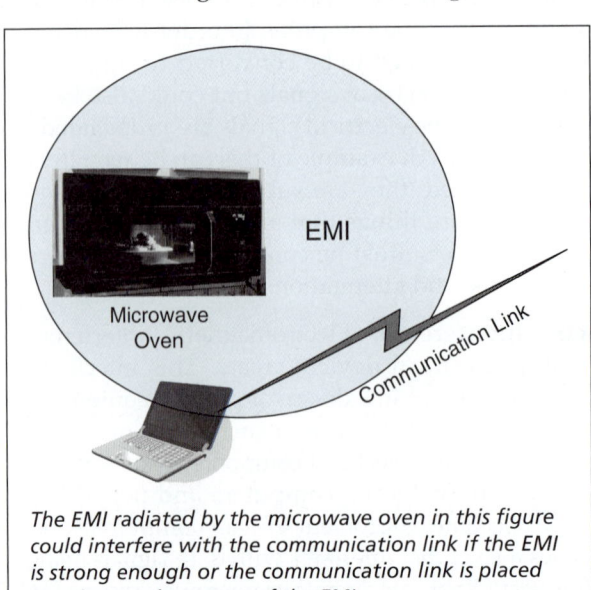

The EMI radiated by the microwave oven in this figure could interfere with the communication link if the EMI is strong enough or the communication link is placed too close to the source of the EMI.

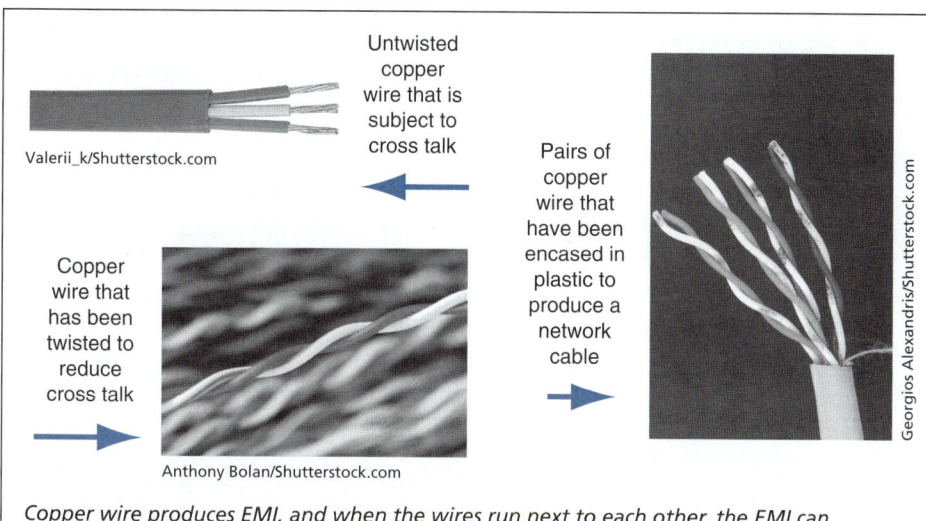

FIGURE 1-9 Twisted-Pair Cable

Copper wire produces EMI, and when the wires run next to each other, the EMI can interfere with the signal on the other wire. Twisting copper wires has a cancelling effect that reduces EMI. To create UTP cabling, once pairs are twisted together, they are encased in plastic to form an 8-conductor (4 twisted pair) network cable.

the room and plays the drums loudly. If you cannot hear the TV clearly because the drums are too loud, then the sound of the drums could be considered noise, and what you hear from the TV may be incorrect. Hearing the TV incorrectly would be an error caused by the noise, or a noise error. Turning up the TV volume would change the ratio of the TV volume to the drum sound, or would change the signal- (the TV sound) to-noise (the drums) ratio. The phenomena of signal-to-noise ratio (SNR) and noise errors in a network can be seen in Figure 1-10. This figure graphically shows attenuation, noise errors, the average noise floor, and the SNR.

Data Communications Techniques

Data communications techniques are ways the propagated signals are modified to create specific kinds of communication. The techniques can be used together to create various types of communications circuits.

SERIAL VERSUS PARALLEL

When propagating a signal it is possible to do so one bit at a time or several bits simultaneously. Transmitting one bit at a time is referred to as serial communications, and

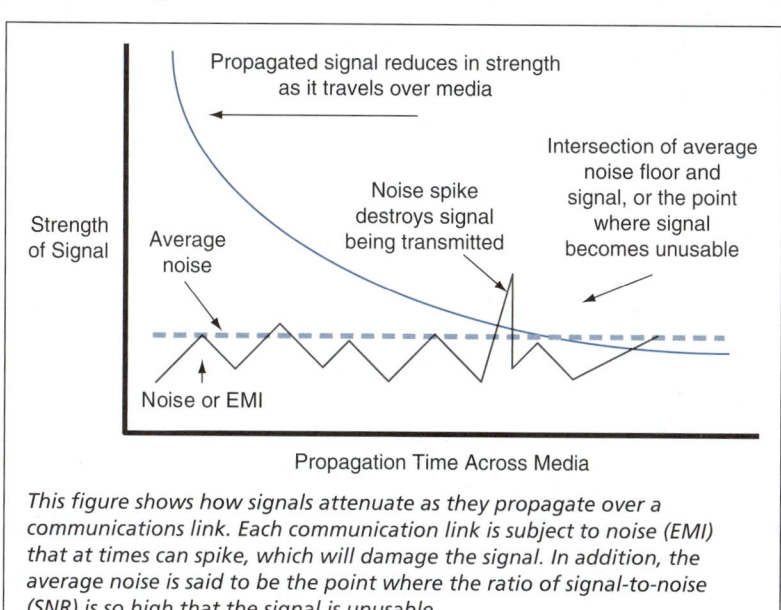

FIGURE 1-10 Attenuation and Noise Effects

This figure shows how signals attenuate as they propagate over a communications link. Each communication link is subject to noise (EMI) that at times can spike, which will damage the signal. In addition, the average noise is said to be the point where the ratio of signal-to-noise (SNR) is so high that the signal is unusable.

FIGURE 1-11 Serial Versus Parallel Transmission

Serial Transmission of *HELLO*	Parallel Transmission of *HELLO*	
0100100001000101010011000100110001001111	H	01001000
	E	01000101
	L	01001100
	L	01001100
	O	01001111
In this serial transmission of *HELLO*, each bit is transmitted one at a time, over a single pair of copper wires	In this parallel transmission, each character of *HELLO* is transmitted over a separate pair of copper wires	

Serial and parallel transmission can use the same character encoding, but in serial transmission a single pair of copper conductors are used to transmit one bit at a time, or in a series. In parallel transmission the message is broken into individual parts, and bits are transmitted in parallel over multiple pairs of copper wires simultaneously.

transmitting several bits simultaneously is referred to as parallel communication. The technology being used dictates whether the communications is serial or parallel. For example, a serial port on a desktop PC transmits one bit at a time, while a parallel printer port transmits several bits simultaneously. Examples of serial and parallel communications can be seen in Figure 1-11.

FULL VERSUS HALF DUPLEX

When two telecommunication devices communicate, it is possible to transmit in either full or half duplex. Both half- and full-duplex communications allow for communication in both directions. The difference is whether you can transmit in both directions simultaneously, or if you can only transmit in one direction at a time. In **half-duplex** communication, only one party can be transmitting at a time, while in **full-duplex** communication both parties can transmit simultaneously. Duplex is shown in Figure 1-12.

FIGURE 1-12 Half- and Full-Duplex Transmission

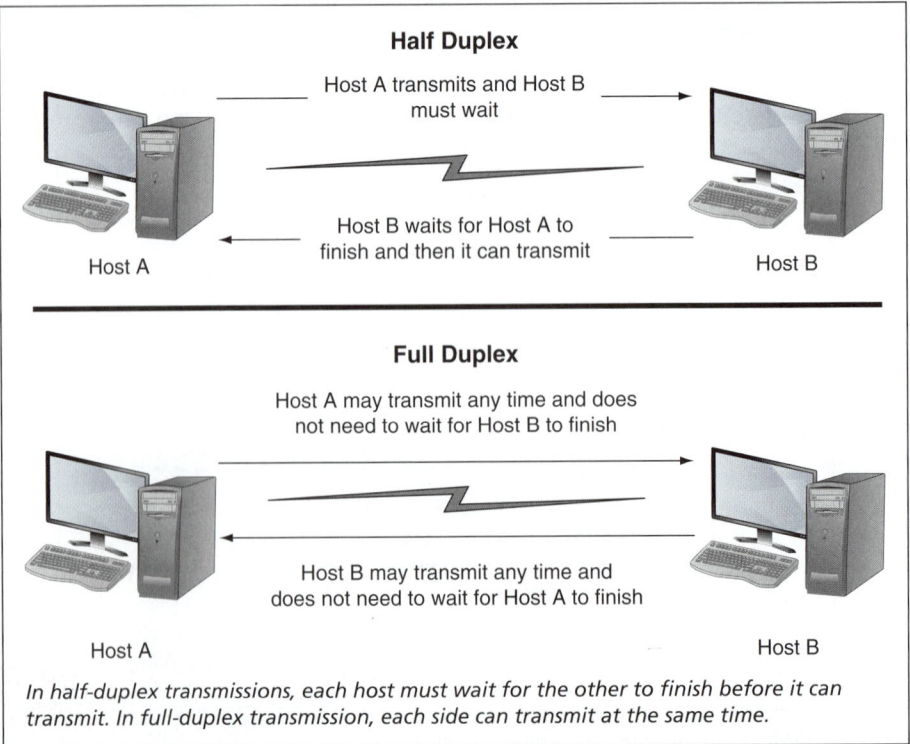

In half-duplex transmissions, each host must wait for the other to finish before it can transmit. In full-duplex transmission, each side can transmit at the same time.

FIGURE 1-13 Data Stream Synchronization Techniques

Example of Synchronous Data Stream	Example of Asynchronous Data Stream
P01110101P01001110P00011110P	01110101010011100001111001010101010101010101
P indicates electrical pulse in data that synchronizes the signal	------------------DATA------------------|----SYNCHWORD--->
	The SYNCHWORD synchronizes the sender and receiver at the start of the message

These two examples show two ways that a sending and receiving computer can synchronize a data stream from one computer to another.

MESSAGE SYNCHRONIZATION

In order for two computers to communicate over media, some method of synchronizing the signals being propagated between hosts or devices is necessary. A rhythm must be established between the computers so the receiver is able to decode what the sender is propagating, and turn it back into useful data. Without this rhythm, the receiving computer will not know where one bit or octet starts and another one ends. Computers use two types of synchronization techniques, referred to as synchronous and asynchronous transmission (See Figure 1-13).

Synchronous transmission involves data being encoded into signals that the media can propagate with some type of pulse signal being included (either on the same wire or an adjacent one) to indicate the start and end of one bit/octet.

Asynchronous transmission involves encoded data as well, but rather than some sort of pulse signal, the data stream is preceded by a bit, octet, or larger more complicated synch word that allows the receiver to synchronize itself to the incoming data stream. An example of this is **Ethernet** that uses multiple octets at the start of a message (i.e., a *synch* word) in a fixed pattern known by the sender and receiver. The receiver expects the synch word and uses it to synchronize itself to the data stream. Synchronous and asynchronous transmission is supported by different standards and different media, depending on factors such as the number of conductors in the media, the need for accurate and fast synchronization between sending and receiving hosts, speed, and cost.

MODULATION AND MULTIPLEXING

In telecommunications, modulation is taking a digital data stream (e.g., 01011101) and turning it into a sound that represents the data, which allows the data to be transferred over voice-grade carrier circuits. **Modulation** (i.e., converting a bit stream to sound) is performed by a device called a modulator, while a demodulator performs demodulation (i.e., converting sound back into digital data). One device that can do both modulation and demodulation is a modem. Computers communicate over telephone lines by using modems that represent digital data streams as tones. Modems are described in Figure 1-14.

Akin to modulation/demodulation is multiplexing. **Multiplexing** is done by a device called a MUX. The **MUX** may use modulation/demodulation in the case of voice-grade circuits, or it may be totally digital if other types of carrier circuits are used. A MUX takes several data streams and combines them into one signal so they can be transmitted over a carrier circuit. This sharing allows several computers to use one carrier circuit, which is cheaper than each device having its own carrier circuit. Multiplexing will not work in all applications and its usefulness is dependent on the bandwidth of the carrier circuit and the amount of data that need to be transmitted from the computers connected to a MUX. Multiplexing is shown in Figure 1-15.

DATA COMPRESSION

When transmitting data, it is possible for a sender and receiver to use compression to reduce the number of bits it takes to transmit a message. When you can reduce the number of bits, you reduce the bandwidth necessary to communicate a message.

14 Unit 1 • ICT Infrastructure Components: A Technical Overview

FIGURE 1-14 **Modems**

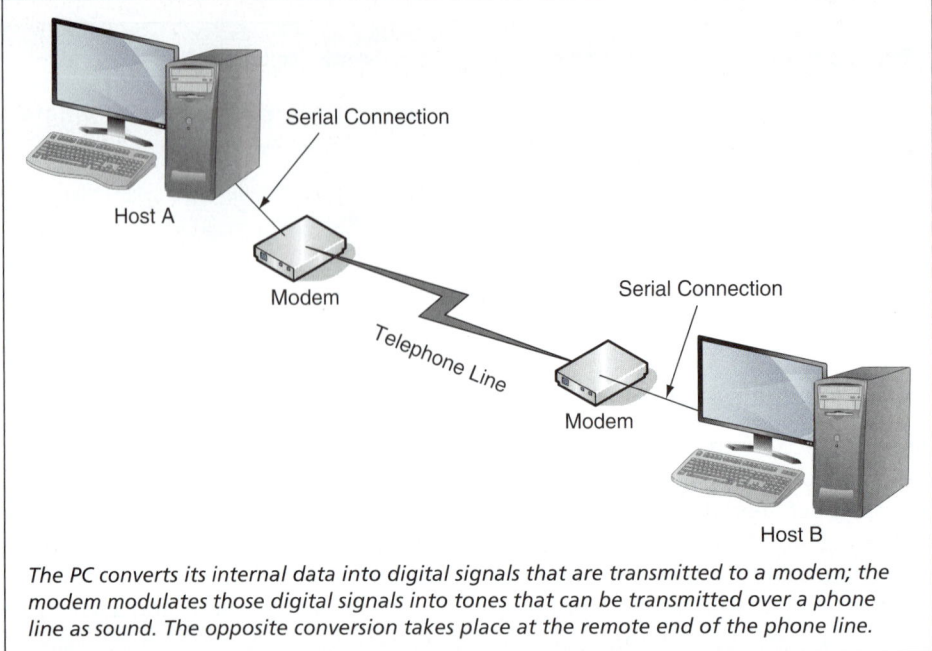

The PC converts its internal data into digital signals that are transmitted to a modem; the modem modulates those digital signals into tones that can be transmitted over a phone line as sound. The opposite conversion takes place at the remote end of the phone line.

Think of it this way, suppose you wanted to transmit the message "Green Apples Are Apples That Only Apple Lovers Will Allow in an Apple Store."

- The sender and receiver agreed that the word Apple(s) could be represented by Ap.
- Then the sentence would read "Green Ap Are Ap That Only Ap Lovers Will Allow in an Ap Store."
- The first sentence contains 75 characters, but the second compressed sentence has only 61 characters, or a savings of 18.7 percent. Spaces are included in these character counts because they take just as many bits to transmit as other characters in a data stream.

FIGURE 1-15 **Multiplexers**

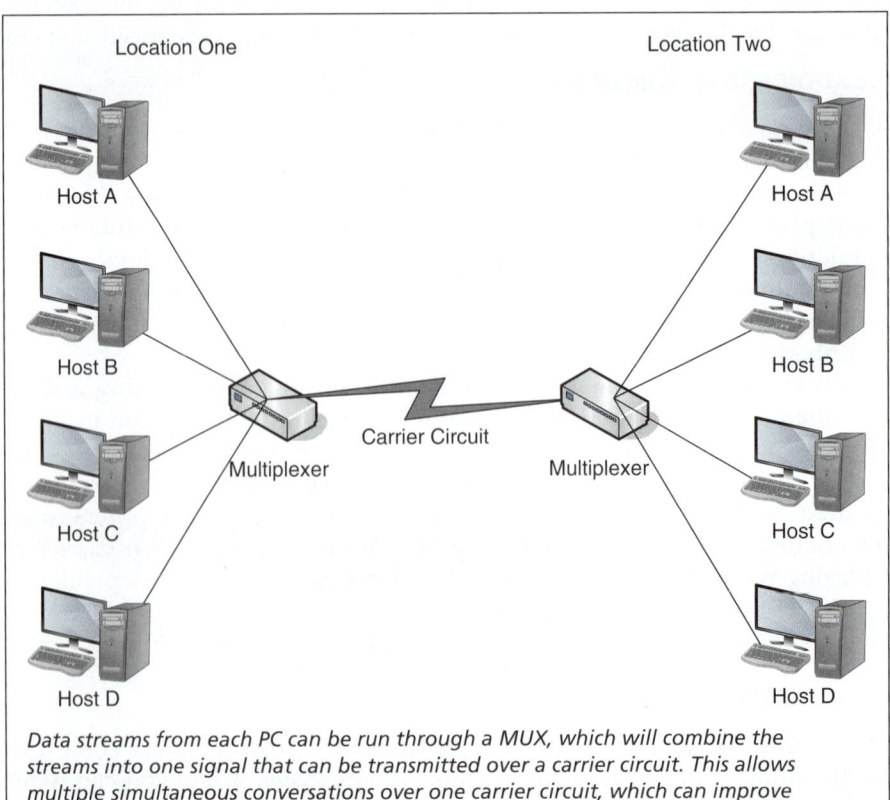

Data streams from each PC can be run through a MUX, which will combine the streams into one signal that can be transmitted over a carrier circuit. This allows multiple simultaneous conversations over one carrier circuit, which can improve overall throughput and efficiency.

Data compression is not as simple as our example, but the example describes the goal of data compression well. The goal is to use fewer bits in a data stream than were in the original message while still allowing the sender to understand the original message.

When transmitting data, the sender and receiver must agree to an encoding scheme that allows the sender to encode a message in some standardized way that the receiver can decode and arrive back at the original message. Compression is useful because it allows carrier circuits (an expensive resource) to carry more data. Many data compression techniques are available; what is important is that the sender and receiver use the same techniques so they can understand each other.

SYMMETRIC VERSUS ASYMMETRIC COMMUNICATIONS

Data circuits have a limit on how much data they can transmit. A DSL circuit may be able to carry 1.5 Mbps. The business systems analyst should ask these questions: Is it necessary that the circuit carries the same amount of bandwidth in each direction? Would it more efficient to divide the communication bandwidth differently?

Think about typical web browser use. Typically, you type in a web address or click a link in a search engine, and then go to a specific web page where you may have graphics, movies, sound, and other large items downloaded to your web browser. The need for bandwidth is not the same for both ends of this transmission: When you enter in a web address you are only sending a few characters (the upstream side or client request), but when you access a web page you are probably downloading a large amount of information (the downstream side or server response). Because these request-response cycles have different data needs, users may be better off if the DSL circuit has different upstream/downstream speeds or is asymmetrical. For that reason, many data circuits offer asymmetrical speeds, where the upstream speed is much slower than the downstream speed. If a DSL circuit is symmetrical (upstream and downstream speeds the same), some amount of bandwidth may be wasted. An example of the request/response bandwidth needs is shown in Figure 1-16.

SPEED MEASUREMENTS AND BANDWIDTH

Telecommunications is measured in bits per seconds. The measurements are multiples of 1,000 bits per second, rather than the 1,024 bits increment used to measure computer memory and disk space. The three common telecommunication speed measurements are kbps (1,000b/sec), Mbps (1,000,000b/sec), and Gbps (1,000,000,000b/sec). Bandwidth can be thought of as how much data can be moved from point A to Point B over a specific period. For example, if a water pipe can carry 5 gallons of water per minute that could be

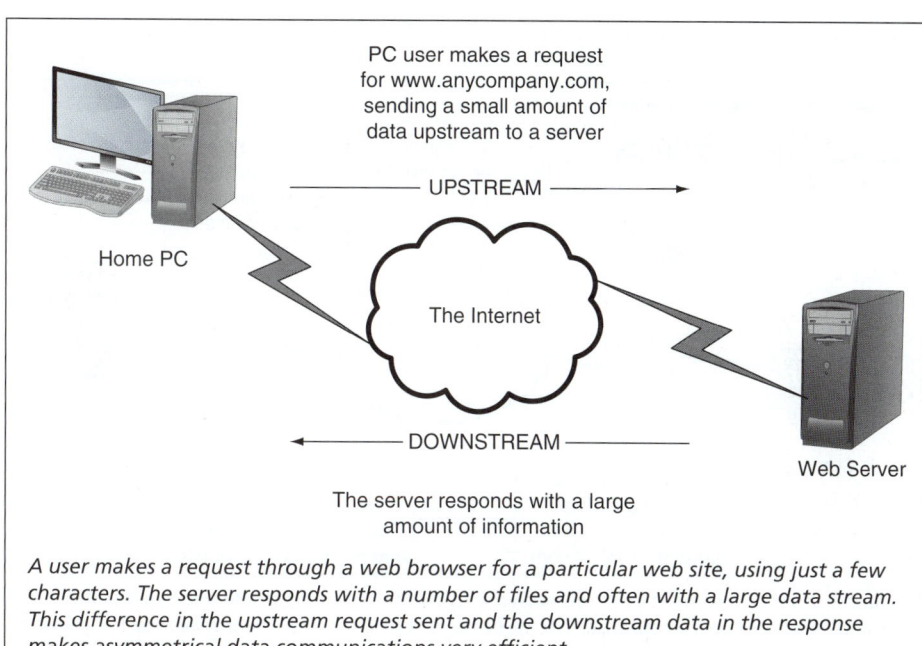

FIGURE 1-16 Response/Request and Asymmetrical Communications

FIGURE 1-17 Broken Water Pipe

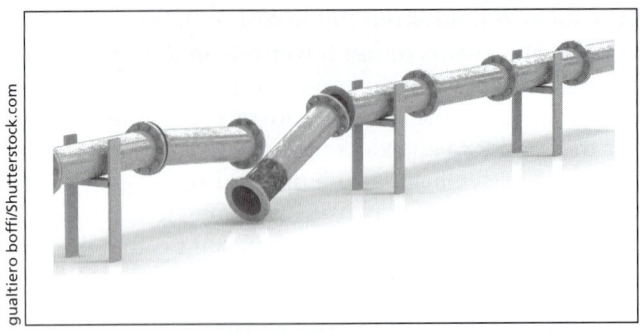

> ### VIGNETTE BOX 1-1
> #### HealthyWay's Need for Bandwidth
> HealthyWay must consider its bandwidth needs so it can properly size its network, select the right technologies, and get the correct carrier circuits to transmit data to its employee Joe Smith. Joe must make sure he has the appropriate hardware to interface with the office.

its bandwidth. If you try to push 6 gallons per minute, the pipe may burst (see Figure 1-17). Although you will not see a data cable burst if you try to push too much data, you will see other problems, such as increased collisions and increased latency. In data communications, if a particular technology can provide 1Gbps and you try to push 1.5Gbps, you may see data discarded, or you may see collisions that prevent any data from getting through. The problems are different between a water pipe and a data cable, but the outcome is the same—you cannot get water or data from Point A to Point B.

When a communication circuit is overloaded, collisions occur. Collisions occur when more demand is placed on a communication circuit or its equipment than it is able to handle. In this case, errors occur and latency is introduced into the circuit. **Latency** refers to a delay in propagated data getting from its source to its destination.

CLIENT-SERVER COMPUTING

The most common form of interaction between two computers today is client-server computing. In **client-server computing**, one computer is the requester of information (the client), and one computer responds with the information (server). This type of request-response cycle governs how most interactions occur across the Internet. Viewing a web page in a browser is a familiar client-server interaction. Client-server computing is described in Figure 1-18.

FIGURE 1-18 Client/Server Request-Response Cycle

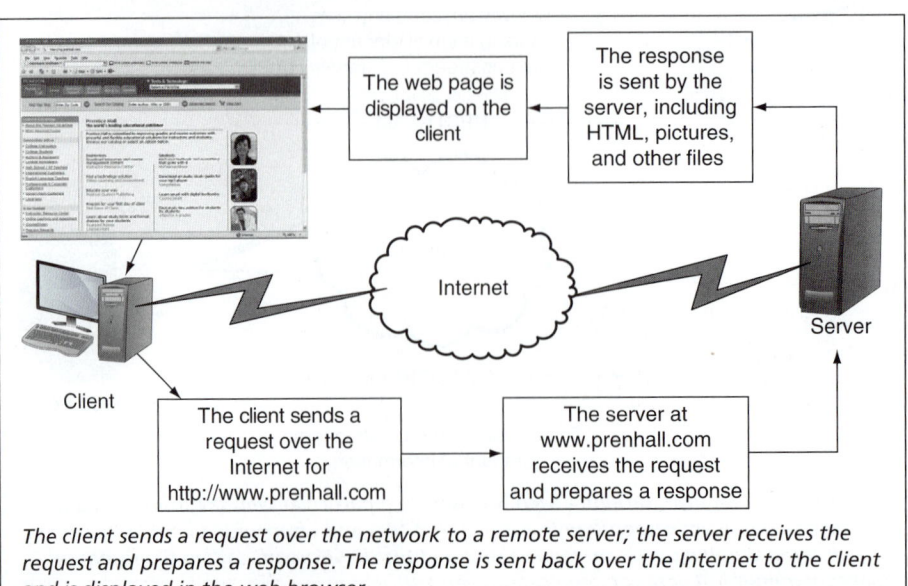

The client sends a request over the network to a remote server; the server receives the request and prepares a response. The response is sent back over the Internet to the client and is displayed in the web browser.

Computer Network and Carrier Concepts

In this section, terms and concepts that relate to computer networks and telecommunication carriers are introduced. These terms describe the concepts of carrier circus, geographic scope, interoperability, and LAN line types.

CARRIER CIRCUITS

When a business wants to communicate from one building to another, and those buildings are not on the same campus (i.e., buildings on land that is physically connected), they need to lease a carrier circuit (e.g., Figure 1-19) from a telecommunications carrier. The carrier has been given special permission from a government agency (e.g., the FTC in the United States) to run cables or use specific wireless frequencies. The carrier is then able to provide leased circuits under a tariff, or regulated pricing structure, to the businesses. Because the carrier has a legal monopoly (i.e., they have exclusive use of wireless frequencies or to cable geographic areas), their pricing structure for long-haul data services is restricted by government regulation. In fact, long-haul data services are the last major vestiges of telecommunications regulation in the United States, while most of the other services provided by carriers, such as voice-grade dial-up and DSL, have been deregulated to provide greater flexibility in pricing and a more competitive market place.

Carrier circuits are available in a number of speeds and types. Some of the most common are digital-grade copper circuits called T-carrier circuits. Businesses commonly lease T-1 circuits that offer 1.544 Mbps, fractional T-1 circuits that offer a portion of full T-1 speed, and T-3 circuits that offer a speed of about 43 Mbps. An example of carrier circuits can be seen in Figure 1-19.

VIGNETTE BOX 1-2

Joe Smith and HealthyWay's Carrier Circuits

Joe Smith from HealthyWay HMO will use a carrier circuit, probably DSL, to connect to the Internet from his home. The office will use a faster circuit, possibly a T1, to connect to the Internet. The Internet will provide the necessary interconnection between Joe and his office so he can access the corporate network from home.

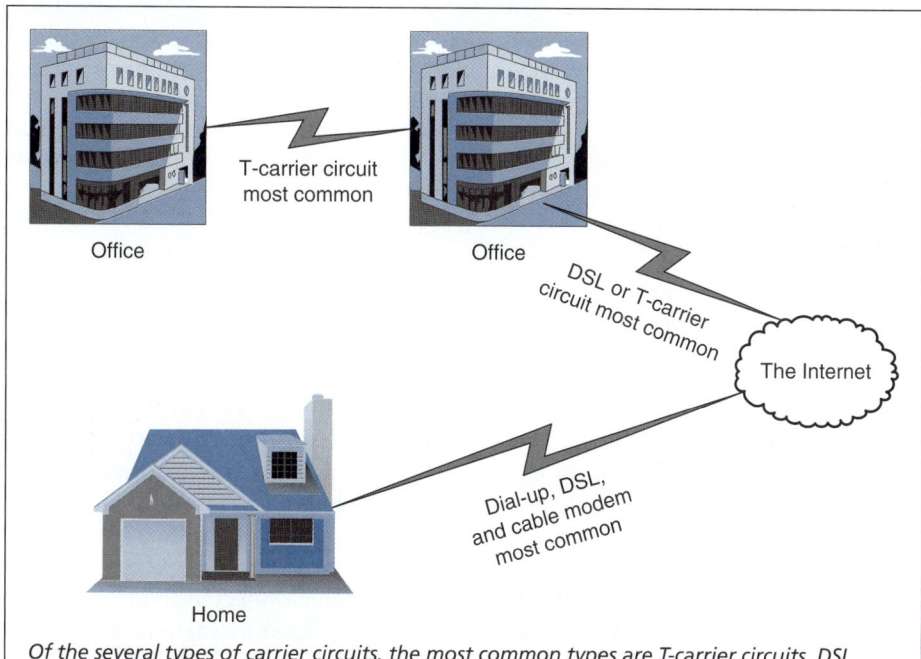

FIGURE 1-19 Common Carrier Circuits Connections

Office — T-carrier circuit most common — Office

Office — DSL or T-carrier circuit most common — The Internet

Home — Dial-up, DSL, and cable modem most common — The Internet

Of the several types of carrier circuits, the most common types are T-carrier circuits, DSL, cable modem, and dial-up. The type of the carrier circuit used is often dependent on available technology, cost, and speed. Between offices, DSL and T-carrier circuits are most common. From the home to the Internet, dial-up, DSL, or cable modems are most common.

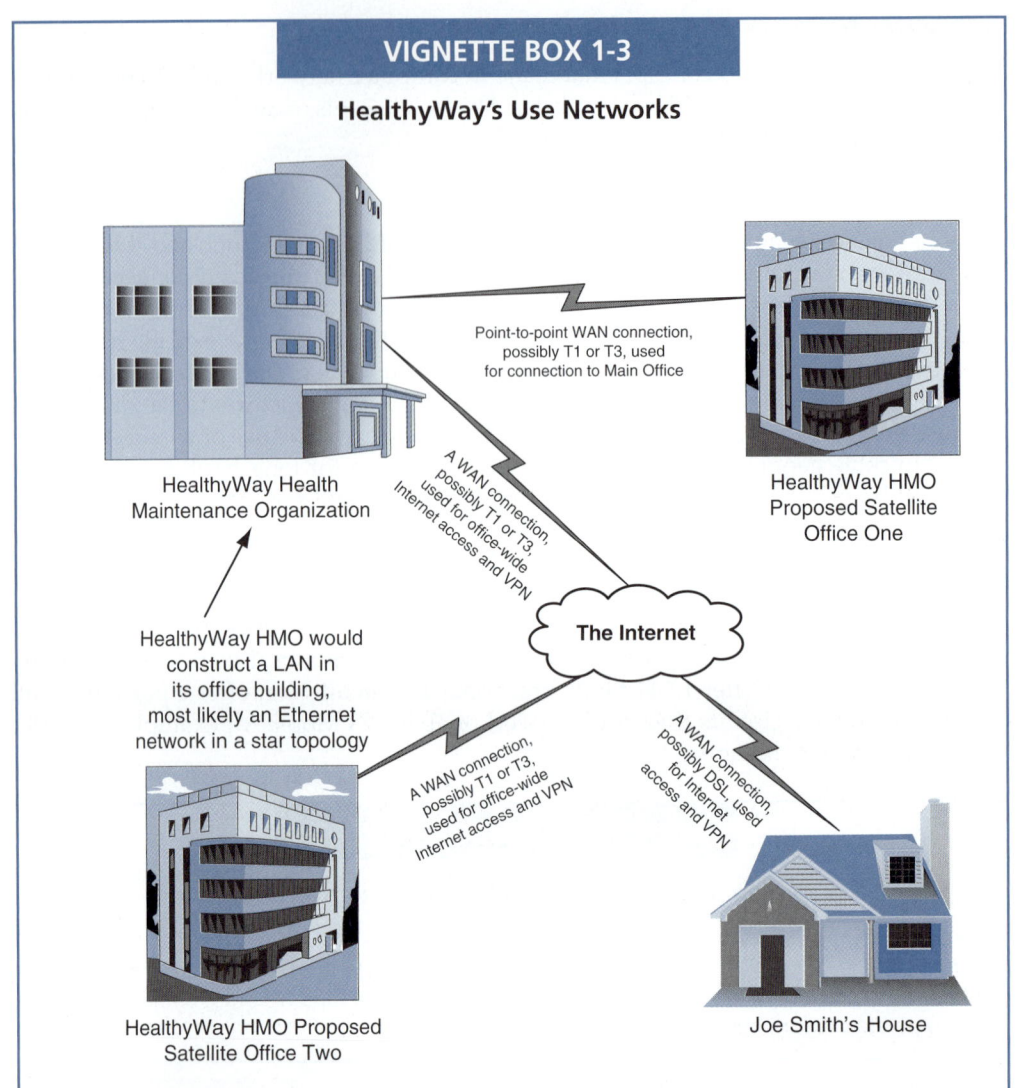

> **VIGNETTE BOX 1-3**
>
> **HealthyWay's Use Networks**
>
> [Diagram showing HealthyWay Health Maintenance Organization connected to HealthyWay HMO Proposed Satellite Office One via "Point-to-point WAN connection, possibly T1 or T3, used for connection to Main Office"; connected to The Internet via "A WAN connection, possibly T1 or T3, used for office-wide Internet access and VPN"; HealthyWay HMO Proposed Satellite Office Two connected to The Internet via "A WAN connection, possibly T1 or T3, used for office-wide Internet access and VPN"; Joe Smith's House connected to The Internet via "A WAN connection, possibly DSL, used for Internet access and VPN". Note: "HealthyWay HMO would construct a LAN in its office building, most likely an Ethernet network in a star topology"]
>
> HealthyWay HMO is leasing space in an office building where it would construct a LAN. The LAN would connect all of its computers, servers, and other devices. HealthyWay would use a WAN connection to connect to the Internet, as would Joe Smith to connect to the Internet as well as establish a VPN connection to the office. HealthyWay HMO could also use other WAN connections if it decided to open a branch office and wanted to connect to it point-to-point (Proposed Satellite Office One) or the other office could connect via a virtual private network (VPN) connection over the Internet (Proposed Satellite Office Two).

GEOGRAPHIC SCOPE

In order to describe the geographic scope of computer networks, we use the following terms:

- **Local Area Network (LAN).** A LAN is a computer network that covers a relatively small geographic area. It could be a single floor in a building, an entire building, or a campus. The area covered by a LAN is physically connected and no carrier circuits (e.g., DSL, T1, T3, etc.) are necessary to interconnect buildings or devices. LANs are normally built using cabling in a building or on a campus, or are wireless.
- **Wide Area Network (WAN).** A WAN is larger in geographic scope and utilizes some type of carrier circuit (e.g., DSL, T1, T3) to interconnect individual computers, buildings, or locations. WAN connections are provided by carriers and are slower and more expensive than LAN connections; therefore, it is important that they be used appropriately. Joe Smith, in our opening vignette, would use a WAN connection to connect back to HealthyWay's office, via a VPN over the Internet.

- **Metropolitan Area Network (MAN).** A MAN is similar to a WAN in that it uses carrier circuits to interconnect networks within a city or metropolitan area. It is optimized for large geographic areas that range from several blocks to an entire city. MANs are owned by individuals or companies, or they are operated as public utilities. MANs use moderate to high-speed data circuits that interconnect locations, but exist within one metropolitan area. MANs are normally shared between multiple companies.

COMMUNICATIONS INTEROPERABILITY

The key to making ICT hardware work is interoperability. Simply put, interoperability means that vendors must build hardware that seamlessly works together. Vendors must follow guidelines, called standards, which dictate how their hardware must operate. The vendor is responsible for the design and manufacture of its equipment, but in order to be interoperable it must operate the same as any other hardware that follows the same standards. Following standards will allow a vendor's hardware to interface with all other similar hardware. For example, an Ethernet 10/100 switch from Vendor A must operate identically to the same type of switch from Vendor B, otherwise interoperability cannot happen. The two switches may have differences in the size of the power supply or vendor-specific options, but in order for switches to interoperate, they must adhere to the Ethernet 10/100 standard. Standards are discussed here in depth, along with how they are created and implemented.

When ICT is built in accordance with existing standards, competition is affected. Standards create a marketplace for hardware and software because multiple vendors offer solutions that do the same or similar functions. These standards force vendors to compete on price, availability of options, and other features. In this competitive market, vendors have an incentive to innovate their products and compete on price. This competitive marketplace is good for consumers because it can motivate vendors to create innovative products as well as cause more attractive pricing.

TRUNK VERSUS DROP LINES

Within a LAN, there are two types of local lines: trunk lines and drop lines. Trunk lines are high-speed cables that interconnect telecommunication devices, and drop lines connect hosts to the network. These elements are described in Figure 1-20.

Introduction to Layering and TCP/IP

When telecommunications is discussed, a layered approach is normally used to describe the technologies. Two major architectures are used in this layered approach: The **Open System Interconnection (OSI)** model promulgated by the International Organization for Standardization (referred to as ISO from the Greek meaning "equal"), and the other a hybrid architecture that combines the lower layers of the OSI model with the **Transmission Control Protocol/Internet Protocol (TCP/IP)** standard promulgated by The Internet Society. This textbook will use that hybrid TCP/IP–OSI architecture.

Regulations, Standards, and TCP/IP

The hybrid TCP/IP–OSI architecture is composed of five layers, which taken together describe telecommunications hardware and software. The ISO portion of the hybrid

---

VIGNETTE BOX 1-4

Why HealthyWay Needs to Understand Standards

As HealthyWay HMO decides on what to purchase for its network, it needs to select devices and vendors that have hardware and software that work together, or interoperate. This means that someone must understand the technology and standards for devices that interoperate as well as understanding the network.

FIGURE 1-20 Carrier Circuits, Trunk Lines, and Drop Lines

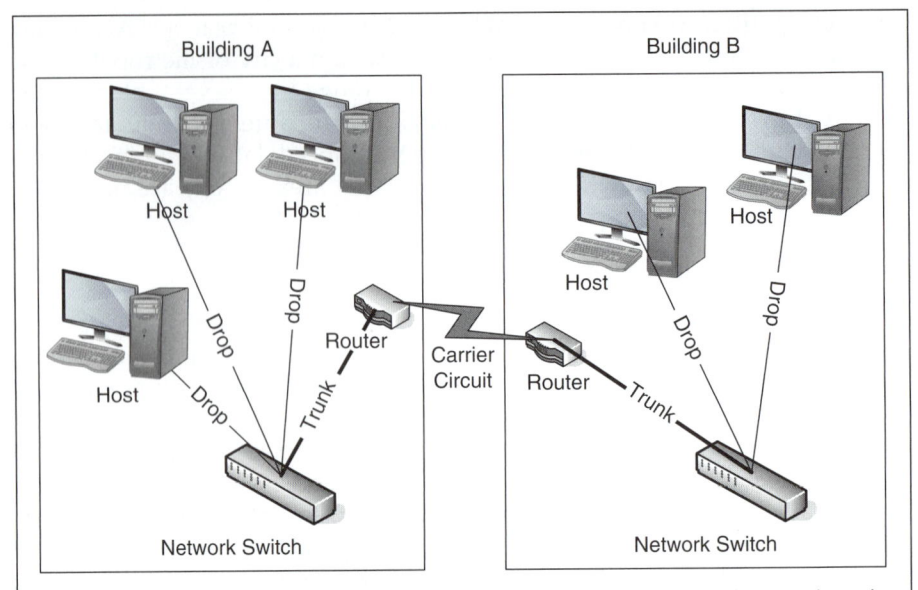

This diagram has two buildings (A and B). Each building contains a small network, and the networks are interconnected through a carrier circuit. Also within the building, the switch and the router are connected with a high-speed trunk line, and the hosts are connected with drop lines.

architecture involves layers one and two, and the TCP/IP standards are concerned with layers three through five (see Figure 1-21). This layered architecture is discussed in depth later in this chapter, but is introduced here so the student has a framework in which to place all the major organizations that create standards.

All of us are subject to regulations and standards, which includes vendors, companies, and individuals. For example, regulations promulgated by the U.S. Federal Communication Commission (FCC) mandate that electronic equipment may not emanate more than a specified level of radio interference. (Computers, and in fact all electronic equipment, produce radio interference.) These guidelines keep hardware from interfering with each other, as well from interfering with other equipment such as FM radio and TV. The FCC also regulates the frequency spectrum (radio waves) that are used for wireless communications, including mobile telephones, TV, and ICT. This will be discussed in greater detail later in this chapter.

Vendors must implement standards so their hardware can interoperate. Vendor compliance with standards is usually voluntary, but if vendors want their equipment to interoperate with other vendors' hardware and be able to sell in the ICT marketplace, they will follow the standards. Consideration of standards also extends to an organization purchasing ICT. If an organization wants a wide audience to have access to its ICT (e.g., think of creating a web site that does not appear on the Internet

FIGURE 1-21 TCP/IP–OSI Hybrid Architecture

	Hybrid Architecture		Protocol Organizations		
Software Standards	Layer 5	Application Layer	World Wide Web Consortium	The Internet Society and its committees: the IETF, IESG, and the IAB	ITU-T and Study Groups
	Layer 4	Transport Layer			
	Layer 3	Internet Layer	MFA Forum		
Hardware Standards	Layer 2	Data Link Layer	ISO		
	Layer 1	Physical		IEEE-SA	

> **VIGNETTE BOX 1-5**
>
> **HealthyWay ICT Components**
>
> As HealthyWay selects its ICT components, it is important to consider hardware and software that is standards based. Attention to this consideration will allow HealthyWay to buy hardware at competitive prices, interoperate with other networks, and maximize the investment into technology.

because it was built with nonstandard hardware, software, or protocols), it should adopt standards-based technology. In addition to enhanced usage, standards-based hardware is easier to maintain and operate due to the availability of technical staff that understands the standards. For a host of reasons, it makes sense to know about and adopt standards.

Global ICT standards are created by six main organizations: the IEEE, W3C, Internet Society (ISOC) and its committees, International Organization for Standardization (ISO), ITU-T, and the MFA Forum. Each of these is described here.

- The Institute of Electrical and Electronics Engineers (IEEE.org, 2011) is an international nonprofit professional organization dedicated to the advancement of technology standards related to electricity. IEEE has a number of purposes, including education, publishing journals, and standards setting. Standard setting is performed through the IEEE Standards Association (IEEE-SA). Networking and telecommunications standards are limited to hardware. A number of notable IEEE-SA standards have been adopted by organizations such as the International Organization for Standardization. This adoption has fueled the use of IEEE standards by vendors.
- "The World Wide Web Consortium develops interoperable technologies (specifications, guidelines, software, and tools) to lead the web to its full potential. W3C is a forum for information, commerce, communication, and collective understanding" (W3C, 2010). The W3C develops such standards as Cascading Style Sheets, Extensible Markup Language (XML), and Hypertext Markup Language (HTML). Many of these standards are implemented in ICT hardware and software and in part are what allow the World Wide Web to interoperate.
- The Internet Society (ISOC) is "a professional membership society founded in 1992 with more than 100 organizations and over 20,000 individual members in over 180 countries. ISOC provides leadership in addressing issues that confront the future of the Internet, and is the organizational home for the groups responsible for Internet infrastructure standards, including the Internet Engineering Task Force (IETF) and the Internet Architecture Board (IAB)" (Bahlmann, n.d.; cf Internet Society, 2011). The IAB is both a committee of the IETF and an advisory body of ISOC. The IAB is responsible for the architectural oversight of the IETF activities and the Internet Standards Process (IAB, 2011). Membership in the IETF, which is open to anyone, includes network designers, operators, vendors, and researchers concerned with the evolution and the smooth operation of the Internet and its architecture. Members of the IETF are concerned with the technical correctness of the standards the IETF promulgates, rather than the preferences of any vendor. The IETF areas of involvement include e-mail, multimedia, Voice Over IP (VoIP), IP v4/v6, as well as a number of routing and security protocols.
- The International Organization for Standardization (ISO, 2011) is a network of the national standards institutes of 155 countries, on the basis of one member per country, with a Central Secretariat in Geneva, Switzerland, that coordinates the system. It is widely known as ISO, after the Greek term that means "equal." ISO is a nongovernmental organization and occupies a position between the public and private sectors, because, on the one hand, many of its member

institutes are part of the governmental structure of their countries or are mandated by their government. On the other hand, other members have their roots in the private sector, having been set up by national partnerships of industry associations. Therefore, ISO is able to act as a bridging organization in which a consensus can be reached. The American National Standards Institute (ANSI) is the U.S. member of ISO. ISO develops a number of standards—from those that define screw threads to petroleum products—created through a variety of technical committees. This textbook is only interested in JCT1, the ISO committee that governs information technology. JCT1 is responsible for layer 1 and 2 standards of the hybrid TCP/IP–OSI architecture (layers are discusses later in this chapter).

- The Telecommunication Standardization Sector (ITU-T) was established in 1993 and is a member of the International Telecommunications Union, which was formed by the United Nations in 1865. The "ITU-T Recommendations (standards) form the foundations of the information and communications technologies of today. Anytime you make a simple telephone call, send a text message to a mobile phone (i.e., short message service (SMS)), or receive streaming video to your mobile phone or computer an ITU-T recommendation will have played a fundamental role. Developed in study groups (SGs) made up of experts from the private and public sectors, ITU-T recommendations help drive the global information society, allowing social and economic development worldwide" (Corporate QA, n.d.).
- The ATM Forum was originally founded in 1991 as an industry consortium to stabilize the implementation of Asynchronous Transfer Model (ATM). In 2004, the ATM Forum joined with the *Multiprotocol Label Switching (MPLS) and Frame Relay Alliance* to form the MFA Forum. "The MFA Forum is an international, industry-wide, nonprofit association of telecommunications, networking, and other companies focused on advancing the deployment of multi-vendor, multi-service packet-based networks, associated applications, and interworking solutions" (Bahlmann, n.d.). The MFA Forum has two committees: the Technical Committee and the Marketing Committee. Together the committees promulgate standards for MPLS, Frame Relay, ATM, and Internet and vendor interoperability.

Together these six agencies promulgate the overwhelming majority of ICT standards. Vendors, government agencies, consumers, and other interested parties are members of these various groups. These standards govern everything from media (e.g., UTP cable, fiber optic, etc.) construction to transmission methods and communication protocols. Even though it is not necessary for the business systems strategist to understand precisely which standards and protocols come from which agency, it is important to have an understanding of standards and their usage.

PROTOCOLS

The various standards organizations control and promulgate protocols. An ICT protocol is a standard set of rules for representing data, signaling, error detection, data formatting, and representation. Protocols are designed by standards agencies so engineers, designers, and developers can know and implement them. Telecommunications hardware today generally implements two protocol architectures: TCP/IP and OSI (the hybrid architecture discussed previously). TCP/IP is promulgated by the IETF, while OSI is promulgated by ISO. In practice, the hybrid five-layer protocol architecture is used to implement and describe ICT hardware, and it will be used as the reference architecture model throughout this textbook.

LAYERS AND HARDWARE

Computers and telecommunications equipment implement the five layers of the hybrid TCP/IP–OSI model in hardware and software. Various standards and protocols are implemented at each layer; the consistent implementation by vendors of those

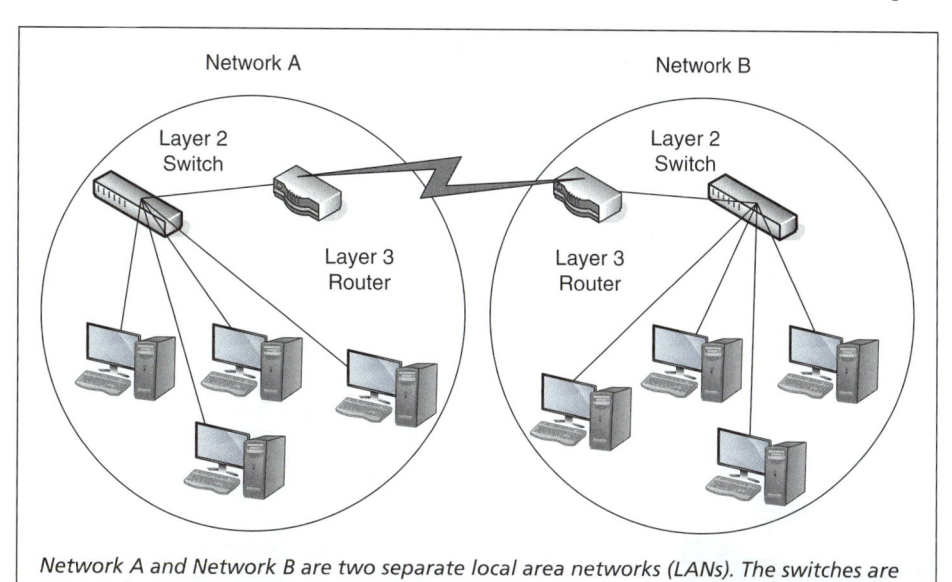

FIGURE 1-22 Layer 2 and Layer 3 Devices

Network A and Network B are two separate local area networks (LANs). The switches are Layer 2 devices and control the network traffic within the network (LAN). The routers are Layer 3 devices, which are capable of moving traffic between two local area networks. Together the two networks create an internet.

standards insures interoperability. Devices can be classified according to two dimensions: (1) the layer at which they operate, and (2) whether they communicate within a local network or operate between multiple local area networks. When you have two local area networks (LAN) that are interconnected by telecommunication devices so they can communicate with each other, you have an internet. The word *internet* means a "network of networks." The world's largest internet is the Internet (notice the capital "I" when referring to the global internet).

A local area network (LAN) is a self-contained set of computers that communicate with each other. Figure 1-22 shows how these interoperate. The LAN includes all hardware up to the router. The router allows communication outside of the LAN to another network. When you have one or more LANs interconnected via routers, you have an internet. The following equipment, summarized in Figure 1-23, is commonly found in a LAN:

- Hosts. These Layer 5 devices, normally configured as either servers and/or clients, are the devices used to perform work by people that access the network.
- Routers. These Layer 3 devices allow communication between LANS.
- Switches. These Layer 2 devices allow communication within a LAN.
- Hubs. These Layer 1 devices allow communication within a LAN.

FIGURE 1-23 Layers and Associated Hardware

TCP/IP–OSI Hybrid Model			Common Communication Devices	
Layer	Layer Name	Function of Layer	Within Networks (LANs)	Between Networks (Intranets)
5	Application	Host Program Interface		Host
4	Transport	Reliability and End-to-End Communication		
3	Internet	Internetwork Communication		Router
2	Data Link	Intranetwork Communication	Switch	
1	Physical	Signal Propagation	Hub	

This table summarizes the equipment that allows between- and within-network communication.

WIRED MEDIA AND NETWORK TYPOLOGIES

Wired Media

Media are used to interconnect devices in all wired typologies. Media are the cables over which data are propagated. Several common types of media are summarized in Table 1-2. Each of these types has particular characteristics, but as stated earlier, the selection of media type is driven by the technology selected based on ICT installation, speed, distance, and cost.

TABLE 1-2 Common Media

	Description	Common Types
Copper Cable	Copper twisted-pair wire is where two conductors are twisted together to cancel out electromagnetic interference. Four pair of twisted wires are bundled together and wrapped in plastic.	Unshielded twisted-pair (UTP) in a number of categories Shielded twisted-pair (STP)
Fiber Optic (FO)	A glass or plastic fiber designed to guide light. In data communications, the light source is normally a light-emitting diode (LED) or a laser, with LEDs being cheaper but not able to transmit as far as lasers (i.e., LED light source is 550 meters whereas laser is up to 10 km). Fiber optic cable has a thin glass or plastic core, surrounded by light-reflecting material known as the cladding. Cladding keeps the light in the core. The cladding is then surrounded by buffer material and a plastic jacket. The outer layers of cladding, buffer, and plastic jacket add strength to the fiber but do not contribute to the optical properties of the cable.	Multimode fiber optic cable is cheaper but only able to carry a signal a short distance. Single-mode fiber optic cable is thinner, more fragile, and more expensive to handle. Although the equipment that it uses and the cable are more expensive, it allows for data transmission over greater distances.
Coax Cable	This is an older cable used in a bus typology. The cable has a center core, insulator, metallic shield, and a plastic jacket. The insulator (or dielectric insulator, which means the same thing) separates the electrical signals of the core from those of the shield.	This media is available in a number of types and is rated as RG-XXX. XXX stands for a number that indicates the type of cable. For example, RG-8/u is known as Thicknet or Thick Ethernet, while RG-58/u is known as Thinnet or Thin Ethernet.

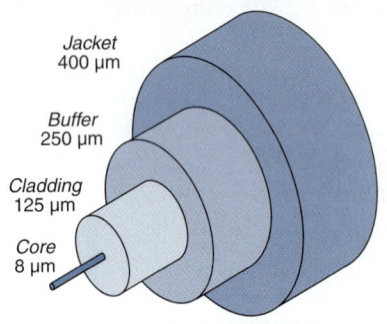

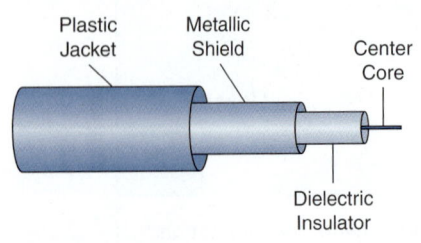

Chapter 1 • ICT Introductory Concepts

TABLE 1-3	Common Typologies
Typology	**Description**
Point-to-Point	A connection that allows two hosts or devices to communicate through a circuit that interconnects the devices
Bus	A network where all hosts are attached to one common bus (media) that allows communication among the hosts
Star	The most common type of LAN typology in which hosts are interconnected through a series of hubs and switches
Ring	A circuit that is fashioned in a ring to allow communication among devices that hang from the ring
Mesh	A series of interconnecting routers that creates multiple pathways between points on a network

Typologies

Networks are built in structured ways, which is to say that they are not built haphazardly. Instead, they are cabled/installed the way they are for specific reasons. Several important things need to be considered when determining how to build a network, including geographic scope, network typology, when to use wired and wireless technologies, and the various types of media you can use to interconnect network devices. Each of these factors is discussed in this section

When a network is created, a typology (see Table 1-3) needs to be selected. This selection is governed by the desired speed, distance, available technology, and financial resources. The common wired typologies are discussed here.

POINT-TO-POINT

Point-to-point is a connection that allows two hosts or devices to communicate through a circuit that interconnects the devices. A dial-up modem connection is a point-to-point typology. A point-to-point connection is shown in Figure 1-24.

BUS

The original Ethernet standard was based on the **bus typology.** It includes the notion that all hosts attach to one common bus (media) that allows communication among the hosts. The hosts connect to the bus using drop cables. This typology (described in Figure 1-25) has largely been replaced for LANs by the star typology.

STAR

The most common type of LAN implemented today is the **star typology.** Hosts are connected to switches through a drop cable and switches are interconnected through a series of trunk lines, most often implemented as an Ethernet network. Originally, when Ethernet was implemented in a star typology, hubs were used instead of switches to reduce costs. The star network is composed of core and workgroup switches. The core is the place that all other switches interconnect, and the workgroup is where workstations connect to the network, as shown in Figure 1-26.

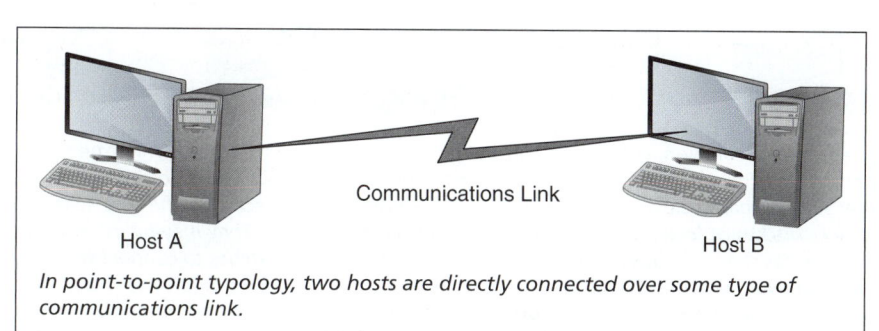

FIGURE 1-24 Point-to-Point Typology

In point-to-point typology, two hosts are directly connected over some type of communications link.

Host A — Communications Link — Host B

26 Unit 1 • ICT Infrastructure Components: A Technical Overview

FIGURE 1-25   Bus Typology

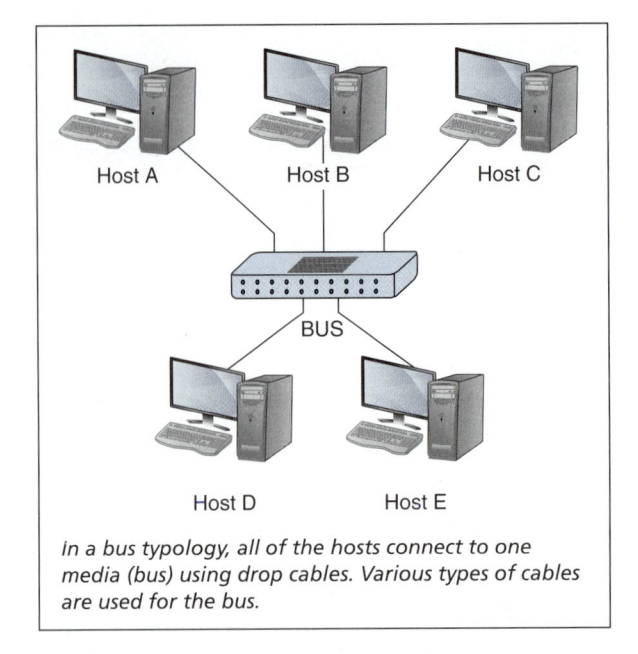

In a bus typology, all of the hosts connect to one media (bus) using drop cables. Various types of cables are used for the bus.

FIGURE 1-26   Star Topology

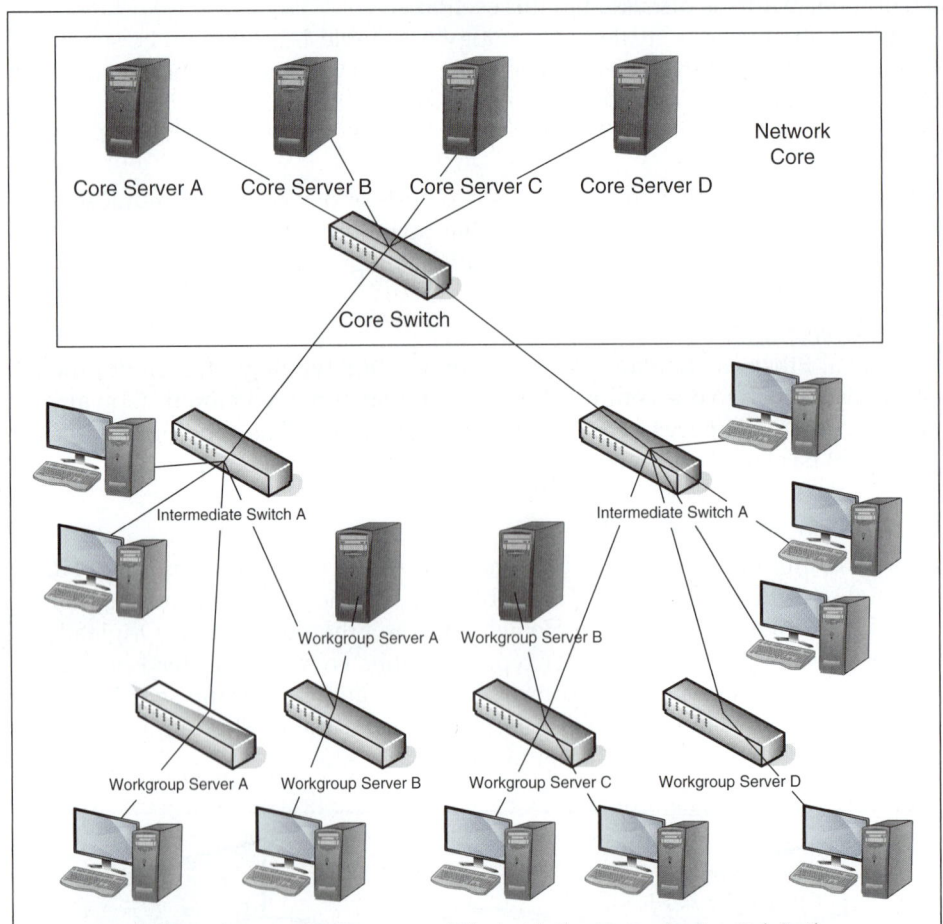

In a star configuration, you have a core switch that is the most robust switch in the network, mainly because all of the network traffic has the possibility of going through that switch; shared servers and other devices are normally connected to the core switch. Other switches of lesser power/speed are connected to the core. They may be intermediate switches (as shown in this diagram), which allow workgroup switches to connect to them, or workgroup switches that connect directly to the core. The workgroup servers and PCs connect to the intermediate and workgroup switches. The number of intermediate and workgroup switches depends on the size and complexity of the network.

FIGURE 1-27 Ring Typology

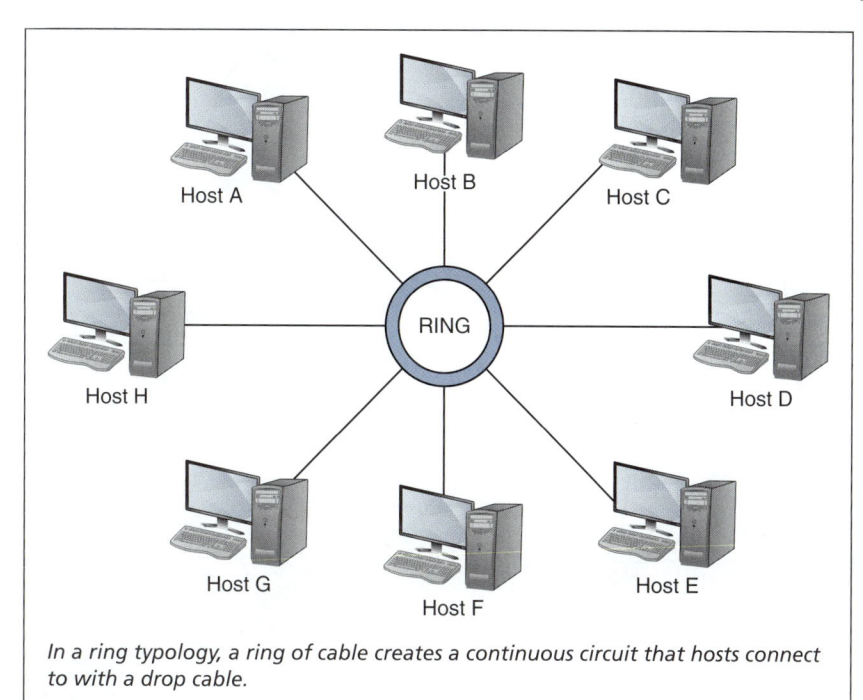

In a ring typology, a ring of cable creates a continuous circuit that hosts connect to with a drop cable.

RING

In a **ring typology,** a circuit is fashioned in a ring and devices hang off that ring, which allows communication among the devices (Figure 1-27). An older technology marketed by IBM was Token Ring, but this has largely fallen into disuse. The most common ring typology today is Sonet/SDH.

MESH

A **mesh typology** consists of a number of devices interconnected with trunk lines or point-to-point carrier circuits (see Figure 1-28). The mesh creates redundancy in the network with multiple paths between hosts in the mesh. Routers are network devices that receive network traffic in a mesh typology and decide which path is best to send the information. The router makes these decisions using many factors including cost, speed, and availability of bandwidth. The Internet is the world's largest mesh network.

SWITCHING HIERARCHIES

There are many similarities between the telephone system over which we make voice calls and data networks. Both propagate signals, and both are responsible for end-to-end communication of a signal. In the case of the telephone system, analog signals (sound) are transmitted from one telephone to another; in the case of data networks, digital data are transmitted from one host to another. Local area data networks have a number of typologies, the most common of which is the star typology. Multiple local area data networks that are interconnected into a wide area network are usually a routed typology. The telephone network is a star typology, but it is a circuit-switched network, whereas data networks are packet-switched networks.

In circuit switching, an electrical circuit is created each time data are sent (either analog or digital). In packet switching, data are broken up into packets and sent over the network, one packet at a time. Those packets can be routed across a mesh typology or switched across a bus, ring, or star typology.

Phone System and Circuit Switching

The worldwide phone system is based on circuit switching. Originally, the phone system was totally circuit switched; however, today portions are digital and use packet switching. Today, the local loop portion of the phone system from the customer premises to the

FIGURE 1-28 Mesh (Routed) Typology

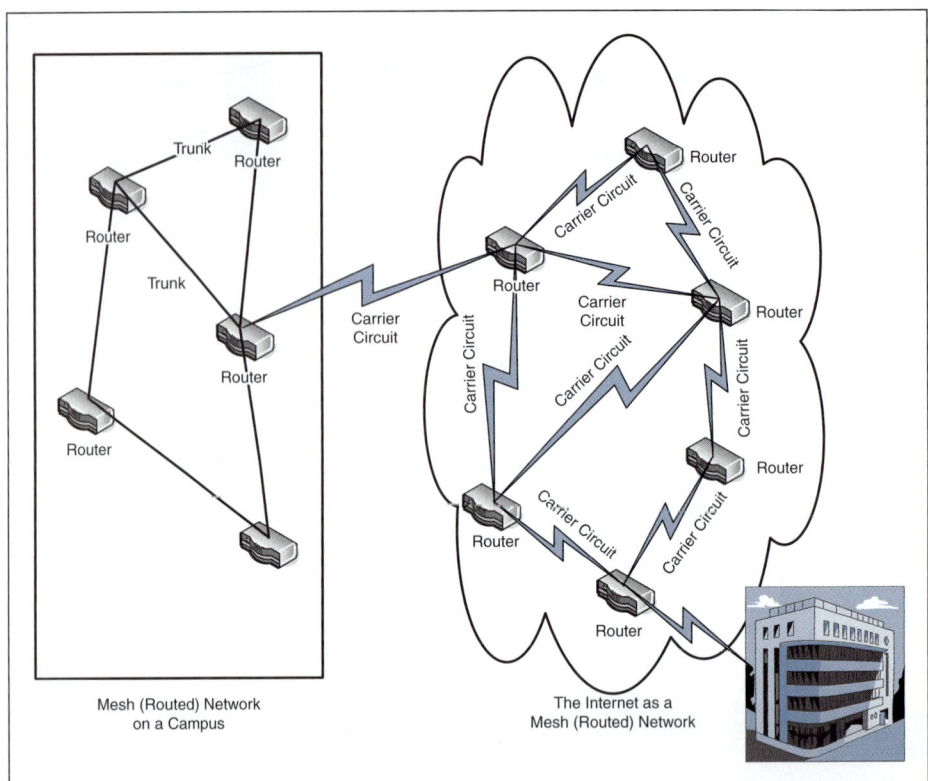

In the mesh typology, routers are used to direct network traffic through the network. It is possible to have a routed network in your office building, between buildings, or in the most ubiquitous network in the world, the Internet. Mesh networks are often shown as a "cloud" in diagrams because you have no idea which path the data take through the network, but rather the only thing you can be sure of is the source and destination host.

local switch (called the central office) is still voice-grade copper and is used for analog signaling. The circuits between switches, however, are digital. In a circuit-switching system, every time data are to be transmitted, a circuit or channel is created to propagate the signal. This circuit is dedicated to that transmission, and the bandwidth taken up by that circuit cannot be used by any other device. The process of dialing a phone number gives the switches in the worldwide phone network instructions to create the electronic circuit. Placing a phone call involves the following steps:

- The caller dials a phone number.
- The first switch determines the call routing (which switches it must contact to complete the call).
- The switches set up an electronic circuit to propagate the call (called provisioning).
- Once the circuit is provisioned, the caller can begin to talk.
- The phone on each end encodes/decodes voice (sound as an analog signal) to an electrical signal.

The copper from the customer premises to the local switch is called the local loop, and the carrier circuits that interconnect switches are called trunk lines (shown in Figure 1-29).

Data Networks and Packet Switching

Data networks propagate signals between two devices, but in the case of a data network the devices are called hosts (Figure 1-30). A host is any computer capable of propagating data. In packet switching, all data are digital, but large messages are broken into smaller messages called packets. The messages are disassembled at the sending host and reassembled at the receiving host. Technically speaking, Layer 5 devices are the only hosts that reassemble packets into complete message. The most common Layer 5 device is a computer.

Chapter 1 • ICT Introductory Concepts 29

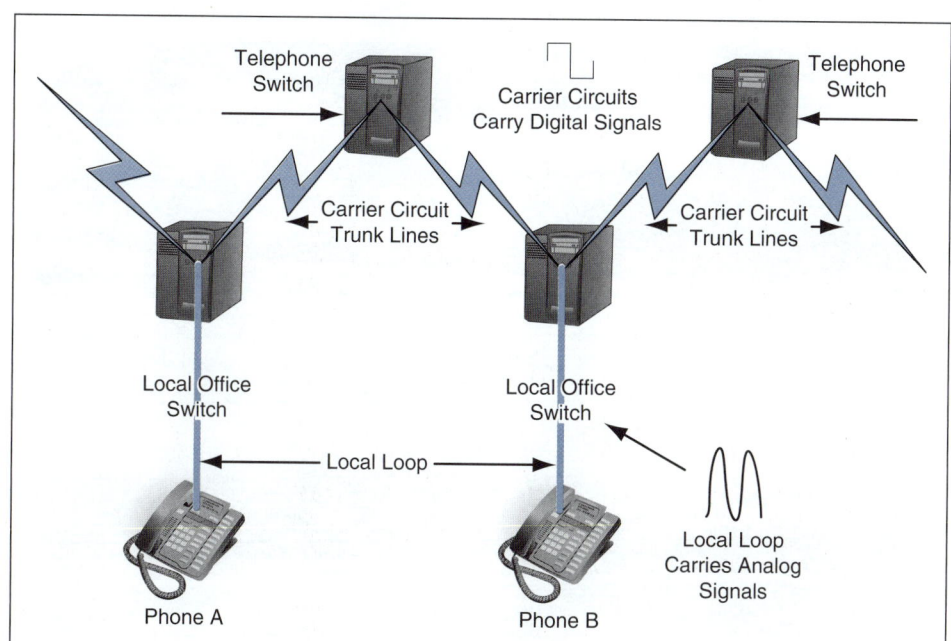

FIGURE 1-29 Phone-Switching Hierarchy

This diagram shows how the telephone network is configured. The local loop is copper from the phone at the customer premises to the local office. The local switching office connects to a number of interconnecting switches through carrier lines. Local loops carry analog data, while the carrier circuits are digital. Dialing a phone number instructs the switches to create a dedicated circuit between the two phones. This process is inefficient because the bandwidth taken by the circuit cannot be used by other calls.

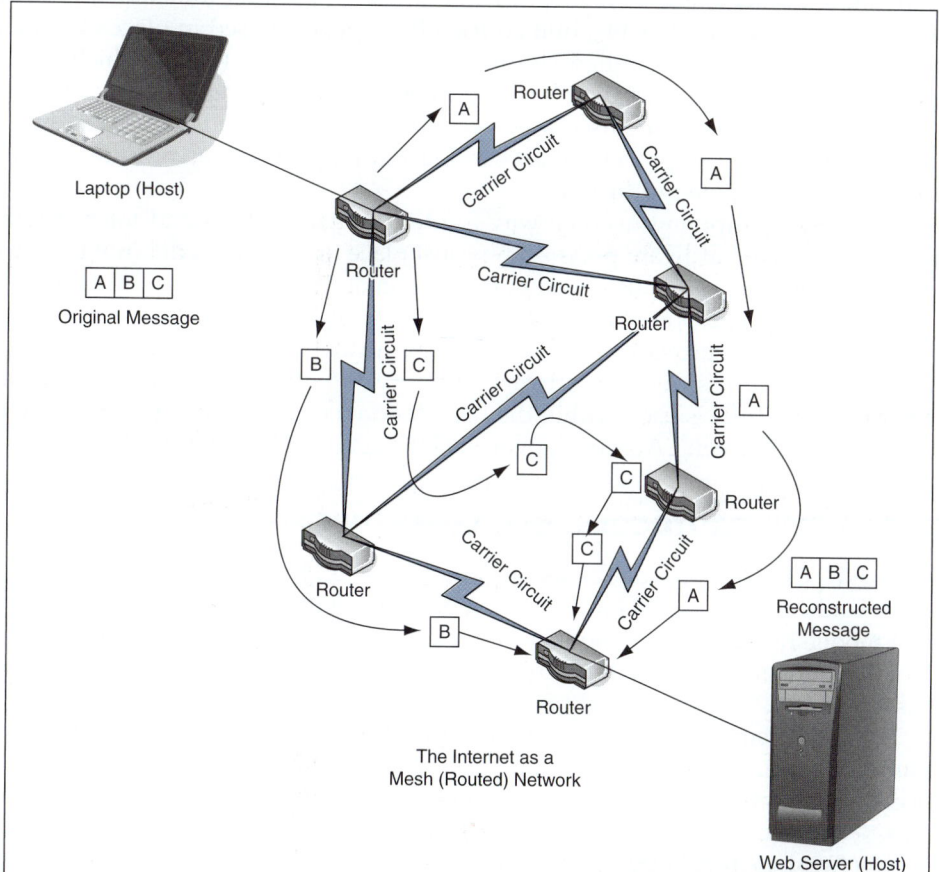

FIGURE 1-30 Packet Switching

In packet switching, the message a host wants to deliver is broken up into packets, which are propagated across the network. No dedicated bandwidth is occupied by any one message; rather, the bandwidth is shared by all hosts communicating on a network. In this routed network, packets may even follow different paths between the source and destination host.

FIGURE 1-31 Switch Hardware Ports

The area shown in the box contains the hardware ports.

Addressing

Humans generally cannot remember long strings of numbers; computers operate by manipulating numbers and remember them quite well. In order to make information (e.g., web pages) easily available, human-friendly names are used in place of numeric addresses. These names are called Uniform Resource Locaters (URL), which include names such as www.microsoft.com or www.prenhall.com, as well as hosts and other names. When these names are used they need to be converted into numeric addresses, called IP addresses. The process of converting human-friendly names into numeric addresses is called **name resolution.**

Computer equipment needs a way to identify itself. Hosts and telecommunication devices have hardware ports—a physical place to plug in media (not to be confused with transport ports (discussed in the section on TCP/IP below). An example of an Ethernet switch and ports can be seen in Figure 1-31. Two addresses are used: hardware addresses and software addresses. The hardware address is the Media Access Control (MAC) address, and the software address is the Internet Protocol (IP) address. The hardware address is used within the LAN for data transmission, and the software address is used between LANs (e.g., over the Internet) for routing of packets.

TCP/IP LAYERS, PROTOCOLS, AND COMMUNICATION

The hybrid TCP/IP–OSI model was introduced earlier. In this section, that model is revisited and expanded to include common protocols that are implemented within the hybrid model. Remember, the model is broken into five layers. At each layer a number of protocols are implemented. Protocols communicate with the layers above and below to pass messages.

TPC/IP is a suite of protocols that operates at Layer 3 through Layer 5 of the hybrid architecture. Within TCP/IP we see a number of standards that allow for interoperability of devices that follow the TCP/IP standard. The most common of these are listed in Figure 1-32.

Layer 5 (Application Layer)

Arguably, when you are browsing the web, the most common protocols at the **application layer** (Layer 5) are the hypertext transfer protocols, HTTP and HTTPS. HTTP and HTTPS are protocols that govern the syntax of web browser messages.

Hybrid Architecture			Common Protocols that Operate at this Layer
TCP/IP Software Standards	Layer 5	Application Layer	HTTP, HTTPS, DHCP, FTP, POP3, SMTP, SNMP, SSH, TELNET, SSL
	Layer 4	Transport Layer	ICMP, UDP, TCP
	Layer 3	Internet Layer	IP, IPSec, ARP, RARP
OSI Hardware Standards	Layer 2	Data Link Layer	ETHERNET, PPP, POPOE, ISDN, MODEMS' Sonet/SDH
	Layer 1	Physical	

FIGURE 1-32 Common Protocols

The difference is that one is an unsecure (HTTP) and the other is a secure (HTTPS) protocol. These protocols are request/response protocols between clients and servers. In other words, the client computer will make an HTTP request, and the server that stores the required information will respond. Several intermediaries are likely between a client and a server and do the message routing across the Internet. The other common protocols are described in Table 1-4.

Layer 4 (Transport Layer)

The most common protocols at the **transport layer** are Transmission Control Protocol (TCP), User Datagram Protocol (UDP), and Internet Control Message Protocol (ICMP). TCP is a reliable protocol in that it does error checking and error correction and is responsible for the end-to-end communications across the Internet. End-to-end communications refers to communications between two hosts. UDP does a similar job to TCP, but UDP is unreliable. Reliable protocols perform error checking and error correction, while unreliable protocols do error checking but not error correction. TCP is suitable for web browsing and e-mail, whereas UDP is often used for voice and video communications in which some lost information may be acceptable. UDP has less overhead than TCP, placing less of a demand on the network, which is why UDP is used for voice and video. However, if network congestion occurs, UDP drops information. TCP, on the other hand, will have the information retransmitted, making it reliable. It is a trade-off between using UDP with its lower network load, and TCP that has a much higher network load that may cause congestion problems but guarantees delivery. ICMP is not used to transmit data, but rather is chiefly used by networked computers to send error messages (e.g., a server is unavailable).

TABLE 1-4 Other Layer 5 Common Protocols

Protocol	Purpose
Dynamic Host Control Protocol (DHCP)	Assigns IP address and other identifiers to hosts (computers on a network)
Domain Name System (DNS)	Converts host names to IP addresses, for example, www.microsoft.com to 207.46.19.180
File Transfer Protocol (FTP)	Files transfer between hosts
Internet Message Access Protocol (IMAP)	Allows a local client to access e-mail on a remote server
Post Office Protocol (POP)	Allows a local client to access e-mail on a remote server
Simple Mail Transfer Protocol (SMTP)	Allows a local client to send e-mail to a remote server
Secure Shell (SSH)	Provides an encrypted connection to a remote computer/device that typically allows login and commands to be executed on the remote computer
Telnet (Telnet)	Provides a connection to a remote computer/device that typically allows login and commands to be executed on the remote computer
Transport Layer Security (TSL) and its predecessor, Secure Sockets Layer (SSL)	Cryptographic protocols that provide secure communications for Internet communications such as web browsing and e-mail

Layer 3 (Internet Layer)

At Layer 3, the **Internet layer,** three common protocols are used: Internet Protocol (IP), IP Security (IPSEC), and **Address Resolution Protocol (ARP).** IP is a packet-switched protocol that is used for communicating between networks. IP provides communication among computers on the Internet using the global network of IP addresses provided by the IETF. IPSEC is a suite of protocols for securing IP communications at Layer 3; other security protocols, such as TSL/SSL, operate at Layer 5, but since IPSEC operates at Layer 3 it can protect protocols above it. However, IPSEC's disadvantage is that it requires configuration and maintenance and is thus more expensive to support. ARP is responsible for converting Layer 3 addresses (e.g., an IP address) to a hardware address (e.g., an Ethernet MAC address).

Layer 2 (Data Link Layer)

The most common Layer 2 protocols are Ethernet, 802.11/Wi-Fi, and Asynchronous Transfer Mode (ATM). Ethernet is a family of connectionless technologies that is standardized as IEEE 802.3 and is the most widespread LAN technology in use today. 802.11 is a set of standards for wireless local area network (WLAN) communications. ATM is a WAN fixed-cell-length, packet-switched technology that uses logical connections. Other **data link layer** protocols are listed in Table 1-5.

Layer 1 (Physical Layer)

Standards at the physical layer govern how data are encoded from internal computer format to signals that can be transmitted. Layer 1 standards include signaling (i.e., how bits are represented), media, and connectors. Media are the vehicles over which signals travel, which are interconnected through network components. (Common media types are presented in Table 1-2 and are arranged in typologies in Table 1-3.) Media are terminated with connectors.

TABLE 1-5 Other Layer 2 Common Protocols

Protocol	Purpose
Worldwide Interoperability for Microwave Access (WiMAX)	Provides wireless data over long distances, including point-to-point access as well as full mobile cellular, with an upper limit on upload/download at 70 Mbps
Token Ring	Older ring typology protocol strongly marketed by IBM; not generally sold or installed today
Fiber Distributed Data Interface (FDDI)	A dual ring topology for LANs that can extend in range up to 200 kilometers (124 miles), which has been made both redundant and expensive by fast Ethernet and gigabit Ethernet
Frame Relay	A WAN technology used to interconnect LANs and uses private lines from a user's site to a Frame Relay node, but is largely being supplanted by native IP-based networks that use cable modems or digital subscriber lines (DSL) for VPN connections
Point-to-Point (PPP)	A data link layer protocol commonly used to establish direct connections between two hosts over a serial cable, phone line, or trunk line, supported by most Internet Service Providers (ISPs) for dial-up connections
Point-to-Point over Ethernet (PPPoE)	A common encapsulated form of PPP used over DSL
Point-to-Point over ATM (PPPoA)	A common encapsulated form of PPP used over DSL
Layer 2 Tunneling Protocol (L2TP)	A VPN tunneling protocol that provides secure connection using UDP at Layer 4
PPTP	A VPN protocol that has been replaced by the standards-based protocols L2TP and IPSEC

Many standards are found at Layer 1, including Ethernet, ATM, and carrier-circuits. Ethernet standards are described in the next chapter. Other common standards are described in Table 1-6.

Layer 1 uses digital signaling. Digital signaling is used translate a message into signals that may be transmitted using a few representative indicators.

TABLE 1-6 Other Common Physical Layer Standards

Standard	Maximum Speed	Media	Comment
Modem	56 Kbps	Dial-Up Voice Grade Carrier Circuit	Standard speed maximum is 56 Kbps; however, achieving that speed depends on the quality of the dial-up circuit (plain old telephone system, or POTS). Data communications can be done over regular voice-grade telephone lines, which is most often done for connection to the Internet.
Integrated Services Digital Network (ISDN)	Max 128 Kbps	Data Grade Carrier Circuits	This circuit-switched carrier circuit, designed to allow digital transmission over regular telephone lines and most commonly used for Internet access, has largely supplanted by DSL.
Synchronous Optical Network (Sonet/SDH)	Various speeds from 48.49 Kbps to 153.994 Mbps	Fiber Optic	Laser-driven or LED-driven optical fiber most often used for carrier interconnection, Sonet is used in the United States and Canada, while SDH is used in the rest of the world. These standards are quite similar.
Digital Subscriber Line (DSL)	Varying speeds: *Asymmetric (ADSL)* ranging from 56 Kbps to multiple Mbps *High Data Rate (HDSL)* 1.544 Mbps *Symmetric (SDSL)* ranging from 56 Kbps to multiple Mbps	Voice Grade Dial-up Carrier Circuit	Speeds depend on the distance from the central office and the quality of voice-grade copper from the customer premises to the central office. This standard is most often used for connection to the Internet.
Cable	Varies, depending on cable company, ranging up to 14 Mbps	Coax cable from cable company	An asymmetric connection to the Internet provided by the cable company. Technically speaking, the cable modem incorporates functionality at Layers 1 through 4. Cable modems are asymmetric (i.e., the upstream and downstream speeds can vary) and most often used for connection to the Internet.
T1	1.544 Mbps	Digital Copper Carrier Circuit	Often used for high-speed connection to the Internet as well as for point-to-point circuits between two locations.
T3	44.736 Mbps	Digital Copper Carrier Circuits	Often used for high-speed connection to the Internet as well as for point-to-point circuits between two locations.
Wireless	Various standards – 802.11a 54 Mbps 802.11b 11 Mbps 802.11g 54 Mbps 802.11n 248 Mbps	Unlicensed Frequency Spectrum	This set of standards operates at different frequencies and can operate at varying distances. The further away a host is from the wireless access point, the slower the transmission. It is most often used in a LAN to provide wireless access to the network.
Satellite	Various	Licensed Frequency Spectrum	Major classifications: • *Low Earth Orbit* (LEO) • *Medium Earth Orbit* (MEO) • *High Earth Orbit* (HEO) sometimes called *Geosynchronous (GEO)* They are used in a variety of applications, including Internet access as well as point-to-point circuits.

FIGURE 1-33 Layer 1 Signal Propagation

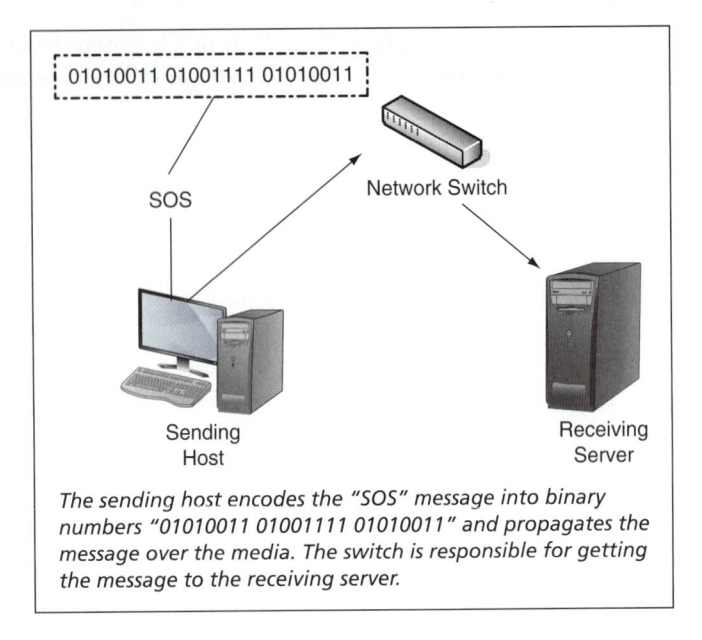

The sending host encodes the "SOS" message into binary numbers "01010011 01001111 01010011" and propagates the message over the media. The switch is responsible for getting the message to the receiving server.

This set of binary numbers must be converted into electrical impulses in order for a computer network to be able to translate them over some type of media, such as UTP cable (see Figure 1-33). Among the many types of character encoding you will find EBCIDIC and ASCII.

TCP/IP–OSI ARCHITECTURE AND HOW IT WORKS

The concepts discussed thus far provide the basis for understanding how ICT networks are built. Now we will pull these concepts together by discussing indirect communications, and expanding the TCP/IP–OSI architecture discussion by showing how it works.

Before discussing specific TCP/IP–OSI issues, several concepts need to be introduced:

- **Encapsulation.** Encapsulation is the process of putting a message inside another message so it can be transmitted; decapsulation is the reverse.
- **Protocol Data Unit.** A Protocol Data Unit (PDU) is a message that has a specific format governed by protocols as discussed earlier. The common format for a message is *message trailer – message body – message header*. (See Figure 1-34.)
- **Transport Port.** At the transport layer, two numbers are added to the transport PDU that indicate the application on the sending host that should receive the response, and the application on the receiving host that should receive the request. Some ports (these are software ports, not to be confused with physical hardware ports) are well known, others are registered, and some are dynamic. There are three types of ports that are generally used:
  - **Well-Known Ports.** Well-known ports are in the range of 0–1023. For example, 20 is used for FTP and 80 is used for HTTP on the receiving server.
  - **Registered Ports.** Registered ports are in the range of 1024–49151. These can be registered with the Internet Corporation of Assigned Numbers and Names and are assigned to certain applications. For example, port 8080 is commonly used for HTTPS (note that the S indicates a secure protocol).

FIGURE 1-34 PDU

| MESSAGE TRAILER | MESSAGE BODY | MESSAGE HEADER |

*The standard format for a PDU is the **message trailer – message body – message header**.*

- **Ephemeral Ports.** Ephemeral ports, sometimes called dynamic or private ports, are in the range of 49152–65535. These are randomly chosen by a host as source ports associated with instances of an application (e.g., if you had two browsers open, an ephemeral port would be associated with each).

When the IP address and the port number are written together, they take the form of IP_ADDRESS:PORT_NUMBER and are called a **socket**. This socket number indicates the IP address of the host and the application on that host (see Figure 1-35).

Indirect Communication

Networks that use the TCP/IP–OSI model work by indirect communication. In other words, the five layers desire to get a message from a sending host to a receiving host with each layer being able to communicate with the same layer on the other end of the communications link. Layer 1 on the sending host wants to talk to Layer 1 on the receiving host; Layer 2 on the sending host wants to talk to Layer 2 on the receiving host; and so on up through the five layers.

At each of the five layers, specific things happen. The layers can be divided into:

- **Within Network Layers.** Layers 1 and 2 (i.e., physical and data link) carry messages within a single LAN. Both layers are needed. As can be seen from the diagram below, as Layers 1 and 2 move the message along, they carry the messages from the layers above.
- **Between Network Layers.** Layers 1 through 3 (i.e., physical, data link, and Internet) are needed to carry a message between networks (e.g., across the Internet). The main device at this layer is a router. The router takes the message from one LAN, decapsulates it up to Layer 3, and based on the IP address decides which LAN to send the message to. In order to send it out, the router must again encapsulate the message from layer three (e.g., a packet) back into a frame.

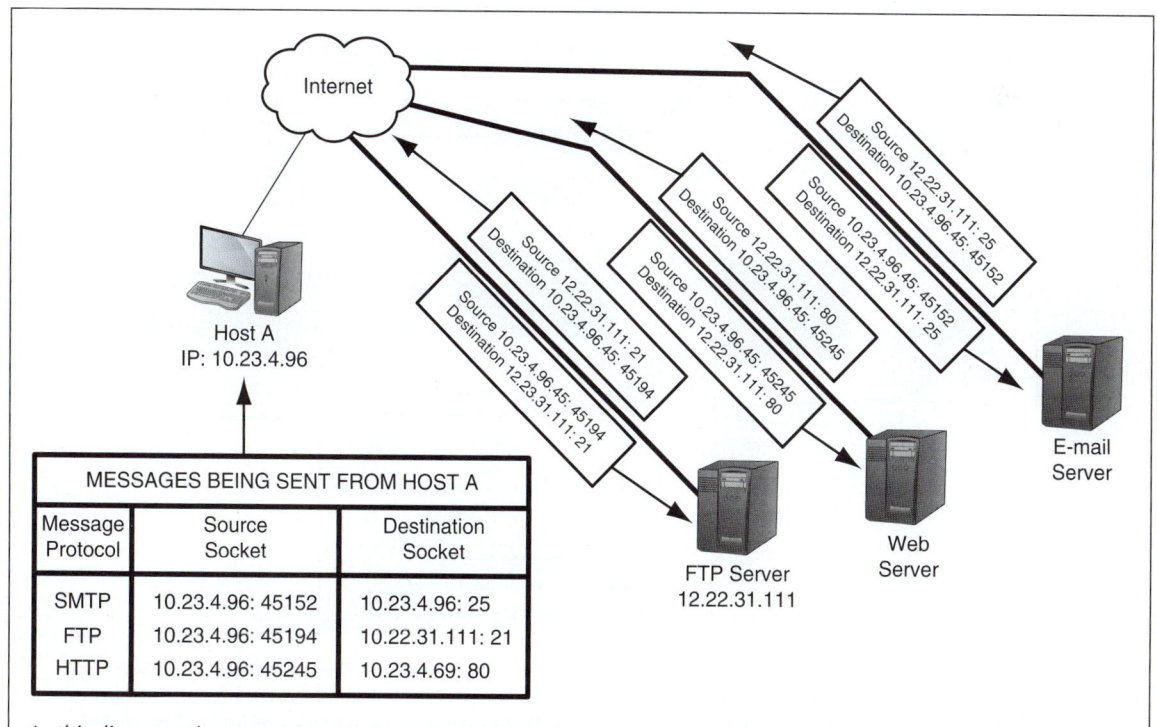

MESSAGES BEING SENT FROM HOST A

Message Protocol	Source Socket	Destination Socket
SMTP	10.23.4.96: 45152	10.23.4.96: 25
FTP	10.23.4.96: 45194	10.22.31.111: 21
HTTP	10.23.4.96: 45245	10.23.4.69: 80

In this diagram, the source, Host A, is sending three messages to three different servers. Each server receives this message (a request), then responds with a message. Notice that the source sockets are reversed on the response so the messages get to the correct application on Host A.

FIGURE 1-35 Transport Port Usage

- **End-to-End Layers.** Layer 4 (transport) is actually the end-to-end layer, because it is responsible for detecting and correcting any errors found in the message from the layers below it. Layer 4 needs Layers 1 through 3 to do propagation, routing, and switching.
- **Client-to-Service Layers.** In order to get a message from a sending host (i.e., the client) to a receiving host (i.e., the server) all five layers are needed (i.e., physical, data link, internet, transport, and application). Layers 1 through 4 have specific jobs to perform as already noted. Layer 5 consists of the application that either generates the application message at the sending host (e.g., web browser, FTP Client, e-mail client, etc.) or the receiving host that will send back a response (e.g., web server, FTP server, e-mail server, etc.).

During encapsulation, we start at Layer 5 of the sending host, where an application message is created. That message is passed to Layer 4 where a transport layer header is appended with the port numbers and the message is processed for error control. The message is then sent from Layer 4 to Layer 3 where IP addresses are added so the message can be moved between networks. The Layer 3 message is sent to Layer 2 where a MAC header and trailer are added with MAC addresses that allow messages to be transferred within a network. Finally, the message from Layer 2 is sent to Layer 1 where it is propagated over the media, as shown in Figure 1-36.

In order to understand encapsulation, a request for a web page (http://www.prenhall.com) will be followed through the process of a client-server request-response cycle in Figure 1-37. This example discusses communication over a routed network, but if the server being contacted is on the same local area network as the requesting host, the same series of steps is followed. These steps are:

FIGURE 1-36 Indirect Communication Between Hosts

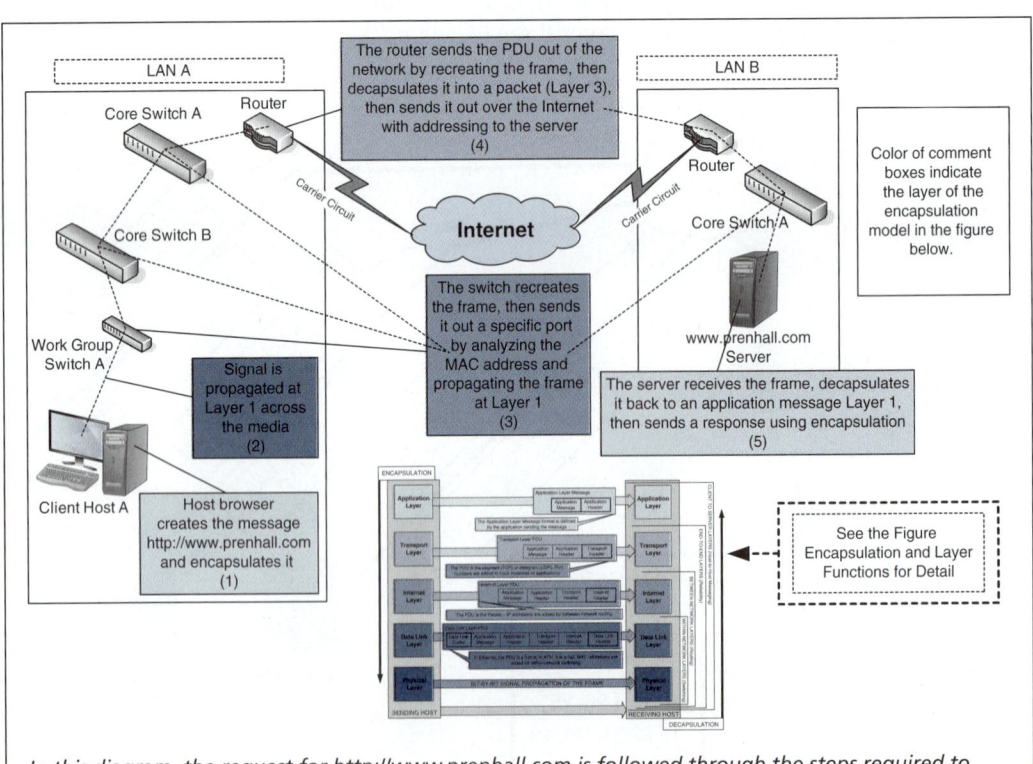

In this diagram, the request for http://www.prenhall.com is followed through the steps required to create the message in the browser, propagate the message across the media, switch the message within the LAN, and route the message between two networks over the Internet. The inset shows details concerning encapsulation and is explored in Figure 1-37.

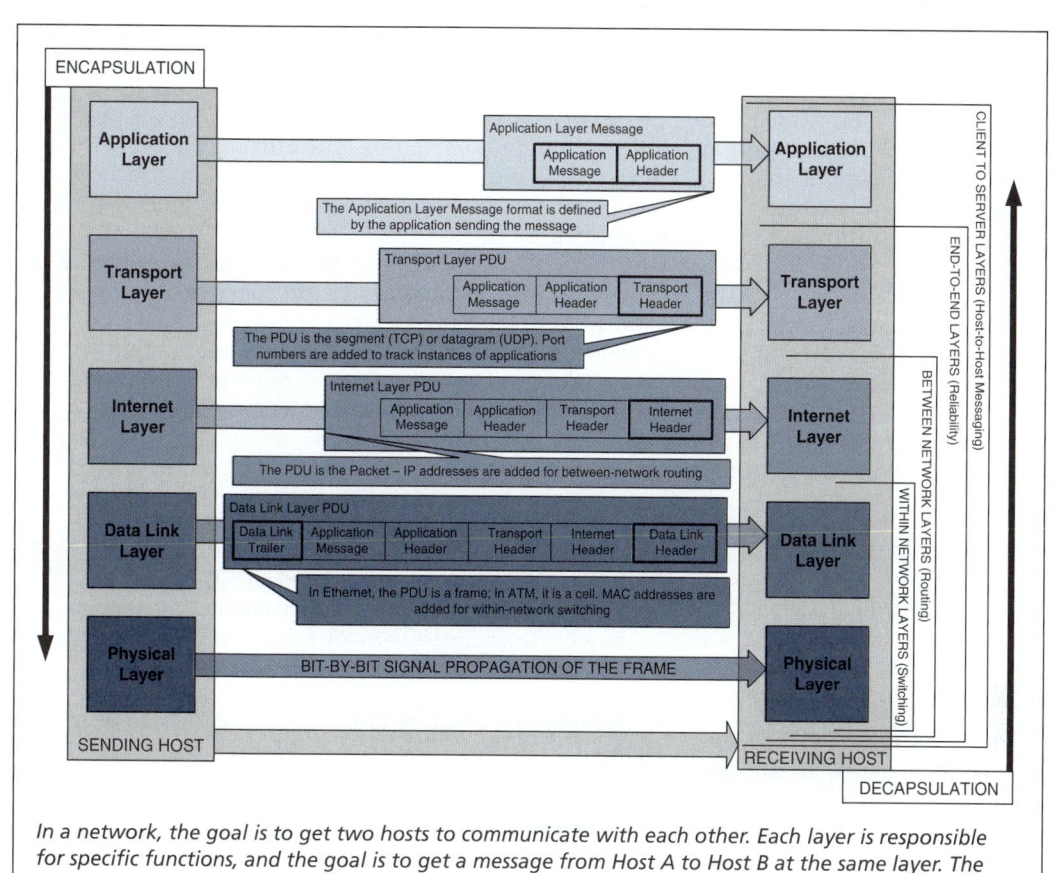

FIGURE 1-37 Indirect Communication

In a network, the goal is to get two hosts to communicate with each other. Each layer is responsible for specific functions, and the goal is to get a message from Host A to Host B at the same layer. The process by which this happens is called encapsulation.

- **Layer 5, the Application Layer.** The sending host (A) would prepare the HTTP Request message at Layer 5, the application layer. The goal would be to get the Prentice Hall web site to send back its web page. The protocol would be HTTP, and the application would be a web browser. Host A would send the message down to Layer 4, the transport layer.
- **Layer 4, the Transport Layer.** The application message received from Layer 5 would be encapsulated into a *TCP segment,* or what the PDU at Layer 4 is called. (If this were some other type of message it might be encapsulated into a *UDP datagram,* but that would be a different type of message.) The Host A transport layer wants to communicate with the transport layer on Host B so it can make sure that the information sent is the same as what is received: Layer 4 is largely responsible for between-network error control.
- **Layer 3, the Internet Layer.** The segment received from Layer 4 would be encapsulated into a PDU called a *packet.* The Host A Internet layer wants to communicate with the Host B Internet layer in order to get the packet from the source to the destination host. Layer 3 is responsible for end-to-end between-network routing.
- **Layer 2, the Data Link Layer.** The packet received from Layer 3 is encapsulated into a PDU called a *frame.* (Remember, the protocol data unit, or PDU, is the specific name given to the messages at each layer of the TCP/IP–OSI architecture.) The data link layer is responsible for communicating within a local area network; Layer 2 handles communication within a single LAN.
- **Layer 1, the Physical Layer.** At this point, we have a frame that needs to be propagated within a network. As discussed earlier, Layer 1 is responsible for this propagation and uses different types of propagation methods based on the technology, protocol, and media used.

Chapter Summary

In this chapter, introductory concepts were discussed so that the business systems analyst would be familiar with basic telecommunications. The concept of interoperability is based on the idea that equipment from different vendors using the same standards should work together seamlessly. Interoperability provides the basis for innovation and competition in the marketplace for ICT equipment. Additionally, this chapter included a lengthy discussion about the TCP/IP–OSI hybrid architecture used in the design of telecommunication systems. Next, the chapter moves on to a discussion of network structures, typologies, and switching hierarchies. The current chapter finished with a review of indirect communication and how it is used within a network to facilitate end-to-end transfer of application messages.

This chapter provides the basis for introducing the hardware and techniques of the network components within Figure 1-1. These concepts will prepare business systems analysts as they make recommendation for ICT infrastructure. The following chapters will discuss how to implement the concepts learned in this chapter.

Vignette Wrap Up

The opening vignette described HealthyWay HMO and Joe Smith's need to get Internet access at home for two PCs, as well as get a connection back to the office. The first thing we will do is create an overview of the two networks: one at HealthyWay and the other in Joe's home. From the discussion of standards, the following are pretty good assumptions:

- The network at HealthyWay will be an Ethernet LAN, with some type of core-to-workgroup arrangement of switches.
- HealthyWay will need a carrier circuit to connect to the Internet, which means it will need an ISP.
- Joe will need a carrier circuit to connect to the Internet, and he will use a wireless network at his home to connect the two PCs and printer so they can be shared.

A high-level diagram of the two networks can be seen in Figure 1-38.

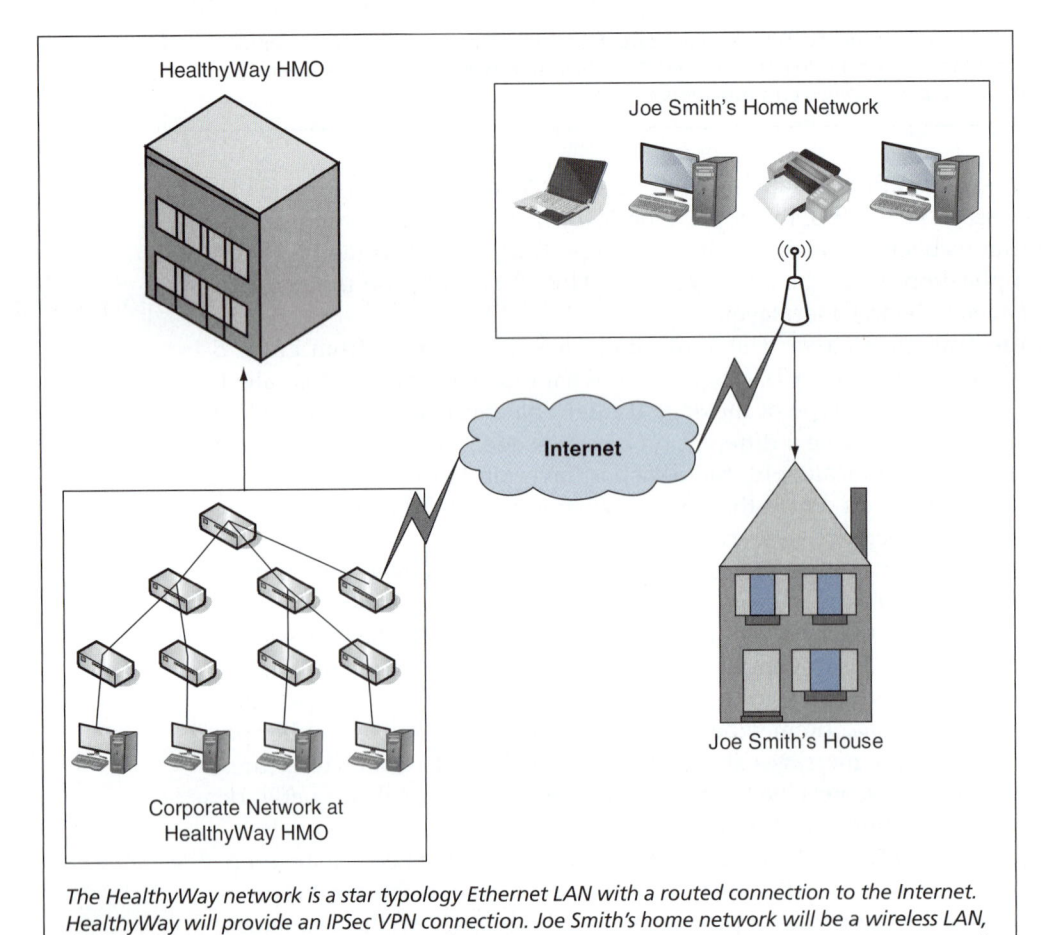

The HealthyWay network is a star typology Ethernet LAN with a routed connection to the Internet. HealthyWay will provide an IPSec VPN connection. Joe Smith's home network will be a wireless LAN, and he will be able to share the Internet connection at his home, as well as share his printer. Joe will use a carrier circuit to connect to the Internet, which will allow him and his family to web surf as well as connect back to HealthyWay over its IPSec VPN.

FIGURE 1-38 Overview of HealthyWay's Corporate Network and Joe Smith's Home Network

End of Chapter Questions/Assurance of Learning

1. Discuss why analog and digital data are important, how they differ, and what the relationship is between them.
2. Think of an office or building you are familiar with. What are the things in that building that would cause major propagation effects for a wired network? What can be done to minimize them? How would a wireless network be any different?
3. Analyze why interoperability is important from the perspective of the customer and vendor.
4. Describe and analyze why the TCP/IP–OSI hybrid model is important to businesses. Do the same for the OSI model.
5. Select an application (e.g., browser, e-mail, FTP, Real Player) and draw the five-layer hybrid TCP/IP–OSI communication model showing how messages are encapsulated through layered communications.
6. Analyze how transport, Internet, and MAC addressing interact to facilitate end-to-end communications, and write a technical description.

Case Exercises

1. Assume that XYZ Inc. wants to build a new Ethernet switch with a number of unique options. (These options do not matter, but the fact that they are not ratified by any standards organization does.) The switch is a 10-gigabit Ethernet switch that comes in several sizes (number of ports). Develop a plan for XYZ Inc. so it can be sure it is building the switch to the appropriate standards. Make sure you answer the following: (a) Which standards bodies would XYZ Inc. have to contact, and what is the process? (b) How should ZYX Inc. handle any proprietary options? For example, should it seek to have its options become standards? (c) Explain the competitive positioning (or lack thereof) that XYZ may have because it uses proprietary options for its hardware; be sure to indicate the benefits and pitfalls it will face.
2. HealthyWay HMO was discussed in the opening vignette. Prepare a brief report and presentation indicating how a LAN can help it attain competitive advantage in the marketplace of HMOs. In your case analysis discuss what things are important for HealthyWay to consider when selecting LAN and WAN technologies.
3. Select a company you are familiar with and write a case analysis that describes its LAN/WAN. Describe which technologies it uses and how those technologies are important to the competitive positioning of that company. Support your analysis by citing Internet and/or print articles (i.e., trade publications, journal articles).

Key Words and Concepts

Address Resolution Protocol (ARP) 32
analog 6
application layer 30
asynchronous transmission 13
attenuation 10
bandwidth 15
bus typology 25
business systems analyst 1
client-server computing 16
client-to-service layers 36
cross talk 10
data link layer 32
digital 6
DSL 2
electromagnetic interference 9
EMI 9
encapsulation 34
end-to-end layers 36
enterprise applications 1
ephemeral ports 35
Ethernet 13

full-duplex 12
half-duplex 12
hardware address 30
HTTP 30
HTTPS 30
hybrid architecture 19
IAB 21
IEEE 21
IETF 21
information and communication technology (ICT) infrastructure 1
Institute of Electrical and Electronics Engineers 21
International Organization for Standardization 21
internet 23
Internet Architecture Board 21
Internet Control Message Protocol 31
Internet Engineering Task Force 21
Internet layer 32

Internet Protocol 30
Internet Society 21
IP addresses 30
IP Security 32
ISO 21
ISOC 21
ITU-T 21
LAN 18
latency 16
local area network (LAN) 18
media 9
Media Access Control 30
mesh typology 27
metropolitan area network (MAN) 19
MFA Forum 22
modulation 13
modulator 13
multiplexing 13
Multiprotocol Label Switching (MPLS) and Frame Relay Alliance 22
MUX 13

name resolution 30
network services 2
network technology 3
networking and telecommunications 1
Open System Interconnection (OSI) 19
packet-switched networks 27
point-to-point 25
propagation effects 9
Protocol Data Unit 34
Protocol Organizations 20
registered ports 34
reliable protocol 31
ring typology 27
routers 27
signal-to-noise 10
SNR 10
Socket 35
Sonet/SDH 27
star typology 25
symmetric vs. asymmetric communications 15

synchronous transmission 13
technology infrastructure 1
Telecommunication Standardization Sector 21
Transmission Control Protocol 31
Transmission Control Protocol/Internet Protocol (TCP/IP) 19
transport layer 31
transport port 34
twisted-pair cable 11
Unicode 7
Uniform Resource Locaters 30
User Datagram Protocol 31
W3C 21
well-known ports 34
wide area network (WAN) 18
World Wide Web Consortium 21

References

Bahlmann, B. (n.d.). All things broadband and more. Retrieved April 4, 2011, from http://www.birds-eye.net/definition/acronym/?id=1160844854ITU. (2011).

Retrieved August 26, 2011, from www.itu.eduIAB. (2011, February). Internet Architecture Board.

Retrieved April 4, 2011, from http://www.iab.org/IEEE.org. (2011). Index.

Retrieved April 4, 2011, from http://www.ieee.org/index.htmlInternet Society. (2011). Home Page.

Retrieved April 4, 2011, from http://www.isoc.org/ISO. (2011). Home.

Retrieved April 4, 2011, from http://www.iso.org/iso/home.htmlW3C. (2010, September 30).

W3C UK and Ireland Regional Office. Retrieved August 22, 2011, from http://www.w3c.rl.ac.uk/

2 BUILDING THE LOCAL AREA NETWORK USING ETHERNET

> **Learning Objectives**
>
> - Understand the technical details of an Ethernet LAN.
> - Apply the typologies learned in the previous chapter to LAN configurations.
> - Understand the differences between the plain old telephone system (POTS), which carries voice and data, and a public switched data network (PSDN).
> - Integrate material about protocols, typologies, the TCP/IP-OSI hybrid model, and other concepts previously introduced with the concepts of LAN and MAN so network structures can be built.
> - Understand VLANs and how they affect the network.

The previous chapter introduced a number of topics that are essential to understanding this chapter. It provided foundational information, while this chapter builds on that foundation. In the current chapter, how LANs are implemented and what they mean for network design are discussed. Specifics about the standard telecommunications infrastructure and network implementation are introduced (see Figure 2-1). The concepts of switching and routing are discussed further, with examples of networks based on the opening vignette being used to illustrate concepts. Students are challenged to understand these implementations of various network topologies and to apply them to the running case in the text. This chapter discusses the specifics of Ethernet as a network component.

INTRODUCTION

Today, Ethernet is the local area network (LAN) technology used most often. The term *Ethernet* is based on *ether*, or a medium that can propagate light. The term *Ethernet* was coined because using that standard, data are propagated across media creating a network; hence we get the term **Ethernet**. The name stuck, and today it indicates the most common form of installed data networking. The rest

ENTERPRISE-WIDE SOFTWARE COMPONENTS — Enterprise-wide software, including ERP, e-commerce/e-business, document management, knowledge management, and other specialized applications	User Components	Items that directly interface with the user, including workstations, printers, scanners, associated software (especially desktop applications), and specialized applications
	Service Components	Those network parts that facilitate network operations with direct user interface, including printing services, inter/intra office communications (i.e., telephone or fax), network attached storage, database/application servers, security servers and appliances, and VPN technology
	Network Components	Those items/concepts traditionally thought of as networking and telecommunications equipment, including network switching and routing hardware, media, outside vendor interconnects (i.e., T1, T3, DSL), and cabinetry, patch panels, and associated items

This figure lists and describes the components of ICT infrastructure architecture from the standpoint of the information technology user. The areas highlighted in blue are covered in this chapter.

FIGURE 2-1 Information Technology Infrastructure Architecture

FIGURE 2-2 Ethernet at Layer 1 and Layer 2

Ethernet Layer 1 Standards: Physical	Ethernet Layer 2 Standards: Data Link (Frame)
• Governs what media is used • Governs signal propagation • Governs speed	There are four, but one is used most often: 1. Ethernet II (used most often) 2. Ethernet Raw 3. IEEE 802.2 LLC 4. Snap

Ethernet standards govern what happens at Layers 1 and 2. In reality the standards can be equated to the media and speed (Layer 1), and the frame type (Layer 2). The Layer 1 standards govern media and technology selection, and the Layer 2 frame type can be configured in the operating system (e.g., Microsoft Windows ® Network Properties). It is important to note that all devices on the same LAN must use the same Layer 1 and Layer 2 standards in order to communicate. It is possible to use a router between two LANs to translate between different Layer 1 and Layer 2 standards; however, absent a router to interpret between the different networks, devices on the same LAN will not interoperate unless they use the same Layer 1 and Layer 2 standards.

of this textbook will focus on the Ethernet LAN standard. Even though other LAN standards exist, none is as ubiquitous as Ethernet. Many of the basic concepts are the same, whether you are discussing Ethernet, Token Ring, or something else—the goal is to allow hosts to communicate.

Remember from our previous chapter, Ethernet standards are implemented in Layer 1 and Layer 2 of the TCP/IP-OSI hybrid model, because the hybrid model and the OSI model share the bottom two layers. Ethernet Layer 1 standards govern what media can be used, how data are signaled, and the speed of the Ethernet LAN. In other words, the speed of an Ethernet network depends on the physical portion of each Ethernet standard. There are multiple Ethernet Layer 1 standards (see Chapter 1 for details).

The four Ethernet Layer 2 (data link) standards include (1) Ethernet II, (2) Ethernet Raw, (3) IEEE 802.2 LLC, and (4) Ethernet Snap (see Figure 2-2). Each standard has a slightly different frame format (remember that frames are the protocol data units at Layer 2). Ethernet II is the most common type of Layer 2 Ethernet frame format. Therefore, we will use the Ethernet II standard in our discussion for the rest of this textbook.

Another concept worthy of reviewing is the difference between routing and switching. Routing is done *between* LANs, and switching is done *within* a LAN. Ethernet networks use Layer 2 switches to communicate within the network. The Layer 2 switch takes frames in one hardware port, decides on a destination hardware port, and sends the frame out that hardware port. This *within*-LAN activity uses the MAC address to switch traffic at Layer 2. When a frame needs to be sent to another network (remember, it is encapsulated in a packet), a router is used between networks to route the traffic using the IP address. The router is capable of translating Layer 1 and Layer 2 standards, so it can take networks that use different standards and allow them to communicate. For example, an Ethernet 100BaseFX (100 Mbps multimode fiber optic) network can communicate with an Ethernet 100BaseTX (100 Mbps UTP) by using a router to translate between the two standards. The same kind of translation can be done over the Internet between two networks that use different standards; for example, an ATM network can communication with an Ethernet 100BaseFX over the Internet.

TYPES OF ETHERNET EQUIPMENT AND MEDIA

Ethernet standards define the media used to interconnect devices, as well as how the devices must function so they can interoperate. Media are introduced in the following text, along with the various equipment necessary to interconnect devices within an Ethernet LAN.

Media

In the previous chapter, various types of media were introduced. Media are mentioned here for the sake of a complete discussion of Ethernet. Within the limitations of each Ethernet standard, UTP and fiber optic are the most common types of media. Even though an Ethernet network can be extended with **wireless standards** (e.g., IEEE 802.11 and 802.16)(IEEE.org, 2011), these wireless standards are technically not Ethernet because they have different frame formats.

When building a LAN, fiber optic is usually used between switches. These between-switch cables are called the **vertical runs** because they often run between floors, interconnecting switches. UTP is normally used from the switch to the user components (e.g., host, printers). These UTP cables are called **horizontal runs** because they often are limited to one floor of an office building and run horizontally between the switch and the device. Horizontal and vertical runs will be covered in detail later in this chapter.

Ethernet requires that there is only one link between any two devices. A typical network configuration is seen in Figure 2-3. Only one path lies between any two devices, and this rule is the same for hubs and switches. It holds true for all Ethernet LANs unless special equipment and protocols are used to provide redundancy.

Adapter Cards: Motherboard Interfaces

Ethernet requires that hosts have Ethernet ports, or places to which a drop cable can connect. The host will either have an adapter card plugged into a card slot, or it will have an Ethernet adapter integrated into its motherboard. Either way, the adapter provides connectivity over the specified media (most often UTP) between the host and an Ethernet switch.

Hubs, Repeaters, and Bridges

Hubs and repeaters are largely outdated devices, but they should be mentioned here for thoroughness. A hub provides for interconnection of Ethernet devices within a relatively low bandwidth network. A hub does not read the frame or attempt to direct LAN traffic; all ports on a hub see all traffic. A repeater can be thought of as a device

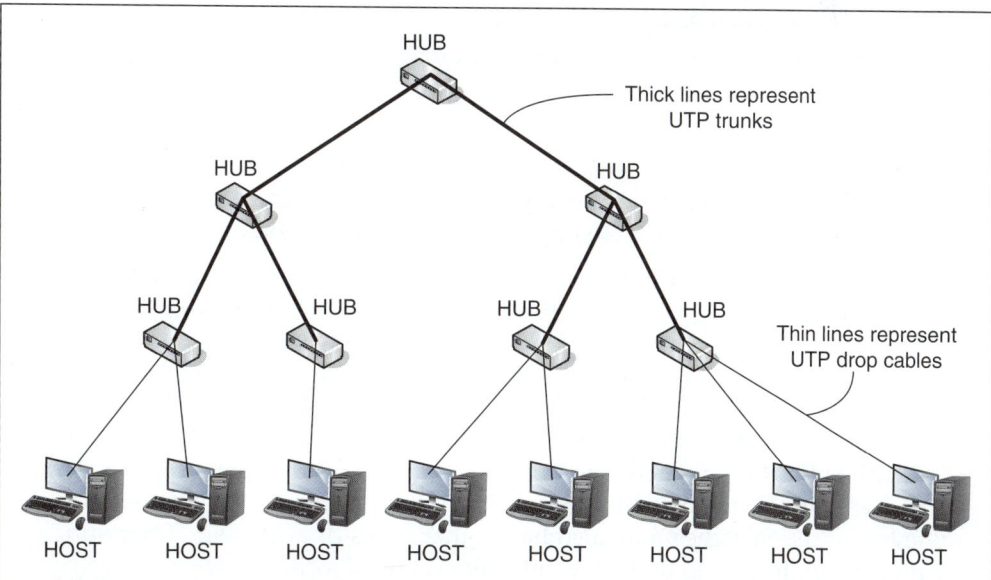

FIGURE 2-3 Hub-Based Star Typology

In this diagram, a star typology hub-based network is depicted—although switches are normally used today rather than hubs, both hubs and switches follow the same star typology requirements. Remember that hubs have the same collision problems as coax-based networks, while switches do not. Connections between hubs (vertical runs) are trunk lines, and from the hub to the workstation are drop lines (horizontal runs). Single points of failure can still occur in this star, but the section of the network can be isolated, which makes the LAN more resilient.

used to extend the limitations on Ethernet media—that is, increasing the length of a cable run from a few hundred feet to much longer. Bridges were created to better handle traffic on an Ethernet LAN. A bridge is a multiport device able to read the frame and then decide which port should receive that frame. Bridges and hubs also provide the signal regeneration of a repeater.

Bridges and Switches

The term *switch* is a manufacturer-created term; the IEEE 802.3 standard refers to bridges. The terms *bridge* and *switch* are interchangeable, but switch is commonly used and thus will be used throughout the rest of this textbook. Unlike hubs, which use shared bandwidth across the bus, switches operate at the designated speeds at each port. A 100 Mbps 8-port switch can operate at 100 Mbps at each port, while a 5 Mbps 8-port hub shares all 5 Mbps with all eight ports.

Early switches were slow devices; in fact, they were slower than hubs. Nevertheless, they gave the advantage of isolation of each device in the LAN and reduced the possibility that a malfunctioning device would cause the entire LAN to malfunction. Over time switches became faster and cheaper, supplanting hubs in the marketplace. Ethernet switches are multiport Layer 2 devices that operate within the LAN, and function as follows:

- When the switch is first turned on, it operates much like a hub and does not know what devices are connected to it. At power on, the switch takes a frame in one port and sends it out all ports of the switch.
- Over time as the switch receives frames, it reads the source MAC address of each frame and creates a switching table. The source address is used because if a frame comes in a particular port, then the switch can assume that it should send all frames with that same MAC address out that same port.
- Once the switch has decapsulated the MAC address, it knows which port to send that frame out of, assuming it has seen a frame with that same MAC address before.
- Periodically, the switch dumps its switching table and starts to rebuild it, which allows the switch to determine any network changes.
- Switches only know that a device with a particular MAC address is out a particular port, but the switch does not know whether the device is directly connected to it or to another switch somewhere else in the LAN. This property is exhibited in Figure 2-4.

Switch Characteristics

This material is a bit technical, but will give you a good understanding of the types of decisions that must be made when building a LAN using switches. A number of considerations are important when purchasing switches for installation.

- **Number/Type of Ports.** Ethernet Switches use ports (i.e., usually UTP) to connect user components (e.g., workstations, printers). When purchasing a switch you need to consider the number of devices that will be connected to the switch, as well as any growth. The ports designed to connect devices accept an RJ-45 terminated UTP cable that runs from the device to the switch (a wall jack may be included, as well as a horizontal run between the switch and the office where a device is located). Switches commonly come as 4-port, 8-port, 16-port, 24-port, and 48-port. Switches with more ports are more expensive than switches with fewer ports. Switches may also have other types of ports (e.g., fiber optic or a proprietary interface) that allow interconnection of switches.
- **Form Factor.** Form factor refers to the physical style of a device. Switches are regularly manufactured as either desktop devices or rack-mounted devices, although it is possible to purchase a chassis-mounted switch for high-end networks. The form factor chosen is determined by whether the switch is to be installed on a desk or in a cabinet. The rack-mounted switch has "ears" that allow it to be affixed to a standard computer rack (see Figure 2-5). The rack and the

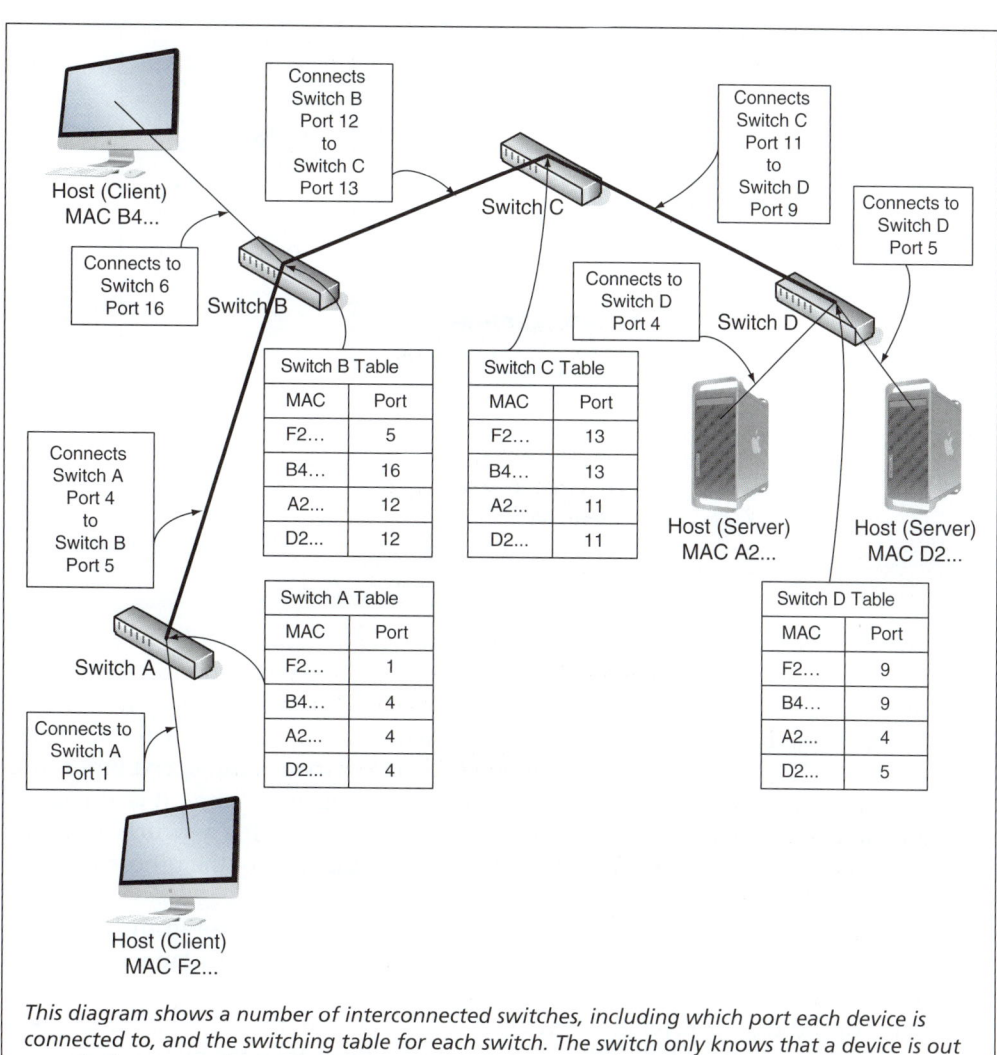

FIGURE 2-4 Ethernet Switching

Switch B Table	
MAC	Port
F2...	5
B4...	16
A2...	12
D2...	12

Switch C Table	
MAC	Port
F2...	13
B4...	13
A2...	11
D2...	11

Switch A Table	
MAC	Port
F2...	1
B4...	4
A2...	4
D2...	4

Switch D Table	
MAC	Port
F2...	9
B4...	9
A2...	4
D2...	5

This diagram shows a number of interconnected switches, including which port each device is connected to, and the switching table for each switch. The switch only knows that a device is out a particular port, and not whether the device is connected directly to that switch, as can be seen in the switching table by tracing a MAC address and seeing that the device is indicated on a different port of each switch. Switching is a within-LAN Layer 2 function. Routing handles the between-network communications.

switch are measured in rack units (RU) or units (U). A unit is an amount of physical height in a rack, so a 2U switch uses two units in a rack, and a 14U rack can hold seven two-unit (2U) switches (7 × 2 = 14).

- **Stackable.** Stackable switches have ports designed to interconnect them. They are stacked on top of each other in a rack, or on a desktop, and have an interconnecting port that connects the switches. The stacking port is usually a proprietary vendor-specific standard, meant for very close connections (i.e., on top of each other). Because the interconnecting port is proprietary, switches from different vendors do not stack together. Interconnecting ports are not meant to connect switches over any significant distance. Switches are stacked so multiple switches can act as one. For example, two stackable 24-port switches can be connected together to make one 48-port switch. This reduces the number of times frames are switched—in theory, switching through one 48-port switch requires half the number of switches, and thus half the amount of time, as switching through two 24-port switches.
- **Ethernet Standard, Media Supported.** Switches can support a number of speeds, most typically 100 Mbps or gigabit speeds. In addition, switches can support various media, the most prevalent of which are UTP and fiber optic. In the previous chapter, the various Ethernet standards, speeds, and media were covered.

FIGURE 2-5 Desktop and Rack-Mounted Switches

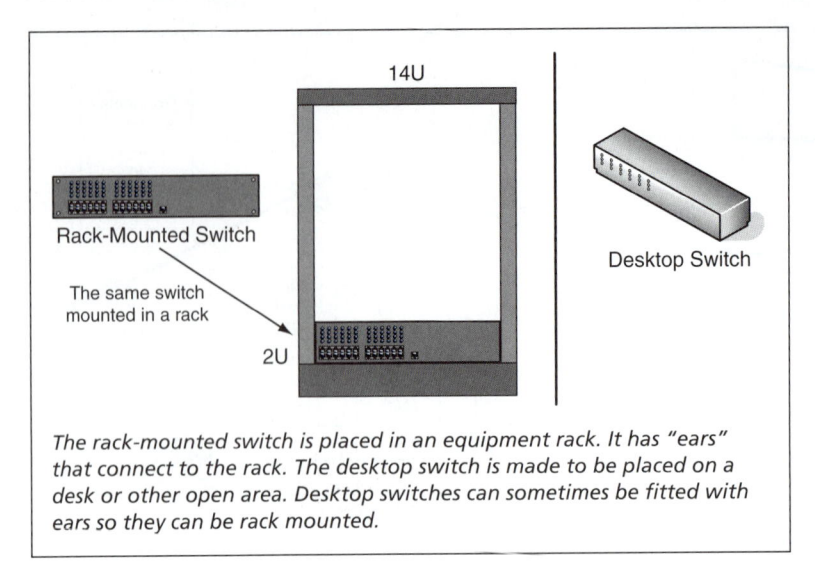

The rack-mounted switch is placed in an equipment rack. It has "ears" that connect to the rack. The desktop switch is made to be placed on a desk or other open area. Desktop switches can sometimes be fitted with ears so they can be rack mounted.

Switch selection needs to include the desired speed and media. UTP is the norm for user devices, while fiber optic ports and media often interconnect switches.

- **Switching Matrix.** The switching matrix of a switch is measured by its blocking factor. A zero blocking factor means that a switch will not block any frames that it receives. The matrix is fast enough to handle simultaneous full-speed input from all ports and subsequent switching without dropping any frames. It is also called a nonblocking switch. The faster the matrix, the less blocking a switch does, and the more expensive a switch is. Matrix speed is a function of the processor in the switch and its memory.
- **Switch Method.** There are various methods a switch can use in the matrix to forward frames, such as cut-through, store-and-forward, fragment-free, and adaptive switching.
  - In cut-through switching, the frame is only read up to the MAC addresses, then the frame is forwarded. If the outgoing port is busy, then the matrix must operate in the store-and-forward mode.
  - A store-and-forward switch reads the entire frame and performs error checking on the frame before it sends the frame.
  - Fragment-free switching attempts to retain the benefits of both cut-through and store-and-forward switches by error checking the first 64 octets of the frame (addressing information is stored within these octets). If those 64 octets are error-free, then the frame is assured to get to its destination.
  - Adaptive switching uses all three switching methods, switching between them as network condition allows.
- **Power over Ethernet (PoE).** Ethernet switches can provide power over UTP directly to devices connected to the switch, eliminating the need for a separate power supply for those devices, and is often used to power wireless access points and IP telephones. Besides the obvious benefit of eliminating the power supply, another benefit is continuous power if the switch is connected to an uninterruptible power supply.
- **Managed Switches.** Managed switches allow for configuration changes remotely, either through a client or through a web interface. Typical switch management features include:
  - **Enabling/disabling ports.** allow ports to be disabled, so if a device connected to a disabled port, it will not function.
  - **Change speed or duplex setting of ports.** ports on switches are rated at a particular speed, and most ports default to full duplex. Sometimes it is necessary to change that speed or duplex (i.e., either half or full) to accommodate specific types of user components or to debug network problems.
  - **Setting port priority.** sometimes it is desirable for frames from a particular port to get a higher priority through the switching matrix.

FIGURE 2-6 Spanning Tree Protocol 802.1D

STP 802.1D allows for a redundant link to be present in the network. That link is normally disabled and is automatically enabled when one of the primary links fails.

- **Instructing a port to filter traffic based on MAC address.** switches that support MAC filtering can be configured to allow a port to accept frames only with a particular MAC address. This useful security feature limits what can be connected to a port and prevents MAC flooding. MAC flooding happens when a switch must deal with many frames each containing a different MAC address, forcing the switch to act like a hub and send all frames out all ports, and then, using special software, sniff the frames for data such as passwords or e-mail.
- **Simple Network Management Protocol (SNMP) monitoring of a switch.** SNMP monitoring is done by client software that monitors the activity of the switch. SNMP checks switch health and reports significant errors.
- **Managing the use of spanning tree protocol (STP).** STP is defined in the IEEE standard 802.1D. STP 802.1D (Figure 2-6) includes redundant links in the network design that become active if the primary link fails. It also manages the multiple links so only one path exists between any two devices on the network.
- **Managing the use of link aggregation.** sometimes it is desirable to have higher speed than what is supported by one port on a switch. Link aggregation, sometimes called bonding, allows multiple ports to act as one, giving the device more bandwidth (Figure 2-7).
- **Setting VLAN parameters.** Ethernet networks suffer from lots of traffic only of interest to specific hosts. An example of this traffic is a server's broadcast message that tells the host it is online and "alive." Only hosts that need to communicate with the server need to know it is "alive." Because Ethernet still retains much of the properties of a broadcast protocol, owing to its roots as a bus network, and because all devices can potentially see all traffic on the network, all

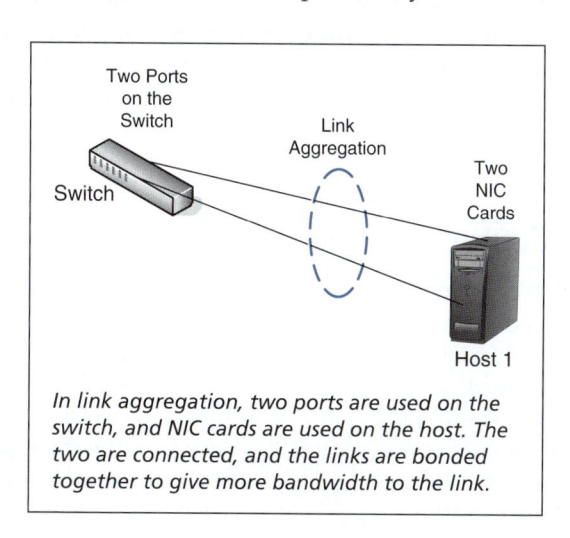

FIGURE 2-7 Link Aggregation

In link aggregation, two ports are used on the switch, and NIC cards are used on the host. The two are connected, and the links are bonded together to give more bandwidth to the link.

FIGURE 2-8 VLANs and Broadcast Messages

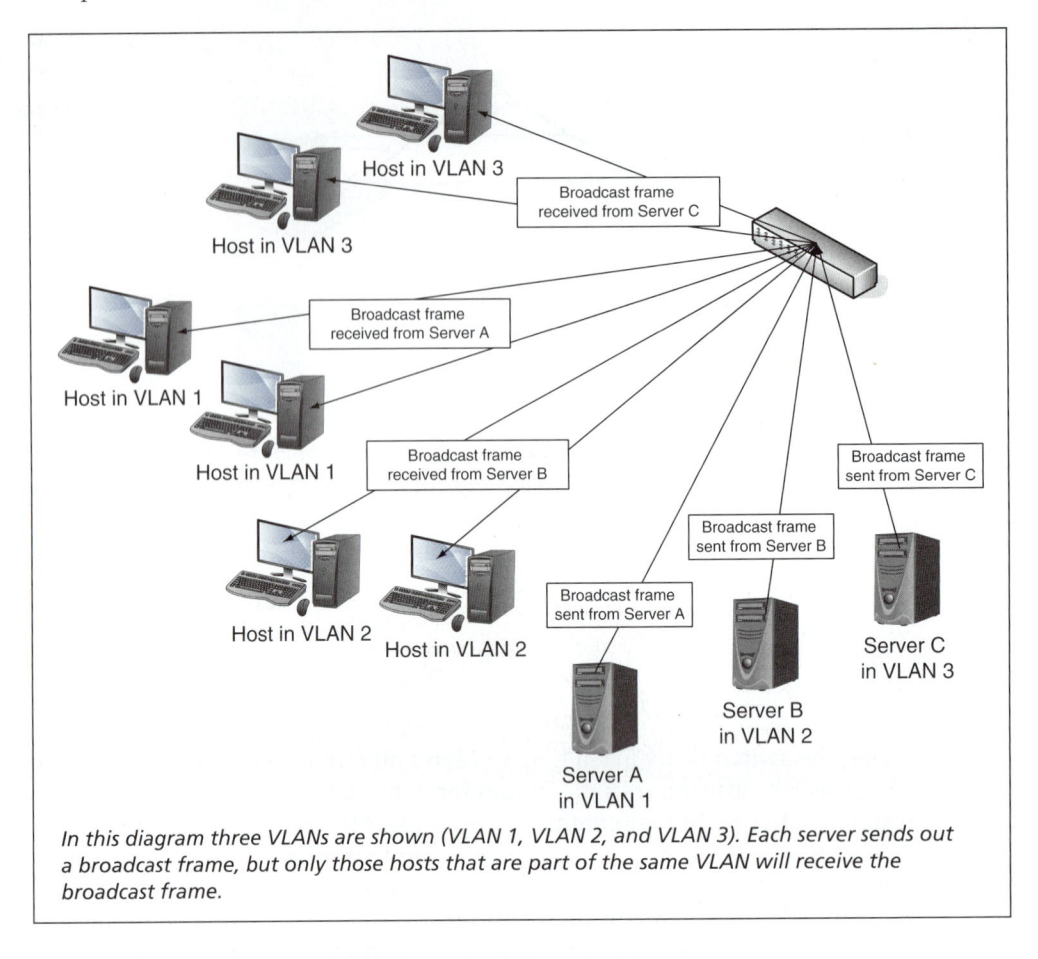

In this diagram three VLANs are shown (VLAN 1, VLAN 2, and VLAN 3). Each server sends out a broadcast frame, but only those hosts that are part of the same VLAN will receive the broadcast frame.

hosts will see these broadcast messages unless a VLAN is set up. Virtual LANs, or VLANs, group devices on the network together so broadcast traffic is limited to a subset of devices, rather than to the entire network (Figure 2-8). This arrangement offers the advantage of limiting network traffic to devices that need to see it, but the disadvantage is that hosts cannot communicate with devices in another VLAN even though all are connected to the same physical Ethernet network.

- **Vendor-Specific Option.** Vendors often offer options that they only provide, such as firewall options, network intrusion detection, and performance analysis modules. Some of these options will only work with other switches from the same vendor, so care must be taken when selecting switches that use vendor-specific options.

Whether a switch is going in the network core or somewhere else determines which of the selection criteria just listed are important. Switches in the network core are at the top of the switching hierarchy and thus have the potential to see more frames than workgroup switches directly connected to user components. For this reason, core switches need to be faster than workgroup switches (i.e., faster switching matrix). The other purchasing considerations are also important and drive switch selection.

ETHERNET: THE TECHNICAL DETAILS OF ITS EVOLUTION

Note: The information contained in this section is largely historical in nature and very technical. It is included for those instructors and students who have an interest in these topics, as well as to round out students' understanding of Ethernet. Courses that are more technical in nature, or are taught within a more technical academic program, will find these materials useful. Others may skip this section. The author of this textbook believes that by understanding this material, students will have a better grasp of how Ethernet operates and be better able to adopt to future changes in Ethernet standards.

Some of the first personal computers were made at the Palo Alto Research Center (PARC, 2011), in Palo Alto, California. Robert Metcalfe was asked to build a network for these computers so they could communicate with each other. The motivation for building the network was to share the world's first laser printer among the computers. It was built over a number of years and was recognized in the late 1970s. This network became the basis for what we know as Ethernet today.

Originally, Ethernet was created as a bus typology that used coax cable to create a trunk line, which connected to each personal computer. With no switches or routers, a bus terminated at each end where personal computers connected to that bus. From the bus typology, Ethernet evolved into a star typology using hubs. This next step in Ethernet LAN typology was the star typology using switches; this is the most prevalent LAN typology in use today The problem with the bus typology was in determining which computer could talk (communicate) when. Think of a crowded room with everyone talking loudly at the same time, making it difficult to discern a single conversation. The same problem exists when multiple computers try to communicate over the same media at the same time. In a room of 20 people talking at the same time it might be called chatter; in a computer network, when multiple computers attempt to communicate at the same time, the result is a collision. The design of Ethernet took into account collisions and had ways to deal with them. The switch-based star typology largely eliminates collisions, but it is possible to mix bus-based and switch-based typologies to support legacy applications, so Ethernet still handles collisions.

Since its inception, Ethernet has gone from thick coax cable in a bus typology to UTP- and fiber optic-based Ethernet in star typology and beyond, with several different network configurations in between (see Figure 2-9). Even so, the Layer 2 frame formats have stayed the same through all the changes, with the main changes occurring at Layer 1. Because the frame formats stayed the same, the interface to higher layers (3 through 5) stayed the same, and thus Ethernet equipment can be readily interconnected, allowing legacy and current equipment to easily interface.

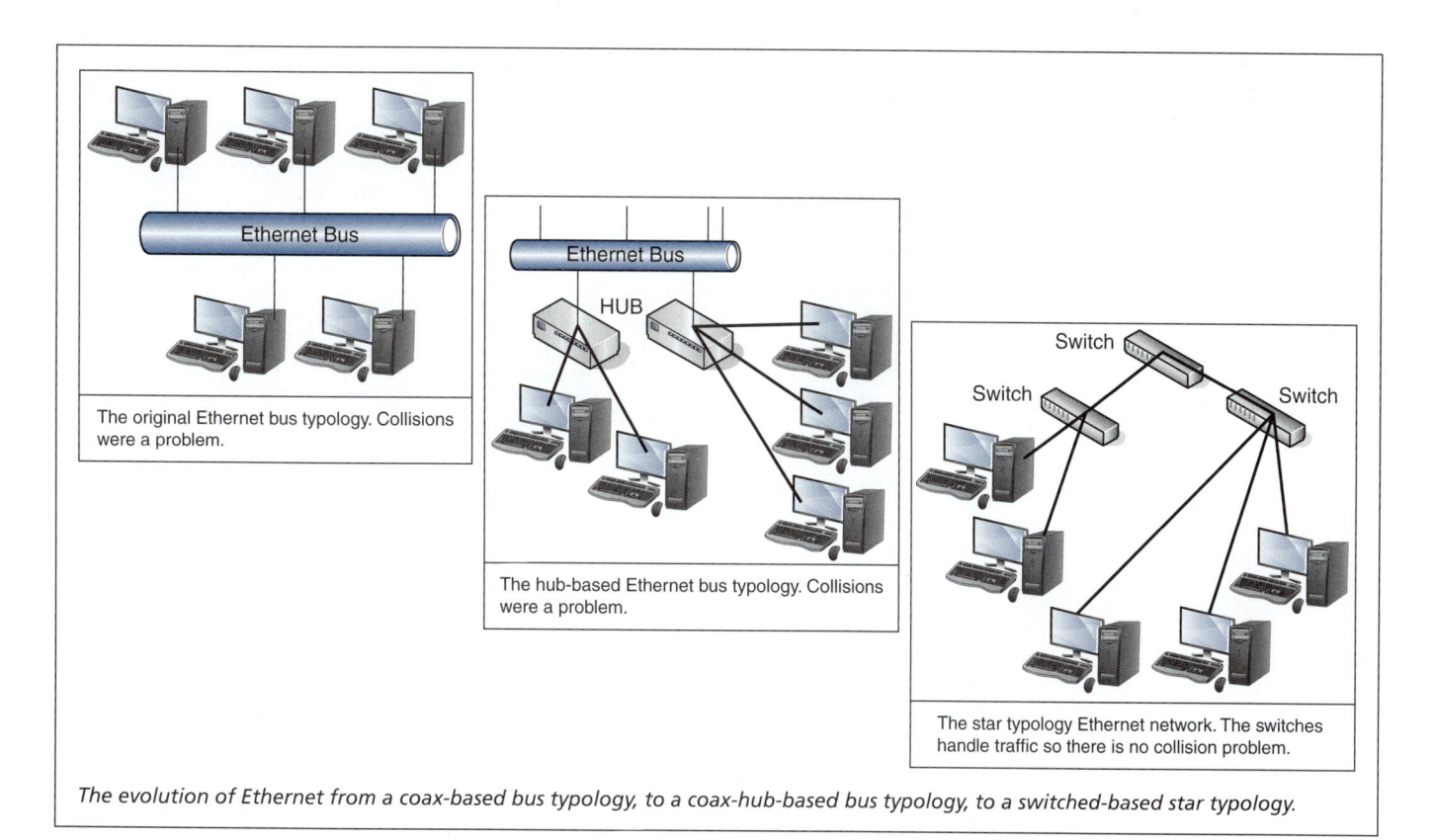

The evolution of Ethernet from a coax-based bus typology, to a coax-hub-based bus typology, to a switched-based star typology.

FIGURE 2-9 Evolution of Ethernet

Multiple Users and the Network

CMSA/CD

Because Ethernet originally used a shared coax cable in a bus typology, a way was needed to determine whether the bus was busy or whether a computer could use it and send a message. A scheme was developed called **carrier sense multiple access with collision detection (CSMA/CD)** as part of the original Ethernet standard. CSMA/CD was simpler than the other major competing network technology—Token Ring—which used a ring typology and a token-passing scheme to control collisions. Ethernet's success in the marketplace is due, in part, to the simplicity of Ethernet. It is simpler and cheaper to install, easier to maintain and troubleshoot, and faster than many other technologies.

CSMA/CD can be broken into two parts: (1) carrier sense multiple access (CSMA), and (2) collision detection (CD). These two procedures—shown in Figure 2-10—create the CSMA/CD scheme. CSMA is an attempt at collision avoidance and is implemented in the host computer Ethernet adapter card. CSMA/CD follows these steps:

- The host computer prepares a frame at Layer 2. Remember, this is an encapsulated PDU that contains the PDUs from Layers 3 through 5.
- The host computer determines whether the transmission medium is busy. It needs to know if another computer is using the media. If another computer is communicating, then the host computer waits a predetermined amount of time, called the interframe gap.
- The host computer then propagates the frame over the media at Layer 1—it starts to communicate.
- If a collision occurs, then the host goes to the collision detection procedure.
- Transmission counters reset, and frame transmission ends.

The collision detection procedure includes the following steps:

- The host continues transmission for a predetermined length of time to be sure all receivers on the bus detect the collision.
- The host computer then increments the retransmissions counter.
- If the maximum number of retransmission attempts has occurred, the host aborts transmission.
- If the maximum number of transmission attempts has not occurred, then the host waits a random amount of time based in the number of collisions.
- The host then restarts the CSMA procedure at the beginning.

FIGURE 2-10 CMSA/CD Flow

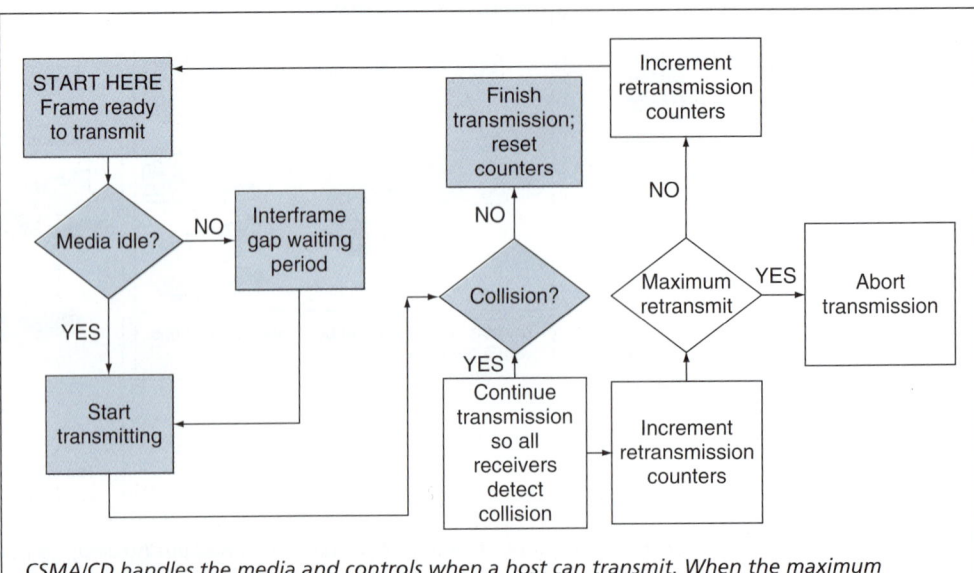

CSMA/CD handles the media and controls when a host can transmit. When the maximum number of transmits are reached, the host aborts the transmission. The blue represents the CMSA process, and the white represents the CD process.

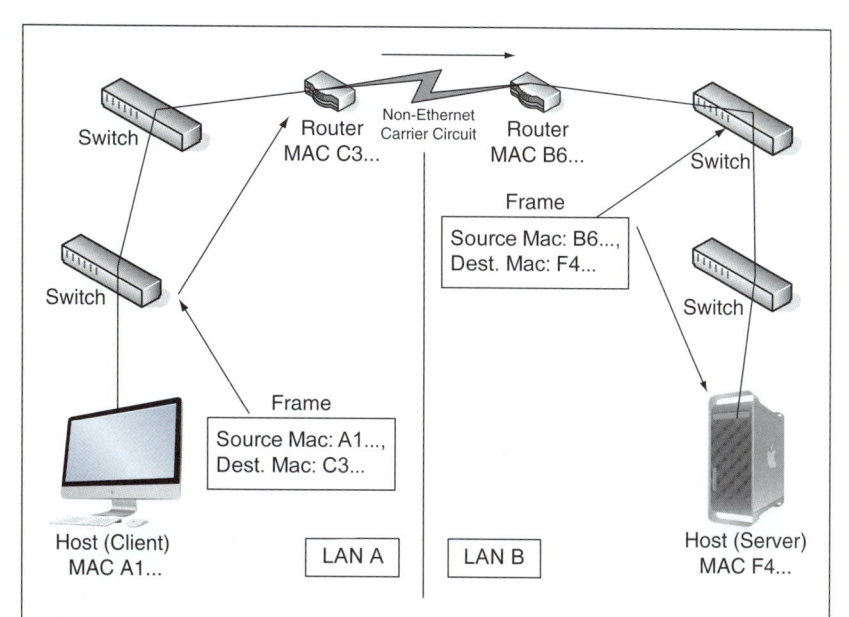

FIGURE 2-11 Frame Propagation by MAC Address

This diagram shows a frame being propagated by a client computer in LAN A with the MAC address A1... (Note that all MAC addresses have been shortened for ease of discussion.) The destination MAC address is the router, because it is the device within the LAN A that needs to get the frame. The router then propagates the frame over a non-Ethernet carrier circuit to another router. The receiving router in LAN B uses its MAC address as the source (B6...) and the host's (server) MAC address (F4...) as the destination, which is where the frame need to go.

When the full room of people are talking we have chatter; the CMSA/CD procedure can be likened to that same room full of people, except with rules that govern when people can talk. All the people are using a common medium (the air) to communicate. If rules are enforced then (1) only one person can be speaking at a time, and (2) if two people start talking at the same time (a collision) then both must wait a random period of time before beginning to talk again, creating a form of collision avoidance and collision detection.

FRAMES AND MAC ADDRESSES

Remember from the previous chapter that frames are the PDU at Layer 2. The frame has the basic format of a Frame Trailer → Frame Data → Frame Header. Ethernet is an asynchronous protocol (meaning that there is no synch signal on the media), and the frame header has the synch word that is used to synchronize the sender's and receiver's clocks so the signals being propagated over the media can be turned back into a frame. The header also has a source and destination MAC address (remember, this is the physical address within the LAN). The source address is the MAC of the sending host or device, and the destination address is the receiving host or device MAC (see Figure 2-11). Remember, MAC addresses are within-network addresses, so the MAC changes as a frame is propagated through a router. MAC/hardware addresses are used by hosts to determine whether a particular frame is meant for it. If a frame is meant for another host (i.e., a different MAC address), then it is ignored.

Physical Layer and Propagation

MEDIA

The physical layer is Layer 1 and is based in the OSI standards. Ethernet has a number of physical standards that are reviewed in Table 2-1. Ethernet started out as 10Base5, and used expensive thick coax cable as the shared medium. Ethernet 10Base2 soon followed and used less-expensive thinner coax cable as the shared medium. Both 10Base5 and 10Base2 were a configured in a bus typology. Soon afterwards, 10BaseT came into use with a star typology, using UTP as its medium.

TABLE 2-1 Common Ethernet LAN Physical Standards

Standard	Speed	Media	Comment
10Base5	10 Mbps	RG-8X	Bus typology; expensive thick Ethernet*
10Base2	10 Mbps	RG-58	Bus typology; inexpensive thin Ethernet*
10BaseT	10 Mbps	UTP	Star typology*
100BaseTX	100 Mbps	UTP	Star typology; Cat 5 required
100BaseFX	100 Mbps	Multimode Fiber Optic	Point-to-point typology; max length 400 meters for half-duplex and 2 km for full-duplex; laser light source
100BaseSX	100 Mbps	Multimode Fiber Optic	Point-to-point typology; max length 300 meters; LED light source; cheaper than laser
1000BaseT	1000 Mbps	UTP	Star topology; CAT5/CAT5e/Cat6 UTP required
1000BaseSX	1000 Mbps	Multimode Fiber Optic	Point-to-point typology; max length up to 550 meters
1000BaseLX	1000 Mbps	Single or Multimode Fiber Optic	Point-to-point typology; multimode max length 550 meters; single-mode max length 2 km, but can be optimized for up to 10 km
1000BaseLH	1000 Mbps	Single-Mode Fiber Optic	Point-to-point typology; max length 100 km
10GBase	10 Gbps	Various	Not often used yet; consists of many different standards (e.g., 10GBaseSR, 10GBaseLX4, etc.)

*Older and largely out-of-use standard

From Table 2-1, it is easy to see that Ethernet speeds vary greatly as do its media. Today, the most common installation uses UTP with modular RJ45 connectors in a star typology for connections between hosts/devices and switches, and fiber optic between switches 100BaseTX, 100Base-?X, 1000BaseT, and 1000Base?X (the question marks represent all of variable forms of the standards) are today's most commonly used Ethernet standards. Each standard is more selective about the grade of UTP used, with 1000BaseT requiring the highest quality and most expensive UTP cable.

Ethernet has fiber optic variants. Fiber optic variants are most often used for Ethernet connections between buildings on the same campus (or geographic space) or between switches in the same building. Fiber optic Ethernet is more expensive to install, but has several advantages over UTP-based Ethernet, including longer distances, higher speeds, and lack of susceptibility to electromagnetic interference. Although it does not have as large an installed base, 10GBase Ethernet is being used in some enterprise-wide and carrier-based applications. Variants of 10GBase Ethernet each use different media; for example, 10BaseSR is designed for short range over multimedia fiber optic media.

The Data Link Layer and Frames

The data link layer is Layer 2 in the hybrid TCP/IP-OSI model. The protocol data unit (PDU) for this layer is the frame, and it is used within the network to transmit data. Remember that a frame has a packet, segment, and application message encapsulated inside it. As discussed earlier, the most common format for an Ethernet frame is Ethernet II. The standard format for an Ethernet II frame can be seen in Figure 2-12.

Frame Check Sequence	Payload (Encapsulated PDUs from Higher Layers)	Ethernet Type	Source Mac Address	Destination Mac Address	Preamble (synchword)
The Ethernet II frame format includes a number of fields that facilitate data transmission within the LAN.					

FIGURE 2-12 Ethernet II Frame

An Ethernet II frame contains a number of fields, which include the following:

- **Preamble.** This field is a synchword and is composed of 64 bits. The first 56 bits consist of an alternating 1 and 0 pattern (i.e., 1010101010101010 . . .), and the last 8 bits consist of the value 10101011 called the Start of Frame Delimiter (SFD). These 64 bits are used to synchronize the clocks of the sending and receiving devices so the propagated signals can be interpreted correctly. Because Ethernet uses a synchword, it is an asynchronous transmission protocol. By the time the SFD is read, the receiving host must be ready to receive data because the destination MAC addresses follows the SFD.
- **Destination MAC Address.** This 48-bit field contains the LAN physical hardware address of the device that must receive the frame. The destination can be a telecommunication device, such as a router that allows between-LAN communication, or it can be the final host. The destination MAC address always contains an address of a device within the LAN that the source host is connected to.
- **Source MAC Address.** This 48-bit field contains the LAN physical hardware address of the device sending the frame.
- **Ethernet Type.** This 16-bit field indicates the type of payload being carried in the frame. Payload types include IPv4, IPv6, ARP, 802.1Q Tagged (used to indicate VLANs), and PPPoE as well as a number of other payload types.
- **Payload.** This variable length field contains the encapsulated PDUs from the higher layers. The payload maximum is 1500 bits.
- **Frame Check Sequence.** This 32-bit field is used in error detection. The sending host computes a value based on the pattern of bits in the frame using an algorithm such as cyclic redundancy checking. That value is stored in the Frame Check Sequence field. The receiving host computes the same value using the same algorithm and compares the sent value to the one computed by the receiving host. If the receiving host determines that the two values are different it discards the frame because it has errors. The actual error correction will occur at Layer 4 of the hybrid model (IEEE.org, 2011).

The data link layer is the interface between the physical layer (Layer 1) and the Internet layer (Layer 3). The data link layer is responsible for transmission within the LAN or physical link. In Ethernet, the data link layer is actually broken up into two sublayers: the MAC sublayer and the Logical Link Control (LLC) sublayer (see Figure 2-13). The MAC sublayer implements CSMA/CD as previously described. The LLC sublayer is the same for Ethernet or any other physical standards such as Token Ring or WiFi, and provides traffic control for the various standards and the media. Although not often implemented, the LLC sublayer optionally provides flow control, acknowledgment, and error recovery. The LLC sublayer provides the interface between the Internet layer and the MAC sublayer. For example, if a host was configured to work with both the IP and IPX (legacy Novell) standards at Layer 3 (i.e., Internet layer), then the LLC would be responsible for taking an incoming frame from the MAC layer and routing it to the correct Layer 3 process.

Ethernet Summary

The IEEE 802.3 standard governs Ethernet physical media and data link layer operations. Today, Ethernet is implemented using UTP and fiber optic media and extended wirelessly. The typical installation uses UTP for horizontal runs (i.e., from the

FIGURE 2-13 LLC and MAC Sublayer Processing

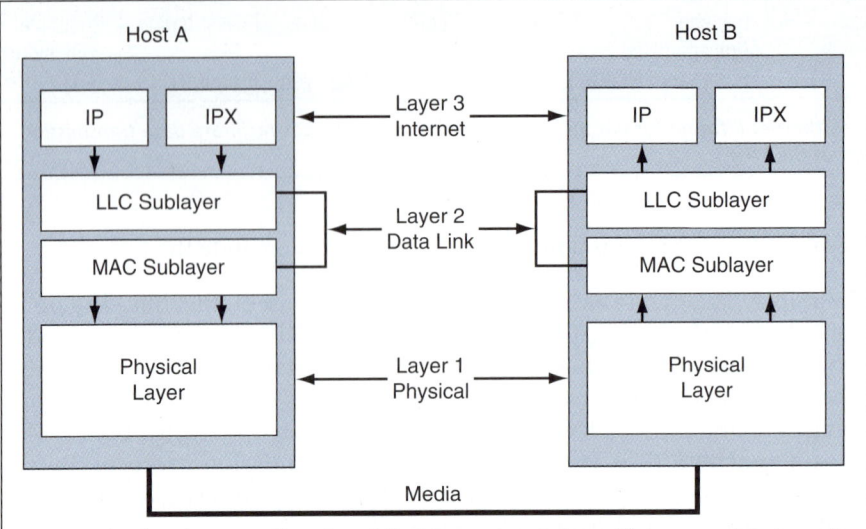

Communications between Host A and Host B occurs as follows: The appropriate Layer 3 process prepares a packet with the between-network addressing (e.g., IP address), then passes it off to the LLC sublayer of the data link. The LLC can be thought of as traffic control, keeping track of which Layer 3 process sends/gets the packet. The LLC passes the packet off to the MAC sublayer, which adds MAC addresses (i.e., hardware addresses) and prepares the frame for propagation. The MAC sublayer passes the frame off to the physical layer for propagation. The receiving host reverses the process.

switch to the desktop/printer) and fiber optic for vertical runs (i.e., between switches). Ethernet is the most ubiquitous LAN technology and has largely replaced competing standards such as Token Ring and Fiber Distributed Data Interface (FDDI). Over the recent past the Ethernet LAN has been extended through wireless IEEE 802.11 devices, which are discussed in the next section of this chapter.

Wireless Technologies

A number of wireless technologies allow an organization to extend its wired network. **Wireless technologies** allow an organization to deploy devices (e.g., computers and printers) without running wires to each location. The advantages of wireless include reduced costs and increased flexibility. With wireless technologies, devices can be placed in locations that might have been previously inaccessible. In order to understand wireless communications it is helpful to understand how wireless works and what the frequency spectrum is.

Frequency Spectrum

Wireless telecommunication devices operate by encoding data streams into radio waves and propagating those data streams at specific radio frequencies. These devices can also decode those same radio waves back into data streams. Frequency is measured in the Hertz (Hz) of the signal. The frequency at which wireless devices operate exist along the **frequency spectrum** (see Figure 2-14), which goes from zero to infinity. The frequency spectrum is broken into two major sections: the licensed portion and the unlicensed portion.

FIGURE 2-14 Frequency Spectrum

Frequency Spectrum Zero Hz to Infinity HZ	Licensed	Cellular Band	Many channels exist within each band. Each channel is a range of frequencies measured in Hz, and each channel has a bandwidth, also measured in Hz.
		PCS Band	
		Microwave Band	
		TV Band	
		AM Radio Band	
		FM Radio Band	
	Unlicensed	Shared Frequency Space	

Within these two major portions of the frequency spectrum sections are dedicated to specific types of signals. These dedicated sections are called bands, and within the bands, **channels** exist. In the licensed band, radio stations, TV broadcast stations, microwave communication users, cellular communications providers, and others apply for a channel license from the government authority (the Federal Communications Commission in the United States) that controls the frequency spectrum (FCC, 2011). In the unlicensed band, devices such as cordless phones, wireless network access points, and walkie-talkie radios can operate without obtaining any licensing. In the licensed band, signals should not interfere with each other, but in the unlicensed band, devices can interfere with each other.

In summary, licensed and unlicensed space exists within the frequency spectrum. The licensed space is broken up into bands, and each band has channels. Channels exist in the unlicensed band as well. A channel starts at a specific Hz, and ends at another. The difference between the high Hz and low Hz of a channel is the bandwidth.

Large-Scale Wireless Technologies

Before moving to LAN-based wireless technologies, it is appropriate to review several technologies that are used by carriers and other large organizations: (1) microwave, (2) satellite, and (3) WiMAX.

MICROWAVE

Microwave communications are used in point-to-point applications. The user must obtain government permission to use a specific microwave channel. Microwave transmission is line of site; in other words, the microwave dishes need to be pointed at each other. The properties of microwave communication are the reason telecommunication carriers and other organizations often use it to provide connection between locations where cabling or carrier circuits are not feasible (see Figure 2-15).

SATELLITE

Satellite communications provide a point-to-point circuit. The three types of satellites are categorized by their altitudes (see Table 2-2). Satellites require an uplink station on Earth that sends the desired signal to the satellite, and a satellite dish at the location receiving the signal. The satellite receives the signal from an uplink station, then reproduces the signal, and broadcasts the signal back to Earth, over a large area. The higher the satellite, the larger the area that is covered (see Figure 2-16). If a satellite is geostationary, it appears over the same location of Earth all the time. If it is not geostationary, the satellite rotates around Earth, and users are passed off from one satellite to another.

WIMAX

Worldwide Interoperability for Microwave Access, or WiMAX, is a protocol that provides mobile and fixed Internet access and is based on the IEEE standard 802.16. It is

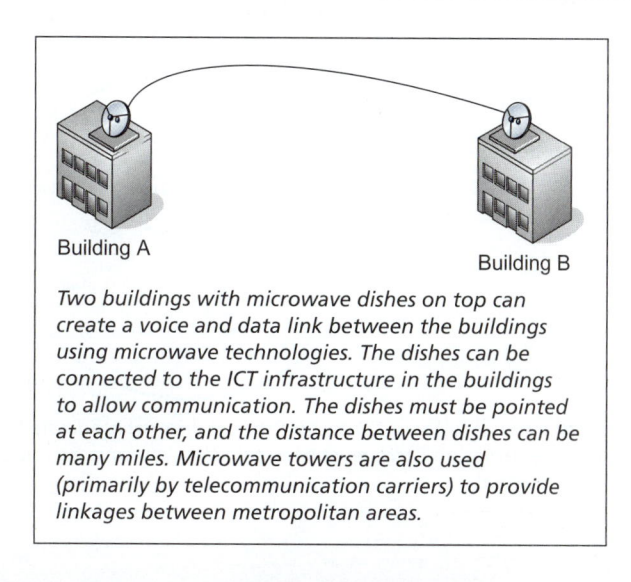

FIGURE 2-15 Microwave Communication

Building A   Building B

Two buildings with microwave dishes on top can create a voice and data link between the buildings using microwave technologies. The dishes can be connected to the ICT infrastructure in the buildings to allow communication. The dishes must be pointed at each other, and the distance between dishes can be many miles. Microwave towers are also used (primarily by telecommunication carriers) to provide linkages between metropolitan areas.

TABLE 2-2 Satellite Type and Altitude

Type	Altitude	
Low Earth Orbit (LEO)	0 to 2000 km	Not geostationary; rotates around Earth about once every 90 minutes. A constellation of LEO satellites is required for continuous coverage. Can be accessed with a small antenna on a handheld device (i.e., omnidirectional antenna).
Medium Earth Orbit (MEO)	2001 km to just below GEO	Not geostationary; rotates around Earth about once every 120 minutes to 12 hours, depending on altitude. A constellation of MEO satellites is required for continuous coverage. Can be accessed with an omnidirectional antenna.
Geostationary Orbit (GEO)	35,786 km	Geostationary with Earth and has a fixed area on Earth to which it broadcasts. Requires a ground station to receive a signal from the satellite.

essentially "broadband wireless access." This technology was promulgated by the WiMAX forum in 2001. WiMAX is described as a standards-based technology that enables the delivery of last-mile wireless broadband access as an alternative to cable, DSL, and satellite. WiMAX is a technology being deployed by telecommunications companies to provide mobile or at-home Internet connectivity at broadband speeds. This technology can be used to support cellular data and voice services, and may even supplant traditional fixed land-based carrier circuits place in the market.

LAN-Based Wireless

LAN-based wireless telecommunication (WLAN) devices are deployed by organizations seeking to allow wireless network access to users of their network. Devices used to support WLAN applications exist in the unlicensed shared frequency space. A wireless network in a corporate application is usually created by attaching wireless access points to a wired network. At home, you would typically attach a wireless access point to a DSL or cable modem, or the wireless access device may be part of the modem itself. The **802.11** series of wireless devices are the most commonly used to create a wireless network, sometimes call WiFi or hotspot.

FIGURE 2-16 Satellite Transmission

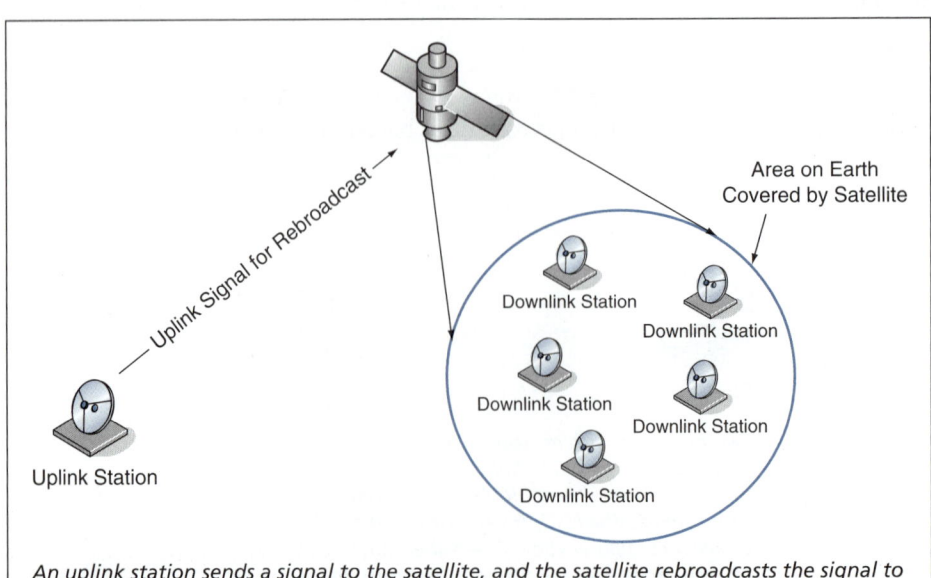

An uplink station sends a signal to the satellite, and the satellite rebroadcasts the signal to an area on Earth. Satellite dishes on Earth must be within the area covered and pointed at the satellite to receive its signal.

Chapter 2 • Building the Local Area Network Using Ethernet 57

> **VIGNETTE BOX 2-1**
>
> **Joe Smith's Home LAN**
>
> Joe Smith may have a wireless network at home. This will allow him to have multiple devices (hosts) as part of his home network. All of these hosts can share one Internet connection.

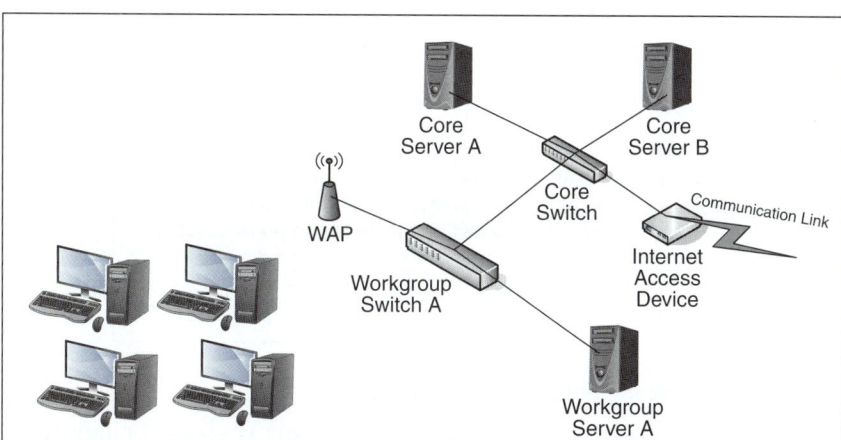

A small LAN with two switches, three servers, a wireless access point (WAP), and some type of Internet access device. The WAP allows hosts with wireless adapters to connect to the network via radio waves. In this example four computers are wirelessly connected to the LAN.

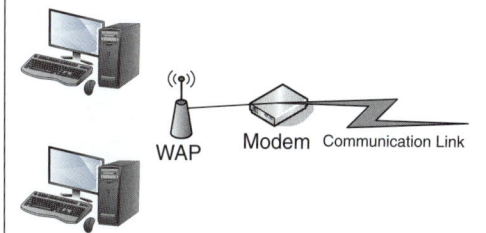

A home network that includes a communication link (possibly DSL or cable modem), a modem, and a wireless access point (WAP). In this example two PCs connect to the modem wirelessly. This configuration is often used for a home network where multiple PCs want to share one Internet connection. Often just one device acts as both modem and WAP.

FIGURE 2-17 Wireless Access Points

WLAN technologies allow *over the air* signal propagation, rather than using wired media. The most prevalent WLAN technology is standardized as IEEE 802.11. The 802.11 technologies can be used to extend the hardwired Ethernet LAN in an enterprise situation or to provide wireless access in the home or small office (Figure 2-17).

A **wireless access point (WAP)** is used to provide wireless network access to hosts, which requires that each host have a wireless access device and the network have at least one WAP (see Figure 2-18 for an example of a WAP). The host connects to the WAP through its wireless access device. The wireless access device can be connected to its host via USB, an Ethernet connection on the host, or an internal card plugged into the host bus. In addition, some host motherboards have internal wireless devices built in.

The WAP can be a stand-alone device that plugs into a network switch, or it can be a multifunction device with switch, router, WAP, and/or modem built into the same unit. The stand-alone WAP is most often used to extend a wired corporate LAN, whereas the multifunction WAP is most often used in small office or home situations to connect to the Internet. WAPs can operate in infrastructure or ad hoc (point-to-point) mode, which is explained in Figure 2-19. Whether the WAP is stand-alone or part of a multifunction device, its purpose is the same—to give wireless access to hosts that have wireless access devices.

802.11 and Ethernet

802.11 LANs are often referred to as wireless Ethernet. Technically, this reference is not correct because 802.11 does not use the Ethernet frame format. However, because it uses the same transmission principles as Ethernet, it is not too much of a stretch to call 802.11 technologies *wireless Ethernet*. Even the creators of Ethernet, notably Bob Metcalfe, support this naming. For clarity's sake, this textbook will refer to the wireless standard as 802.11, which is the IEEE working group in control of this standard.

This device contains a Layer 3 router, a 4-port Ethernet Layer 2 switch, and a wireless access point. It is often used in home networks connected to a DSL or cable modem for Internet access.

FIGURE 2-18 Multifunction Wireless Access Point

FIGURE 2-19 WAP Infrastructure vs. Ad Hoc (Point-to-Point) Mode

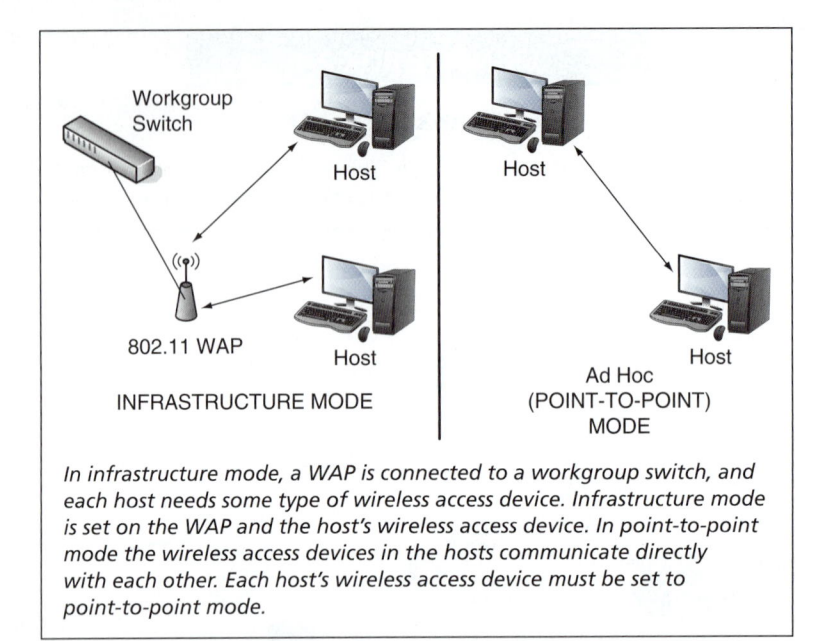

In infrastructure mode, a WAP is connected to a workgroup switch, and each host needs some type of wireless access device. Infrastructure mode is set on the WAP and the host's wireless access device. In point-to-point mode the wireless access devices in the hosts communicate directly with each other. Each host's wireless access device must be set to point-to-point mode.

IEEE 802.11 Wireless Access: The Technical Details

The most frequently installed wireless devices use the IEEE 802.11 standard. In order to better understand how WAPs are used to extend the wireless network and to understand how multifunction wireless devices operate, a review of the technical details of 802.11 follows.

The IEEE 802 working group has promulgated a number of standards, including 802.11a, 802.11b, 802.11g, and 802.11n. There are other 802.11 standards but these are the most common, with 802.11b, 802.11g, and 802.11n being the ones used most often today All of these standards use unlicensed frequency spectrum, and therefore do not need any special regulatory permission to set up or use. However, care must be taken because some wireless devices, such as older cordless phones, use the same frequency spectrum as 802.11 devices, leading to conflict between devices.

802.11 FREQUENCY SPECTRUM AND CHANNELS

IEEE 802.11 devices use **radio frequency modulation** techniques to propagate signals between WAPs and the host's wireless access device. 802.11 devices draw on a number of modulation techniques, each of which has particular properties including the range (distance) of the device. The devices also use a specific part of the frequency spectrum for signal propagation. 802.11a devices use the 5 GHz band, 802.11/b/g devices use the 2.4GHZ band, and 802.11n devices can use either 2.4 GHz or 5 GHz band within the frequency spectrum. The band and range can be seen in Table 2-3.

802.11 b/g devices using the 2.4 GhZ spectrum divide it into 14 overlapping channels. Due to technical and regulatory limitations, the number of useable overlapping channels in the United States is 11, and the number of nonoverlapping channels is 3

TABLE 2-3 IEEE Wireless Standards

IEEE Standard	Speed	Unlicensed Frequency Spectrum	Indoor Range (Distance)	Outdoor Range (Distance)
802.11a	54 Mbps	5 GHz	35 meters	120 meters
802.11b	11 Mbps	2.4 GHz	38 meters	140 meters
802.11g	54 Mbps	2.4 GHz	38 meters	140 meters
802.11n	248 Mbps	2.4 GHz or 5 GHz	70 meters	250 meters

(channels 1, 6, and 11). Nonoverlapping channels are used most because channel overlap on devices close to each other can cause unacceptable signal degradation. In other countries the number of available channels and those used most often can differ; for example, in European Union countries the maximum number of channels is 13, and the channels normally used are 1, 5, 9, and 13. WAPs and host access devices must use the same channel to communicate.

SERVICE SET IDENTIFIER

Multiple wireless LANs can operate in the same geographic area because the 802.11 standards require all 802.11 frames to contain a **Service Set Identifier (SSID)**. The SSID is a string of up to 32 alphanumeric characters that all wireless access devices and WAPs that wish to communicate with each other must have in common. The SSID is manually entered into the WAP. WAPs can be configured to broadcast their SSID so nearby clients can automatically attach to them, or not broadcast their SSID as a weak form of security. The client can be either manually configured or automatically detect available WAPs that are broadcasting their SSID, as in Figure 2-20. Advanced WAPs provide client isolation, preventing clients from communicating with each other.

WIRELESS SECURITY

Because wireless connection to a WAP does not require a physical media (e.g., UTP), wireless access presents particular security issues. The first and most obvious security measure is to not broadcast the SSID; however, because the SSID is transmitted in clear text in each frame it would be easy for a hacker to detect. Over time, from the original introduction of 802.11 to now, several security protocols have emerged. Initially, the Wired Equivalent Privacy (WEP) used RC4 (a security algorithm) for encryption. WEP was easy to hack into so the IEEE 802.11 working group began to devise new security specifications, 802.11i. As a stopgap measure the Wi-Fi Alliance (an industry trade group) announced an interim specification based on an IEEE 802.11i wireless security draft called WI-Fi Protected Access (WPA), while waiting for IEEE to announce the a new security specification. Vendors began to implement WPA in products around mid-2003, prior to the actual ratification of the 802.11i standard. When the final 802.11i specification was ratified in 2004, devices already existed with WPA security standard. The ratified new 802.11i became known as WPA2 and used Advanced Encryption Standard (AES) rather than RC4. Many

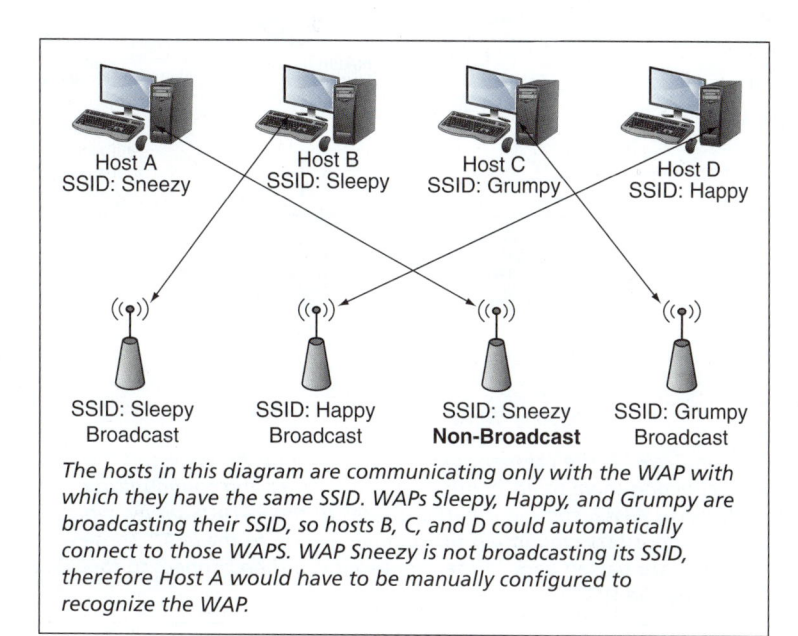

FIGURE 2-20 SSIDs

The hosts in this diagram are communicating only with the WAP with which they have the same SSID. WAPs Sleepy, Happy, and Grumpy are broadcasting their SSID, so hosts B, C, and D could automatically connect to those WAPS. WAP Sneezy is not broadcasting its SSID, therefore Host A would have to be manually configured to recognize the WAP.

FIGURE 2-21 802.11 Security Standards

Current Wireless Security Standard	What Organization	Comments
WEP	Original IEEE 802.11	Used RC4 security algorithm; easy to hack
WPA	Stopgap standard, introduced mid-2003 by *Wi-Fi Alliance*, based on IEEE 802.11i draft	Partially implements the actually 802.11i security standard based on a draft before official ratification by IEEE; between the draft and final ratification the standard changed considerably. WPA uses the easy-to-hack RC4 algorithm
WPA2	IEEE 802.11i Security Standard, introduced in 2004	Implements the fully ratified 802.11i security standard that uses AES, a government-strength security algorithm

clients and WAPs support all three security standards, WEP, WPA, and WPA2 (Figure 2-21). WPA2 is the current standard.

WPA2 operates in two modes: Enterprise and Personal. Enterprise WPA2 uses a RADIUS server, and Personal WPA2 uses a preshared key. Personal WPA2 requires that a key (i.e., a string of alphanumeric characters) be entered into the WAP, and the same key be entered in the hosts. That key is used by the WAP and the host to authenticate to each other and to encrypt data as it is transmitted wirelessly.

Enterprise WPA2 uses a RADIUS server that provides authentication services. RADIUS servers are officially known as Remote Authentication Dial in User Service (RADIUS) from this protocol's early roots as a dial-up authentication server; however, today the RADIUS server's function has expanded to include authentication to a number of network-based services, including 802.11 WAPs. Clients must be configured to use a RADIUS server for WAP authentication. The RADIUS server allows the client to authenticate to it, and then the RADIUS server provides the security credentials necessary for the client to authenticate to the WAP (see Figure 2-22).

FIGURE 2-22 Personal and Enterprise WPA2

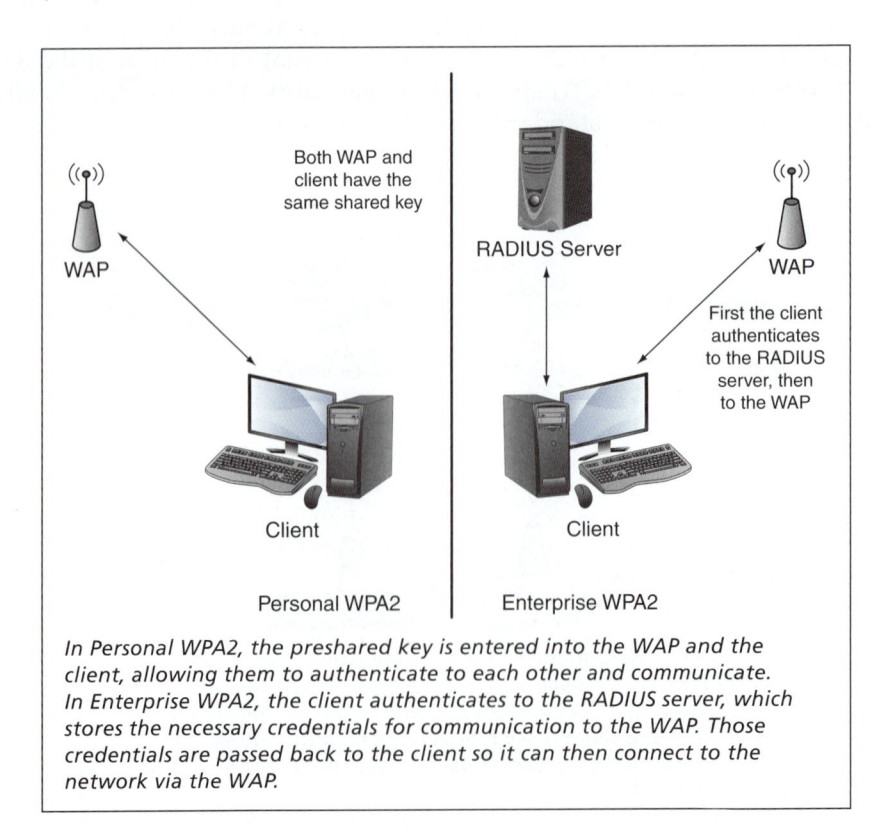

In Personal WPA2, the preshared key is entered into the WAP and the client, allowing them to authenticate to each other and communicate. In Enterprise WPA2, the client authenticates to the RADIUS server, which stores the necessary credentials for communication to the WAP. Those credentials are passed back to the client so it can then connect to the network via the WAP.

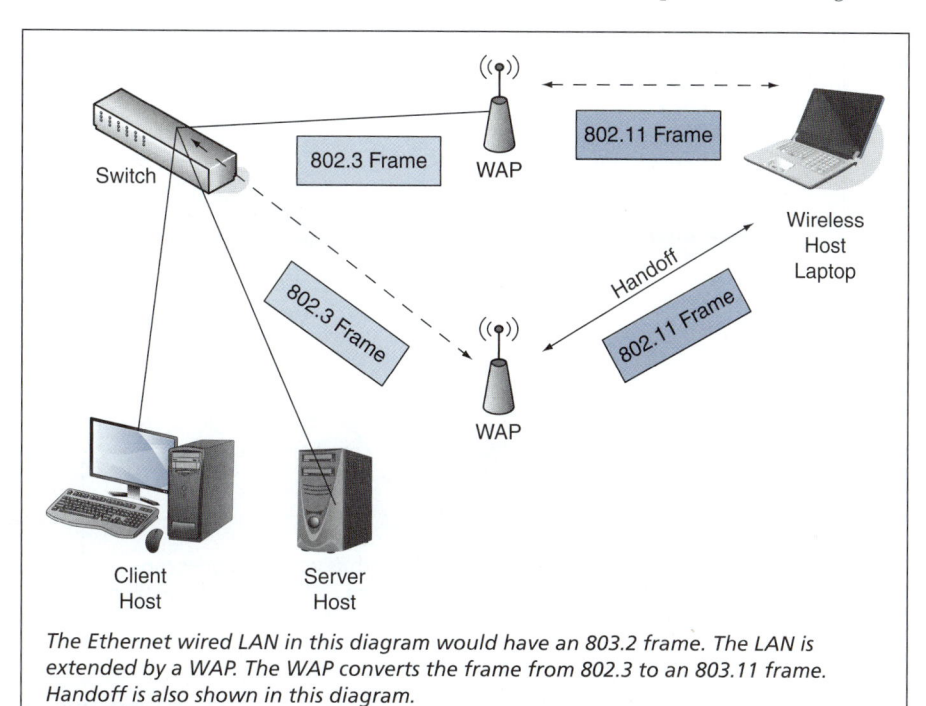

FIGURE 2-23 Frame Conversion in a Wired LAN Extended by a WAP

The Ethernet wired LAN in this diagram would have an 803.2 frame. The LAN is extended by a WAP. The WAP converts the frame from 802.3 to an 803.11 frame. Handoff is also shown in this diagram.

HANDOFF

Figure 2-23 shows a wireless laptop being handed off between two WAPs. **Handoff** occurs when a mobile client travels too far from an access point, and an access point with the same SSID is closer to the client. This functionality was standardized as IEEE 803.11f in 2003; however, vendor interoperability can be limited.

MULTIPLE USERS

WAPs can provide connectivity to a number of clients simultaneously; however, only one client can transmit at a time, otherwise their signals will overlap and be unintelligible. Therefore, it is necessary that WAPs implement flow control. 802.11 devices implement **carrier sense multiple access with collision avoidance + acknowledgment (CSMA/CA+ACK)** to control traffic between WAPs and clients.

Let's assume that a WAP is connected to a wired LAN. In the wired LAN, the 802.3 (Ethernet) frame format is used, and that 802.11 frame is sent to the WAP. The WAP converts that 802.3 frame into an 802.11 frame for wireless transmission via CSMA/CA+ACK.

The CMSA/CA process, diagrammed in Figure 2-24, proceeds as follows:

- The sender (WAP or client wireless access device) listens for traffic.
- If it hears traffic, it sets a random timer and waits.
- If there is no traffic, it then checks the last time it heard traffic.
  - If the elapsed time since the last time the sender heard traffic is less than the elapsed-time-since-last-transmit value, the sender waits a random amount of time. It then sends traffic if no sender is transmitting.
  - If the elapsed time since the last time the sender heard traffic is greater than the elapsed-time-since-last-transmit value, the sender transmits.

The ACK process proceeds as follows:

- The receiver immediately sends back an acknowledgment.
- If the sender does not receive an acknowledgment, it retransmits using CSMA/CA.

FIGURE 2-24 CMSA/CA+ACK Flow

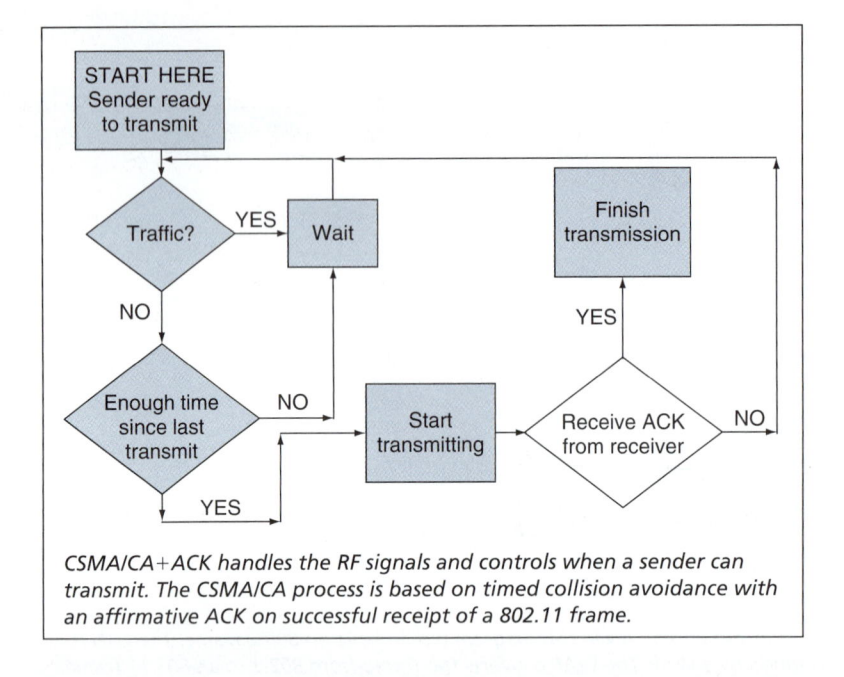

CSMA/CA+ACK handles the RF signals and controls when a sender can transmit. The CSMA/CA process is based on timed collision avoidance with an affirmative ACK on successful receipt of a 802.11 frame.

In addition to CSMA/CD+ACK, the 802.11 standard includes the option of implementing a request-to-send/clear-to-send (RTS/CTS) form of flow control. CSMA/CD+ACK is mandatory, but RTS/CTS is optional, although it is often used. In RTS/CTS the sender sends an RTS to a specific receiver, and waits for a CTS from that receiver. The RTS/CTS is transmitted over the wireless RF (radio frequency) link between the WAP and host wireless access device. RTS/CTS has been shown to slow throughput, and because it is optional it should be used in situations where it is truly needed. When 801.11b (11 Mbps) stations and 802.11g (54 Mbps) stations share the same access point, the 802.11g stations must use RTS/CTS.

WIRELESS PROPAGATION PROBLEMS

Wireless signal propagation suffers from propagation problems, although they are different problems than those experienced by wired propagation. Wireless propagation problems are tricky to diagnose because different clients accessing the same WAP can experience different problems. We will review the most common ones, which include those illustrated in Figure 2-25.

FIGURE 2-25 Wireless Propagation Effects

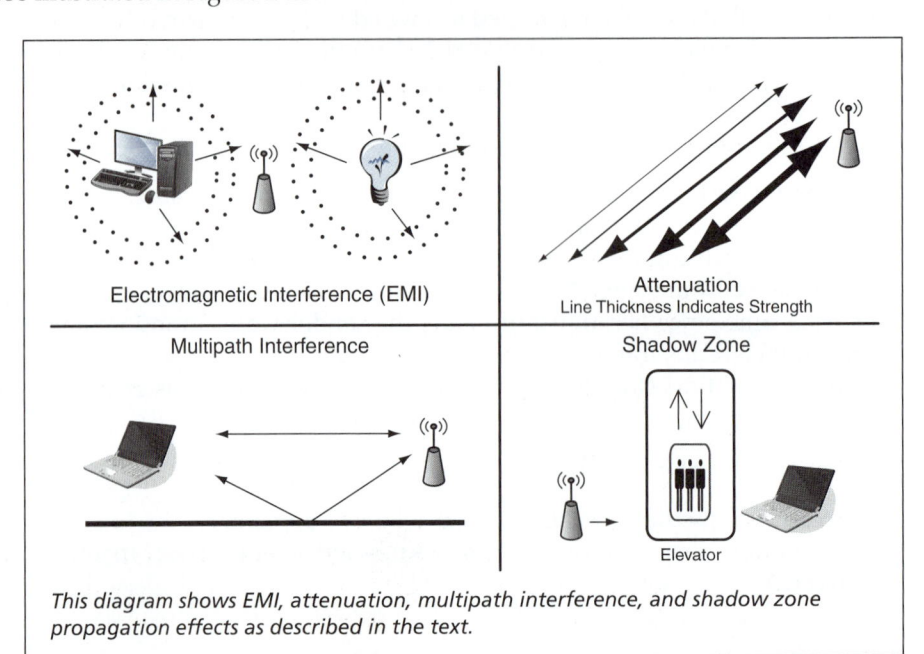

This diagram shows EMI, attenuation, multipath interference, and shadow zone propagation effects as described in the text.

Dead Spots/Shadow Zones Dead spots or shadow zones are areas where radio signals are poorly received because they are blocked by objects. Radio waves can go through or around some objects, but not all. It could be a building, elevator, very thick wall, or other dense object that prevents or slows radio wave transmission. If you have ever had problems using a cellular phone inside a building, but had it work outside, you are familiar with this sort of problem

Rapid Attenuation The strength of radio signals attenuates (reduces) much faster than signals propagated over wire or fiber optic cable. This phenomenon is referred to as the Inverse Square Law Attenuation. Basically, it means that signal strength rapidly declines the farther you get from the antenna, and that the receiver must be close to the antenna or that signal strength must be high. This factor greatly influences how far WLAN transmission can propagate.

Electromagnetic Interference As discussed in an earlier chapter, electromagnetic interference (EMI) is caused by motors and other electrical equipment, such as florescent lights or microwave ovens, that radiate electrical energy. Sometimes the radio frequency energy that is radiated is at the same frequency as the WLAN transmission, and if the EMI is close enough or powerful enough, it can interfere with WLAN performance.

Multipath Interference Radio signals can bounce off walls, floors, and other objects that are between the sender and the receiver (remember, radio signals are propagated in a sphere), which can cause the receiver to receive two or more signals that are *out of phase* with each other. *Out of phase* means that the signals arrive at the receiver at slightly different times, making it difficult, if not impossible for the receiver to understand the garbled signal.

Frequency Effect on Propagation Problems As was just discussed, different wireless standards operate at different frequencies. This is an important point because the frequency of the signal can affect the signal's ability to propagate. Slower frequency signals have a greater ability to flow around objects than faster ones. That means that 802.11b (2.4 GHz) and 802.11g (2.4 GHz) have a greater ability to travel around objects than 802.11a (5 GHz). Slower signals also have better attenuation properties and therefore experience less rapid attenuation than faster signals.

Personal Area Network: Short-Range Wireless

Another type of network is the **personal area network (PAN)**. WLAN technologies are a good solution for extending the Ethernet network or providing wireless access in a small office/home office environment, whereas PAN technologies are a good solution for replacing cables in your personal area. Bluetooth is the most prevalent PAN technology, with its range limited to 10 meters and a maximum speed of 722 kbps. This makes Bluetooth short range and slow when compared to 802.11 WLAN technologies. Bluetooth has the advantage of being simpler and cheaper to implement. It should be noted that Bluetooth is subject to the propagation effects of other radio frequency networking technologies.

A few important features in Bluetooth are not offered in 802.11 technologies:

- Bluetooth is low power when compared to 802.11, which means that Bluetooth drains batteries on wireless devices less than 802.11 wireless network adaptors. This lower power use means longer battery life.
- Bluetooth uses application profiles; 802.11 technologies do not. Application profiles are predefined configurations that allow devices to work together. For example, a Bluetooth-enabled notebook computer and printer may be able to work together as soon as they recognize each other. 802.11 LANs require configuration for devices to work together. Although Bluetooth does not support many devices, those that it does support should work together seamlessly.
- Bluetooth supports users in an attempt to eliminate cable connections for their personal devices, including PCs, printers, cell phones, and fax machines. Many devices are Bluetooth-enabled. 802.11 does not support this same type of personal cable reduction.

BUILDING A LAN

With the basic technical materials to build a wired and wireless LAN covered, this chapter will move into a discussion of what it takes to build a local area network, extend it with wireless access, and create a home network. The unit opening vignette, HealthyWay HMO, will be used for the Enterprise LAN, and Joe Smith's house will be used for the home network. To facilitate the discussion of building the LANs, some assumptions will be made. (Note: In Unit Three we will turn out attention to building LANs for competitive advantage.)

In this section, the student is introduced to the basic concepts in building a LAN. First, a comparison is made between building a voice telephone system and LAN wiring. The HealthyWay's LAN and Joe Smith's home network will be used as examples. A link between the corporate LAN and the Internet will be shown as a wide area network (WAN) communication link, but the details of how to build the WAN and VPN connections will be covered in the next chapter.

LAN Wiring

Building telephone wiring is based on UTP cabling. The cabling is normally UTP Category 3, which is only sufficient to carry slow Ethernet signaling. The concepts discussed in this section for building a telephone network and LAN are based on a number of standards from the Telecommunications Industry Association (TIA) and the Electronic Industries Alliance (EIA). TIA is a U.S.-based trade association that represents about 600 telecommunications companies and was formed in 1988 as an offshoot of EIA. The standards define techniques for building and campus telecommunication cabling infrastructure are known as **structured cabling**. This discussion is technical and included so the business student understands and is able to communicate with the engineers and other technical staff.

STRUCTURED CABLING

Structured cabling is based on a number of well-defined subsystems that together form the infrastructure necessary to create a unified phone or data network. The structured cabling standards outline the use of fiber optic and shielded/unshielded twisted pair cable (STP/UTP). Because Ethernet uses UTP and fiber optic, the following discussion will be limited to those cable types. The major subsystems in a structure-cabling plan include:

- **Entrance Facility.** Here is where the internal network interfaces with the outside world. In telephone and data networks, this demarcation block or termination equipment is usually provided by a telecommunication carrier. It normally connects to a modem or some other channel service unit/data service unit (CSU/DSU), which then connects to a router (or firewall). The router is then connected into the Ethernet network.
- **Backbone Cabling (Vertical Cabling/Runs).** Backbone writing runs up through the floors of a building, or through what is called the vertical riser space. It provides interconnections for equipment rooms. The cable length limitations depend on the type of cable and the equipment it connects. Fiber optic cable is often used.
- **Horizontal Cabling (Horizontal Runs).** The cable subsystem runs from each telecommunication closet to the work area components (wall boxes/faceplates). The maximum cable distance from the telecommunication closet to the work area components is dependent on the technology and standards implemented, including the category/type of UTP.

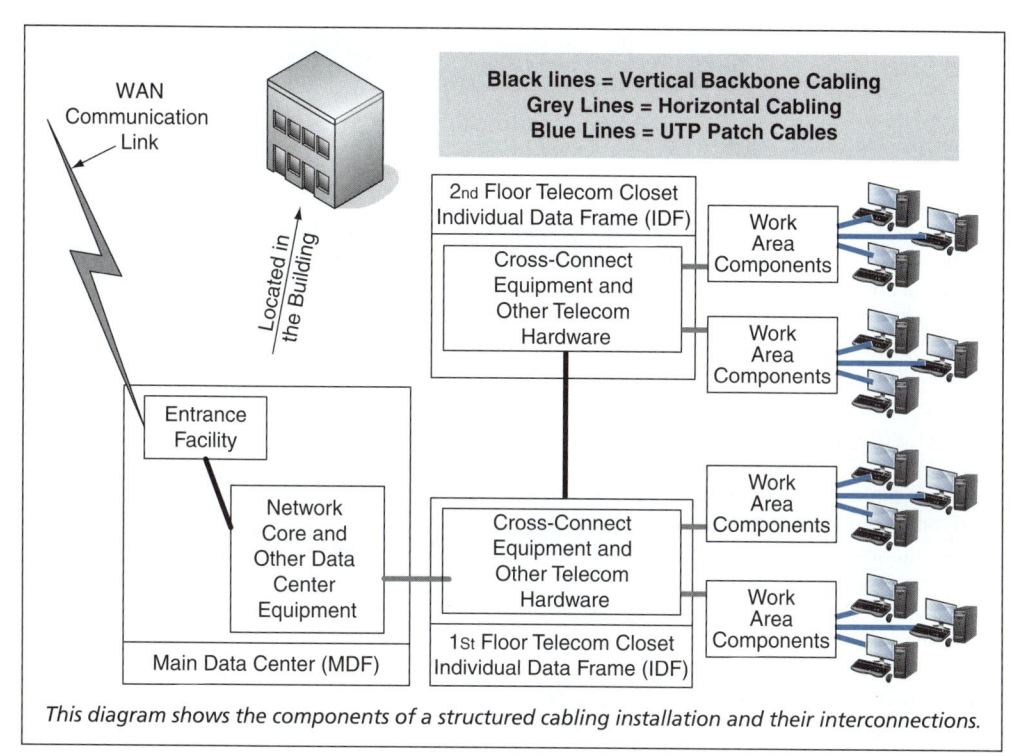

FIGURE 2-26 Structured Cabling

This diagram shows the components of a structured cabling installation and their interconnections.

- **Equipment Rooms.** The location where telecommunication and data equipment reside and where vertical and horizontal cabling interconnects can be one of two types:
  - **Main Cross-Connects (e.g., Data Center, Main Data Frame (MDF)).** Here the vertical cabling interconnects and provides connectivity to all of the telecommunication closets. A single building installation usually has one main cross-connect room, which for data LANs is often called the data center and houses the network core. In a campus (multibuilding in one geographic area) environment, it is common to find a data center that houses the network core and a main cross-connect in each building to interconnect the telecommunication closets on each floor of the building to each other, as well as back to the main data center.
  - **Telecommunication Closets (e.g., Telecom Closet, Individual Data Frame (IDF)).** The telecommunications closet houses equipment and connections for vertical and horizontal cabling. The vertical connections create the backbone of the network, and the horizontal connections provide linkages from the workgroup switches to the work area components. Large organizations often require a number of telecommunications closets. Depending on the floor plan and network size, some buildings may even have multiple telecommunications closets for each floor, with a cross-connect for each floor as well.
- **Work Area Components.** These communication outlets and writing/connectors are needed to connect user components (e.g., computers, printers) to the network. The communication outlets are wall boxes and faceplates, and the wiring/connectors consist of cables used between two devices or ports to interconnect them.

Using the structured cabling nomenclature (i.e., naming scheme), a block diagram of how cabling plans fit together is given in Figure 2-26.

> # VIGNETTE BOX 2-2
>
> ## LAN Assumptions
>
> - Two installations will be completed: one for the corporate office, and one for the home network of Joe Smith.
> - A structured cabling plan will be used to identify all of the subsystems in this implementation. All networking components will be included, except the WAN connection to the Internet. WAN connections are discussed in the next chapter.
> - The enterprise LAN will be a star typology Ethernet LAN, supporting 100 Mbps to the desktop. This speed is assumed to be enough to support the applications of HealthyWay.
> - The vertical backbone will be fiber optic using the IEEE 802.3 Ethernet standards, which supports 1 Gbps full-duplex.
> - The horizontal runs will be Cat5e UTP.
> - A data center with the network core will be installed, as well as WAN entrance facilities to provide Internet access to all employees, as well as e-mail, collaboration, application data, and database support to the entire organization.
> - The number of network drops will be established by the number or employees, printers, and the needs of the data center.
> - A telecom closet will be placed on each floor:
>   - First Floor—the data center and all telecommunications will originate from this location for the first floor. The first floor telecom closet will be named the Main Data Frame (MDF). All first floor cross connects to work group equipment located on the first floor will originate from the MDF.
>   - Second Floor—the second floor data closet will provide connectivity to the fiber backbone and a point of connection for vertical runs between the first and third floors, along with interconnection for horizontal runs on the second floor. It will be known as the Individual Data Frame Two (IDF2) because of its location on the second floor.
>   - Third Floor—the third floor data closet will provide connectivity to the fiber backbone and cross-connection for the horizontal runs that deliver Internet access to the third floor. It is called IDF3.
> - All equipment in the data center and the telecom closets will be rack-mounted.

HEALTHYWAY LAN

The design discussed here will include a number of assumptions based on our opening vignette for this unit. The first step will be a discussion of each subsystem of the structured cabling plan. We will start with the corporate network at HealthyWay, Inc., and then move to the home of Joe Smith, the chief operating officer of HealthyWay.

BUILDING THE STRUCTURED PORTION OF THE LAN

Technologies are selected to support the amount and type of network traffic. Earlier, various characteristics about switches were covered so that appropriate switches can be selected. A number of assumptions were also provided for this HealthyWay network. Those assumptions can be used in equipment selection. When selecting the

FIGURE 2-27 The Entrance Facility

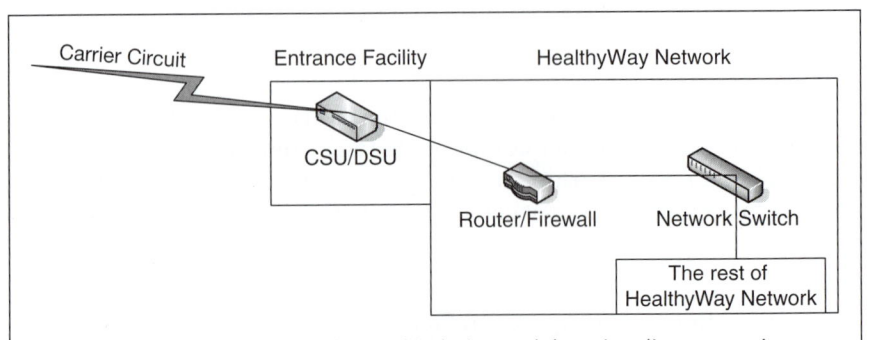

The entrance facility provides electrical isolation and data signaling conversion between the carrier and the LAN through the CSU/DSU. The CSU/DSU provides the appropriate interface for the LAN. This interface needs to be routed, and that device often provides firewall functionality. The router/firewall is then connected to the Ethernet switch for Internet connectivity to the LAN.

VIGNETTE BOX 2-3

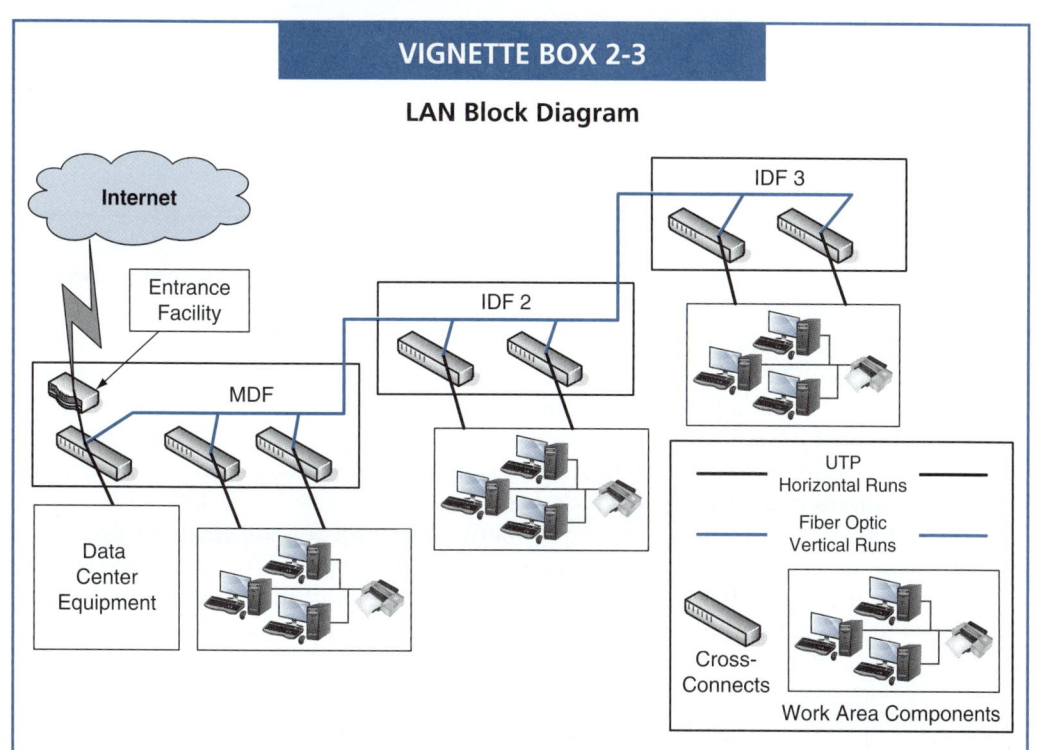

LAN Block Diagram

This diagram represents HealthyWay's structured wiring plan for its corporate network. It consists of an entrance facility that provides Internet connectivity (WAN connectivity is discussed in the next chapter), as well as three equipment rooms: MDF, IDF2, and IDF3. The MDF is contained on the first floor and is in the data center. The MDF provides network connectivity to the data center itself as well as the first floor work area equipment. IDF2 and IDF3 provide work area equipment connectivity to the second and third floors, respectively. The vertical fiber optic backbone runs are indicated in blue, and the UTP horizontal runs are indicated in black. The vertical runs provide connectivity between the floors and the data center, and the horizontal runs provide network connectivity back to the cross-connects where patch panels and switches are located. The work area components are at the end of the horizontal runs and provide a place for workgroup equipment to connect.

equipment, it is important to remember the characteristics of switches and other telecommunications equipment.

Entrance Facility The entrance facility provides an interface between the corporate network of HealthyWay and the telecommunications carrier that delivers Internet access to the company. It includes a demarcation block where the carrier terminates its incoming cable and provides an interface that can be connected to the HealthyWay network. The facility will provide a channel service unit for electrical isolation between the carrier's network and the HealthyWay network. It also provides a data service unit that translates the carrier's data signaling into one compatible with HealthyWay's network. Options for these connections are discussed in Chapter 3.

Equipment Rooms The HealthyWay configuration includes three equipment rooms, MDF, IDF2, and IDF3, in which all equipment is to be rack mounted. When selecting a location for an equipment room it is best that the room have easy access to AC and power for environmental conditioning, and vertical and horizontal cable runs. Within the equipment room, equipment racks or cabinets are used to mount equipment and associated cables.

VIGNETTE BOX 2-4

Entrance Facility

Specifics of the HealthyWay entrance facility will be covered in the next chapter on WAN connectivity.

VIGNETTE BOX 2-5

Equipment Rooms

HealthyWay will have three equipment rooms: a data center with the MDF, and one on each of the second (IDF2) and third (IDF3) floors.

Building Equipment Racks The standard equipment rack is 19 inches wide and is specified in the EIA standards. It holds equipment designed to be rack- or chassis-mounted. In addition to the equipment itself, a number of other items are put in the rack, including cabling management systems, shelves to hold non–rack-mountable equipment, power distribution and conditioning equipment, and cooling fans. Racks are sold according to size (i.e., number of rack units) and based on options (e.g., whether it is lockable or has power distribution built in). The most common rack size is 42U, which will hold 42 1U (one rack unit) devices. The sample rack diagrammed in Figure 2-28 is 42U.

Cooling is a concern for the equipment room and for the racks in the room. Cooling can be handled through the room air conditioning and/or a separate cooling unit built into the rack. It is necessary to consider the heat output of all equipment to be mounted to the rack and to assure adequate airflow so no equipment overheats.

FIGURE 2-28 Rack Configuration

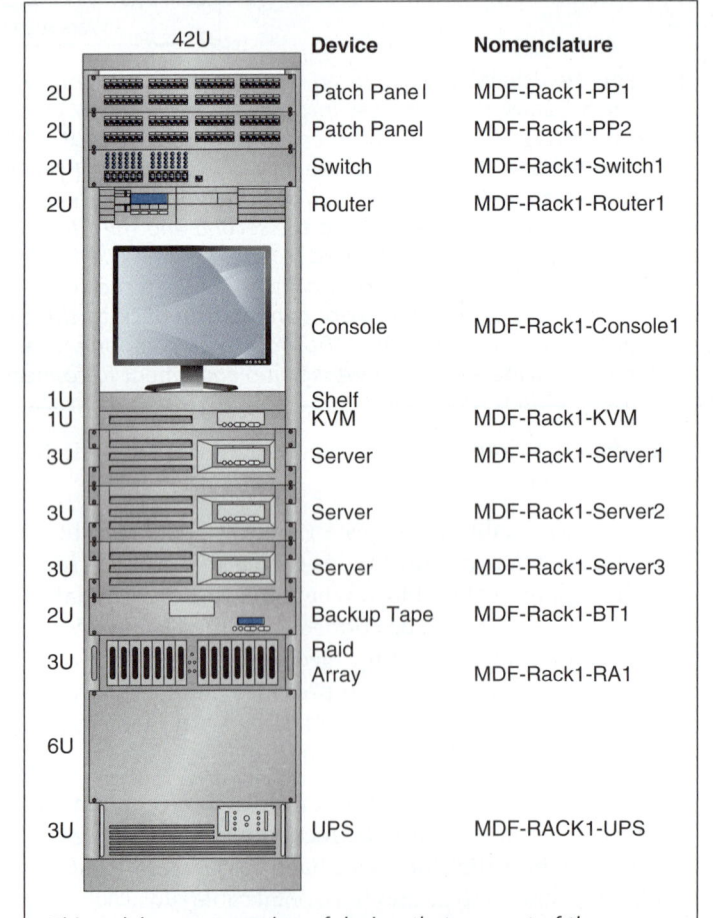

Size	Device	Nomenclature
2U	Patch Panel	MDF-Rack1-PP1
2U	Patch Panel	MDF-Rack1-PP2
2U	Switch	MDF-Rack1-Switch1
2U	Router	MDF-Rack1-Router1
	Console	MDF-Rack1-Console1
1U	Shelf	
1U	KVM	MDF-Rack1-KVM
3U	Server	MDF-Rack1-Server1
3U	Server	MDF-Rack1-Server2
3U	Server	MDF-Rack1-Server3
2U	Backup Tape	MDF-Rack1-BT1
3U	Raid Array	MDF-Rack1-RA1
6U		
3U	UPS	MDF-RACK1-UPS

This rack houses a number of devices that are part of the HealthyWay network. It is just a sample rack that includes power conditioning (USP), disk storage (RAID array), a backup tape drive, three servers, a KVM, a shelf for the console, the console, an Ethernet switch, and two patch panels that connect the Ethernet switch to the horizontal runs on the floor. Note that this 42U rack currently has a total of 33U for the devices (and the blank panel) in the rack.

VIGNETTE BOX 2-6

Equipment Racks

HealthyWay will use lockable 19-inch equipment racks. The standard rack will include a UPS, KVM/console if necessary, and patch panels. The MDF will be built using standard 42U racks.

Similar rules hold true for power needs in a rack. The power consumption of all equipment in the rack needs to be considered, along with whether the rack is adequately powered for the equipment to run properly. In addition to power consumption, power quality considerations are important. The electric grid that provides power to commercial buildings is often subject to voltage and other variations in the power supplied. Designs for the data center and equipment rooms need to accommodate the quality of the incoming power and include devices that compensate for the power quality variations. Power conditioning devices can also provide backup power. A device that provides both is called an Uninterruptible Power Supply (UPS). The devices come in whole building, room, and rack sizes. Often a data center will have a whole room UPS, while an IDF equipment room will have a UPS mounted in the rack. Lastly, whatever power conditioning is chosen, appropriate power distribution within the rack must be installed.

If the rack contains multiple servers it is often desirable to use just one keyboard, mouse, and monitor (i.e., the console) to control them. It is possible to use a keyboard-video-mouse (KVM) switch that allows a single console to control multiple servers, reducing the rack space necessary for consoles to just one. Several types of KVMs are available; some are hardwired to the servers and others operate over IP.

Data Center Of special note is the data center, where the software applications that provide core business services are housed. The network core and the interface to all other services normally reside in this equipment room. Here we typically see servers, storage devices, the interface to the entrance facility, extensive power conditioning and environmental controls, and special room security. The goal is to provide a centralized location where the operating environment (i.e., power and cooling) can be controlled and a place for the main cross-connect where vertical runs interface with each other. The data center also provides a centralized place for information technology staff to monitor and control equipment and to ensure maintenance and uptime of enterprise-critical equipment. Data center design, construction, and operation has been standardized through organizations such as the Telecommunications Industry Association (TIA), and anyone considering building a data center should consult those standards.

Cabling (Vertical and Horizontal Runs) As indicated, backbone cabling or vertical runs provide interconnection between the MDF, IDF2, and IDF3. In the case of HealthyWay,

VIGNETTE BOX 2-7

Data Center

An external data center contractor could be brought in to design and construct HealthyWay's data center on the first floor. Some important parts of the design would include the following:

- Redundant air conditioning to provide continuous heat and humidity control
- Redundant power conditioning equipment and backup power (Uninterruptable Power Supply) to clean electrical power provided by the utility company and to provide an orderly shutdown of equipment in case of power failure
- Raised flooring to provide space for air to circulate as part of the air conditioning system, and a space to run power and network cabling
- A fire suppression system designed to control electrical fires
- A physical intrusion alarm system to control and record access to the data center

> **VIGNETTE BOX 2-8**
>
> **Cable Runs**
>
> The HealthyWay backbone (vertical runs) will be built using Ethernet standards with fiber optic cable used between equipment rooms. The horizontal runs will be UTP from the patch panel to the work area wall plates. From the work area wall plates, UTP patch cables will be used to connect user components (e.g., workstations and printers).

fiber optic cable will connect to the network core, as well as to the workgroup switches in each IDF. More correctly the cable will connect to a patch panel. Each equipment rack will have a fiber patch panel where the vertical run will connect, and then a fiber patch cable will be used to connect to the switch, as shown in Figure 2-29.

Work Area Components Work area components are the communication outlets and writing/connectors needed to connect user components (e.g., computers, printers) to the network. The communication outlets are wall boxes and faceplates, with wiring/connectors consisting of patch cables used between devices or ports to interconnect to the wall plate. Each UTP connection is often referred to as a drop, is pulled through a wall box, and is connected via an RJ45 jack. Due to the proliferation of UTP-based IP devices, it is customary for wall plates to have more than one network drop.

Nomenclature By now anyone reading this textbook realizes that networks involve a lot of components, cables, and equipment. The key is keeping it all straight, and in order to do that you need to develop logical naming conventions for everything. A little bit of these conventions were already introduced when we talked about MDF,

FIGURE 2-29 Horizontal and Vertical Runs

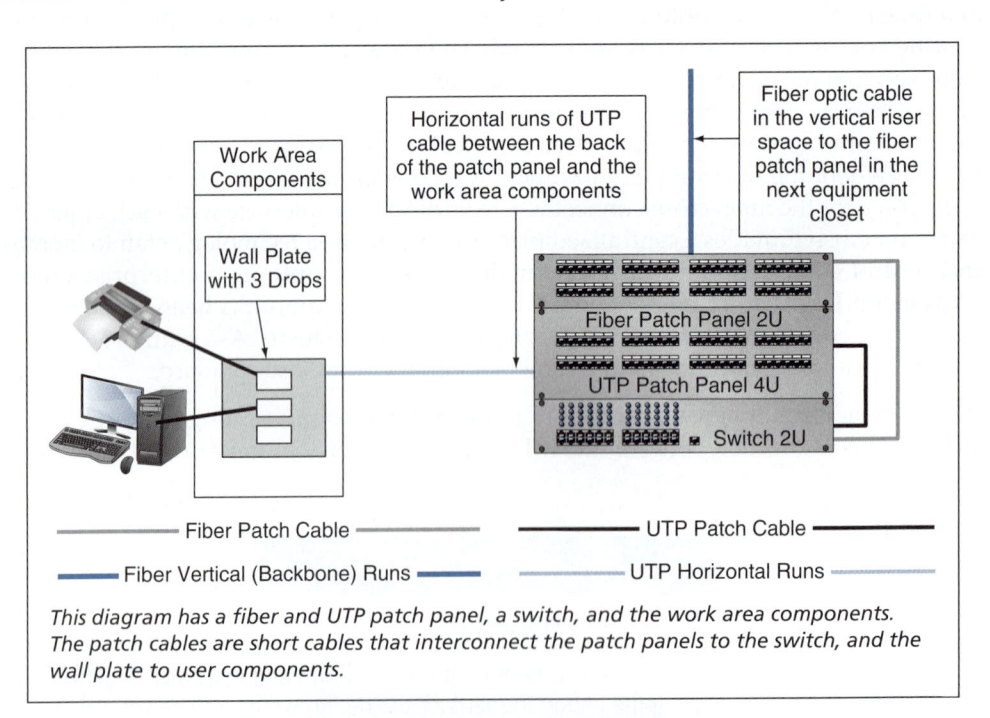

This diagram has a fiber and UTP patch panel, a switch, and the work area components. The patch cables are short cables that interconnect the patch panels to the switch, and the wall plate to user components.

> **VIGNETTE BOX 2-9**
>
> **Work Area Components**
>
> HealthyWay will have three drops per wall plate, and a wall plate at each desk/office. This configuration will allow for shared printers and other devices to be connected as well as for expansion.

> ## VIGNETTE BOX 2-10
>
> ### Nomenclature
>
> HealthyWay will use the following nomenclature:
>
> - The main equipment room (data center) will be named the Main Data Frame (MDF).
> - The second and third floor will have equipment rooms called Individual Data Frames (IDF), IDF2, and IDF3, respectively.
> - Within each room there will be equipment racks, which will be named by room. There will be MDF-Rack#, IDF2-Rack#, and IDF3-Rack#, where # is the sequential number of each rack in that room. For example, MDF-Rack1, MDF-Rack2, and so on.
> - Each device in a rack will get a unique name indicating the type of device, and a unique numeric identifier.
>   - For example, MDF-Rack1-PP1, MDF-Rack1-PP2, MDF-Rack1-Switch1, MDF-Rack1-Console1, MDF-Rack1-Server1, MDF-Server2, and so on
> - Each UTP patch panel will have a number of ports. The RJ45 ports are numbered from one to the maximum number of ports on that patch panel. Each port will correspond to a network drop that appears on a wall plate. The wall plates will be numbered by floor, wall plate, and RJ45 jack in the plate. For example, floor three, wall jack 5, drops 1, 2 and 3, would be numbered respectively FL3-WJ5-1. FL3-WJ5-2, and FL3-WJ5-3. A table will be kept indicating the Rack-Patch Panel-Port Number to Floor-Wall Jack-Drop.
>   - For example, Rack1-PP2-Port22 to FL3-WJ5-Port2

IDF2, and IDF3. It was decided that all equipment rooms would be called "data frames," and that the data center would contain the "main data frame," and the equipment closets on the second and third floors would be called "individual data frames." The individual data frames were given the number corresponding to their floor so they would be easy to locate. By mutual understanding, the MDF is in the data center. But what do you do if a given floor contains multiple IDFs? The solution is fairly simple problem if they are labeled in a consistent way, such as simply appending a letter after the floor number (e.g., IDF2A, IDF2B, etc.). This same labeling extends to equipment racks and the equipment in them. For example, what if there were three racks in the MDF? You could label them MDF-Rack1, MDF-Rack2, and MDF-Rack3. The same is true for each switch in the rack—you could use a similar sequential naming scheme so you can document equipment. The key is to name/number everything so it can be uniquely identified.

SERVICE COMPONENTS

The student should now understand what it takes to build out a structured cabling plan. The WAN portion was not covered in this chapter, but will be covered in Chapter 3. However, before finishing the discussion of the HealthyWay Corporate LAN a discussion of service components of the information architecture is in order. First some of the typical service components will be reviewed, and then a recap of what HealthyWay will install is given.

Many types of service components can be considered for an enterprise. Remember, **service components** are those parts of the network that facilitate network operations and with which the user may directly interface, including printing services, inter/intra office communications (i.e., telephone or fax), and network assessable storage. Several service components will be discussed here (e.g., file server, print services, and database/application server); others include network accessible storage (NAS), IP-faxing, and RADIUS services for remote user authentication. User access to service components is controlled through the Security Service Component, a discussion of which is covered in another chapter.

File Services It is possible to create file shares on servers. Those file shares point to directories on the server that are made accessible to users over the network. Access to file shares

FIGURE 2-30 File Services

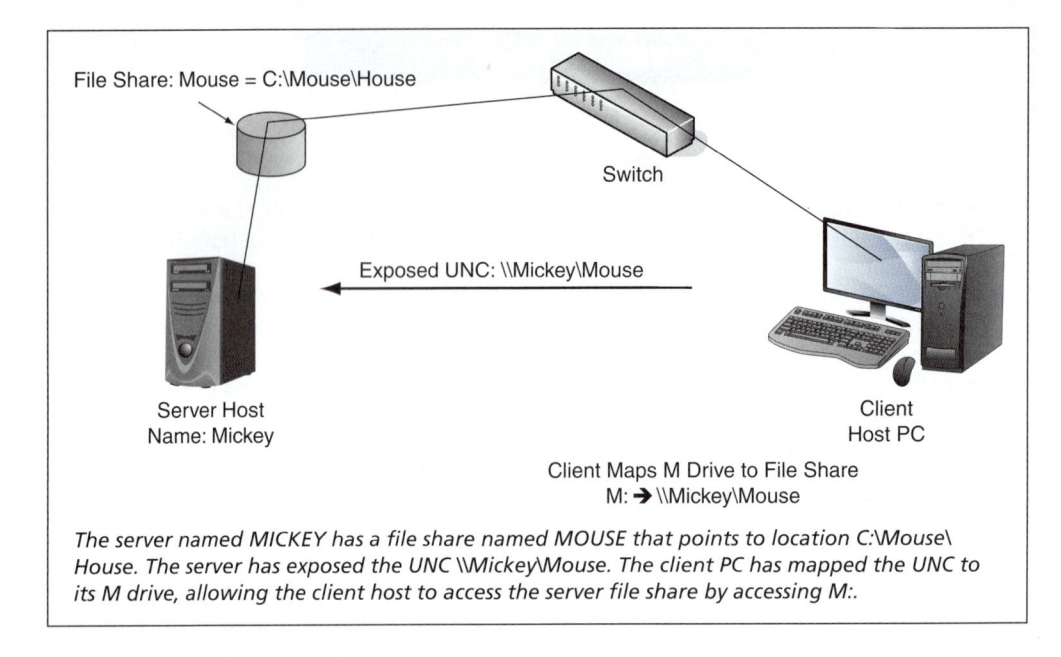

The server named MICKEY has a file share named MOUSE that points to location C:\Mouse\House. The server has exposed the UNC \\Mickey\Mouse. The client PC has mapped the UNC to its M drive, allowing the client host to access the server file share by accessing M:.

is controlled through the Security Service Component. When a file share is created, a server exposes a universal naming convention for the file share. The standard format for the UNC is \\HostName\ShareFolder\Resource. A host client can then access the UNC through the appropriate program. (Note: On a Windows® client, the appropriate program would be File Explorer.) The UNC can also be mapped to a drive letter on the host client making the file share appear to be disk drive, as illustrated in Figure 2-30.

Print Services Servers can run print services that allow multiple users to share the same printer without conflicting with each other. Several components make print services work, including the server-based print services and its spooler, the printer and its associated print server, and the client host configuration, shown in Figure 2-31.

The server-based print service has a spooler or temporary disk storage that holds print jobs until the printer is available. The printer requires a print server that communicates with the server-based print services and controls printer availability. The client actually communicates with the server print services, and it is those services that communicate with the print server.

FIGURE 2-31 Print Services

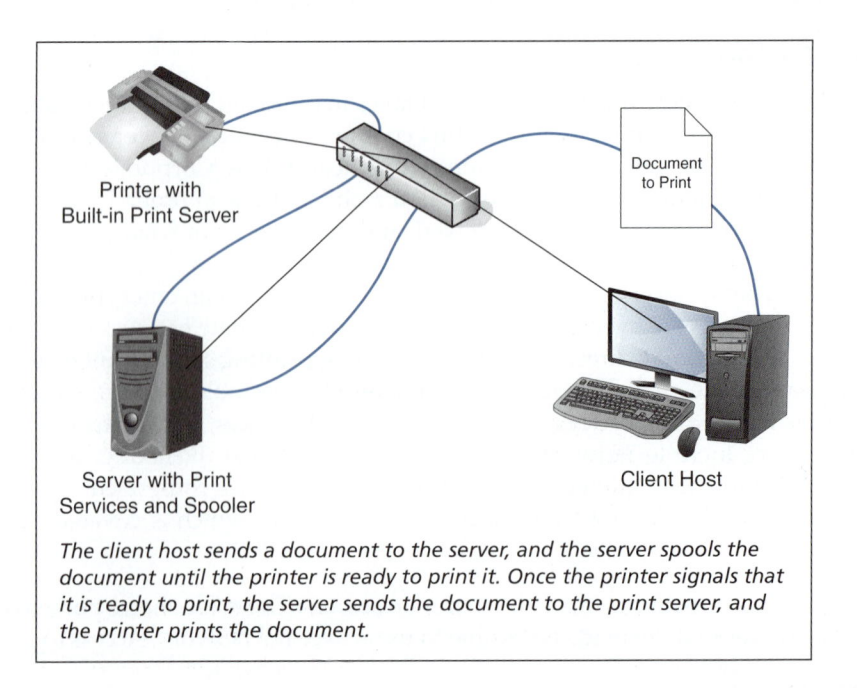

The client host sends a document to the server, and the server spools the document until the printer is ready to print it. Once the printer signals that it is ready to print, the server sends the document to the print server, and the printer prints the document.

Application Servers Historically, application servers are named after the application they provide, for example, Microsoft provides the Internet Information Server, while Sun provides the J3EE® Server (Java Platform–Enterprise Edition). Both of these servers provide environments that can be used to develop applications that are run on the server, and are accessed by the client computers. These two application servers often provide application through a web browser interface. The application server will be programmed with the business logic, while the client computer will provide a graphical interface.

Database Servers Database servers provide database services to host computers in a client-server environment. They provide a database management system (DBMS) such as Microsoft SQL®, MySQL®, or Sybase® to the other hosts, and allow the database to be shared with multiple hosts simultaneously.

Network Attached Storage Network attached storage (NAS) is similar to the file server technology already discussed. An NAS device is an appliance that attaches to the network. It is considered an appliance because it has limited functionality and typically does not have a console (i.e., keyboard/mouse/monitor). Rather, an NAS has a web-based interface accessible through a browser that is used to monitor and manage the storage. The NAS appliance contains one or more hard drives, often arranged into redundant storage arrays. The major purpose of an NAS appliance is to remove the responsibility of file services from other servers, reducing the load on otherwise already busy servers. The NAS appliance connects to the network switch just like any other host through a UTP or fiber optic connection. Client hosts in a LAN are made aware, when accessing data on an NAS appliance, that they are accessing remote storage.

Storage Area Networks A host that has a disk drive installed in it accesses the disk drive in block mode, rather than through file services mode provided by a network file server. Block mode is considered a low-level access method because the host is reading directly from the disk drive, and the host is required to manage a file system and any concurrent access to information on the disk drive. In file services mode, the device

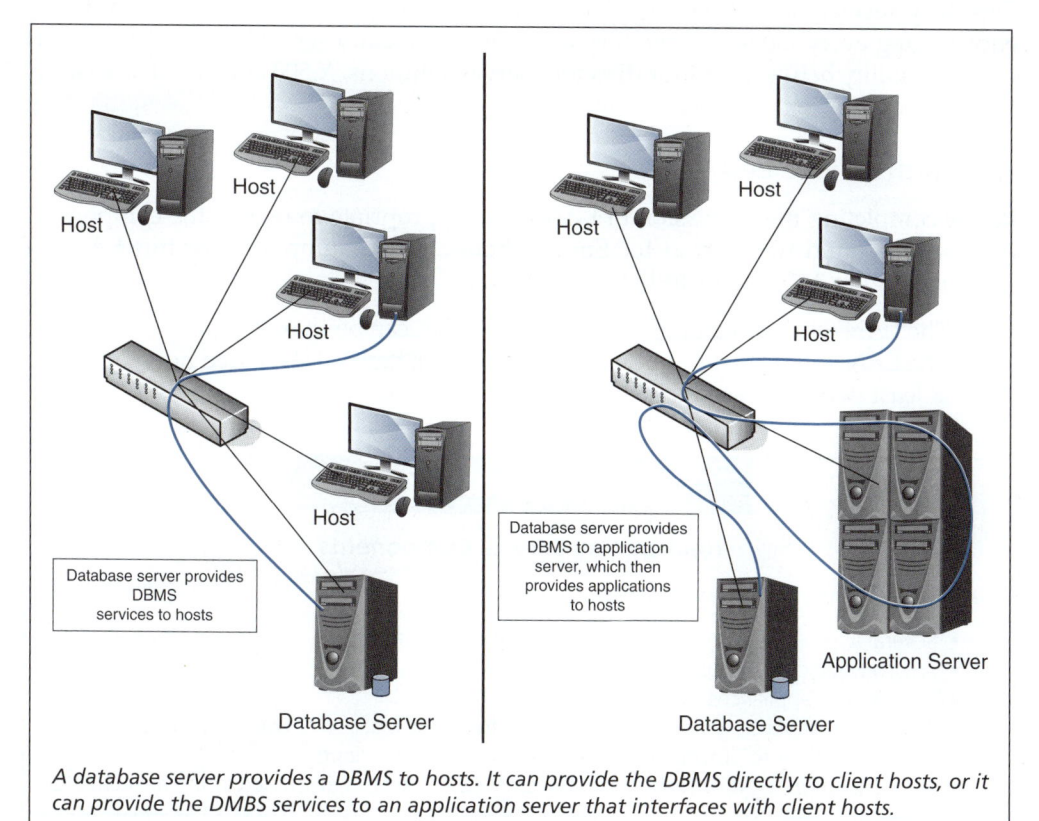

FIGURE 2-32 Database and Application Servers

A database server provides a DBMS to hosts. It can provide the DBMS directly to client hosts, or it can provide the DMBS services to an application server that interfaces with client hosts.

(e.g., NAS) containing the data is responsible for the file system on its disk drives and for concurrent access. Block mode requires the host to maintain a file system, whereas file services mode leaves the maintenance of a file system to the file-serving device.

A storage area network (SAN) is a block mode storage device that connects storage devices (i.e., disk arrays, tape libraries, optical media) to the network in such a way that clients and servers think they are directly connecting to a disk drive on the host. In other words, the disks in a SAN appear as if they are locally attached to the host, but in fact the disks are part of a large high-speed network usually located in the data center. SAN implementations are found in large enterprise LANs and are cost prohibitive for smaller installations.

In the past, it was common for enterprise LANs to have application/database servers with high performance storage. Each sever was dedicated to a particular application and was visible as a number of "virtual hard drives" over the LAN. In these solutions, the device kept track of who was accessing it and of the file system on the device. The SAN is different. In the SAN, disk storage is tied together over a high-speed network connection, and the host is responsible for managing the file system on the SAN, versus the virtual hard drive managing the file system itself. NAS appliances manage the file systems on their hard drives and are preferable to SAN solutions for many applications due to the block-level access and file system management that a SAN requires.

E-Mail Server An e-mail server is a host that is responsible for transferring e-mail from and to clients, and between other e-mail servers. The e-mail server uses two protocols, SMTP and POP. POP is responsible for transferring e-mail from the e-mail server to the local client so the user has access to e-mail. SMTP is responsible for outgoing e-mail, and takes the e-mail a user sends and transfers it over the Internet to the receiving SMTP server at the destination.

Directory Server A directory server stores and organizes information about a network's users and resources. It controls access to network users and resources, and allows that access to be managed in one place. The directory server creates an interface between the user and the resource (e.g., storage, VPN access, printing), and controls access to those same resources. A number of directory services are offered by various vendors. Directory services are often proprietary and vendor specific. A campaign by ISO is encouraging everyone in the industry to agree on directory server standards, allowing interoperability between vendor directory server solutions. X.500 and LDAP are two of those standards.

Joe Smith's Home LAN

Before completing the discussion of LANs, it is appropriate to review the components necessary to build the LAN at Joe Smith's house. The assumptions for this LAN are shown in Figure 2-33 and include the following:

- The LAN will need an Internet connection that can be shared.
- The LAN will need the ability to share a printer, have a UTP wired host client, and at least two wireless notebooks.

VIGNETTE BOX 2-11

HealthyWay Service Components

HealthyWay will use the following service components:

- Several applications servers and database servers to support the HMO business applications
- A server dedicated to print services
- Several NAS appliances to handle file services
- A directory server to authenticate users and track privileges to network resources
- An e-mail server to provide e-mail services to connected clients
- A VPN solution to allow secure remote access by employees (discussed in the next chapter)

Chapter 2 • Building the Local Area Network Using Ethernet 75

> **VIGNETTE BOX 2-12**
>
> **Joe Smith's Home LAN**
>
> In order to meet the needs of this home-based LAN in Joe Smith's house, a DSL connection will be procured from the local phone company. The local phone company will provide a device that has a DSL modem, WAP (i.e., 802.11b/g), Ethernet switch (i.e., 100BaseT), and an IP router built in. Each notebook must have a wireless network interface (i.e., 802.11b/g/n), and the wired host must have a UTP wired network interface (i.e., 100BaseT). The printer will be connected via USB to the wired host, and shared through the wired host to provide spooling and print services.

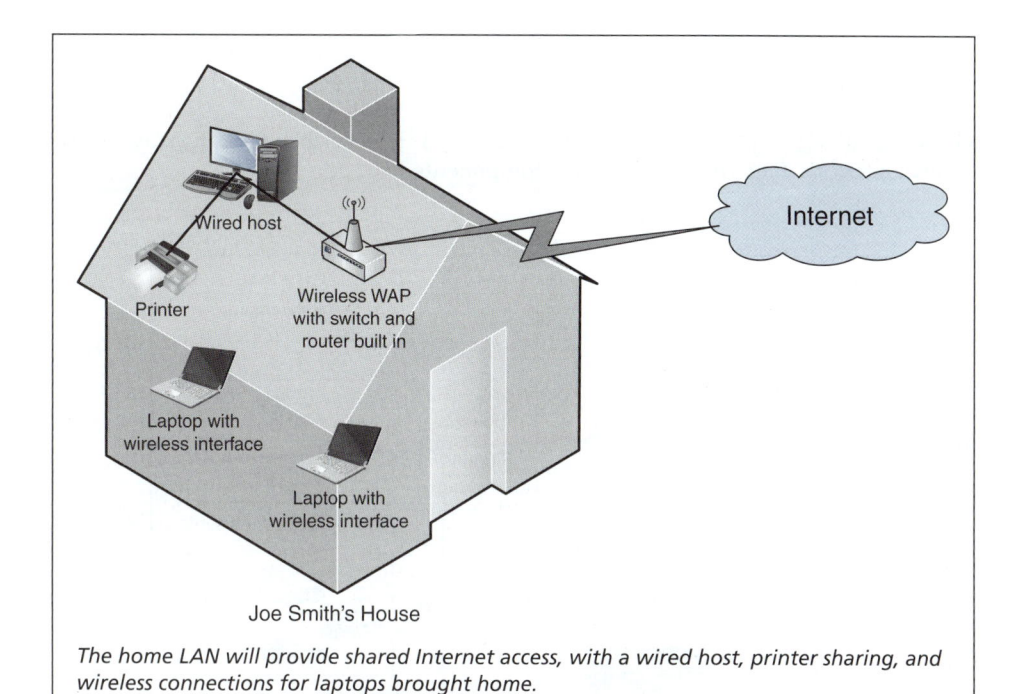

FIGURE 2-33 Joe Smith's Home LAN Using DSL

The home LAN will provide shared Internet access, with a wired host, printer sharing, and wireless connections for laptops brought home.

Chapter Summary

This chapter started out with a discussion of Ethernet media, including categories of UTP as well as fiber optic cable. The most commonly installed UTP is Cat5e, and the newest is Cat7. Fiber optic cable comes in multimode and single mode, with multimode being slower and supporting less distance than single mode. However, both the equipment that supports multimode fiber optic cable and the cable itself are less expensive than single-mode equipment and cable. The chapter next reviews Ethernet interfaces, hubs, and switches. The various host-based interfaces include two major types: those that support wired LAN standards and those that support wireless LAN standards. Hubs are broadcast devices, whereas switches direct traffic using the MAC address of the Ethernet frame. Hubs have largely fallen into disuse.

Next the technical details of Ethernet were discussed, with a substantial amount of time devoted to carrier sense media access/collision detection (CMSA/CD). CMSA is how Ethernet decides which host in a LAN has control over the media and is allowed to transmit. CD determines what an Ethernet device (e.g., host, switch) does when it accidentally transmits at the same time another device is already transmitting. Next, the chapter covered Ethernet frame formats, and then described what a MAC address is and its function. A summary of Ethernet covered media and propagation.

Wireless LAN (WLAN) technologies were covered next. A significant amount of time was spent discussing 802.11 WLAN standards and technical details. The frequency spectrum was introduced, along with the channels within the frequency spectrum dedicated to WLAN transmission. The Service Set Identifier (SSID) is a way to identify a WLAN and how a WLAN could either broadcast or not broadcast the SSID as a way to "hide" the WLAN from detection by hosts. Wireless security and how WAPs hand off hosts were also discussed. WLANs that use the 802.11 standards handle multiple uses through carrier sense multiple access with collision avoidance + acknowledgment (CSMA/CA+ACK) to control traffic was included. The section of 802.11 included a discussion of wireless propagation problems such as dead spots/shadow zones, rapid attenuation, EMI, multipath interference, and the effect signal frequency has on signal propagation. Personal area networks (PANs) were also introduced.

Structured cabling plans are an orderly way to build the wiring infrastructure of a LAN. They are composed of a number of components. The entrance facility is where any connection to other buildings or carrier circuits enter the building. Telecommunication equipment and cabling cross-connects are located in the equipment room. The data center is a special room in a structured cabling plan that contains the network core. Cabling, referred to as horizontal runs, goes from the equipment room to the work area components, and vertical runs interconnect equipment rooms. Work area components include the wall boxes, faceplates, and other cabling that terminate the horizontal runs and allow user components to connect the LAN. It is important that naming conventions are used for everything in the structured cabling plan, as well as for all devices in the LAN. This naming convention is called the *nomenclature*. The various components of the structured cabling plan were used to build a LAN for the company in the opening vignette, HealthyWay.

Vignette Wrap Up

The last part of this chapter covered the HealthyWay LAN in some depth. In this wrap up a high-level network diagram is given in Figure 2-34. It describes HealthyWay's network and service components.

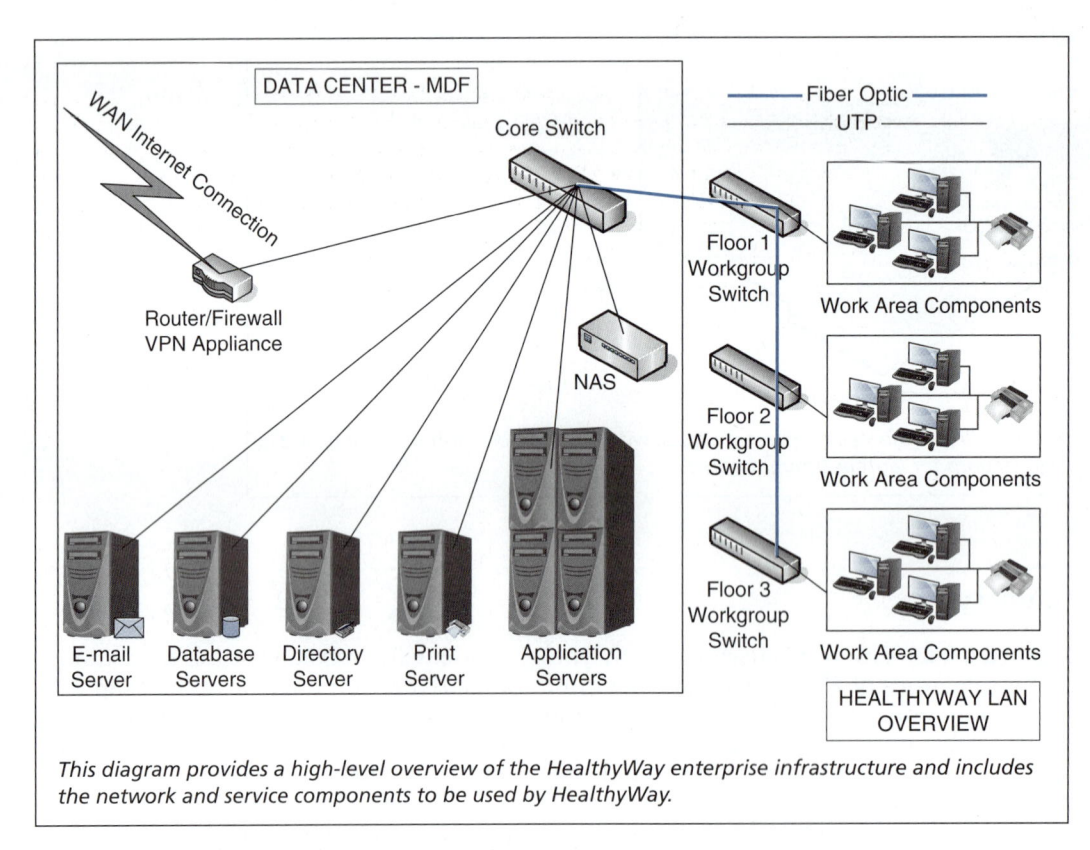

This diagram provides a high-level overview of the HealthyWay enterprise infrastructure and includes the network and service components to be used by HealthyWay.

FIGURE 2-34 High-Level HealthyWay Infrastructure Diagram

End of Chapter Questions/Assurance of Learning

1. Design a network for HealthyWay and select all of the components for the structured cabling plan and the associated network and service components to support the assumptions in the unit opening vignette.
2. Develop a cost list of the components in the preceding question.
3. Describe CSMA/CD and CSMA/CA+ACK and how they differ. Discuss why CSMA/CA+ACK is used in wireless technologies rather than CSMA/CD.
4. Describe wired and wireless propagation effects and analyze what they mean for installing a LAN.
5. Discuss the differences in wired and wireless LAN technologies, and when it is appropriate to use them.

Case Exercises

These exercises build on the case exercises from Chapter 1.

1. The switch built by XYZ Inc. had a number of standards-based options and a few options not yet ratified by the standards bodies (e.g., IEEE working groups). HealthyWay is considering purchasing this switch because it is interested in these new unratified options. Analyze the situation and make a recommendation about how HealthyWay should proceed.
2. HealthyWay HMO was discussed in the unit opening vignette. Use a product such as MS-Visio to recreate the HealthyWay LAN diagrams, and elaborate on the HealthyWay LAN services required for the LAN implementation to be successful. Prepare a brief report and presentation indicating how a LAN can help the company attain competitive advantage in the marketplace of HMOs. In your case analysis discuss what factors are important for HealthyWay to consider when selecting LAN and WAN technologies. Incorporate what you have learned in this chapter.
3. Select a company you are familiar with and write a case analysis that describes its LAN, expanding it with the new information you learned in this chapter. Describe the technologies used and how they are important to the competitive positioning of that company. Support your analysis by citing Internet and/or print articles (i.e., trade publications, journal articles).

Key Words and Concepts

802.11 56
adapter card 43
carrier sense multiple access with collision avoidance + acknowledgment (CSMA/CA+ACK) 61
carrier sense multiple access with collision detection (CSMA/CD) 50
channels 55
Ethernet 41
Ethernet Layer 2 42
frames 42
frequency spectrum 54
geostationary 55
handoff 61
horizontal runs 43
LAN wiring 64
media 43
microwave 55
personal area network (PAN) 63
radio frequency modulation 58
satellite type and altitude 56
service components 71
Service Set Identifier (SSID) 59
structured cabling 64
switch characteristics 44
TCP/IP-OSI hybrid model 42
vertical runs 43
wireless access point (WAP) 57
wireless signal propagation 62
wireless standards 43
wireless technologies 54

References

FCC. (2011, April 4). *Home*. Retrieved April 4, 2011, from http://fcc.gov/

IEEE.org. (2011). *Index*. Retrieved April 4, 2011, from http://www.ieee.org/index.html

PARC. (2011). *Home*. Retrieved April 4, 2011, from http://www.parc.com/

3 EXTENDING THE LAN THROUGH WAN CONNECTIONS

> **Learning Objectives**
>
> - Understand the technical details of WAN technologies.
> - Apply the typologies leaned in the previous chapter to WAN configuration.
> - Understand the public switched data network (PSDN) and public switched telephone network (PSTN), as well as their similarities.
> - Integrate material about protocols, typologies, the TCP/IP-OSI hybrid model, and other concepts previously introduced with the concepts of WANs so network structures can be built.
> - Understand the basic concepts of ATM and Frame Relay as WAN technologies.

The previous chapters explained LANs and general network concepts. Those network concepts covered technology from the network core to the demarcation point where the LAN connects to a WAN. This chapter looks at the WAN, including the topics of ATM, Frame Relay, wide-area Ethernet, and other technologies. The goal is to inform students (i.e., future business strategists) about the technologies so they can understand what the network engineer builds. A business strategist needs to understand how WAN connections are used to interconnect LANs not located on the same campus, as well as how to connect LANs to the Internet. Numerous options are available for WAN connections, many of which are covered in this chapter.

WANs are part of the network components of the information technology infrastructure architecture, along with LANs. They are discussed in this chapter separate from LANs because of the extensive amount of information that must be conveyed. In addition to the WAN connections themselves, public switched data networks and public switched telephone networks are discussed. It is important to note that some service components of the information technology infrastructure architecture (most notably Internet access and VPN services) use the WAN connection to interoperate.

INTRODUCTION

Although LANs were built to allow data communication within a local geographic area not requiring carrier circuits to interconnect endpoints, WANs are the technologies that allow the interconnection of endpoints across cities, states, or around the world. WAN technologies are provided by carriers that own or lease data circuits that allow this vast interconnection.

LAN vs. WAN Pricing

Historically, a wide gap separated the price per megabyte transmission costs of a LAN versus a WAN, with LANs being much cheaper. Although the gap still exists today—prices for LAN hardware have fallen and LANs do not require carrier circuits—LAN and WAN technologies are converging, and the gap is shrinking. A major part of any price difference can also be understood in the genesis of LAN and WAN technologies. LANs began in the computer industry and were built for the specific purpose of data communications. WANs grew out of the telecommunication industry and were adaptations of technologies originally designed to transmit voice, which means that WANs are more expensive per megabyte transmitted. For these reasons, most organizations opt for relatively low-speed WAN connections. To see the difference, you only have to compare a T1 WAN connection at 1.544 mb/second with a LAN operating at 1 gb/second.

ENTERPRISE-WIDE SOFTWARE COMPONENTS Enterprise-wide software, including ERP, e-commerce/e-business, document management, knowledge management, and other specialized applications	User Components	Items that directly interface with the user, including workstations, printers, scanners, associated software (especially desktop applications), and specialized applications
	Service Components	Those network parts that facilitate network operations with direct user interface, including printing services, inter/intra office communications (i.e., telephone or fax), network attached storage, database/application servers, security servers and appliances, and VPN technology
	Network Components	Those items/concepts traditionally thought of as networking and telecommunications equipment, including network switching and routing hardware, media, outside vendor interconnects (i.e., T1, T3, DSL), and cabinetry, patch panels, and associated items

This figure lists and describes the components of ICT infrastructure architecture from the standpoint of the information technology user. The areas highlighted in blue are covered in this chapter.

FIGURE 3-1 Information Technology Infrastructure Architecture

Types of Connections

It may seem like an outlandish statement, but all wide area network (WAN) connections start out as **point-to-point (POP) connections**—the actual connection between two locations is from Point A to Point B. What happens at the connections is what makes the difference. Here are some examples:

- A company wants to connect two buildings across town. It uses a T1 carrier circuit to interconnect the two buildings. You have a point-to-point connection between the two buildings.
- A company wants to connect to the Internet. The company uses a T3 carrier circuit to connect from its building to its Internet service provider (ISP). The ISP interconnects the company to the Internet.

The idea is that WANs are made of point-to-point connections, with the difference being what is at each point. In the first example, the company is providing interconnection between two of its buildings with routers providing connection to the LAN in each building. In the second example the company is using a point-to-point connection to an ISP, and the ISP in turn connects to the Internet. The important idea is that point-to-point connections provide the interconnections in the WAN, it's just what those point-to-point connections connect to that matters. In the first example there is a simple routed connection between two buildings, and in the second example there is a routed connection from the building to the Internet via an ISP (see Figure 3-2).

This simplistic view of WAN connections provides the basis for all types of WAN connections that are available. If an enterprise wants to interconnect its buildings or if it wants to connect to the Internet, it must start with point-to-point connection.

Points of Presence

ISPs provide Internet connectivity through points of presence (POPs) where they allow companies to connect for a fee. A company will purchase a particular type of connection to a POP. Fees vary based on the type and speed of the connection. The POP is a physical location where the ISP has servers, routers, and other communications hardware that allow

---

VIGNETTE BOX 3-1

HealthyWay's Connection to Its ISP

HealthyWay wants to connect to the Internet. It will have to decide what type of connectivity it needs. Considering its size, a T1 line that connects it to its ISP will probably be sufficient.

FIGURE 3-2 WAN Point-to-Point Circuits

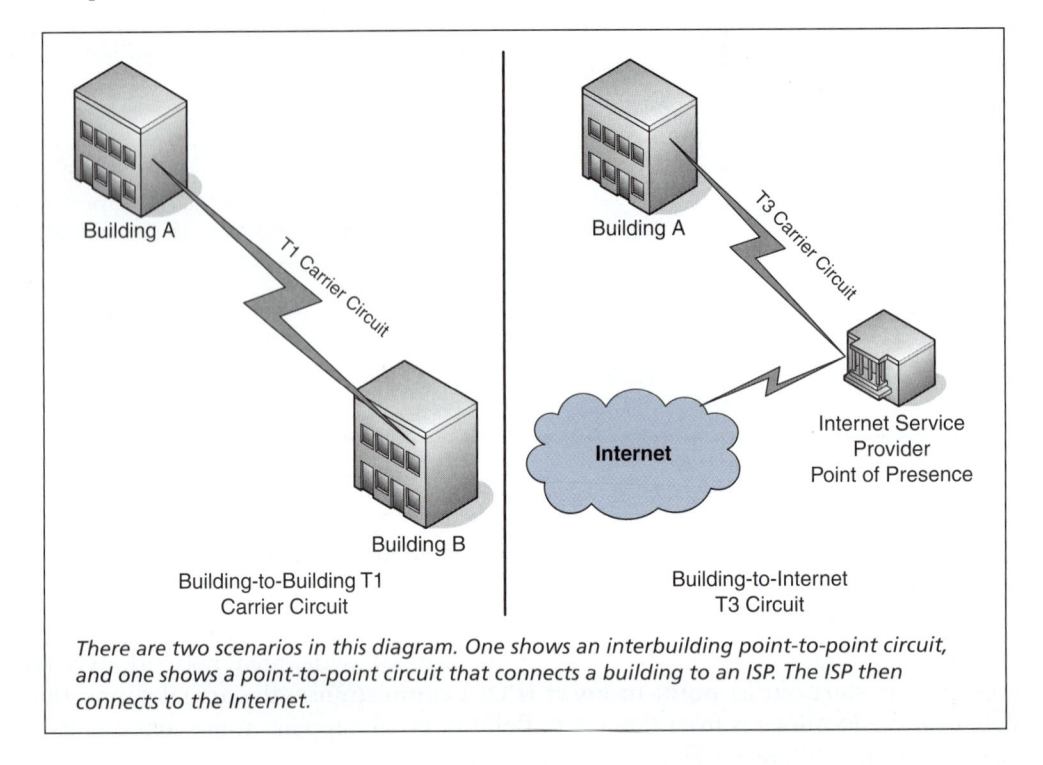

There are two scenarios in this diagram. One shows an interbuilding point-to-point circuit, and one shows a point-to-point circuit that connects a building to an ISP. The ISP then connects to the Internet.

its customers to connect. The larger the ISP, the more POPs it will have. Customers must purchase a point-to-point circuit that goes from their location to the ISP's POP. Sometimes that point-to-point connection is bundled in the price of the POP connection fee.

PSDN

Sometimes ISPs provide public switched facilities that allow the customer to connect via a POP. These facilities are called **public switched data networks (PSDNs)**. PSDNs are different from the worldwide **public switched telephone network (PSTN)**. The PSDN is packet switched (i.e., routed), while the PSTN is circuit switched (see Figure 3-3). Remember from the earlier discussion of packet versus circuit switching that packet

FIGURE 3-3 PSDN

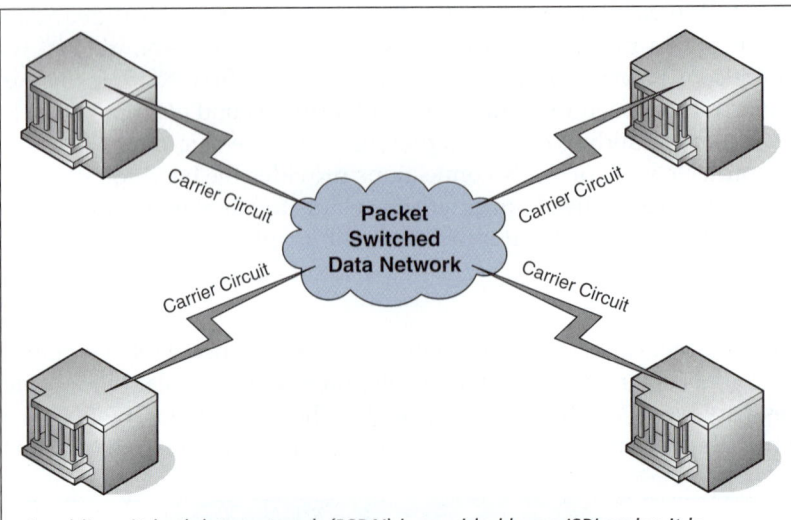

A public switched data network (PSDN) is provided by an ISP/carrier. It is separate from the public switched telephone network (PSTN). The PSDN provides packet switching between locations through POPs. The PSDN is shown as a cloud in this diagram because it is packet switched, and when a company purchases connections and bandwidth the company does not have any control, nor does it necessarily know how its traffic travels between its locations.

VIGNETTE BOX 3-2

HealthyWay's Use of a PSDN

As HealthyWay expands and opens new buildings in different locations it may want to become part of a PSDN. It will still need leased lines from each building to a POP and pay PSDN charges, but those charges will probably be less than running leased lines directly between its buildings, especially if HealthyWay has buildings that are geographically far apart.

switching is better for data than circuit switching because circuit switching ties up the available bandwidth for the entire connection time, while packet switching allows multiple data streams to share bandwidth.

The PSDN should not be confused with integrated services digital network (ISDN) or digital subscriber lines (DSL). ISDN and DSL use circuit switching over the PSTN to communicate, whereas the PSDN is a private network that uses packet switching.

The PSDN can be built using a number of technologies, including Asynchronous Transfer Mode (ATM), Frame Relay, Internet Protocol (IP), and General Packet Radio Service (GPRS), as well as a number of other packet-switched techniques (see Figure 3-4). The following description of these technologies begins with permanent and switched virtual circuits.

PCV and SVC

Permanent virtual circuits (PVCs) and **switched virtual circuits (SVCs)** are virtual channels that provide a connection-oriented communication service that is delivered through packet mode communication. These circuits are established between two hosts or buildings. SVCs are dynamically established for the duration of a call (or connection) and disconnected when the call is terminated. PVCs are established for a long period and act like a traditional carrier circuit. PVCs provide a dedicated circuit link between two facilities and are normally preconfigured by the ISP. PVCs are seldom broken or disconnected, unlike SVCs that are disconnected at the end of each connection An organization would choose a PVC if it wanted a continuous "always on " connection

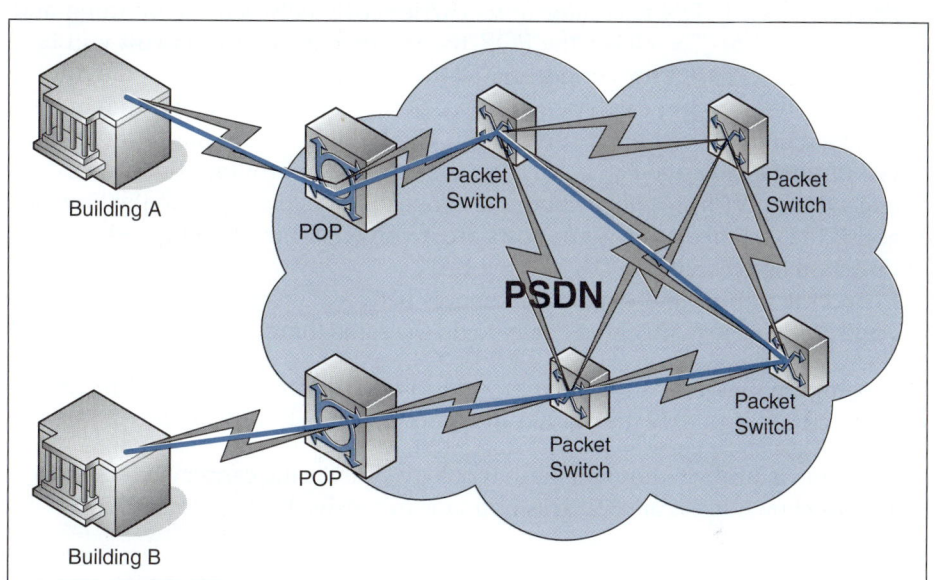

FIGURE 3-4 Virtual Circuits

This diagram shows a virtual circuit over a PSDN. The customer usually has no idea how the virtual circuit is established, and the PSDN is normally just shown as a cloud, but the actually routing is shown here for illustrative purposes. The virtual circuit follows a path through the PSDN based on a number of factors including available bandwidth, network latency, as well as quality of service guarantees given by the PSDN. In this diagram, the blue line represents the virtual circuit. It can be either switched (temporary) or permanent. Note that the PSDN is a routed (e.g., packet-switched) network.

> **VIGNETTE BOX 3-3**
>
> **HealthyWay's Use of VCs**
>
> The virtual circuits in Figure 3-4 could represent two buildings owned by HealthyWay. Using the PSDN, HealthyWay could add more locations and set up VCs between those buildings, creating a packet-switched network that acts like a dedicated T1 or T3 line.

between two locations, and would choose an SVC when a continuous connection is not needed. It's probably apparent that an SVC would be cheaper than a PVC because the PVC provides a higher level of service.

The availability of SVCs and PVCs differs among technologies. Frame Relay is typically used to provide PVCs, while ATM provides both PVCs and SVCs. X.25 also provides PVCs and SVCs but will not be discussed here because it is largely considered legacy technology. Even though PVCs and SVCs are being discussed in the context of PSDN and WAN technologies, PVCs and SVCs can also be used in LAN implementations that use ATM, Frame Relay, or X.25. In other words, PVCs and SVCs apply to many different packet-switched technologies, not just **WAN and PSDN** connections.

Pricing WAN and PSDN Connections

In a review of the pricing of WAN and PSDN connections, the easiest pricing is the point-to-point circuit that is used to connect two buildings. The pricing normally consists of three components: (1) the cost of the circuit provided by the carrier, (2) the cost of equipment to connect the WAN connection to the LAN, and (3) the costs to maintain the connection. These components are listed in Figure 3-5. The cost of the circuit is based on the distance between the points being connected, the speed of connection, and the quality of service guarantees expected. Sometimes the cost of equipment that connects the carrier circuit to the LAN is included in the monthly fee, and sometimes the company must purchase the equipment that allows connection. The same is true of the cost to maintain and configure the connection. Whether the costs are bundled or individual, it is important that all costs be considered when installing these types of circuits.

Pricing of the PSDN is similar in its carrier costs between the building and the POP (see Figure 3-6). The closer the POP, the cheaper the carrier circuit will be. Port charges that are assessed for connecting to the POP are more expensive with higher bandwidths. The port and carrier circuit speeds must be high enough to handle all of the virtual circuits that come into a building. The ISP will charge based on the number and type of virtual circuits. PVCs are more expensive but provide continuous "always on" connectivity. SVCs are cheaper, but the connection is slower due to the time needed to establish the virtual circuit. Some costs are involved in maintaining and configuring the connection between the PSDN and the LAN.

In order to understand the cost differences between a company using multiple carrier circuits to create a WAN and a PSDN to do the same thing, consider this example:

> A company has four buildings located in four different towns. It needs a fully redundant WAN that allows interconnection between all offices.

The first option is a fully redundant mesh typology WAN using carrier circuits between all buildings, as shown in Figure 3-7. This option is expensive because it involves six leased

FIGURE 3-5 Carrier Circuit Costs

Item	Cost
Equipment to Connect Carrier Circuit to LAN	May be bundled with carrier circuit costs or purchased separately
Carrier Circuit Costs	Costs depends on speed, distance, and quality of service
Maintenance/Configuration Costs	Company must provide engineer to maintain connection from carrier circuit to LAN

FIGURE 3-6 PSDN Costs

Item	Cost
Equipment to Connect Carrier Circuit to POP	May be bundled with carrier circuit costs or purchased separately
Carrier Circuit Costs	Costs depends on speed, distance, and quality of service: the closer the POP is to the building, the cheaper the circuit will be
POP Costs	Cost depends on the speed of the port used (obviously you do not want to use a port speed greater than your carrier circuit)
VC Costs	PVCs are more expensive but provide continuous "always on" connectivity, whereas SVCs are cheaper, but have a slower connection due to time to establish the virtual circuit
Maintenance/ Configuration Costs	Company must provide an engineer to maintain connection from carrier circuit to LAN

lines of sufficient speed to provide connectivity backup to all the offices. It is also expensive from the configuration/management standpoint. The company must configure, run, and maintain the mesh, which requires staff, hardware, and software. In some installations this option makes sense due to internal company needs (e.g., security, quality of service, etc.).

Another option for this company is to use a service provider that manages a PSDN. In that case, the company would need a carrier circuit from the company building to a POP on the PSDN (see Figure 3-8). Only one carrier circuit is needed from each building because redundancy is provided by the PSDN, instead of multiple circuits required by a mesh typology. There may be a need for faster carrier circuits due to multiple PVCs, but that cost should be outweighed by the shorter distance to POPs, and the fewer carrier circuits needed. The diagram below shows four carrier circuits, and three PVCS, however because all buildings are attached to the PSDN, all buildings could have virtual circuits.

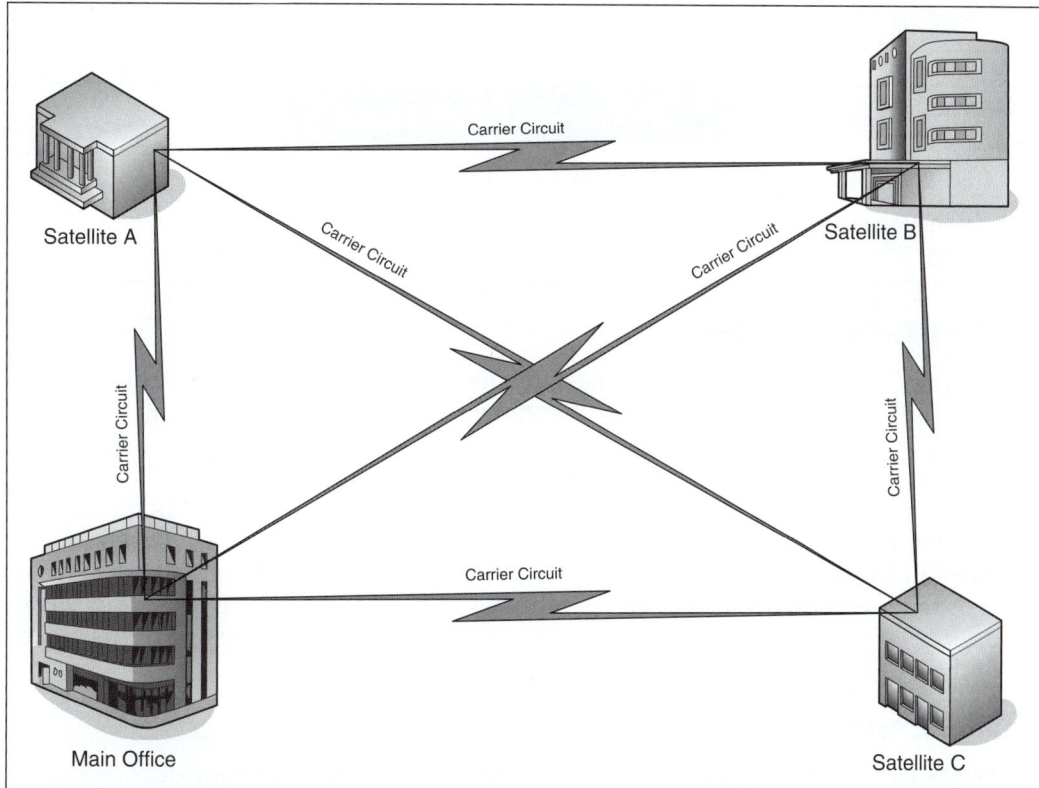

FIGURE 3-7 Mesh of Carrier Circuits to Provide Redundancy

A mesh of carrier circuits can be used to provide redundant connectivity between the main office and the three satellite offices. In order to provide full redundancy, many carrier circuits must be provisioned, which increases costs dramatically.

FIGURE 3-8 PSDN WAN

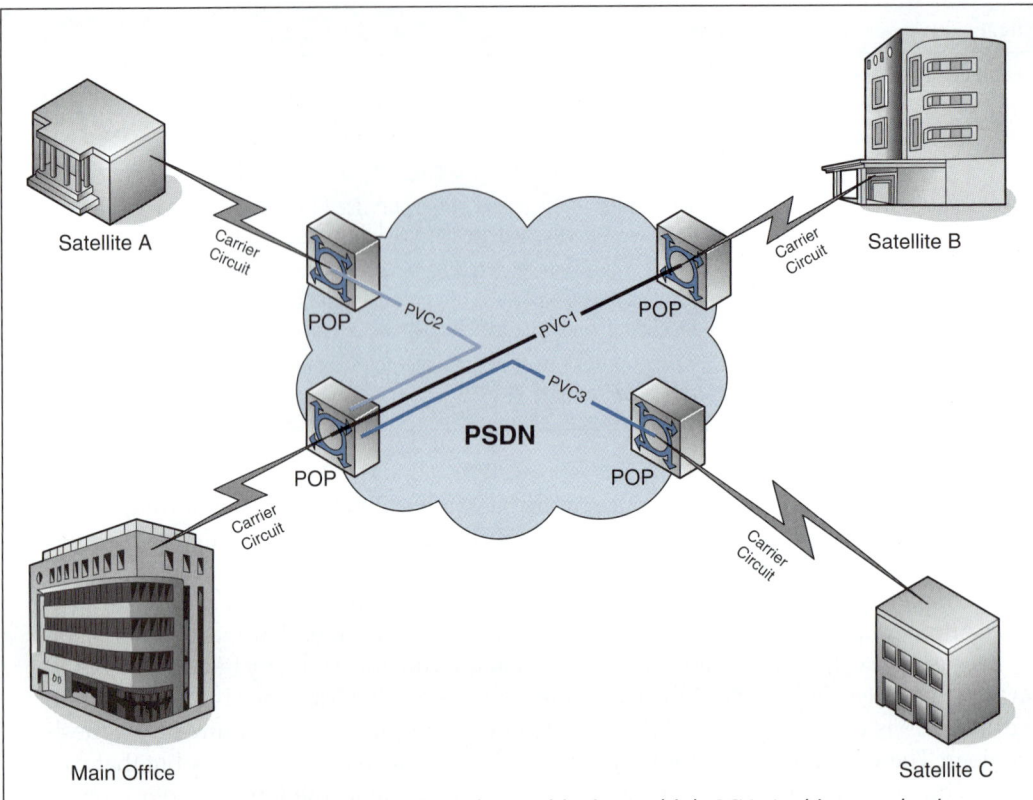

A company can create a WAN through a PSDN by provisioning multiple PCVs. In this example, the main office is connected to each satellite office through the PSDN. PVC1 is 64 kb, the PVC2 is 128 kb, and the PVC3 is 256 kb. With this configuration, each satellite building must have a carrier circuit capable of handling the speed of the PVC. The main office must have a POP port and a carrier circuit capable of handling the aggregate speed of all three PVCs (64 kb, 128 kb, and 256 kb) totaling 448 kb, or a fractional T1 line.

VIGNETTE BOX 3-4

HealthyWay's Connection to Its ISP

HealthyWay would need to determine the most cost-effective way to interconnect its buildings: using dedicated leased lines and creating its own mesh typology, or using a PSDN.

WAN TECHNOLOGIES

A number of technologies can be used to build a WAN. Many of these same technologies can also be used within organizations to build campus-based networks. For example, ATM may be used to build a network within your campus, or it may be used to connect to a PSDN and create permanent virtual circuits. The point is that while these technologies are used to build WANs, they also have other uses. In this section, Asynchronous Transfer Mode (ATM), Frame Relay, General Packet Radio Service (GPRS), Multiprotocol Label Switching (MPLS), and some of the newer Ethernet standards will be discussed. Just remember that these technologies have multiple uses. They will be discussed in the context of WANs but it is possible to use many of them in a LAN as well (www.broadband.com, 2011).

Frame Relay

Frame Relay is a stripped-down version of the X.25 protocol and provides connection-oriented data link layer communications. Frame Relay is not reliable; it detects errors but does not correct them, rather it drops the frame. It is Layer 1 (physical) and Layer 2 (data link) technology originally designed for use over ISDN. However, today it is used over a variety of network interfaces. Frame Relay is a packet-switched technology that provides WAN services.

FIGURE 3-9 Frame Relay and Hybrid TCP/IP-OSI Model

This diagram shows multilayered communication between Host A and Host B. Layer 2 is Frame Relay, while Layer 1 is the physical link, Layers 3 and 3 are TCP/IP, and Layer 5 is the application layer.

FRAME RELAY TECHNICAL DESCRIPTION

A packet-switched technology is often displayed as a cloud in network diagrams. As a packet-switched technology, Frame Relay allows the network medium to be shared (contrast that with a circuit-switched technology where the network medium is dedicated to one call at a time). Frame Relay uses variable-length packets for efficient data transfer and use of the medium. Frame Relay is a Layer 2 protocol and requires other protocols at Layers 3 through 5, and a physical connection at Layer 1 to create end-to-end interoperability (see Figure 3-9). The upper layers normally are TCP/IP, but could be any other suitable protocol. Frame Relay is standardized by the ITU-T internationally and ANSI in the United States.

Committed Information Rate Frame Relay connections often give a **committed information rate (CIR)**. They also often allow for extendable information rates (EIR). The CIR is a rate that is guaranteed—think of this as the lowest possible speed or the floor. The EIR is the maximum speed a connection will support, in short burstable time periods. Packets sent at the CIR are guaranteed to get through, while packets sent at the EIR are marked "discard eligible (DE)" and are the first to be dropped if network congestion occurs.

Virtual Circuits Frame Relay supports virtual circuits. Remember that virtual circuits allow defined communication paths between pairs of devices. These circuits are created by using a connection identifier. Frame Relay provides both SVCs and PVCs. The virtual circuits are identified with a Data Link Connection Identifier (DCLI) as shown in Figure 3-10. The DCLI identifies the circuit on the local LAN, but not over the WAN.

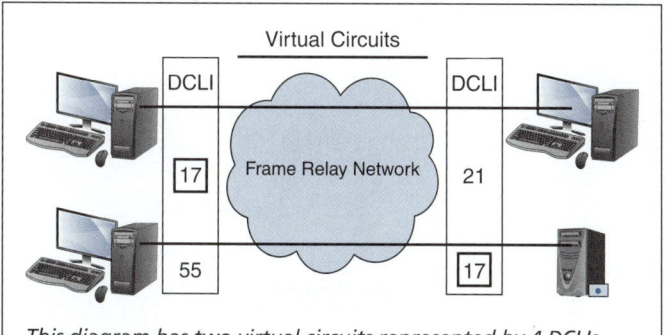

FIGURE 3-10 Frame Relay DCLIs

This diagram has two virtual circuits represented by 4 DCLIs (17, 17, 21, 55). Note that two of the DCLIs are duplicated (17), which is possible because the DCLIs are significant to the LAN, but not to the Frame Relay WAN.

FIGURE 3-11 Frame Relay PDU

| FCS | PAYLOAD | FECN, BECN, DE BITS | DCLI | ADDRESS FIELD | FLAG FIELD |

This diagram shows the format of the Frame Relay PDU.

Frame Relay PDU Frame Relay is an encapsulated protocol, which takes the packet from Layer 3 and places it into a frame at Layer 2. The frame is then physically propagated at Layer 1. The **Frame Relay PDU** (Figure 3-11) contains the following fields:

- Flag field: a synchword used to synchronize clocks between senders and receivers
- Address field: a variable-length address field, depending on the range of addresses in use
- Data Link Connection Identifier: identifies virtual circuits
- FECN, BECN, DE: used to report congestion
- Payload: the packet encapsulated into this frame from Layer 3
- Frame check sequence: a cyclic redundancy check designed to catch single bit errors

Frame Relay and Multiprotocol Environments Because Frame Relay is implemented at Layer 2, other protocols and devices are able to be used at other layers. For example, it is possible to intermingle Ethernet, Token Ring, and so on using multiplexing. (See the example in Figure 3-12.)

FRAME RELAY COMPONENTS AND PRICING

In Frame Relay parlance, LANs are known as data terminal equipment (DTE), and the point of presence (POP) to which the DTE device connects is known as data circuit-terminating equipment (DCE). The DTE that connects a LAN to the Frame Relay

FIGURE 3-12 Frame Relay and Non-Frame Relay Devices

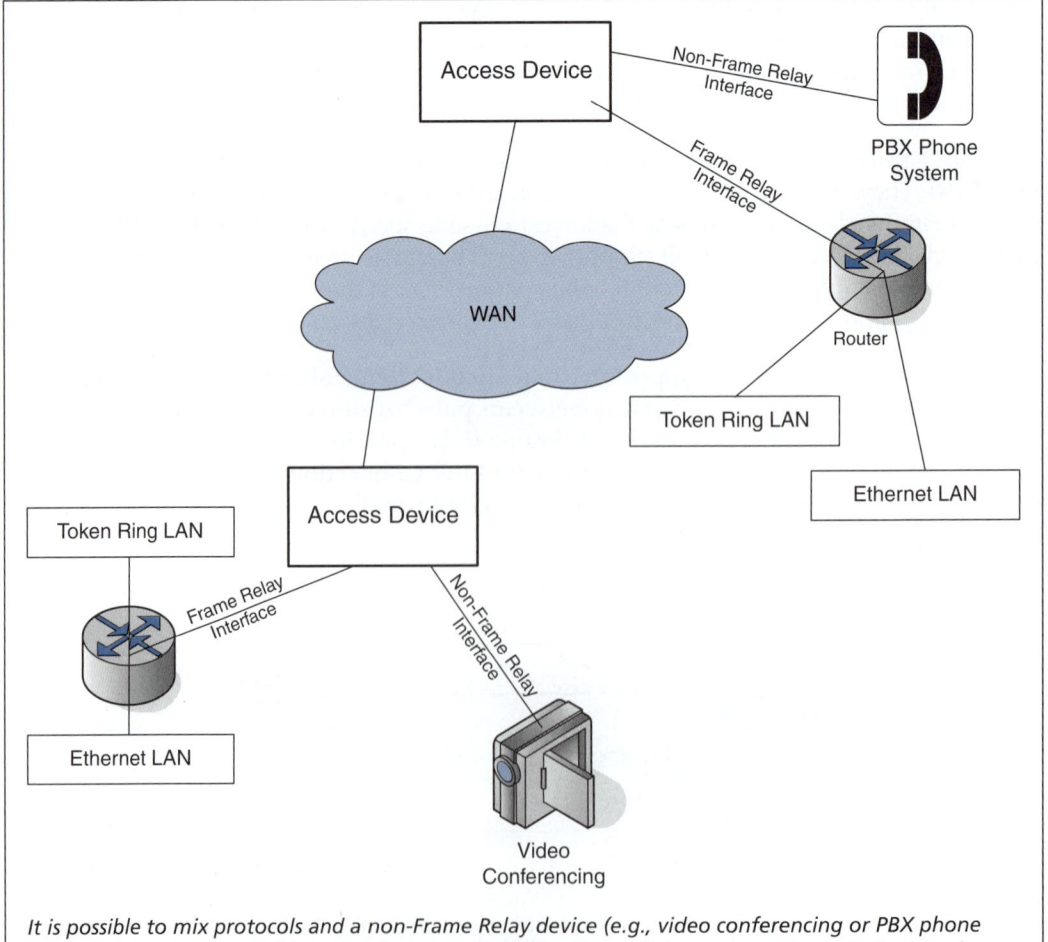

It is possible to mix protocols and a non-Frame Relay device (e.g., video conferencing or PBX phone system) across the WAN with access devices that support Frame Relay and non-Frame Relay interfaces.

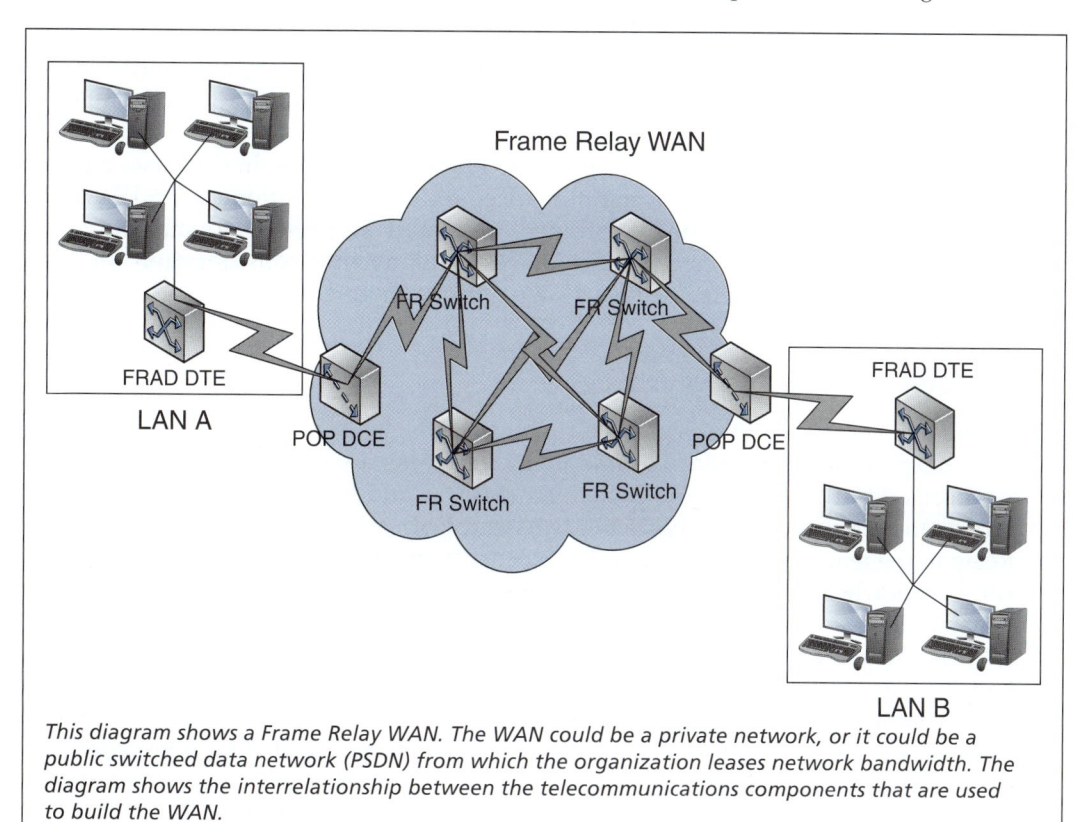

FIGURE 3-13 Frame Relay Network Components

This diagram shows a Frame Relay WAN. The WAN could be a private network, or it could be a public switched data network (PSDN) from which the organization leases network bandwidth. The diagram shows the interrelationship between the telecommunications components that are used to build the WAN.

WAN is known as a Frame Relay Access Device (FRAD). Between the FRAD and the POP/DCE the customer will need a point-to-point connection. So to recap, connection to a Frame Relay WAN requires the following:

- A Frame Relay Access Device that interconnects the LAN to the WAN
- A point-to-point circuit that interconnects the FRAD to the point of presence
- A port on a POP that provides interconnection to the Frame Relay WAN

The Frame Relay WAN is made up of a number of Frame Relay switches that are interconnected in a mesh typology. When an organization wants to create its own Frame Relay WAN, it needs to purchase a number of Frame Relay switches and point-to-point circuits that interconnect the switches. When a company wants to connect to a Frame Relay PSDN, it needs to purchase the FRAD, lease a point-to point circuit between the FRAD and the POP, and lease the port on the POP. (See Figure 3-13.) Frame Relay port and network usage pricing is governed by quality of service guarantees, port speeds, and number and type of virtual circuits.

PUBLIC VERSUS PRIVATE FRAME RELAY NETWORKS

Carriers offer Frame Relay networks. In those cases, the carrier is responsible for all network hardware and the circuits that are used to create the WAN. The carrier charges for the WAN components. In a public carrier–provided WAN, all switching

---

VIGNETTE BOX 3-5

HealthyWay's Possible Use of Frame Relay

Using all of the components of **Frame Relay pricing**, HealthyWay would have to determine how much Frame Relay would cost. It would also have to determine whether Frame Relay can give it the needed level of service and appropriate service level guarantees through a negotiated service level agreement (SLA).

equipment is located at the office of the telecommunication carrier. Customers who use the WAN pay lease fees and are called subscribers. Subscribers are charged based on their use but are relieved from the maintenance and administration of the Frame Relay network.

Organizations can also create a Private Frame relay WAN. In this case, they are responsible for all equipment, maintenance, and administration of the WAN. All equipment is owned by the customer, and staff is needed to maintain and administer the WAN. A cost-benefit analysis, taking into consideration the total cost of ownership, of the lease-versus-own options should be done before a decision is made.

THE FUTURE OF FRAME RELAY

Frame Relay was initially designed to run over ISDN; however, with the advent of fast and inexpensive alternatives, Frame Relay networks are being displaced. IP-based networks, Multiprotocol Label Switching (MPLS), and VPNs, along with dedicated broadband services such as cable modems and DSL, are gradually displacing Frame Relay in the marketplace for fast and inexpensive always-on connections. However, in rural areas where these displacing technologies may not be available an organization may still chose a 64 kb Frame Relay circuit as its best option.

The largest Frame Relay provider in the United States is AT&T. As of June 2007 it had POPs in 22 states, plus connections to national and international networks. As Frame Relay contracts expire (for AT&T and others), the number of POPs and network connections is expected to decrease dramatically. Customers are expected to migrate to other services such as MPLS over IP. It is expected that this migration will reduce the costs and improve manageability and performance of those organizations' WANs.

ATM

Asynchronous Transfer Mode (ATM) was originally designed to provide faster data, video, and voice services over ISDN. In 1988, the ITU-T designated ATM became the universal network transport service for data, voice, and video. Like Frame Relay, ATM originally evolved from the need for faster and more reliable data, voice, and video transport. ATM is a packet-switching protocol that operates at the data link layer of the five-layer TCP/IP-OSI model.

ATM TECHNICAL DESCRIPTION

Specifically, ATM provides data link layer services that are propagated over a physical layer link (see Figure 3-14). In ATM, the PDU is called a "cell." ATM is a connection-oriented protocol and establishes a connection between two endpoints (hosts or networks) before actual communication starts. This section describes ATM and its functionality.

ATM Cells ATM uses fixed-length cells, rather than variable-length frames. (Notice that the PDU at Layer 2, the data link layer, is called a cell rather than a frame.) Fixed-length cells are used because they provide faster switching at each node of an ATM network. The fixed-length cell also reduces the variability in transmission delay; fixed-length cells make the delay more predictable. Reduced jitter is especially important when transmitting voice or video to make the digital encoding/decoding of voice and video more predictable.

Encapsulated data from Layers 3 through 5 are passed to ATM at Layer 2. Layer 2 creates an ATM cell with a 48-octet payload. In other words, the data packet from the upper layers is broken into 48-octet chunks that are encapsulated into the payload of the ATM cell. The ATM cell has an overall size of 53 octets that include header information. Of the two types of cells (UNI and NNI), UNI is the most widely used. The UNI cell is composed of the following fields, as indicated in Figure 3-15:

- GFC: generic flow control (4 bits); all four bits must be set to zero by default
- VPI: virtual path identifier (8 bits); used for ATM virtual circuits

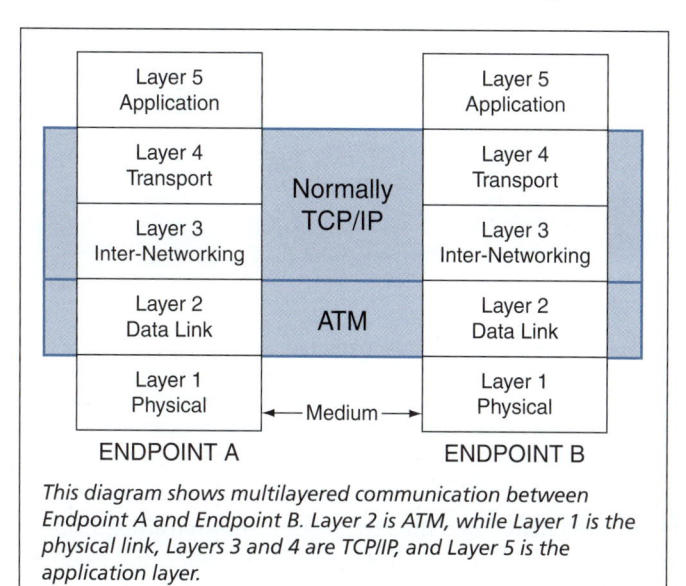

FIGURE 3-14 ATM and Hybrid TCP/IP-OSI Model

Layer 5 Application		Layer 5 Application
Layer 4 Transport	Normally TCP/IP	Layer 4 Transport
Layer 3 Inter-Networking		Layer 3 Inter-Networking
Layer 2 Data Link	ATM	Layer 2 Data Link
Layer 1 Physical	←Medium→	Layer 1 Physical
ENDPOINT A		ENDPOINT B

This diagram shows multilayered communication between Endpoint A and Endpoint B. Layer 2 is ATM, while Layer 1 is the physical link, Layers 3 and 4 are TCP/IP, and Layer 5 is the application layer.

- VCI: virtual channel identifier (16 bits); used for ATM virtual circuits
- PT: payload type (3 bits)
- CLP: cell loss priority (1 bit); controls the probability of a cell being discarded if a network becomes congested
- HEC: header error correction (8-bit CRC); able to correct single-bit errors and detect many multi-bit errors
- Payload: data from upper layers (384 bits/48 octets)

Virtual Circuits ATM implements both static (permanent) and dynamic (switched) virtual circuits. Permanent virtual circuits (PVCs), sometime referred to as permanent virtual paths in ATM, require that the network provider (e.g., carrier) provision a series of network segments to create the PVC. Because nearly every virtual circuit implemented today is a PVC, the rest of this discussion will center around them. ATM can support switched virtual circuits; however, they are rarely implemented.

ATM's implementation of PVCs uses virtual paths and virtual channels (Figure 3-16). The ATM header discussed previously has a virtual channel identifier (VCI) and a virtual path identifier (VPI), and together these form the basis for ATM's channel-based communications. The ATM cell is examined at each switch in a network, and the VCI and VPI are used to make forwarding decisions. It should be noted that even though ATM networks are typically in a **mesh typology**, the ATM implementation of PVCs does not allow for rerouting of a PVC in the event of a network error.

ATM Traffic ATM implements quality of service (QOS) in what are called *traffic contracts*. When a virtual circuit is provisioned each switch is informed of the class of traffic. This information forms the basis of the traffic contract for the circuit. The four basic types in ATM each describe a circuit:

- Constant bit rate (CBR): specifies the circuit's peak cell rate.
- Variable bit rate (VBR): specifies the maximum cell rate and maximum interval allowed

FIGURE 3-15 ATM PDU

| PAYLOAD | HEC | CLP | PT | VCI | VPI | GFC |

This diagram shows the format of the ATM PDU.

FIGURE 3-16 ATM Paths and Circuits

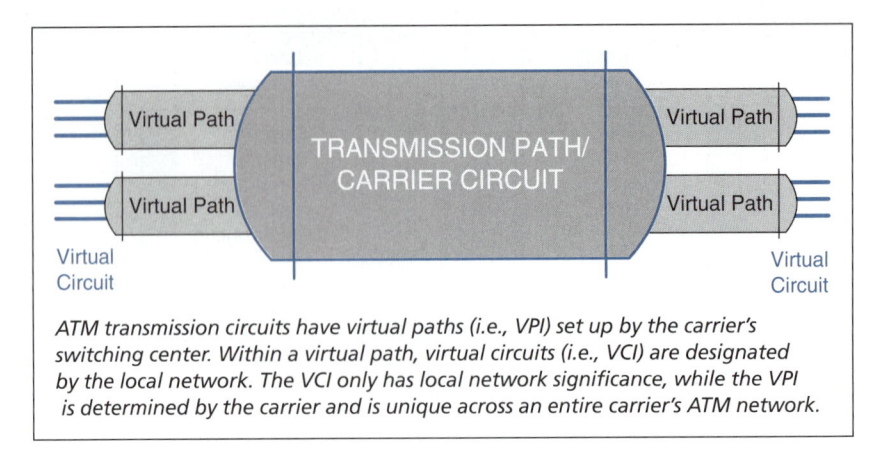

ATM transmission circuits have virtual paths (i.e., VPI) set up by the carrier's switching center. Within a virtual path, virtual circuits (i.e., VCI) are designated by the local network. The VCI only has local network significance, while the VPI is determined by the carrier and is unique across an entire carrier's ATM network.

- Available bit rate (ABR): specifies the minimum guaranteed cell rate
- Unspecified bit rate (UBR): specifies traffic that is allocated to unused transmission capacity.

Taken together these traffic types, their parameters, and the various subtypes create traffic contracts and the basis for QOS guarantees in ATM.

ATM also supports traffic shaping. Traffic shaping is an attempt to control network traffic in order to optimize and guarantee QOS. Basically, traffic shaping may impose delay or constraints on certain categories of traffic in order to give other traffic priority in the network. For example, because of their time-sensitive nature, voice or video are given priority over other types of data in an ATM network. Traffic shaping is normally done at the point of entry (i.e., the first switch) in an ATM network.

A final mechanism used by ATM is traffic policing. Traffic policing is performed by ATM switches, where they look at cells in a virtual circuit and compare them against the circuit's traffic contract. Cells that exceed their traffic contract can have their cell loss priority (CLP) bit set, indicating that they can be dropped if congestion gets too severe.

ATM and Multiprotocol Environments ATM functions similarly to Frame Relay in a multi-protocol environment. As a Layer 2 data link layer protocol, ATM relies on Layer 1 to provide signal propagation, and Layers 3 through 5 to provide the encapsulated data that transmits over the network. ATM creates/manages cells and virtual circuits, and provides traffic control with QOS guarantees (Figure 3-17).

ATM COMPONENTS AND PRICING

ATM requires similar components to Frame Relay but is more expensive. Many carriers offer both Frame Relay and ATM services because they serve different markets. ATM services a market that needs higher QOS guarantees than Frame Relay users. Because of the overhead and expense of providing QOS guarantees, ATM is more expensive.

Connection to an ATM WAN requires the following:

- An ATM access device that interconnects the LAN to the WAN
- A point-to-point circuit that interconnects the access device to the point of presence
- A port on a POP that provides interconnection to the ATM WAN

The ATM WAN is made up of a number of ATM switches that are interconnected in a mesh typology. However, the ATM network will provide virtual circuits, not packet switching. The mesh allows for flexibility in creating virtual circuits, but does not provide for traffic rerouting to accommodate network errors or congestion.

Similarly to Frame Relay, when an organization wants to create its own ATM network, it needs to purchase a number of ATM switches and the point-to-point circuits that interconnect the switches. When a company wants to connect to an ATM

FIGURE 3-17 ATM Network

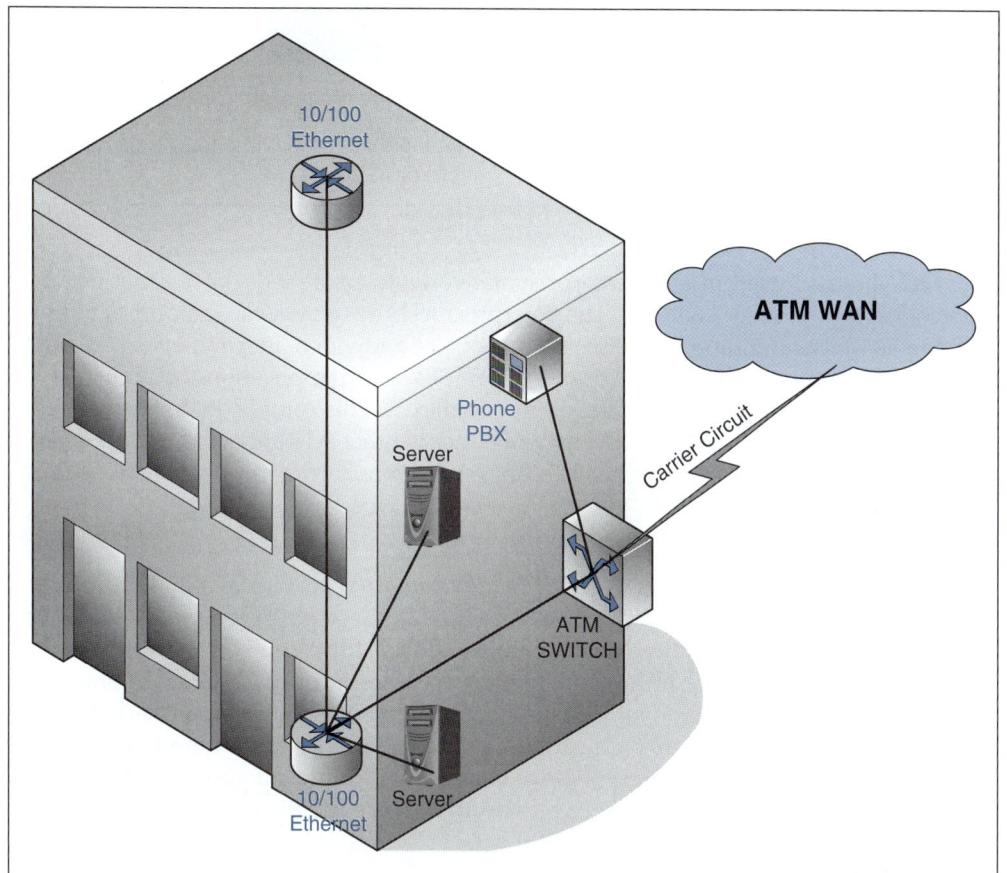

The LAN within this building is attached to an ATM switch that has the carrier circuit interface built in. The phone PBX is also attached to the ATM switch, allowing phone calls to be transported over the same ATM WAN as data. This configuration could also include video conferencing.

PSDN, it needs to purchase or lease the access device, lease a point-to point circuit between the access device and the POP, and lease the port on the POP. ATM port and network usage pricing is governed by quality of service guarantees, port speeds, and number and type of virtual circuits. ATM will offer high levels of QOS.

ENTERPRISE USE OF ATM

Many organizations use ATM as a key enabling technology to facilitate interconnection of company locations to allow voice, video, and data communication. One key reason organizations use ATM is because of the QOS guarantees ATM offers. Carriers are responding to enterprise customers' needs for fast, reliable communication both nationally and internationally. Enterprises are leasing time on carrier-based ATM networks to create virtual circuits between their facilities that carry voice, video, and data.

VIGNETTE BOX 3-6

HealthyWay's Possible Use of ATM

Using all of the components of **ATM pricing**, HealthyWay would have to determine how much ATM would cost. Considering the extent of ATM service level guarantees available, HealthyWay can probably negotiate a service level agreement (SLA) that would give the necessary services levels, but it comes at greater cost than Frame Relay. HealthyWay would have to do a cost analysis of Frame Relay, ATM, and any other available technology before making a decision about which technology best serves its needs and is the most cost-effective.

> **VIGNETTE BOX 3-7**
>
> **HealthyWay's Possible Use of Frame Relay**
>
> If HealthyWay provides mobile telephone service to its employees, it will have to consider whether they need Internet and/or e-mail service on their mobile devices.

ATM is also used in large enterprise networks to create a backbone that provides interconnection to other switches. The enterprise ATM networks can support data transmission as well as multimedia services such as voice and video. In summary, ATM can be used in long haul as well as local area and campus-based applications. Although it is a sophisticated technology, its drawback is its complexity. This complexity has to be figured into the total cost of owning an ATM network and whether ATM network management is best kept in-house or done through a telecommunications carrier–provided network.

General Packet Radio Service (GPRS)

General Packet Radio Service (GPRS) is a mobile data service available to users of Global System for Mobile Communications (GSM) telephony. Outside of the United States, GSM telephony is the most popular standard for mobile phones worldwide. Today, a number of carriers in the United States are adopting the GSM standard, making GPRS more ubiquitous. The GPRS standard allows data transmission through a GSM cellular network, providing data services virtually anywhere GSM cellular exists. This capability makes GSM/GPRS telephony providers a good choice when an enterprise wants to extend its WAN's reach and provide mobile roaming data services.

TECHNICAL DESCRIPTION

GPRS is a packet-switched technology that operates at Layer 2, the data link layer. It provides relatively slow data transmission, but the advantage of packet switching. Users are only charged for actual data transmitted. With traditional circuit-switched telephony, the user would be charged for the entire time a connection was made. GPRS can be used for Wireless Application Protocol (WAP) access, Short Message Service (SMS), Multimedia Messaging Service (MMS), and for Internet communications services such as Web browsing (e.g., http) or e-mail (e.g., POP/SMTP). GPRS was originally going to be extended to cover other cellular standards; however, networks are being converted to GSM, and GSM is the only type of cellular network where GPRS is being used.

GPRS is a wireless technology that uses channels within the GSM frequency band. Layer 1 physical signal propagation is wireless via GSM, and Layer 2 data link framing is handled by GPRS. GPRS provides a data uplink and down link, which use time domain statistical multiplexing (i.e., packet switching). This allows multiple users to share the same frequency channel, thus increasing efficiency of GPRS.

GPRS Connectivity A GSM/GPRS mobile phone can be used to connect a PC to a GPRS network. Depending on the mobile telephony carrier's service offerings, the GPRS network will allow connection to the Internet or to its own WAN or both. The PC would normally connect to the GPRS-enabled mobile phone via a universal serial bus (USB) connection or have a network interface card (perhaps a PC card) that connects direct to their laptop. The mobile phone or network interface card would provide an IP tunnel between the phone and GPRS network. The phone/network interface card would provide wireless connection to the cellular network, with handoff and roaming to allow continuous connectivity as the mobile PC moves from location to location.

GPRS and the Enterprise GPRS requires a GSM cellular network to provide data connectivity. The cellular network receives that GPRS data stream and multiplexes it over the GPRS backbone IP network, which in turn provides interconnection to the Internet or a corporate network, as shown in Figure 3-18. This relatively low-cost mobile connectivity for mobile

FIGURE 3-18 GPRS Network

The mobile user connects to a GSM/GPRS-enabled cellular phone via USB or through a GSM/GPRS network card that plugs directly into the user's laptop. The phone/interface card provides connectivity to the cellular network. The network is then responsible for routing GPRS data through the GPRS core IP network, which then transmits the data over the Internet or to a corporate network. This technology is useful for a company's staff members who are often mobile but require access to the Internet or corporate network.

network users has the advantage of being able to provide connectivity anywhere it can connect with a compatible cellular tower.

WiMAX

Worldwide Interoperability for Microwave Access (WiMAX) is a Layer 1/Layer 2 standard that has been codified by the IEEE 802.16 subcommittee. WiMAX is also referred to as *wireless metropolitan area network*, or WirelessMan (see Figure 3-19). The name WiMAX was created by the WiMAX forum, which is an industry group that certifies the WiMAX readiness of telecommunications equipment. The original standard was ratified by IEEE as 802.16-2004, then subsequently amended as 802.16e-2005. WiMAX is used to deliver point-to-point circuits from an ISP to an end user (WIMAXforum.org, 2011). It also has back-haul applications for cellular providers.

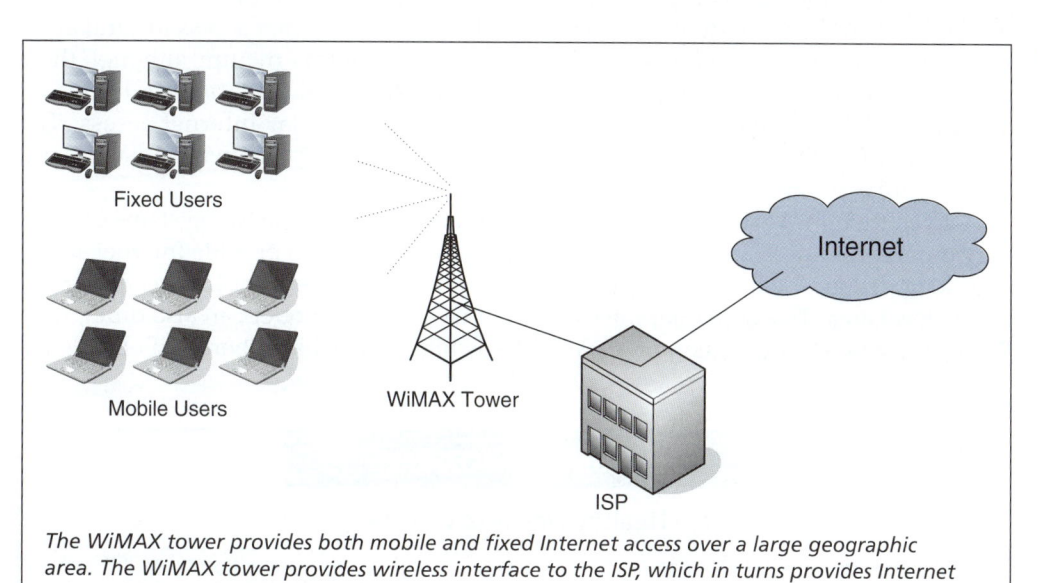

FIGURE 3-19 WiMAX

The WiMAX tower provides both mobile and fixed Internet access over a large geographic area. The WiMAX tower provides wireless interface to the ISP, which in turns provides Internet connectivity.

TECHNICAL DESCRIPTION

WiMAX is available as fixed WiMAX and mobile WiMAX. Mobile WiMAX can provide either a point-to-point circuit as well as nomadic roaming capabilities that allow a user to move around the area covered by multiple WiMAX towers provided by the same carrier. Mobile WiMAX implements the newer 802.16e-2005 standard. Fixed WiMAX supports the older 802-16-2004 standard and does not support nomadic roaming.

WiMAX Subscriber Stations/Units WiMAX requires that the user has a subscriber unit. The subscriber units allow wireless connectivity between the host (or the local network) and the WiMAX network. Traditionally, WiMAX subscriber units come in three forms: indoor, outdoor, and mobile. The indoor and outdoor units are used for fixed WiMAX installation, with the outdoor subscriber unit being more expensive to purchase and install. Mobile WiMAX subscriber units are being built into a number of devices, include headsets, PC network interface cards, and even some consumer electronics such as game consoles and MP3 players.

WiMAX at Layer 1 and Layer 2 At Layer 2, WiMAX subscriber stations compete for a time slot at their initial entry into a WiMAX network. The procedure uses a scheduling algorithm to determine the priority of traffic generated by the subscriber station. The time slot (i.e., think of a particular amount of bandwidth) remains constant unless enlarged by a QOS guarantee. This preassigned time slot is not available to other subscriber stations for their use, and protects the user against the WiMAX network becoming oversubscribed or too congested. This procedure is very different from a WiFi network where all packets compete for available bandwidth.

WiMAX has a number of sublayers at Layer 2 that describe how wired technologies (e.g., Ethernet, ATM, IP) are encapsulated for transmission over Layer 1. They also describe other features such as QOS, security, and encryption. The MAC layer also has power-saving mechanisms built.

At the physical layer, WiMAX typically uses licensed frequency spectrum for transmission. However, it is possible to use unlicensed frequency spectrum space. Most commercial installations use the higher frequency licensed space to avoid the rapid signal attenuation that occurs in the lower unlicensed frequencies. The licensed frequency spectrum yields better range and better penetration through shadow zones such as buildings or typographic changes in the landscape.

COMPARING WiMAX TO OTHER TECHNOLOGIES

It may appear that WiMAX, GPRS, and WiFi serve the same need. It is true that WiMAX and GPRS do compete with each other; however, they reach a different market. WiMAX is often deployed to provide broadband Internet access in rural areas where it would be difficult and expensive to build wired infrastructure, although there is a recent uptick in the number of metropolitan WiMAX installations. GPRS is an add-on to GSM cellular and is geared toward mobile cellular Internet access. The emergence of mobile WiMAX may stimulate greater competition between WiMAX and GPRS cellular providers.

Even though WiMAX may appear to compete with WiFi, the two systems provide very different services. WiMAX is a long-range system meant to provide Internet access over long distance, whereas WiFi is normally used to provide local LAN connectivity with a local area. The QOS guarantees that WiMAX and WiFi offer can also differ, with WiMAX giving stronger guarantees. WiMAX is highly scalable, where WiFi LANs are

---

VIGNETTE BOX 3-8

HealthyWay and WiMAX

WiMAX provides a good alternative to HealthyWay for high-speed connection to its ISP and is another technology that should be considered when analyzing costs of Internet connectivity.

FIGURE 3-20 WiMAX and WiFi Comparison

	WiMAX	WiFi
Range	Long-range system designed to cover many kilometers	Short-range system designed to cover hundreds of meters
QOS	Provides strong QOS guarantees based on packet scheduling	Provides weak QOS guarantees based on relative difference between packets
Scalability	Highly scalable from small-scale fixed installation to large-scale fixed/mobile installations	Somewhat scalable, but covers short distances
Frequency Spectrum	Usually licensed spectrum	Always unlicensed spectrum
Usage	Used to provide access to the Internet	Used to directly access a LAN

built to provide local area access within a small geographic area (e.g., think of a WiFi hotspot in a coffee shop). Although WiMAX can be deployed using the unlicensed frequency spectrum, it is normally deployed in the licensed frequency spectrum. WiFi is always deployed in the unlicensed frequency spectrum, meaning that other unlicensed wireless devices can interfere with the WiFi connection. In a comparison of the two, WiMAX could be equated to a mobile cellular phone whereas WiFi would be equated to a cordless home phone (see Figure 3-20).

DSL was previously discussed as a WAN technology, and WiMAX competes with DSL in certain markets. WiMAX has become available in a number of metropolitan markets and will undoubtedly become available in many more. It is unclear which technology will win out in the marketplace for Internet connectivity; however, both technologies provide similar services and each have certain advantages. WiMAX provides connectivity into geographic areas where DSL is not feasible due to distance from the Telco switching office or inadequate wired infrastructure. However, if the Telco wired infrastructure is adequate, DSL may be a better option. WiMAX is designed around QOS guarantees, whereas DSL depends on the protocols at the upper layers to provide those guarantees. WiMAX requires a licensed frequency spectrum, whereas DSL employs existing phone lines (see Figure 3-21).

When deciding between WiMAX, WiFi, and DSL, one should consider the previously mentioned factors as well as a thorough cost-benefit analysis. Clearly, WiMAX is suited to providing long-distance Internet access, whereas DSL is suitable for providing Internet access to end users reachable by the local Telco phone network. WiFi has its strongest place in providing multiple end users access through extending the reach of a wired LAN in the enterprise.

FIGURE 3-21 WiMAX and DSL Comparison

	WiMAX	DSL
Range	Long-range system designed to cover many kilometers	Uses existing copper local loop; range is limited from customer premises to central switching office, about 2 kilometers
QOS	Provides strong QOS guarantees based on packet scheduling in a Layer 1 and 2 standard	A Layer 1 standard with QOS guarantees that depend on what is being used at higher layers
Scalability	Highly scalable from small-scale fixed installation to large-scale fixed/mobile installations	Not applicable because DSL is used for point-to-point circuits between the host and the Digital Subscriber Line Access Multiplexer (DSLAM)
Frequency Spectrum	Usually licensed spectrum	Not applicable because it uses existing Telco copper; however, transmission is based on the quality of the local loop copper between the Telco switching office and the customer premises
Usage	Used to provide access to the Internet	Used to provide access to the Internet

FIGURE 3-22 MPLS Network

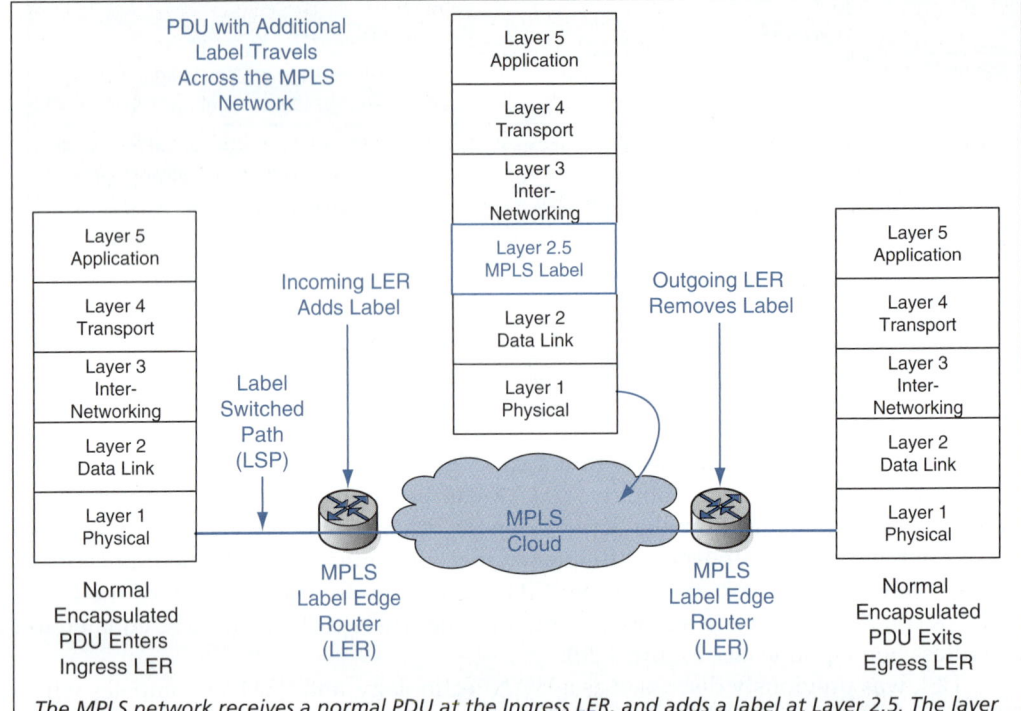

The MPLS network receives a normal PDU at the Ingress LER, and adds a label at Layer 2.5. The layer is removed at the Egress LER, and the normal PDU is passed to the receiving network/host.

Multiprotocol Label Switching (MPLS)

Multiprotocol Label Switching (MPLS) is a packet-switched networking technology that exists at "Layer 2.5" of the hybrid OSI-TCP/IP model (see Figure 3-22). It is generally considered to be between Layer 2 (data link) and Layer 3 (IP). MPLS can carry virtually any kind of traffic. If an MPLS network is passed a properly encapsulated protocol data unit (PDU), the MPLS network will append the appropriate labels and transport the PDU over the MPLS network. MPLS is able to carry IP packets, as well as **ATM cells**, and SONET and Ethernet frames.

TECHNICAL DESCRIPTION OF MPLS

The entry and exit points of an MPLS network are called leading edge routers (LERs) or label switch routers (LSRs). An LER can support multiple protocols, while an LSR supports only MPLS; this book will use the term *LER* exclusively. MPLS takes encapsulated frames from a network via an incoming LER and adds an MPLS header called a label. This header is added between Layers 2 and 3 of the PDU. In some applications like IP-VPNs, multiple MPLS headers can be added. The new header contains four fields:

- MPLS Label: 20-bit value indicating the path through the MPLS cloud; this is the equivalent of a permanent virtual circuit (PVC) in ATM and Frame Relay. Multiple labels can be added to an encapsulated PDU to support applications like MPLS VNPs.
- QOS Priority: experimental 3-bit quality of service field; not widely implemented yet.
- Bottom of Stack Flag: Because multiple MPLS labels can support applications like IP-VPNs, this 1-bit field indicates whether this label is the last one for this PDU.
- Time-to-Live (TTL): This 8-bit field indicates the maximum number of LERs that can be traversed in the MPLS cloud before the encapsulated PDU is discarded. This TTL value is only used in the MPLS cloud and does not affect any IP TTL value that is encapsulated in the PDU. When the encapsulated PDU leaves the MPLS cloud, the IP TTL value should be the same as when it entered the MPLS cloud.

When an unlabeled PDU enters an ingress router to be transported over the MPLS cloud, the leading edge router (LER) determines the label switched path (LSP) the PDU will travel over (i.e., which MPLS LERs the PDU will traverse from ingress to egress), and then inserts the appropriate labels into the MPLS header. The newly encapsulated PDU then is passed to the next hop LER for the label switched path (LSP) specified by the label. This operation occurs successively for each LER in the MPLS cloud until the PDU reaches the egress router. A number of operations occur within the cloud, including label swapping, label pushing, and label popping:

- **Swapping** removes the topmost label and adds a new one to cause the PDU to traverse a new path in the MPLS cloud. A new label means a new LSP.
- **Pushing** places a new label into a PDU, in addition to any other label that might already be there and is used in applications like MPLS VPNs.
- **Popping** removes a label from the PDU, possibly revealing another label. This process is also known as decapsulation.

When the labeled PDU is received by an LER, the top MPLS label is examined. Depending on the content of that label and the location of the LER (i.e., ingress, egress, or within the MPLS cloud itself), the LER will do a swap, push, or pop operation and then pass the PDU off to the next LER, host, or network.

BENEFITS

MPLS allows network resources to be managed and used efficiently. It has the benefit of being able to carry IP traffic as well as providing a connection-oriented service like ATM. MPLS can work with both variable-length PDUs such as Ethernet and fixed-length PDUs such as ATM. MPLS allows tunneling to support things like VPN technologies. MPLS is a good technology to support converged video, voice, and data application by using a class of service tagging mechanisms.

VIGNETTE BOX 3-9

HealthyWay's MPLS

The use of MPLS may provide HealthyWay with alternatives that other technologies lack. HealthyWay executives should consider this technology when looking into remote connectivity between locations. The executives should consider the need for QOS and associated cost when making the decision to implement MPLS or any other technology.

Metro Ethernet

Carrier Ethernet or **Metro Ethernet** is a technology provided by large telecommunications carriers, harmonized around the Ethernet (IEEE 802 workgroup) standards. Although Carrier Ethernet class service has some similarities to LAN-based Ethernet, it is different in some important ways: carrier class service provides Ethernet over a carrier-based network, is highly scalable, provides a higher level of reliability and quality of service, and has extensive service management components. All of these services are provided via direct connection of an Ethernet LAN to the Carrier LAN.

DESCRIPTION AND BENEFITS

Metro Ethernet can be deployed in a number of typologies including a traditional Ethernet hierarchy, but it can also be deployed using hub-and-spoke and mesh typologies. Each implementation has drawbacks and benefits. Obviously the greater the benefits, the greater the cost. Pure Ethernet MANs are the least expensive, while SONET/SDH-based and MPLS-based MANs are more expensive but give greater flexibility and options. The following discussion covers two common types of Metro Ethernet MAN: Pure Ethernet and MPLS.

Pure Ethernet MANs A pure Ethernet MAN uses Layer 2 switches through the MAN in a relatively simple and inexpensive design. Think back to earlier chapters and the shortcomings of Ethernet that include shared bandwidth, multiple opportunities for data collision, little provision for service level guarantees, switching tables that must track endpoint MAC address, little opportunity for traffic engineering and shaping, and lower network stability compared to other Metro Ethernet techniques. Taken together, these shortcomings point to the fact that Ethernet is not well suited to carrier-level operations. For these reasons, pure Ethernet MANs are a less-desirable choice for large-scale metropolitan production MAN applications when compared to the other Metro Ethernet implementation. To ease connectivity as well as decrease cost, a Pure Ethernet design may be found at the endpoints of a Metro Ethernet MAN where user intranets connect.

MPLS-Based MANs MPLS-based MANs implement MPLS over Ethernet and provide the customer with either a fiber or copper connection between the customer intranet and the MPLS-based MAN. Although it may sound strange, what you really have is Ethernet over MPLS over Ethernet—that is, Ethernet frames from the customer, MPLS labeling at the point of entry into the MAN, then encapsulated into an Ethernet frame to traverse Metro Ethernet MAN. This approach gives the following advantages: scalability, network resiliency, and availability of increased service level guarantees.

VIGNETTE BOX 3-10

HealthyWay's Use of Metro Ethernet

If HealthyWay has multiple buildings in the same metropolitan area, but not on the same campus, Metro Ethernet technologies may be a good alternative to things like PSDN or individual leased lines. Metro Ethernet could provide seamless connectivity between these buildings at lower costs than other technologies. It will be important to select/lease a Metro Ethernet MAN that uses a technology (e.g., pure Ethernet MAN, MPLS MAN, etc.) that supports the service level HealthyWay needs. It is also important to know what types of services are available in the geographic areas where HealthyWay's buildings are located—if there is no Metro Ethernet MAN, then that will not be an option. Understanding what is available and most cost effective takes market research.

VIRTUAL PRIVATE NETWORKS

In technical terms, a virtual private network (VPN) is a communication network, tunneled through another network. Tunneling refers to creating a secure channel over an existing network by using encryption algorithms to encapsulate and secure data to only be read by hosts at the end of the tunnel. Businesses often use tunneling protocols over the Internet to provide secure remote access from employees' homes back to the enterprise LAN. VPN tunneling protocols can also be used over WAN connections (i.e., provided by telecommunication carriers) between a company's buildings to secure information as it travels over the WAN.

VPN Types

A typical VPN transmits data using the Internet as represented by the cloud in Figure 3-23. This figure shows **site-to-site** VPN implementation between buildings and **remote access** VPN implementation that allow users to gain secure access to the organization's network resources. In the site-to-site VPN, each location has a VPN gateway that secures communication between the gateway, but not within the buildings. In the remote access VPN, the location to which the user is connecting (e.g., the main office) has a VPN gateway, and users have software on their PCs that allows them to create secure connections. In the remote access scenario, VPN is a service component that users interact with and gain access to network resources.

Note that the cloud in Figure 3-23 could represent the Internet or a PSDN that has a contract with the company. VPN technology can also use carrier-based leased lines to

Chapter 3 • Extending the LAN through WAN Connections   99

interconnect buildings and to increase security over the leased lines. Whatever networking technology is used, one of two types of secure data pathways is implemented, a site-to-site VPN or a remote-access VPN.

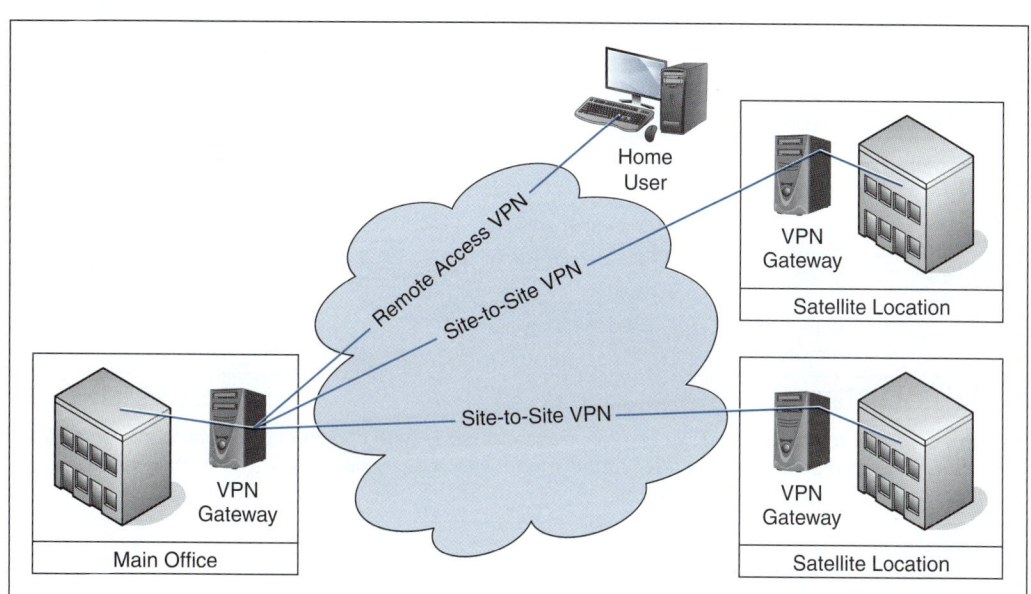

FIGURE 3-23 VPN

In this diagram, two satellite locations and one home user need a secure connection back to the main office. A secure connection is accomplished using VPN technology that creates secure data pathways between the users and the main office. In fact, two types of pathways, each of which will be discussed in the following section, can be used.

VIGNETTE BOX 3-11

Overview of HealthyWay's VPN

Each client that wishes to access a corporate network over a VPN needs a VPN client that takes care of encryption and authentication to the VPN appliance at the corporate office. Normal IP traffic from Joe Smith's home is not secure; however, when a VPN tunnel is used a secure communication channel between the laptop and the office is created, allowing the laptop to largely act like it is directly connected to the HealthyWay LAN.

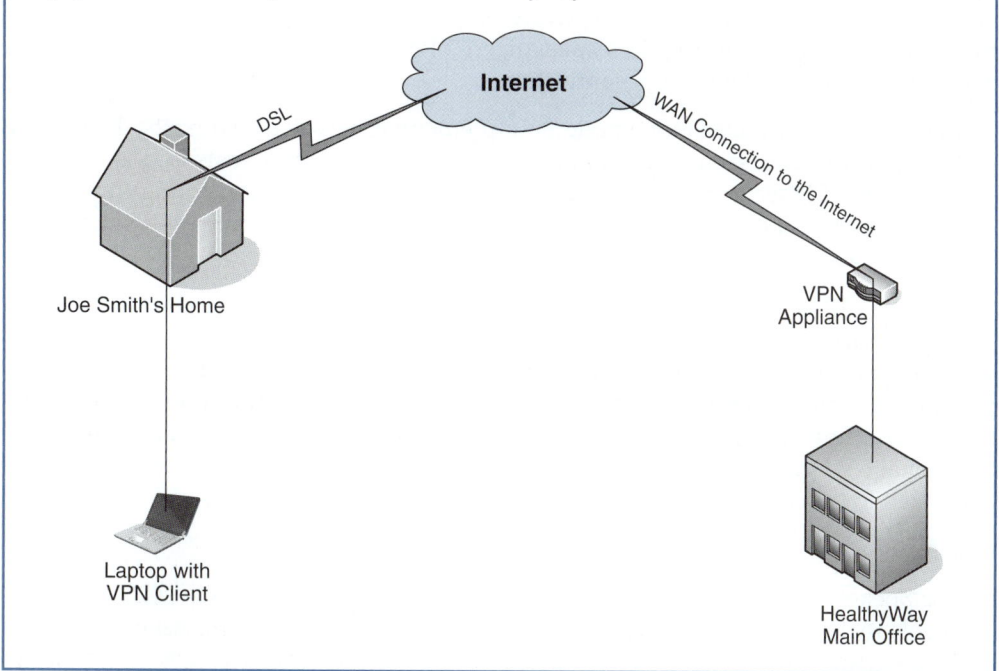

FIGURE 3-24 IPsec Transport and Tunnel Modes Compared

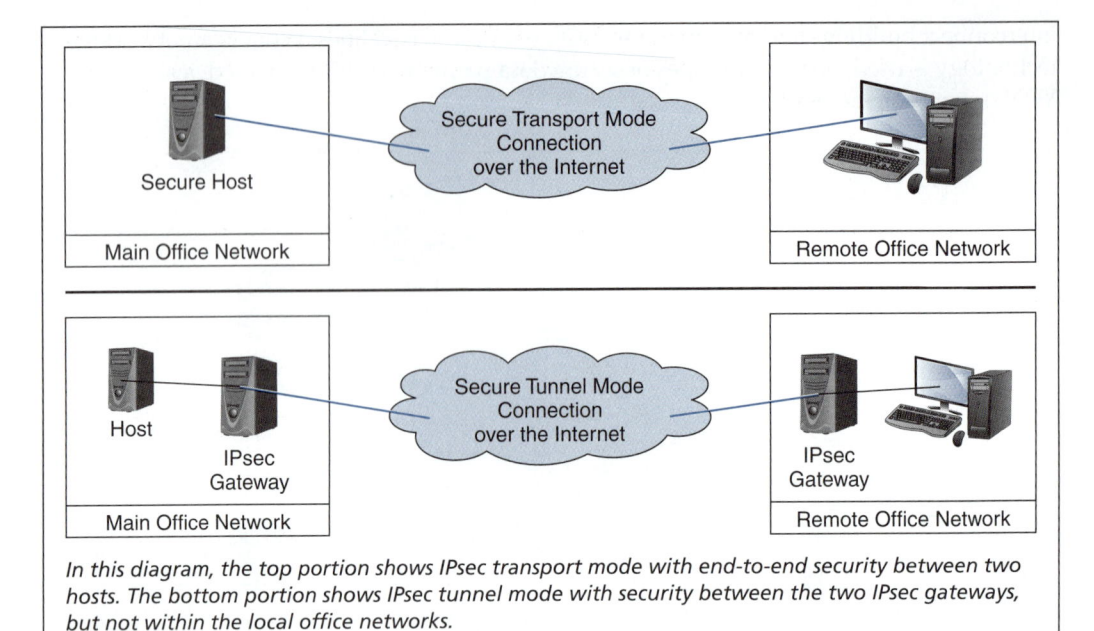

In this diagram, the top portion shows IPsec transport mode with end-to-end security between two hosts. The bottom portion shows IPsec tunnel mode with security between the two IPsec gateways, but not within the local office networks.

VPNs IPsec and TLS/SSL

VPNs are implemented within two major standards groupings. The first and most secure includes VPNs implemented within the IP suite of protocols (Layer 3), and other is implemented within the TLS/SSL (Layer 5). Each will be discussed in the following sections.

IPsec VPN

An **IPsec** VPN operates at the Internet (3) layer of the hybrid TCP/IP-OSI model. As such, it provides security to all the layers above it, which means that it protects everything within the IP packet (e.g., transport and application layer parameters and payloads). Even though IPsec VPNs provide the strongest security and data protection, they do have the drawback of being expensive and complex to implement and manage as compared to TLS/SSL VPN technologies. IPsec allows two modes of operation: **transport mode** and **tunnel mode**, which are shown in Figure 3-24. Transport mode requires special software on the hosts involved in the VPN connection, while tunnel mode requires specialized VPN gateway servers at each location connected by a site-to-site VPN connection.

Transport Mode IPsec transport mode is implemented between two hosts. This mode provides end-to-end secure communications between the two hosts and is the most secure mode of IPsec. It requires a digital certificate and additional configuration that make transport mode expensive to implement and manage. However, when complete end-to-end security is needed, transport mode is preferred.

Tunnel Mode IPsec tunnel mode is used to implement a VPN border-to-border between two sites. Each site has a VPN gateway at its border that communicates and creates a secure connection with the VPN gateway at the border of the other site's network. This provides a secure connection over a shared network such as the Internet or PSDN. In this configuration, only the two IPsec gateways need digital certificates and additional configuration, reducing the cost to implement and manage tunnel mode as compared to transport mode.

TLS/SSL VPN

Secure Socket Layer (SSL) and its successor, Transport Layer Security (TLS), are both protocols that support VPN connectivity. An organization that allows users to connect to the company network using a web browser will have a **TLS/SSL VPN** device. Users can then access network resources on the organization's network and perhaps even appear as a peer on the network (see Figure 3-25). Although the TLS/SSL VPN is less robust than IPsec, the TLS/SSL VPN is easier to deploy and maintain, making it a less-expensive alternative. The major decision to be made is whether the increased security of IPSec justifies the increased costs.

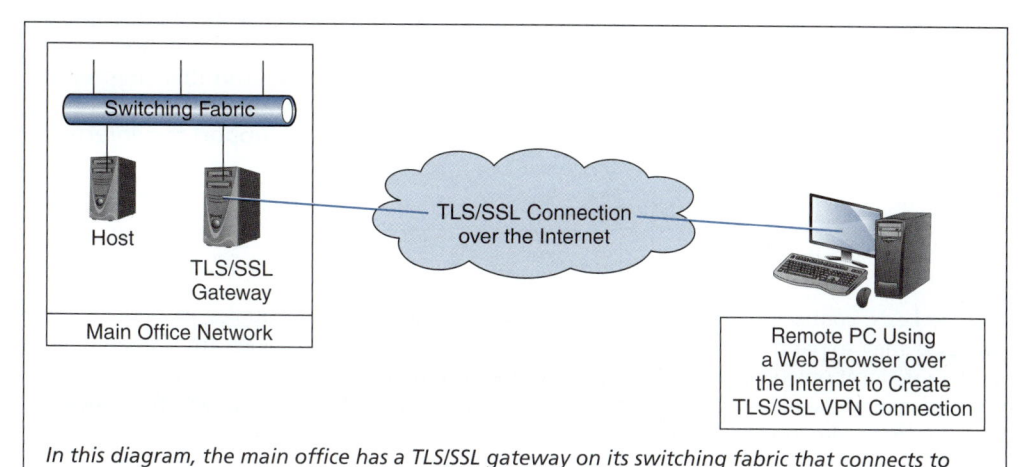

FIGURE 3-25 **TLS/SSL VPN**

In this diagram, the main office has a TLS/SSL gateway on its switching fabric that connects to the Internet. This gateway allows remote PCs using a web browser access to the main office network through a secure VPN connection. The connection provides remote users access to network resources and makes the remote PC appear as a peer on the main office network.

VIGNETTE BOX 3-12

HealthyWay VPN Connections

HealthyWay has space in its main office building where it would construct a LAN. It would use the main office LAN to interconnect all company computers, servers, and other devices. HealthyWay would use a WAN connection at the main office to connect to the Internet, as would Joe Smith. The main office is likely to be a T3 leased line, while Joe Smith's home office is likely to be DSL.

HealthyWay could also use other WAN connections (probably T1 leased lines) for any satellite offices it wishes to connect to the Internet. All connections to the Internet could be used to set up VPN connections back to the home office network (see the VPN secure channels in the diagram). Perhaps HealthyWay would choose an IPsec VPN for interoffice connection, and a TLS/SSL VPN for individual user connection back to the home office.

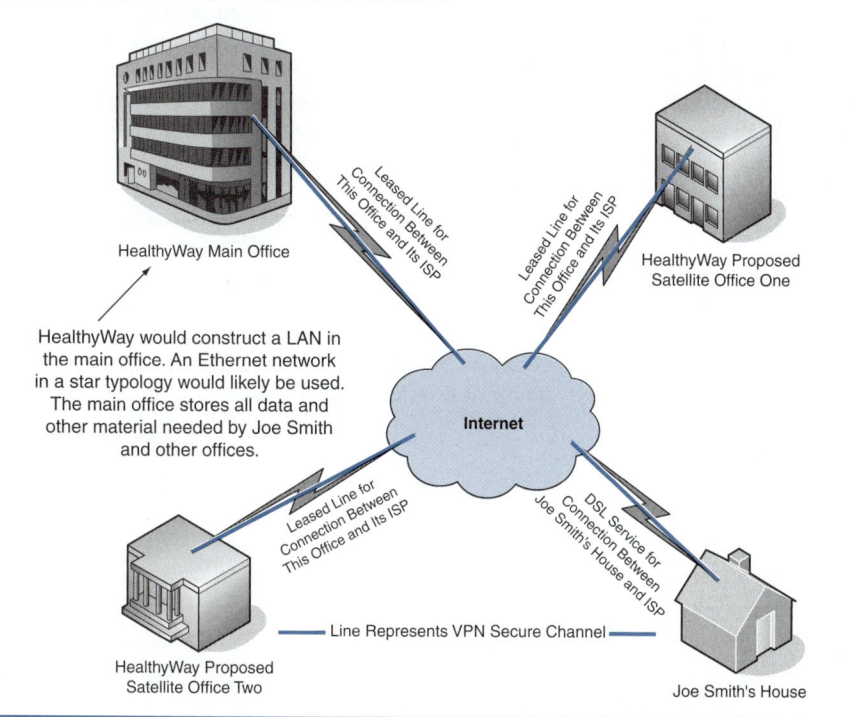

HealthyWay would construct a LAN in the main office. An Ethernet network in a star typology would likely be used. The main office stores all data and other material needed by Joe Smith and other offices.

Chapter Summary

This chapter covered ways of extending the reach of a LAN through WAN technologies. This chapter is not exhaustive, but it is meant to give the student the necessary knowledge to understand current WAN technologies as well as an understanding of new WAN technologies as they emerge. The chapter provided some introductory knowledge about **LAN versus WAN pricing**, as well as some technical details. Then the chapter turned to a description of various WAN technologies, including Frame Relay, ATM, GPRS, WiMAX, and Metropolitan Ethernet. Where appropriate, technical details, benefits, and pricing considerations were given. With the information contained in this chapter, the student should have an understanding of WAN technologies and where they can be used to support the enterprise.

Vignette Wrap Up

This chapter focused on how to extend the LAN, connect to an ISP, interconnect HealthyWay buildings if they expand, and provide connectivity for employees at remote locations (i.e., at home or away on travel). Extensive examples in vignette boxes were given through the chapter to explain how HealthyWay might implement the various WAN technologies available. It is important to note that not all technologies are available in all marketplaces, and often the driver for selecting a specific technology is that it is offered in each geographic location where it is needed.

End of Chapter Questions/Assurance of Learning

1. Prepare an analysis of the various WAN technologies presented in Chapter 3. Emphasize the business and cost benefits of each. Specifically focus on the business benefits of each technology and when they would be implemented.
2. Analyze the business benefits of IPSEC and TLS/SSL VPN technologies.
3. Write a brief paper comparing the similarities and differences of the PSDN and PSTN.
4. Select ATM, Frame Relay, or Metropolitan Ethernet and write a brief report and presentation on that technology.

Case Exercises

These exercises build on the case exercises from previous chapters.
1. XYZ Inc. wants to build a new CSU/DSU/firewall/router and to include options that will make the device competitive. It has heard of new standards being discussed by IEEE. Develop a plan for XYZ Inc. so it can be sure it is building the router to use appropriate current and emerging standards. Make sure you address the following issues:
   a. Which standards bodies would XYZ Inc. have to contact, and what is the process XYZ would follow?
   b. Explain the competitive positioning (or lack thereof) that XYZ may have because it wants to employ new and emerging standards.
   c. Make recommendations that will help XYZ keep its device current as new standards emerge.
2. HealthyWay HMO was discussed in the unit opening vignette. Use a product like MS-Visio to recreate the HealthyWay LAN diagrams. Recommend new WAN services that will aid HealthyWay in its search for competitive positioning. Prepare a brief report and presentation indicating how WAN services can help it attain competitive advantage in the marketplace of HMOs. In your case analysis discuss what things are important for HealthyWay to consider when selecting WAN technologies. Incorporate what you have learned in this chapter.
3. Select a company you are familiar with and write a case analysis that describes its WAN (or make recommendations for new WAN services). Describe which technologies it currently uses, or should use, and how they are important to the competitive positioning of that company. Support your analysis by citing Internet and/or print articles (i.e., trade publications, journal articles).

Key Words and Concepts

Asynchronous Transfer Mode (ATM) 88
ATM cells 96
ATM pricing 91
ATM traffic 89
committed information rate (CIR) 85
Frame Relay 84
Frame Relay PDU 86
Frame Relay pricing 87
General Packet Radio Service (GPRS) 92
IPsec 100
LAN versus WAN pricing 102
mesh typology 89
Metro Ethernet 97
Multiprotocol Label Switching (MPLS) 96
permanent virtual circuit (PVC) 81
point-to-point (POP) connections 79
public switched data network (PSDN) 80
public switched telephone network (PSTN) 80
remote access VPN 98
site-to-site VPN 98
switched virtual circuit (SVC) 81
TLS/SSL VPN 100
transport mode 100
tunnel mode 100
WAN and PSDN pricing 82
WAN connection types 79
Worldwide Interoperability for Microwave Access (WiMAX) 93

References

WIMAXforum.org. (2011). *Home*. Retrieved April 4, 2011, from http://www.wimaxforum.org

www.broadband.com. (2011). *Home*. Retrieved April 4, 2011, from http://broadband.com/

4 WRAPPING UP SERVICE, USER, AND ENTERPRISE COMPONENTS

Learning Objectives

- Understand what service, user, and enterprise-wide components are.
- Apply concepts from earlier chapters to service, user, and enterprise-wide components.
- Understand how and when service, user, and enterprise-wide components are used.

Earlier chapters introduced basic networking concepts and included a discussion of some service components. In this chapter, service components will be reviewed more fully, as will user components and enterprise-wide components. Service components provide the user with technical services and facilitate the network functions in the following ways:

- Print spooling and shared printers
- Database services where users store information
- Application servers that allow sharing of business logic instantiated in executables
- Intranet and Internet web servers that allow web page hosting
- File services that allows individual and shared storage space
- Storage area networks that allow vast amounts of data and file storage
- Backup and recovery services that archive data and files

User components are those components that the user directly interfaces with, especially those things that appear on the user's desktop: user workstations, desktop productivity software, printers, scanners, and specialized applications.

Enterprise-wide components include enterprise resource planning systems (ERP), document management application, knowledge management solutions, and a host of other specialized enterprise-wide applications. What sets the enterprise-wide components apart from user components is that enterprise-wide components cut across the organization and, rather than working within one

ENTERPRISE-WIDE SOFTWARE COMPONENTS Enterprise-wide software, including ERP, e-commerce/e-business, document management, knowledge management, and other specialized applications	**User Components**	Items that directly interface with the user, including workstations, printers, scanners, associated software (especially desktop applications), and specialized applications
	Service Components	Those network parts that facilitate network operations with direct user interface, including printing services, inter/intra office communications (i.e., telephone or fax), network attached storage, database/application servers, security servers and appliances, and VPN technology
	Network Components	Those items/concepts traditionally thought of as networking and telecommunications equipment, including network switching and routing hardware, media, outside vendor interconnects (i.e., T1, T3, DSL), and cabinetry, patch panels, and associated items

This figure lists and describes the components of ICT infrastructure architecture from the standpoint of the information technology user. The areas highlighted in blue are covered in this chapter.

FIGURE 4-1 ICT Infrastructure Architecture

department of the company, enterprise-wide components provide a unified application that brings together organizational information into one system.

INTRODUCTION

ICT infrastructure uses network components as the basis for providing communication among and between hosts within a LAN, and is extensible to users outside the local area through WAN connectivity. These components provide the basis for data communications, but they need other components to make data communications truly usable. One such service component is the VPN, which gives users remote access to the network, but just being able to communicate data without some purpose is not very useful. Those things that make the network truly useful to the user and the organization are service components, user components, and enterprise-wide components. First we turn our attention to some basic concepts of PC hardware.

PC HARDWARE

Hardware platforms include Apple, Intel, Sun, and various mainframe technologies. Apple, Intel-based, and SUN platforms are used in server and desktop configurations, while mainframe computers are used in large transaction processing systems. Because Intel-based (and compatibles such as AMD-based) desktops and servers dominate the market, we will focus our discussion on them. Specifically we will cover the Intel and AMD processor architectures, but first we look at ATX factor form, which is the most prevalent today.

Factor Form

Notwithstanding blade servers, laptops, and application delivery through products such as Citrix® that use thin terminal client devices, the most prevalent Intel-based or compatible (e.g., AMD) desktop and server devices in use today are based on the ATX motherboard factor form. The ATX motherboard comes in fairly standard sizes but is not so standard in its options. Most of these options are transparent to the purchaser of desktop devices. The ATX factor form PC will support an Intel or compatible CPU.

The cases that house the ATX motherboard and other components (e.g., disk drives, RAM, CPU) come in desktop, tower, and rack-mount factor forms. Each offer distinct advantages. Note that the case factor form drives the size, shape, and robustness of the device due to available size and options, but whether the device is used as a server or a workstation largely depends on the operating system and other software on the device, not the factor form. The major advantages and uses of each are reviewed in Figure 4-2.

Blade servers, shown in Figure 4-3, are a different configuration from devices that use the ATX factor form. Blade servers, like the Dell PowerEdge® series, use a chassis that is rack-mountable. A blade server has the same types of options for memory and other peripherals as ATX-based devices, but it supports multiple motherboards in the chassis. With server virtualization each blade can act as one or many servers.

Laptops refer to thin portable computers that normally have an LCD screen. They offer the same options as listed in the next section, except they do not offer PCI slots. The size and specialized options offered on laptops vary by manufacturer, but the basic device runs an operating system and applications like a PC.

PC Options

When buying a desktop PC or a server, a number of options need to be considered, including the following:

- **Number of PCI Slots.** Does the device have enough PCI slots to allow the necessary devices to be installed? Those devices include modems, network adaptors, and video adaptors, as well as a number of specialized PCI devices that users may want.
- **CPU Type and Speed.** Is the CPU fast enough to give the performance needed for the applications being run?

Case Type	Description	Use	
Desktop PC	The desktop PC comes in a variety of sizes. The size is normally governed by the amount of disk space, memory, and number of card slots for PCI cards.	These devices are normally used at the user's desk.	
Tower	The tower PC comes in a variety of sizes that range from a mini tower to a full-sized tower. The size is indicative of the number and type of options that may be used in the device.	The mini tower is often used for desktop clients, while the full-sized tower is often used as a server in a small installation.	
Rack-Mount	As the name implies, these devices are meant to be installed in a standard equipment rack. They tend toward the higher end devices with more options and higher cost.	The rack-mounted device is most often installed in an equipment rack and used as a server. It is often installed with other servers and network devices such as switches, routers, and network accessible storage (NAS).	

FIGURE 4-2 Computer Case Type

- **Disk Size and Type.** Is disk space adequate for the data and software stored on the device? Is the disk type/configuration right (e.g., SATA, RAID)?
- **Random Access Memory (RAM).** Does the device have enough RAM for the operating system, applications, and number of external connections being made to it?
- **Video Adaptor.** Is the video adaptor high enough in resolution and speed to support the monitor and graphics that will be used? Is the video adaptor fast enough, with enough memory, to support the types of applications to be used with the device (i.e., some applications are graphic intensive and need more robust video adaptors to run successfully)?
- **Monitor.** Is the monitor of sufficient size and resolution to support the intended applications?
- **Universal Serial Bus (USB) Connections.** Does the device have enough USB ports and power to support the hardware that will be plugged into it (e.g., printers, mice, keyboards, external hard drives, etc.)?
- **Network Adaptor.** Is the network adaptor of sufficient speed (e.g., 100 Mbps) and of the correct media type (e.g., UTP, wireless 802.11 b/g/n)?
- **Power Supply.** Will internal power supplies provide sufficient voltage for the devices being installed?
- **Built-In Adaptors.** Although a move to have certain adaptors built-in to the motherboard of the device has been made to save cost, sacrifices are usually involved. For example, built-in video adaptors are often of lower resolution or "steal" RAM or process time from the device in order to operate, making them deliver lower quality than their counterparts that plug into an open PCI slot.

Processor Speed

Processor speed and type appear to be a confusing array of names and numbers. Not all PC motherboards will run with all Intel and AMD CPUs. Thankfully, unless you are building your own devices, you do not need to be concerned with this detail. However, it is helpful to know which processor is best for which application. The main way that processors are rated is in Gigahertz (GHz) and number of cores. GHz refers to the speed of the processor, while multicore refers to two or more

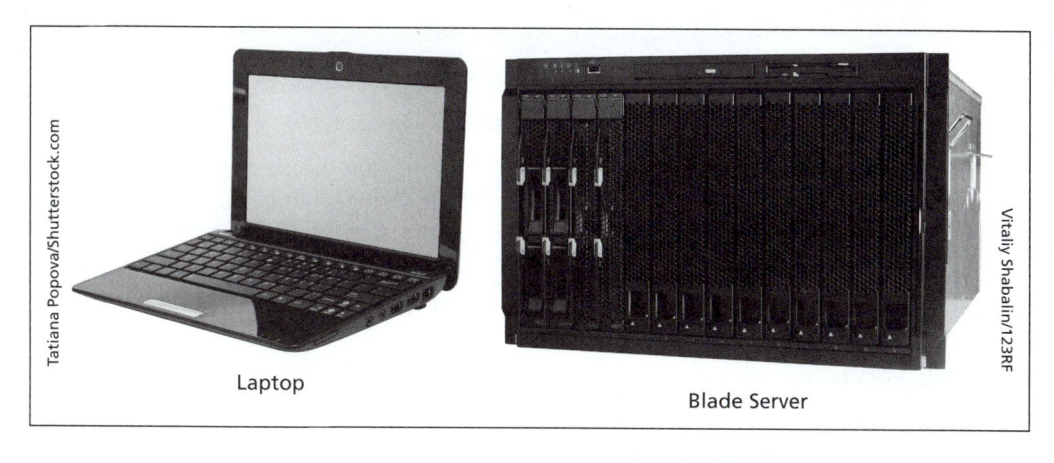

FIGURE 4-3 Laptop and Blade Server

VIGNETTE BOX 4-1

HealthyWay's Use of Thin Clients

HealthyWay may want to use thin clients, but that decision needs to be part of a larger discussion about virtualizing applications and desktops.

---

independent CPUs on a single chip. The combination of speed and the number of cores on a single CPU chip can significantly improve performance.

Summary of PC Selection

Remember, PCs can be used as workstations or as servers based on the operating system and software installed on the device. Normally desktop devices are not as robust as servers. Where servers might have redundant power supplies, fiber optic network connections, larger disk arrays, and more memory, PC selection is primarily driven by form factor (e.g., rack, desktop, etc.), operating system selection (e.g., MS-Windows™, Unix™, etc.), and applications used on the device. Software vendors like Microsoft will specify minimum hardware required to run a specific application or operating system. Keep in mind that those are minimums, and in most cases faster and bigger is often needed. It comes down to the cost benefit of buying a more robust device and the value of the increased speed the extra investment will yield.

Thin Clients

Although not a true personal computer, **thin clients** are part of a larger infrastructure deployment in which the client device consists of a small component with monitor, keyboard, mouse, network, and USB connections. It has limited memory, processing power, and graphics capabilities. A thin client device is used in a server-centric environment where the server is responsible for the processing of business logic or applications, and the thin client is responsible for the input (e.g., keyboard/mouse) and output (e.g., monitor or printer) functions. These thin clients are used in the application distribution and virtual desktop infrastructures discussed later in the chapter.

SERVICE COMPONENTS

Service components are what make the network components useful to the user. As soon as this book is printed new service components will be created, therefore it is impossible to cover all types of service components. The same is true of all components—vendors are always attempting to gain market share by creating new options and offering new components. The components covered in this section are representative of what is currently available and most common among service

> **VIGNETTE BOX 4-2**
>
> **HealthyWay's Use of Service Components**
>
> The business system analyst who reviews the ICT infrastructure needs of HealthyWay must consider what services are needed to make the ICT infrastructure useful.

components. Just remember this list is not exhaustive, but rather representative and meant to teach how service components work and what they are.

Printing Services

Users often have printers connected directly to their desktop PC, which allows one user to access that printer, and anyone else that wants to use that printer must bring their file to that PC or be networked peer-to-peer. Additionally, the PC must have the correct software installed. For example, if a coworker wants to use the printer connected to your PC and there file is a Microsoft Excel® spreadsheet, you need to have software that will open that spreadsheet. It also means that you cannot use your PC while your coworker is printing. Shared printers and a network-based service component called print services provide an alternative to having each user have his or her own printer.

Print services allow multiple PCs to share one printer. Print services support is implemented using a server that captures printer output from multiple PCs over the network, and then redirects those output jobs to a print server attached to the printer. The job of the server is to manage a print queue that keeps the printer output from each PC in order and feeds that output to the print server when it is ready. (See Figure 4-4.)

> **VIGNETTE BOX 4-3**
>
> **HealthyWay and Shared Printing**
>
> Shared printing services will help HealthyWay to optimize its investment in printers by allowing users to share large high-quality printers from a central location. It will mean less staff time servicing the printer. Also, printing documents on larger printers can cost less per page. Having shared printers does not mean that certain employees will not have personal printers. Sometimes special application printers (e.g., printing in color) are needed to facilitate certain tasks.

FIGURE 4-4 Shared Printing Using a Server

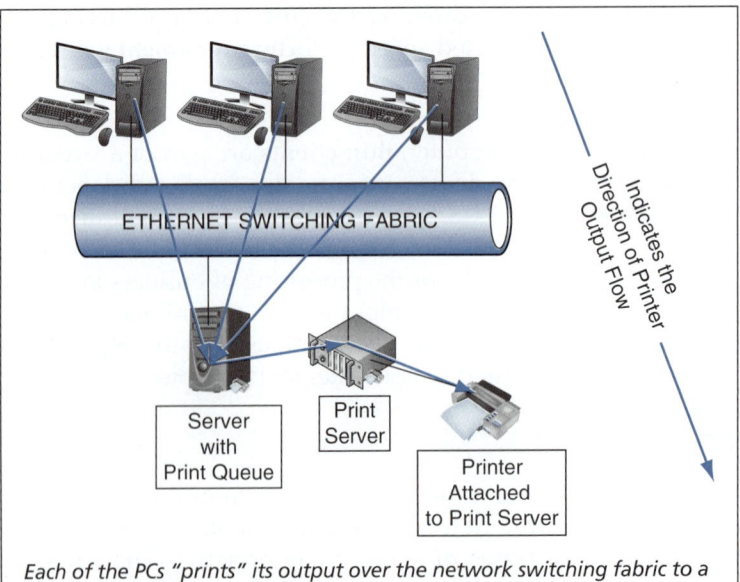

Each of the PCs "prints" its output over the network switching fabric to a server that manages a print queue. The server sends the output from its print queue to a print server over the switching fabric. The print server monitors the output and tells the server when it is ready for more output to print. This technology allows multiple PCs to share one printer.

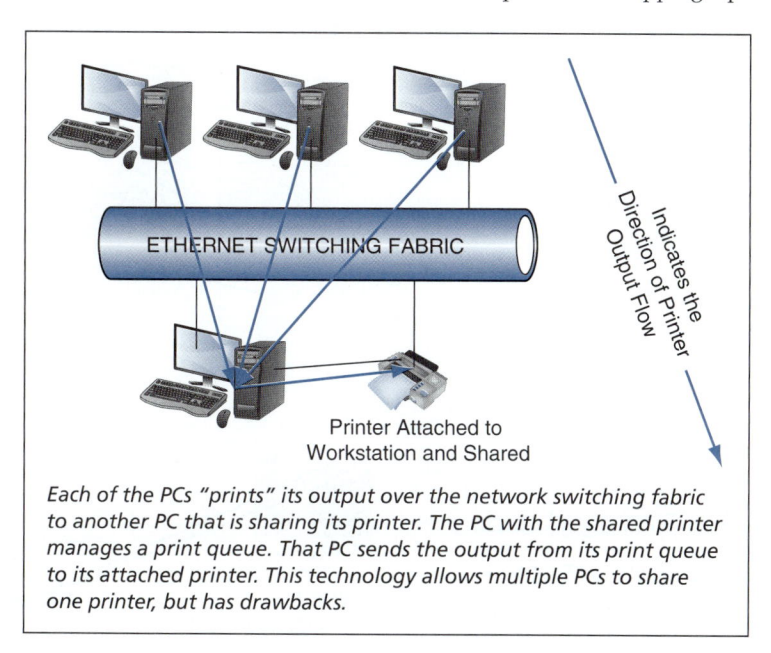

FIGURE 4-5 Shared Printing Using a Workstation

Each of the PCs "prints" its output over the network switching fabric to another PC that is sharing its printer. The PC with the shared printer manages a print queue. That PC sends the output from its print queue to its attached printer. This technology allows multiple PCs to share one printer, but has drawbacks.

VIGNETTE BOX 4-4

Sharing Printers Through a Workstation

Departments within HealthyWay may want to share an individual's printer through that person's workstation. This situation is not an ideal situation for larger departments or organizations, but it may facilitate some operations. It is a viable alternative to purchasing individual printers for every user, and for a small organization it may be more effective than having print services through a server. It is usually considered a viable option for home networks.

In addition to sharing printers using a separate server to manage the print queue, it is possible to share a printer using peer-to-peer networking technologies, which is often the case in small organizations where print volumes are not large. This setup basically works the same as server-based print sharing (see Figure 4-5); however, it has two major drawbacks: (1) the user who is sharing his or her printer must leave that workstation turned on for other users to share their printer, and (2) a large print job sent through a user desktop PC to the printer can make that PC very slow.

Inter/Intra-Office Communications

Another inter/intra-office communications service component worth mentioning is **Voice over IP (VoIP)** telephony. This technology supports both voice and faxing. VoIP uses packet-switched networks to facilitate communications within and between offices, and to non-VoIP locations via the Public Switched Telephone Network (PSTN). The key driver for VoIP is reduced cost because VoIP does not rely on the PSTN for the bulk of its communication. It's cheaper to communicate over a packet-switched network than over the PSTN.

The basic flow when originating a phone call over a VoIP network involves conversion of analog voice into a digital format, encapsulation of the digital data into IP packets, transmission over the packet-switched network, and reversal of the process at the other end. In the situation where only one end of the communication is VoIP, the PSTN is involved at the other end. While similar processing occurs, the remote end process will be slightly different because the VoIP call will connect back to the PSTN rather than to another VoIP-enabled network.

VoIP can be implemented in hardware in the organization that uses a VoIP-enabled PBX to connect to a packet-switched network (e.g., the Internet) to make calls,

FIGURE 4-6 Types of VoIP Calls

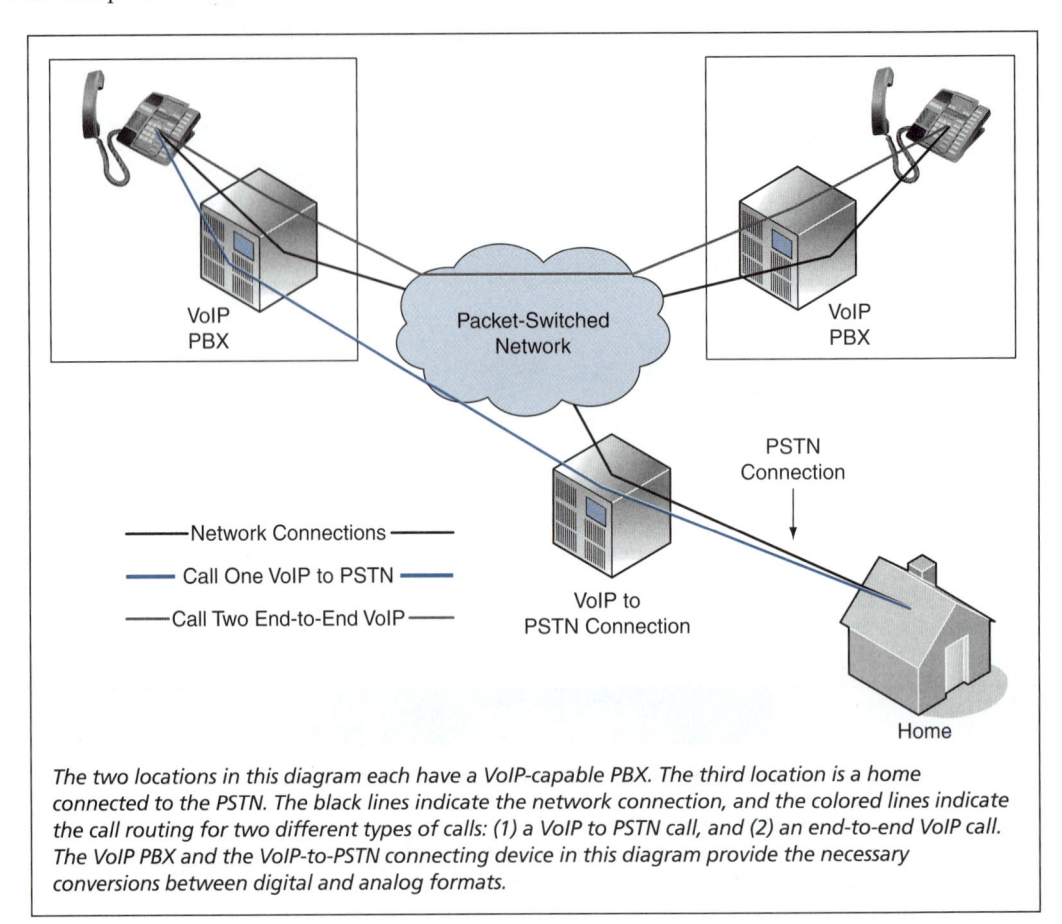

The two locations in this diagram each have a VoIP-capable PBX. The third location is a home connected to the PSTN. The black lines indicate the network connection, and the colored lines indicate the call routing for two different types of calls: (1) a VoIP to PSTN call, and (2) an end-to-end VoIP call. The VoIP PBX and the VoIP-to-PSTN connecting device in this diagram provide the necessary conversions between digital and analog formats.

as a server-based solution, and through mobile phones (see Figure 4-6). It can also be implemented in a "softphone" approach where the software necessary to initiate a VoIP call is installed on a PC, and the user can either communicate with the computer's microphone and speakers or use a phone that connects direct to the PC (e.g., connection via USB). "Softphone" clients include AOL® Instant Messenger, Skype®, and Vonage® to name a few. PBX solutions are provided through the PBX vendor and their associated service providers, while server-based solutions are available for many platforms, including Microsoft Windows, Linux, and Mac servers.

BUSINESS BENEFITS OF VoIP

VoIP can reduce a business's operational costs by eliminating the need to implement and manage both data and voice networks within the organization. In addition, the cost of calling can be significantly less using VoIP technologies rather then PSTN call services due to the way VoIP calls are routed via the Internet and how Internet access is billed, compared to regular phone calls. Lastly, VoIP can provide free or low-cost access to premium services such as conference calling, call forwarding, caller ID, and other features for which the traditional telephone company normally charges.

VoIP may provide flexibility that a PSTN connection does not. For example, a VoIP connection will be able to multiplex multiple phone calls over one data connection, while an analog PSTN connection requires one circuit for each incoming or outgoing call. It is easier to provide security around telephone calls when using VoIP because you are dealing with packetized data rather than analog voice signals. VoIP can also give location independence in that only an Internet connection is needed. All of this adds up to flexibility for the VoIP user, as well as the potential for greatly reduced communication costs.

> ## VIGNETTE BOX 4-5
>
> ### Inter/Intra-Office Communications
>
> HealthyWay is large enough that it will have a phone system with a PBX for call routing within the organization. That same PBX can connect to a VoIP provider of low-cost, long-distance VoIP-based phone connectivity between remote offices, and VoIP-based connectivity to the PSTN allowing low-cost local calls anywhere the provider has connectivity to the PSTN.

VoIP SHORTCOMINGS

VoIP has several notable shortcomings, primarily quality of service (QOS) issues. Since analog data are digitized and communicated over the Internet, phone calls can sometimes be jittery due to network latency and congestion. Some of these problems can be alleviated through service level agreements (SLA) with your ISP, but others cannot. VoIP is susceptible to power failures; the PSTN provides its own power whereas VoIP devices are powered by the local electric power provider. When the lights go out in your area you probably will not be able to make a phone call if you are using VoIP. If you are using the PSTN, however, its likely that you will still be able to make a phone call. Another issue is access to local emergency services through dialing your local emergency service access code (e.g., 911 in the United States). Due to the nature of VoIP telephony your location may not be identified to the emergency service. (Note: enhanced 911 services in many areas deals with the geo-location issues of VoIP.)

SAN and NAS

Storage area networks (SANs) are technology that provides storage (e.g., disk arrays, tape libraries, optical devices) to network users. SAN storage appears as if it is local storage to the user, and the user can access one specific block of a file rather than the whole thing. This approach to providing shared storage solutions to users is uncommon outside large organizations. It is expensive technology to deploy and maintain. In contrast, **network attached storage (NAS)** is much more common. NAS technologies (Figure 4-7) are based on file-oriented protocols such as the network file system. These protocols require the user to request an entire file from the NAS rather than just part of a file. Although the difference may be transparent to the user, speed of access and the impact on network resources should be considered.

NAS has several advantages:

- **A large amount of disk space can be made available.** It allows the network administrator to make a large amount of disk storage available to network users and simplifies the infrastructure requirements in doing so.
- **Hardware redundancy is increased.** NAS facilitates making redundant storage solutions (e.g., RAID-5 disk arrays) accessible to many users simultaneously, giving the advantage of increased redundancy at a cost cheaper than deploying that same solution to everyone's desktop.
- **It is easier to share files.** It allows users to share the same files, thus simplifying some operations within the office.
- **Disaster recovery is simplified.** Files are stored on a location that is easy to back up and manage, which allows network administrators greater control over recovery of files.

SAN and NAS devices are evolving. Currently vendors provide mapping of physical storage devices (e.g., a disk drive) to logical storage (e.g., the "C" drive on a PC) through their own proprietary protocols if the disk is attached directly to a PC or attached via network connection through a SAN or NAS. As we move from physically connecting disk drives to a PC to a NAS configuration, the goal is to provide pools of physical storage that can be mapped to logical storage accessible by the user. Even though little vendor interoperability is available today, greater standardization of

FIGURE 4-7 Network Attached Storage

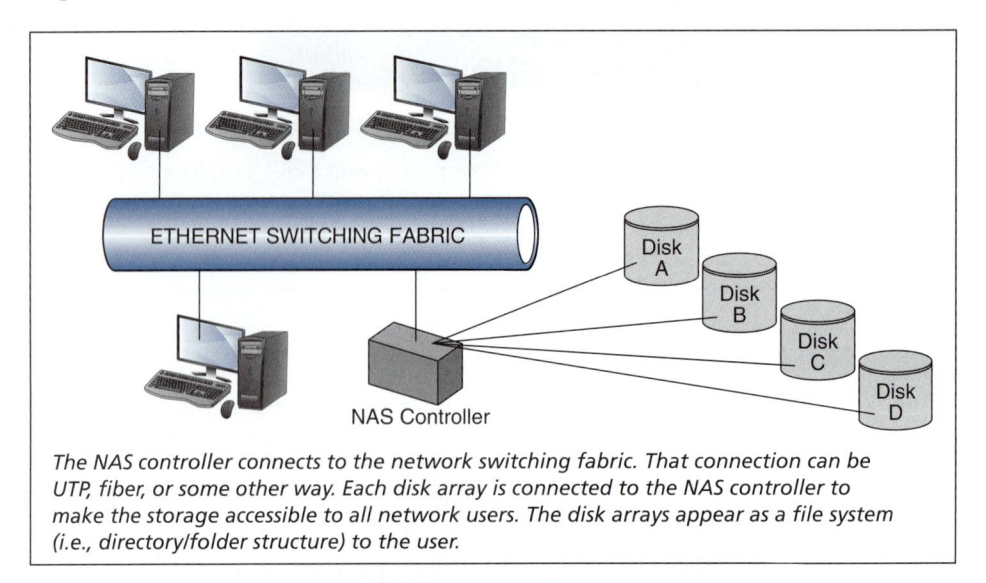

The NAS controller connects to the network switching fabric. That connection can be UTP, fiber, or some other way. Each disk array is connected to the NAS controller to make the storage accessible to all network users. The disk arrays appear as a file system (i.e., directory/folder structure) to the user.

VIGNETTE BOX 4-6

HealthyWay's NAS

HealthyWay should consider network attached storage (NAS) that will allow individual file shares as well as shared storage for users. A benefit of NAS is that it provides a single place for users to store files at the same time that it gives network administrators greater control of disk space quotas and backup capabilities. In other words, NAS provides increased user functionality and decreased cost of administration.

---

protocols as this technology evolves will allow for more interoperability among vendors that provide SAN and NAS solutions.

Web Server

Web servers are devices that accept HTTP requests from user clients and respond to those requests with an HTTP response message. The user client runs a web browser. Organizations with Internet connectivity can run their own web servers; however, it is often more cost-effective to use a hosted solution. Hosted solution providers supply the user organization with a web address (e.g., www.anycompany.com) and network administration, while the user organization provides the content and business logic. This arrangement is easiest when the hosted solution does not need information behind the organization's firewall to implement business logic. When information from behind the organization's firewall is needed to complete business logic it is often best for the organization to invest in the Internet connectivity and ICT infrastructure necessary so it can host its own web site, as shown in Figure 4-8.

A web server can host web pages that are simple and provide information to users at a specific web address (e.g., www.anycompany.com) or at an intranet web site within the organization's network. Web servers can also host complex pages that provide functionality like accessing an organization's business logic or data. The type of web site deployed is determined by the functionality that remote users require.

VIGNETTE BOX 4-7

HealthyWay's Web Server

HealthyWay will need to determine if it is more cost effective to use an internal web server or hosted services. Much of that decision rests on whether the website will need access to business logic and other resources that are found behind HealthyWay's firewall, and the cost/benefit to develop such connectivity.

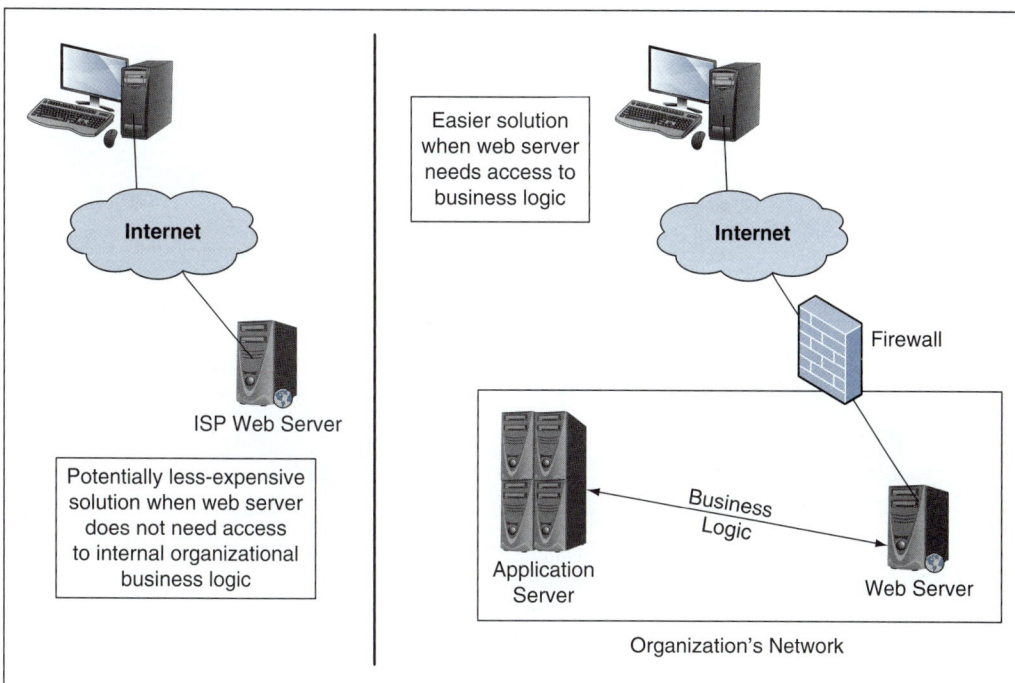

FIGURE 4-8 Web Server Usage

When a web server needs access to business logic, it is often easier to implement the web server as part of the organization's network. Even though access to business logic is not impossible over the Internet, it is often simpler and cheaper when accessed within the organization's network. However, for a stand-alone web site (i.e., does not need access to resources within the organization's network), it is often simpler and cheaper to implement on an ISP's web server.

E-Mail Server

A common application that users need is e-mail. Often that service is hosted by the organization's ISP; however, it is possible for an organization to host its own e-mail with an **e-mail server**. Incoming POP e-mail is received using the **Post Office Protocol v3 (POP3)**, and outgoing e-mail is sent using **Simple Mail Transfer Protocol (SMPT)**.

TABLE 4-1 POP3/SMTP and IMAP Comparison

POP3/SMTP	IMAP
Users download e-mails from server, and e-mail is usually deleted from the server. E-mail is sent via SMTP.	Normally, all e-mail is stored on the server, and client mailbox (i.e., cache) is synchronized with the server mailbox.
Clients normally work offline, and then send e-mail via SMTP. The e-mail originates from a specific client and a copy stays in that client's "sent items folder," not on the server who it was sent from.	Can work when the client is connected (i.e., synch local mailbox to the server) or disconnected (i.e., store and forward) from the Internet.
Only one client can be attached to a POP3 mailbox at a time.	Allows multiple clients to simultaneously connect to the same mailbox (e.g., mobile phone and desktop user).
E-mails are searched on the client system after they are downloaded.	Supports server-side searches.
Fairly easy to implement.	More difficult to implement due to the more complex nature of this protocol (e.g., allowing multiple users to access the same mailbox).
Implemented in virtually all e-mail clients.	Implemented in virtually all e-mail clients.

FIGURE 4-9 POP and IMAP E-Mail

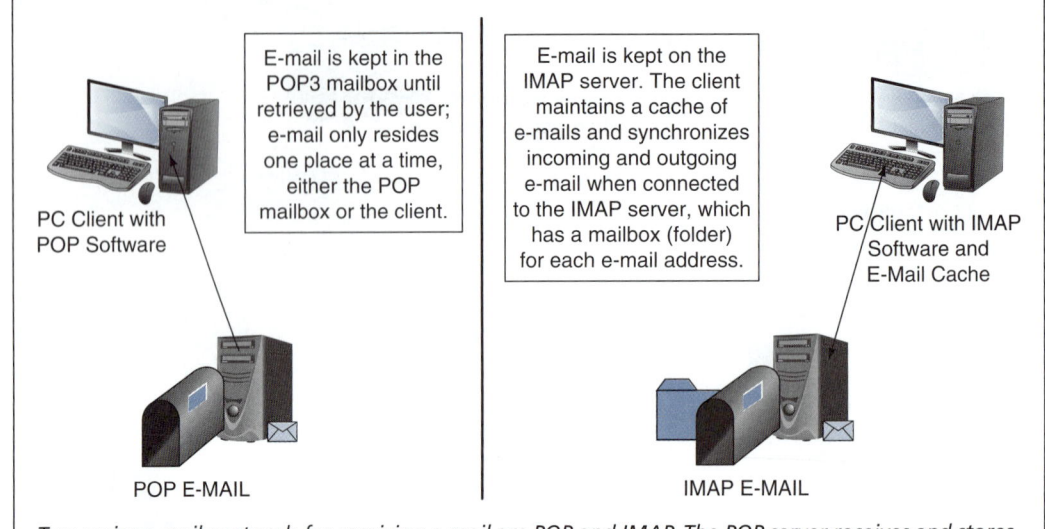

Two major e-mail protocols for receiving e-mail are POP and IMAP. The POP server receives and stores all e-mails until a client retrieves them. In the case of an IMAP server, the server is the authoritative source for all e-mail, and the client maintains a cached copy of the server. When the client connects, it synchronizes the client cache with the server, retrieving a copy of all incoming e-mail and sending all outgoing e-mail to the server.

POP3 and SMTP are the most common e-mail transfer protocols and are used to transfer e-mail over the Internet. **Internet Message Access Protocol (IMAP)** can also be used to transfer e-mail. Each protocol has its advantages.

POP3 and IMAP protocols are dominant on the Internet. POP3's major advantage is the ease with which it is configured as compared to IMAP, making POP3 a more cost-effective solution in many cases. However, when you have a user that needs access to a mailbox from a mobile phone, PDA, home, and office desktop simultaneously, IMAP may make more sense. (See the comparison in Figure 4-9.)

Application Servers

Large organizations often have **application servers**. These servers expose application program interfaces (APIs) that can be used by software within the organization to standardize business processes (Figure 4-10). In order for software to use APIs from an application server, the software must be designed to do so. For example, a desktop application such as word processing would probably not use an application server, but an enterprise resource planning system that processes data for a large company might use an application server. Some of the more common application server architectures include Java Application Server, and Oracle WebLogic Suite.

BENEFITS OF APPLICATION SERVERS

An application server's benefits to the organization include the following:

- **Standardize Business Logic.** Application servers allow organizations to standardize how business logic is processed. By having all the program code in one place and processes standardized, businesses are better able to control how business issues are handled.
- **Manageability.** As business logic changes, the application only needs to be updated in one central location, thus lowering management costs.
- **Strong Support for Client-Server Computing.** Using an application server approach, a network can provide stronger support for client-server computing by providing APIs that implement business logic.
- **Total Cost of Ownership (TCO).** By combining all of the benefits listed here, TCO can be reduced.

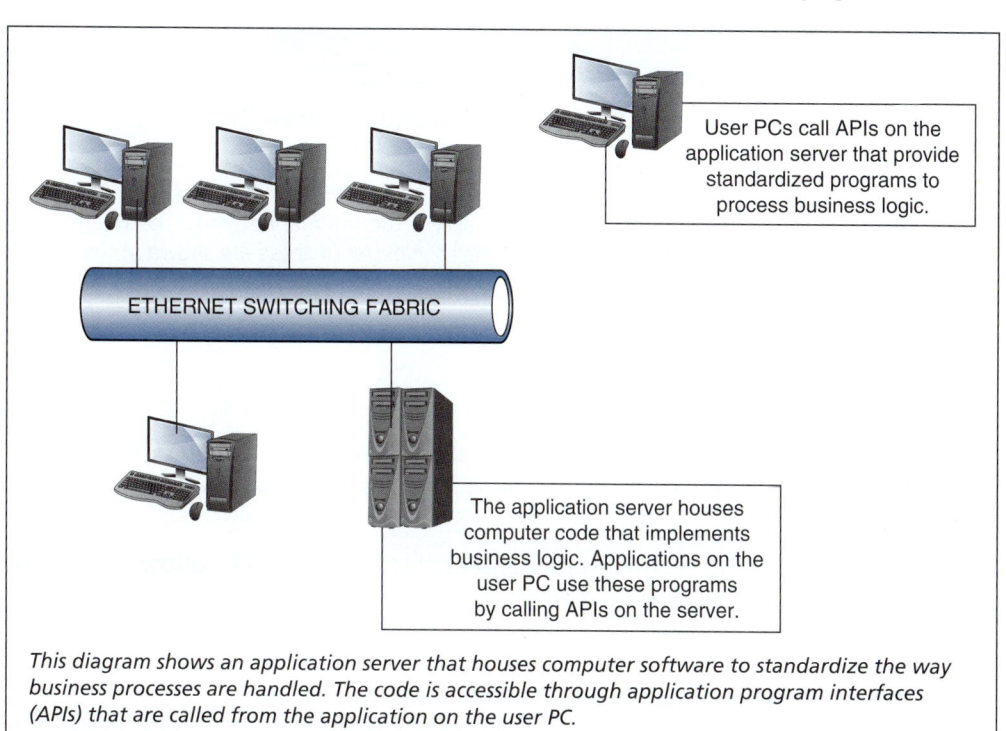

FIGURE 4-10 Application Servers

This diagram shows an application server that houses computer software to standardize the way business processes are handled. The code is accessible through application program interfaces (APIs) that are called from the application on the user PC.

Database Servers

Database servers provide a centralized place for organizations to store their data, and give access to users and applications on the network. The database server will run a database management system (DBMS), such as Oracle or MS-SQL, that handles/stores the database transactions as well as provides an interface for software on the network to access the databases (see Figure 4-11). The database server is a back-end function that does the actual data manipulation and storage, while the user PC acts as a front end and runs client applications.

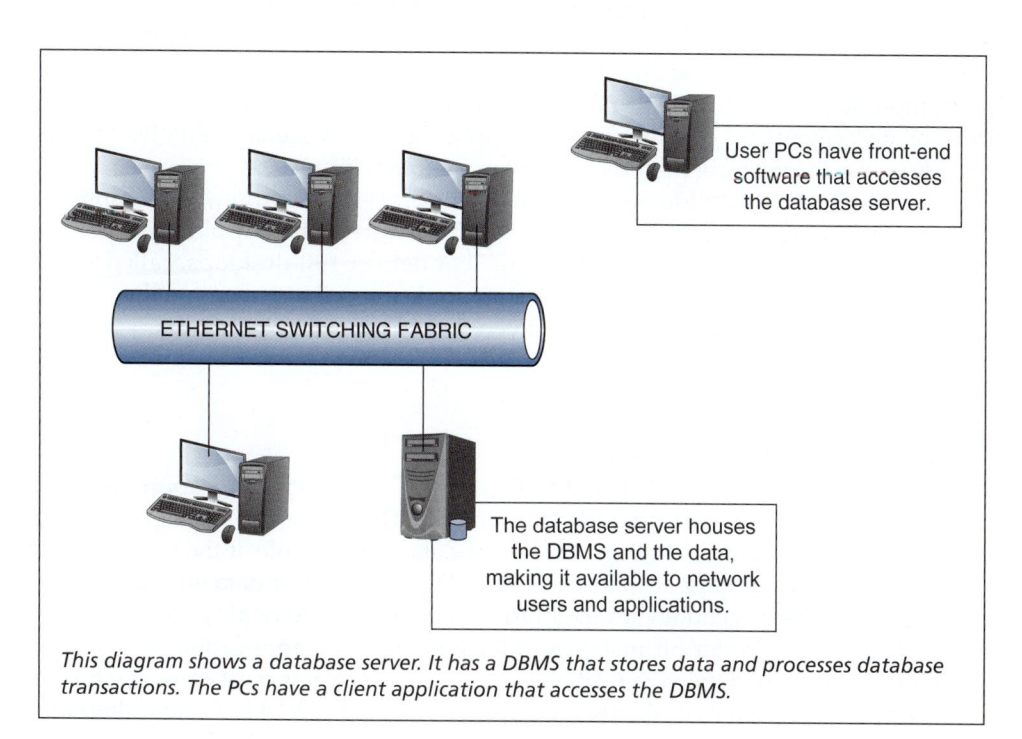

FIGURE 4-11 Database Server

This diagram shows a database server. It has a DBMS that stores data and processes database transactions. The PCs have a client application that accesses the DBMS.

> ## VIGNETTE BOX 4-8
>
> ### HealthyWay's Use of Application and Database Servers
>
> HealthyWay will probably run an enterprise-wide application which requires an application server and a database server. It will probably also have a Web Server and VPN-gateway. The VPN-gateway would allow remote users to access the internal network. The HealthWay installation will undoubtedly include an IMAP email server. All of these are shown in the block diagram in the Vignette Wrap Up.

BENEFITS OF A DATABASE SERVER

Database servers provide several benefits to the organization. Although they are not typically implemented in small organizations, benefits of database servers include the following:

- **Centralized Storage and Management.** Database servers allow data to be stored, shared, and managed from one location, simplifying backup and other operations such as database resizing and moving databases to new, larger storage facilities.
- **Increased Processing Power.** Because the database server is handling data retrieval, sorting, and filtering, the client is relieved of that processing, potentially freeing it up to do other things.
- **Concurrent Access to Data.** A database server allows multiple users to access data concurrently, as well as allowing more than one person to simultaneously access the same information.
- **Increased Data Security.** Data integrity and security are enhanced because data are stored centrally and under the control of database staff.

Application and Desktop Virtualization

Virtualization refers to the decoupling of a user's desktop and applications from the actual hardware. The virtual environment can exist alongside the user's regular PC operating system, or it can be implemented via a thin client. VMware® is an example of a virtualization platform commercially available (VMWare, 2011).

Software can be distributed in a number of ways. In addition to simply installing it on the desktop PC, it can be virtualized. Software virtualization technologies facilitate application delivery to the client PC, while preserving the integrity of the application licensing agreement and offering the same application to a virtually unlimited number of users across the network (assuming you have enough licenses).

An easy way to divide software distribution (virtualization) technologies is by those technologies that deliver application software, called application delivery infrastructure (ADI), and those applications that deliver full desktops, called virtual desktop infrastructure (VDI). Whether it's an application that is being delivered to a client PC or a complete desktop being delivered to a thin client, both are server-centric models. (See Figure 4-12.)

Benefits

The number one limitation of ADI and VDI is sizing the infrastructure appropriately to the applications that are being deployed. ADI and VDI may not be appropriate for an application that must process a large amount of data. For example, if the user desires to run a statistical analysis application that uses a large amount of data and takes a long time to process, these technologies may not be the best way to deploy the application; the user is probably better off installing a local copy of the application on his or her desktop PC. However, if the organization wants to reduce its total cost of ownership and be better able to manage its desktops and applications, ADI or VDI is a viable alternative

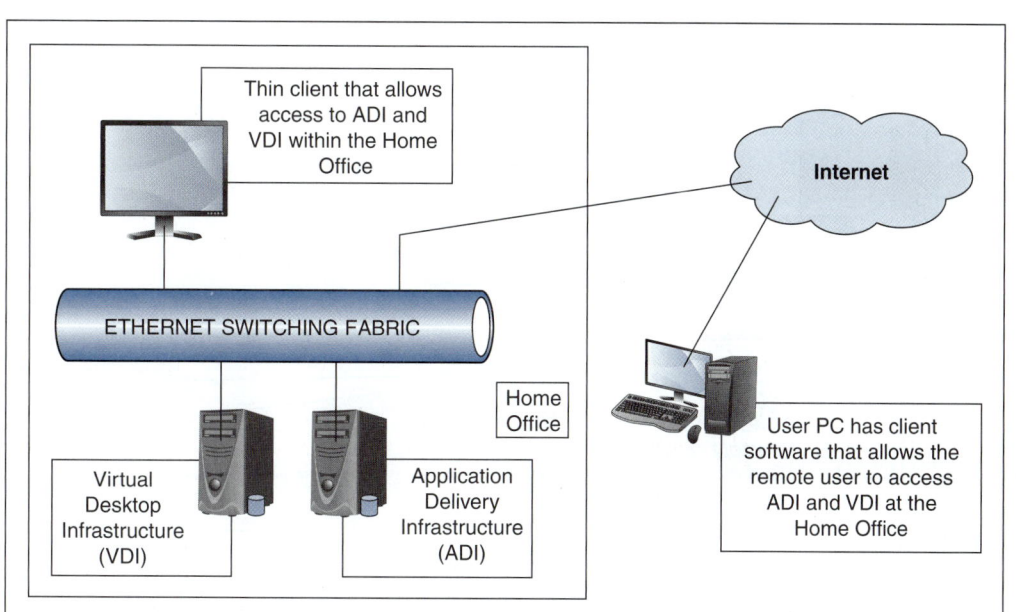

FIGURE 4-12 Application Distribution and Virtual Desktop Infrastructures

This diagram shows the Home Office with a virtual desktop infrastructure (VDI) and an application delivery infrastructure (ADI). The Home Office has a number of thin clients that allow users to access the VDI and the ADI. Remote users can also connect to the Home Office via the Internet; a remote user can access both the VDI and the ADI offsite. It is not necessary to have both VDI and ADI, but they can coexist within the same infrastructure.

for appropriately sized installations. Some of the benefits of virtualization via ADI and VDI include the following:

- **Easier and More Efficient Management of Applications and Desktops.** Using these technologies makes it easier and faster to make changes to a number of applications and desktops used by multiple users. Changes would only need to be made to one installation on a virtualization server rather than requiring an update to each user's PC. Users will get the updated application or desktop when they log in.
- **Quicker Recovery from Hardware Failures.** Because the user is not tied to one specific workstation, if that workstation fails the user can just move to another one.
- **User Flexibility.** The user is able to log in to any workstation or thin client attached to the ADI/VDI infrastructure and get to needed applications, including remote locations.
- **Reduced Hardware Costs.** Because most processing occurs on the server, users do not need a very robust PC to access applications. This capability can extend the desktop refresh cycle (time between when desktop PCs are replaced due to obsolesce) significantly. Additionally, because applications and desktops are accessible via an inexpensive thin client, many users will only need the thin client rather than a more expensive PC, thus reducing hardware costs.

VIGNETTE BOX 4-9

HealthyWay's Virtual Delivery of Desktops and Applications

HealthyWay should consider implementing virtual desktops to be delivered to users via thin clients that only need access to standardized applications (e.g., the enterprise-wide software front end and some desktop productivity software). Desktop virtualization could reduce the total cost of ownership for desktops requiring specific functionality. HealthyWay should also consider offering application virtualization for those users who have PCs and need access to the HealthyWay enterprise-wide front end. Additionally, consideration should be given to making both the virtual desktop and virtual applications available to remote users through the VPN gateway.

118 Unit 1 • ICT Infrastructure Components: A Technical Overview

FIGURE 4-13 Directory Server

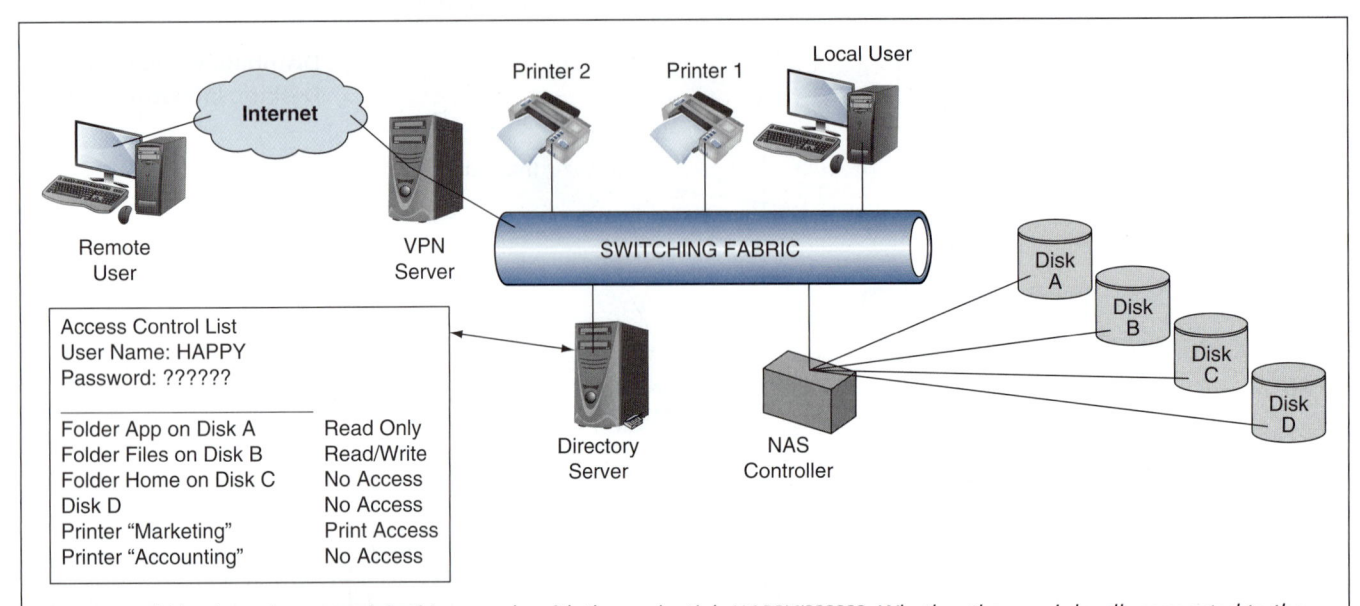

A user would log into the network in this example with the credentials HAPPY/??????. Whether the user is locally connected to the network or connecting remotely from offsite, that user's level of access would be the same. The directory server would be checked for the existence of these credentials, then the access control list (ACL) for those credentials would be loaded. The user HAPPY would be given access level to the resources specified in the ACL, and the directory server would know where those resources are located (i.e., provide a mapping to those resources). The VPN server would communicate with the directory server using RADIUS protocol for authentication and to obtain access information.

Security and Policy Services

Users interact with a number of services, but they are probably unaware of their existence. These services normally fall under the purview of the network engineer as do many network service components, but the business systems analyst needs to be aware of these services and their uses.

DIRECTORY SERVER

From the users' perspective, identity management is often their first indication that they are connected to a network. The user identity is managed through the user credentials (i.e., user name and password) they are assigned by the network administrator, and those credentials are linked to an access control list (ACL) that specifies which network resources the user has access to. The ACL also specifies the level to which the user can interact with network resources. The **directory server** maintains the list of credentials and associated ACLs, along with a mapping of logical names of resources to actual physical locations. (See Figure 4-13.) The directory server and ACLs are normally part of a network's operating system and reside on one centralized server. In large installations with many users and resources to manage the directory server is actually a separate device. The directory server may also be referred to as a **policy server**. In large organizations, the directory and policy server are often separate devices.

VIGNETTE BOX 4-10

HealthyWay's Directory Server

HealthyWay will have a directory server in place that will authenticate users, as well as provide mapping between the user and the devices on the network. This is common in all organizations today.

Summary of Service Components

Service components are what make the network infrastructure work for the user. Many of the components we discussed are transparent to the user, but the business systems analyst and network designer need to be familiar with them. User components and enterprise-wide components often use service components, and these services are often imbedded in network products. Still, it is necessary that those doing the specification, design, and purchasing are able to conceptualize these various types of components.

USER COMPONENTS

User components are those things that the user interacts with on a PC desktop; you could say that the user components are what expose all other services of the network to the user so he or she can interact with them. Consider how, without a workstation or thin client, a user could interact with a database or application server, or how a user could run a word processor. In these instances, the user components come into play. The design of a network needs to take into account the user components that facilitate the work of the user both at the desktop and through a connection to the network

The Desktop

The PC desktop is what you see on the monitor when you turn on the PC. How that desktop looks and what it allows you to do is largely dependent on the operating system that is used, and the login credentials and associated ACL that controls the PC. A Microsoft Windows desktop (Figure 4-14) that provides a graphical user interface (GUI) looks very different from a desktop (Figure 4-15) running in command mode. However, both are desktops.

The desktop can be driven to the PC or thin client from a virtual desktop infrastructure (VDI), or it can be part of the local operating system installed on the PC. Often, a large installation or sophisticated users will run a local desktop as well as run a virtual desktop that has been generated via a VDI.

FIGURE 4-14 Microsoft Windows Desktop

This Microsoft Windows desktop provides the user with a graphical user interface. It allows the user to interact with the local workstation and network resources using the mouse and a "click and do" interface.

FIGURE 4-15 Command Mode Desktop

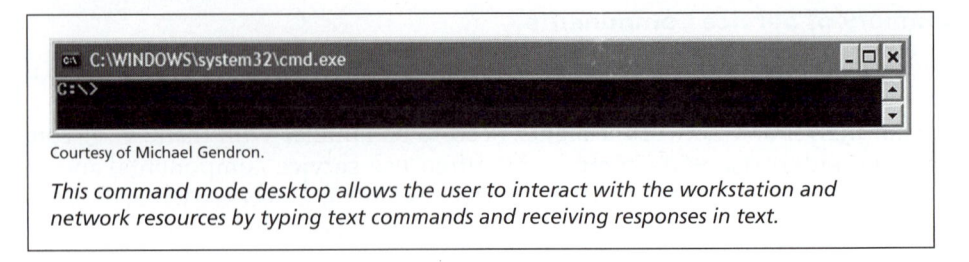

Courtesy of Michael Gendron.

This command mode desktop allows the user to interact with the workstation and network resources by typing text commands and receiving responses in text.

PC

Users need some type of device that allows them to run programs and attach to and use network resources. That device is often a personal computer (PC). As discussed earlier, the PC has a variety of options, and the selection of those options depends primarily on the operating system being run, the types of applications being used, and the connection type to the network. All these factors drive the robustness, and therefore the cost, of the desktop.

As an example of operating systems, let's focus on Microsoft products. Microsoft offers Windows 7 in several levels for the user. The more options Windows 7 has, the more memory and the faster the processor that are needed. Ten years ago the processor speed and amount of RAM made a significant difference in price. However, as speed increased and the market became diluted, the price of a PC became lower. Even though cost is always a concern, the issue for the business analyst is to make sure you have the right PC with the right options to support the user.

When it comes to desktop applications, it is important to remember that the more processor and memory intensive an application is, the more robust the PC must be. Go back to the example of a user who needed to run statistical analysis on a large data set. That user will need a robust PC in order to accomplish the work in a reasonable period of time.

Lastly, desktop connection to the network is a function of the ICT infrastructure and the amount of data the user has to move between the user's PC and the network. This must be considered when specifying ICT infrastructure.

The axiom "more is better" generally holds true for the PC and extends the useful life of the PC. The faster the processor, and the more RAM that is installed, the higher the likelihood the PC will have a longer useful life.

Thin Client

As discussed earlier, thin clients are part of an ADI/VDI infrastructure. These relatively inexpensive devices allow the ADI/VDI infrastructure to drive an application or full desktop to the thin client. It is also possible to run a software client on a network-attached PC that gives the user access to applications and desktops run via ADI/VDI. (For an interesting comparison, see Figure 4-16.)

FIGURE 4-16 Thin Client vs Traditional Tower PC

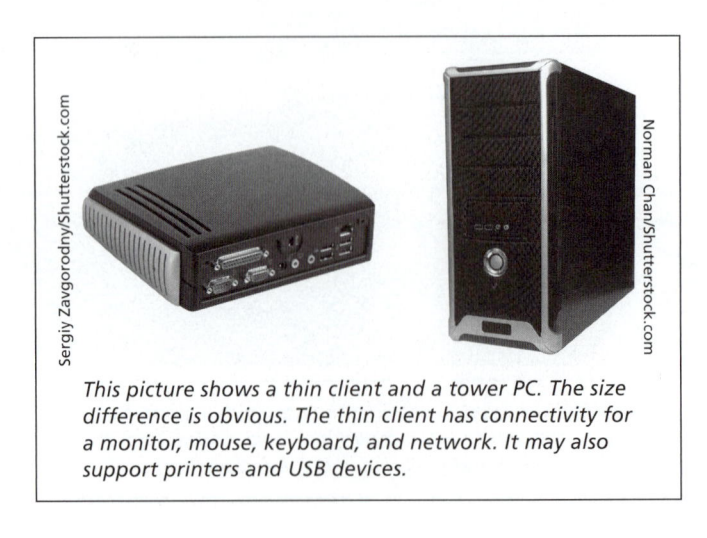

This picture shows a thin client and a tower PC. The size difference is obvious. The thin client has connectivity for a monitor, mouse, keyboard, and network. It may also support printers and USB devices.

FIGURE 4-18 **Laser Printer**

This laser printer has a single paper tray. Many other manufacturers and models are available.

Laser printers (shown in Figure 4-18) are often shared over the network in an office and have a relatively low cost per printed page. A reasonably sized laser printer is robust enough to handle the output level when shard among several users. Laser printers offer two important options beyond color versus monochrome printing. First, multiple paper trays, available on some laser printer models, allow different types of paper to be simultaneously accessible to users (e.g., one tray has letterhead and another has plain paper). Another option is duplex (two-sided) printing, with its potential to cut paper usage in half.

Many large organizations need to print great quantities of documents efficiently and have turned to office document management centers. Many people think of a document center as just a photocopier. However a document management solution normally prints very fast (upwards of 100 pages per minute); has the ability to collate, staple, and bind documents; and is often network accessible.

SPECIALTY PRINTERS

Dye-sublimation, or dye-sub, printers use a heat process to transfer dye to paper or some other flat surface such as card stock or plastic. These printers are used when an especially high level of print quality is needed for applications such as a marketing department might require or when printing photographs. These printers were once only found in high-end print shops, but due to the decreased costs, they are now found in offices with high-quality printing needs. Decreased cost is relative, however, and the per-page cost of dye-sub is still much greater than traditional office printers, as is the purchase cost.

VIGNETTE BOX 4-12

HealthyWay's Printing Solution

PCs in the HealthyWay ICT Infrastructure will probably all have access to printing. Some will have their own printer, while others will use shared printing services through the network. Those that have their own printer will be given either a desktop laser or a desktop inkjet. Which printer they receive will be a function of their job role (e.g., administrative assistants may get laser jet printers, while executives may get inkjet printers that also allow them to print in color). Shared printing will most likely be available through large document center printers.

VIGNETTE BOX 4-11

HealthyWay's Use of PCs and Thin Clients

Organizations like HealthyWay will usually implement GUI desktops at all locations. They will use PCs in locations where users require fast access to large applications on the desktop, such as desktop productivity software or analytical software that requires a large amount of resources. Thin clients can be used in locations where users need access to a standardized desktop and to the organization's enterprise-wide software front end. These users need the flexibility of being able to log in to any thin client and get the same desktop, but application access will be restricted to software that is part of that desktop (ADI/VDI).

Desktop Optical Devices

Optical devices such as the CD, DVD, and CD/DVD are common in today's desktop PC. They can be either read only (e.g., CD-ROM) or read/write (e.g., CD-RW), and can support CD, DVD, or both. The type and amount of data being stored on the optical media and the cost of the media are factors to consider when selecting which optical device to purchase. Today, desktop applications are regularly delivered to the desktop on CD or DVD for installation. DVDs are often necessary because of the size of the installation image.

Printers

Printers allow the user to create hard copies of documents from their workstation. These printers can be shared over the network (as described in the section on Printing Services), or they can be directly attached to the PC. In the past, parallel cables were traditionally used to connect printers directly to the workstation. More recently, however, USB connections have become the way printers are direct-connected. When selecting a printer, three things are usually considered initially: (1) whether the printer can print in color or just monochrome; (2) the printer resolution, especially for color printing; and (3) the speed of the printer, normally measured in pages per minute. However, other considerations are also important. Printers can be grouped into specialized printers and traditional office printers.

TRADITIONAL OFFICE PRINTERS

Two printers immediately come to mind when thinking about traditional office printers: the laser printer and the inkjet printer (shown in Figure 4-17). Both are available in color and monochrome, although color printers cost more, both initially and per printed page. These printers are most often used attached to a PC for individual use.

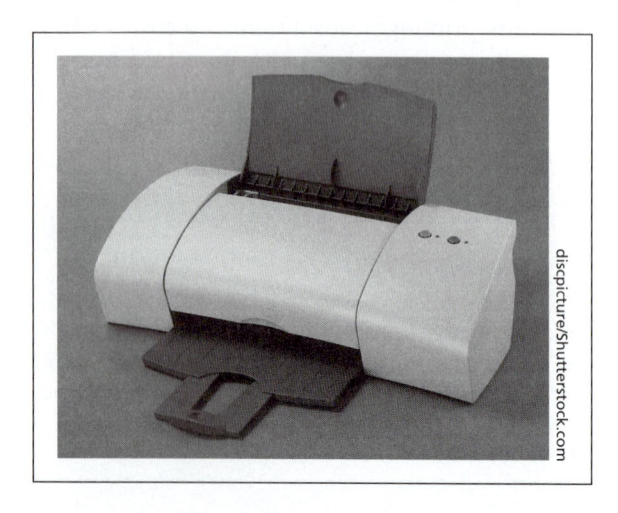

FIGURE 4-17   Inkjet Printer

Chapter 4 • Wrapping Up Service, User, and Enterprise Components **123**

FIGURE 4-19 **Label Printer**

Thermal printers use heat to create monochrome text and images on special paper. These printers are used in ATMs, cash registers, and for gasoline pump receipts. Some older fax machines also use this technology.

Label printers (Figure 4-19) use special label paper or strips to print a limited amount of information on labels. They are often used in hospitals to print a patient's name and medical record number, as well in any other situation in which labels would be useful to a business process.

Plotters are vector graphic devices that operate by moving a pen over the surface of the paper. Plotters are used in computer-aided drafting and design applications to print blueprints, and in cartography applications to print maps. The plotter accommodates a wide format and often prints from rolls of paper, making the plotter ideal for banners and other large items (see Figure 4-20).

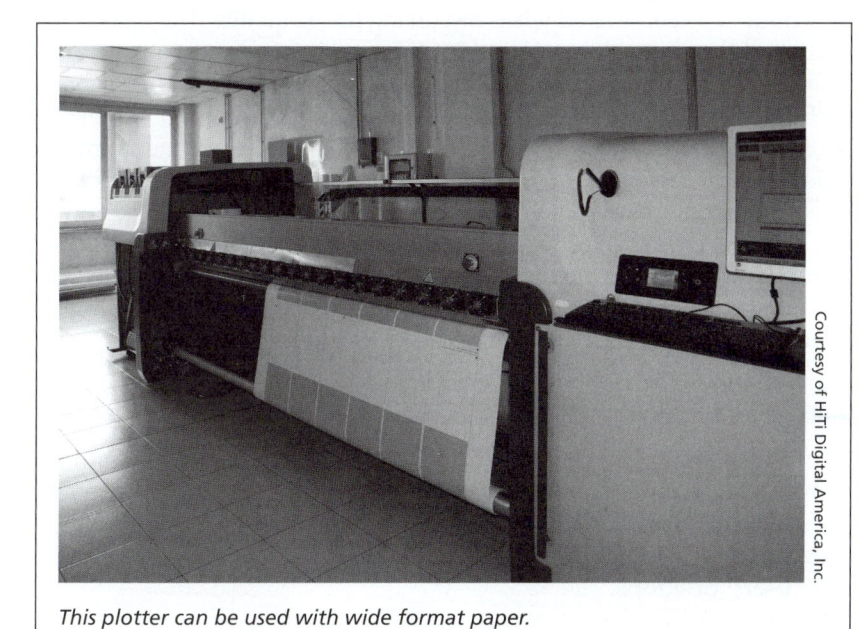

FIGURE 4-20 **Plotter**

This plotter can be used with wide format paper.

FIGURE 4-21 **Flatbed Scanner**

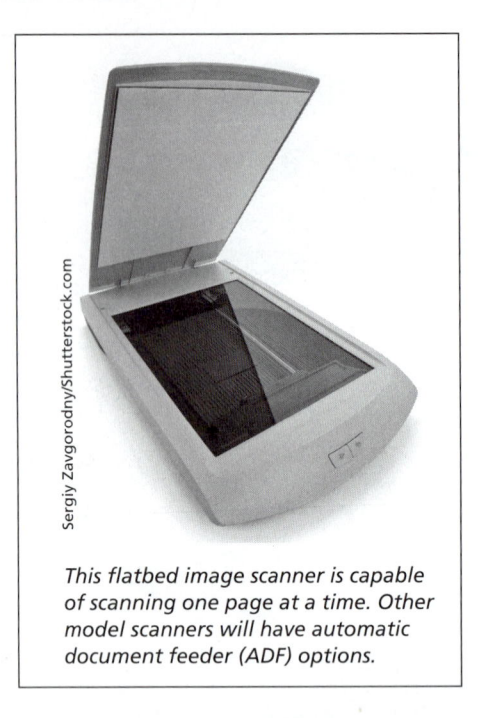

This flatbed image scanner is capable of scanning one page at a time. Other model scanners will have automatic document feeder (ADF) options.

Image Scanners

Users often need to convert hardcopy images and text documents into digital format. A scanner allows for that type of conversion. A user may want to create an image file from a picture, create an Adobe® Portable Document Format (PDF) file from a printed document, or even convert a printed document into text for editing. All of these functions are possible with the right image scanner and software. A number of factors are important to consider: (1) How large of an image can the image scanner accommodate? (2) Can the image scanner scan one page at a time, or does it have an automatic document feeder? (3) What is the image quality of the scanner? (4) What software is needed to support the scanner?

IMAGE QUALITY

Two things need to be considered when discussing image quality. The first consideration is the resolution of the scanner. Resolution is measured in pixels per inch (PPI). The higher the PPI, the better the image quality. Good flatbed scanners range from about 1600 PPI to 3200 PPI. The other consideration is color depth. Color depth is measured in the number of bits—the more bits of color depth, the more colors the scanner can read. A color depth of 24 bits is normal, whereas color depths greater than 48 bits provide much better images. Greater resolution or color depth results in bigger images when digitized. Larger digital images take longer to manipulate, which means a more expensive PC is needed to manipulate them. Scanners with a large PPI and color depth bits allow users to set parameters to a lower value to accommodate the scanning quality and file size required.

SOFTWARE

When selecting a scanner you need consider the application software and drivers that come with it. Some scanners offer the ability to increase resolution through software interpolation. Some manufacturers provide software for image manipulation and for converting images to text. These options are important to consider when selecting a scanner for users' desktops.

> **VIGNETTE BOX 4-13**
>
> **HealthyWay's Image Scanners**
>
> HealthyWay should provide image scanners to those staff members who have PCs and need scanning capabilities for their job.

Multifunction Devices

Devices that support printing, scanning, copying, and faxing are referred to as **multifunction devices**. Vendor-specific options can integrate these functions into the desktop, allowing the user to automate many tasks. For example, the user could send or receive a fax without ever leaving his or her desk.

Desktop Productivity Software

Users often need **desktop productivity software** to make their workstation useful on the job. The most common form of this software is referred to as an office suite. It includes a word processor, electronic spreadsheet, and presentation software. Sometimes, a desktop database application is included as well. Proprietary desktop productivity software includes Corel WordPerfect Office® and Microsoft Office®. Open source software includes solutions like OpenOffice. All of these packages offer similar functionality. Cost, vendor-specific functionality, and cross-vendor interoperability are all things to consider when selecting desktop productivity software.

Specialized Applications

Organizations need specialized applications to get their work done. Sometimes it is an off-the-shelf application to support computerized drawing, statistical analysis, or some other function. And sometimes it is a custom-written application, such as those used for claims processing at an insurance company. Software is what facilitates doing the work of the organization.

ENTERPRISE-WIDE COMPONENTS

Large organizations often have software applications that unify the organization called **enterprise-wide components**. A large law firm may have a consolidated attorney billing system, a hospital may have a hospital information system, or a manufacturing firm may have an **enterprise resource planning (ERP) system**. Many smaller companies still use individual workstation-based applications. For example, the accounting department might use accounts payable and receivable systems, along with electronic spreadsheets, to manage their work, while the sales department might have an order entry processing and inventory system, and the marketing department may simply require user desktop productivity applications to do its work. The problem with such an approach is that often one department does not know what the other department is doing, and reconciling those activities is

> **VIGNETTE BOX 4-14**
>
> **HealthyWay's Applications**
>
> As mentioned previously, HealthyWay will provide desktop productivity software to all PCs as well as enterprise-wide front end to all PC users and all thin clients.

often a manual process. In short, this scheme creates data silos. An enterprise-wide approach breaks down data silos and allows departments to share their resources with each other.

Enterprise-wide components require a new way of thinking about the organization. Think of the organization as a whole, rather than a collection of individual departments. That is what an enterprise-wide approach does. The departments are interdependent parts of the whole organization, rather than constituent parts that each has their own unique computer-based and network-based needs. An enterprise-wide approach to computer software is referred to as an enterprise resource planning (ERP) system.

An ERP uses a service-oriented architecture. The ERP is composed of a number of different services/modules that interoperate to communicate data among each other. The goal is data and information sharing across business processes and breaking down data and information silos. An ERP takes what were once independent processes, and, through ERP's service-oriented architecture, loosely couples those services together. The services provide individual business processes, while the ERP meshes them together to provide end-to-end data and information management. The services are offered through an individual or unified set of databases that minimally cover manufacturing (production), human resources (HR), customer relationship management (CRM), supplier relationship management (SRM), and financial management. All of the primary and secondary value chain (see the next chapter) functions are covered in the ERP.

As an example of how an ERP facilitates a customer phone call to order a "widget," let's look at the potential services involved. The services involved might include the following:

1. The customer relationship management process is queried to get the previous order history.
2. The order entry process captures the new order.
3. The inventory control database is queried to see if the "widget" is available.
4. The order fulfillment process is enacted if the "widget" is available, or a backorder process is evoked if the "widget" is not available.
5. The accounts receivable process generates an invoice if the order is filled, or a supplier management module is invoked to tell the supplier that more "widgets" are needed.

Through an enterprise-wide approach to handling that customer order, the system can bring together the services of the company so the entire transaction can happen in one phone call. Whereas using a departmental approach, it may take several phone calls, faxes, and other interactions to perform the same transaction, potentially resulting in an unsatisfied customer.

Another aspect of enterprise-wide components is that they offer best practices. Whether it's an ERP that promotes compliance with the Sarbanes-Oxley legislation, ISO quality standards, or general accepted accounting practice (GAAP), the ERP often has best practices built in as part of its implementation.

Probably the most well-known enterprise application is SAP (SAP, n.d.). SAP offers a business suite composed of customer relationship management, enterprise resource management, product life cycle management, supply chain management, and supplier relationship modules. Taken together these modules cover most of the services that a large commercial organization needs. SAP offers software for the large enterprise as well as for the small and medium-sized business. Other vendors of enterprise-wide applications include Oracle® PeopleSoft for the large enterprise and SunGard Banner® for higher education.

Enterprise-wide components and ERPs exist for many types of organizations. A hospital-wide information system (i.e., Health Information Systems) provides interoperability and unified medical records among hospital units including the emergency department, the surgical suite, and laboratory. An academic institution may use an ERP to record and control the flow of information from the moment a

> **VIGNETTE BOX 4-15**
>
> **HealthyWay's ERP**
>
> HealthyWay's enterprise-wide application will be an ERP. It will provide a front-end application that can be distributed as a PC client and a thin client virtual application.

student applies to the institution through graduation and on indefinitely through career and alumni tracking. What all ERP implementations have in common is a holistic view of the enterprise, rather than a silo or departmental view.

Benefits of an Enterprise-Wide Component

Enterprise-wide components bring a functional view of the business, rather than a departmental view. This perspective allows the enterprise to optimize its processes, increase customer satisfaction, and hopefully have a positive influence on the bottom line. All of these services come at a cost. Enterprise-wide solutions are expensive to purchase and to implement. An ongoing investment is necessary to ensure training of the technical staff as well as the organization's operational staff. The organization also needs to increase its vigilance in maintaining data security and integrity now that many staff members potentially have access to data that was once housed within departments.

Chapter Summary

This chapter introduced a number of new technical concepts related to service, user, and enterprise-wide components. The goal was not to make the student an expert in any one area, but to increase students' breadth of knowledge and ability to explore and recommend technical solutions. Specifically, the following components of ICT infrastructure were covered:

- **PC Hardware.** PC hardware was introduced as a foundation for the discussion of desktop and user components.
- **Service Components.** The concept of service components and their role as parts of the network that deliver usability to the user were addressed. Those components include printing, communications, network storage, application and database servers, and application and desktop virtualization. The service components presented in this chapter are meant to be a representative list rather than an exhaustive one. Vendors and standards workgroups develop and offer new hardware and options almost daily. It is important that the business systems analyst know what service components are and how they provide usability.
- **User Components.** User components provide the interface between the user and all other components of ICT infrastructure. The desktop, thin clients, desktop optical devices, printers, and image scanners, along with desktop productivity and specialized software, all come together to facilitate user interaction with ICT.
- **Enterprise-Wide Components.** Enterprise-wide components, especially the enterprise resource planning (ERP) system, provide a way to look at the enterprise through a service-oriented architecture. Viewing the organization through its transactions and business processes, rather than from a departmental (e.g., accounting, marketing, etc.) approach, allows organizations to better design and deliver services to meet the needs of the customer.

Reviewing these topics provides a foundation for understanding the components of ICT infrastructure. Unit Two looks at the organizational factors that drive hardware selection, while Unit Three discusses techniques for understanding organizational ICT Infrastructure needs.

Leaving this chapter, the reader should note a few important things. Selecting infrastructure components is an exacting task and the business systems analyst must understand the business processes that drive ICT selection. Selecting desktop applications to enhance user productivity is important, whether these applications are productivity tools or a specialized application that is part of an enterprise solution. The next unit discusses what drives an organization and how that affects technology selection. Taken together, technical knowledge of ICT components and what intra- and interorganizational factors drive the selection of ICT will enable the business systems analyst to deliver solutions that enhance competitive position of the organization.

Vignette Wrap Up

HealthyWay has robust ICT infrastructure needs that include the following service, user, and enterprise-wide components. These components are also summarized in the block diagram found in Figure 4-22:

- **User Components**
  - **PCs.** User PCs can be onsite or remote. All PCs will have a DVD, and some will have local printers. Other PCs will print to the shared printer. Each PC will have desktop productivity software as well as the HealthyWay enterprise-wide front-end application. The processor speed, random access memory, and disk size will be sufficient to support the selected operating system and installed software. Remote PCs will access the network via the VPN gateway at HealthyWay, while local PCs will be directly connected to the network via a workgroup switch. All PCs will have access to the Internet.
  - **TCs.** User thin clients (TCs) can be onsite or remote. Each TC will be able to run a desktop provided by the virtualization server. The TCs will not have DVD drives or disk drives, but will run the operating system desktop provided by the virtualization server. Enterprise-wide front-end software rather than desktop productivity tools will be provided on the virtual desktop. Remote TCs will access the network via the VPN gateway at HealthyWay, while local TCs will be directly connected to the network via a workgroup switch.
  - **Shared Printers.** A number of shared printers at HealthyWay will use the print server to provide queuing services.
  - **Desktop Productivity Software.** Each PC will have a desktop productivity suite containing word-processing, spreadsheet, and presentation software.

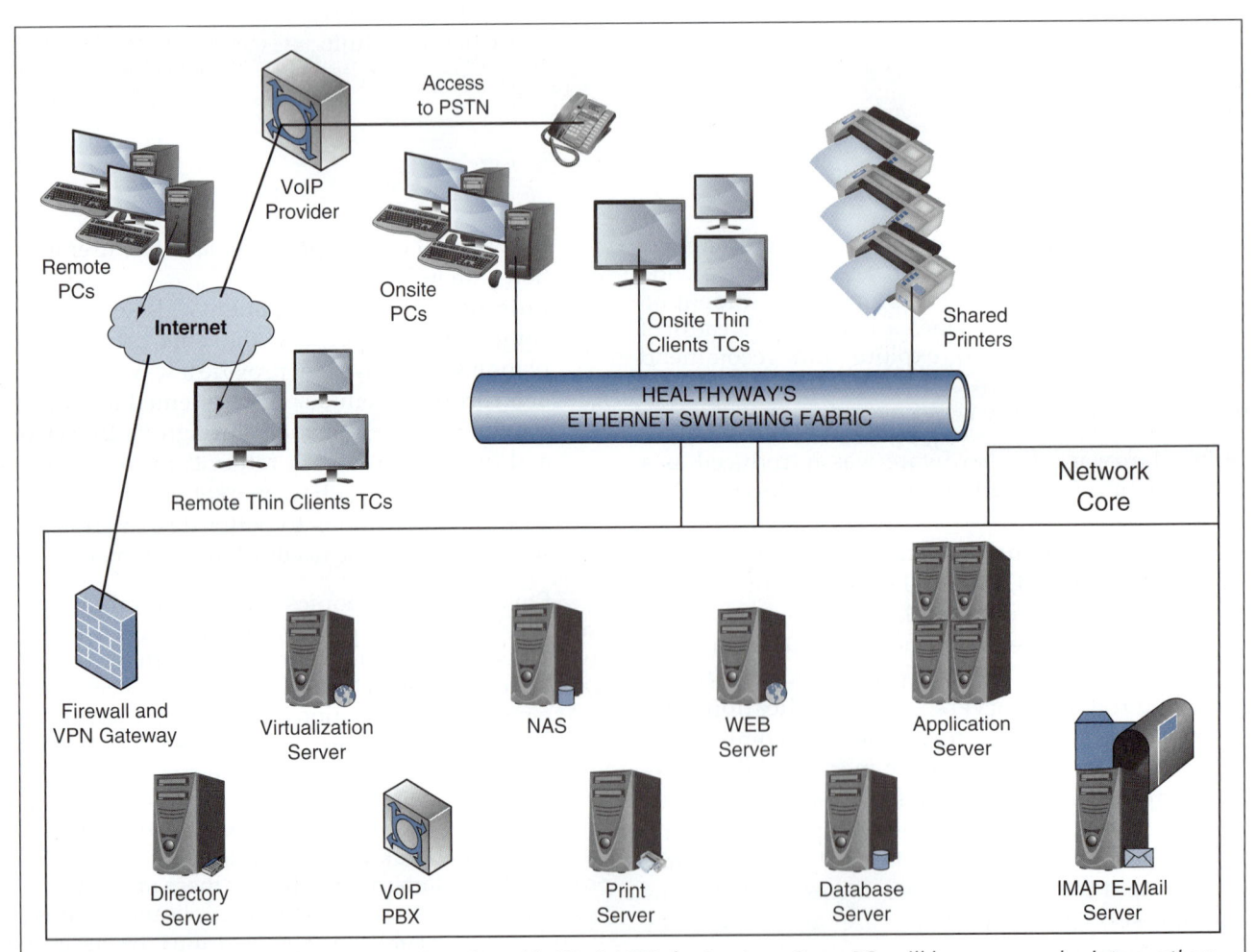

This diagram shows a block representation of HealthyWay's ICT infrastructure. Some PCs will have personal printers; others will share a printer. All PCs will have DVD drives for installing software. The network will support both onsite and off site connectivity via PCs or TCs. The VPN and virtualization server provide all enterprise-wide front-end software at all locations, as well as a full desktop to TCs.

FIGURE 4-22 HealthyWay's Infrastructure Block Diagram

- **Service Components**
  - **VPN Gateway.** The VPN gateway will provide secure IPsec tunneling services to remote users, allowing them authenticated access to the HealthyWay network.
  - **Directory Server.** This server will provide authentication services to the network, including the VPN server, as well as mapping resources on the network so the user knows how to access the resources. It will also implement policies regarding storage limits and other resource utilization.
  - **Virtualization Server.** The virtualization server will provide virtual desktops and applications for use on the TCs and PCs.
  - **VoIP PBX.** The VoIP PBX will provide call routing within HealthyWay as well as between HealthyWay and the PSTN via the VoIP provider's PSTN access.
  - **NAS.** The Network Attached Storage (NAS) device will provide 1 TB of file-based storage to the users at HealthyWay. They will be able to use it for personal file storage, shared file storage, and for storing databases accessed via the database server. All of these storage needs are subject to the policies implemented via the directory server.
  - **Print Server.** The print server will control printing to shared printers and provide queue services so jobs submitted to the print server can be printed in order or prioritized.
  - **Web Server.** HealthyWay will run its own web server, allowing them to deploy web-based applications to their remote users. These remote applications can use the business logic provided by the application server.
  - **Application Server.** The application server provides software that performs business logic as part of the HealthyWay ERP.
  - **Database Server.** HealthyWay ERP requires a database server to process its data storage needs. The database server offloads data retrieval and update processing, freeing the PC or TC to perform user-oriented tasks. The actual database will be stored on the NAS, whereas the database server will provide the processing power to keep the database updated.
  - **E-Mail Server.** An IMAP-capable e-mail server will be used to allow HealthyWay employees the benefits of Internet e-mail, with the robust feature set IMAP provides. Users can access their e-mail from their mobile phone, PDA, PC, or TC, whether they are onsite at HealthyWay or remote from it.

- **Enterprise-Wide Components**
  - HealthyWay will run an enterprise-wide application that provides support for its core business processes: claims processing, actuarial analysis, premium billing, membership processing, and provider relations, as well as utilization assurance and review. The enterprise-wide solution will use a database server to store and retrieve data, and an application server to implement business logic. The application's front end will provide access to the services afforded by the enterprise-wide solution. The front end can be deployed direct to the PC or via a virtualized environment.

End of Chapter Questions/Assurance of Learning

1. Describe service, user, and enterprise-wide components and their application to the organization.
2. Develop a block diagram and list of components for an organization you know as was done in Figure 4-22 from the Vignette Wrap Up. Describe the organization, develop the list of components, and then draw a block diagram with a desktop tool such as Microsoft Visio®.
3. List the all the user, service, and desktop components you can think of and indicate why and when they would be used by an organization. Your list must include components in addition to those listed in this chapter.

Case Exercises

These exercises build on the case exercises from previous chapters.

1. XYZ Inc. is a hardware company that builds network hardware and it wants to expand its product offerings to ensure it is a viable alternative to other network hardware manufacturers. The mission of XYZ Inc. is to create innovative hardware solutions that are both standards-based and have innovative options that make them unique in the marketplace. Develop a plan for XYZ Inc. that will ensure it is offering solutions that will gain market share. Make sure you address the following issues:
   a. How will XYZ Inc. be sure it understands the customers' needs?
   b. Which standards bodies would XYZ Inc. have to contact, and what is the process?
   c. Explain the competitive positioning (or lack thereof) that XYZ may have because it wants to employ both new and emerging standards.
2. HealthyWay HMO was discussed in the opening vignette. Prepare a brief report and presentation that indicate how service, user, and enterprise-wide components can assist HealthyWay in attaining competitive advantage in the marketplace of HMOs. In your case analysis, discuss what factors are important for HealthyWay to consider when selecting/recommending these components.
3. Select a company you are familiar with and write a case analysis that describes its service, user, and enterprise-wide components (or make recommendations for new components). Describe which technologies the company does/should use, and how those technologies are important to the competitive positioning of the company. Support your analysis by citing the Internet and/or print articles (i.e., trade publications, journal articles).

Key Words and Concepts

application servers *114*
application virtualization *117*
ATX *105*
database servers *115*
desktop *119*
desktop optical devices *121*
desktop productivity software *125*
desktop virtualization *116*
directory server *118*
dye-sublimation *122*
e-mail server *113*

enterprise resource planning (ERP) system *125*
enterprise-wide components *125*
factor form *105*
image scanner *124*
Internet Message Access Protocol (IMAP) *114*
inkjet printer *121*
Intel or compatible *105*
inter/intra-office communications *109*
label printers *123*
laser printers *122*

multifunction devices *125*
network attached storage (NAS) *111*
office document solution *122*
PC hardware *105*
PC options *105*
PCI slots *105*
plotters *123*
policy server *118*
Post Office Protocol v3 (POP3) *113*
printers *121*
printing services *108*
rack-mount *106*

RAM *106*
scanner *123*
service components *107*
Simple Mail Transfer Protocol (SMTP) *113*
storage area network (SAN) *111*
thermal printers *124*
thin clients *107*
universal serial bus (USB) connection *106*
user components *119*
virtualization *116*
Voice over IP (VoIP) *109*
Web servers *112*

UNIT 1

SUMMARY

The overriding goals of Unit 1 were to introduce ICT infrastructure and to present a framework in which to understand the design of that infrastructure. The framework, called the **information and computer technology infrastructure architecture** (see Figure 4-23), presents ICT infrastructure as a series of interconnected components that provide the user with various functionality. In order to understand the framework, this unit introduced numerous technical concepts.

Earlier chapters focused on the network components of the ICT Infrastructure architecture. Chapter 1 introduced standards and protocol, and discussed why they are important. It also covered introductory TCP/IP concepts, and encapsulated/layered communications so the business systems analyst would have a working knowledge of those concepts. Within- and between-network addressing were also covered. Even though it is not necessary for the business systems analyst to be an expert in these topics, familiarity with them helps the business systems analyst intelligently convey information to network engineers.

Chapter 2 covered the some of the technical details of Ethernet, and introduced VLANs and WANs. The plain old telephone system (POTS) was compared to data networks and examples given to help the student integrate material about protocols, typologies, the TCP/IP-OSI hybrid model, and many other concepts previously introduced.

Chapter 3 delved further into WAN technologies to assist the student in applying the typologies learned in the previous chapters. The public switched data network (PSDN), and public switched telephone network (PSTN) were compared, and their similarities and differences were considered. The basic concepts of ATM and Frame Relay as WAN technologies were covered to help the student apply these concepts.

Chapter 4 introduced the student to the devices and services that make up the service, user, and enterprise-wide components. Although the chapter introduced these components and gave extensive examples of what they contain, the chapter is not meant to be exhaustive. Taken together, these first four chapters provide the student with a convenient way to conceptualize ICT infrastructure as a foundation from which to recommend and design infrastructure from a business-driven perspective.

Enterprise-wide, user, service, and network components make up ICT infrastructure. In order to use this information in the process of designing and writing specifications for ICT infrastructure, a business

ENTERPRISE-WIDE SOFTWARE COMPONENTS — Enterprise-wide software, including ERP, e-commerce/e-business, document management, knowledge management, and other specialized applications	User Components	Items that directly interface with the user, including workstations, printers, scanners, associated software (especially desktop applications), and specialized applications
	Service Components	Those network parts that facilitate network operations with direct user interface, including printing services, inter/intra office communications (i.e., telephone or fax), network attached storage, database/application servers, security servers and appliances, and VPN technology
	Network Components	Those items/concepts traditionally thought of as networking and telecommunications equipment, including network switching and routing hardware, media, outside vendor interconnects (i.e., T1, T3, DSL), and cabinetry, patch panels, and associated items

This figure lists and describes the components of ICT infrastructure architecture from the standpoint of the information technology user.

FIGURE 4-23 ICT Infrastructure Architecture

systems analyst needs to ask certain questions. Those questions are summarized in Figure 4-24. These questions should lead the business systems analyst to other questions that are important in preparing a basic design for a network engineer to "flesh out" and implement. In other words, these questions start the discussion. The questions in the Figure 4-24 are not discrete to just one component—in other words, there is quite a bit of overlap. For example, the VPN question affects network, service, and user components, as does the virtualization question.

Network Component Questions	• What is the **scope** of the network? • How many **locations/LANs**? • Are **interbuilding** LAN connections needed? • What **carrier-based services** will be needed? • What level of **security and firewall** will be needed? • If **Internet access** is needed, how much bandwidth is required? • What types of LANs will be used? • How much ICT infrastructure is in place and can be reused? • Do users need **wireless** access? • Can the **telephone network and data network** use the same infrastructure? Is so, how? • Will external users need **VPN** access?
User Component Questions	• Will a **virtualized ICT environment** serve the users best? • What **desktop productivity applications** will the user need? • Will the system **use thin clients with virtual desktops and/or desktop PCs** with installed applications? • Do any **users need** personal printers? Optical devices? Image scanners? Multifunction devices?
Service Component Questions	• Are **shared printing services** needed? • How closely, if at all, do the **telephone network and data network need to interoperate**? • Do any **applications need** an application server? Database server? • How, if at all, is **virtualization implemented**, and how does it affect other components in the ICT infrastructure? • Will the **organization** run its own web server? E-mail server? • Is **shared storage needed** (e.g., SAN or NAS)? • Is a large amount of **network accessible storage** needed (e.g., SAN or NAS)?
Enterprise-Wide Component Questions	• Will the organization benefit from **enterprise-wide software (e.g., SAP)**? • What enterprise-wide application should be considered, and how does that consideration affect the other components of the ICT infrastructure?

This diagram provides initial questions to ask when recommending and designing ICT infrastructure.

FIGURE 4-24 Questions to Ask When Designing ICT Infrastructure

UNIT 2

Additional ICT Concepts

Unit Purpose

Because a number of additional and emerging ICT topics did not fit well into the structure of Unit 1, they can be found here in Unit 2. This textbook covers a lot of material, and it may border on too much material for a traditional semester-length course. Therefore, this separate unit can be included in those academic programs where it is needed, or skipped by those programs that have separate courses covering this material. The material in this unit is essential for business systems analysts to understand, so if they are not getting it elsewhere, this unit should be covered.

Unit 2 includes two topics: cloud computing and security. Cloud computing allows an organization to share information, software, and hardware resources over the Internet. Instead of being concerned with the technical details inside the "cloud," the user/developer/business analyst can focus on what services are available, how they can be used to solve business problems, and how the services offered in the cloud can support the competitive positioning of their organization. By incorporating these services in new and unique ways, an organization increases its ability to create competitive advantage in the marketplace and capture market share. A high-level introduction into the technical details of cloud computing, along with some examples, are the substance of Chapter 5.

Another major area that some may argue is outside of the technical framework presented in Unit 1 is security. Many schools have separate courses on security and may not want to cover this chapter, but in the absence of a specialized course, Chapter 6 will provide the necessary information.

Security must be understood at several levels. At the physical level the security of laptops and other devices that can be easily stolen or damaged is essential. Security at the LAN level must also be considered, including ways to control access to the LAN. Security between partners sharing information and other resources must also be implemented as we move to greater reliance on things such as digital transactions and cloud-based computing.

Unit Objectives

Unit 2 has the following objectives:

Knowing what cloud computing is and having a high-level technical understanding of cloud-computing concepts.

Analyzing when cloud computing is beneficial to an organization's competitive position and when it is best for the organization to implement solutions in-house.

Understanding the importance of security and why proper security measures must be taken.

Relating cloud computing to client-server computing.

Understanding issues that surround implementation of security in an ICT environment, including physical and ICT access security.

Being able to create security policies that make sense for your organization.

Vignette

This unit uses several organizations to explicate this unit's concepts. Chapter 5's cloud-computing concepts will be discussed using several cases that include products from Microsoft, Amazon, and Google. Security in Chapter 6 will be discussed using the vignette from Unit 1, HealthyWay HMO. The unit vignettes are done in this fashion to allow for the flexibility to seamlessly include Chapter 5 and Chapter 6 as appropriate to your course.

Chapter 5 Vignettes/Cases

Amazon.com as a consumer service and Amazon Web Services (AWS) as a commercial provider of cloud-based solutions will be introduced. According to its web site, AWS provides (1) application hosting, (2) backup and storage, (3) content delivery, (4) e-commerce, (5) high-performance computing, (6) media hosting, (7) search engines, and

(8) web hosting. These services are provided to a number of companies,[1] including Amazon.com. We will use AWS and Amazon.com as examples for clouding computing.

A number of Microsoft® products will be examined, including (1) Healthvault, a personal health record management system, and (2) the Azure™ platform that provides cloud-based Windows™, SQL service, and AppFabric™ as a platform for combining web services from various cloud vendors. Additionally, Sopima, a company in Finland that uses cloud-computing solutions to provide a "contract bank," will be discussed.

Chapter 6 Vignette, HealthyWay HMO

You can find all of the details of Joe Smith's need for remote access to his office LAN at HealthyWay HMO, and HealthyWay's LAN and WAN needs, in Unit 1. In addition to these needs, HealthyWay needs security policies to govern employee access to its LAN via a VPN, data transfer, and local authentication. Chapter 6 will give a high-level overview of the policies and technologies needed to accomplish security best practices for HealthyWay HMO. As a refresher, here are the details of Joe Smith and HealthyWay HMO:

- HealthyWay insurance has 125 employees. Its chief executive officer, chief financial officer, chief information officer, chief operating officer, and director of marketing each has a private office, with a secretary, arranged in one suite. In addition to c-suite members, HealthyWay has eight operational managers/assistant managers who are responsible for the various units of the organization. There is one secretary for every two operational managers. The managers report to the various executive suite members. The organizational units include the following staff:
  - Finance: 6
  - Marketing: 4
  - Operations: 75
  - Information Systems: 12
  - Human Resources: 3

  HealthyWay leases 150,000 square feet in an executive park building.

- Joe Smith is the chief operating office of HealthyWay and lives in a residential area outside of the city where HealthyWay is located. At his home he has two PCs for which he needs Internet access. Joe also bring a laptop computer home from work, which needs Internet access. All computers in Joe's home will share a printer located in his home office. Joe is fortunate because he has dial-up, DSL, and cable Internet available to him. He has to weigh the options and choose the correct type of Internet connection. Chapter 6 will deal with Joe's need for connectivity to HealthyWay HMO. That need was already discussed in Unit 1.

---

[1] All case information comes from http://aws.amazon.com/solutions/case-studies/ unless otherwise indicated by footnote or other reference.

5 OBTAINING SERVICES THROUGH CLOUD COMPUTING

> **Learning Objectives**
>
> - Understand the basic architecture and characteristics of cloud computing.
> - Apply business and economic considerations to decisions related to cloud computing.

The Internet and its protocols and standards are the basis for what is called **cloud computing**. In other words, cloud computing is the evolutionary product of the Internet and its growth. The plain old telephone system (POTS) was referred to as a cloud for many years, owing to the fact that a person would pick up the phone and dial, but not know the route their call would take to make it to its destination. The Internet has that same quality: a user enters a web address without knowing what route that data will follow getting from the user's desktop computer to the host computer being contacted. This phenomenon is the basis for representing the Internet as a cloud symbol too. The next evolutionary step, cloud computing, moves services from the desktop and other on-premises computers to the Internet cloud. This chapter introduces the basic architecture and other characteristics of cloud computing, along with business and economic considerations for selecting cloud-based services.

The framework for all technical discussions in this textbook are based on Figure 5-1. Cloud computing covers all aspects of the ICT infrastructure covered in this framework while allowing for that same infrastructure to be disaggregated into a number of services. Everything from infrastructure-as-a-service or database-as-a-service (e.g., largely the network and service components of the ICT infrastructure architecture) is available in the cloud, as are any of the services necessary to power and build user and enterprise-wide components. Cloud computing is not just a traditional networking and telecommunications topic; instead, it encompasses all aspects of the ICT infrastructure architecture as well as systems analysis and design, application development, and database management. In fact, few ICT services or concepts have *not* been envisioned and delivered over a cloud-computing platform. The only question that remains is what will be the evolutionary step after cloud computing. This question and many others are the substance of this chapter.

ENTERPRISE-WIDE SOFTWARE COMPONENTS Enterprise-wide software, including ERP, e-commerce/e-business, document management, knowledge management, and other specialized applications	**User Components**	Items that directly interface with the user, including workstations, printers, scanners, associated software (especially desktop applications), and specialized applications
	Service Components	Those network parts that facilitate network operations with direct user interface, including printing services, inter/intra office communications (i.e., telephone or fax), network attached storage, database/application servers, security servers and appliances, and VPN technology
	Network Components	Those items/concepts traditionally thought of as networking and telecommunications equipment, including network switching and routing hardware, media, outside vendor interconnects (i.e., T1, T3, DSL), cabinetry, patch panels, and associated items

This figure lists and describes the components of ICT infrastructure architecture from the standpoint of the information technology user. The areas highlighted in blue are covered in this chapter.

FIGURE 5-1 ICT Infrastructure Architecture

INTRODUCTION

Larry Ellison, CEO of Oracle, said that cloud computing can be defined as "everything we already do." He went on to say that cloud computing will basically just "change the wording on some our ads" (Ellison, 2008). Others have had similar comments, but we must dig deeper, past the sound bites and buzzwords. As we proceed through this chapter, the substance to cloud computing that goes beyond the media hype will become evident. Cloud computing may be a term that repackages what the Internet has already enabled, but the term *cloud computing* has come to have meaning.

The major issue that challenges the emergence of cloud computing is a lack of standards. Almost every day a new cloud-computing initiative or product is announced, and some of those initiatives are based on proprietary rather than standards-based solutions. Solid growth in cloud computing will happen as organizations such as OMG, ITU, or IEEE develop and ratify standards for cloud computing. The student may ask why study this topic. The answer is simple: Cloud computing is an emerging technology that students should understand. It seems cloud computing, or its next evolutionary cousin that is yet unnamed, is here to stay, which makes it important that the student understand the concepts and business implications of this technology. Just one warning: because the only standards that exist are those that underpin and define the Internet and its associated technologies, and because no specific cloud computing standards have been established, the terms used in this chapter may not concur with what vendors offer. The concepts will be the same, but the terms and descriptions may be different. Do not be mistaken; there are many standards used in cloud computing, but the world's standards bodies have yet to standardize the definition of cloud computing.

What Is Cloud Computing?

When a home owner hires someone to mow the lawn, seal the driveway, or fix the furnace, the home owner is purchasing a service from someone else. This same theory applies to services from the cloud. We pay for others to do what we cannot or do not want to do. An example would be a web site that wants another vendor to do credit card processing. Perhaps the web site operators do not have the expertise or the technologies to do the credit card processing. Whatever the reason, they can turn to the cloud to buy the services they need.

Cloud computing is defined by layers of abstraction; by that we mean that developers or users may not know the specific technologies that are employed in the cloud, but they know the service they want performed. Take the furnace repair example: you may not know or care what brand of tools the repair person uses, but you need to feel comfortable that the repair person knows how to repair the brand of furnace you own. The furnace repair is the service you are purchasing, but the tools and other methods are abstract from the person requesting the repair service. The same is true of cloud computing. An organization may purchase a service from the cloud, but it will probably not know much about the technology used by the cloud vendor. All the organization really cares about is whether the cloud vendor can deliver the requested service. (Okay, there may be some who want or need to know the technical details, but they are probably in the minority in your organization and are probably members of the technical IT staff.)

When purchasing services from a cloud vendor the user/developer does not necessarily know what technologies are driving the service that the organization is consuming. An organization enters into a contract to purchase a service, such as credit card authorization/processing, but often that contract does not include the specific technical details of the cloud-based infrastructure. The user/developer consumes a service through some type of application program interface (API), and the service vendor communicates with the necessary systems and databases to obtain the desired results—in this case, an authorized/processed/declined credit card. Everything behind the service is said to be abstract, as shown in Figure 5-2.

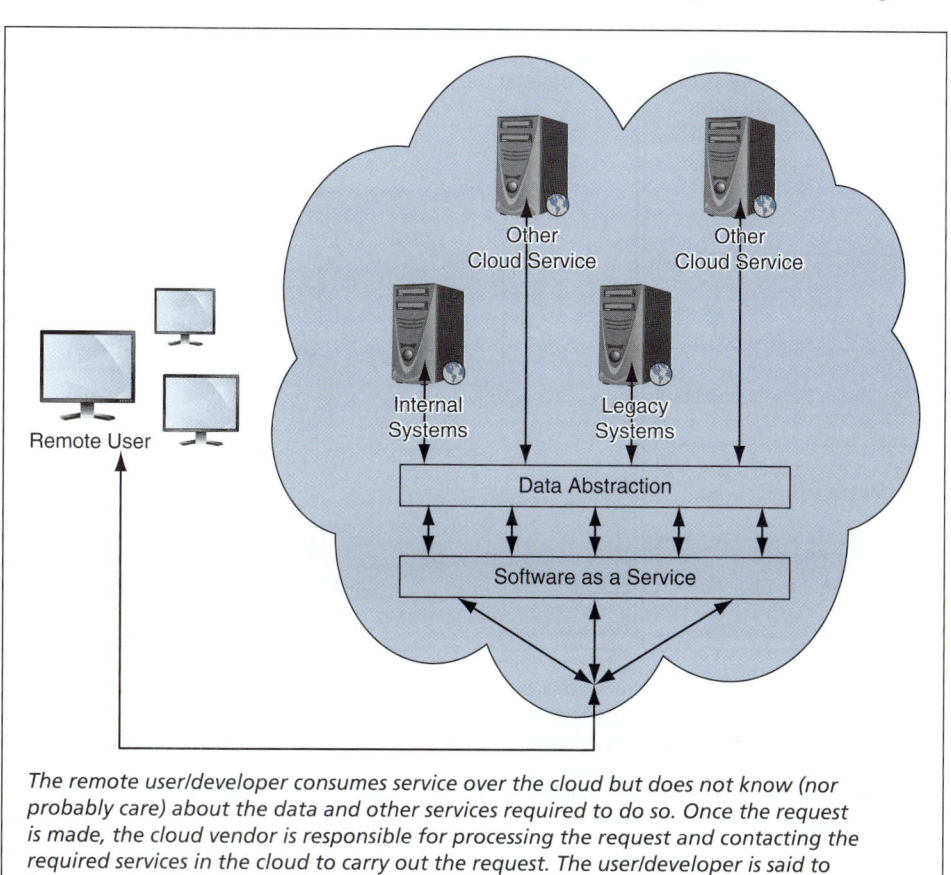

FIGURE 5-2 Cloud-Computing Abstraction

The remote user/developer consumes service over the cloud but does not know (nor probably care) about the data and other services required to do so. Once the request is made, the cloud vendor is responsible for processing the request and contacting the required services in the cloud to carry out the request. The user/developer is said to be consuming the service, and the process by which the service is carried out is said to be abstract to the user/developer.

HOSTED APPLICATIONS VS. CLOUD COMPUTING

What is the difference between hosted applications and cloud computing? **Hosted applications** have been around since the beginning of the Internet and were referred to as client-server computing. A client (e.g., a web browser, e-mail client, etc.) is used to access the hosted application, giving users access to remote servers. As clients evolved, the concepts of object-oriented programming—**service-oriented architecture (SOA)** and **software as a service (SaaS)**—also evolved. Object-oriented programming is about reusing objects within or between applications, while SOA is about reusing services across the network and SaaS is defined as software on demand.

SOA moved software design from writing applications to do just one specific thing to designing applications to use a loosely coupled set of services that interact to provide the application. A simple example of this can be seen in Figure 5-3. SOA is much more complicated than this simplistic view, but this view gives an introduction to SOA and its impact on cloud computing. SOA is about system design principles, while SaaS is about software designed to be delivered over the Internet or from behind the firewall on a LAN. SOA and SaaS are at the heart of cloud computing—that is, offering software that allows applications to be developed using modular components from various vendors.

Steve Ballmer, CEO of Microsoft, gives perhaps the best description of cloud computing when answering the question: Why have hosted servers not historically been called "cloud computing"? He postulates that hosted servers are not called cloud computing because they have not been re-architected to include scaling, fault tolerance, geo-replication, and security in an environment where information is being shared across the cloud. He further implies that because things are happening "outside the firewall," the re-architecture must occur (Ballmer, 2008). Since Ballmer gave that explanation in 2008, it is safe to say that today we have seen much of this re-architecture. In the current Internet Age, we often participate in cloud-computing environments without even realizing it. It seems that cloud computing has become ubiquitous.

FIGURE 5-3 Service-Oriented Architecture

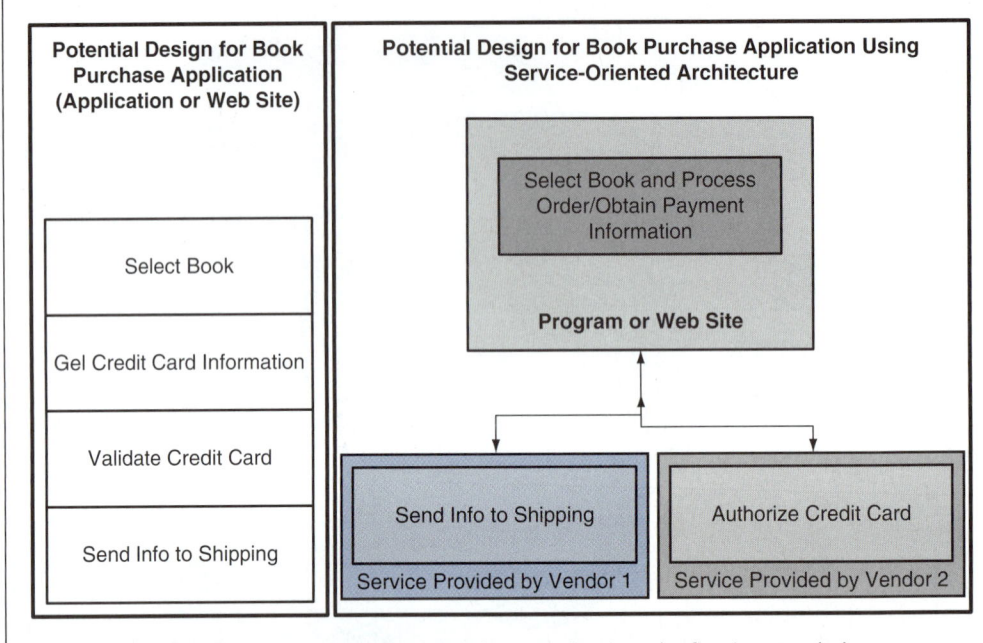

Potential Design for Book Purchase Application (Application or Web Site)	Potential Design for Book Purchase Application Using Service-Oriented Architecture
Select Book	Select Book and Process Order/Obtain Payment Information
Gel Credit Card Information	**Program or Web Site**
Validate Credit Card	Send Info to Shipping — Service Provided by Vendor 1
Send Info to Shipping	Authorize Credit Card — Service Provided by Vendor 2

Of these two different designs for a book purchase application, the first is a stand-alone application. It may be a program or individual web site that does everything necessary for the book purchase process. The second is a book purchase application that uses services from other vendors to authorize the credit card and to manage distribution/warehouse activities. This (simplistic) look at online book purchasing makes the point that the application uses the services of other vendors to fulfill the order.

CORPORATE LAN-BASED APPLICATIONS VS. CLOUD APPLICATIONS

Let's take the example of an application offered by a company's data center to remote users on the Internet. It does not matter what the application is; it could be a web site, payroll application, or something that supports another business process. In outward-facing corporate LAN-based applications, the company must maintain internal infrastructure with various servers, firewalls, and other technologies to create, enable, and support the application. They must also have a connection to the Internet that allows remote users to access the application. The organization must maintain the technology and the staff that supports it. This approach to offering the application to remote users is resource-intensive. What happens when this application is moved into the cloud? Can resource requirements be reduced and potentially increase uptime?

Moving the corporate LAN-based application to the cloud yields some advantages. By purchasing the necessary services from one or more vendors, a user/developer can reduce the local resources necessary for deployment of the application. Then, the organization can consume the resources it needs as the demand for the application increases and only pay for the resources it actually uses, potentially reducing upfront costs for deploying the application. Examples of a corporate LAN-based deployment and a cloud-based deployment can be seen in Figure 5-4. Before discussing the attributes of cloud computing, let's first look at 6waves's implementation of cloud-based games on Facebook.

> 6waves, a venture backed company, is the leading international publisher of gaming applications on the Facebook platform. Through partnerships with top developers, 6waves aims to publish the next generation of social games to cover every genre, language, and platform. To date, we have over 30 million monthly active players playing our games and applications, a number that continues to grow daily (6Waves Limited, 2011).

6waves uses Amazon's Elastic Compute Cloud (EC2), Simple Storage Service (S3), Elastic Block Store (EBS), and Elastic Load Balancing to enable its gaming application. Cosmos Tong, system administrator for 6waves, describes how the services fit into the company's

This figure shows two different designs for an application: The corporate LAN-based application runs on the corporate LAN and is offered to remote users over the Internet. The other design, a cloud-based application, resides on the Internet, and users access it directly without the need for a corporate LAN. The entire infrastructure necessary to maintain the application and associated services is obtained through a cloud vendor.

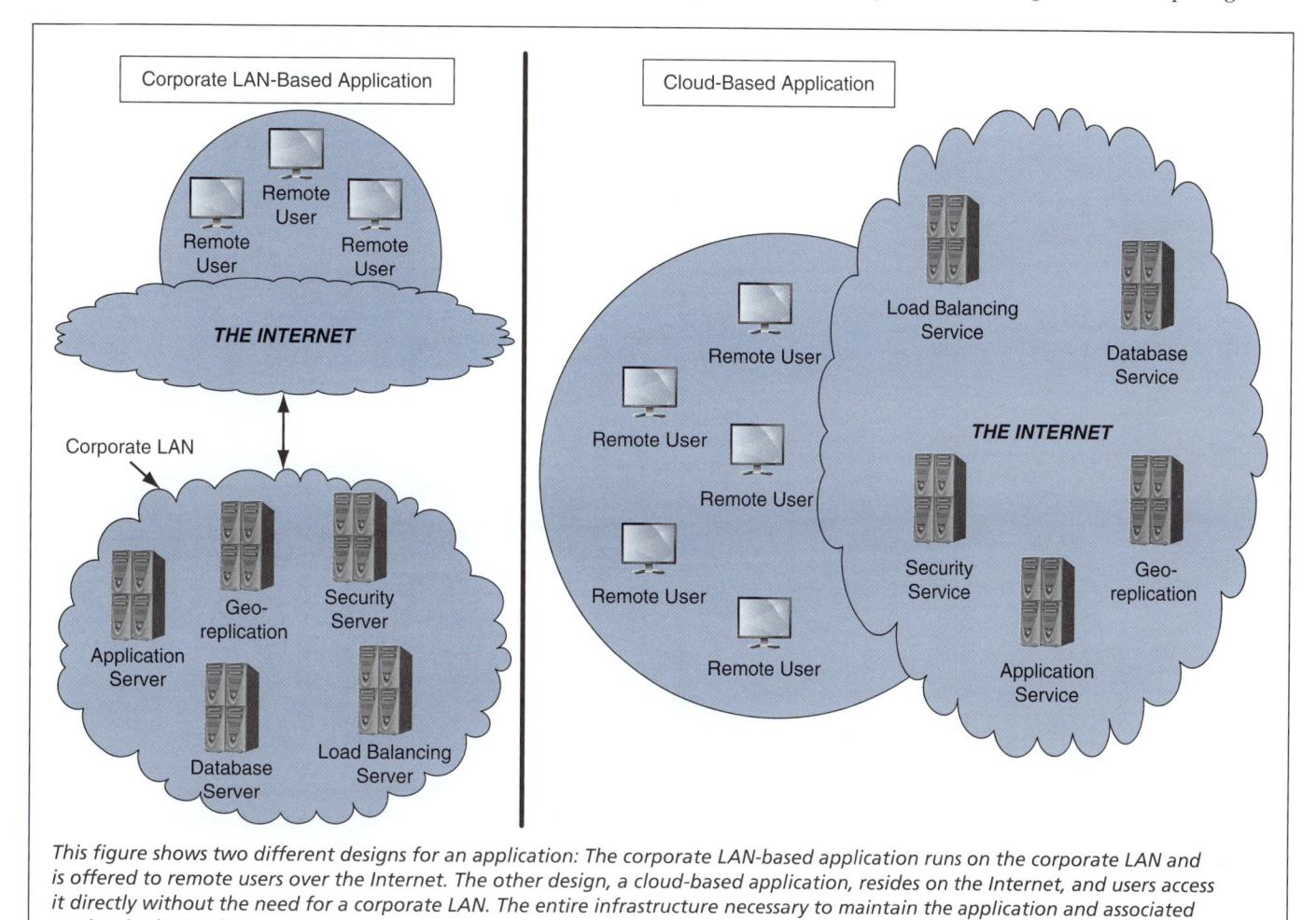

FIGURE 5-4 Cloud vs. Corporate LAN Applications

architecture. "As the games we publish are relatively independent, we group servers of different games into separated AWS [Amazon Web Services] accounts and use [Elastic Load Balancing] to set up load balancing and AWS security groups to control access." He further states that using AWS simplifies the deployment of new games. This saves 6waves time and money. An overview of the architecture can be seen in Vignette Box 5-1.

Attributes of Cloud Computing

Cloud computing is offered by many vendors. Even though the technologies that underpin cloud computing are normally standards-based, cloud computing itself does not have any industry-ratified standards (e.g., the IEEE has not promulgated any standards). Therefore, we turn to what industry leaders say about cloud computing and how they define its attributes. Specifically, we will use the attributes as defined by the Gartner Group and Microsoft.

The Gartner Group has highlighted five attributes of cloud computing (Gartner, Inc., 2009). According to Gartner, cloud-computing applications must be (1) service-based, (2) scalable and elastic, (3) shared, (4) pay as you use (metered use), and (5) Internet-based technologies. The Gartner group goes on to elaborate on each of these:

- **Service-Based**: Being service-based means that consumer concerns are abstracted from provider concerns through service interfaces that are well-defined. In other words, the person using/buying the service is not concerned with how the service is delivered (e.g., what specific technologies are used to deliver the service), but rather consumers are concerned with the correct functioning of

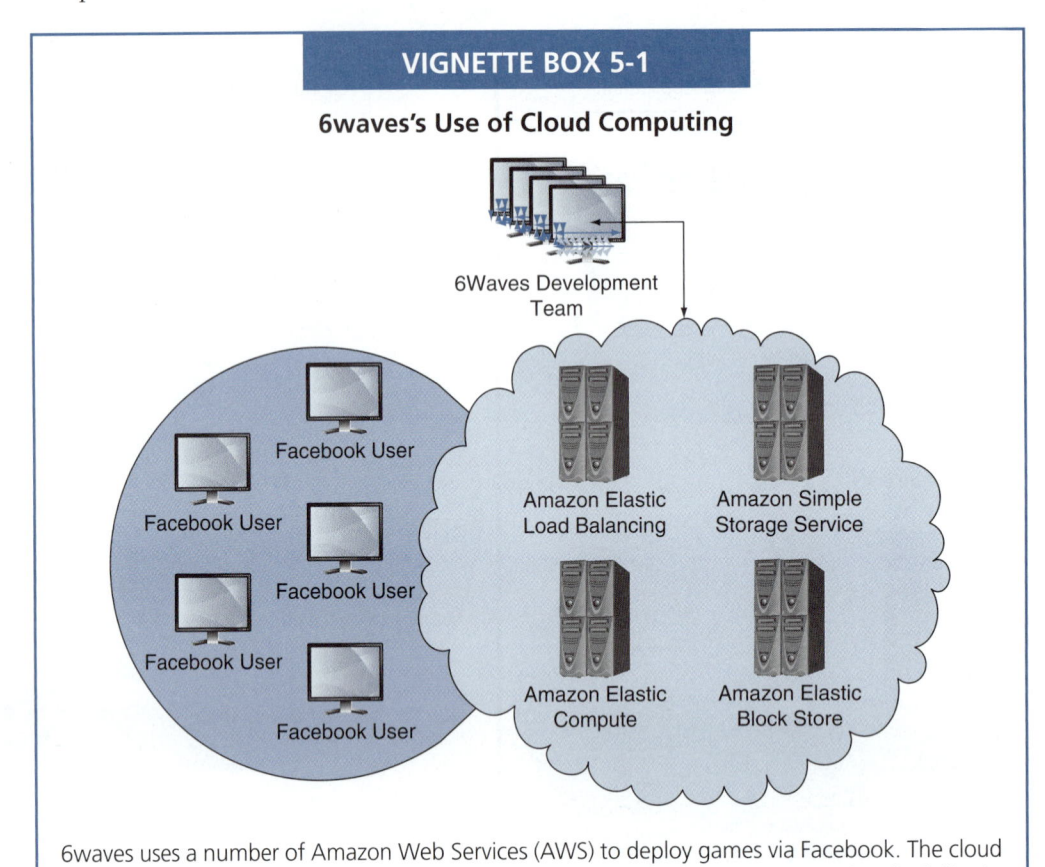

> **VIGNETTE BOX 5-1**
>
> **6waves's Use of Cloud Computing**
>
> 6waves uses a number of Amazon Web Services (AWS) to deploy games via Facebook. The cloud arrangement allows 6waves to decouple the underlying hardware and provides flexibility in implementing high-quality services to its customers. Amazon has a number of services available in the cloud to the 6waves developers and Facebook users.

the service. The interface hides the implementation details and enables a completely automated response by the provider of the service to the consumer of the service. The service could be considered "ready to use" or "off the shelf" because the service is designed to serve the specific needs of a set of consumers, and the technologies are tailored to that need rather than the service being tailored to how the technology works. The articulation of the service feature is based on service levels and IT outcomes (e.g., availability, response time, performance versus price, and clear and predefined operational processes), rather than technology and its capabilities. What the service *needs to do* is more important than *how the technologies are used* to implement the service.

- **Scalable and Elastic**: The service can scale capacity up or down as the consumer demands change and can do it at the speed of full automation, which may be seconds for some services and hours for others. Scaling refers to a system or network ability to adapt and continue to provide services as the demand for its services increases. This increase can be measured as an increase in the number of users, calls to the service, or some other increase in demand. Scaling should occur gracefully, if not automatically. In other words, the service should respond to increased demand by providing increased resources. In an ideal situation, the user will not experience any slowdown as the service responds to the increased demand. Elasticity is a trait of shared pools of resources. Scalability is a feature of the underlying infrastructure and software platforms. Elasticity is associated not only with scale but also with an economic model that enables scaling in both directions—adding or removing resources as needed—in an automated fashion.
- **Shared Resources**: Services share a pool of resources to build economies of scale. IT resources are used with maximum efficiency. The underlying infrastructure,

software, or platforms are shared among the consumers of the service (usually unknown to the consumers), enabling unused resources to serve multiple needs for multiple consumers and all working at the same time.
- **Metered by Use**: Services are tracked with usage metrics to enable multiple payment models. The service provider has a usage accounting model for measuring the use of the services, which could then be used to create different pricing plans and models. These plans may include pay-as-you go plans, subscriptions, fixed plans, and even free plans. The implied payment plans will be based on usage, not on the cost of the equipment. The amount of the service used by the consumers can be measured in terms of hours, data transfers, or other use-based attributes delivered.
- **Uses Internet Technologies**: The service is delivered using Internet identifiers, formats, and protocols, such as URLs, HTTP, IP, and representational state transfer web-oriented architectures. Many examples of web technology exist as the foundation for Internet-based services. Google's Gmail, Amazon.com's book buying, eBay's auctions, and Lolcats' picture sharing all use Internet and web technologies and protocols.

Balmer of Microsoft indicates (2008) that in order to be considered cloud computing, vendors' services should include scaling, fault tolerance, geo-replication, and security. These last three attributes are in addition to those included in the Gartner Group's model and are defined as follows:

- **Fault Tolerance.** Hardware failure is probably inevitable. A fault-tolerant system will adapt to hardware failure and have sufficient capacity and redundancy to respond to hardware faults. The user will experience minimal interruption in service. Because software is designed and created by humans, software failure is also probably inevitable. Fault-tolerant software is able to handle software bugs, correcting them where possible and notifying the user of the errors the system/service cannot handle. Cloud-based services should offer fault tolerance to its users and developers so that (1) when hardware failure occurs, the service is automatically moved to other hardware, and (2) when software errors occur, the system either automatically corrects the error or does extensive reporting so the user/developer can correct the error.
- **Geo-replication.** Geo-replication is a way to improve access time and the user experience by distributing servers across a network geographically so the content is closer to the user. In a geo-replicated system, content is replicated and kept up to date across a number of distributed servers. In cloud computing, it might mean having geo-replicated services that appear in each major country in the world.
- **Security.** Security exists at the physical and IS levels. At the physical level, the data center and the assets housed within it must be protected from intrusion and attempts at destruction. At the IS level, policies and safeguards must exist that prevent unauthorized and/or malicious attempts to change data or interrupt the functioning of the information system. IS security includes computing and network security. Cloud computing must encompass both physical and IS security. Security is such an important topic that all of Chapter 6 is dedicated to it.

The attributes of cloud computing are summarized in Figure 5-5.

Examples of Cloud-Computing Vendors

As we saw in the 6waves example, it is possible to have an application exist in the cloud. It is also possible to have the application exist on local servers. Next, we examine a number of cloud-computing vendors so the student can begin to understand the breadth of cloud services. For illustrative purposes, two major cloud offerings will be reviewed: the HealthVault offering from Microsoft and a suite of applications from Google (Google Apps). Using these vendors in this textbook is not meant to indicate that they are the only cloud-service vendors, nor is it meant to indicate that they are the best vendors; rather, they provide a good sample of vendors so the student can understand the number and type of services that are offered.

Internet Technologies	Services-Based	Scalability and Elasticity	Shared Resources
• Services are delivered using Internet technologies and protocols.	• Customers are only concerned with the software interface to the service, not the underlying technology.	• The service can add and/or delete technology capacity as needed to accommodate demand, and that change in technology capacity is transparent to the customer.	• Services share a pool of technology resources that allow customers to have on-demand access to a highly efficient infrastructure.
Metered Use	**Fault Tolerance**	**Geo-replication**	**Security**
• Customers are charged through multiple payment models that are based on usage.	• Technologies used to deliver services can adapt to and compensate for hardware and software faults.	• Technologies, data, and services are replicated in various geographic locations to maximize response time.	• Security is in place at the physical and information system levels to ensure protection from intrusion and attempts at destruction.

FIGURE 5-5 Cloud-Computing Attributes

HEALTHVAULT

According to Microsoft, "HealthVault is a health application platform, a set of platform services, and a catalyst for creating an application ecosystem that lets consumers collect, store, and share health information online. The HealthVault platform provides a privacy-enhanced and security-enhanced foundation that can be used to store and transfer information between a variety of providers' health services and health devices" (Microsoft, 2011). HealthVault provides a set of services that web developers can use to store and exchange data between patients, physicians, and other healthcare providers. It gives patients the ability to have a secure location to enter their health information including allergies, medical conditions, health history, and medical device measurements. The patient can then share that information with designated individuals and have access to that information in any number of applications that they authorize. Medical devices that interface directly with HealthVault include at-home devices like blood pressure monitors, blood sugar meters, weight scales, and pedometers.

Vendors create web-based applications that use HealthVault for secure storage of health information. Each vendor has some type of value added. Let's examine a few of these vendors, and then see how they might fit together to access and use HealthVault services in the cloud:

- *ActiveHealth Management* offers *ActivePHR,* which can be used to organize your family's medical information—prescriptions, test results, immunizations, and family medical histories. It also offers a patented monitoring system that "alerts you about opportunities for improved care" (ActiveHealth Management, 2010).
- The *American College of Cardiology* offers *CardioSmart,* which provides the patient and physician a way to work together to manage hypertension. *CardioSmart* offers tools that track blood pressure, medication, and other relevant information.
- *CVS Caremark* offers a product that allows mail-order prescription management.

A patient could set up a HealthVault account, then set up accounts with several health-related web sites, such as ActivePHR to manage personal health records, CardioSmart to manage blood pressure information, and CVS Caremark to manage prescriptions. Patients could then give all of their health-related web sites permission to store and retrieve data from HealthVault. Having a central repository of health-related data means a patient only has to enter the data once. Finally, the patient could also give access to his or her healthcare providers. The health web sites provide tools for the patient and physician to manage the patient's healthcare (a cloud-based service), while HealthVault provides a secure central data storage and retrieval repository. This scenario can be seen graphically in Vignette Box 5-2.

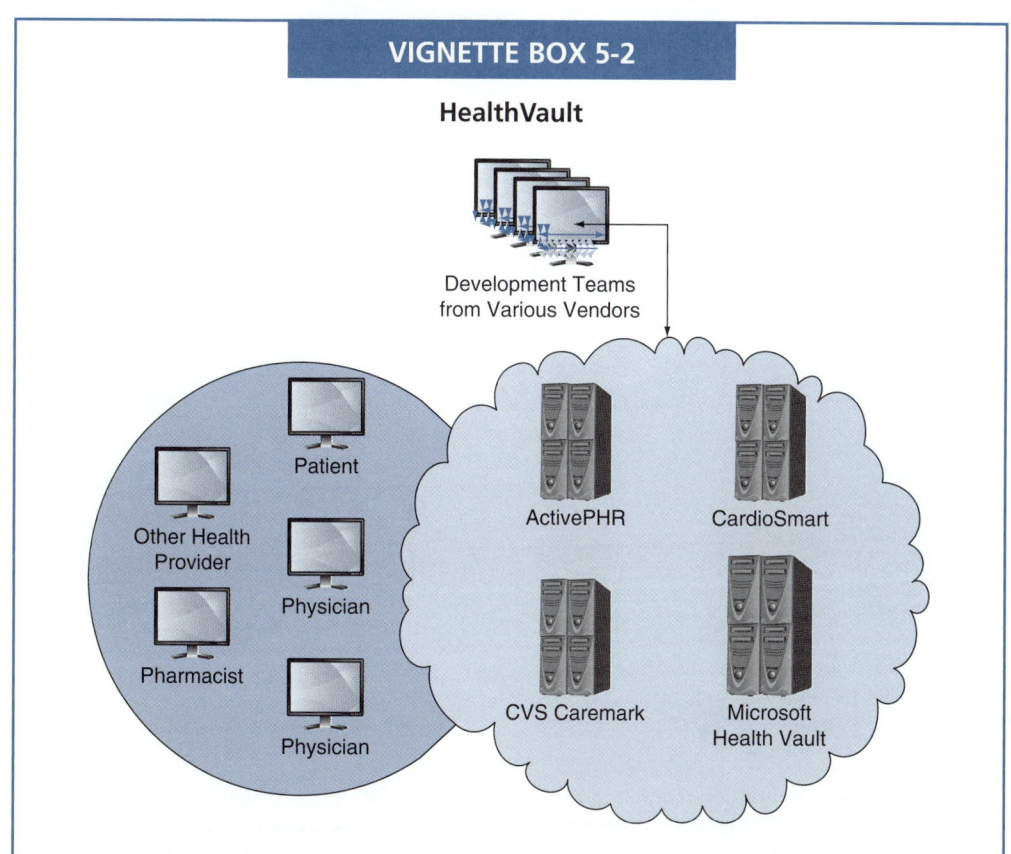

> **VIGNETTE BOX 5-2**
>
> **HealthVault**
>
> Development Teams from Various Vendors
>
> Patient, Other Health Provider, Pharmacist, Physician, Physician
>
> ActivePHR, CardioSmart, CVS Caremark, Microsoft Health Vault
>
> A number of users (e.g., patient, physician. pharmacist) use the Web sites of ActivePHR, CardioSmart, and CVS Caremark. For these web sites, Microsoft HealthVault provides the services that store and retrieve data. Each vendor's development team creates its web sites and software services. These development teams integrate HealthVault into their applications as a secure place to store and retrieve data. Note that the web sites and the HealthVault are all "in the cloud" and the main interface is a web browser.

GOOGLE APPS

Google Apps is a service offered by Google that provides several Google products over the web. The functionality offered is similar to a desktop office suite of software, except it is delivered through the web browser and is offered over the cloud. Google Apps is branded several ways, including Google Apps for Business and Google Apps for Education. The business version is sold on a per-user basis and has storage limits (the storage limits appear to be so large that most users would probably never approach them). The education version is free (and ad-free) and is broken into apps for K–12 schools and universities. Google Apps are also offered to personal users. The major difference in the product offerings are the fee structure, SLA guarantees (e.g., uptime), and other technical limitations. However, all Google Apps services are offered over the cloud. Technical limitations of Google Apps can be summarized as different levels of technical infrastructures as you go from free to pay services.

    Services like Google Apps afford the user (and the user's IT staff) a solution that is delivered using an Internet connection, desktop PC, and a web browser. The mechanics of software version control, upgrades, and infrastructure creation and maintenance are left to Google. Google takes care of security, storage, applications, and the ICT infrastructure necessary to run its applications, leaving the user (and its IT staff) with support for its local hardware needs, potentially saving the user's organization substantial resources. For the purposes of this textbook we will focus on Google Apps for Business and specifically examine the infrastructure and benefits of the Gmail, Google Calendar, and Google Docs applications.

VIGNETTE BOX 5-3

Google Apps

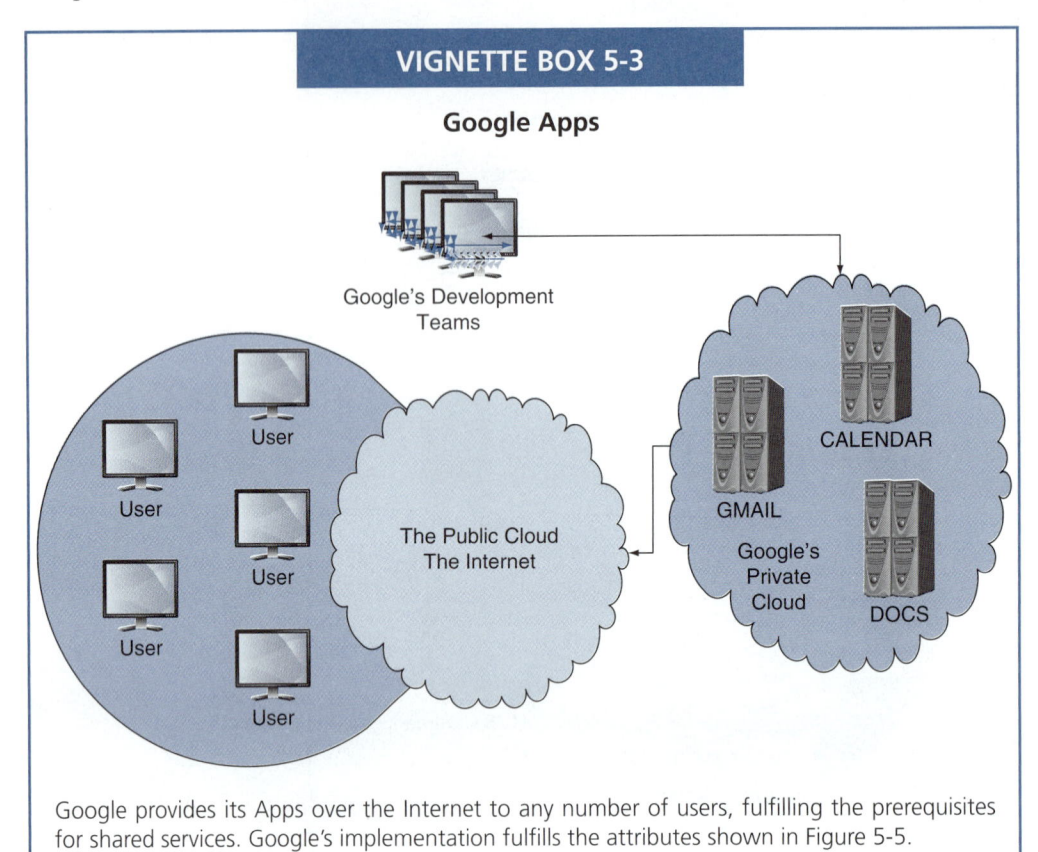

Google provides its Apps over the Internet to any number of users, fulfilling the prerequisites for shared services. Google's implementation fulfills the attributes shown in Figure 5-5.

Google provides applications over the Internet that are service-based, scalable, geo-replicated, and co-located. Users access shared resources that are available as required; users can create new accounts, allowing them to scale their consumption of resources to meet their needs. Looking at Vignette Box 5-3, we see that these applications are available over the Internet, and that Google runs its own private cloud that interfaces to the Internet, allowing Google to manage the infrastructure while at the same time providing Google Apps as a service to users.

DEVELOPING IN THE CLOUD

Developing cloud-based applications requires a number of existing standards, combined and offered in new ways. Building a cloud application can employ Internet computer protocols and standards such as HTTP, FTP, TCI/IP, XML, SOAP, and UDDI. It also uses a development language such as VB, APSX, C, or C#. The plethora of existing standards for Internet technologies and the lack of existing standards for cloud computing make this a new frontier. Using Microsoft Azure©, we explore an example of cloud-computing application development. Other cloud vendors include Google, Oracle, and SalesForce.

Private vs. Public Cloud

The term *cloud* can have a variety of connotations. The unifying thought, however, is that a user connects to the cloud to get services of some type. The user does not necessarily know how the ICT infrastructure of the cloud is configured or the technologies that enable the service the user is accessing, nor does a user necessarily care. What the user does know is that the service is available when needed. This point is: the user does not know what is going on inside the cloud, but knows that the cloud-based service vendor provides what is needed when it is needed.

We saw in Vignette Box 5-3 that it's possible to have private clouds that exist inside the Internet. By **private clouds** we mean networks (usually networks with some type of routing) that provide services or connectivity available to external users either directly connected to the cloud (e.g., connected to the organization's private cloud via a leased line) or via the Internet. Organizations can use multiple private clouds connected to the Internet to accomplish redundancy, geo-location, and other attributes of cloud computing.

Vignette Box 5-4 shows a number of users connected to the Internet, which allows them to connect to the Google private cloud. They undoubtedly connect to www.google.com/apps or some other similar address and are redirected to the appropriate Google Private Cloud. We only show two private clouds in this diagram for sake of simplicity, but a number of private clouds are run by Google. These private clouds allow Google to scale, handle geo-replication, and provide fault tolerance. The **public cloud** or the Internet provides connectivity at a low cost per bit transmitted for a large number of users.

A user—whether a single user or an entire organization—may also have a secure VPN tunnel into one of Google's clouds. What should be understood is that secure connectivity through the public and private clouds is available using VPN technologies discussed in earlier chapters. The diagram also shows a leased line connection direct to one of Google's clouds. Here, Google Apps is only an example of the types of public and private clouds and their connections. These connections may not exist in reality.

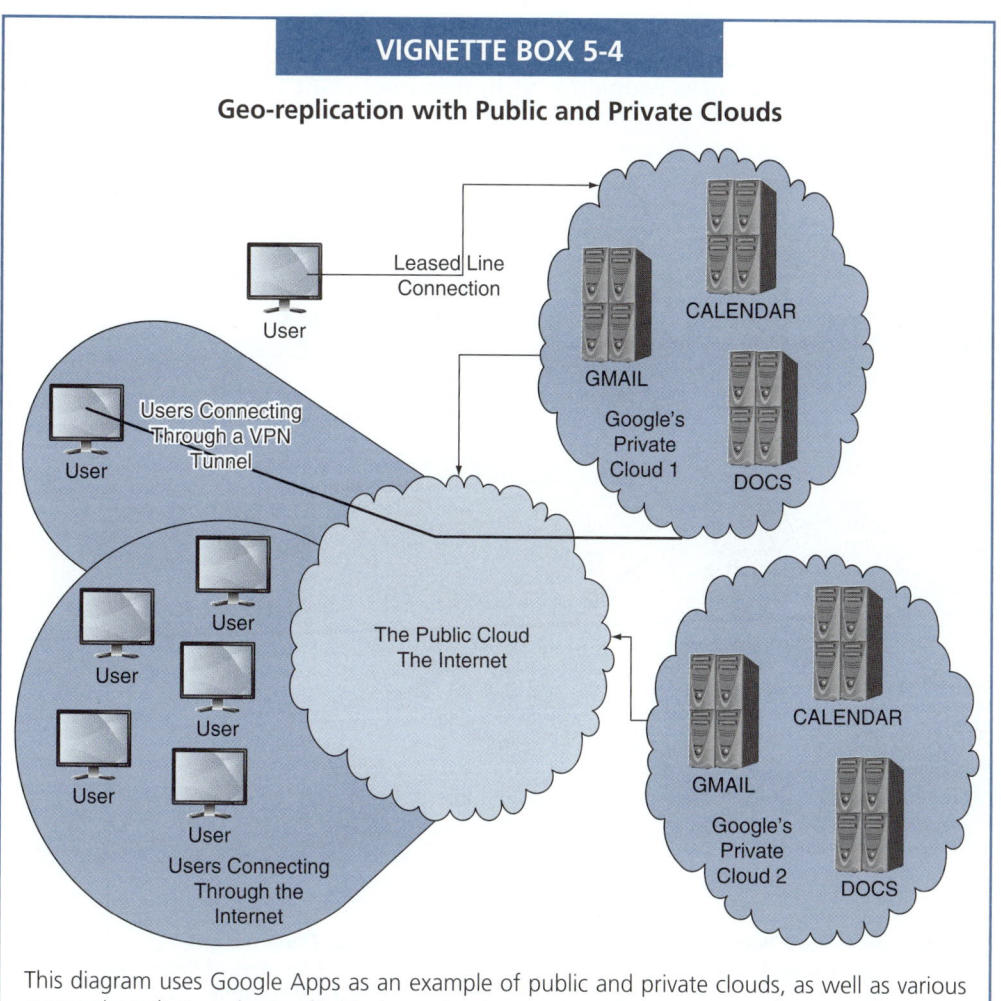

VIGNETTE BOX 5-4

Geo-replication with Public and Private Clouds

This diagram uses Google Apps as an example of public and private clouds, as well as various connections that can be used with those clouds.

Service Types in the Cloud

A complete list of services that can help the developers, users, and business analysts understand what is available over the cloud has been proposed by David Linthicum (2010). Linthicum identified the following eleven services:

1. Storage-as-a-service
2. Database-as-a-service
3. Information-as-a-service
4. Process-as-a-service
5. Application-as-a-service
6. Platform-as-a-service
7. Integration-as-a-service
8. Security-as-a-service
9. Management-as-a-service
10. Testing-as-a-service
11. Infrastructure-as-a-service

In a private cloud-computing environment or within the public cloud, these services are available (see Figure 5-6). The user is normally unaware of where these services exist, but rather just knows that they are accessible. Developers use these services to create applications that solve business problems, and users consume these services in the course of doing business. Think of these services as building blocks that are independently fitted together to solve business problems. This list of services is not exhaustive, but rather representative of what is available today to create cloud-computing applications. Surely as soon as this service list is created, some clever developer will envision new and innovative ways to implement technology that solves unrealized business problems. Still, it is important to define these services (Linthicum, 2010).

Linthicum identified the eleven services described in this chapter that exist within the cloud. These services are used by developers to create applications that solve business problems and are consumed by users of those applications. These services might be used independently or together to create cloud-based applications.

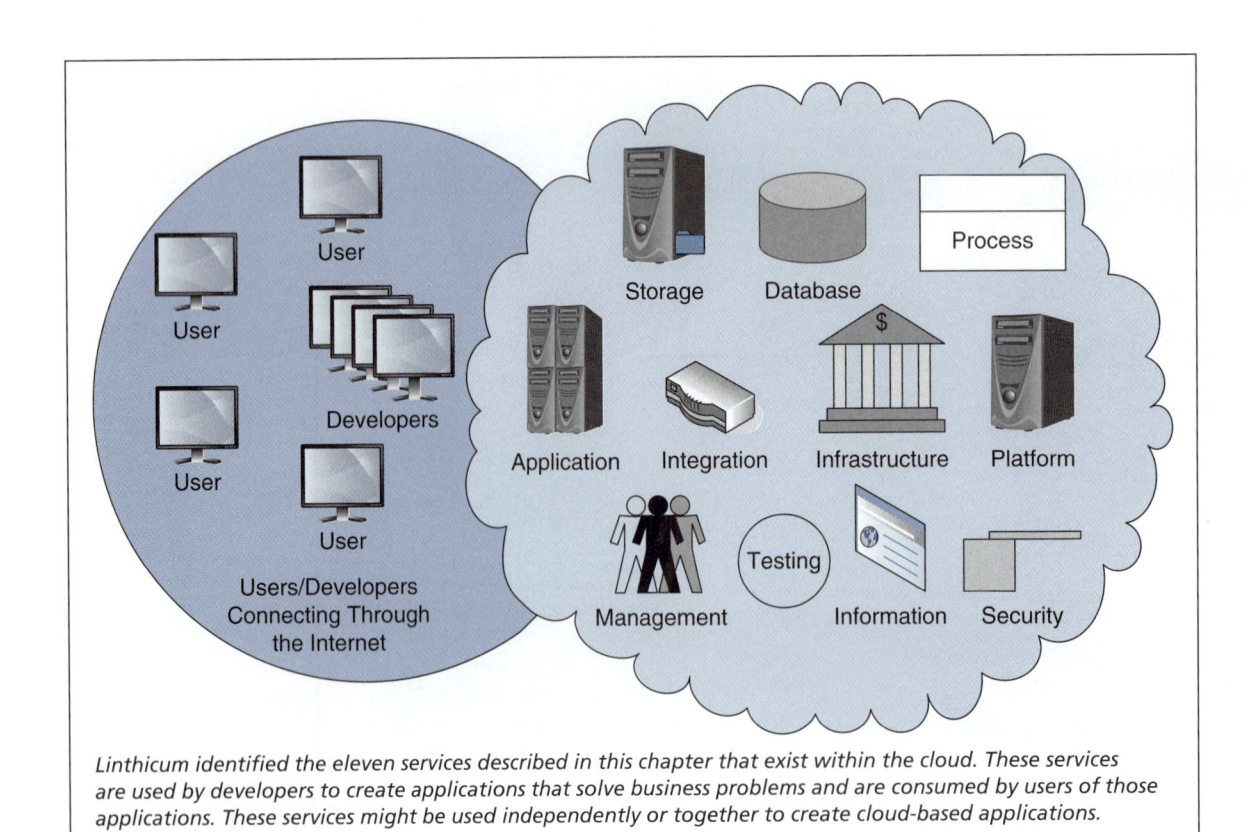

FIGURE 5-6 Cloud Services

- **Storage-as-a-service** (also known as disk on demand) is the ability to leverage storage that physically exists at remote locations but logically appears as local storage to any application that requires storage. Storage-as-a-service is a fairly low-level cloud-computing service often consumed by other services in this list. Amazon S3 is a cloud-based storage service that is available to web sites and other applications to provide remote storage. Storage-as-a-service is economical to the consumer of this service because the initial capital expenses and ongoing operational expenses are borne by the provider. The consumer pays for storage used and transactions that store and retrieve data. The product Allway Sync uses Amazon S3 to allow consumers to store data in the cloud and retrieve it at will.
- **Database-as-a-service** allows developers and consumers to use database services of a provider on a "pay-as-you-go" basis, rather than incur up-front capital expenses to set up the servers and databases. Often, database-as-a-service providers offer a number of different database management systems (DBMS) so the application can utilize the one that best fits the application. You might see the same service provider offer MS-SQL™, MYSQL™, and Oracle™, to name a few. It is possible that database-as-a-service providers will offer the DBMS and either offer the storage themselves or use a storage-as-a-service provider. For example, Amazon's offering of its Relational Database Service (RDS) provides a MYSQL™ DBMS stored in the Amazon cloud using Amazon S3 (a storage-as-a-service offering).
- **Information-as-a-service** refers to any cloud-based service that provides an application programming interface (API) or other similar method that allows an application to use/consume information. Examples include providers that offer credit card verification. These providers will allow you to pass credit card details to them for verification of card number and amount of purchase. Some service providers will also process the bank transactions necessary to secure funds from the bank issuing the credit card. Quicken™ is an example of this. In addition to many other credit card processing providers, numerous information providers offer information/services such as stock prices and address verification.
- **Process-as-a-service** supports business processes through combining other services to create meta-applications. The application at www.salesforce.com delivers service over the cloud that supports the customer relationship management process of an organization. Salesforce offers these applications: Sales Cloud™ to support the sales processes in an organization, Service Cloud™ to support the customer service processes in an organization, Chatter™ to support collaboration between colleagues in real time, and Force.com™ as a cloud platform for custom application development.
- **Application-as-a-service** is any application that is delivered through a browser to an end user's PC. Salesforce falls into this category as does Google Apps. Google Docs, Google Calendar, and Gmail are applications delivered as a service. These examples use other services (e.g., storage, process, etc.) from their private cloud or services that are available over the public cloud.
- **Platform-as-a-service** is a subscriber-based service delivered to customers. It typically includes application, interface, and database development, along with storage, testing, and other technologies. Platform-as-a-service delivers its services from cloud-based hosted data centers. Red Hat™ delivers platform-as-a-service solutions "that can be deployed or offered through a public or private cloud to build, deploy and manage applications across their lifecycle" (Red Hat, Inc., 2011).
- **Integration-as-a-service** includes the features traditionally found in enterprise application integration but delivered as a service. Cloud integration services are offered by companies such as SnapLogic, Boomi, and Cast Iron Systems. Integration-as-a-service offers solutions and services that assist companies in their quest to integrate in-house and cloud-based solutions. These integrators provide consulting, training, and service solutions within vertical markets or horizontally across business processes.
- **Security-as-a-service** "is simple. Rather than acquiring your own security software tools and the technical expertise to administer them internally, you contract with

security vendors to have a turnkey service of virus defense, firewall management, and e-mail filtering. Outsourcing cyber security eliminates all the labor and infrastructure, while still giving you the state of the art in anti-virus, firewall, and spam-fighting technologies" (McAfee, Inc., 2010). Virus defense, firewall, management, and e-mail filtering is offered by vendors such as McAfee, while more sophisticated services like identity management are offered through directory services available online (e.g., www.accenture.com).

- **Management-as-a-service** refers to any "on-demand service that provides the ability to manage one or more cloud services. These are typically things such as typology, resource utilization, virtualization, and uptime management. Governance systems are becoming available as well, offering, for instance, the ability to enforce defined policies on data and services" (Linthicum, 2010). An example would be the company Softchoice, which offers IT Asset Management (ITAM) as a service.
- **Testing-as-a-service** providers offer the ability to test applications through cloud-delivered testing algorithms that can test web sites, applications, and other software that do not require an on-premise footprint to carry out the testing. Hewlett-Packard offers quality management solutions using "a service model that accelerates the implementation of your quality center of excellence" (Hewlett-Packard Development Co., L.P., 2011).
- **Infrastructure-as-a-service** refers to actually having a data center-as-a-service. The difference between this approach and others discussed in this textbook is that rather than having a service exposed for the consumer to use, the consumer will place its servers in someone else's data center (or lease a server from the data center) and connect to the infrastructure. The data center's infrastructure will then attach to the public cloud. This service is often referred to as dedicated hosting, and companies such as Lunarpages and Go Daddy offer these dedicated hosting or infrastructure-as-a-service solutions.

A number of services are offered in the cloud. The services discussed in this chapter are meant to give examples of the types, breadth, and depth of services that are offered over the cloud. By using cloud-based services individually or combining them in unique and innovative ways, the developer can build robust applications at relatively low cost to enhance an organization's competitive positioning.

Cloud Development: Microsoft Azure and Sopima

Below we will give a high-level definition of Microsoft Azure™, and then we will turn our attention to Sopima (Sopima Oy, 2011), a Finish software company that has used Azure™ to create an online contract bank. First, let's turn our attention to Azure™ and whether to build a local application or move it to the cloud.

The decision to develop a local application or build local infrastructure has many facets. Some would say that the decision comes down to resources (aka money). But that is a simplistic view of a decision that involves many somewhat complicated issues. These are covered in detail later in this chapter. For now, let's assume that we have decided to develop in the cloud. Further, let's assume that we will use Microsoft Azure™ as the development platform. (This is just an example, and there are a number of cloud-computing vendors you could use.) The decision of which to select depends on the type, sophistication, and service-level required and is beyond this textbook. However, it is safe to say that decision must be driven by the organizational needs and the needs of the customers. Sopima and Azure were chosen to demonstrate cloud-based application development and deployment because they are straightforward, easy to understand, Sopima is totally cloud-based (Azure™) (Microsoft, 2009), and together they give a very good example of cloud-computing development and deployment.

AZURE

Azure is a cloud-computing platform that provides the technical infrastructure so an organization can "**focus on solving business problems and addressing customer needs**" (Microsoft, n.d.). Many of the technical details of the infrastructure are transparent to the developer and the user. Azure is a development platform and environment that allows organizations to develop web services or applications. "For some applications, both code and data might live in the cloud, where somebody else manages and maintains the systems they use. Alternatively, applications that run inside an organization—on-premises applications—might store data in the cloud or rely on other cloud infrastructure services" (Chappell, 2010).

In a totally on-premises application—one developed and executed on infrastructure owned by the organization—the technologies such as servers, development environments, and more are housed and maintained by the organization. Moving an application to the cloud means deciding which parts of the application will stay on-premises (if any) and which parts will be moved to the cloud. The Microsoft Azure™ platform offers Azure Platform AppFabric, SQL Azure, and Windows Azure. These parts of the platform provide services to the user/consumer:

- **Windows Azure** provides a Windows-based environment for running applications and storing data in Microsoft data centers located in the cloud. This is a remote Windows™ session hosted in a Microsoft© data center.
- **SQL Azure** provides data services in the cloud based on Microsoft© SQL Server. Again, this is a remote service, consumed by the user/consumer, and all infrastructure for the SQL server is in a Microsoft© data center.
- **Azure Platform AppFabric** provides cloud services for connecting applications running in the cloud or on-premises. AppFabric provides access control through on-premises enterprise directories like Microsoft Active Directory™ or web-based identity providers like Windows LifeID™, Google™, Yahoo™, and Facebook™. AppFabric also provides a service bus that allows applications

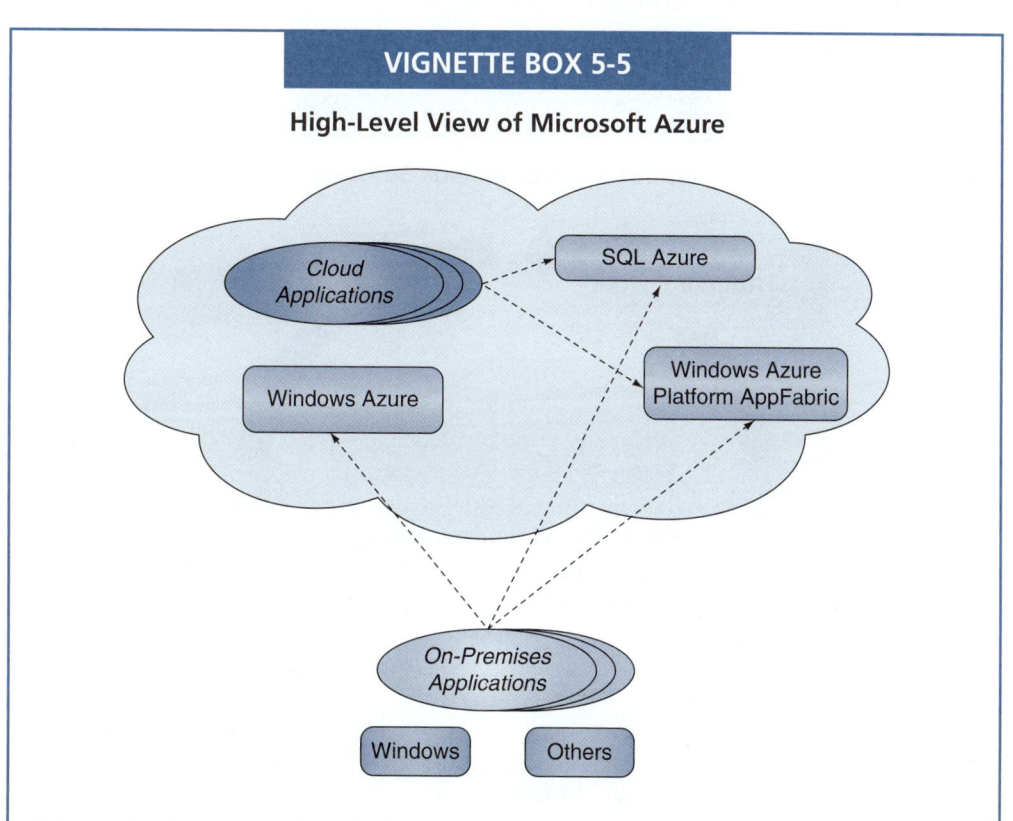

VIGNETTE BOX 5-5

High-Level View of Microsoft Azure

This graphical representation of Microsoft Azure shows a cloud-based platform that allows developers to create and deploy cloud-based applications to users. The applications can run on Microsoft Windows or other platforms on-premises, or they can exist totally in the cloud and run over a web browser.

Source: www.microsoft.com.

and services on any Internet-connected network to register with the service bus and interoperate in accordance with access rules and account restrictions between those applications and services.

Each of the components of Azure offers its own part in creating the Microsoft Azure cloud-based application environment. These components offer services that are essential to application development and deployment in a cloud-based environment. They support the integration of on-premises applications, Azure™ cloud-based applications, and applications and services from other cloud service vendors. AppFabric™ acts as the glue that holds together all these services and components. The cloud components in Vignette Box 5-5 could be exploded to show that Azure runs on a large number of machines in Microsoft data centers geo-located across the globe. Together these data centers create the services available through the Azure platform.

SOPIMA'S CLOUD SOLUTION

Sopima, a Finnish software company, uses Azure to create an online contract bank (Sopima Oy, 2011). Sopima provides online cloud-based contract management solutions throughout the contract lifecycle as shown in Vignette Box 5-6. Sopima's support for the contract lifecycle includes business development, administrative, production, and customer contracts. Sopima provides the following services:

- Draft initial contracts
- Handle negotiations of contract terms
- Manage acceptance and signing of contracts
- Handle initial execution and follow-up
- Provide ongoing analysis, reporting, and alerts
- Manage renewal and termination of contracts

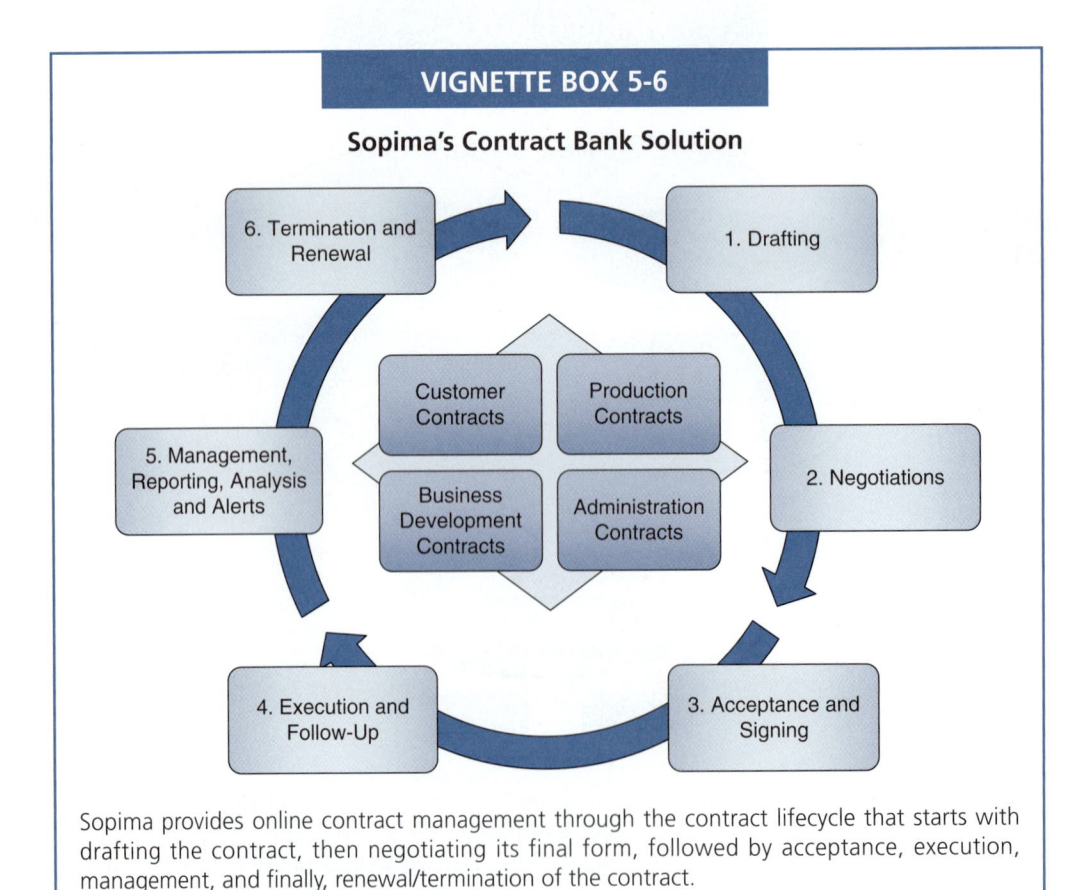

VIGNETTE BOX 5-6

Sopima's Contract Bank Solution

1. Drafting
2. Negotiations
3. Acceptance and Signing
4. Execution and Follow-Up
5. Management, Reporting, Analysis and Alerts
6. Termination and Renewal

Customer Contracts
Production Contracts
Business Development Contracts
Administration Contracts

Sopima provides online contract management through the contract lifecycle that starts with drafting the contract, then negotiating its final form, followed by acceptance, execution, management, and finally, renewal/termination of the contract.

Source: www.sopima.com/en/solutions (2010).

Sopima wanted to provide global online-accessible contract management tools but did not have an IT staff or infrastructure to provide this service. It turned to the Microsoft Azure platform.

Markus Mikola, a partner in Sopima, stated that "as a small company in a time of recession, we [Sopima] have built a global solution with minimal investment. If we [Sopima] hadn't used the Windows Azure platform, we wouldn't have been able to launch this service [Sopima's contract solution] at all" (Microsoft, 2009). In other words, Sopima may not have been able to surmount the barriers to entry, such as the cost to build the necessary infrastructure, necessary talent, and so on, which would have prevented Sopima from building and launching a globally accessible service.

Sopima evaluated a number of cloud-service vendors (Microsoft, 2009), and in March 2009 selected the Windows Azure platform from Microsoft. Sopima did not want to administer individual parts of service-based products purchased from different vendors, but rather wanted a "platform-as-a-service" approach that moved all ICT administration from Sopima to a single vendor that Sopima paid on a "pay-as-you-go" basis. For example, Sopima could have used a storage-as-a-service provider such as Amazon Elastic Compute Cloud (EC2) or Google Apps, but in Sopima's opinion "neither provided the full-scale platform and service management capabilities that the company [Sopima] was looking for." After analyzing its needs and the services offered by various cloud vendors, Sopima chose Microsoft Azure.

Sopima uses Microsoft SQL Azure, a cloud-based relational database platform that is built on Microsoft SQL Server technologies, to manage contracts and contract information. Using SQL Azure, Sopima also stores all deadline and project milestone reminders for users involved in the contract creation process. As part of the Windows Azure platform, SQL Azure provides automated management capabilities, including built-in data protection, self-healing, and disaster recovery—features that Sopima's management found crucial for safeguarding customers' data. "SQL Azure relieves Sopima of the database management aspect, which would otherwise require a huge investment of resources. [Antti Makkonen, Research and Development Lead at Sopima]

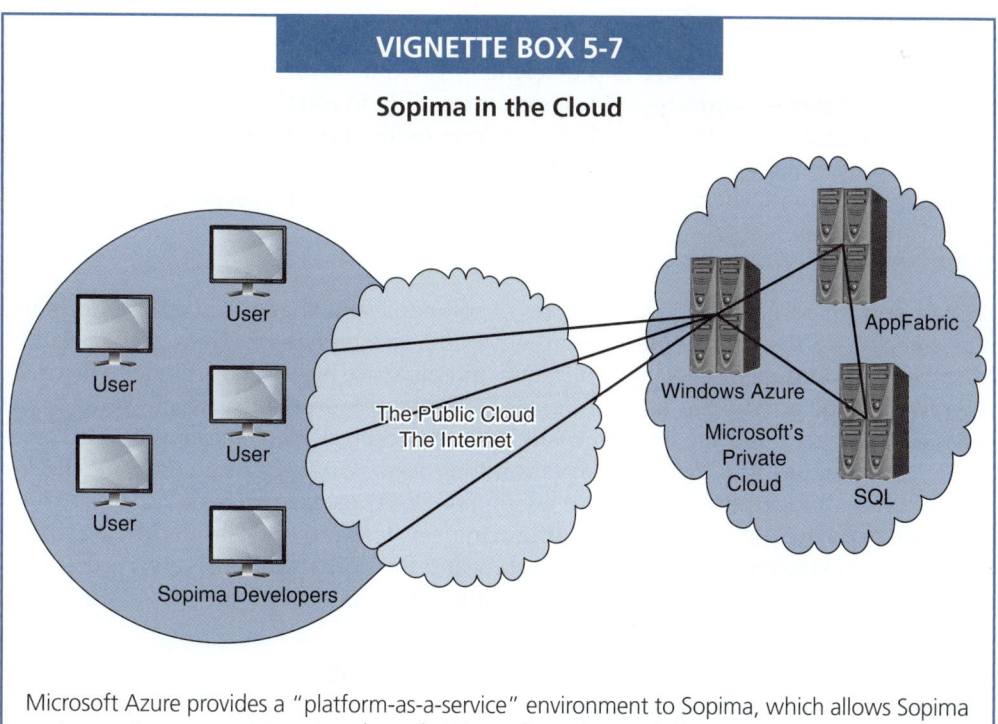

VIGNETTE BOX 5-7

Sopima in the Cloud

Microsoft Azure provides a "platform-as-a-service" environment to Sopima, which allows Sopima customers to consume resources through Microsoft services and data centers. This service gives Sopima the ability to pay on a usage basis rather than have the initial resource outlay to build the necessary ICT infrastructure.

FIGURE 5-7 Using Services from Several Vendors

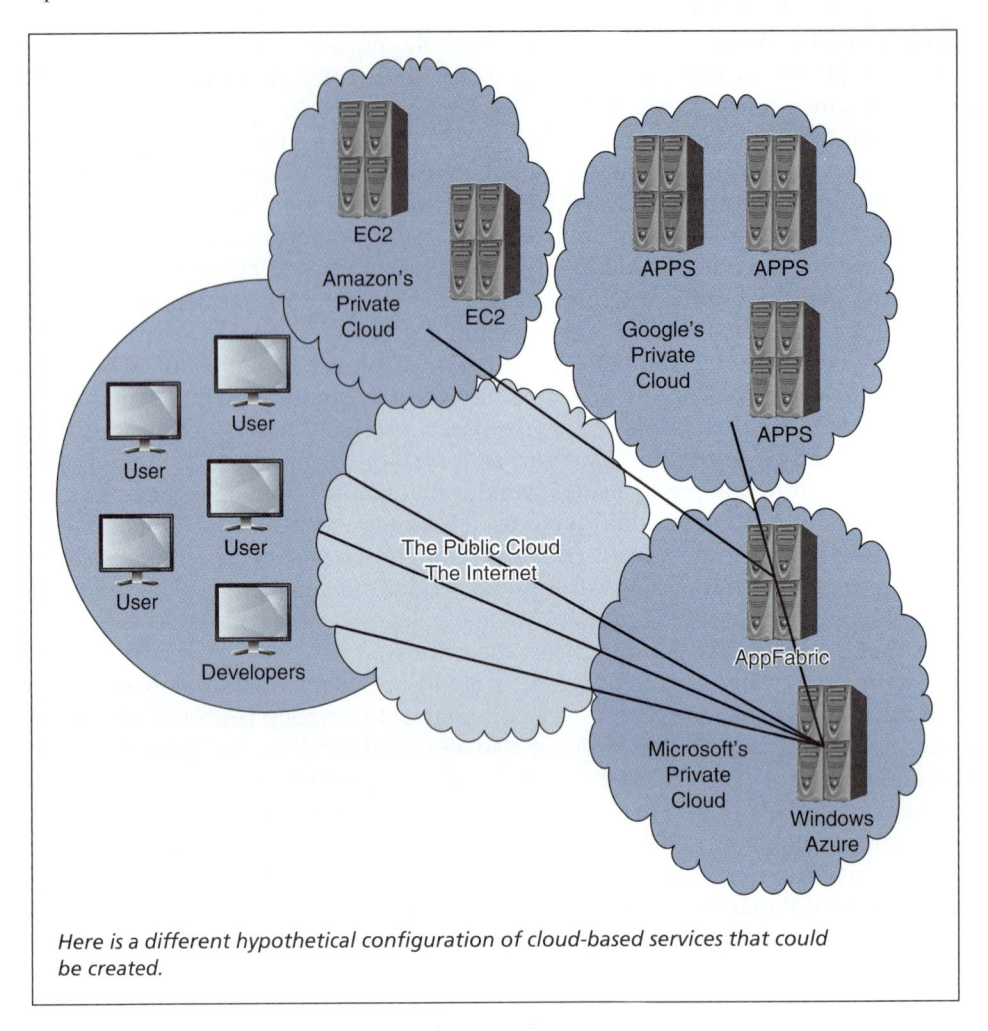

Here is a different hypothetical configuration of cloud-based services that could be created.

estimates that they would have had to spend approximately $20,000 annually in server licensing, and pay several support salaries amounting to roughly $300,000 in savings." The expense of these resources could be a strong motivation for moving an application into the cloud. Further details about Sopima can be found at www.sopima.com and further details about Microsoft Azure can be found at www.microsoft.com/azure.

SUMMARY: BUILDING IN THE CLOUD

Sopima and Microsoft Azure are examples of companies that have built applications and offer services in the cloud, and made them publicly available. In the case of Sopima, Microsoft provides the necessary application and database hosting (see Vignette Box 5-7). It would also be possible to use a different service configuration in which cloud-based services are aggregated together to create a single application. For example, Microsoft Azure could be used to host an application that used Windows Azure and AppFabric Azure™ to pull together those services with Google Apps and Amazon EC2, as shown in Figure 5-7. The possibilities for configuring services are only limited by available technology and the creativity of the developers and their organization. Note, Figure 5-7 is meant to be illustrative and not exhaustive of those possibilities.

BUSINESS CONSIDERATIONS OF CLOUD-BASED APPLICATIONS AND SERVICES

At first, it may seem like a simple question: Do we build applications using our own ICT infrastructure, purchase services from vendors in the cloud, or implement some combination of both? Building its own ICT infrastructure will give the organization the most control

- **Leverage Existing Resources:** Can your organization leverage existing staff or ICT infrastructure when it moves into the cloud?
- **Type of Services:** Is your organization looking to build an application using services from a number of vendors, or does it want a "platform-as-a-service" approach that allows it to have a unified cloud-based environment and "pay-as-you-go"? Will the application be used by enough people to justify moving the application to the cloud?
- **Capabilities:** Does the organization have the technical capabilities in-house, or will it be necessary/preferable to obtain them?
- **Infrastructure:** Is the current ICT infrastructure and Internet connectivity robust enough to support the application the organization wants to build or is it more cost efficient to develop in the cloud?
- **On-Premises or Off:** Does the application need to be built on-premises, should the organization build in the cloud, or should it take a hybrid approach in which some of the applications/data are on-premises and some in the cloud?
- **Management Costs:** Is it more cost effective to build and manage the application on-premises or in the cloud?
- **Geo-replication:** Does the organization need the application co-located in various geographic regions to provider faster access or redundant data storage?
- **Capital vs. Operational Expenses:** Are the capital expenditures too high when considering whether to build on-premises infrastructure? Is it more cost effective to build an application in the cloud where a service provider has the up-front capital expenditure and your organization pays on a usage basis?

Here are some of the major considerations when deciding whether to build an application and ICT infrastructure in-house, in the cloud, or a combination of both.

FIGURE 5-8 Considerations for Developing in the Cloud

over its applications and data, but at what cost? Building applications in the cloud and storing data there may be an organization's most cost-effective solution, but what other "costs" need to be considered? Those are the questions that this section will attempt to answer.

Clearly, an organization faces trade-offs between building applications on premises and building applications in the cloud. Financial considerations include how to pay for application and ICT development and deployment. But other considerations have their trade-offs as well. The decision is not just financial; the many facets that must be considered are summarized in Figure 5-8.

On-Premises or the Cloud?

The decision to build everything on premises versus paying a vendor for services consumed is complex. It could be that your organization has excess capacity on its ICT infrastructure or excess capacity in its technical staff (which is unlikely since there always seems to be too few technical staff members and too many ICT projects), so the organization may decide that it wants to leverage its existing resources rather than move its application to the cloud.

A major factor in deciding whether to build an application locally is whether your organization has the resources to do so. These resources include the capital to build the necessary infrastructure and the technical staff to build and maintain the application and infrastructure. The decision to leverage existing resources, build ICT infrastructure, or hire the required staff must be based on adequate fiscal, risk, and resource analyses. Fiscal analysis can be fairly straightforward, and the analysis of capital versus operational resource outlay is discussed next. Although fiscal analysis is an important factor it is not the only factor.

Capital outlay or the investment of staff time to build an application is risky. This risk is based on many factors, including the organization's past ability to build similar ICT applications and/or willingness to expend the resources necessary to build the ICT infrastructure and hire the necessary technical staff. The organization must assess its willingness to take on this risk, and whether it is less risky to use cloud services. A thorough risk analysis should be performed before an organization embarks on building

ICT infrastructure, hiring ICT staff, or moving an application to the cloud. This analysis must include a thorough analysis of your organization's industry, your organization's strategy, and an understanding of how an on-premises or cloud-based application fits within that strategy. Making the wrong decision about whether a major application should be built in your own infrastructure versus in the cloud can be costly.

Capital vs. Operational Expenditures and the Cloud[2]

When analyzing ICT expenditures to determine whether in-house or cloud-computing solutions will be deployed, we need to divide the expenditures into capital and operational expenditures. According to Generally Accepted Accounting Principles (GAAP), when a business incurs an expense it should be allocated over the entire period that expense will benefit the company. This GAAP rule is an attempt to match revenue with expenditures. It will be helpful to look at an example: an organization purchases $200,000 in ICT with an expected life of 5 years (this can be negotiated; some would say the expected life is 7 years). If you were using straight-line depreciation that expenditure should be expensed $40,000 per year, reducing the organization net income by that same $40,000 per year. This would be done to match the expense to any revenue generated during the same period.

Now consider that the same organization has $15,000 in start-up costs in year 1, a yearly maintenance expenditure of $2,200, and $175,000 per year in personal costs to maintain the equipment. This first-year expense of $220,200 that includes the ongoing annual expenses for personnel and maintenance costs would need to be figured with an average percentage increase in years 2 through 5 to account for cost-of-living increases. This calculation does not consider any electrical or other utility costs. Note: 6 percent is selected for illustrative purposes, and your organization may choose a different percentage.

If we move the same application to the cloud we *may* incur lower expenses. Assume that in order to develop this application we would need initial ICT costing $60,000; incur setup costs of $75,000; and have personnel costs of $75,000, ICT maintenance costs of $1,100, and cloud-computing service costs of $22,000. In this scenario the five-year costs would go from $1,213,893 (in-house ICT infrastructure) to $687,999 (cloud-based infrastructure). This cost comparison is shown in Figure 5-9.

This example leaves the reader believing that the major benefit from moving to a cloud-computing environment is cost savings, but other benefits need to be considered, including availability and marginal cost of consumption ("pay as you go").

Cloud Computing and Its Impact on the Organization

Moving an application to the cloud will change your organization, and your organization must consider these potential changes when deciding to adopt a cloud-computing approach. Cloud computing involves a number of potential risks and benefits that may require a delicate balance (Hinchcliffe, 2009).

NEW GENERATION OF PRODUCTS AND SERVICES

An obvious benefit is that cloud computing allows for the creation of a new generation of products and services that previously did not exist. In part, this new generation of products and services is enabled by the emergence of the Internet, but it goes further because organizations are now able to create products and services that were not possible in the past. Some technologies that exist today did not exist 30 years ago, 20 years ago, 10 years ago, or even possibly yesterday. As organizations harness these new technologies they are able to create new products only limited by their vision and strategic implementation of these technologies. At issue is whether the

---

[2] Thanks to Monique O. Durant, JD, CPA, LLM for reviewing this example for correctness and adherence to GAAP rules.

| | Initial Costs | YEAR ||||||
		ONE	TWO	THREE	FOUR	FIVE
In House Infrastructure Budget						
Initial Hardware Costs	200,000	40,000	40,000	40,000	40,000	40,000
Setup Costs	15,000	3,000	3,000	3,000	3,000	3,000
Personnel		175,000	185,500	196,630	208,428	220,933
ICT Maintenance Costs		2,200	2,332	2,472	2,620	2,777
Annual Costs →		220,200	230,832	242,102	254,048	266,711
Total Five-Year Costs →						1,213,893
Cloud Computing Budget						
Initial Hardware Costs	60,000	12,000	12,000	12,000	12,000	12,000
Setup Costs	75,000	15,000	15,000	15,000	15,000	15,000
Personnel		75,000	79,500	84,270	89,326	94,686
ICT Maintenance Costs		1,100	1,166	1,236	1,310	1,389
Cloud Service Costs		22,000	23,320	24,719	26,202	27,774
Annual Costs →		125,100	130,986	137,225	143,839	150,849
Total Five-Year Costs →						687,999

This five-year budget illustrates what might happen if an application is moved from an in-house infrastructure to a cloud-based infrastructure. A similar analysis should be done before any in-house or cloud-computing application implementation is considered.

FIGURE 5-9 In-House vs. Cloud Computing Budget Example

organization takes a "field of dreams approach—if we build it they will use it" or they take a strategically measured approach to building cloud-based applications. Organizations have to find that delicate balance between wanting to be first with a product or service and wanting to be a fast follower.

NEW PARTNERSHIPS, LESS OVERHEAD

Today's cloud-based infrastructure enables new lightweight partnerships between organizations: organization A and organization B can now communicate easier than ever before. The new cloud-based paradigm allows organizations to communicate and interoperate more easily than in the past, reducing interaction costs and making those interactions lightweight. As a result, organizations can realize new opportunities for business processes such as end-to-end supply chain management solutions that allow monitoring and control of goods from the raw materials that make up products to the shipping that delivers those finalized products to the customer. We also see offerings such as end-to-end customer relationship management from

- New generation of products and services
- New partnerships and less overhead
- Leveraging Internet resources
- Integration of on-premises and cloud-based resources
- Shifting of reliance on IT staff to user skills
- Increased experimentation (and innovation)

This list summarizes some of the factors to be considered when moving applications into the cloud.

FIGURE 5-10 Organizational Considerations in Moving to the Cloud

companies like Hexaware (Hexaware Technologies, n.d.). The new lightweight partnerships are not limited to suppliers and industry partners, but those same lightweight interactions can occur between an organization, its customers, and its cloud-based service provider.

LEVERAGE INTERNET RESOURCES

It's safe to say that in the past many developers never considered the World Wide Web as serious computing. Most serious computing was done using local hardware and software, but the emergence of the Internet, cloud computing, and Web 2.0 has brought a paradigm shift. We see robust services being offered using the software as a service (SaaS) platform, allowing complex computing applications to be built on the Internet backbone and enabling organizations to leverage Internet resources to fulfill strategic business needs. The challenge is for organizations to determine how to best position themselves using the Internet and cloud-based resources at their disposal. Proper implementation and exploitation of those resources could lead to better competitive positioning, while poor implementation is likely to mean lost market share.

INTEGRATION OF ON-PREMISES AND CLOUD-BASED RESOURCES

Choosing to move applications to the cloud means that the existing applications within the organization will probably need to be integrated with those applications moved to the cloud. This integration requires specialized skills and knowledge for modifying existing ICT architecture to allow for that integration. The organization will need to determine whether it has the skills to allow for this integration, or if it has the resources to obtain those skills. In other words, all organizations must consider resource commitments when making the decision about moving into cloud computing.

SHIFT FROM RELIANCE ON IT STAFF TO USER SKILLS

As a results of shifting to the cloud, many organizations experience less reliance on their own internal IT staff. Instead, users develop their own skills or contact the cloud vendor's IT staff for support. An example would be the organization that uses on-premises Microsoft Exchange Server and Outlook for calendaring. When a problem occurs with that application, the users would probably contact the internal IT help desk to get a resolution. Now consider that same firm moving calendaring (and e-mail, too) to Google Apps. Who will the users need to contact to get support, the local IT help desk or Google Apps technical support? This shift may cause a resource reallocation in the organization that results in needing less IT help-desk support personnel and more money put into buying additional support from Google. The result could be greater self-service by the business side of the organization (users) and less reliance on the internal IT support function (technical staff), creating a culture change that needs to be managed within your organization.

INCREASED EXPERIMENTATION

Because it may be cheaper to roll out new applications in the cloud, organizations may be more tolerant of innovation. The lowering of technical and resource-based barriers to creating innovative processes should make organizations more nimble. Organizations should be better able to experiment with new applications and experience less risk when they deploy a new solution. For example, if your organization wants its customers to schedule service appointments over the web, but is unsure about whether customers would use this ability, your organization may decide to deploy a web service–based scheduling application. Your organization may find that it costs hundreds of thousands of dollars to create the application itself, but that a cloud-based scheduling web service is available for just $100 per month. Would the organization be more willing to experiment with online appointment scheduling if the cost was low?

Making a Business Case for Cloud Computing

Making a business case for cloud computing involves a number of steps, not unlike making a business case for any infrastructure, application, or other ICT project. Making a business case for ICT infrastructure is the basis of this textbook. The steps are discussed in Units 3 and 4 and involve the strategic alignment of business strategy and IT. In summary, these things should be considered when making a business case for a cloud-based application:

1. Your organization needs to understand its competitive positioning within its industry. Michael Porter's competitive forces and competitive strategy models provide a good place to start this analysis. The information that comes out of this analysis should lead your organization to adopting a more competitive strategy.
2. Your organization's competitive strategy should lead to the creation of a value chain. The value chain will help your organization understand the business processes that must be created in order to fulfill your organization's strategy.
3. Having created a value chain (or value web) your organization should understand how it will create value for its customers, and how each activity in the value chain adds marginal value to your organization's products and services. This value chain becomes the basis for your organization's competitive strategy (i.e., can your organization fulfill its desired competitive strategy with the proposed/existing value chain?).
4. Having completed the industry analysis, selected a competitive strategy, and created a value chain, your organization is now ready to create business processes. For existing organizations you would create "as-is" and "to-be" processes (discussed in Unit 3). Having created a final set of "to-be" processes, the business systems analyst is ready to determine which technologies are needed to fulfill the organization's competitive strategy and its value chain. The business systems analyst may be called on to develop a number of alternative "to-be" business processes and provide cost estimates for each.
5. At this point, technical, economic, and business considerations of moving the application to the cloud must be considered. The impact on the cost/benefit must be assessed as must the impact on organizational culture. Moving to the cloud may be one of the "to-be" process models that are analyzed.
6. The organization is now ready to document its ICT design, including the "to-be" processes finally chosen. This step includes process and technology documentation, covered in Unit 4.
7. Lastly, the organization must consider implementation planning for the chosen ICT infrastructure along with a post-implementation review so the organization can keep ahead of competitive changes in its industry, all of which affect the organization's ability to gain/retain market share.

Utilizing cloud-based services requires the same careful analysis as building on-premises systems. In fact, assessing and monitoring the cloud-based services your organization is purchasing present a whole new set of challenges because the ICT infrastructure and services are largely out of the control of your organization. This will present a whole new set of challenges, including how to assess and monitor the cloud-based services that your organization is purchasing.

Deciding if and when to move into a cloud-computing environment requires substantial analysis. Your organization needs to decide whether its culture, staff, resources, and infrastructure are ready to make that shift. Like any major organizational change, moving into cloud computing requires careful analysis and thought, and that change must be managed. Fortunately, you can move slowly into cloud computing and expose your organization to little risk in doing so. No imperative states that if an organization does not adopt cloud computing, then it will close its doors. But an organization must be vigilant, watch technical trends, and decide if and when the time is right. Some organizations are on the "bleeding-edge" of technical change and desire to be there; others are on the "leading-edge" and are comfortable there; still others are "fast followers" that want other organization's to prove a technology before they adopt it. Whatever your organization's culture, it is important that the organization understands technical trends so it can maintain its competitive position in the marketplace.

Chapter Summary

In this chapter, a business-oriented view of cloud computing was discussed. Moving infrastructure and applications to the cloud is a complicated decision that affects both ICT infrastructure and organizational culture. Moving to a cloud-computing platform should be given the same consideration as any other large ICT infrastructure project. In fact, making that move may blur the lines between application creation/support and ICT infrastructure, creating a whole new paradigm for organizational IT departments to reckon with.

The ICT infrastructure issues are fairly easy to envision. For example, if you move an application or organizational service to the cloud, the business systems analyst should be able to quantify the impact of that move fairly easily. The need for new ICT infrastructure or the obsolescence of existing infrastructure can be given a dollar value fairly quickly, as shown in the example given in this chapter.

Assessing the organizational cultural impact of moving to cloud-based computing may be a bit more difficult. Your staff may feel changes that affect their ability to envision and create new products and services. Your organization may see cloud computing as a way to create new industry partnerships due to lower overhead, or it may see some of its small partners not able to connect to the cloud because they do not have the technical expertise in-house. The decision to integrate on-premises systems with cloud-based resources can be complicated and take resources your organization does not have. Moving to the cloud may cause users to troubleshoot their own problems rather than rely on the on-premises IT department for support. All of these issues and other considerations must be taken into account when moving to cloud-based computing.

Vignette Wrap Up

Multiple companies were reviewed rather than just one specific vignette for this chapter. They present a number of lessons learned. Several Microsoft products providing cloud-based services were reviewed. HealthVault provides a service-based personal health record repository accessible to health providers, patients, and other cloud vendors, while Microsoft Azure provides cloud services for application development and storage. Amazon offerings were reviewed, and how they could be used to build applications was discussed. Google Apps were introduced. The cases of Sopima and 6waves were covered as were the decision processes they had to go through to select their cloud vendor.

End of Chapter Questions/Assurance of Learning

1. Describe the differences between hosted applications and cloud computing. Discuss the benefits of each.
2. Select a cloud-computing vendor and describe what that vendor provides, its industry segment, and its pricing structure. Analyze how the business solution it provides will enhance another organization's competitive positioning.
3. Select a number of services offered in the cloud. Find three vendors for each and describe their offerings, pricing structure, and how they can affect an organization's competitive advantage.
4. Review the Sopima case and determine whether any other cloud solutions would be useful/better to support its business strategy.
5. Select a business you are familiar with and prepare a report that reviews how cloud computing would affect that organization.

Case Exercises

These exercises build on the case exercises from previous chapters.
1. The company XYZ Inc. (see the case exercises in earlier chapters) desires to find out whether cloud computing could benefit its organization. Its major customers are companies like HealthyWay HMO. Review XYZ Inc. (it is fictitious so you can make some of this up) and develop a business strategy for XYZ to move into cloud computing. Prepare an industry analysis and other appropriate analyses (e.g., value chain) to support your strategy and how a cloud-computing solution can aid XYZ in retaining its market share.
2. HealthyWay HMO, the opening vignette from Unit 1 desires to move its data services to the cloud. What are the implications for a healthcare organization, and how will that move support its business strategy? Prepare a presentation and report.
3. Work together in a small group with classmates to select an organization you are somewhat familiar with. Using that organization's mission statement, vision statement, or other strategy documents, craft a cloud-computing strategy for that company. Select the cloud solutions/services the organization would use and diagram the solution it would want to build. Prepare a report and presentation for this company as it attempts to gain funding from its board of directors for this project.

Key Words and Concepts

ActiveHealth *142*
application-as-a-service *147*
attributes of cloud computing *139*
Azure Platform AppFabric *149*
CardioSmart *142*
Caremark *142*
cloud-based applications *144*
cloud computing *135*
cloud-computing abstraction *137*
database-as-a-service *147*
Google Apps *143*
HealthVault *142*
hosted applications *137*
information-as-a-service *147*
infrastructure-as-a-service *148*
integration-as-a-service *147*
integration of on-premises and cloud-based resources *156*
management-as-a-service *148*
Microsoft Azure *148*
platform-as-a-service *147*
private cloud *145*
process-as-a-service *147*
public cloud *145*
security-as-a-service *147*
service-oriented architecture (SOA) *137*
software as a service (SaaS) *137*
Sopima *150*
SQL Azure *149*
storage-as-a-service *147*
testing-as-a-service *148*
Windows Azure *149*

References

6Waves Limited. (2011). *AWS Case Study: 6 Waves Limited Rides the AWS Wave*. Retrieved April 3, 2011, from http://aws.amazon.com/solutions/case-studies/6waves/

ActiveHealth Management. (2010). *ActivePHR from Active Health Management*. Retrieved April 3, 2011, from http://www.healthvault.com/details.aspx?PartnerID=activehealth+management&EntryID=activephr&type=application

Ballmer, S. (2008, September 29). *Steve Ballmer on Cloud Computing*. Retrieved April 3, 2011, from http://www.youtube.com/watch?v=ODE8-D-ABb0

Chappell, D. (2010, October). *Introducing the Windows Azure*. Retrieved April 3, 2011, from http://www.microsoft.com/windowsazure/Whitepapers/introducingwindowsazureplatform/default.aspx

Ellison, L. (2008, September 25). *Larry Ellison—What The Hell Is Cloud Computing?* Retrieved April 3, 2011, from http://www.youtube.com/watch?v=0FacYAI6DY0

Gartner, Inc. (2009, June 23). *Gartner Highlights Five Attributes of Cloud Computing*. Retrieved April 3, 2011, from http://www.gartner.com/it/page.jsp?id=1035013

Hewlett-Packard Development Co., L.P. (2011). *HP Testing-as-a-Service*. Retrieved April 3, 2011, from https://h10078.www1.hp.com/cda/hpms/display/main/hpms_content.jsp?zn=bto&cp=1-23%5E42007_4000_100__

Hexaware Technologies. (n.d.). *Enterprise Solutions: CRM*. Retrieved April 3, 2011, from http://www.hexaware.com

Hinchcliffe, D. (2009, June 5). *Eight Ways That Cloud Computing Will Change Business*. Retrieved April 3, 2011, from http://www.zdnet.com/blog/hinchcliffe/eight-ways-that-cloud-computing-will-change-business/488

Linthicum, D. S. (2010). *Cloud Computing and SOA Convergence in Your Enterprise: A Step-by-Step Guide*. Boston, MA: Addison-Wesley Professional.

McAfee, Inc. (2010). *Security-as-a-Service*. Retrieved October 17, 2010, from http://www.mcafee.com/us/products/security-as-a-service/index.aspx

Microsoft. (n.d.). *Focus on Your Application. Not the Infrastructure*. Retrieved September 15, 2010, from http://www.microsoft.com/windowsazure/

Microsoft. (2011). *Microsoft HealthVault*. Retrieved April 3, 2011, from http://msdn.microsoft.com/en-us/healthvault/default.aspx

Microsoft. (2009, November 17). *Sopima: Software Firm Launches Business Contract Service with Lean Staff, Low Investment*. Retrieved April 3, 2011, from http://www.microsoft.com/casestudies/Case_Study_Detail.aspx?CaseStudyID=4000005881

Red Hat, Inc. (2011). *Platform as a Service Solution*. Retrieved April 3, 2011, from http://www.jboss.com/solutions/PaaS/?s_kwcid=TC/8574/platform%20as%20a%20service||S||5856738441

Sopima Oy. (2011). *Home*. Retrieved April 3, 2011, from http://www.sopima.com/

6 SECURITY

Learning Objectives

- Understand organizational security policies, what they are and how they are created.
- Know how ICT security operates at the physical, local authentication (LAN), and Internet levels.
- Be able to develop ICT-related security policies as part of an integrated security system within your organization.
- Understand the importance of virus and malware protection and how that protection fits into an organization's security structure.
- Describe responses to security threats.

This chapter is about infrastructure security. By the end of this chapter, readers should understand the key aspects of ICT security and what is required to create appropriate security policies for their organizations. This chapter covers physical security of data centers and hardware, LAN security (local authentication), and wireless security—the convergent security disciplines that directly affect ICT infrastructure.

Security is defined as "measures taken to guard against espionage or sabotage, crime, attack or escape" (Merriam-Webster, 2011). In the context of ICT infrastructure architecture (see Figure 6-1), according to this definition, security is protection created through structures and processes that decrease the likelihood a malicious individual or organization could do intentional or unintentional harm to an organization's ICT resources. Historically, organizations normally had various security-related units (IT security, police, fraud protection, etc.) that often do not cooperate to maintain seamless organizational security. Today, however, we see more of a convergence of these security-related units through organizations such as Alliance for Enterprise Security Risk Management (AESRM). This chapter will focus on ICT security-related concepts that can be incorporated throughout an organization's security-conscience departments and into an organization's security policies.

ENTERPRISE-WIDE SOFTWARE COMPONENTS Enterprise-wide software, including ERP, e-commerce/e-business, document management, knowledge management, and other specialized applications	**User Components**	Items that directly interface with the user, including workstations, printers, scanners, associated software (especially desktop applications), and specialized applications
	Service Components	Those network parts that facilitate network operations with direct user interface, including printing services, inter/intra office communications (i.e., telephone or fax), network attached storage, database/application servers, security servers and appliances, and VPN technology
	Network Components	Those items/concepts traditionally thought of as networking and telecommunications equipment, including network switching and routing hardware, media, outside vendor interconnects (i.e., T1, T3, DSL), cabinetry, patch panels, and associated items

This figure lists and describes the components of ICT infrastructure architecture from the standpoint of the information technology user. All areas of the Architecture as impacted by security.

FIGURE 6-1 **ICT Infrastructure Architecture**

INTRODUCTION

Security is an issue for organizations no matter what their size. The organization needs to be concerned with the security of its physical assets (e.g., data centers, ICT infrastructure, laptop and desktop computers, etc.) and digital assets (i.e., data, software, and information stored on the physical assets as well as security of cloud-based/virtualized assets). Organizations need to prevent intrusion, as well as detect malicious tampering with assets. These tasks require a unified set of technologies and security policies that work together to protect assets against intrusions (a.k.a. cybercrime).

Cybercrime includes illegal or malicious activities that use personal computers, corporate or personal networks, or the Internet to perpetrate illegal activities, including illegal physical and digital access or alteration. Cybercrime is the fastest-growing form of crime in the world (Joffee, 2010). It is an international phenomenon costing large sums of money. For example, in a 2010 survey of large British companies, it was estimated that hacking attacks cost those companies € 10 billion (euros) per year, about double the cost of 2008 (Palmer, 2010). Vendors such as McAfee are calling for a more proactive strategy for fighting cybercrime. "Cybercriminals prosper because they have very little reason to fear the consequences," said Jeff Green, senior VP of McAfee Labs. McAfee also has called on ICANN (the Internet Corporation for Assigned Numbers and Names) to take a stronger stance against cybercrime (Schwartz, 2010). All of which comes down to the fact that the business systems analyst must be cognizant of the threats against corporate assets, as well as measures and policies to protect those assets. This chapter will give the reader an overview of those technologies and policies necessary to combat the threat of cybercrime.

If the statistics are to be believed, virtually all organizations will be hit by some type of cybercrime. Therefore, all organizations should have policies and technologies for protecting their assets as well as policies and technologies for responding to attacks. Organizations need to understand what should be protected and decide on what policies and technologies to put into place to effectuate that protection. Figure 6-2 illustrates the cyclic flow in which many organizations deal with security. These steps include:

- **Create/Update Policies.** The organization must have a systematic way to determine where it is vulnerable to cyber attack and create policies that thwart those attacks.
- **Policy Documents.** Organizations must create and maintain policy documents that describe all aspects of security from acceptable use policies, through virus and malware protection, to ICT credentials. These policy documents must describe the technologies and personnel needed to implement the policies.
- **Implement Policies.** It is essential that the policy documents detail who is responsible for policy and technology implementation of thwarting cyber attacks.
- **Surveillance.** After policies are created and technology is implemented, it is essential that those individual(s) and department(s) in the organization responsible for monitoring compliance actually do so.
- **Response to Attack.** The individuals or department responsible for responding to a cyber attack must be identified in the policy documents as well as specific steps that should be taken by the response team.
- **Post Attack.** Periodically or when an attack occurs, the response team should document the attack and review policies and technologies to see if the likelihood of subsequent attack can be reduced.

VIGNETTE BOX 6-1

HealthyWay's Security Policies

HealthyWay HMO needs to have strong security policies and technologies to guarantee the integrity of its data and to protect patient privacy. Therefore, HealthyWay must have security personnel in place for implementing those policies and technologies, ensuring that the correct surveillance and response occur.

FIGURE 6-2 Policies/Implementation/Respond Cycle

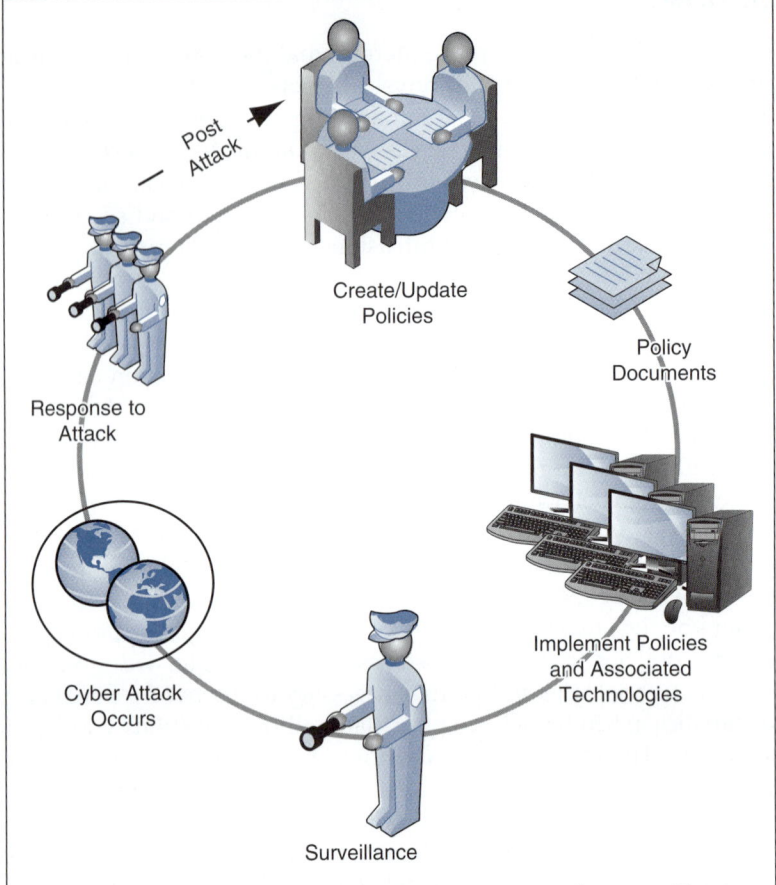

All organizations should attempt to maintain a secure environment. The way an organization must prepare policies and technologies that protect its ICT assets, implement those policies and technologies, and have policies in place to deal with threats when they occur follows a cyclic format.

TYPES OF ATTACKS AND THREATS

Before discussing technologies and policies to thwart threats, it is necessary that the types of threats are understood. This section will review the typical types of attacks and threats that an organization may encounter and the technologies that can be put in place to prevent them. Cyber attacks are of three major types: (1) attacks against physical assets, (2) attacks by/against software that disrupt operations, and (3) attacks against data. Crossover of attacks often occurs—for example, a virus (software) may be aimed at disrupting operations by destroying data.

System-Fault-Risk Framework

Following on the work of Ye, Newman, and Farley (2005), which describes the **System-Fault-Risk (SFR) framework**, a cyber attack and its effects are called an incident. That incident, then, is composed of a threat and the actual attack. Those threats and attacks have a cause and effect. The incident, threat, attack, cause, and effect are defined by the following characteristics:

- **Objective.** The attacker's objective in carrying out the cyber attack could be to spy, perpetrate crimes with financial objectives, cyberterrorism, corporate rivalry, cracking, vandalism, etc.
- **Propagation.** The cybercrime could be spread by humans or it could be spread autonomously by software.

- **Attack Origin.** The cybercrime could be from a local machine or it could be remote to the hardware/software being attacked.
- **Action.** Attacks use a number of activities to accomplish their objectives, including probing, scanning, flooding, data modification, etc.
- **Vulnerability.** Cyber attacks are perpetrated against ICT infrastructure with a misconfiguration or a specification/design flaw that leaves it open to potential attack.
- **Asset.** The resource under attack can be physical or digital, including hardware, software, business processes, data/information, or users.
- **State Effects.** A cybercrime affects the state of an asset, including its availability, integrity, and confidentiality. It is also possible that a cyber attack would collect information unobtrusively (e.g., spying) rather than affect the state of any asset.
- **Performance Effects.** Cybercrime can affect the performance of ICT assets, including the speed, accuracy, and precision of business processes.

The interplay between the incident, threat, attack, cause, and effect can be seen in Figure 6-3. When analyzing ICT infrastructure or security risk, the SFR framework posits a good starting place. By analyzing these areas the business systems analyst will have a thorough idea of the impact of cybercrime on his or her organization.

Whether creating policies and implementing technologies to prevent cybercrime, or dealing with an incident that has already occurred, it is helpful to classify those incidents using the SFR (or some other) framework. Examples of classification using the SFR framework can be seen in Figure 6-4. This documentation can be used to create policies and craft technologies to thwart future attacks.

Types of Attacks

As you can see from the SFR framework, cyber attacks can be understood from a number of vantage points. It is important to understand, first of all, the reason why the attack was perpetrated (sometimes it's "just because," with no real apparent reason). If the business systems analyst can determine why the attack was perpetrated, he or she has a better chance of creating policies and implementing technologies that will thwart future attacks.

In the time it takes you to read this chapter, new types of cyber attacks will be perpetrated; some may build on existing cyber attack technologies and others will be brand new. Whenever new software or hardware is created, new vulnerabilities will also be created, and types of cyber attacks are only limited by the human imagination. Therefore, this chapter can only be representative of the types of attacks that exist today. All organizations must be diligent in keeping abreast of cybercrime and its organizational and societal impact.

Cyber attacks are always against people, whatever the objective—the outcome is that people are affected by the attack. Cyber criminals may think that they are just affecting hardware or software, but any attack that causes a system to operate differently than intended will affect people. Whether it's spying to get credit card information or flooding a server so it stops accepting requests from users, people are affected. Some specific attacks, such as social engineering, directly affect or use people; however, even attacks that target only technology eventually impact people. (Securing Our eCity, n.d.). In the remainder of this section, various types of cyber attacks will be described.

VIGNETTE BOX 6-2

SFR Implementation

HealthyWay should implement a framework like SFR to be sure its analysis and response to threats cover the necessary areas of its physical and digital assets.

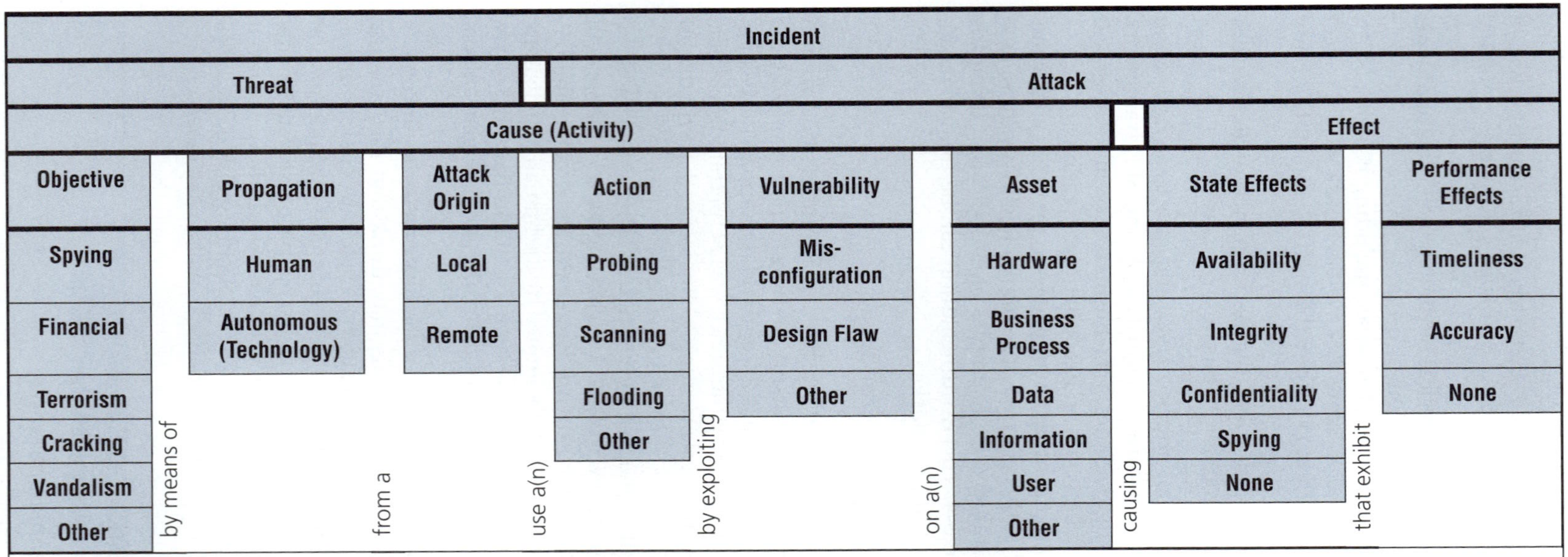

FIGURE 6-3 Adapted SFR Framework

A cybercrime is defined as an incident with threats, attacks, causes, and effects.

Incident = Threat (by means of) + Cause (Activity) [from a (Attack Origin) use a(n) (Action) by exploiting (Vulnerability)] + Attack (on a(n) Asset causing) + Effect (that exhibit)

- **Threat — Objective**: Spying, Financial, Terrorism, Cracking, Vandalism, Other
- **Threat — Propagation**: Human, Autonomous (Technology)
- **Cause — Attack Origin**: Local, Remote
- **Cause — Action**: Probing, Scanning, Flooding, Other
- **Cause — Vulnerability**: Misconfiguration, Design Flaw, Other
- **Attack — Asset**: Hardware, Business Process, Data, Information, User, Other
- **Effect — State Effects**: Availability, Integrity, Confidentiality, Spying, None
- **Effect — Performance Effects**: Timeliness, Accuracy, None

164

Attack Name	Objective	Propagation	Attack Origin	Action	Vulnerability	Asset	State Effect	Performance Effect	Action/Remedy/Comments
Worm	Cracking	Autonomous	Remote	Other	Design Flaw	Hardware (Network)	Availability and Integrity	Accuracy	Complete as appropriate for your organization
Virus	Financial	Human	Local	Scanning	Misconfiguration	Hardware (Servers)	None	None	Copy credit card account records to perpetrate a crime

This table shows how the SFR framework might be used to document an attack (potential or real). This information can be used to craft policies and select technologies to thwart attempts of the same or similar cyber attacks.

FIGURE 6-4 Sample SFR Attack Documentation

PHYSICAL-FOCUSED ATTACKS

Numerous physical attacks can be perpetrated against physical assets. These acts include outright terrorism and vandalism (in this context we are referring to attacks that damage or deface physical assets). Vandalism attacks have the goal of destroying or defacing physical property, usually with little or no intention of disrupting technology-based services or causing fear. However, even though that is not the intention, it is often the outcome.

In terrorism, the physical attacks are perpetrated to "bring about terror." In other words, physical assets are attacked in order to evoke fear in people who use the physical assets and potentially send a message through the attack. In the world we see acts of terrorism through suicide bombers or atrocities like the 9/11 attacks on the World Trade Towers. In the world of technology and the Internet, we see acts of terrorism through disabling, disruption, or destruction of technology (e.g., Internet hardware, data centers, electrical grid, etc.) for the purpose of furthering a political or personal agenda, or "just because."

Protecting physical assets of an organization requires the unified efforts of the entire organization. Although it is true that the IT department must be involved in protecting technology assets, they are but one group. Depending on the size of the organization, other departments need to be included: security (e.g., police or other security-related group), plant management (e.g., those involved with maintaining the physical plant of an organization), and senior/operational management, to name a few. Policies regarding how and when hardware can leave your facility, who gets access to data centers and associated locations, and what security systems are put in place to protect assets (even whether food and drink can be brought into certain locations) are all related to the physical security of an organizations assets.

TECHNOLOGY-FOCUSED CYBER ATTACKS

Attacks that focus on the technology through the Internet abound. Those attacks are normally launched via e-mail or web sites and often require that users do something that allows the attack, whether it's lending someone a flash drive, opening an e-mail, or installing software. The major types of these attacks are discussed in this section.

Malware **Malware** is short for "malicious software," which includes viruses, Trojan horses, worms, and any other software designed to attack an organization's or person's

---

VIGNETTE BOX 6-3

Physical Attacks

HealthyWay needs to be sure its security approach covers physical attacks. These attacks can be just as devastating as cyber attacks. Physical security of its assets (e.g., buildings, data centers, etc.) is just as important as cyber security.

> **VIGNETTE BOX 6-4**
>
> **Types of Attacks**
>
> HealthyWay will be open to each type of cyber attack. Once an organization's personnel use the Internet to communicate, the organization is open to cyber attacks.

technology. Because malware encompasses all software-based attacks, it is safe to say that all companies will experience one or more malware attacks each year.

Sometimes malware is designed to use a specific vulnerability or design flaw in software or hardware. When that occurs, vendors will usually issue a patch (a small program to update the software or hardware) to correct the vulnerability or design flaw. When malware attacks a vulnerability or a design flaw before the patch can be issued it is called a **zero-day attack**.

Malware can be designed so that it does not require a vulnerability or design flaw. This type of malware, referred to as universal malware, is generally delivered via an e-mail (by simply opening the e-mail) or a web site by simply visiting it.

Adware Technically, **adware** is any software that automatically displays advertisements to your computer. The purpose of adware is normally to generate revenue for a software author, but since it is often packaged with spyware and other software that invades the privacy of the user, it has become known as a type of cyber attack.

Spyware **Spyware** is software that collects information about the user and transmits that information to a third party without the user's knowledge or consent. The information collected can be anything from user keystrokes to Internet surfing habits. A user can install a number of free proprietary software solutions on his or her computer to detect and remove spyware.

Trojan Horse A **Trojan horse** is software that appears to perform a desirable function but in reality allows unauthorized access to a user's computer by the creator of the software. Adware is often delivered via a Trojan horse. For example, suppose you receive an e-mail promising that when you click a certain link your computer will be scanned for malware. However, in order to do the scan the web site needs to install software on your computer. Let's say you allow the web site to install the scanning software, only to find out that once installed the software not only does the scan but forces advertisements for virus scanners on your monitor and initiates strange network activity. Eventually you find out that an unauthorized individual has accessed your computer via a Trojan horse. One famous Trojan horse was named Back Orifice and, according to the Symantec's Security Response web site (Symantec.com, 1999), it allowed the perpetrator to execute programs, record key strokes, access files, and restart an infected computer.

Viruses A **virus** is malicious software that can replicate itself and is often malicious code that attaches itself to existing legitimate software on a computer system, thus modifying the files on the system. Over the past 30 years we have seen viruses such as Elk Cloner that attached itself to Apple Dos 3.3, ©Brian that attached itself to software to protect its author's intellectual property, and various macro viruses that attached themselves to products such as Microsoft Word and Excel.

Many types of malicious software are erroneously called viruses, like malware or spyware, but they are not viruses because they cannot replicate themselves. In order to be classified as a virus, software must be able to autonomously spread itself from one computer to another in executable code. Viruses were a problem long before computers were networked. Today however, with the prevalence of networks, viruses can replicate themselves over the network using shared file systems and storage with relative ease.

Viruses are created to achieve any number of objectives. Some viruses are created to slow performance, others to destroy data, and some do nothing but replicate themselves. Viruses may have symptoms noticeable to the user, like slowing down the user's computer, while others have no noticeable effects at all. The function of the virus is determined by its author and the objective may be to just disrupt network or computer operations. The key distinction between a virus and other malware is the virus's ability to autonomously self-replicate.

Viruses use a number of strategies to infect a network or computer. In order to infect its host and replicate itself, the virus must have access to the system so it can execute code, write to memory, and attach itself to files. Often, a virus only replicates itself or performs a designated malicious task when its host application is executed. For example, suppose Microsoft Excel is infected with a virus—somehow malicious code attaches itself to the Excel executable file. When the user executes Excel the malicious code may simultaneously execute, do its job (whatever that is), and replicate itself (e.g., by attaching itself to the saved Excel file that is then e-mailed to another user). In this example, Excel is the vector used to infect the computer and replicate the virus. Possible vectors and infection strategies include the following:

- **Executable Files.** A virus may attach itself to an executable file and when that file is run, the virus will execute, perhaps go unnoticed, and replicate itself to another user.
- **Master Boot Record.** The Master Boot Record (MBR) is the first thing executed when you turn on a computer; the MBR is what defines your computer hard drive and causes the operating system to execute. A virus can imbed itself in the MBR and thus is very difficult to eradicate.
- **General Purpose Scripting.** A virus may infect a general purpose script file such as batch files in MS-DOS or shell script files in Unix.
- **System Specific Scripting.** Files like autorun.inf that are used by Microsoft Windows to automatically start applications on USB devices or CDs can be infected by a virus.
- **Network Device Infection.** With the increasing functionality and complexity of network devices comes more dynamically written memory that can be infected; an example might be the virus infection of the routing tables on a router.

In addition to these ways in which a virus can infect a computer or a network, viruses can also exploit software bugs and allow the virus to use system resources or damage data. It falls to the software designer to minimize those bugs so the number of potential exploits can be minimized. Software designers will often distribute patches to eliminate known bugs and minimize virus and other cyber attacks. Any good cyber attack prevention policy will include language regarding patch installation and maintenance.

Worm   A computer **worm**, like a virus, is self-replicating. The major difference is that a worm does not attach itself to another program on the host computer but is a standalone program that depends on security shortcomings of the target computer. Worms have been created with good and bad intent. Xerox PARC and Microsoft have both tried to create benevolent worms that would deliver patches to host computers using the security vulnerability they intended to patch. These patches were never well received because they consumed network bandwidth and often rebooted user systems during the course of the patch, all without the consent of the user. Worms are generally regarded as malware no matter their intent.

Many worms are created just to spread. They do not attempt to alter the systems they are using to spread themselves. One such worm that had devastating results was the Morris Worm, written in 1988. The worm was written as an intellectual exercise to determine the size of the Internet. However, that worm was able to replicate itself at such a rate that it made many computers unusable because of the processor cycles it used. The end result of the Morris Worm was to turn a harmless intellectual exercise into a powerful denial-of-service cyber attack. The Morris Worm had no payload, but other worms do.

When a worm has a payload, it carries code designed to do more than replicate itself. The purpose of the payload depends on the objective of the worm. The payload may delete files on the host system, send e-mail to everyone in the computer's address book, or install a backdoor onto the host computer that allows the worm author to gain access to the computer. It is not uncommon for networks of computers to be exploited to allow spammers to send out their spam via the host infected with the worm.

Denial-of-Service (DoS) and Distributed Denial-of-Service (DDoS) Denial-of-service (DoS) cyber attacks originate from a single source. The objective of a DoS attack is to overwhelm the target system, thereby blocking it or a web site hosted on it from receiving or responding to requests from legitimate users. It prevents the target system from exchanging data with other systems or using the Internet. A variant of the DoS attack is the **distributed denial-of-service attack (DDoS)** cyber attack. A DDoS attack originates from a number of coordinated sources, rather than from a single source. A DDoS attack often makes use of worms to spread its payload to various systems that will then simultaneously attack and overwhelm the target system.

Logic Bombs When a programmer inserts code into software that is triggered when certain criteria are met, a **logic bomb** is created. This type of cyber attack comes from inside the organization responsible for designing the software. The logic bomb can be something as trivial as a message that occurs when the right conditions are met, or as devastating as deleting files. What sets a logic bomb apart from other malware and cyber attacks is that it is created by a programmer as part of a legitimate application, and is activated usually by some external event. For example, software that displays a message every Friday the 13th, or the banking software that deposits the rounded pennies on all transactions into a designated account whenever the transaction results in fractional penny transactions (this is presumed to be an urban myth) are logic bombs.

Sniffer A **sniffer** is also known as a packer sniffer. The sniffer intercepts data in IP packets and examines each packet in search of the desired information. Sniffers have legitimate uses, such as debugging network problems. But sniffers also have more nefarious uses like scanning packets that are transmitted as clear text in an attempt to find information such as passwords or other sensitive data.

HUMAN-FOCUSED CYBER ATTACKS

All cyber attacks affect people in some way, as indicated in the SFR framework. Still, a few cyber attacks use technology to directly impact people. These types of attacks are largely based on social engineering and can result in identity theft.

Social Engineering **Social engineering** refers to a cyber attack that manipulates people to divulge confidential information rather than using techniques such as worms, viruses, or scanning to gain access to that information. Basically, social engineering is a fancy name for tricking people into doing what you want them to do. E-mail with a fraudulent link is an attempt at social engineering. For example, an e-mail that asks you to go to a web site and verify banking details may be an attempt to manipulate the unwitting user into divulging personal banking details to a nefarious third party. Another example would be manipulating a user into giving his or her username and password to a secure web site.

Phishing and Vishing In the form of social engineering known as **phishing**, the user receives an e-mail that appears to come from a legitimate business. The e-mail requests verification of some confidential information and warns of some undesirable consequences if the request is not followed (e.g., your account will be closed in 10 days if you do not respond). **Vishing** is a method of phishing that specifically uses voice-over-Internet Protocols (VoIP) and exploits call center software.

VIGNETTE BOX 6-5

Human-Focused Attacks

Having policies and procedures that protect the organization from human-focused attacks is essential for HealthyWay. Education of personnel is often the best defense against human-focused cyber attacks, and HealthyWay should have policies, practices, and technologies in place to ensure that the organization's personnel are educated and protected.

Spam **Spam** is unsolicited commercial e-mail and is probably the most annoying type of cyber attack or malware. Users' e-mail inboxes are flooded with e-mail that they have no interest in receiving. Almost half of all e-mails are reported as unsolicited (Spamlaws.com, 2009). In fact, spam is so troublesome that many countries have created laws that make unsolicited e-mails illegal.

Identity Theft When a cyber attacker collects enough information about the identity of another and uses it, that attacker has stolen the target's identity—in other words, he or she has perpetrated **identity theft**. The stolen information can include the target person's name, Social Security number, bank account information, credit card numbers, and/or date of birth. When someone with less-than-honorable intentions has collected enough information about another individual, the identity thief can engage in serious crimes such as opening fraudulent credit cards or bank accounts. Cases of someone fraudulently buying property using another's identity have even been reported.

Human Break-Ins (Hacking) Another form of human-centered cyber attack is **hacking**. It is not human-centered in the sense that it necessarily focuses on directly affecting human behavior, but rather it is human-centered because it is interactively performed by a person, not autonomously by software as is done by malware. Hackers (those performing the hacking) are people committed to circumventing computer security. There are black hat hackers who break into a computer via a network or the Internet in order to gain access or do damage to the target computer, white hat hackers who debug or repair vulnerabilities, and grey hat hackers that are morally ambiguous. The bottom line is that any unauthorized access to a computer or a network is a crime.

A subculture within the hacking community, known as **script kiddies**, includes people who practice hacking by using scripts or software written by other people and do not precisely know how the script or software works.

EXPLOITS

The purpose of some attacks is to capture data and allow potential cyber attackers to learn about vulnerabilities. This activity includes exploit tools, wardriving, and hacking. Make no mistake, these are cyber attacks. They often do not leave any trace of the attack, but rather gain information to be used in future, more damaging attacks.

Exploit Tools Although not officially classified as a cyber attack, **exploit tools** are publicly available software tools that allow would-be intruders to determine the vulnerabilities of a computer system or network. Examples include vulnerability scanners such as NMAP or Firestorm, which are a network intrusion detection system. Many tools can be used to assist potential intruders in finding the vulnerabilities in systems.

Wardriving **Wardriving** is a method of gaining entry into wireless computer networks using a remote device such as a PDA or a laptop. It involves patrolling locations to gain access. A commonly discussed example in the late 1980s was the cyber attacker who would drive or walk by a department or grocery store with a wireless device to attempt to gain access to the stores wireless cash registers. The cyber attacker's hope was to capture credit card numbers transmitted in clear text.

Methods of Delivery

Cyber attacks can be delivered in a number of ways. They can be as simple as people who directly manipulate the behavior of others as in social engineering, or as complex as a distributed denial-of-service or large-scale virus attack. Attacks can come via e-mail in the form of spam or phishing, or be delivered on media used on a computer. It is possible to insert a USB flash drive into a computer and unknowingly propagate a virus onto that computer. The point is that it is important to know the source of any e-mail, message, file, website or device you access via your computer.

STOPPING CYBER ATTACKS

Security is about stopping cyber attacks and, if they happen, about responding to them appropriately. Below, ways to stop cyber attacks are introduced, as well as what to do in case an attack occurs. Two models introduced earlier in the text will be used: Figure 6-2 provides the basis for policy creation and implementation, and Figure 6-3 is used for crafting a response to a cyber attack. First, we review the impact of good planning and policies on thwarting cyber attacks.

Planning and Policies

Organizations should plan for and have strong policies that create a cyber defense fabric to protect them from cyber attackers. A top-to-bottom commitment to creating, implementing, and carrying out security policies is critical, whether the security function resides within the IT department or is a coordinated effort between a number of departments within the organization. Some type of security statement, memo, or manifesto from senior management will indicate their commitment to the security policies created by the organization's security function. A security statement indicates what technologies will be put in place and what policies will be created to protect the physical and digital assets of the organization. The Certified Information Systems Security Professional (CISSP) framework specifies several domains/categories within ICT security policy ((ISC)^2, 2011):

- Access Control
- Application Development Security
- Cryptography
- Information Security Governance and Risk Management
- Legal, Regulations, Investigations, and Compliance
- Operations Security
- Physical (Environmental) Security
- Security Architecture and Design
- Telecommunications and Network Security

Within these categories, appropriate polices and technologies can be put into place to protect the assets of the organization. Planning and policies within these areas is essential.

All digital assets exist on physical assets (technology). Even when processes or files are moved into a cloud environment, someone must mind the physical technology. The physical security considerations should include policies about where technology is stored and who gets access to it, who is allowed to "jack into" the organization's network, who is allowed to take technology off site, and how the physical state of the organization's technology will be audited. All policies must include mechanisms for gaining permission and technology to engage in an activity that is "at odds" or varies from the policy (e.g., your organization prevents USB devices from be inserted into your computers, but you have a legitimate reason to do so and need permission/access).

Access Control

Access control is common. A locked door, an ATM PIN, and a username/password all control access to resources. **Access control** protects confidential, important, or secure information. It also is used to control access to network and other specific resources.

VIGNETTE BOX 6-6

CISSP

In an organization like HealthyWay, it is important to have trained staff members who understand the various aspects of cyber security. Industry certifications such as the CISSP are good indicators of an individual's understanding of security policies and technologies. It is important to have personnel who are knowledgeable and can recommend the correct security measures for an organization.

ICT access control is implemented through credentials that identify the user. Simple credential mechanisms include usernames and passwords. Smart cards, fingerprint scanners, or biometric locks provide more sophisticated access controls. Whatever the credential mechanism, access controls allow the security function within an organization to maintain access control lists (ACLs) that tie the credentials to network devices to which the user can have varying levels of access.

Access control is done through some method of authentication; these methods are usually grouped into (1) things that you know, (2) things that you are, and (3) things that you have. *Things that you know* include usernames and passwords, personal identification numbers (PINs), and challenge questions. *Things that you are* include your fingerprint, voice, or retinal characteristics; and *things that you have* include security devices (tokens), pass cards, or smart cards. A large number of authentication methods can be used. *Things that you know* depend on the user to keep the things that they know secret or hidden. *Things that you are* depend on no one being able to replicate your personal characteristics. *Things that you have* depend on the user being able to keep possession of the items. The strongest authentication is when all three types of authentication methods are combined so a user must have a security token, know a password or the answer to a challenge question, and has the right physical (biometric) characteristics. Note that the length and complexity of *things that you know* (e.g., PINs, passwords, challenge phrases, etc.) are directly proportional to their ability to protect corporate assets.

Once access is grant through the selected methods (know, have, are), then the type of access to the desired resource can be determined. Three types of access are typically granted: read, write, and read/write. Operating systems may provide greater granularity of access—for example "a specific user can add or delete files"—but in the end, access is determined to be read, write, or read/write. Operating systems also often extend access to *List Directory content*, *Add Files*, *Delete Files*, or *Execute*. However, these are variations or extensions of basic read/write access.

Encryption

Another way to control access to information is through encryption. Encryption can protect data being transferred over a network or stored on a particular technology, safeguarding the confidentiality of information. However, encryption does not guarantee the authenticity of a message (i.e., who sent it). Other techniques, such as digital signatures, are needed for that.

Encryption changes the information, using some type of algorithm, into a form that is unintelligible to anyone who does not possess the algorithm. The information can be stored on a hard disk or transmitted over a network. The algorithm, called a cipher, is software and some type of key possessed by the person or system encrypting the information. The result is referred to as **ciphertext**—that is, information that has been processed through a cipher to create the ciphertext. The information can then be decrypted using the ciphertext as input into the appropriate algorithm/key combination to recreate the initial information. An example is shown in Figure 6-5.

KEYS

Keys are information needed by an encryption algorithm (cipher). These parameters are used to transform plain text into ciphertext, and conversely from ciphertext into plain text. Keys are also used in digital signatures. Keys are bits of information that are meant to be kept secret. If a key is found out, it can be used to decrypt information inappropriately. Keys are of a specific length, measured in bits, and generally the longer

---

VIGNETTE BOX 6-7

Certificate Authorities

If HealthyWay wants to use encryption for its web site or e-mail, it will probably have to purchase a certificate from a certificate authority (e.g., VeriSign, Go Daddy, Comodo).

FIGURE 6-5 Overview of Encryption

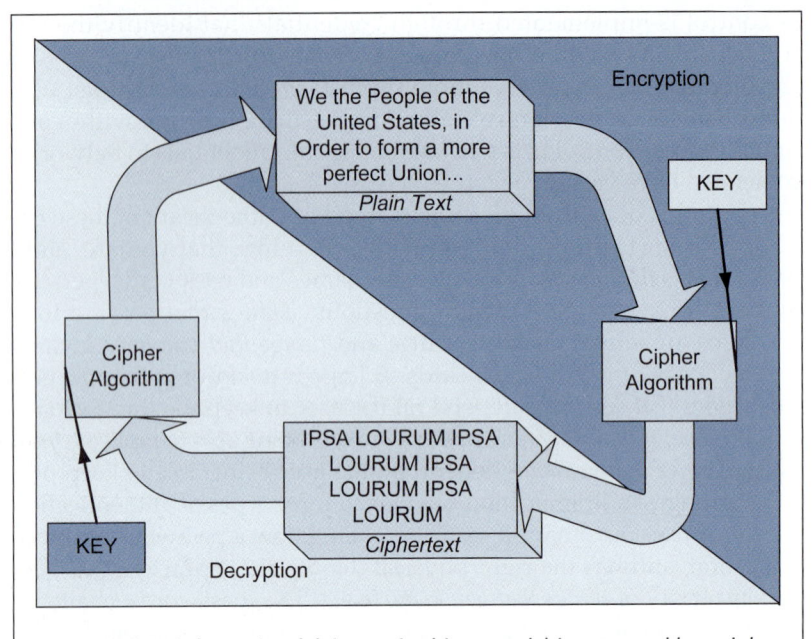

In encryption, information (plain text in this example) is processed by a cipher algorithm and turned into ciphertext. A key is used by the cipher to encrypt the information. The ciphertext is decrypted by an algorithm using a key. The ciphertext and key are used as input to the algorithm, and the original information is recreated. The process of encryption and decryption protects information.

the key, the stronger the encryption. For example, an encryption algorithm that uses a 256-bit key is considerably stronger than an algorithm that uses a 128-bit key, because a brute force attack on a 128-bit key algorithm would yield 16,384 combinations, while an attack on a 256-bit key algorithm would yield 65,536 combinations, or 4 times the key combinations.

The two types of key algorithms are symmetric key algorithms and asymmetric key algorithms. Symmetric key algorithms use the same key to encrypt and decrypt information, while asymmetric key algorithms use one key for encryption and another for decryption. Symmetric key algorithms require that the individual encrypting the information and the individual decrypting both have the key. Asymmetric key algorithms allow for anyone to have a public key so they can decrypt data, and the individual wishing to encrypt the data can have a private key so only they can encrypt the data. Symmetric key encryption is simpler, but depends on one single sharable, losable, possibly easily known key, whereas asymmetric encryption is much stronger but complex and potentially costly. All of that said, symmetric key encryption is the norm for securing Internet communications; however, many software packages and vendors have implemented asymmetric key algorithms due to their potential to protect confidential information.

SSL/TLS

Transport Layer Security (TLS), and its predecessor **Secure Sockets Layer (SSL)**, are cryptographic protocols that provide secure communications over the Internet. TLS and SSL provide encryption to the layers (see the TCP/IP-OSI hybrid model in Unit 1) above the transport layer. TLS is the IETF protocol and uses a symmetric key algorithm (http://tools.ietf.org/html/rfc5246). The IETF states that the TLS protocol has two basic properties:

1. The connection is private. Symmetric cryptography is used for data encryption using protocols such as Data Encryption Standard (DES) or RC4. The keys for this symmetric encryption are generated uniquely for each connection and are based on a secret negotiated by another protocol (such as the TLS Handshake Protocol).

In other words, TLS uses a private connection and symmetric cryptography based on a number of encryption standards.

2. The connection is reliable. Message transport includes message integrity providing error checking and reliability. Secure hash functions are used to accomplish this reliability (http://datatracker.ietf.org/doc/rfc2246/?include_text=1).

TLS provides private, reliable connections between two hosts. The most frequent way users will encounter the TLS protocol is through an HTTPS:\\ call in their web browser.

The ITEF goes on to say that TLS provides connection security that has three basic properties:

1. TLS has a method to authenticate a host's identity. Even though TLS uses symmetric cryptography, the host's identity can be authenticated using asymmetric, or public key, cryptography. This authentication is optional, but is generally required for at least one of the peers.
2. The negotiation of the symmetric key is secure. It is negotiated by the hosts and is unavailable to eavesdroppers, and for any authenticated connection the key cannot be obtained, even by an attacker who can place himself in the middle of the connection.
3. The negotiation is reliable. No attacker can modify the negotiation communication without being detected by the parties to the communication.

Using all of the properties just described (reliability, authentication, key security, and connection security/privacy), TLS has four goals:

1. **Cryptographic Security:** TLS provides secure connection between two hosts.
2. **Interoperability:** TLS provides transparency in that two programmers writing code that uses TLS do not need to know each other's code, just that it is TLS compliant.
3. **Extensibility:** TLS seeks to provide a framework into which new public key and encryption methods can be incorporated as necessary.
4. **Relative Efficiency:** TLS is designed to reduce the amount of network activity required to accomplish the properties listed above.

This example of TLS handshaking will describe how the protocol works and its security features. A simple example of a secure session using TLS proceeds as follows:

- **Negotiation Phase:** The originating host (i.e., client) sends a message to the receiving host (i.e., server) specifying the highest-level TLS protocol version it supports, a list of suggested authentication methods encryption message authentication code, and compression algorithms. The server responds with the selected set of algorithms. If the algorithms require a certificate, it is also sent by the server. The server will also send a DONE message to indicate that the handshaking negotiation is complete. The client and server then together communicate to create a unique secret symmetric key.
- **Client Change Cipher Specification Phase:** The client sends a message to the server telling it that everything from now on will be encrypted and that all future messages will be authenticated. The client also sends a FINISH message. The server will attempt to decrypt the authentication message, and if the decryption fails the connection will be shut down.
- **Server Change Cipher Specification Phase:** The server sends a message to the client telling it that everything from now on will be encrypted and that all future messages will be authenticated. The server also sends a FINISH message. The client will attempt to decrypt the authentication message, and if the decryption fails the connection will be shut down.
- **Application Phase:** After the client and server have successfully decrypted the FINISH messages and no connections were shut down, the connection then enters the application phase. This means that the Handshake and Client/Server Change Cipher Specification phases were completed successfully. Now the application (typically a web browser) can exchange authenticated and encrypted messages between the client server.

Figure 6-6 depicts the simple TLS session.

FIGURE 6-6
TLS Descrpition

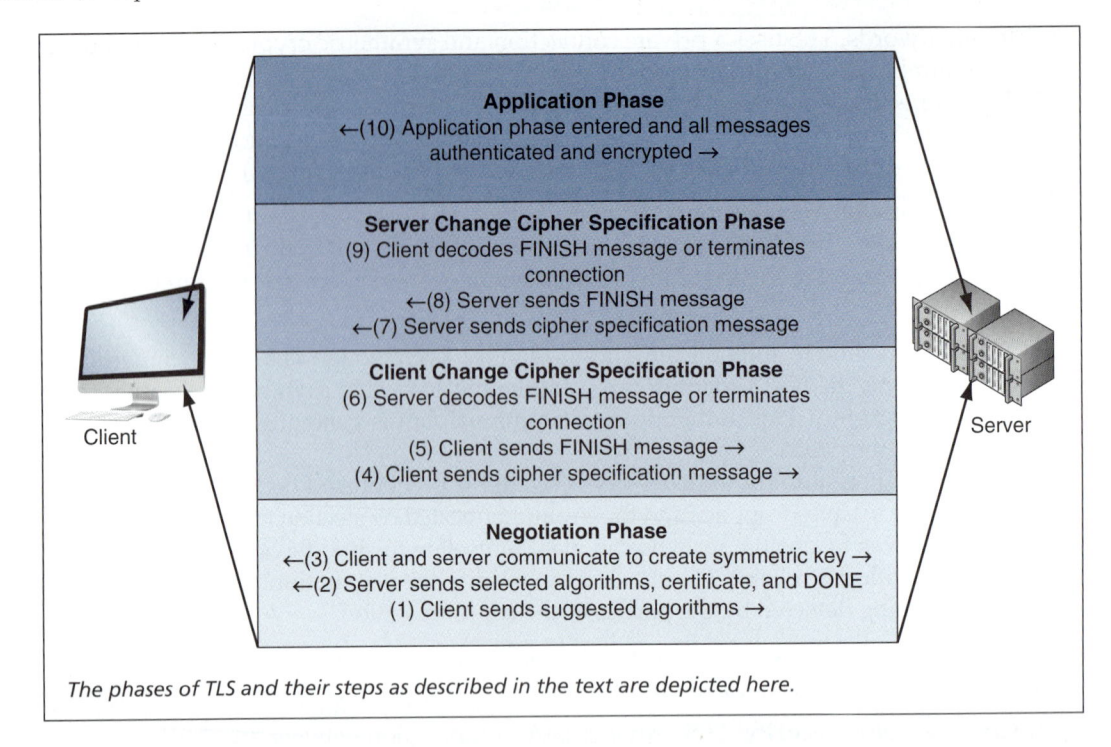

Application Phase
←(10) Application phase entered and all messages authenticated and encrypted →

Server Change Cipher Specification Phase
(9) Client decodes FINISH message or terminates connection
←(8) Server sends FINISH message
←(7) Server sends cipher specification message

Client Change Cipher Specification Phase
(6) Server decodes FINISH message or terminates connection
(5) Client sends FINISH message →
(4) Client sends cipher specification message →

Negotiation Phase
←(3) Client and server communicate to create symmetric key →
←(2) Server sends selected algorithms, certificate, and DONE
(1) Client sends suggested algorithms →

Client   Server

The phases of TLS and their steps as described in the text are depicted here.

TLS is one method of protecting data during transmission across the infrastructure. TLS protects all data at the transport layer and above, meaning that transport and application layer data are protected from a cyber attack. The authentication mode of TLS also protects an open connection between two hosts from another party interjecting itself within the connection stream to capture information or injecting/modifying data in the stream.

Client Host Solutions

The client host is a logical place to defend against many cyber attacks. The most common ways for a cyber attack on a client host to occur are through the web browser and e-mail. TLS was just discussed as a way to protect browser communications; next we will discuss e-mail. E-mail is potentially the most common way to communicate in business today, even outpacing telephone and traditional mail services (Edwards, 2008). As such, any sensitive information transmitted via e-mail needs protection. E-mail is often bombarded with spam or used as a mechanism for delivery of viruses and malware. Concern for the integrity of e-mail and any attachments has led software and hardware designers to develop a number of ways to protect against viruses, phishing schemes, spam, and other attacks.

Corporate client hosts often have a number of software applications installed to protect network communication. The most well-known application is probably virus protection software; however, a number of functions are delivered through e-mail

---

VIGNETTE BOX 6-8

Security Suite

Undoubtedly, HealthyWay will need to install a suite of desktop security software on its client hosts. These programs will provide a line of defense against cyber attack for HealthyWay's client hosts and, ultimately, the network and its servers.

clients and security suites offered by software vendors (e.g., McAfee, Norton) and include such functionality as:

- **Client Security:** Virtually all major e-mail clients now offer security settings, anti-spam tools, phishing filters, and other features designed to snare and isolate dangerous messages before they can inflict harm. E-mail users should investigate all of these features and use them as their first line of defense.
- **Client Software Firewall:** A client-side software firewall can bolster e-mail security by filtering out malware-laden attachments and other types of unwanted material that don't meet preconfigured rules. Large corporations often have a number of policies that indicate how often the user is notified of spam that has been captured, what types of e-mails are captured as spam, and other security information.
- **Encryption:** Rendering messages indecipherable to unauthorized recipients is a popular way of protecting outbound e-mails. Encryption is imperfect, slow, and with enough time can be broken. Encryption algorithms use processor speed and memory, and users can lose or forget passwords. It is possible to use certificates or digital IDs to store ciphers used during encryption and decryption of data, but then the IDs and certificates require protection from prying eyes.
- **Anti-Virus Tools:** A number of software tools offer anti-virus protection. These tools need to be configured to do "on-access" scanning and/or periodic disk and memory scans. These software tools generally do a good job of spotting and removing viruses, worms, and Trojan horses from incoming e-mail messages or when a user visits a web site. However, new malware is being created every day, and it is important that the software's signature files are updated often so that new cyber attack attempts can be identified.
- **Anti-Spam Filters:** A well-configured spam filter can differentiate between legitimate e-mail and spam, freeing a user's inbox from mounds of digital debris. A drawback to this technology is that a poorly configured spam filter, or one that has not been properly tuned, will remove a certain number of legitimate e-mails from a user's view while letting some spam pass through to the user's inbox. Improved spam-recognition technologies are making spam filters more accurate—most vendors now promise 99 percent-plus accuracy rates—but even the best spam filter will incorrectly categorize at least some e-mails. Using an anti-span filter means that users will need to check e-mail caught by the filter periodically so they can ascertain whether legitimate e-mails are being caught.
- **Digital Signatures:** Digital signatures are used in e-mails and other digital documents. They employ a type of asymmetric cryptography, using both a public key and private key. Digital signatures also can provide nonrepudiation (proof of the integrity and origin of a message), meaning that the signer cannot say he or she did not sign the e-mail/document as long as the signer's private key remains secret. Digital signature algorithms include RSA-based schemes, DSA, and ElGamal. The processes of document signing and verification are described in Figure 6-7.

Network Solutions

First and foremost in network security is identity management and authentication, described earlier as a Directory Server. Those functions attempt to keep would-be cyber attackers and others with malicious intent from accessing network resources. Authentication verifies that the user has valid access to the network and identifies which network resources the user is authorized to access. Having strong authentication (e.g., enforcing strong passwords that are changed frequently), identity management (e.g., no one gets access to network resources without first identifying themselves and having the appropriate authorizations in place), and directory-based access (e.g., users only get access to network resources for which they have been authorized) systems that align user authorization and identity with resources-based

Signing

Digital Message → **Signing/Hash Algorithm** (with *Private Key* input) → *Encrypted Signature with Hash* → **Attach Signature to Data** → *Digital Signed Message*

Verification

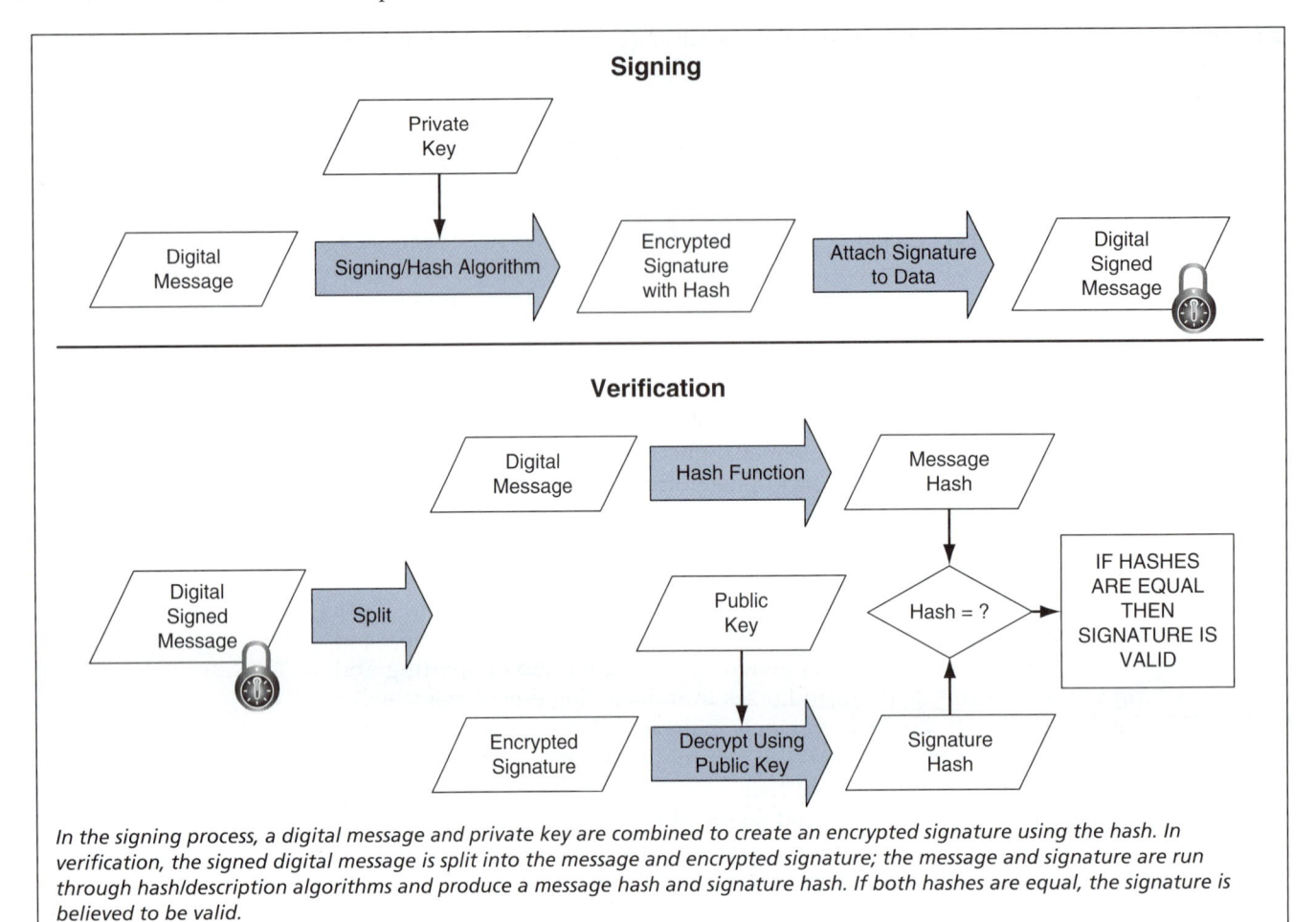

Digital Signed Message → **Split** → *Digital Message* → **Hash Function** → *Message Hash* → **Hash = ?** → IF HASHES ARE EQUAL THEN SIGNATURE IS VALID

Encrypted Signature + *Public Key* → **Decrypt Using Public Key** → *Signature Hash* → **Hash = ?**

In the signing process, a digital message and private key are combined to create an encrypted signature using the hash. In verification, the signed digital message is split into the message and encrypted signature; the message and signature are run through hash/description algorithms and produce a message hash and signature hash. If both hashes are equal, the signature is believed to be valid.

FIGURE 6-7 Digital Signature Signing and Verification

access are the first line of defense to network security. A number of other systems and protocols add to the security of the network environment.

WIRED

Computer networks can be built using wired and wireless technologies. Wired LANs, which use cables and hardware to facilitate communications, prompt four major security concerns: (1) protecting the physical assets and resources of the LAN, (2) protecting access to LAN digital resources, (3) protecting data during transmission across the LAN and to hosts outside the LAN, and (4) providing secure remote access to the LAN.

Protecting the physical assets of a LAN is often the combined job of the IT staff and security services in an organization. At a minimum, it includes physical access devices in computer rooms and associated telecommunication closets and requires organizational policies that determine who gets access to physical assets. The physical

---

VIGNETTE BOX 6-9

Wired and Wireless at HealthyWay

Based on its size and needs as described in the opening vignette, HealthyWay will most likely install wired and wireless LANs. The security of both is essential to HealthyWay's data integrity.

security systems may include biometric devices, locks, and associated security equipment (e.g. alarm systems or cameras). The goal is to create a unified set of physical security policies and technologies that protect the LAN assets from harm by cyber attackers. As previously discussed, access to network resources through some protection scheme and directory service will protect network digital resources from unauthorized use.

Protecting data as they are transmitted across a LAN is accomplished through protocols like TLS. TLS was discussed in detail previously in this chapter. Another method of protecting data during transmission between hosts outside the LAN is the Virtual Private Network (VPN). Technology used in Virtual Private Networks was discussed earlier in this textbook. The technologies of IPsec and TLS-based VPNs were covered in this earlier chapter, but because VPN technologies provide secure remote access, it is important that VPNs are mentioned here as well. As a security method to protect against cyber attacks, VPNs provide technologies that a network designer can use to create a secure, but accessible environment.

Aside from authentication and resource-based access directory services, the main security device that protects a wired LAN is the firewall. The firewall provides a demarcation point between the external world (i.e., the Internet or an intranet connection) and the LAN. The firewall is a PC or other device that sits between the LAN and a connection to external network, normally a carrier connection to an organization's ISP (see Figure 6-8). As the firewall examines each incoming packet, it looks at the source and destination IP addresses and/or the protocol of the packet. Organizations develop rules that instruct the firewall to filter packets of information and allow or deny their access to the network. A typical rule may say something like DENY IP ADDRESS 10.1.1.4, which would instruct the firewall not to allow communications between the LAN and any packet that has a source or destination of 10.1.1.4. Firewalls are also equipped to handle events such as denial-of-service attacks (i.e., DoS or DDoS); IP addresses or protocols used for that or other nefarious purposes can be programmed into the firewall rule set to prevent attacks.

Large organizations often use a multi-tiered approach when implementing firewalls. For example, a public firewall may create what is known as a demilitarized zone (DMZ). The purpose of the DMZ is to expose portions of the organization's LAN to potentially untrusted individuals. It is analogous to organizations that have some type of public area. The front door allows people to enter the business's common area (i.e., lobby). A receptionist, security guard, or some other mechanism screens who gets access to the inner offices of the building. Similarly a DMZ may allow certain traffic into

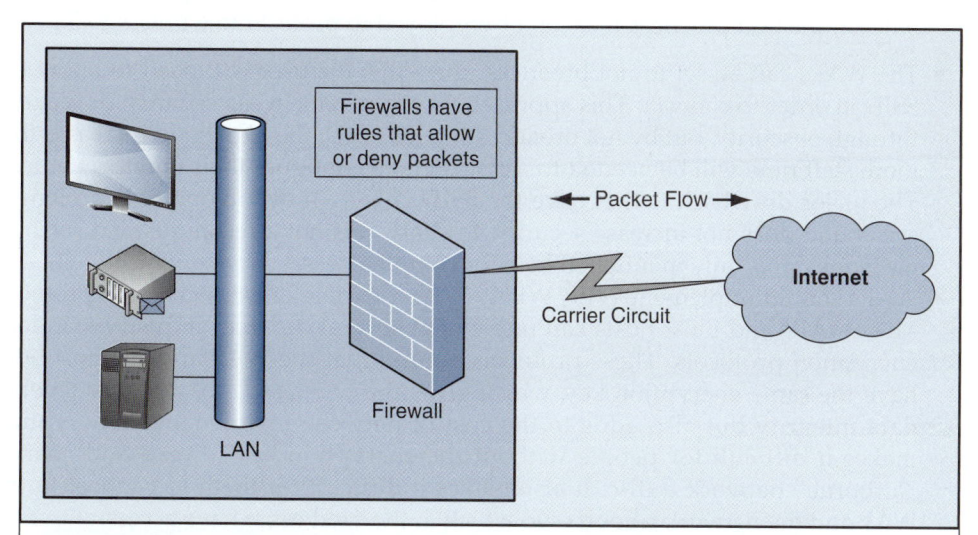

FIGURE 6-8 Firewall Description

This LAN's firewall sits on the edge of the network and controls packet flow into and out of the network. The firewall is configurable with rules that define protocols and IP addresses that are allowed/denied.

FIGURE 6-9 Two-Tiered Firewall

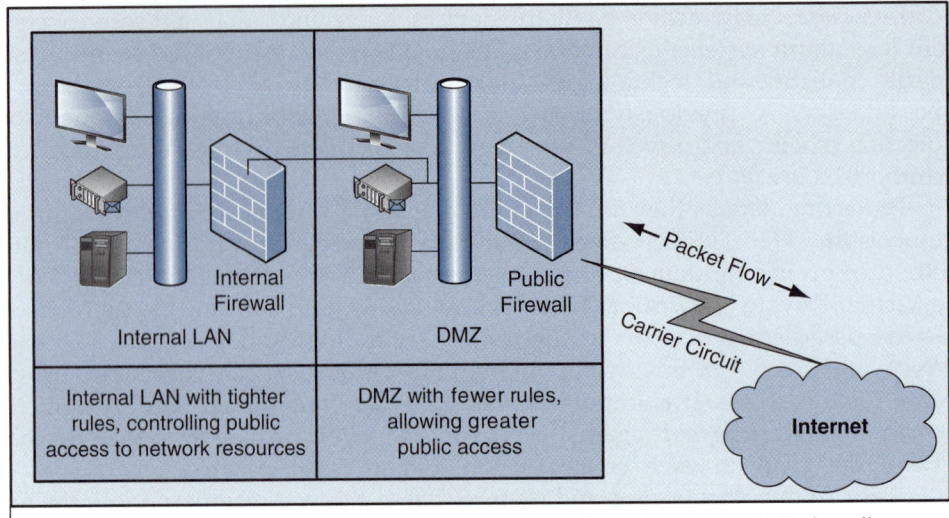

This LAN has a two-tiered firewall implementation. One firewall creates a DMZ that allows greater public access, while the internal firewall restricts public access.

a public portion of a corporate network, but the internal firewall is more restrictive in allowing traffic into and out of the internal LAN, as shown in Figure 6-9.

WIRELESS SECURITY

Wireless access points are used to extend wired LANs by allowing mobility. In a wired LAN, hosts need to be plugged into the network infrastructure, whereas wireless access points obviate the need to plug in. Rather, the host only needs a wireless NIC to connect. Because wireless access points do not require hosts to plug in, hosts do not need direct physical access to the LAN. It also means that wireless access poses some unique security risks. Wireless connections will still need to use any enforced authentication, but the fact that wireless access points are omnidirectional (and probably make the network accessible outside the physical LAN) means that anyone with a wireless NIC can attempt connection to the wireless access points. Also, because the network traffic is "airborne," anyone with a wireless NIC can potentially read the information being transmitted. So the question is: What can be done to secure wireless access points?

The technologies were covered in earlier chapters, but it is appropriate to mention here some simple best practices that can be employed to protect the wireless LAN:

- The WAPs can be set to not broadcast the SSID; the user will need to know the SSID in order to connect. This approach provides some weak security, or security through obscurity. But by not broadcasting the SSID, the likelihood increases that more staff time will be needed to assist users to configure their wireless devices. The major drawback is that once the SSID is known by anyone, it is no longer secret and does not increase security. In short, it is not a recommended security measure and is only mentioned here for completeness.
- WAPs should implement WEP, WEP2, WPA, or some other encryption protocol. Most WAPs and most hosts can implement several different industry-standard encryption protocols. These protocols require that the WAP and the host both have the same encryption key, which gives the wireless LAN a higher level of data integrity but also adds to the cost of network maintenance. Encryption makes it difficult for people without the encryption key to read and change "airborne" network traffic. It also makes it difficult for them to connect to the WAP and the network resources to which authorized users have access.
- In a large network with WAPs, the WAPs can be firewalled into its own DMZ, allowing the network administrator to give appropriate access to those who connect wirelessly, while protecting the internal corporate LAN (see Figure 6-10).

FIGURE 6-10 Two-Tiered Firewall with Wireless

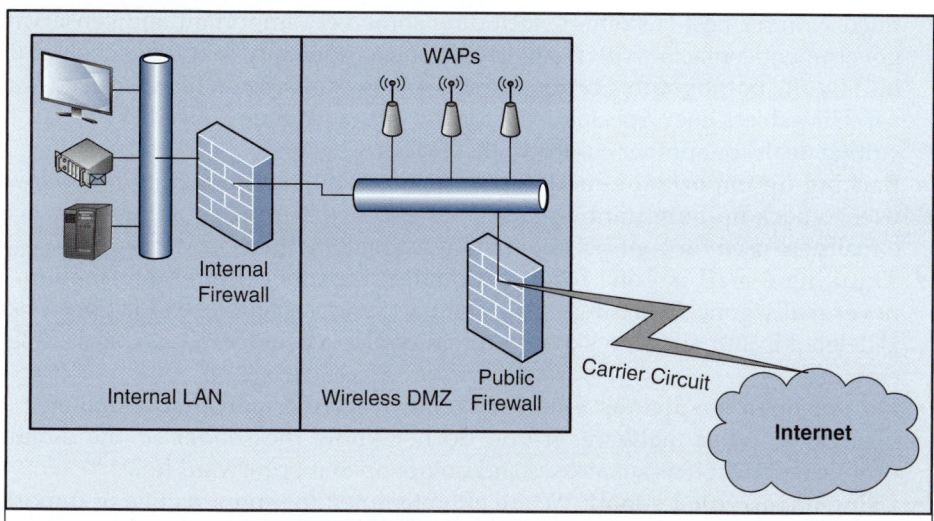

In this LAN with a two-tiered firewall implementation, one firewall creates a wireless DMZ while the internal firewall restricts public access.

Many different configurations of firewalls and encryption can be employed when considering wireless security. It is best to use encryption at the access point, firewalls with wireless DMZs, network authentication, and resource-based access lists (i.e., a Directory Server).

Educating the User

Educating the user is potentially the most important way to safeguard against cyber attacks. Some of the best practices a user could be taught include the following:

- **Browsers and history:** Closing browsers and deleting browser history and cache after logging off a web site so the connection between the user and the web host is deleted, and so any information stored in the browser cache and history are expunged.
- **E-mail security:** Employ e-mail security for e-mails that contain sensitive information.
- **Using the telephone:** Unless you need a written record of something, use the telephone. A phone conversation may require a few extra minutes, but a phone call often is far more secure.
- **Using BCC:** Use the blind carbon copy (BCC) option when sending out e-mail to a number of users. This approach protects user privacy because e-mail addresses are not made public to all recipients. In addition, recipients do not have to wade through a long list of "TO" e-mail addresses to get to the actual message.
- **REPLY ALL vs. REPLY:** Carefully consider whether to use the REPLY ALL versus REPLY button when responding to e-mail. The REPLY ALL button sends everyone on the e-mail the response, while the REPLY button sends the response only to the originator of the e-mail. Including individuals who were not intended to be included on the reply can have disastrous consequences. An example: "A very successful salesman at our networking company had a large e-mail address book

---

VIGNETTE BOX 6-10

HealthyWay Employee Education

As mentioned earlier, HealthyWay should undertake a strong employee education program in an attempt to get its personnel to guard against cyber attacks. Educated employees are the first and most effective defense against malicious attack.

filled with his best customers, including some very important and conservative government contacts. With a single click, he accidentally sent a file chock-full of his favorite pornographic cartoons and jokes to everyone on his special customer list. His subject line: 'Special deals for my best customers!' Needless to say, he's cutting deals for another company these days."

- **Backing up important e-mail:** Most e-mail clients have a facility that allows a user to back up important e-mails. This practice is especially important when e-mails are used for contract negotiations or making financial decisions.
- **Thinking e-mail is gone forever:** E-mails, like other digital information, are never really gone. Thinking that an embarrassing e-mail thread is gone once it is deleted is unrealistic. A skilled professional can usually recover those deleted e-mails.
- **Do not open suspicious e-mails:** We all receive e-mail that contains spam, viruses, or other malware. If you do not know the sender or the e-mail is unsolicited, treat it as suspicious and do not open it or forward it.
- **Using unencrypted e-mail:** We are often tempted to send sensitive or important financial information by e-mail. Bad idea! Normal e-mail is sent using plain text and can be intercepted easily. You should use encrypted e-mail if your message contains any sensitive information.
- **Encrypting wireless connections:** Cyber attackers can gain access to information and networks through wireless access points that are not encrypted. Users need to turn on encryption when using wireless network connectivity. This extra layer of encryption protects communications before they enter the wired network. Wireless communication is easier to capture than wired communications because wireless cyber attackers only have to "listen" to find wireless communications whereas a cyber attacker must gain physical access to capture data on a wired network.
- **Using digital signatures:** Today, e-mail is often recognized as an important form of communication for major financial or other undertakings. Contracts can be negotiated and funds transferred (see www.ingdirect.com for transferring funds by e-mail). In these types of e-mails it is important to confirm the identity of the person sending an e-mail. Identification can be confirmed through the use of digital signatures. Users should be encouraged to obtain digital signatures and to use them to authenticate any sensitive e-mail.
- **Using fake answers to challenge questions:** Today it is common for web sites with accounts to use challenge questions to verify someone's identity. Questions like "The name of your first pet?" or "What street is your office on?" are often used. Frankly, the answers to these questions are often easily discovered by would be attackers. One potential way to thwart would-be attackers is to use fake answers to the challenge questions. For example, for the question "What street is your office on?" you could use an answer like "YY77UU55" rather than "Main Street." This approach takes a little more effort on the user's part, but it would provide more security. (ITSecurity, 2007)

Chapter Summary

In addition to an overview of security, both physical and digital, this chapter discussed methods of thwarting cyber attacks. First, threats to security were covered, including physical-, technology-, and human-focused cyber attacks. Physical-focused attacks are directed toward the physical assets and are often thought of as terrorist attacks. Technology-focused attacks and human-focused attacks are what are traditionally described as cyber attacks. The final attack covered in this chapter is exploits. Exploits often leave no traces and may be used to gather data for a full-on cyber attack. Next this chapter covered ways to thwart cyber attacks. The need for policies, planning, access, and control were covered. Encryption was described, using TLS/SSL as an example to describe encryption techniques. Finally client, wired, and wireless network solutions to stop cyber attacks were discussed.

Vignette Wrap Up

HealthyWay has both legal and ethical imperatives to maintain the integrity of patients' healthcare data. This necessitates strong security policies and technologies to protect the organization's digital assets. The SFR framework (or something similar) should be used to assess the likelihood of cyber attacks, as well as how to respond to them if they occur.

HealthyWay is vulnerable to physical and nonphysical cyber attacks and must have people, policies, and technologies in place to thwart those attacks. The first line of defense against attack is the people in the organization, and thus employees should be properly educated and trained, especially in ways to handle e-mail threats.

End of Chapter Questions/Assurance of Learning

1. List the security policies that most organizations should have, and define who in the organization should be involved in the creation of each policy.
2. Write a research paper to extend the information in the chapter that describes physical, local authentication, and Internet security policies and technologies.
3. Select one major Internet security technology, research that technology, and prepare a presentation and paper about it. Give the presentation to the class to teach them about the policy.
4. Write a paper that describes a major government's (e.g., UK, Australia, United States) response to cyber attacks. Describe the policy and legal ramifications.
5. Select three of the security threats described in this chapter, and develop user education, technology, and policies for each that would thwart those threats.
6. Create a recommendation for a three-tiered firewall infrastructure that supports VPN, DMZ, wireless, and internal wired LAN. Select the hardware to implement this configuration, along with a budget and set of diagrams. Lastly, prepare a document explaining the benefits of your configuration.

Case Exercises

These exercises build on the case exercises from previous chapters.

1. The company XYZ Inc. (see the case exercises in earlier chapters) desires to develop strong security policies and a plan to implement those policies. Its major customers are companies like HealthyWay HMO. Review XYZ Inc. (it is fictitious so you can make some of this up) and develop a set of technology policies and implementation plans XYZ can use for providing service to its customers while protecting its data. Prepare a report for the board of directors of XYZ, detailing the policies and technologies that should be used to secure the XYZ LAN, WAN, and cloud environments.
2. HealthyWay HMO, the opening vignette from Unit 1, desires to provide remote services to its customers and major providers. What are the security implications for a healthcare organization, and how will that move support its business strategy? Prepare a presentation and report.
3. Work together in a small group to select an organization with which you are familiar. Using its mission statement, vision statement, or other company strategy documents, craft LAN and WAN security recommendations to ensure communications integrity. Select the technologies the company would use and diagram the solution it would want to build. Prepare a report and presentation for the purposes of securing funding for this project from the company's board of directors.

Key Words and Concepts

access control *170*
adware *166*
anti-spam filters *175*
anti-virus tools *175*
Certified Information Systems Security Professional (CISSP) framework *170*
ciphertext *171*
cybercrime *161*
denial-of-service (DoS) *168*
digital signatures *175*

distributed denial-of-service attack (DDoS) *168*
encryption *171*
exploit tools *169*
firewall *177*
hacking *169*
human-focused cyber attacks *168*
identity theft *169*
keys *171*
logic bomb *168*
malware *165*

network solutions, wired and wireless *175*
phishing *168*
physical-focused attacks *165*
script kiddies *169*
Secure Sockets Layer (SSL) *172*
sniffer *168*
social engineering *168*
spam *169*
spyware *166*

System-Fault-Risk (SFR) framework *162*
technology-focused cyber attacks *165*
Transport Layer Security (TLS) *172*
Trojan horse *166*
vectors and infection strategies *167*
virus *166*
vishing *168*
wardriving *169*
worm *167*
zero-day attack *166*

References

(ISC)², Inc. (2011). *CISSP: Certified Information Systems Security Professional*. Retrieved April 3, 2011, from https://www.isc2.org/cissp/default.aspx

Edwards, J. (2008, May 15). *The Essential Guide to Email Security*. Retrieved April 3, 2011, from http://www.itsecurity.com/features/essential-guide-email-security-051508/

ITSecurity. (2007, February 28). *The 25 Most Common Mistakes in Email Security: 25 Tips To Bring Newbie Internet Users Up To Speed So They Stop Compromising Your Network Security*. Retrieved April 3, 2011, from http://www.itsecurity.com/features/25-common-email-security-mistakes-022807/

Joffee, R. (2010). Cybercrime: The Global Epidemic at Your Network Door. *Network Security*, 2010 (7), 4–7.

Merriam-Webster. (2011). *Security*. Retrieved April 3, 2011, from http://www.merriam-webster.com/dictionary/security

Palmer, M. (2010, April 27). Rising Cybercrime Costs UK Pound(s)10bn a Year. *FT.com*.

Schwartz, M. J. (2010, August 10). McAfee Says Security Industry Failing on Cybercrime. *InformationWeek–Online*.

Securing Our eCity. (n.d.). *Protect Your Computer From Cyber Threats and Learn How To Be Safe Online*. Retrieved November 21, 2010, from http://securingourecity.org/

Spamlaws.com. (2009). *Spam*. Retrieved April 3, 2011, from http://www.spamlaws.com/spam.html

www.symantec.com (1999). *Symantec First to Provide Immediate Cure for Back Orifice 2000 Trojan Horse*. Retrieved April 2011, from www.symantec.com/about/news/release/article.jsp?prid=19990712_01

Ye, N., Newman, C., & Farley, T. (2005, June 1). A System-Fault-Risk Framework for Cyber Attack Classification. *Information Knowledge Systems Management*, 5, 135–151.

UNIT 2

SUMMARY

Unit 2 covered additional ICT concepts that extended the introductory information about ICT infrastructure building given in Unit 1. Chapter 5 discussed the attributes of cloud computing including the need for the cloud-based service to have the following characteristics: (1) be Internet-based, (2) be service-based, (3) be scalable and elastic, (4) use shared resources, (5) have metered use, (6) possess substantial fault tolerance, (7) be geo-replicated, and (8) have adequate security for physical and digital assets.

After introducing and defining cloud computing, examples were given. These examples included Microsoft HealthVault and Google Apps. Methods of developing in the cloud were discussed and illustrated by cases that included Azure and Sopima and the technologies used to launch cloud-based services.

A substantial portion of Chapter 5 was devoted to the business considerations of launching cloud-computing services. The business case for application development on-premises or in the cloud was covered along with extensive discussion of cloud-based computing's impact on the organization. Even though cloud computing may not be the right answer for all software, it does offer a number of business advantages that include the following:

- New generations of products and services
- New partnerships with less overhead
- Leveraging Internet resources
- Integration of on-premises and cloud-based resources
- Shifting of reliance on IT staff to user skills
- Increased experimentation (and innovation)

Chapter 5 wrapped up with a discussion of the business case for cloud computing.

Chapter 6 gives the student an overview of physical and network security. This chapter spent a considerable amount of time discussing the types of attacks and how they are delivered. Attacks were broken into physical, technology, and human-focused attacks, and exploits. Physical-focused attacks are those attacks you might traditionally think of as terrorism, and are focused on doing physical damage to a building, or organizational asset. Technology-focused attacks are traditionally thought of as cyber attacks and include malware, adware, spyware, Trojan horses, viruses, worms, DoS and DDoS, logic bombs, and sniffers. Human-focused attacks include social engineering, phishing and vishing, spam, identity theft, and hacking. Exploits are attacks that allow cyber attackers to learn about vulnerabilities, and usually do not leave any trace of the attack. The purpose of the exploit is information to be used in future, more damaging attacks.

With the description of cyber attacks completed, the focus of Chapter 6 changed to ways to stop cyber attacks. Emphasis on planning, policy, and the Certified Information Systems Security Professional (CISSP) framework was covered. That framework includes:

- Access Control
- Application Development Security
- Cryptography
- Information Security Governance and Risk Management
- Legal, Regulations, Investigations, and Compliance
- Operations Security
- Physical (Environmental) Security
- Security Architecture and Design
- Telecommunications and Network Security

Encryption as a way to increase data integrity was introduced, and symmetrical and asymmetrical encryption techniques were discussed. A discussion of the use of keys, ciphers, encryption algorithms, and SSL/TLS provides students with an understanding of the complexities brought about by encryption.

Next, Chapter 6 described client host software solutions for protecting users and their PCs. The user is the front line of defense against cyber attacks. Wired and wireless security were described, including the prominence of the firewall in a network security scheme. Ways to create a DMZ and a protected wireless network were presented. This chapter closed with the notion that user education is a primary way to thwart cyber attacks.

UNIT 3

Understanding the Business of Infrastructure Design

Unit Purpose

This unit moves away from the technical topics in earlier units and turns to the topic of ICT infrastructure strategy and the enterprise. Business and technology strategy concepts are reviewed, and the importance of technology infrastructure to the enterprise is explained. Business process and functional views are discussed as well as how infrastructure and technology strategy are concerned with more than just networking and telecommunications, but rather must be part of the overall business strategy. The ICT infrastructure architecture enables the student to see how ICT can be driven by the business imperatives, and how technology must support those imperatives. Understanding the competition, knowing your enterprise's internal business processes, and turning that knowledge into technology infrastructure recommendations are tantamount to creating competitive advantage.

Unit Objectives

Understanding why management must be involved in system design and technology infrastructure building.

Defining competitive advantage and ways of creating it through technology infrastructure.

Comprehending the role of management in technology infrastructure decisions.

Understanding the importance of technology infrastructure to the enterprise.

Relating business-driven infrastructure design (BDID) concepts to sustained competitive advantage.

Vignette

FedEx, UPS, and the Shipping Industry

United Parcel Service (UPS) worked steadily through the 1980s to transition itself from a common carrier using a paper-based system for package tracking to an overnight package carrier with electronic tracking. It did so, in part, by expanding its technology infrastructure to enhance its competitive advantage and gain market share. It has virtually replicated the services provided by FedEx, including Saturday morning package delivery. Other airfreight companies, including Airborne Freight, DHL, and Emery, also emulated the services that brought FedEx its competitive advantage. For these companies, continued innovation affected competitive advantage, caused mergers, and drove market share. If we look at UPS in particular we see that it had to change the way it did business so it could stay in business; it changed its business processes to technology-based systems that allowed it to process transactions faster and more accurately and to give customers better service. In other words, it changed its technology infrastructure. Only through understanding the relationships among business processes, innovation, technology infrastructure, and market share could UPS regain its position in the shipping industry and maintain market share.

FedEx was the first mover in the next-day shipping marketplace. The founder of FedEx, Fred Smith, saw the organization's core competencies as essential to success: logistics with speed, reliability, and customer service. Instituting these core competencies through ICT infrastructure led to a positive net income in FedEx's financials through 1985, but in the years 1986–1991 they experienced a continuous fall caused by competition from other carriers, most notably UPS. FedEx's worst net income losses during that time were in 1985 and in 1991. What happened during those years to cause the losses? Simply put, emulation of FedEx's business process engineering and infrastructure building allowed FedEx's competition to take market share away. What did UPS do during this time that allowed it to take market share from FedEx? Those questions are the substance of this unit.

7 INFRASTRUCTURE AND THE ENTERPRISE

> **Learning Objectives**
>
> - Understand why management must be involved in ICT infrastructure building.
> - Define competitive advantage and ways of creating it through use of ICT infrastructure.
> - Understand the importance of ICT infrastructure to the enterprise.
> - Relate the concepts of business-driven infrastructure design to sustained competitive advantage.

This chapter reviews business and technology strategy concepts and explains the importance of technology infrastructure to any enterprise. Business process and functional views are discussed as well. The text explains how infrastructure and technology strategy are concerned with more than just networking and telecommunications and are actually key aspects of overall business strategy. Information and communication technology (ICT) infrastructure can be viewed as a multilayered architecture, driven by the business imperatives of the enterprise and the technologies that must support them. Understanding the competition, knowing the internal business processes of your enterprise, and turning that knowledge into technology infrastructure recommendations are tantamount to creating competitive advantage. Within this chapter, the various conceptual frameworks that underpin appropriate business-driven infrastructure design (BDID) are specifically addressed.

DEFINITION OF TECHNOLOGY INFRASTRUCTURE

The introduction to ICT infrastructure technologies in Unit 1 described the framework used throughout this book. Management information systems students often take a course in networking and telecommunications to learn technical concepts, but that course doesn't always offer a business-driven focus. The technical information taught in these courses is essential to those students, especially with the ubiquitous nature of the Internet as the primary global communications medium. Still, a greater business-driven focus is needed. The external impact of technology infrastructure is most often seen in business relationships with suppliers/distributors or directly with the customer. External technology infrastructure can often be seen as sustaining or disrupting technologies (Christensen, Bohmer, & Kenagy, 2000). A new customer service that is offered may not be viewed as a technology; however, many services are indeed enabled by technology. For example, next-day shipping is a service that did disrupt the traditional shipping marketplace, and even though it was not an information technology as traditionally described, next-day shipping was still disruptive and required a large ICT infrastructure to support it and make it work.

Disruptive technologies provide a new way of doing things that does not initially meet the needs of the market, or is a product for which a market may not currently exist. This "new way" can overturn the dominant technology in the marketplace even though the new concept may be radically different from current leading technologies. In fact, disruptive technologies initially often perform worse than the leading technology in the field they are trying to change. Disruptive technologies come to dominate existing markets by filling a role in new markets or by successfully capturing market share through market performance improvements. Some examples of disruptive technologies are included in Figure 7-1.

FIGURE 7-1 Examples of Disruptive Technologies

Disruptive Technology	Displaced / Potentially Displaced Technology	Description
Semiconductors	Vacuum Tubes	Electronic systems built with semiconductors required less energy and were smaller and more reliable than systems with tubes. This new technology allowed semiconductors to disrupt the vacuum tube market.
Personal Computers	Minicomputers, Workstations	Workstations still exist, but are increasingly assembled from high-end personal computer parts, and the distinction is fading. Minicomputers are largely extinct and have been replaced by personal computers. Personal computers' cost, reliability, ease of use, and the level of control they give users over their own work (which leads to many positive benefits) allowed personal computers to disrupt the minicomputer/workstation marketplace.
Minicomputers	Main Frames	Although main frames survive in a niche market that persists to this day, minicomputers have largely displaced them.
Desktop Publishing	Traditional Publishing	Early desktop-publishing systems could not match high-end professional systems (e.g., manual type settings and professional-grade computerized publishing systems) in either features or quality. Nevertheless, desktop systems lowered the cost of entry into the publishing business, and the economies of scale eventually enabled them to match and then surpass the functionality of the older, dedicated publishing systems.
Digital Photography	Chemical and Instant Photography Technologies	Classic chemical photography required a stand-alone camera and processing by a processing lab. That technology was somewhat disrupted by instant photography. Digital photography is now disrupting both chemical and instant technologies.

A number of technologies were supplanted by disruptive technologies. A brief description of the disruption is also given.
Source: Adapted from Wikipedia, 2006.

Sustaining technologies are usually introduced by incumbent companies and offer newer, better, or cheaper ways to do the same task. Sustaining technologies refer to those successive incremental improvements to performance that market incumbents incorporate into their existing products.

The opening vignette discusses FedEx's introduction of package tracking, which was disruptive to the shipping marketplace. FedEx management had no guarantee that customers would pay a premium for overnight shipping with exacting standards for package tracking. However, the company believed its business strategy was good and thus created a technology infrastructure based on the analysis. FedEx's read of the marketplace proved to be correct, and it was successful in creating a market for next-day package delivery. After FedEx's successes, UPS, an incumbent company in the traditional shipping marketplace, capitalized on FedEx's first-mover, next-day shipping methods by offering the same service, but at cheaper rates. Thus, FedEx originally created the disruptive technology/service (next-day shipping), whereas UPS created a competing/sustaining duplicate of the same technology, becoming a fast follower. Whether it is a product that sustains a marketplace or a product that disrupts that marketplace, organizations need ICT infrastructure to support their business processes and products. That infrastructure must be part of the business strategy that sustains/enhances competitive advantage.

It is essential that today's information systems graduate be prepared to take a high-level view of the organization, including its business processes, products, and the technologies needed to support those processes. These graduates do not necessarily need to understand all the subtle nuances of hardware and software, but they must understand the linkage among business strategy, technology infrastructure, and organizational success in order to be a positive part of the team that drives strategic discussions within an enterprise. Frequently, hardware engineers are making the decisions about which technologies to use, whereas the **business systems analyst** is ensuring that all the technologies fit together to support the business processes and products of the organization. The business systems analyst needs to have an understanding of the technologies and their capabilities, although the subtleties of individual technologies often remain the purview of the engineer. The business systems analyst specifies what needs to be done and at a macro level determines how it is to be done, while the engineer handles the specifics of doing the tasks. This text focuses on the skills needed by the business systems analyst.

ICT infrastructure consists of user, enterprise, service, and network components which include all the components of the networking and telecommunication system from user desktop to data center servers; the physical cabling/media necessary to interconnect the technologies; and the external services necessary to support the business processes and organization's products. Most important is that all decisions about hardware, software, interconnecting media, and external services must be driven by a business systems analyst who understands the organization's overall business strategy.

INFORMATION TECHNOLOGY INFRASTRUCTURE AND STRATEGY

Organizations are directed by management, and information systems exist under the direction of that same management. Information systems are used by the organization to bring efficiencies to business processes and create new products. In the view taken by this textbook, these systems have three major components: staff, business processes, and business outcomes. Each component is interlinked through a technology infrastructure that includes user interface software, enterprise applications, network services, and network technology. Staff performs and manages the business processes, and those processes yield business outcomes that affect the competitive positioning of the organization. All these outcomes are directly or indirectly enabled by ICT infrastructure.

It is important that business systems analysts understand the relationship between the technology infrastructure components and business processes. Without that understanding, the business systems analyst cannot build a technology infrastructure that will support the business processes and enable the desired business outcomes to occur. Comprehensive planning is the most effective way to support both goals by facilitating appropriate changes in that process design (Mitchell & Zmud, 1999).

How successful would FedEx have been if it did not understand its business strategy, affected business processes, staffing needs, or the information technology infrastructure it needed to reach its goals? Could it have accomplished its stated business strategy without the technology that linked together those elements? FedEx had to hire the correct staff to support its business strategy, and those staff had to understand the business processes. The technology had to be created to tie staff and the business processes together to create the specific business outcome FedEx wanted.

Understanding the relationship between staff, business processes, and business outcomes is essential to successful implementation of technology infrastructure (Figure 7-2). Information technology infrastructure supports staff efforts to effectively manage processes and attain the desired business outcomes (e.g., products of higher quality, faster cycle times, better product delivery).

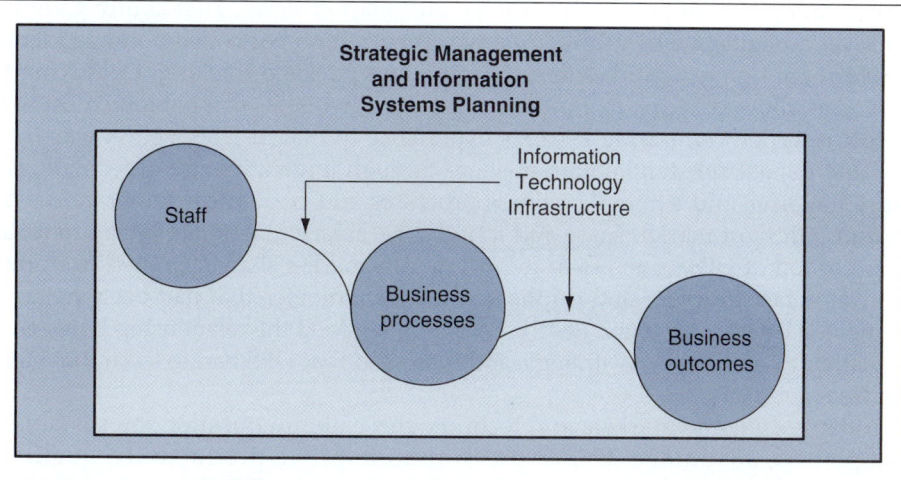

FIGURE 7-2 Relationships Among Staff, Processes, Outcomes, and Technology

*This diagram shows the linkages among an organization's staff, business processes, and business outcomes via information technology infrastructure. These linkages are immersed in the **Strategic Management and Information Systems Planning** functions of the organization.*

Strategic Management and Infrastructure Decisions

Do strategic managers, business systems analysts, and information systems staffs all need to be involved in strategy and technology infrastructure building? Is strategy the purview of the business systems analysts at all, or should this planning be left to senior levels of management? Are business processes important to technology infrastructure decisions and organizational success? The answer to all these questions is an overwhelming **YES!** As we look at how organizations manage themselves as well as the roles of managers and the part they play in technology decision making, it becomes evident that these interactions greatly influence competitive advantage. Below we introduce several theories necessary to understand the place of technology strategy within the general business strategy. We will spend time reviewing the theories necessary to create successful ICT infrastructure, a process that then leads to an organization's competitive advantage. These theories will set the stage for understanding business-driven infrastructure design, a concept developed throughout this textbook.

Introduction to Business and Technology Strategy

> Note: *This section is a good review for students with a background in organizational behavior, management, and technology policy. This review is not meant to be an exhaustive study of these topics, but rather an overview of key points as they relate to technology infrastructure design. Those interested in intensive study of business strategy would be best served by a course or book on that topic.*

Information technology has become a commodity. In and of itself, information technology provides no competitive advantage, and because of its commodity status, it is relatively easy to amass large quantities of technology cheaply (M. Porter, 1996). This was true in 1996 when Michael Porter penned that idea, and is more true today. Absent a sound business use for technology, even in the hands of the most skilled engineer, large amounts of technology will not yield competitive advantage. What will then? Technology infrastructure that is implemented as a result of technology recommendations driven by good business strategy will yield competitive advantage. FedEx clearly saw the need to incorporate a technology strategy into its business strategy. In short, FedEx saw the linkage between the two strategies. Although it was not necessary for managers to understand all the aspects of the technology implementation, it was necessary for them to understand how the technology fit into their ability to sustain FedEx's operation, create innovative products, and gain competitive advantage and market share. That ability gave FedEx **first-mover advantage** when the company capitalized on bar-coded package identification, overnight delivery, and online shipping and package tracking. Deploying these technologies allowed FedEx to garner market share, while its competitors, most notably UPS, lost it. When comparing FedEx's experience to that of UPS, FedEx was the first mover and gained substantial market share through innovative use of technology that enhanced internal and external business processes and created consumer value. At the same time, UPS lost market share and found it necessary to emulate FedEx to regain it. A large portion of UPS's success in recapturing its market share stemmed from the fact that it was a **fast follower** and duplicated the technologies that had been created and implemented by its competitor, FedEx. FedEx understood the relationship between technology strategy and business strategy, and it seemed that UPS had to learn that valuable lesson from FedEx.

Today's dynamic markets and technologies call into question the sustainability of competitive advantage. Under pressure to improve productivity, quality, and speed, managers have embraced such business tools as TQM, benchmarking, and reengineering (Lee & Asllani, 1997). Dramatic operational improvements have resulted, but rarely have these gains translated into sustainable profitability. Gradually business tools can take the place of strategy within many organizations. As managers push to improve on all fronts, they often move further away from viable competitive positions by depending on business tools alone to achieve those positions. These pressures for process efficiency can often act as blinders to the larger goal of improving competitive positioning; thus, technology is often seen solely as process efficiency enhancement rather than a cornerstone of real identifiable competitive advantage.

Michael Porter argues that operational effectiveness, although necessary to achieve superior performance, is not sufficient to achieve competitive advantage in and of itself (M. Porter, 1985). Competitors can use techniques such as TQM, benchmarking, and reengineering as strategic initiatives to bring about their own operational efficiencies. In contrast, the essence of any exceptional business strategy is choosing a unique and valuable position rooted in systems of activities that are much more difficult to duplicate. So if process improvements are not a strategy, then what is? A strategy is a plan. A business strategy is a well-articulated vision of where a business seeks to go and how it expects to get there. Management constructs those plans in response to internal and external forces including market forces, customer demands, and organizational capabilities. In other words, businesses must sense the market. Customer demands and organization capabilities must drive an organization's fundamental strategy and its ICT infrastructure. FedEx sensed that the market was ready for next-day delivery of the type it positioned itself to offer. The company also knew that it either already had or could create the organizational capabilities to deliver this new service. It is helpful to have a framework within which to understand these factors, namely, the marketplace, competitive forces, and the needed organizational capabilities. This textbook uses the work of Michael Porter to provide this framework. Other frameworks are mentioned in this text (e.g., the hypercompetition model, D'Aventi, 1994); however, this text mainly uses the Porter models and their terms. Porter captures the essential components necessary to understand sound business strategy and its linkage to technology infrastructure. Additionally, Porter's work is generally well known and accepted in the business community.

Porter states that the fundamental basis for long-term, above-average performance is sustainable competitive advantage. Further, he states that an organization can take an industry-wide or focused approach to strategy to achieve this long-term, above-average performance. Using an industry-wide approach, the organization attempts to attain a competitive position within an entire industry; when using a focused approach, an organization attempts to gain position within a specific segment of an industry. Developing technology infrastructure requires an understanding of your organization's use of these approaches to the market.

Two Approaches to Strategic Initiatives: Industry-Wide and Focused

An **industry-wide approach** to strategic initiatives occurs when an organization implements strategies that produce an industry-wide solution while maintaining quality. FedEx took an industry-wide approach when it positioned itself through appropriate technology deployment to gain competitive advantage by creating the overnight shipping industry. FedEx saw a need for next-day package delivery and then created the business and technology strategy to fill that need. Those strategies led to the creation of a technology infrastructure that supported both strategies. On closer examination, you will see that FedEx had to create all the components of the technology infrastructure (user, enterprise, service, and network components) to achieve its desired competitive position. FedEx developed an entire architecture that gave birth to what we know today as the next-day shipping industry, but ICT infrastructure alone was not the only factor that fostered the creation of that industry.

FedEx had to look at the marketplace, determine what would serve the customer best, and then provide what the customer wanted. It did so as new technologies became available while always keeping its business strategy and resultant technology ahead of the technology curve. In a direct strategic move, FedEx decentralized technologies and placed them in the hands of the customer to give them a sense of control and empowerment, which contributed to FedEx's success in the logistics marketplace.

In its industry-wide approach, FedEx developed the next-day shipping industry and then proceeded to add services to expand its offerings. This approach allowed the company to stay ahead of its competitors (mainly UPS, which kept trying to catch up) and attract new customers. Throughout this process, it was essential that FedEx's technology strategy closely parallel the business strategy of the company.

In a **focused approach** to achieving long-term and above average-performance, a company needs to choose a strategy that impacts a specific area of its business, but may not necessarily impact an entire industry. Take, for example, the high-end hotel industry. Management of a high-end hotel chain may believe that process improvements through the installation of a speedy-checkout kiosk system will bring about efficiencies and cost savings. However, a speedy-checkout kiosk may seem untoward in a high-end hotel like the Ritz-Carlton in New York City where customers expect a high level of personal service, not a self-service kiosk. Although a business might prefer immediate online access for information about packages it ships, rather than contacting a call center to obtain that information, would a customer at a high-end hotel be as willing to use a speedy-checkout kiosk rather than personal service at a checkout desk? That question can only be answered by knowing the customer and sensing the marketplace.

When developing ICT infrastructure, the business systems analyst must consider market research. Guests paying high nightly rates at a high-end hotel might prefer a customer relationship management (CRM) system that knows their preferences and has prepared their rooms as they like, rather than providing speedy checkout kiosks. They might like the personalization of a CRM, but may not like the impersonal checkout process using a kiosk. It is important that ICT resources are placed to maximize customer satisfaction. To realize a focused approach to strategy, Porter explains that creating a successful strategy involves knowing current and potential customers. As he notes, narrow focus alone will not guarantee above-average performance, but product differentiation from the rest of the industry is important and may achieve that performance:

> The focuser can thus achieve competitive advantage by dedicating itself to segments exclusively. Breadth of target is a matter of degree, but the essence of focus is merely the exploitation of a narrow target's differences from the balance of the industry. Narrow focus in and of itself is not sufficient for above-average performance. (M. Porter, 1996)

FIGURE 7-3 Competitive Strategies

	Cost Leadership	Product Differentiation
Industry-Wide	Strategies that produce an industry-wide low-cost solution while still maintaining quality	Strategies that produce products unique to an industry-wide marketplace at a price that is fair to the customer
Focused	Strategies that produce an industry-segment product that is a low-cost solution while still maintaining quality	Strategies that produce products unique to an industry-segment marketplace at a price that is fair to the customer

Overall competitive business strategies can be viewed as the intersection of industry-wide/industry-segment focus and cost leadership/product differentiation.

Cost Leadership and Differentiation

Within the various industry-wide and focused approaches, competitive advantage can be achieved in two ways: cost leadership and product differentiation (Figure 7-3). Business strategy needs to determine which approach is appropriate, and the business systems analyst needs to recommend the technology that supports that decision. The two strategies of cost leadership and product differentiation can be described as follows:

- **Cost leadership** occurs when an organization aims to be the lowest-cost producer in the marketplace (either industry-wide or focused) and attain that goal without sacrificing product quality. Cost leadership can be achieved through operational efficiencies, mass distribution, economies of scale, and so on. Information technology can be the foundation for many of these strategies (e.g., cost reduction through process efficiencies and shortened cycle times, implementation of technical solutions that reduce costs through electronic marketplaces, etc.). Competition based on cost leadership is fierce and can result in lost market share due to price wars and customer price sensitivity. This kind of competition is especially fierce when more than one organization attempts to be the cost leader of the same industry at the same point in time.
- **Product differentiation** (either industry-wide or focused) is when an organization positions its products to make them appear different in the marketplace. Differentiation often allows an organization to charge a higher price, but the price must seem fair to the customer. FedEx differentiated itself by offering extensive online product tracking along with overnight delivery service while its competitors offered overnight delivery with less-easy access and less-detailed package tracking.

Business strategies can be grouped into cost leadership and product differentiation, each having either an industry-wide or industry-segment focus. The goal of such strategies is for the organization to perform well and gain market share, leading to increased profitability. FedEx followed an industry-wide product differentiation strategy by offering next-day package delivery with extensive package tracking. The company took a risk by first assessing the marketplace and then bringing a new next-day delivery service to the market. FedEx had to create a value chain to deliver the service and then create the associated ICT infrastructure. The risk paid off, and FedEx became the first mover in the next-day package delivery service by adopting an industry-wide product differentiation strategy.

Business strategies must influence an organization's technology strategy to create a business and technology relationship (Figure 7-4). Any business strategy must include details on what technology can do for the organization. To do so, an organization needs to understand its marketplace, the competition, and the type of customers. Remember that the organization must first choose its business strategy to use as a base, and then the organization should create technology strategies that relate to its business strategy. Once this is accomplished, the organization is ready to consider competitive and operational technologies based on those strategies.

ICT strategy includes competitive and operational technologies. Operational technologies include those tasks that must be done for the organization to run and produce

FIGURE 7-4 The Business/Technology Relationship

```
┌─────────────────────────────────────────────────┐
│  ┌───────────────────────────────────────────┐  │
│  │           Business Strategy               │  │
│  │  ┌─────────────────────────────────────┐  │  │
│  │  │          ICT Strategy               │  │  │
│  │  │  ┌───────────────────────────────┐  │  │  │
│  │  │  │ Competitive and Operational   │  │  │  │
│  │  │  │        Technologies           │  │  │  │
│  │  │  └───────────────────────────────┘  │  │  │
│  │  └─────────────────────────────────────┘  │  │
│  └───────────────────────────────────────────┘  │
│                                                 │
│  In the relationship among information          │
│  technologies, ICT strategy, and business       │
│  strategy, the focus of an organization should  │
│  be on its business strategy. An organization's │
│  operational and technology strategies must be  │
│  linked to its overall business strategy, and   │
│  the actual technologies implemented should be  │
│  a result of that linkage.                      │
└─────────────────────────────────────────────────┘
```

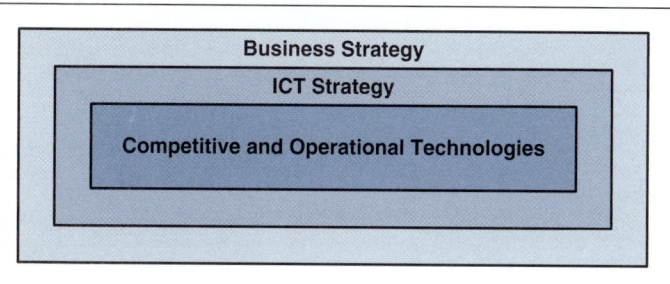

operational efficiency (e.g., online transaction-processing systems such as accounts payable or payroll). Competitive technologies should be implemented to bring about advantage in the marketplace (e.g., FedEx technologies to support next-day package delivery and package tracking).

ORGANIZATIONS AND TECHNOLOGY

Organizations have long struggled with the issue of how best to use technology to improve business processes. The opening vignette discussed how FedEx was the first mover in the overnight package delivery business and provided extensive customer service through its unique system of package tracking. Being the first mover in this market, the company garnered market share; however, as UPS caught up technologically, FedEx lost market share and thus revenue. This scenario is a common problem in business. The first mover has a good idea, implements it, and finds that its competitors may emulate its success. All organizations, including first movers and those that emulate them, must constantly monitor their competition, as well as their internal businesses processes and the relation of those processes to technology changes, in order to maintain ongoing competitive positioning.

As organizations embark on technology projects, they must determine appropriate business and technology strategies, articulate goals, identify distinctive competencies, and assess strengths, weaknesses, opportunities, and threats (SWOT) within the environment. They must also perform internal and external analyses (e.g., value chain, supply chain, etc.), leading to business process improvements and innovations that are implemented in part through technological changes. During this course, it will often be necessary to move between articulation of goals and determination of strategy in an iterative fashion before a viable strategy can be obtained. This approach ensures the best outcome for the organization. This iterative approach can be seen in Figure 7-5.

THE MANAGEMENT ROLE IN TECHNOLOGY DECISIONS

It is not necessary for managers to have extensive technical knowledge to participate in technology decision making, but rather they must be able to analyze those processes they manage (i.e., be a business systems analyst). In fact, being too technical and not strategy and business-process minded enough could result in missed strategic opportunities. For the business systems analyst/manager to be involved, he or she must participate in three ways: (1) be a visionary, (2) have interpersonal skills that let the manager be a informational resource, and (3) have structured skills (i.e., project management, analytical, organization, and planning) (Perlison & Saunders, 2006). By participating in these three ways, managers can set organizational direction and influence technical decision making that supports the core competencies of the organization (Figure 7-6).

In terms of the visionary role, it is necessary that the technology manager be creative. A manager must be able to take the resources in his or her environment and create something new for the organization. An example of this creativity is what FedEx

FIGURE 7-5 The Information Technology Planning Process

Articulate Goals

Assess Internal and External Environments

Identify Distinctive Core Competencies

Determine Business and Technology Strategies

Implement Process and Technology Changes

Perform internal and external business analyses, including SWOT, value chain, and supply chain, to support these activities

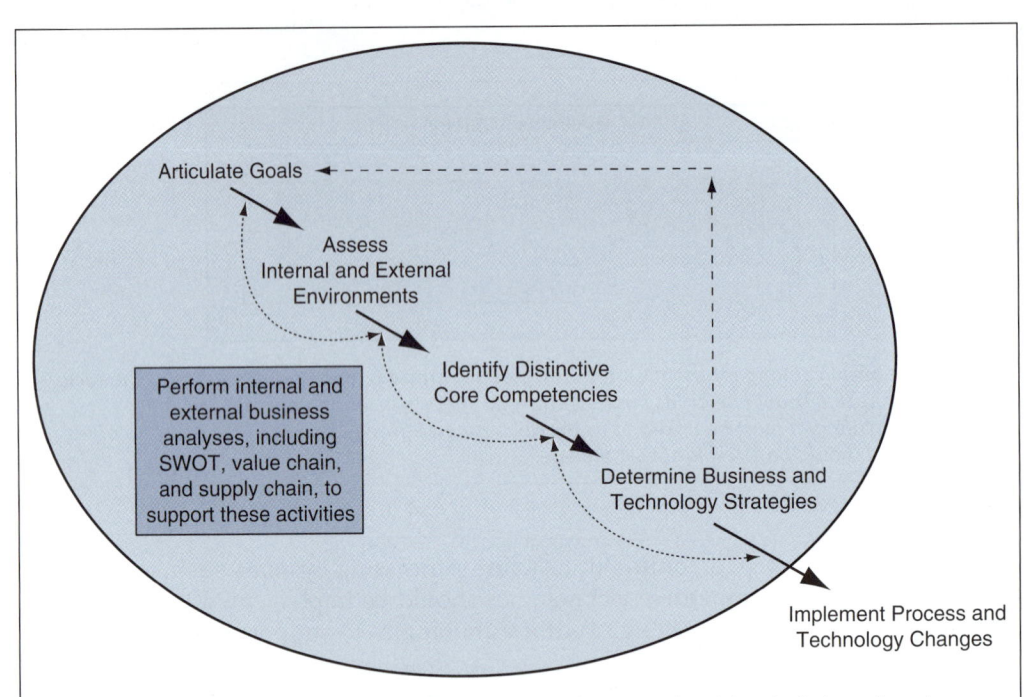

The technology planning process should occur in the following order: (1) articulation of goals, (2) assessment of the internal and external environments, (3) identification of an organization's core competencies, (4) determination of business strategies and technology strategies, and (5) business process and information technology changes. The diagram points out that planning and strategies must be based on a sound understanding of the internal and external environment through business analysis, and that the process of strategic technology planning is iterative—once strategies are developed, goals should be reexamined and rearticulated.

FIGURE 7-6 The Functions of Management in IS Projects

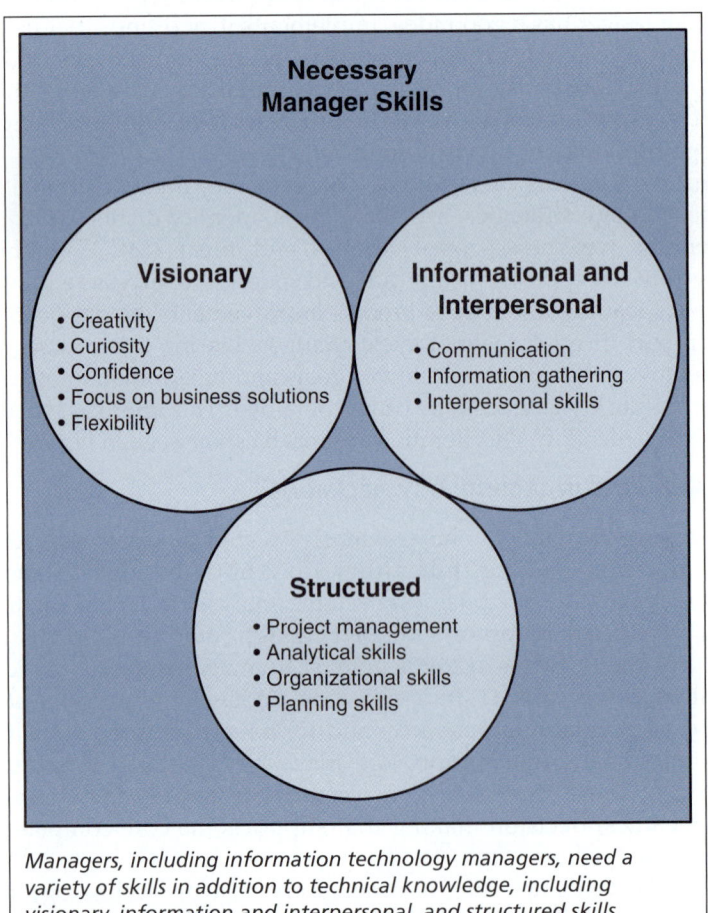

Necessary Manager Skills

Visionary
- Creativity
- Curiosity
- Confidence
- Focus on business solutions
- Flexibility

Informational and Interpersonal
- Communication
- Information gathering
- Interpersonal skills

Structured
- Project management
- Analytical skills
- Organizational skills
- Planning skills

Managers, including information technology managers, need a variety of skills in addition to technical knowledge, including visionary, information and interpersonal, and structured skills.
Source: Based on Perlison and Saunders, 2006.

management envisioned when they saw the current state of the package shipping industry, evaluated the company resources at their disposal, and created the next-day package delivery industry. A visionary manager must also be curious about the business environment and be willing to look into current situations and develop new ways of doing things. Confidence is also important; managers must be confident in their skills as well as confident that they can bring their ideas forward at the proper time in an appropriate way. The manager's previous experience is important also, giving the manager a valuable background from which to draw. Lastly, as a visionary, managers must be flexible—with themselves as well with the people and processes they manage—and able to adapt to changes in their environment. When the competition changes or the enterprise refocuses its goals, the manager must be flexible enough to change as well.

Next, managers must have informational and interpersonal skills. They must be good communicators, as well as have precise information about the projects they are managing. Interpersonal skills are important, because managers must be able to cooperate on a team and across the organization's chain of command to achieve the desired results. Managers cannot be an island within an organization; they must operate within the full organization, applying a variety of methods to the intended strategy—including ICT infrastructure projects—to realize the organization's goals.

Lastly, managers must possess skills that bring structure to a project. They must be able to plan, organize, direct, and control the resources of the enterprise that are necessary for successful completion of the project. These resources include personnel as well as technology. The ability to break down large projects into smaller elements for ease of understanding, analysis, design, and implementation is essential. The manager must then be able to bring those smaller parts back together and combine them into an effective whole. To carry out all these functions, the manager needs to plan, consolidate ideas, and communicate effectively and easily.

Note that the technical abilities of the business systems analyst/manager are only one aspect of the long list of necessary skills. Managers must first know the business that they manage, be a visionary with interpersonal skills, and be able to plan. Information technology skills are necessary, but they are not the only skills a manager or business system analyst must have to be successful.

TECHNOLOGY INFRASTRUCTURE, INFORMATION SYSTEMS, AND PLANNING

Organizational Views

It is possible to analyze an organization in the functional view and the business process view. The functional view looks at the organization as departments or functional units, while the business process view collapses organizational processes into a series of activities that add value to the materials used to create that organization's products or services.

FUNCTIONAL VIEW OF THE ORGANIZATION

The functional view sees the organization as layers of management and individual departments that cut across layers of staff. The following layers are part of that functional view:

- **Strategic Management.** Managers at this level are responsible for determining strategy and setting subsequent business policy for the entire organization. At a high level, the strategic manager determines a business's critical success factors and its operational policies and decides how the organization will employ technology to become both competitive and effective.
- **Management Level.** These staff members are responsible for implementing the business strategies determined by strategic management. They then monitor the progress of business processes and their associated technologies. It is their job to ensure that chosen policies, technology, and monitoring are successfully implemented.

- **Knowledge Level.** These employees include those who create, analyze, and report information and knowledge. This staff can include financial analysts, engineers, market analysts, human resource staff planners, and information technology systems engineers. They are typically high-level users of information technology.
- **Operational Level.** Staff members at this level include those who perform the day-to-day operations of the organization, such as bookkeepers, manufacturing assembly line staff, human resources clerks, and perhaps customer service personnel.

Each of these levels within an organization cuts across functional areas to create activity-centric groups. The functional areas and examples of the activities of these various groups include:

- **Sales and Marketing.** order processing, market and price analysis, sales forecasting
- **Manufacturing.** engineering, production, operations, plant and machine control
- **Finance and Accounting.** accounts receivable and payable, investment portfolio analysis and control, budgeting
- **Human Resources.** training and development, compensation market analysis, succession planning

These staff levels and functional areas contribute to the functional view of the organization (Figure 7-7). By looking down these levels and across the functional areas, we can map the information technology infrastructure to its user base. Some examples might include the following:

- A supply chain management system could involve operational and knowledge levels with sales and marketing, manufacturing, and finance departments.
- A customer relationship management system might involve operational and knowledge levels within the human resources, accounting, and finance departments.
- An enterprise knowledge management system might involve all levels, but just within the manufacturing, finance, and accounting departments.

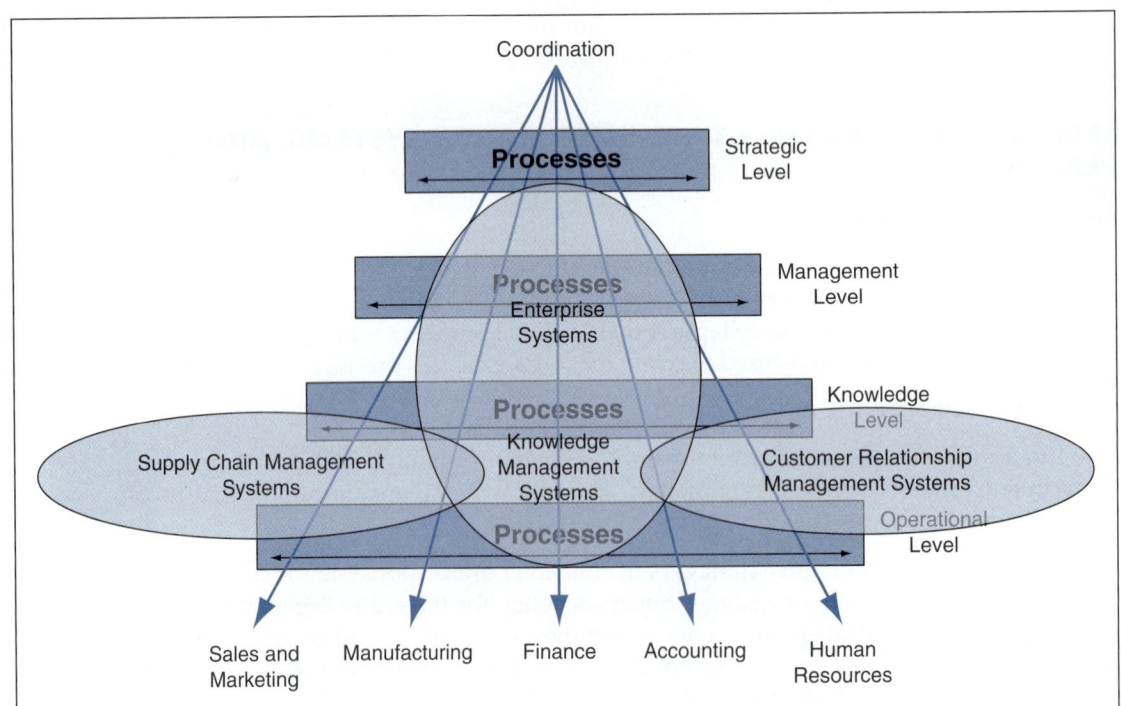

A functional view of an organization shows management layers broken into functional areas, and it indicates how business processes can overlap the functional areas and management levels.

Source: Adapted from Laudon, Kenneth C.; Laudon, Jane, Management Information Systems, 8th Edition, © 2004, p. 27. Reprinted by permission of Pearson Education, Inc., Upper Saddle River, NJ.

FIGURE 7-7 A Functional View of the Organization

At a minimum, what each system affects within an organization is a function of the type of organization, organizational culture, and organizational structure. For example, an enterprise system in an organization involved in manufacturing might involve different departments than an enterprise system in another organization involved with creating software. Organizational culture and structure in large part determine which levels and which departments are involved in which systems. For example, an organization with a highly bureaucratic or control-oriented culture may limit which departments have access to management-oriented sections of an enterprise resource planning system, while a flat egalitarian organization may make those same functions and software widely available. It is important that decisions about technology consider many different organizational factors including the type and culture of the organization.

BUSINESS PROCESSES VIEW OF AN ORGANIZATION

In order to implement ICT strategy, it is helpful to view an organization as processes and break the organization down into smaller units. This breakdown can help in understanding the organization more clearly and in identifying organizational needs. When breaking an organization into smaller units, it is possible to take either a functional or process view. As already discussed, in the functional view of any enterprise, work occurs in activity-centric units (e.g., accounting, finance, operations, marketing, human resources). These functional areas each contain operational-level, knowledge-level, management-level, and strategic-level staffs that exchange information to perform interfunctional area decision making. Viewing an organization functionally can reveal a highly bureaucratic structure, and opportunities for synergy may be missed, whereas a process view can uncover those same opportunities. These missed opportunities often occur in the functional view because information flow is typically vetted through a functional unit's own hierarchy and is often shared only at senior levels of management, effectively creating silos of information.

Compare the functional view to the process view. The business process view sees the organization as composed of primary and support activities (processes) that when taken together create a value chain (Figure 7-8). The primary activities of inbound logistics, operations, outbound logistics, marketing/sales, and service influence the inputs (raw materials) to the enterprise and add value to its eventual output (product) (M. E. Porter, 1990). Information technology is a support activity that ties the data and information needs of the value-creating processes together and

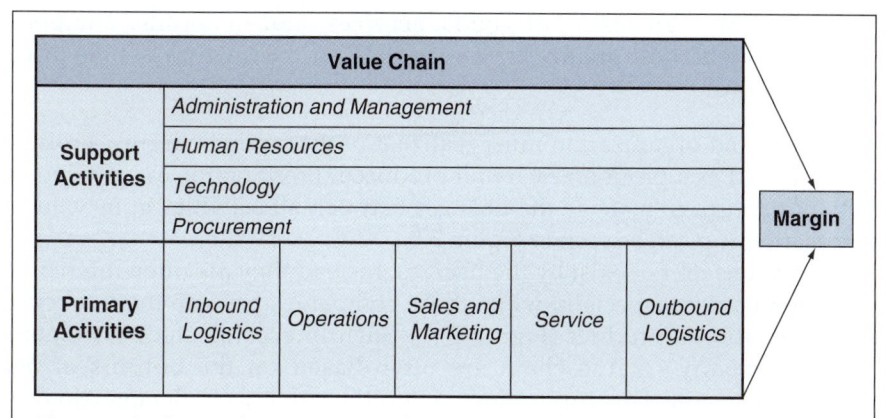

FIGURE 7-8 Porter's Value Chain

Value Chain					
Support Activities	Administration and Management				
	Human Resources				
	Technology				
	Procurement				
Primary Activities	Inbound Logistics	Operations	Sales and Marketing	Service	Outbound Logistics

Margin

The organization can be seen as a set of supporting activities and primary activities that work together to generate profit to the organization for each unit of a product sold. This generic model can be modified to suit a particular situation.

in information-producing organizations is the technology that makes primary processes possible. Those value-creating processes can be described as follows:

- **Inbound Logistics.** Materials are received from the organization's suppliers and are inventoried until needed by production/operations. One can think of this as a process of the organization rather than of a specific department within the enterprise. Take special note that in information-product-producing enterprises, inbound logistics may seem unnecessary. Information-producing organizations (e.g. a newspaper) do still take "raw materials" from their environment, and while inbound logistics in this case may be obscure, it still does exist.
- **Operations.** Materials are processed or assembled for creation of the final product. This assembly process could be analysis, design, and programming in a software development company or an actual assembly line within a manufacturing plant.
- **Outbound Logistics.** The products are sent out to the supply chain where they are distributed to the customer.
- **Marketing/Sales.** Here marketing communications and promotion of the product takes place. These processes prepare the organization's products for presentation to the targeted customers.
- **Service.** This refers to installation, after-sales service, complaint handling, training, and other aspects of the process responsible for customer interaction, as well as the primary post-sales interface with customers.

Those processes that cut across the primary activities and provide service to the primary activities are called support activities. Support activities include administration and management (e.g., legal department, senior management, etc.), human resources (HR) management, technology development, and procurement. Support activities include the following:

- **Administration and Management.** Composed of corporate or strategic planning that includes senior information technology management as well as other management (e.g., accounting, finance, etc.) necessary for planning and control.
- **Human Resources.** Includes recruitment and selection, training and development, and remuneration of employees. The strategy is to fulfill the mission and objectives of the organization through application of effective HR management.
- **Technology.** The creation and management of production technology and information technology.
- **Procurement.** Purchasing of goods, services, and materials. The goal is to purchase the highest-quality "raw materials" at the lowest possible price with the best terms.

To perform well, an organization must realize a profit on the margin. "Profit on the margin" is defined as a profit on each unit produced. Profit on the margin depends on the ability of the firm to manage the linkages between all activities in its value chain. This interrelationship can be seen in Figure 7-8.

Organizations do not exist by themselves. Instead they are often interconnected with other companies, especially when those companies become the final customer for the organization's product (Figure 7-9). Such interconnectedness means that inputs to a company's value chain are often based on the outputs of another company's value chain. This connection creates the value web. Boeing Aircraft is an example of this principle. They buy millions of parts (e.g., switches, gauges, controls, etc.) from smaller suppliers for the aircraft they build. Each of these smaller suppliers has its own value chain and its own outbound logistics that feeds the Boeing value chain. As these interconnected value chains form a value web, each company provides the products that move into another company's value chain and eventually to the end consumer.

FIGURE 7-9 The Value Web

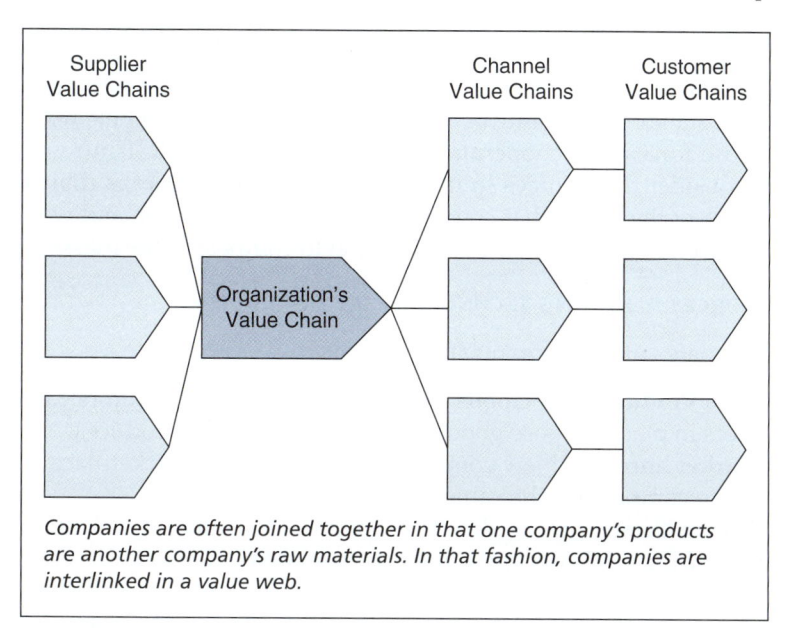

Companies are often joined together in that one company's products are another company's raw materials. In that fashion, companies are interlinked in a value web.

COMPARISON OF THE FUNCTIONAL AND PROCESS VIEWS

When describing ICT infrastructure, the functional and business process views provide different organizational information. Take, for example, an accounts payable system:

- **Functional View.** The accounting functional area (department) of an organization tracks the invoices received and the subsequent payments with an accounts payable system. The accounting department will verify receipt of the materials with the shipping/receiving department before payment is made. Management then reviews reports generated by this system to ensure that payments are appropriately processed. Information about payments is then shared with other functional areas, such as logistics. Applying this functional view, we are able to develop department-centric infrastructural needs and associated cost data that can help with budgeting.
- **Process View.** Taking accounts payable as part of the procurement process allows us to take a process view. Accounts payable must involve inbound logistics to know when materials are received and also to link with operations; in that way, inventory levels can be tracked. In a process orientation, information is freely shared to allow the process to function more effectively and efficiently. Other outputs from this process might include inventory reports and payment reports, so vendor invoices and payments can be tracked.

Both the functional and the process views have merit; however, the process view probably has greater strategic merit. Organizations attain the highest level of efficiency and competitive advantage by viewing technology infrastructure across business processes. While both views tell us something different about a business and both allow us to describe internal business activities, the process view provides stronger strategic information. When developing an ICT infrastructure, with its associated information systems, it is necessary to look at the enterprise using both functional and process views, allowing the business systems analyst to find and make use of efficiencies. The functional view assists in implementation and costing decisions, while the process view assists in setting strategy.

The functional view of an organization is hierarchical in nature, whereas the process view sees an organization as a set of activities that create value. In the functional view, information technology infrastructure provides services to the organization. In the process view, technology is an important supporting function within the organization. It is important in both views that information technology is seen as an essential part of business strategy. Technology is not just a support activity, nor is it just an aspect that underlies the organizational structure; technology must be seen as a key factor in developing business strategy and considered when that business strategy is set.

The Effect of External Forces on Infrastructure

External to any organization are forces that should affect ICT infrastructure decisions. From a strategic standpoint we must evaluate those forces that compete with the organization and those forces that cooperate with it. When creating ICT infrastructure, it is necessary to consider these forces to make sure the infrastructure is robust enough to handle the needs of the forces that cooperate with the organization and well as support the business processes that allow the organization to compete in the marketplace.

COMPETING FORCES AFFECTING TECHNOLOGY INFRASTRUCTURE

Forces that compete with the organization include:

- **Substitute Products and Goods.** Items produced by competitors can be used by consumers in place of those goods that the organization produces.
- **New Market Entrants.** New competitors not yet in the marketplace still have the potential to compete for the same customers.
- **Suppliers.** Although not in direct competition with the organization, suppliers provide raw materials to competing organizations.
- **Customers.** Consumer preferences and choices must be considered when designing ICT infrastructure to support business processes. A good example is the high-end hotel discussed earlier. The hotel may be better using its ICT resources on a CRM system rather than an kiosk to enable speedy checkout.
- **Direct Competitors.** It is usually possible to identify direct competitors of an organization. Carefully reviewing the top competitors often yields strategic initiatives, business processes, and outcomes that can be incorporated into the organization to improve its competitive positioning. Although one organization may have "first-mover" advantage, a competing organization can garner or regain market share through emulating the first-mover's successes and avoiding its failures, as did UPS. Direct competitors are often *fast followers* in the race of competition.

Competitive forces must be carefully examined when making ICT infrastructure recommendations so that the organization is positioned within the marketplace to achieve competitive advantage (see Figure 7-10). It is only when business strategy gives way to information technology strategy and when organizations build ICT infrastructure based on those strategies that the organization can achieve the desired competitive positioning through ICT.

FIGURE 7-10 The Competitive Forces

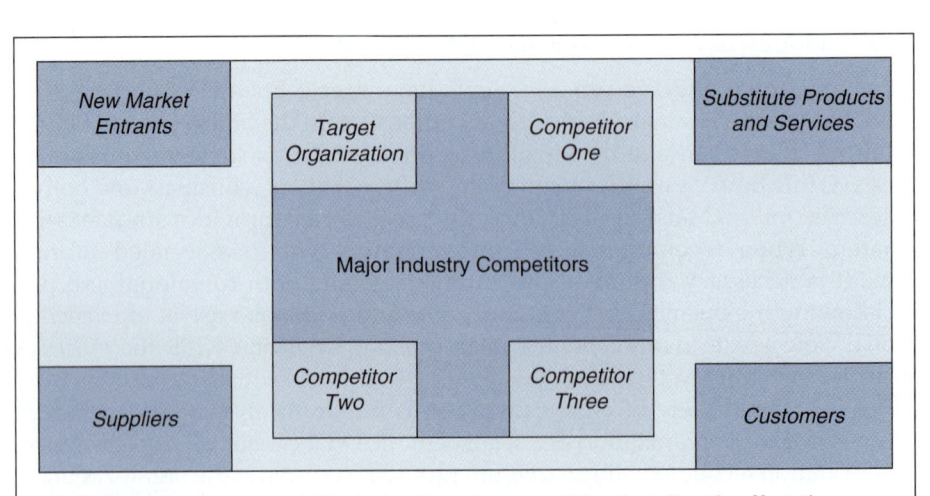

The competitive forces model includes the external entities that directly affect the organization and must be taken into account when building ICT infrastructure. This diagram provides a generic model that can be modified to suit a particular situation and used for analysis of a business. Note: The "Target Organization" is the organization for which the competitive forces analysis is being done.

FIGURE 7-11 The Supply Chain Model

Supply Chain				
Supplier	Manufacturing/Operations	Distributor	Retail Outlet	Customer

For purposes of business analysis, this generic model of the standard supply chain with its various components can be modified to reflect a particular situation.

COOPERATING ORGANIZATIONS: THE SUPPLY CHAIN

It is important to look at those entities that cooperate with the organization when building ICT infrastructure. Often it is a question of building ICT infrastructure that integrates the operations of the entities that cooperate with the organization by building a supply chain management system. That supply chain (Figure 7-11) consists of:

- **Suppliers** supply raw materials to producers of goods and services.
- **Manufacturers** produce the goods and services sold in the marketplace.
- **Distributors** take those goods produced by the manufacturer and get them to retail distribution.
- **Retail outlets** receive the goods through retail distribution and sell them to customers.
- **Customers** purchase the goods or service produced by the organization.

Organizations can be involved in manufacturing hard goods (e.g., clothes, furniture, cars, etc.), producing information goods (e.g., search engines, online databases, private investigators, etc.), providing services (e.g., financial services, janitorial services, Internet service providers, etc.), or any combination. Whatever their product or service, however, all organizations have a supply chain.

When considering information technology infrastructure recommendations for an organization's supply chain, be sure to consider the flow of products, information, and finances. Product flow includes the movement of goods from suppliers to manufacturing/operations, distribution, retail outlets, and eventually to the customer. The supply chain management infrastructure tracks raw materials, their transformation into products, distribution to retail outlets, and the final purchase by the customer. This tracking can be accomplished through a supply chain management system, possibly in conjunction with such technologies as RFID.

Technology Infrastructure Project Planning

Planning for information technology infrastructure is an important undertaking. Information technology infrastructure recommendations must flow from business strategy. The infrastructure must meet the business outcomes specified by the organization's business strategy. ICT infrastructure planning also must occur at the strategic-level of management to ensure that it appropriately meshes with and supports the business strategy goals.

Using appropriate analysis tools, such as value chain or supply chain modeling, the needs of an organization can be understood. Those types of tools should be used by strategic management in their decision making regarding business strategies. The business systems analyst can use the same tools, but from an ICT perspective, to create ICT recommendations that follow the business strategy. Senior management takes a high-level view to set organizational direction and explicate strategy, whereas business systems analysts plan with an eye on business strategy and take an ICT implementation view. The business models are helpful when making ICT infrastructure recommendations. As discussed earlier, the business systems analyst/manager must have both visionary and planning skills to carry out successful ICT infrastructure recommendations.

Traditionally, the design of information technology infrastructure has neither been well structured, nor has planning for that infrastructure had best practices that were widely promulgated and accepted. It has been common that network design activities (these processes were not then called ICT infrastructure design activities) were largely of the ilk that "if we build it, they will use it." Those activities were often not based on well-defined business needs, but rather on pragmatism fostered by technology changes. More often than not, the philosophy was to *build a solution that exploited the available technology rather than first determining whether a business need existed.* Value-proposition-driven information technology infrastructure design, as a strategic imperative also at the center of efficient process design, must be an integral part of an organization's vision to achieve competitive advantage. It cannot be merely an afterthought.

Value-Driven Business Modeling

A primary precept of information technology infrastructure design must be that all implementations necessarily provide tangible value to the organization and its customers. Using business modeling techniques and analyzing the organization internally and the competitive marketplace externally, business systems analysts can extend an organization's business strategy into ICT infrastructure recommendations. A successful design must take into account the general needs of the industry as well as the specific needs and characteristics of the organization. For example, the banking industry requires (in part due to regulations) strong ICT security measures, while a particular bank might require a specific type of web site or configuration of automated teller machines. With information gained from thorough analyses, the business systems analyst is better prepared to design an infrastructure that will provide the necessary technology to fulfill internal operational needs, external industry mandated functions, and at the same time support the value propositions of the organization. A **value proposition** is a clear statement of what an organization can provide to its customers. Some examples of clear value propositions include increased revenues, decreased cycle times (i.e., faster time to market), increased market share, and improved operational efficiency (Konrath, 2006). When business systems analysts create ICT infrastructure, they must remain mindful of the value propositions the infrastructure is trying to fulfill.

Business modeling motivates an analysis of the organization and the industry, maximizing the probability that internal business processes are supported, external forces are considered, and value propositions are fulfilled. This analysis must be aligned with the business strategy before ICT recommendations are determined. Such alignment is accomplished if the business systems analyst does his or her modeling from an ICT infrastructure perspective. Such modeling includes the following:

- Competitive forces modeling mandates the identification of all significant stakeholders and highlights the specific activities of those stakeholders that influence the competitive positioning. This information facilitates the creation of an infrastructure that optimizes the competitive positioning of the company.
- Internal organizational modeling (value chain) identifies the major processes within the company and promotes a design influenced by value propositions.
- Supply chain modeling identifies stakeholders, but differently from competitive forces modeling; supply chain modeling assists in identifying end-to-end supplier-to-customer issues.
- Strength, weakness, opportunities, and threat (SWOT) modeling identifies the competitive position of the company and facilitates recommendations that will enhance competitive advantage.

Each of these modeling techniques is used in the business-driven infrastructure design methodology presented in this textbook.

AN OVERVIEW OF THE BUSINESS-DRIVEN INFRASTRUCTURE DESIGN (BDID) METHODOLOGY

Business-driven infrastructure design (BDID) consists of a series of phases that may appear like a waterfall approach, but in reality has a fair amount of overlap (Figure 7-12) and the steps are cyclic. In this sense, BDID is an intellectual offspring of the System Development Life Cycle (SDLC). Both BDID and SDLC are phase-based, and both

	Project Start				Project End
Analysis	■	■			
Design		■	■		
Implementation Planning			■	■	
Post-Implementation				■	■

BDID flows somewhat like a waterfall, with overlap that occurs during the various steps. The BDID processes also exhibit a cyclic nature.

FIGURE 7-12 BDID Steps and Overlap

assume the iterative approach characterized by a fair amount of "going back-and-forth." Where the two approaches differ is in the methods they apply to address domain-specific issues. SDLC focuses primarily on software design, whereas BDID concentrates on ICT infrastructure. ICT infrastructure includes software functionality as a component part of the overall design, but not the specific analysis and design of software.

The BDID steps include:

- **Analysis.** The analysis step facilitates an understanding of the company and the industry for which the ICT infrastructure is being implemented. In effect, it sets the stage for integration with the organization's business strategy. Standard business-modeling tools are used to analyze company needs and develop an understanding of the industry from the ICT perspective. The goal is to create ICT value propositions on which to base process change initiatives and ICT infrastructure recommendations. These propositions and the resultant recommendations must tie directly back to the organization's business strategy.

  Using the ICT value propositions uncovered during the analysis phase, along with business process selections, ICT recommendations are made within the layers of the *technology infrastructure architecture*: user, enterprise, services, and network components. For example, the FedEx business strategy was to create the next-day package shipping industry. It required specific technical recommendations at each component layer and specific technical solutions with support and ongoing maintenance requirements. These recommendations also necessitated growth and upgrade projections. Analysis is part business analysis and part technical analysis—both parts create analytical outputs that, when taken together, should allow the business systems analyst to make solid and appropriate recommendations.

- **Design.** Reconciling business analysis phase recommendations, business systems analysts, network engineers, software developers, and other designers document business processes for creation/innovation/improvement and hardware/software solutions that create the final design of the ICT infrastructure. These recommendations include hardware selection to support the various components of the ICT infrastructure architecture. The business systems analyst works with other technical staff to perform site surveys to assess appropriateness (e.g., necessary AC power, space, air conditioning, etc.) and to make recommendations for the required infrastructure components. Final design documents are created and validated against the Analysis Phase (just discussed above) recommendations of the BDID cycle. Throughout the design phase, the business systems analyst must keep an eye on the total cost of ownership of the technologies being recommended.

- **Implementation Planning.** An implementation plan is created to describe how process change will be carried out with the recommended technologies. This plan is the blueprint used to change business processes and deliver the value proposition to the customer. Once engineers have built and tested the new infrastructure, it is ready to hand over to the users.

FIGURE 7-13 The FedEx Technology Timeline

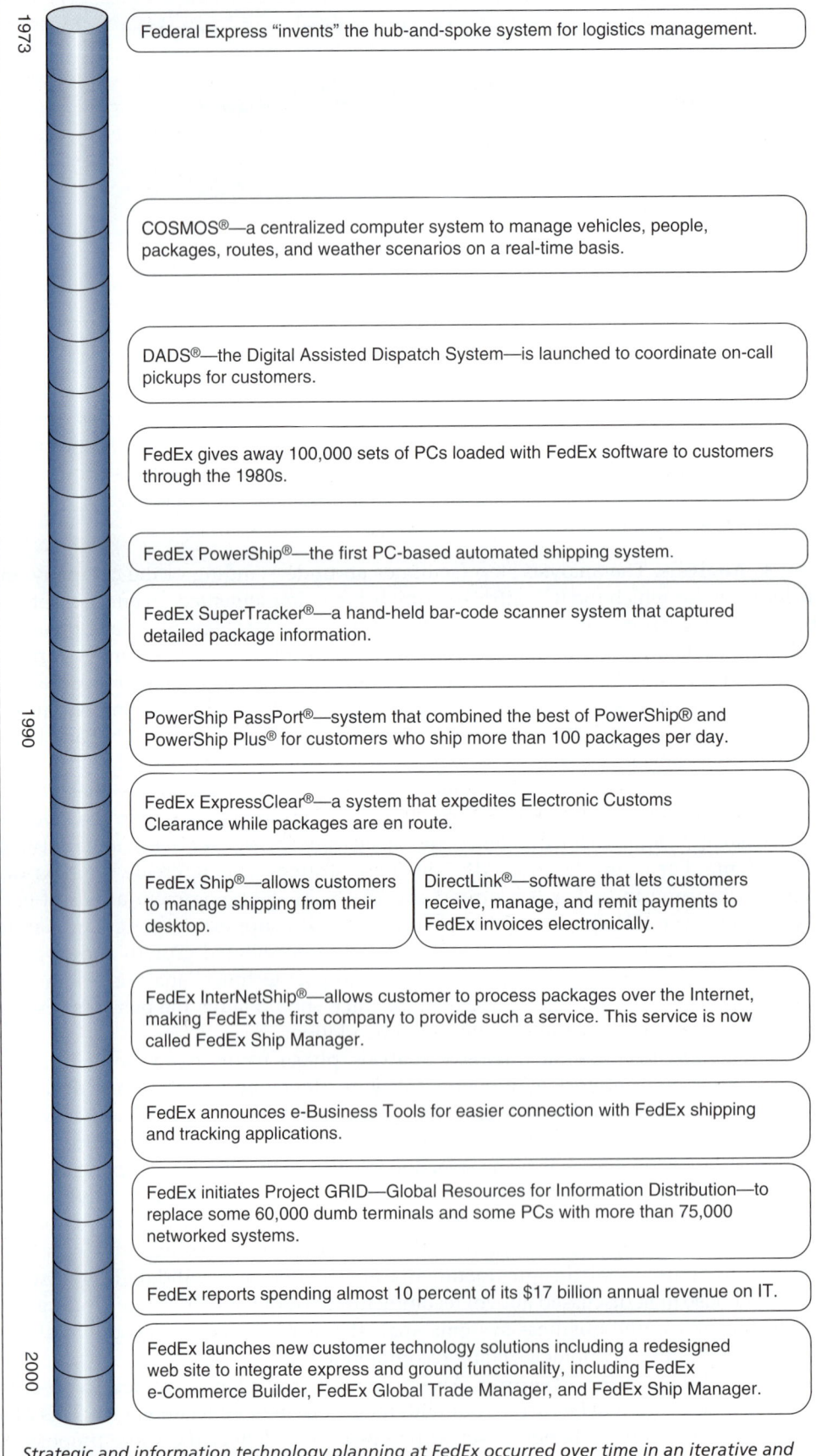

1973 — Federal Express "invents" the hub-and-spoke system for logistics management.

COSMOS®—a centralized computer system to manage vehicles, people, packages, routes, and weather scenarios on a real-time basis.

DADS®—the Digital Assisted Dispatch System—is launched to coordinate on-call pickups for customers.

FedEx gives away 100,000 sets of PCs loaded with FedEx software to customers through the 1980s.

FedEx PowerShip®—the first PC-based automated shipping system.

FedEx SuperTracker®—a hand-held bar-code scanner system that captured detailed package information.

1990 — PowerShip PassPort®—system that combined the best of PowerShip® and PowerShip Plus® for customers who ship more than 100 packages per day.

FedEx ExpressClear®—a system that expedites Electronic Customs Clearance while packages are en route.

FedEx Ship®—allows customers to manage shipping from their desktop.

DirectLink®—software that lets customers receive, manage, and remit payments to FedEx invoices electronically.

FedEx InterNetShip®—allows customer to process packages over the Internet, making FedEx the first company to provide such a service. This service is now called FedEx Ship Manager.

FedEx announces e-Business Tools for easier connection with FedEx shipping and tracking applications.

FedEx initiates Project GRID—Global Resources for Information Distribution—to replace some 60,000 dumb terminals and some PCs with more than 75,000 networked systems.

FedEx reports spending almost 10 percent of its $17 billion annual revenue on IT.

2000 — FedEx launches new customer technology solutions including a redesigned web site to integrate express and ground functionality, including FedEx e-Commerce Builder, FedEx Global Trade Manager, and FedEx Ship Manager.

Strategic and information technology planning at FedEx occurred over time in an iterative and growth-oriented manner.

Source: Based on SRI, 2006.

- **Post-Implementation.** Whereas implementation planning is about getting an infrastructure in place, post-implementation is about forward thinking after the initial implementation. Information gathered during the previous phases regarding expected growth is now used to create a plan for network upgrades. Once future business growth is understood, the infrastructure designer should return to the analysis stage, revisit the business strategy on an ongoing basis, update the business models, develop value proposition models and infrastructure recommendations, and continue forward through the study and design processes. This is an ongoing function that will keep infrastructure abreast of changes in the organization and business environment. Post-implementation feeds back directly to the earlier BDID phases. Such post-implementation activity is seen in FedEx's constant vigilance to keep abreast of technology (Figure 7-13).

Even though systems analysis and design methodologies have matured and become generally accepted, ICT infrastructure, including network design, remains largely an afterthought and has never been widely standardized. Technology infrastructure design must be accomplished from an enterprise perspective, and infrastructure design and implementation processes must be based on organizational and industry value propositions. This approach takes into account the core competencies of the organization as well as industry technical imperatives and stakeholder concerns. Further, network design must be set within the larger context of the strategy-driven management of the enterprise. The phases of business-driven infrastructure design are more fully covered in the following chapters.

Chapter Summary

Information technology infrastructure is defined as four interconnected components: user, enterprise, service, and network components. User components include technologies that the user directly interfaces with; enterprise components include applications that provide enterprise-wide functionality; service components are those parts of the network that facilitate its operations; and network components include typology and its associated equipment.

In order for an ICT infrastructure to provide desired business outcomes, the management of the organization must be involved in ICT infrastructure decision making. Management must set overall organizational business strategy, and that strategy must drive ICT infrastructure resource allocation. Those organizational members who are responsible for ensuring that technology infrastructure supports business goals must view the enterprise both internally and externally. They must also participate in valued-based business modeling as part of a structured planning methodology. Business-driven infrastructure design, or BDID, is such a methodology.

The business-driven infrastructure design methodology will be covered fully in later chapters. The methodology is composed of several phases or steps:

Analysis. The analysis step facilitates an understanding of the company for which the ICT technology infrastructure is being implemented and its industry, setting the stage for integration with the organization's business strategy. Using the value propositions described in the analysis phase, ICT recommendations are made within the components of the technology infrastructure architecture.

Design. Reconciling business analysis and **ICT** infrastructure recommendations, designers select hardware/software solutions to create the final design of the infrastructure. All final design documents are validated against the analysis recommendations.

Implementation Plan. The implementation plan describes how the selected equipment will be installed. This plan is the blueprint used to build the ICT infrastructure, change business processes, and deliver value propositions to the customer. Once engineers have built and tested the network, it is ready to hand over to the users.

Post-Implementation. Post-implementation is about forward thinking after the initial implementation. Information gathered during the previous phases regarding expected growth is now used to create a plan for network upgrades. Once future business growth is understood, the infrastructure designer should return to the analysis stage, revisit the business strategy on an ongoing basis, update the business models, develop value proposition models and infrastructure recommendations, and continue forward through design phases. This is an ongoing function that will keep the infrastructure current with changes in the organization and business environment. Post-implementation feeds back directly to the earlier BDID phases.

Vignette Wrap Up

UPS and FedEx are titans of the consumer shipping market. They have battled for years for preeminence in that market. When looking at next-day shipping, FedEx had the first-mover advantage when it created the information technology infrastructure to deliver a new product (next day shipping) and support a new market. The core business of FedEx is still logistics—moving shipments from point A to point B. The strategies set forth by Fred Smith, the founder of FedEx are still in place. These strategies include shipping fast and reliably while providing excellent customer service. These strategies were coupled with the continued need to minimize the cost of operations, thereby making ICT strategy and resultant ICT infrastructure essential to organizational success. It has been and still is essential that FedEx employ advanced technologies to support its strategies.

A key reason for FedEx's success is that it was built upon an information-driven architecture and fashioned itself as a provider of technological solutions rather than just a logistics company. The company continues to do the same today. Over the years, FedEx has defined the major items of the four components of information technology infrastructure for its organization:

- **User and Enterprise Components.** PowerShip®, Super Tracker®, PassPort®, Ship®, FedEx.com, COSMOS®, DADS®, ExpressClear®, InterNetShip®, PowerShipMC®, 10,000 workstations, 50,000 Wintel PCs, terminals in 100,000 customer sites, and giving proprietary software to 650,000 customers.
- **Service Components.** Data centers that process 20 million transactions daily, database servers that house 3,000 databases and handle more than 100 million requests daily, extensive printing, network accessible storage, file-storage, web, FTP, etc.
- **Network Components.** The largest digital network of any company worldwide, the most extensive private client-server network worldwide, and the third largest private computer network worldwide with 1,000 LANs and 2,500 servers.

FedEx has 5,500 information technology staff located worldwide to support its 260,000+ employees. That staff is charged with maintaining and creating technology to support the company's core business process—logistics—and support the stated business outcomes, namely providing logistical services that are fast, efficient, and reliable while providing excellent customer service. All this service to the customer must be provided while the organization continues to minimize its cost of operations.

End of Chapter Questions/Assurance of Learning

1. Select one of FedEx's technical initiatives, research that initiative, and come up with examples of the various components of information technology infrastructure.
2. Describe the difference between networks and ICT infrastructure, and explain why ICT infrastructure is important to sustain competitive advantage.
3. Compare the job of management within and outside of information technology, and discuss whether both groups should be involved in system and ICT infrastructure design and implementation. Be sure to include specifics on why or why not.
4. Discuss the different types of organizations and what organization type means for building ICT infrastructure.

Case Exercises

These exercises build on the case exercises from previous chapters.
1. XYZ Inc. is a hardware company that builds network hardware and wants to expand its product offerings to ensure it is a viable alternative to other network hardware manufacturers. Develop a plan for XYZ Inc. so it can be sure it understands its customers (think CRM). How should XYZ Inc. proceed with its business plans to ensure that it can meet its customers' needs today and in the future? Develop a brief report and presentation on this topic.
2. Prepare a brief case analysis and presentation that describes HealthyWay HMO (as described in previous vignettes) from a functional view and process view. In your case analysis, discuss what things are important for HealthyWay to consider when designing its business processes. Emphasize how HealthyWay should proceed in respect to its competition.
3. Select a company you are familiar with and write a case analysis that describes it from process and functional views. Make recommendations showing how it can improve its competitive positioning by changing its business processes through ICT. Support your analysis by citing Internet and/or print articles (i.e., trade publications, journal articles).

Key Words and Concepts

business-driven infrastructure design (BDID) 202
business processes view of the organization 197
business systems analyst 188
cost leadership 192
disruptive technologies 186
external forces affecting infrastructure 200
fast follower 190
first-mover advantage 190
focused approach 191
functional view of the organization 195
industry-wide approach 191
product differentiation 192
sustaining technologies 187
SWOT 193
value-driven business modeling 202
value proposition 202
visionary role 193

References

Christensen, C. M., Bohmer, R., & Kenagy, J. (2000). Will disruptive innovations cure health care? *Harvard Business Review*.

D'Aventi, R. (1994). *Hypercompetition: Managing the dynamics of strategic maneuvering*. New York: Free Press.

Konrath, J. (2006). *How to write a strong value proposition*. Retrieved March 3, 2006, from http://www.sideroad.com/Sales/value_proposition.html

Laudon, K., & Laudon, J. (2004). *Management information systems*. Upper Saddle River, New Jersey: Prentice Hall.

Lee, S., & Asllani, A. (1997). TQM and BPR: Symbiosis and a new approach for integration. *Management Decision, 35*(6), 409–416.

Mitchell, V. L., & Zmud, R. W. (1999). The effects of coupling IT and work process strategies in redesign projects. *Organization Science, 10*(4), 424–439.

Perlison, K., & Saunders, C. (2006). *Managing & using information systems: A strategic approach*. Hoboken, NJ: Wiley

Porter, M. (1996). What is strategy? *Harvard Business Review*.

Porter, M. E. (1990). *The competitive advantage of nations* New York: Free Press.

Porter, M. (1985). *Competitive advantage: Creating and sustaining superior performance*. New York: Free Press.

SRI. (2006). *Global impacts of FedEx in the new economy* Washington: SRI International.

8 BUSINESS PROCESSES

> ### Learning Objectives
>
> - Define a business process, its objectives, and its attributes.
> - Understand how a business process can extend across operations, management, and strategic layers of management.
> - Know the key factors involved in process change and how to use them.
> - Understand how to select processes for change.
> - Clarify the role ICT plays in product innovation.

This chapter covers business process improvement and innovation through the strategic alignment of IT with business strategy. This is done in order to bring about positive changes to business processes that can create and sustain competitive positioning. Existing processes and new processes within a business need to add value and must be competitively positioned to do so. In order to be able to change processes to maximize value, the business systems analyst must understand what a business process is and how to make it a value-creating process. This chapter discusses these topics.

INTRODUCTION

Information technology (IT) staff needs to become part of the business rather than be treated as something like *those people in the backroom who are only needed to keep the systems running*. IT staff needs to do more than keep the e-mail flowing or keep the hardware running or build systems that managers request. IT staff must be an integral part of the organization and be aligned closely with the business and its mission. Organizational success can only be enhanced for those businesses that make IT managers an integral part of defining business opportunities and not simply the builders of other managers' solutions (Sauer & Yetton, 1997). Alignment of business strategy with ICT infrastructure requires a highly integrated strategic management process. Strategic alignment of IT infrastructure requires both integration and interplay between business strategy, organizational structure, and organizational processes (Henderson & Venkataman, 1991). This integration enables the organization to align its strategies, structure, and organizational processes, using both internal conditions and the external environment, while at the same time recognizing that both can have an effect on ICT infrastructure choices. In today's web-enabled era, the role of a business systems analyst should be to seek business innovation and use the unique opportunities created by technology. The key objective is to drive strategy (Hansell, 2000). This objective would suggest that the business systems analyst (this term is used for the CIO, CKO, or other persons responsible for strategic alignment IT and business strategy) must work closely with the chief executive officer (CEO) to continuously develop business strategies (Smaczny, 2001). In order to develop business strategies, the business systems analyst must identify processes within the organization that are amenable to improvement or innovation and then understand just how that improvement or innovation will result in new positive outcomes for the organization (e.g., increased market share, improved products, process efficiencies).

The strategic alignment of information technology and its associated systems, and their ability to enhance organizational performance, have been frequently studied. The literature is replete with examples of research that report varying levels of support for information technology being used as a strategic tool. One approach taken in the literature is a resource-centered perspective that usually considers IT hardware and software a strategic resource when properly combined with other strategic resources (Oh & Pinsonneault, 2007). Further, this view assumes that the association between the scale (size, resource commitment, amount, etc.) and scope (uniqueness, type, etc.) of the IT investment are positively associated with organizational performance. (See, for example, Barua, Kriebel, & Mukhopadhyay, 1995; and Dehning, Richardson, & and Zmud, 2003.) Another view of the strategic alignment of IT is the contingency perspective in which IT resources are believed to add little value unless they are planned to support a firm's main strategic objectives (Chan, Huff, Barclay, & Copeland, 1997). The contingency view is taken in this book and is based on the belief that the greatest impact on organizational performance can be realized by utilizing IT resources to support strategic objectives, and by understanding the organization's strategy and where IT can support it.

Why Is ICT Implemented?

The notion of organizational "fit" is key to defining strategic alignment and has been explicated in several ways to include adaptation (personal–environmental fit), compatibility (individual–organizational fit), assimilation (organization–organization fit), and coupling (internal–external fit). "In the context of organizational research, the construct is generally understood as 'congruence, match, agreement, or similarity between two conceptually distinct constructs'" (Oh & Pinsonneault, 2007). This book takes the approach that the strategic alignment of IT is the fit between the objectives of an organization and how the organization proposes to meet those objectives using IT. The "fit" comes when the business systems analyst is able to envision the organization, align IT implementation with organizational objectives, and cause IT to augment the organization. Along the lines of the primary strategic orientation of firms (Porter, 1990), IT is implemented for three reasons—*cost reduction*, *quality improvement*, and *revenue growth*—each of which has been shown to have varying impacts on organizational performance.

- **Cost Reduction.** Firms can attempt to achieve market leadership by reducing cost through a number of strategies. These strategies can include, for example, waste reduction, lower inventories, increasing productivity, and reducing cycle times. In any cost reduction strategy, the overarching objective is to reduce costs while not sacrificing quality and thus be able to maintain a cost-leadership position within the marketplace. IT can be leveraged in a number of ways to affect this strategy, including, for example, supply chain management, inventory control, or ERP systems.
- **Quality Improvement.** It is possible for a firm to gain market share by producing higher-quality goods at the same or higher costs as their competitors. Using this product differentiation strategy (Porter, 1990), firms seek to distinguish their products from others in the marketplace, while at the same time increasing market share and maintaining marginal revenue. In the marketplace, the perception of value needs to be created, allowing for higher price and increased market share. IT can be used to improve product quality through manufacturing improvements, and to enhance product perception in the marketplace (e.g., CRM).
- **Revenue Growth.** In the marketplace, revenue growth strategies focus on increased sales and profits. This approach requires using IT to create/enhance products, allowing for a wider variety of product offering, and/or to enhance sales, while at the same time maintaining market share. Perhaps a revenue growth strategy is easiest to conceive in online companies such as Amazon, Google, or e-Bay.

Process Change

One of the jobs of a business systems analyst is to recommend process innovations and improvements that can be accomplished through use of **enablers** such as information and communication technology (ICT), structural organizational change, and cultural/organizational change. These enablers are discussed in detail later in this chapter. Suffice it to say, however, that the business systems analyst must work closely with the organizational

FIGURE 8-1
ICT Infrastructure, Business Strategy, and Processes Change

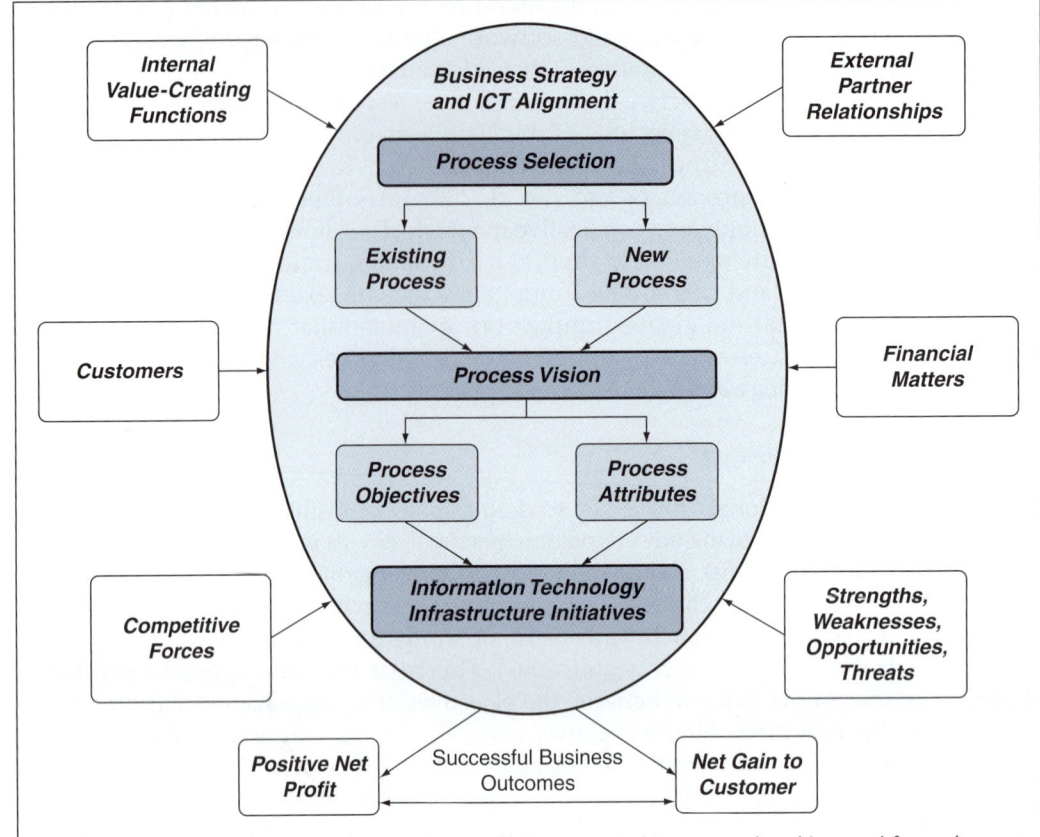

Today's digitally enabled organization must make strategy and its external and internal forces known to all parts of the organization and especially to those who recommend ICT infrastructure. Planning for ICT investments must be driven by sound strategy and based on process improvements within the organization. Those ICT-mediated process improvements must be perceived by the consumer as product enhancements and must also provide a path to a gain in net profit.

senior strategist—whether that person is the CEO or some other staff member—to capitalize on the organizational investment in ICT. The business systems analyst must employ strategies that allow for the recognition of opportunities for process change initiatives and then drive/guide those recommendations through the various obstacles that may thwart success. The interplay among business strategy, process selection, and ICT selection is essential for any ICT initiatives to be successful. (See Figure 8-1.)

The major **informational inputs** needed to align technology with business strategy and select business processes for innovation can be culled from business analysis (introduced in the previous chapter). The information required to align IT with strategy and select business processes for change includes (1) internal value-creating activities of the organization; (2) external partnerships; (3) competitive forces; and (4) strengths, weakness, opportunities, and threats of competitors. By evaluating the information that these inputs provide, a business systems analyst can better offer strategic recommendations for ICT infrastructure. Each of the those informational inputs is necessary:

- **Internal Value-Creating Activities of the Organization.** These activities in Porter's value chain represent the processes that take raw materials into the organization, somehow convert them to add value to the organization's products, and then deliver product to the customer. The value chain is composed of primary and secondary activities.
- **External Partner Relationships.** Porter's supply chain assists in identifying those partners that cooperate with the organization as the organization creates products. Understanding the relationship between these partners and the organization and the level of control the organization has over its partners can assist the business systems analyst in knowing which business processes are particularly amenable to change.

- **Competitive Forces.** In addition to direct competitors that exist in the same marketplace as the organization, other forces affect a company's ability to compete in that marketplace. Those other forces include substitute products and goods, new market entrants, suppliers, and customers—all represent forces that can have an effect on the company.
- **Comparative Analysis of Strengths, Weaknesses, Opportunities, and Threats.** A comparative analysis of the strengths, weaknesses, opportunities, and threats (SWOT) of an organization's major competitors allows the business systems analyst to identify the organization's current competitive position and possibilities for potential competitive changes. SWOT analysis also allows the business systems analyst to see where the organization may possibly be a "fast follower" of a competitor's successful technology. The SWOT analysis additionally allows for identification of organizational strengths and weaknesses within the organization as well as threats from the external environment.

These informational inputs must feed into a clear alignment of technology with business strategy. The business systems analyst must interpret these inputs and use that interpretation to drive the selection of business processes for change initiatives. Identification of processes for change initiatives, the creation of a process vision, and the understanding of process objectives and attributes should lead to clear IT infrastructure initiatives. Those recommendations must provide a positive net gain to the customer and a positive net profit to the organization. The diagram in Figure 8-1 shows this alignment between business strategy and ICT.

Process View of the Organization

Both the functional view and the process view of an organization are useful. As discussed in the previous chapter, in the **functional view**, the organization is broken into functional areas, namely finance, sales and marketing, manufacturing, accounting, and finance. Each functional area is divided into levels of management that include strategic, management, knowledge, and operational levels. Information systems are assumed to support all levels and all functional areas. The functional view allows for departmental and management-level definition, while the **process view** allows for organizational process identification. The functional view is helpful in delineating departmental and managerial hierarchy, while the process view allows cross-departmental processes to be defined. This process view is essential to implementing improvement and innovation; thus, the rest of this textbook applies the process view. The process view used here is based on the work of Michael Porter and Thomas Davenport. Their approaches are combined to provide a unified way to understand process improvement and the innovation prerogatives of information systems infrastructure.

The process view can look both internally and externally. The internal process largely is based on the value chain, while the external view is based primarily on the supply chain. The supply chain consists of linkages between suppliers, distributors, marketing outlets, customers, and the organization. The value chain consists of primary and supporting activities of an organization. The primary activities take raw materials from the environment and then process these materials to add value to the consumer. The supporting activities provide ancillary services necessary to run the organization. Rather than looking at functional areas within the organization as silos where information flows are vetted at the highest levels of management and then sent down their respective functional (departmental) silos or channels, the process view transcends those silos and looks at value-producing processes at the precise points where work and information are shared across departmental lines. These value-producing processes must be part of the strategic direction of the organization in order to produce competitive advantage. Therefore, it is imperative that ICT planning occurs at the strategic level of the enterprise to maximize return on technology investment.

ICT operations must necessarily be concerned with making the technology function properly and often implement what might be called nonstrategic IT—that is, information technology that does not add direct value to the products of the organization (e.g., some regulatory agencies can mandate information reporting systems). All too often, the IT department only sees itself in one of these roles:

- Maintaining technology
- Performing nonstrategic IT implementation
- Developing IT infrastructure only at the behest of other managers

Instead, the IT staff must see themselves as part of a team that defines strategy and its resultant processes, recommends technological solutions to optimize those processes, and brings about competitive positioning. The previous chapter discussed some of the strategic theories and ways that technology could be used to support organizational strategy.

To make a substantial change in processes in an organization, it is important for the business systems analyst to know the key factors involved in process change. That person must understand which process levers drive process change and understand the specific nature of those levers. Then the analyst will be able to develop ICT strategies for process change and recommend how to implement that change.

ICT Impact on Economic Outcomes

ICT impact must be seen in two ways: (1) an increase in net profit to the organization, and (2) an increased perceived benefit to the customer. The process view assists ICT in being able to yield net economic value to the company and net perceived benefit to the customer. All ICT change initiatives must meet this "economic benefit test." A supply chain management initiative (see Figure 8-2) illustrates this point as follows:

- An organization desires to implement a supply chain management initiative and considers it in alignment with its business strategy.
- The organization is analyzed internally and externally, from the perspective of the ICT initiative, using the supply chain and value chain models. Processes requiring change are identified. The objectives and attributes for each process are also identified.
- The linkage between the ICT initiative, process change, and net economic benefit is articulated. The net economic benefits to the organization (i.e., net profit) and the customer (e.g., decreased product lead time) must be identified.
- The relationships among the ICT initiative, process change, and economic benefits are essential to any change initiative's successes.

Any ICT initiative needs to include process changes that maximize economic outcomes for the organization and the consumer. A real-life supply chain management initiative

FIGURE 8-2 ICT Initiative to Economic Outcome

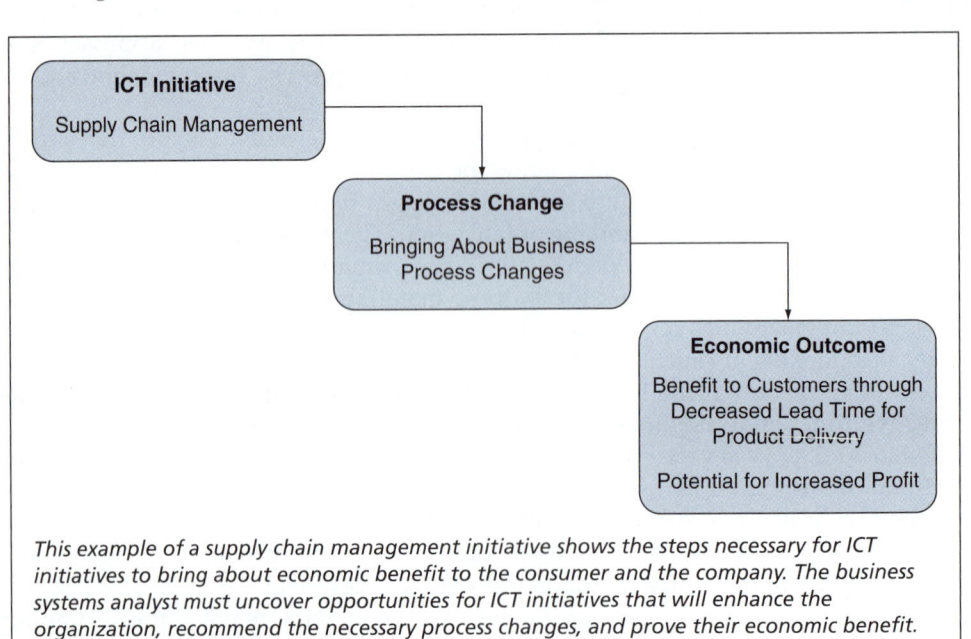

> **ICT Initiative**
> Supply Chain Management
>
> **Process Change**
> Bringing About Business Process Changes
>
> **Economic Outcome**
> Benefit to Customers through Decreased Lead Time for Product Delivery
>
> Potential for Increased Profit
>
> *This example of a supply chain management initiative shows the steps necessary for ICT initiatives to bring about economic benefit to the consumer and the company. The business systems analyst must uncover opportunities for ICT initiatives that will enhance the organization, recommend the necessary process changes, and prove their economic benefit.*
> *Source:* Based on Davenport, 1993.

would of course be more elaborate than our example. Further discussion of the payoff of such ICT investments will be discussed in other chapters.

Information and Communication Technology Use

Before diving into the details of process improvement and innovation, it is helpful to understand how information systems are used. Four types of ICT implementation typically occur within organizations: (1) cost reduction, (2) management support, (3) strategic planning, and (4) competitive thrust. When the business systems analyst recommends or implements technology, that analyst should be aware of the type of project he or she will be working on. The project type often drives specifics such as project priority and available resources. These types of implementations have also been used to study IT use by organizations (Boynton, Zmud, & Jacobs, 1994). The types include:

- **Cost Reduction.** ICT can be used to reduce costs in an organization. By making processes more efficient through ICT-mediated process change, the costs of producing products can be reduced.
- **Management Support**. Information systems can be used to assist in monitoring, controlling, and designing business activities. Systems designed to support management often take data from the organization's transaction-processing systems and transform them into reports and information that enable managers to do their jobs.
- **Strategic Planning**. ICT that supports strategic planning is included in this type of system implementation. These systems can assist in the formulation of business strategy and often include both management reporting as well as "soft" competitive data gathered from sources external to the organization.
- **Competitive Thrust**. Using information systems to develop competitive positioning in the marketplace is essential. It is just one of several major reasons to implement ICT. ICT infrastructure can be directly used to establish competitive advantage in the marketplace.

These four types of information systems (shown in Figure 8-3) are created to support the enterprise, and all types are useful. When the motivation for creating ICT infrastructure

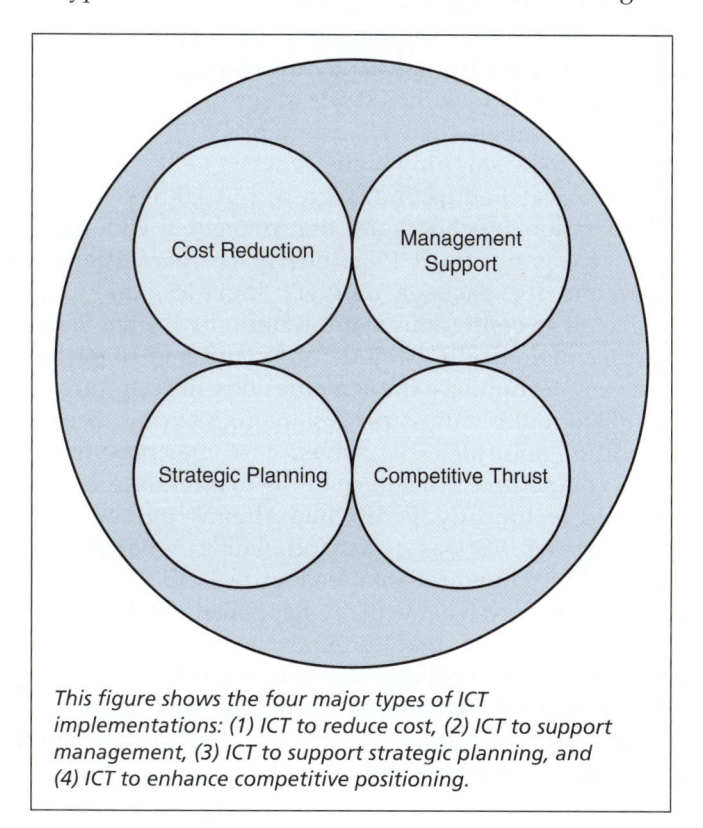

FIGURE 8-3 Types of ICT Implementations

This figure shows the four major types of ICT implementations: (1) ICT to reduce cost, (2) ICT to support management, (3) ICT to support strategic planning, and (4) ICT to enhance competitive positioning.

is combined with the way systems are used, the business systems analyst is positioned to maximize the impact of ICT resource expenditures.

PROCESSES IN AN ORGANIZATIONAL CONTEXT

Organizations consist of departments, and business processes often cut across departments. The process nature of business can be seen within the value chain. Today, virtually all business processes are supported by an ICT infrastructure. It is important for the business systems analyst to be able to identify these processes and make recommendations about which technology can best be used to enhance the organization. To do that job, the business systems analyst must understand how to break the organization into smaller units, so he or she can make the right recommendations.

Existing Infrastructure versus New Infrastructure

Distinct advantages can come from creating a new ICT infrastructure within an organization. It is true that changing business processes that already exist presents unique challenges over the creation of new processes. The business systems analyst must approach both issues, however, from the same vantage point—business strategy. But he or she may need to incorporate different levers for each situation. In fact, it is important for the business systems analyst to sense the ongoing environment, whether building technology infrastructure for new processes or using that infrastructure to change existing processes. In each case, the business systems analyst must be astute enough to determine what is necessary for process implementation/change success. The primary goals for all ICT implementations is to solve business problems, enhance business processes, and increase net profit.

FedEx and UPS offer two outstanding examples of new versus existing process implementation. As a start-up, FedEx was able to develop a strategy that included ICT infrastructure at its core. In fact, FedEx considered technical ability to be a critical success factor and built the company around it. If we look back at the history of FedEx, we see a company that developed itself by focusing on technology and then used technology to reach its strategic goals. FedEx management was astute enough to garner a first-mover advantage by creating the next-day shipping industry (Krause 1999) and then continued on that "technology glide path" by constantly developing new technological solutions to fulfill emerging and already identified needs of customers.

It is interesting to compare the UPS experience with that of FedEx. UPS was an existing company within the shipping industry when FedEx became a new entrant in the marketplace. UPS watched as FedEx grew, but UPS was fettered by existing information and operational technologies that prevented UPS from capitalizing on new technologies. It was not until 1985, nearly 12 years after FedEx created its hub-and-spoke system for package delivery logistics, that UPS had next-day delivery available to all 48 contiguous states within the United States. UPS was thus operationally and technologically behind FedEx and had to perform considerable restructuring and new technology implementations to recapture its market share, which required substantial business process reengineering. FedEx, however, was successful in providing solutions that solved customer problems, which allowed FedEx to exploit its competitive advantage in the marketplace. As UPS was catching up operationally and technically, FedEx had already moved on to exploit other competitive advantages. UPS was a fast follower in what D'Aventi (1994) calls hypercompetition and the counterattack (see Figure 8-4).

In terms of the history of what actually happened, FedEx launched its next-day shipping service and exploited that competitive move. UPS counterattacked by becoming a fast follower in the next-day shipping marketplace. UPS's becoming a fast follower meant that FedEx's competitive advantage was temporary. To sustain its competitive position, FedEx was forced to bring new technologies to the marketplace to retain its market share. FedEx could only do so by sensing customer needs. It appears

FIGURE 8-4 FedEx and UPS in Hypercompetition

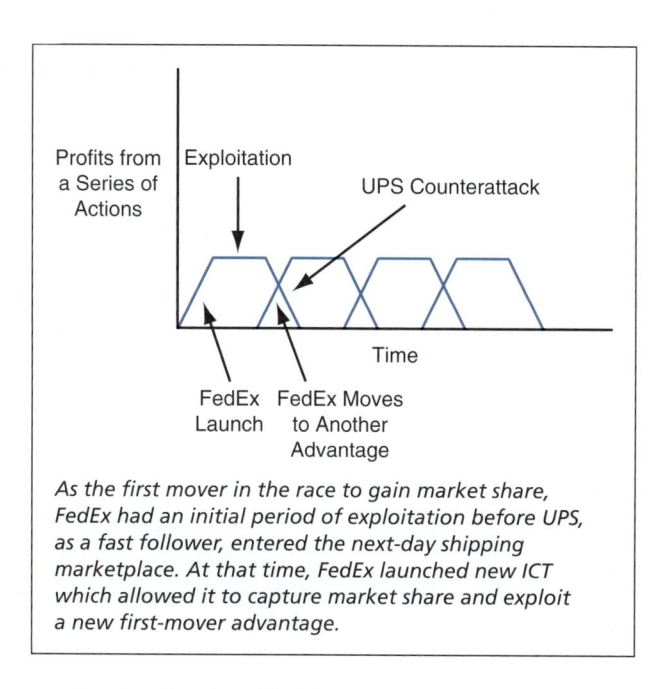

As the first mover in the race to gain market share, FedEx had an initial period of exploitation before UPS, as a fast follower, entered the next-day shipping marketplace. At that time, FedEx launched new ICT which allowed it to capture market share and exploit a new first-mover advantage.

that FedEx, an organization built with ICT as a core strategic competency, was more nimble than UPS and thus able to create processes to meet needs in the marketplace. UPS again had to play catch-up.

Whether an initial mover in competitive strategy or a fast follower, those in an organization must realize that it is imperative to sense customer preferences and bring about process changes that will increase net profit or increase customer perception of the organization's products. The remainder of this chapter discusses such business process improvement and innovation and how ICT infrastructure can be instrumental in sustaining competitive advantage. It is important for the business systems analyst to be ever mindful of the competition, and what it takes to sustain competitive positioning. A solid idea that increases competitive position but that can be easily emulated in a counterattack by the competition needs to be quickly followed up with the next competitive idea. The organization must always be positioned to find and implement its next competitive idea to sustain its marketplace position.

Organizational Types and Their Processes

When discussing processes, you might assume that they only exist in manufacturing companies. It is easy to conceptualize a process in a pharmaceutical manufacturing company where raw materials are taken from the environment, for example, flowers collected with medicinal properties. Those flowers are transformed into pharmaceutical compounds and then pills. In your mind, you can easily see employees collecting the flowers, as well as other employees processing them into pharmaceutical compounds and pills. The supply chain (Figure 8-5) and value chain (Figure 8-6) are easy to conceptualize in this example, and the processes are apparent. Conceptualizing nonmanufacturing processes can be more difficult, especially when you are analyzing an organization that provides services or produces information products. They too have supply chains, value chains, and processes.

SERVICE PROVIDERS AND THEIR PROCESSES

Wireless telecommunications companies provide services, and the complexity of those services is increasing due to convergence. **Convergence** is defined as "the merging of distinct technologies, industries, or devices into a unified whole" (Merriam-Webster Online Dictionary, 2006). Convergence characterizes wireless communications providers today: They provide hardware (telephones), infrastructure (wired and wireless network), and information (sending of news and information services directly to mobile devices). In short, telecommunication providers as well as many other

FIGURE 8-5
The Pharmaceutical Company Supply Chain

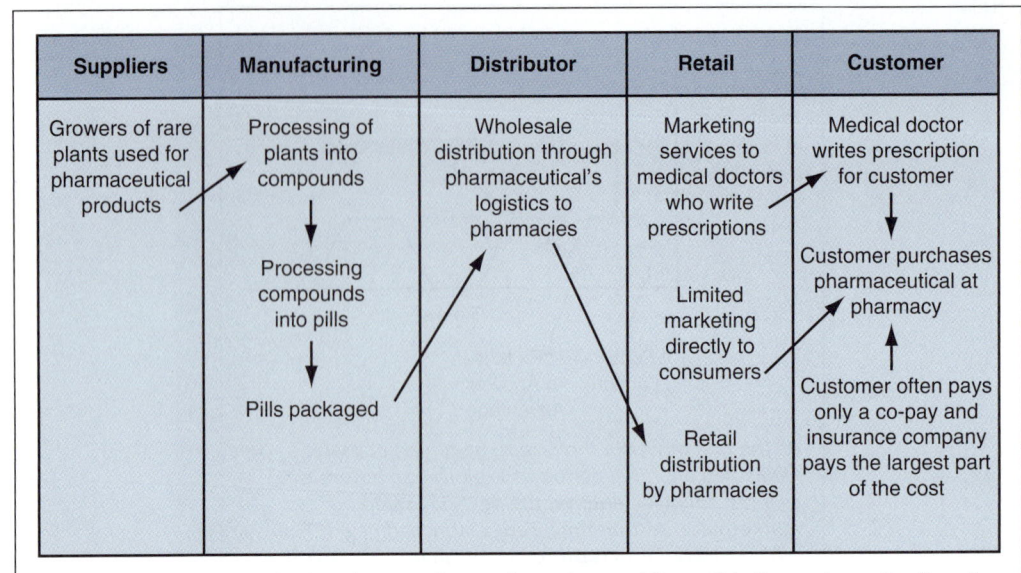

Suppliers	Manufacturing	Distributor	Retail	Customer
Growers of rare plants used for pharmaceutical products	Processing of plants into compounds Processing compounds into pills Pills packaged	Wholesale distribution through pharmaceutical's logistics to pharmacies	Marketing services to medical doctors who write prescriptions Limited marketing directly to consumers Retail distribution by pharmacies	Medical doctor writes prescription for customer Customer purchases pharmaceutical at pharmacy Customer often pays only a co-pay and insurance company pays the largest part of the cost

The manufacturing supply chain has a rather easily understood flow. This figure shows the flow for a hypothetical pharmaceutical manufacturing company.

companies' products and services are converging into a complex set of interrelated customer-centric products and process. In order to illustrate this phenomenon, the wireless telephony service business will be examined. A highly collapsed version of a wireless provider's supply chain (see Figure 8-7) might include the following:

- **Suppliers.** The two major telephony suppliers are landline telecommunication carriers that provide the ability for call completion via landline phones and cell towers from other providers that offer roaming services. Although many other suppliers do exist, this diagram concentrates on the pure telephony suppliers.
- **Manufacturing/Operations.** This wireless provider maintains its own network of cell towers and uses cell towers from other providers when subscribers roam. These logistics mean that the wireless provider must build and maintain its own infrastructure as well as route calls and provide billing services. The utilization of the cell towers of other providers must also be tracked.

FIGURE 8-6 The Pharmaceutical Company Value Chain

Support Activities	*Administration and Management:* Handles strategic and operational planning/control functions
	Human Resources: Hires staff to run business to fulfill mission of the company
	Technology: Supports internal business reporting and call routing
	Procurement: Purchases landline connections and phones

	Inbound Logistics	Operations	Outbound Logistics	Sales and Marketing	Service
Primary Activities	Receipt of raw materials (plants)	Processing of plants into compounds Processing of compounds into pills Pills packaged	Wholesale distribution through pharmaceutical logistics to pharmacies	Marketing services to medical doctors who write prescriptions	Resolution of medical doctor and pharmacy issues

The value chain for a pharmaceutical manufacturing company is relatively easy to envision. This process-oriented view gives the business systems analyst places to make ICT recommendations.

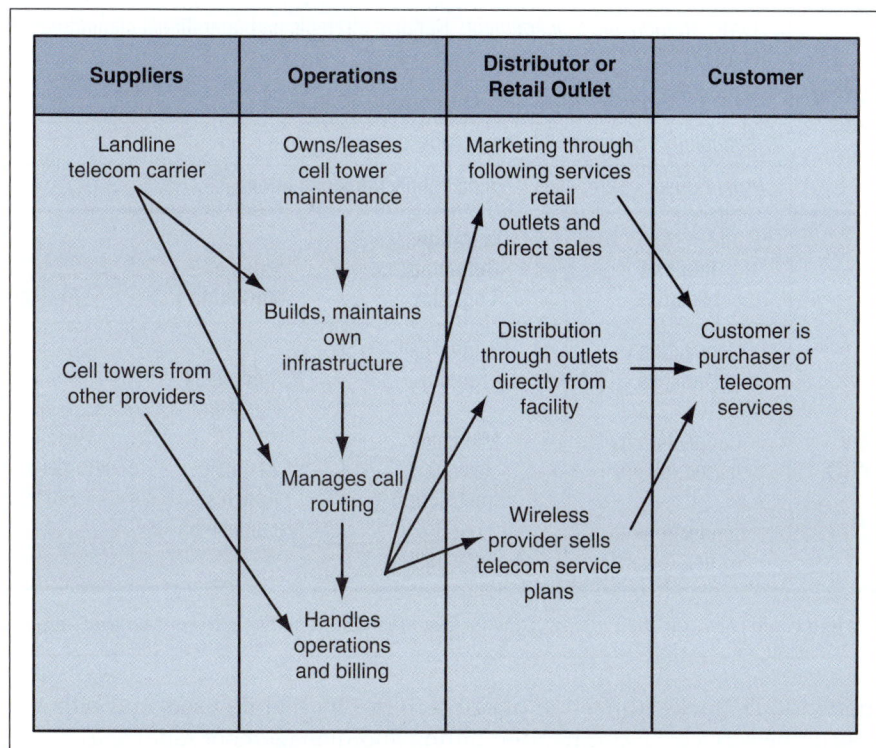

FIGURE 8-7 An Example of a Wireless Provider Supply Chain

Suppliers	Operations	Distributor or Retail Outlet	Customer
Landline telecom carrier	Owns/leases cell tower maintenance	Marketing through following services retail outlets and direct sales	Customer is purchaser of telecom services
Cell towers from other providers	Builds, maintains own infrastructure	Distribution through outlets directly from facility	
	Manages call routing	Wireless provider sells telecom service plans	
	Handles operations and billing		

This fictitious wireless provider's supply chain contains numerous linkages among the major activities in that supply chain.

- **Distribution and Retail.** Distribution and retail are collapsed in this supply chain model and include the internal marketing services of the provider through company-owned retail sales outlets, franchised sales outlets, the Internet, and direct 1-800 sales. Distribution occurs through these outlets as service plans for mobile service. The wireless provider sells those mobile telecommunication services through "fixed-length," "prepaid," and "pay as you go" plans. Some of these plans require contracts, and others just require the purchase of a phone and required services (e.g., airtime minutes, GB of data download).
- **Customer.** The customer is the purchaser of the service plan and the telecommunications services of the provider.

The value chain (see Figure 8-8) for a wireless service provider might include the following:

Support Activities

- **Administration and management** oversee operational and strategic planning (e.g., IT, accounting, finance, etc.), as well as other functions necessary for planning and control.
- **Human resources** recruits and selects employees in line with the organization's mission. HR also does training and development and handles remuneration of employees.
- **Technology** maintains/designs hardware and software to handle routing of telephone calls, utilization tracking by mobile users, billing, and management reporting.
- **Procurement** handles the purchasing of landline connections, leasing of cell towers, and other telephony services to maintain the highest quality at the lowest cost.

Primary Activities

- **Inbound logistics** handles connections to landlines and cell towers, as well as other providers.
- **Operations/outbound logistics** handles routing of telephone calls (operations) between wireless and landline callers, within and outside the wireless provider's

FIGURE 8-8 The Wireless Provider Value Chain

Supporting Activities	colspan across: *Administration and Management:* Handles strategic and operational planning/control functions			
	Human Resources: Hires staff to run business to fulfill the mission of the company			
	Technology: Supports internal business reporting and call routing			
	Procurement: Purchases landline connections and phones			
Primary Activities	**Inbound Logistics**	**Operations/ Outbound Logistics**	**Sales and Marketing**	**Services**
	Connection to landlines Connection to leased towers Connections to owned towers	Handles call routing Maintains telecom infrastructure Handles billing	Direct retail marketing Maintain franchise relationships	Resolves customer issues

A proposed value chain for the wireless provider example would be likely to contain these elements.

network. IT tracks utilization of call facilities by mobile users and bills them for use of the service. IT also handles billing and management reporting.

- **Sales and marketing** creates service plans for sale to mobile users through direct retail, franchise, and Internet channels.
- **Service** handles customer issues, such as billing credits for incomplete calls, poor data connections, etc. Service also handles plan contract administration.

Keep in mind that the supply chain and value chain examples given here are only for the telephony/data transmission portion of a fictitious wireless provider's business. The value chain that includes sale of mobile devices and interactive/news services would be much more complex in a real situation. The telephony portion should make a profit on each call placed through the network. In other words, a profit on the margin should be the goal. Marginal profit means that for each unit of a company's product that is produced, a profit occurs. For the wireless provider in this example, each unit is either a service contract (monthly, annual, or other time period) or an individual call that is placed (one-time). In order to generate profit on the margin, business processes must be efficient and cost-effective. The supply chain indicates how calls (a unit of production) are produced and services contracts (another unit of production) are sold—the ways in which the value chain generates marginal profit.

At many different points within the supply chain and value chain, the business systems analyst has an opportunity to increase operational efficiency and support competitive position. These opportunities can be attained by providing technology solutions that are part of strategic initiatives and fill perceived customer needs. Some examples of process innovations that will increase profits include managing the supply of landline connections and the relationships with other wireless providers or incorporating the "most cost-efficient" methodology to route calls across the network and through landline providers. Reviewing value chain processes for operational and strategic improvements and implementing those improvements will affect the bottom line. Process enhancements require that the business systems analyst understand the nuances of the supply chain and the value chain as well as the information technologies that are available to facilitate any process innovation.

INFORMATION PROVIDERS AND THEIR PROCESSES

Companies that provide search engine results, news, and software are examples of information providers. They all produce information products. A news provider might have as its mission the goal to "publish the region's most vital regional news using the

Internet." Its mission statement would drive the company's supply chain, value chain, and business processes. A highly collapsed version of such a company supply chain is shown in Figure 8-9 in which the company uses a third party to host its web site. This example also assumes a small company with about 10 employees and a large number of freelance contractors. The supply chain (Figure 8-9) might contain the following elements:

- **Suppliers.** Like a traditional newspaper, the online version needs news suppliers and must sell advertisements to generate profit. The news suppliers are information sources that include government filings, other news sources such as Reuters, companies and individuals that report news directly to the newspaper, and a number of freelance reporters who provide stories on a per-story fee basis. Classified ads would be supplied by individuals and companies that want their advertisements to run on the web site. The hosting service for their web site might also be seen as a supplier.
- **Operations.** The operations section of the supply chain might include:
  - Staff and contract reporters who write news stories specific to their area of expertise (e.g., sports, travel, etc.)
  - Staff editors who take stories from the writers and prepare specific sections of the online newspaper (e.g., editorial, business news, sports, etc.)
  - Web developers who create the electronic version of the newspaper for the company's web site
- **Distribution/Retail.** Such an organization might do direct marketing via e-mail and inserts in other companies' direct mail (i.e., direct mail circulation agencies). Using these primary marketing methods also creates retail channels for the web-based product. Actual product distribution is accomplished through a web site hosted by an Internet service provider (ISP). The ISP is paid a monthly fee. Web developers on staff at the newspaper accomplish all development of the web site.
- **Customer.** The customers receive marketing materials over the Internet and in print and subscribe to the web version of the newspaper over the Internet.

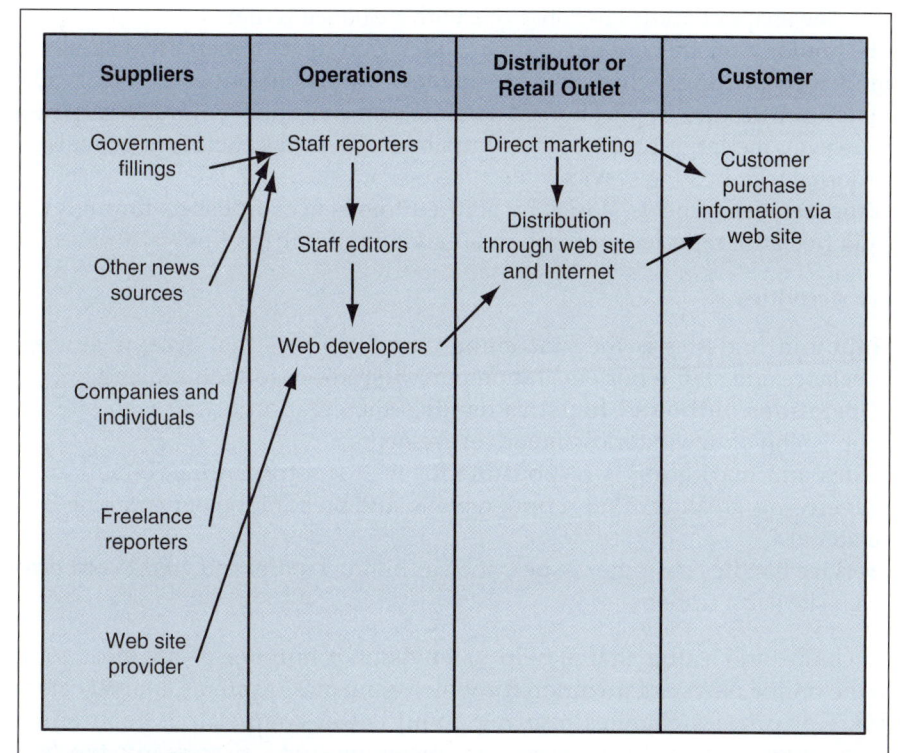

FIGURE 8-9 The Newspaper Web Site Supply Chain

A fictitious web-based newspaper supply chain would likely include these major activities and linkages between those activities.

FIGURE 8-10 The Newspaper Value Chain

Supporting Activities	*Administration and Management:* Handles strategic and operational planning/control functions			
	Human Resources: Hires staff to run business to fulfill the mission of the company			
	Technology: Supports organization's network of desktops and does web development			
	Procurement: Handled by reporters who procure stories or by tips to editors			
Primary Activities	**Inbound Logistics**	**Operations/ Outbound Logistics**	**Sales and Marketing**	**Services**
	Incoming stories	Editorial review Web site development	Internet marketing Subscription plans	Resolves customer issues

This proposed value chain could apply to the newspaper provider in the text example.

Keep in mind that this company is small—the value chain (Figure 8-10) for this information provider thus might include:

Support Activities

- **Administration and management** might include a few senior mangers/editors who set the operational and strategic direction. These same managers might be responsible for budgeting and financial control.
- **Human resources** in this example would handle recruitment and selection of employees through an outside placement service. Training and development are the responsibility of the employee, and remuneration is outsourced. Senior managers have the final say on all hires. The editor of the appropriate section of the newspaper handles negotiations with freelance writers.
- **Technology** for this organization includes web development, which is in-house, and web hosting, which is outsourced. A small in-house network supports employee desktop applications. Therefore, some technology is necessary in-house; however, the largest part of the company's ICT infrastructure is provided by an external web-hosting service.
- **Procurement** of news stories by staff editors is accomplished through the staff and freelance reporters or through anonymous or citizen tips.

Primary Activities

- **Inbound logistics** is the "incoming story" process that accepts stories from freelance and staff reporters and prepares the stories for editorial review.
- **Operations/outbound logistics** handles the creation of the web site and the publishing of news stories and advertisements.
- **Sales and marketing** is responsible for web site formatting, e-mail and other advertising, creation of subscription plans, and preparation of marketing collateral materials.
- **Service** handles customer issues, such as billing credits and credit card errors for web site subscriptions.

Supply chains and value chains help us envision a number of business processes within the online news organization for which a business systems analyst can recommend ICT or process changes to bring about better competitive positioning. For example, it might be possible to merge the "incoming story" process into the "editorial review" process. This change may reduce actual time to "print" by having fewer stories needing "incoming story" processing. When you delve deeper into the supply chain and the value chain and uncover all of the business processes of an organization, you will find many opportunities for positive business process changes, whether they are improvements or innovations.

BUSINESS PROCESSES WITHIN THE ORGANIZATION

From the examples given, you can see that across different types of organizations, all organizations have processes. Whether an organization is an information provider, service provider, or a manufacturing facility, each has a supply chain and a value chain. The supply chain and the value chain describe/define the business processes. When you model a supply chain or a value chain, you sometimes find that sections are so intermingled that it is prudent to collapse them (e.g., putting operations and outbound logistics together). In addition, sometimes it is necessary to add more detail to various sections. In all cases, business processes can be identified within these models. The business systems analyst must work diligently to understand the organization, so the analyst can make process recommendations alongside ICT recommendations. All recommendations of course need to be driven by sound business strategy and support the competitive positioning of the organization.

Defining a Business Process

Taking a process view of an organization requires the business systems analyst to spend time delving deeply into the organization. The business systems analyst may feel that creating a process view is painful—it can indeed be a painstaking process, but one well worth the effort. The business system analyst must identify process information that contains elements of structure, focus, measurement, ownership, and the customer base. The analyst should keep in mind that a process is simply a structured, measured set of activities designed to produce a specified output for a particular customer or market. A **process** has known inputs, is a defined set of work activities, and has known outputs. A process orientation needs to place strong emphasis on *how* work is done within an organization, in contrast to a product focus that emphasizes *what* is produced. In this chapter we focus on *process innovation* and *process improvement* as discussed by Thomas Davenport (Davenport, 1993).

The structure of a process is what distinguishes it from the functional view of an organization, which focuses on departments and hierarchy. Even though the organization may contain a hierarchy and departments within that hierarchy, a process transcends that hierarchy. Structure cuts across hierarchical and department boundaries to describe/identify how the process incorporates the appropriate constituent parts of an organization. Think of process as a dynamic view of an organization that incorporates cost, time, output quality, and customer satisfaction. A process focus examines how things/tasks are done within the organization, as opposed to a product focus, which examines the quality of the final product. The functional focus examines departments. A process focus means that the business systems analyst must look across and into an organization to envision whole processes, rather than only seeing separate departments or functional units. The business systems analyst then must reduce the business process into smaller units to understand clearly how the processes operate and what can be done to enhance those processes.

Contrast the process focus with a product focus. The product focus will ascertain the quality of final products, and then examine the departments that directly contribute to the creation of the product to look for opportunities to increase product quality and reduce costs. In a process focus, we concentrate on the steps within the process that create the final product, understanding that if those steps are more efficient and have higher quality, then the output will commensurately also be of a higher quality. The process focus is forward looking throughout the workflow (and across departmental boundaries), creating quality as part of that workflow; in contrast, a product focus looks back from product quality to determine what went wrong in the actual making of that product. You might say that a product focus is "reactive" while a process focus is "proactive."

Processes that are structured and whose inputs, workflow, and outputs are understood are usually easy to measure. The quality of inputs and outputs can be measured, as can the steps that take those inputs and transform them into products (output) for the customer. Some of these measurements can include quality of inputs, freedom from defects, and cycle times. These measurements can be used to track the effect of any process changes. This topic is so important that the next chapter is entirely devoted to measurement plans.

Process ownership (i.e., who manages the process) is sometime difficult to define because processes often cross traditional hierarchal and department lines. Yet it is important to define these owners, even if groups of department managers share ownership. In that case, a cross-functional team should be created to head the process and any process change initiatives. Identifying process owners allows those who manage the activities within the processes to champion processes changes and bring about positive effects for the organization from those changes.

All process change initiatives must keep an eye on the customer. It goes without saying that without customers to buy its products or services, an organization will go out of business. A focus on customer preferences keeps the business systems analyst alert to product quality and customer-driven product changes. Customer preferences must be considered before process change initiatives are undertaken, as well as after the processes are changed, so the organization can stay current with any changes in those preferences.

An example of a process is the FedEx "logistics process"—a high-level process with many activities. The identification of those processes and activities is the job of the business systems analyst. A high-level view that examines how things are produced allows the business systems analyst to maximize the organization's investment in IT infrastructure without regard for departmental obstacles. Using the high-level view, we can see that FedEx redesigned its linear/grid network cargo movement logistics into a hub-and-spoke logistics system. FedEx had to fuse the processes of package delivery with information and delivery technologies to create the hub-and-spoke delivery system. We can see that fusion in this description:

> FedEx began its operations with the technological capabilities of aircraft and delivery trucks in existence at that time, but immediately fused them with the "hub-and-spoke" system that now dominates the transportation and logistics industry. Since then, FedEx has continued to pioneer the application of newly available technologies from its centralized computer system to manage operations (COSMOS®) in 1979, to the FedEx SuperTracker®, the hand-held bar-code system that captures detailed package information in 1986, to its launch of Internet-based customer services in 1994. (SRI, 2006)

Through implementing its organizational change to hub-and-spoke logistics, FedEx understood the process of logistics well enough to measure the activities of the process and bring about what the customer wanted—fast, reliable, inexpensive overnight shipping with in-depth accurate package tracking information. It took a number of years for FedEx to attain its desired level of overnight package delivery services with extensive accurate tracking and easy customer access to that tracking information, but the company kept clearly focused on customer preferences and created the mega-logistics company that we know today.

PROCESS MEASUREMENT

Processes are amenable to measurement. In fact, if you cannot establish appropriate metrics to identify the impact of process change, you probably have not identified the process correctly. For example, it is possible to measure the following aspects:

- Steps within the process itself—that is, you measure the individual activities that make up the process (e.g., how long a particular step takes or the quality of the output of that step)
- The overall organizational impact of the process through changes apparent in net profit

- External impacts through changes in market share or customer satisfaction
- The time or cost for implementation of a change or the cycle time to market

For ICT to be implemented to support competitive positioning of an organization, the usual metrics include net profit, market share, and customer satisfaction. For an information system that supports noncompetitive operations (e.g., systems mandated by government regulation), you might use changes to net profit, because even noncompetitive implementations cost money and thus affect the bottom line.

Technology that supports noncompetitive initiatives is important and makes up a fair amount of technology implementations. Noncompetitive technologies are often mandated by government regulations (e.g., Sarbanes-Oxley) or are otherwise a requirement of being in business. It is important to be careful—all systems influence or are affected by competitive positioning, even those mandated by government regulations. For example, a Sarbanes-Oxley–compliant accounts receivable system that is part of an outbound logistics system can affect competitive position. If your accounts receivable system were to routinely overbill customers and then send those same customers to a collection agency when they do not pay the incorrect bill, your competitive position would be affected. Unhappy customers may "see another company to buy from." In the remainder of this textbook, technology that directly supports competitive positioning is discussed; nevertheless, when "noncompetitive" technology, such as an *Occupational Safety and Health* monitoring system, is implemented, the impact of that noncompetitive technology on competitive positioning also needs to be considered

Processes affected by ICT projects need to be measured so that the impact of the ICT investment can be ascertained. For example, let's say that new technology is being considered by an insurance company to produce ID cards. Will the faster production of ID cards (i.e., more cards produced per day) be enough to justify the expense? Alternatively, will faster production mean more satisfied customers because the lead time from ordering replacement cards has been reduced by 70 percent? Will more satisfied customers mean better customer retention, which will reduce marketing costs? On the one hand, we measure ID card production per day, and on the other we look for a change in customer satisfaction and increased customer retention due to the technology implementation. Both of these approaches are important. Two major ways are used to measure change brought about by IT infrastructure implementation. They are (1) the variance approach to determining IT payoff, and (2) the process approach to IT payoff. This is discussed more fully in the next chapter which is fully devoted to measurement.

PROCESS OWNERSHIP

"Processes also need clearly defined owners to be responsible for execution and for ensuring that customer needs are met" (Davenport, 1993). When the business systems analyst identifies processes as targets for change, the analyst must be aware of who owns the process. A process owner is someone who is responsible for the operation and output of the process. Within an organization, the owners of a process can be instrumental in the eventual success of the change initiative. Resource allocation for the change initiative can also be affected by where the process owner is located within the political and/or organizational structure. Someone well placed may be better able to garner resources due to their position, while someone who is not so well placed may not have the authority to access the same resources. It is also to be expected that processes will cross department/functional lines in the organization. This cross-departmental alignment may cause political issues, a power struggle, and budgetary difficulties, especially if the process change initiative is actually caught up between departments that are vying for resources or do not see the possible positive synergies to be achieved through interdepartmental cooperation. These situations are complications that the business systems analyst must address. A change initiative may fail because the process owner(s) does not have sufficient authority or the desire to bring about the intended change.

PROCESS LEVERS

Any process involves a number of levers. **Levers** are those forces that influence the success of a process change initiative. It is incorrect to think that only an ICT infrastructure can bring about process change or that ICT infrastructure alone will bring about competitive positioning. Numerous forces (levers), both external and internal, in any organization influence the success of that organization. These forces were described earlier within the context of Porter's business modeling techniques (i.e., supply chain, value chain, competitive forces analysis). Delving even deeper into an organization and looking to utilize organizational resources, the analyst will find that it is the combination of levers, including ICT infrastructure, human capital (employees), organization capabilities, and internal change agents (process owners), that can/will bring about successful process change initiatives. The business systems analyst must bring these major internal process levers together for a process change initiative to be successful.

ORGANIZATIONS, VALUE CHAINS, AND PROCESSES

As was shown above, all organizations have supply chains and value chains. Within its own value chain, an organization can have a number of processes that add value by processing raw materials into final products. Those materials are processed into products through a "value-added" effect. Those processes will represent specific core competencies within the organization. When you compare the supply chain of an organization to its value chain, you will nearly always find an overlap. A supply chain includes the supplier of raw materials, manufacturing/operations, distribution, retail outlets, and of course, customers. Sometimes the supply chain is created by a number of partners (other external organizations) that are providing services to the organization. Sometimes many segments/aspects of the supply chain are performed within the organization itself. The supply chain reach of an organization may extend/vary from being its own supplier of raw materials to having its own retail outlets and dealing directly with customers.

Reach is largely a function of the type and size of an organization and the core competencies of that organization. Reach affects which business processes should come under the scrutiny of the business systems analyst. If the supply chain is largely composed of external partners that interact with the organization, then the organization may have little control over its supply chain operations. For this reason, some organizations bring external parts of the supply chain in-house in order to exercise greater control over their products and thereby affect their competitive position positively.

As stated previously, the value chain consists of support activities (administration, human resources, technology, and procurement) and primary activities (inbound logistics, operations, sales and marketing, service, and outbound logistics). An organization's value chain can actually include any number of supply chain activities. FedEx's value chain includes distribution and retail outlets (parts of the supply chain) as part of its value chain while the company's supply chain includes suppliers (makers of airplanes, computers, packing materials), internal operations (operations, distribution, and retail outlets), and of course, customers. The reach of this supply chain might necessitate that a supply chain management solution in FedEx be very different from a supply chain management solution placed in a shipping organization dependent on its external partners for its retail activities. The supply chain and value chain models thus give the analyst different ways to examine how the various processes in an organization can be interconnected organizationally and externally.

When defining processes, it is possible to examine (1) over arching business processes (e.g., customer relationship management, which cuts across an organization's functional units), (2) activities (e.g., service as established within the value chain), and (3) operating procedures (e.g., handling of customer complaints). (See Figure 8-11.) Examining business processes will probably yield the greatest benefit from ICT implementations, while concentrating on activities is likely to yield much smaller benefits. The way a business systems analyst views processes and activities is an essential component in determining the level of process change that the analyst can

FIGURE 8-11 Processes, Activities, and Procedures

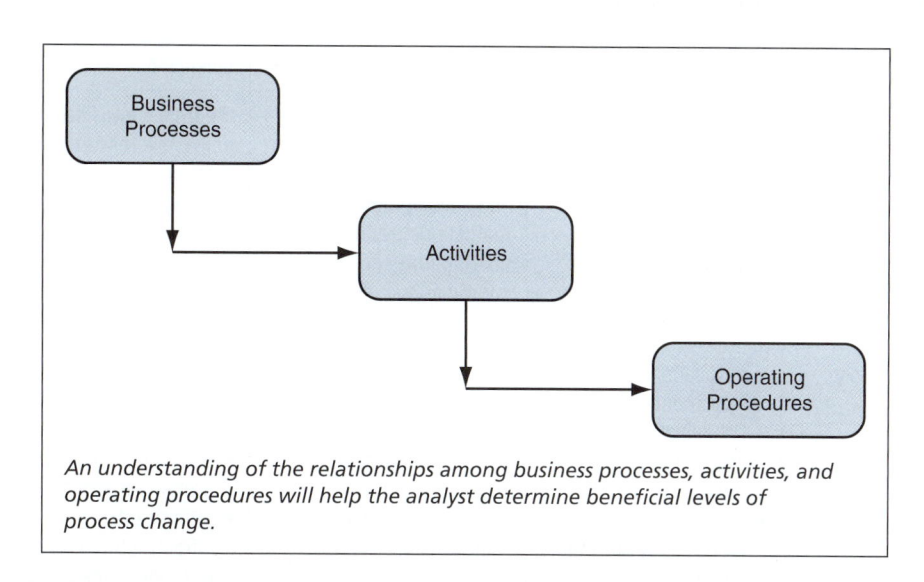

An understanding of the relationships among business processes, activities, and operating procedures will help the analyst determine beneficial levels of process change.

bring about and the benefit that can be brought to the organization. It is essential that the business systems analyst take a high-level and broad view of business processes in order to maximize the investment in IT infrastructure.

A VISION FOR PRODUCT INNOVATION

Much of the discussion in this chapter is on process innovation from the customer's point of view. Every process implementation has an impact on the customer. The customer's view of an organization is created by the products that a company provides, especially any new products brought to market. The business systems analyst must understand how the organization produces its products, what innovations need to occur, and which competencies must exist to ensure the success of any innovation. Product innovation requires a vision for process innovation. Bringing new products to market means generating ideas for new products, as well as enhancement to current products. "Generating lots of creative business ideas is one thing—unless you make money from the innovation, it's just another expense. . . . Companies often select the wrong approach to commercialization of products" (Andrew & Sirkin, 2003). So, what are the right approaches to take to achieve product innovation? Andrew and Sirkin (see Figure 8-12) identify the following three approaches to product innovation, and all can be enabled through IT infrastructure:

Integration The company manages and controls each step required to develop and take a product to market. Integration requires the greatest level of process innovation because the integrator is responsible for the entire process. As a company that invests heavily in semiconductor research; manufactures products at its own facilities; and manages the marketing, branding, and distribution of its products, Intel is an integrator. Innovation at a large integrative organization like Intel requires major investments, strong cross-functional teams, and strong organizational capabilities. Being an integrative enterprise usually works best when:

- Innovation is incremental (i.e., computer processor chips will produce an increase in speed).
- The market position of the organization is already strong.
- Customer preferences are well known.
- The organization's product is a proven one.
- Product life cycles are long.

Orchestration The firm focuses on certain parts of the commercialization processes (i.e., bringing new products to market) and collaborates with its partners on the rest. Porsche uses the company Valmet in Finland to manufacture one of its cars—the Boxster Coupe—rather than setting up a new facility to meet intense market demand for the car.

FIGURE 8-12 Organizational Approaches to Product Innovation

	Integration	Orchestration	Licensing
Investment Required	**Large:** Performs all value-producing functions in-house (i.e., research and development, manufacturing, marketing, branding, distribution)	**Medium:** Performs some value-producing functions in-house (e.g., research and development, marketing, branding and distribution) and requires coordination with partners	**Medium-Low:** Performs only basic research and creation of licensable intellectual property in-house (e.g., research and development)
Works Best When . . .	• Innovation is incremental • Organization has strong market position • Customer preferences are well known • Products are proven • Product life cycles are long	• Product is breakthrough • Competition is intense • Technology is new • Time-to-market is critical • Partners and suppliers are capable	• Market is new • Brand recognition is not important • Licensor's intellectual property is protected • Significant infrastructure is needed to produce the product
IT Infrastructure Can Be Used to Enable . . .	The entire set of internal value-producing activities as well as their supply chain activities	Those value-producing activities done in-house; requires IT to coordinate among partners and suppliers (e.g., supply chain management)	Research and development of products, internal licensor operations, and licensee contract management

Organizations create products. The type of product and the organizational approach to product innovation are summarized in this table.

Using Valmet did not require a large investment of Porsche's physical resources because Valmet had to bear the costs of setting up the manufacturing facility. However, Porsche did have to make a substantial investment in managing the supply chain. A complex project management system across the two companies, Porsche and Valmet, had to be created as well. Porsche provided brand management, customer insight, and distribution, while Valmet provided manufacturing. Such product orchestration (i.e., having several partners involved in the value chain) works best when:

- An innovation is a breakthrough one.
- Competition is intense (with strong substitute products).
- Technology is nascent or just coming into use.
- Time-to-market is critical.
- Partners in the "orchestra" are capable and able to deliver their part.

Licensing The firm sells or licenses new products or ideas to another organization, which then handles the entire commercialization process. GlaxoSmithKline was a licensor when it transferred the patents, technology, and marketing rights for a new antibiotic to Affinium in exchange for an equity stake in that company and board seats. GlaxoSmithKline's costs were lower because it did not have to set up the manufacturing facility, nor did it have to do any marketing—those aspects were done by Affinium. GlaxoSmithKline provided the basic research and solid intellectual property, and then it licensed product manufacturing and distribution rights to Affinium. The substantial expense incurred in research and the creation of intellectual property were paid by Affinium through the license fees. Licensing works best when:

- The market is new to the organization.
- Brand recognition is not important to the licensor.

- Intellectual property of the licensor is protected.
- A significant manufacturing infrastructure is needed to produce the product.

When the business systems analyst selects processes for innovation, it is important that he or she understands how the organization in question approaches product creation.

Process Objectives and Attributes

When creating process innovation initiatives, the business systems analyst must understand the process thoroughly and identify the current objectives and the attributes of the process. The analyst must also know how the process will work after the process innovation initiative is completed, along with the objectives of that initiative, before any process changes are undertaken.

Business processes have objectives. An objective is something the organization is trying to accomplish. When MasterCard deployed its web service–based ATM locator solution in 1997 at MasterCard.com, it had specific objectives. The company wanted to accomplish the following:

- Create revenue by making it easier for customers to find ATMs for cash withdrawals
- Decrease technology duplication (MasterCard had 2 ATM locator systems—one phone-based and the other web-based)
- Implement technology that would allow growth in ATM locator services (e.g., use GPS-enabled phones to allow automatic location of ATMs) (Chen, 2005)

A **process attribute** describes a process and indicates how it should function. Some of the attributes of the original (before process innovation) ATM locator services included (1) two technology implementations of the ATM locators (one phone and one web); (2) different databases and different software for each ATM locator, which sometime resulted in different results for the same query; and (3) current software written in-house. The objectives for the web-services initiative were to (1) create a solution that used one database, (2) provide a software interface that allowed future products to interface with the locater services, and (3) develop a solution that was scalable.

MasterCard settled on the Envisa Location Platform from MapInfo. MasterCard believed that selecting a vendor for the software application to support the process innovation meant selecting a partner. MasterCard retooled its current locator applications to use Envisa and was able to meet the objectives of its web-services initiative. MasterCard created revenue through this web-services initiative by generating an estimated 1,152 percent return on investment in the first six months alone. MasterCard was able to reduce technology duplication by maintaining only one database, and through Envisa's interface, MasterCard became poised to implement technology that would allow corporate growth in ATM locator services (see Figure 8-13).

Attributes of Original Processes	Objectives of Change Initiative	Required Attributes of New System	Results of Change Initiative
• Two technology implementations • Different databases and different software • Current software written in-house	• Create revenue • Decrease technology duplication • Implement scalable technology	• One database • One technology solution with accessible interface • Support of scalability through software/hardware solution	• Envisa selected as solution • One database Web-service interface for application development • Estimated 1,152% ROI through increased revenue during first 6 months alone
MasterCard's ATM locator change initiative included process attributes, objectives, and required attributes of change and led to the results listed here.			

FIGURE 8-13 MasterCard Change Initiative Objectives and Attributes

Identification of process objectives and attributes is essential to securing resources for process change initiatives. It is important that processes, which are amenable to change, be selected for innovation. Part of determining whether a process is amenable to change is to understand the objectives and attributes of that process completely. Selecting appropriate processes and completely defining the objectives and attributes of a selected process naturally leads to creating attainable objectives. Identification is a crucial step in attaining customer-centered, product-focused, and profit-focused process innovation. Those innovations are needed so organizations can maintain competitive positioning.

Infrastructure Implementation and the Value Chain

THE SUPPLY CHAIN AND THE VALUE CHAIN

When implementing ICT infrastructure, it is necessary to understand which business processes the ICT solution impacts. The larger in scope the ICT implementation is (i.e., the number/scope of the business processes involved), the greater the potential for that implementation to influence competitive positioning. However, as the number of processes and activities within processes increases, so does the complexity and scope of the implementation and the possibility for failure of the initiative. For example, if you were to implement a customer relationship management (CRM) system in a large organization, you might impact the following activities: administration and management, technology, sales and marketing, service, and outbound logistics. A CRM solution in a different organization, however, might impact different departments. (See Figure 8-14.)

CRM can be viewed as a high-level process that maps to departments and their operating procedures. CRM implementation can impact large parts of the organization and can be mapped to the value chain. That mapping can assist with identifying value-producing activities, and the operating procedures within those activities. Once you have mapped the CRM processes (or any other processes) to the value chain, it is possible to look within each activity and identify affected activities or operating procedures. For example, in our fictitious CRM implementation, if we were to look inside the service activity, we might see complaint handling operating procedures. It is important that the business systems analyst identify the activities and operating procedures affected by the proposed implementation and then involve all of the process owners from those activities in the planning and implementation of a CRM system. Such an identification and analysis process will increase the likelihood of improvement/innovation success.

FIGURE 8-14 A Hypothetical CRM Value Chain Impact

	Value Chain Customer Relationship Management Implementation					
Support Activities	Administration and Management					
	Human Resources					
	Technology					
	Procurement					
Primary Activities	Inbound Logistics	Operations	Sales and Marketing	Service ↓ Customer Complaint Handling Process	Outbound Logistics

For this hypothetical company, a CRM implementation may include support activities of administration and management and technology and the primary activities of sales and marketing, service, and outbound logistics. A CRM implementation in another company may include different activities that largely depend on organization type, core competencies, and so on.

Because all organizations are unique, an organization different from the hypothetical example in Figure 8-14 may implement a CRM solution that incorporates different value chain activities. These differences in implementation may be due to the size, scope, or industry segment of the organization. A company that specializes in shipping as FedEx does would include inbound logistics as part of its CRM solution because that activity directly interfaces with the customer and the product that FedEx sells. Whichever processes are affected by a specific ICT implementation, the business systems analyst must identify those activities, then determine the impact on the activities, and bring the managers of those activities onto the project team to ensure the success of the implementation.

Always Keep the Customer in Mind

Impact on the customer and customer satisfaction must be considered in all ICT implementations that change an organization's products or services. The earlier example of the high-end hotel chain that was deciding between kiosks for speedy checkout or a CRM system that knows a customers' preferences is a good example. A high-end hotel should understand customers' preferences concerning new ICT options before the organization invests in technology. If the customers prefer a speedy checkout, then the high-end hotel should provide it. However, if the customer prefers a CRM system that has a customer's room ready to satisfy personal preferences, then the high-end hotel should provide that. Also, remember that customer preferences do change; initially, customers may want CRM, but in the future they may prefer speedy checkout kiosks. Because customers' preferences can change, it is important that the high-end hotel stays informed about those preference changes and makes technological changes that support changing customer preferences. In that way, the high-end hotel will have a greater chance of maintaining its market share.

What Is a Process? A Summary

A process has the following characteristics:

- Processes can be mapped to value-producing activities within an organization, and within those activities, operating procedures can explain the individual steps that will be taken.
- A process is a structured, measured set of activities designed to produce a specified output or outcome for a particular customer or market segment.
- A process has known inputs, a defined set of work activities and operating procedures, and known outputs.
- A process is a high-level view of an organization that transcends the organizational hierarchy and its departments or parts. This high-level view includes activities and associated operating procedures.
- Cost, time, quality, and customer satisfaction are all measurable attributes of processes. Processes should also be measured in terms of organizational payoff.
- For process change initiatives to be successful, all the characteristics of a process must be identified and dealt with appropriately within a specific time and organizational framework. These tasks include the following:
    - The impact a process change will have on an organization's products and customer preferences should be assessed before beginning a process change initiative.
    - Once a change initiative is completed, customer satisfaction should be measured along with other aspects, such as return on investment, product quality, and product-to-market cycle time.
    - Determine who the process owners are; those owners can champion or kill a process change initiative.
- Process levers are important. Levers are those activities and events that must go right for a process to have a positive impact on the overall organization.

ENABLERS OF PROCESS CHANGE

Information systems and ICT have long been expected to bring about process improvements in organizations. In the late 1960s, help-wanted advertisements in newspapers indicated that systems analysts were the first to recommend changes in procedures and then apply those technology changes. A typical description of systems analysis from that era was the "study and analysis of operations performed by qualified individuals in factories and offices" (Graham, 1972). From that period until today, the expectations for process change have become the "bread and butter" of the business systems analyst. Remember that we have used the term *business systems analyst* to refer to anyone in an organization (whether CEO, CIO, CKO, or systems analyst) who is responsible for technology innovation.

As stated previously, the business systems analyst must have the ability to understand business processes and their impact on organizational products and customers. The analyst also must have the ability to identify organizational change agents, know when to innovate a process, understand organizational politics, and have sound technical knowledge about ICT infrastructure. These skills will assist all stakeholders in the organization to bring about successful process changes that will enhance the organization's products and customer satisfaction, and thus its overall competitive positioning.

Innovation vs. Improvement

Process change initiatives can be either improvements or innovations. **Improvements** are changes of a smaller scope than innovations. Improvements are small incremental changes that look to modify existing processes, and may be one-time or incremental/continuous. Improvements are generally conceived or implemented in a "bottom-up" approach throughout the organization. For example, changing the way an auto insurance company produces insurance cards might be an improvement to that specific operating procedure, whereas changing the way policies are issued (which includes insurance cards) will probably require innovation.

An **innovation** is a large one-time initiative that creates a new process or examines existing process for opportunities to enhance its output in a dramatic way. Innovation utilizes a clean slate approach and is thus larger in scope than a process improvement. The clean slate approach means that even the existing processes are reviewed for innovation. New processes can be created or existing processes can be scraped/redesigned to improve process output. Because of the clean slate approach, which can sometimes be quite radical, process innovation is more risky than process improvement. Process improvements usually require a "top-down" management approach to ensure their success—you need top management buy-in and support for risky innovation to be successful. These differing qualities of process improvement and process innovation are summarized in Figure 8-15.

FIGURE 8-15 Process Improvement versus Process Innovation

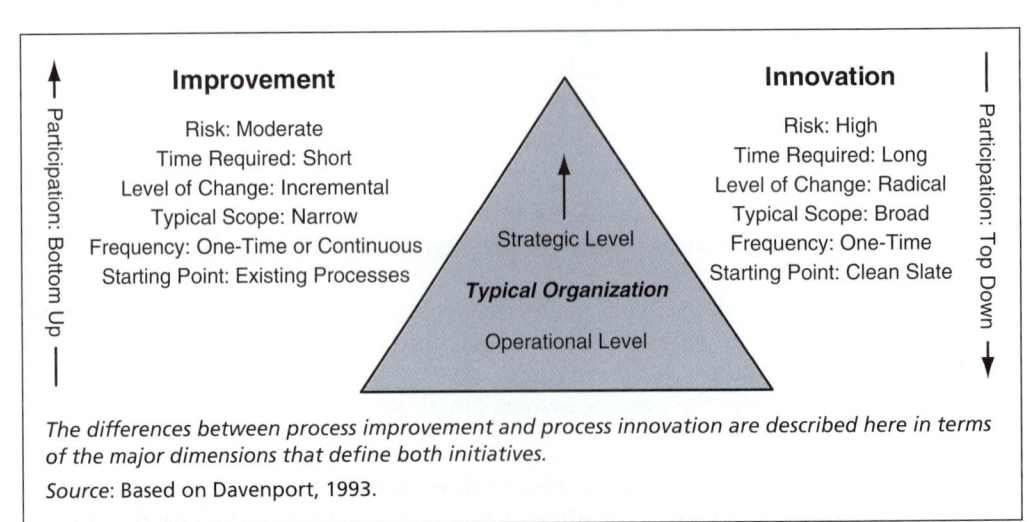

Improvement (Participation: Bottom Up)
- Risk: Moderate
- Time Required: Short
- Level of Change: Incremental
- Typical Scope: Narrow
- Frequency: One-Time or Continuous
- Starting Point: Existing Processes

Typical Organization
- Strategic Level
- Operational Level

Innovation (Participation: Top Down)
- Risk: High
- Time Required: Long
- Level of Change: Radical
- Typical Scope: Broad
- Frequency: One-Time
- Starting Point: Clean Slate

The differences between process improvement and process innovation are described here in terms of the major dimensions that define both initiatives.

Source: Based on Davenport, 1993.

Deciding on process improvement or process innovation is complex and requires much analysis. After assessing the process itself, the business systems analyst will be able to determine whether the process can best benefit from incremental changes that bring about positive net benefits to the organization or if it will instead take innovative changes to yield the maximum amount of benefit from ICT implementation. When deciding whether to recommend improvement or innovation, the business systems analyst must consider the following factors:

- Is the process amenable to starting with a clean slate to bring about maximum benefit to the organization or must the analyst make incremental changes to achieve the desired goal? Business systems analysts must define the starting point in process change (innovation or innovation): clean slate vs. modification of existing processes.
- Business systems analysts must determine whether they have support from those managers "who own the process" and thus the support to bring about the recommended process change. Support and authority from appropriate senior management must also be determined. This support will determine who participates in the process and ultimately drive the success of any process change initiative.
- It is important to determine the amount of risk an organization is willing to take during a process change initiative. One organization may believe that implementing an enterprise resource planning solution that costs $5 million will cause disruption in product production for 30 days but is worth the risk to gain future market share, while another organization may not make the same decision. Many factors play into the perception of risk, including internal cash reserves, current market share, and organization culture and politics.

Once a process starting point is determined (i.e., a clean slate vs. modifying existing processes), the appropriate level of management support and the amount of acceptable risk for the process are also determined. The business systems analyst must then be ready to recommend innovation or improvement. If a process is to be improved, the level of change will be incremental and of a smaller scope than if a large innovation initiative is chosen.

Improvement, as in continuous quality improvement programs, will require small change(s) over time with periodic measurement of the output that have resulted from changes to the process. On the other hand, innovative process changes will be large in scope, start with a clean slate approach to change, take a much longer time to implement, and require measurement of all activities and procedures within the process, as well as a measurement of the total output of the process. Process change initiatives can also add measurements within processes, such as measuring the quality of a specific activity and or just monitoring the existing process metrics. The same initiatives can also monitor overall organizational metrics, for instance ROI or customer satisfaction.

It is important that the business systems analyst identify whether process innovation or process improvement is appropriate. Innovative change is expensive and risky. The scope, risk, and amount of resources required by innovation all contribute to a greater chance of failure. That is not to say that innovative changes mediated by ICT should not be undertaken, but rather that the business systems analyst must be fully aware of the associated risks to the whole organization and make others aware of those risks. It is imperative that all risks and benefits are understood clearly. Process innovation will probably require a greater sales job to management and staff than will process improvement. Also, be forewarned that the business systems analyst should not oversell the benefits of innovation to management, but rather sell innovation only when the payoff from innovation is truly attainable and likely.

Organizational Enablers

ICT is rarely the only enabler that is necessary to bring about successful process improvement or innovation. Typically, ICT infrastructure, the information that the infrastructure supports, and organizational changes must be well aligned to bring about successful process change. In order to achieve this alignment, a business systems analyst cannot be just a technocrat. The analyst must interact with the entire organizational structure, know how to garner resources, work within the organization to mediate and advocate for change, and be a party to setting the strategic direction of the organization.

Organizational enablers fall into two categories, namely structural and cultural (Davenport, 1993). The major structural enabler used in process improvement/innovation is to set up cross-functional (department) teams that bring sets of skills to change initiatives that aid in its success. Teams can facilitate the following activities:

- Brainstorming, decision making, and structured decisions
- Group communication (e.g., using face-to-face meetings, groupware, teleconferencing, electronic mail, and electronic decision groups)
- Input of the group through documents produced for the change project
- Analyses of processes, activities, and operating procedures of the organization through creating teams with representation from all areas to be affected by the process change initiative

These cross-functional teams are essential to the success of a process change initiative.

An organization's culture can enable or hamper process change. Attributes of organizational culture will affect the success of process change initiatives and include organizational hierarchy, level of employee empowerment, and the participatory nature of the organization. The more bureaucratic and hierarchical an organization is, the more difficult innovation or improvement will be. Bureaucratic organizations tend not to empower staff to make decisions and tend not to have a participatory culture. Organizations that are flatter (i.e., less bureaucratic and hierarchical) offer employees greater empowerment to make decisions, and thus they expect their employees to participate in decision making. When selecting process improvement via ICT infrastructure changes, all attributes of organizational culture must be considered.

Another enabler of change is organizational politics. "Organizational politics can be broadly defined as actions taken outside the formal power structure on an individual or coalition level that are designed to influence others, especially those at higher levels, to promote or maintain one's vital interest" (Pan & Flynn, 2003). Organizational politics can bring about project success through favorable resource allocation if the project is thought to be career enhancing. Organizational politics can also bring about project failure if resources are withheld because the project does not serve the interests of project stakeholders. When stakeholders put their interests above the interests of their organization (e.g., achieving competitive positioning), politics becomes a driving issue. Such political issues have been shown to cause project abandonment, possibly before the project even starts, in the following ways:

- Political distrust among project stakeholders can lead to stakeholders' suspecting each other of ulterior (self-interested) motives. Mutual trust among project stakeholders is essential to the success of any process change initiative.
- Formation of opposing coalitions where stakeholders see their interests being threatened by a change initiative can lead to resistance to the change initiative. All members of a cross-functional team must be on board, recognize the organizational good in a change initiative, and satisfy their own personal ambitions through a reasonable discussion of issues.
- Threats of retaliation can occur when a stakeholder threatens a negative action in response to a project proposal. For example, a supplier might threaten to stop providing materials to an organization if a particular system implementation is undertaken, such as a supply chain management system. These types of threats are destructive, and the cross-functional team must heed all such threats and communicate the benefits of the process change initiative. This should allow stakeholders to see how they can personally benefit from the change.
- Failure to obtain continued political support from top management increases the risk of project abandonment. If top management does not support a change

project, the project will likely fail. Project management needs the authority and support of top management to ameliorate political obstacles.

A political campaign to promote a change initiative that is known to be politically sensitive can be crucial. All stakeholders, not just those on a cross-functional implementation team, must understand how the change will benefit them. They must see the change as a win-win. It is important that the cross-functional team, top management, and the business systems analyst all campaign to convince stakeholders that the change is in their best interest.

Political insensitivity can be detrimental to project success. An insensitive member of the cross-functional team or an insensitive business systems analyst can cause a project to fail. When stakeholders threaten or coalitions form, those responsible for the change initiative must view the project from the perspective of stakeholders and devise strategies to counteract any negative political impacts. The business systems analyst must be politically sensitive as well.

Political issues can be found within any organization as well as outside it. Suppliers can feel threatened if they believe a change to an organization will affect the supplier's revenue. Distributors can have issues when new ICT systems are put in place, especially those that impact logistics. Internal managers can form coalitions against a change project when they feel the project may change or eliminate jobs. It is especially important that a political analysis be included as part of the business analysis and that it be completed before any process improvement/innovation initiative actually begins.

ICT as an Enabler

ICT can be used as an enabler of process change. While a process is being evaluated for change opportunities, it is also important to consider ICT as well. ICT infrastructure should be factored into the process improvement/innovation analysis. Any consideration of changing business processes should articulate both the opportunities and constraints placed on the organization by ICT. ICT can enable new process design, but when ICT is introduced into the process initiative, a business systems analyst gains both opportunities and constraints. ICT is usually implemented through modeling tools such as systems engineering techniques (Figure 8-16). ICT can assist in process change as well as be changed itself through effective process design.

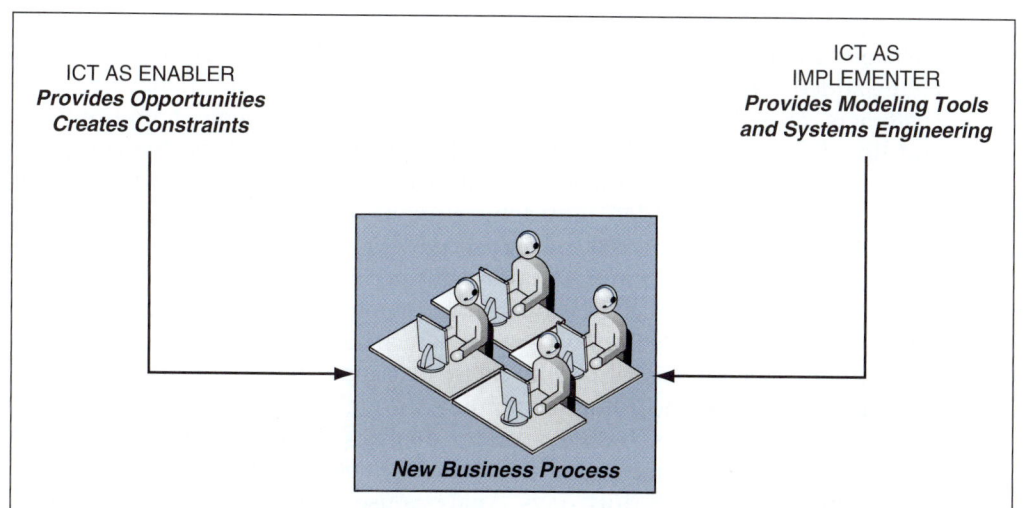

FIGURE 8-16 The Role of ICT in Process Innovation

As new processes are designed within an organization, opportunities for ICT infrastructure implementation should drive the process design. ICT places constraints on process design that need to be considered. Once opportunities and constraints are incorporated in to a process design, ICT can be used to implement that process change through modeling tools and systems engineering techniques.

Source: Based on Davenport, 1993.

ICT infrastructure can enable a host of opportunities for improvements/innovations including:

- **Automation.** Automation removes human labor from a process. Automation will be most often recognized as a manufacturing benefit of ICT where technology is used for applications that involve robotics and process control. However, many examples show the ability of ICT to eliminate steps in business processes. Knowledge workers use high-end workstations to automate design activities within organizations, reducing the number of times that products have to be reworked. For example, automobile knowledge workers use workstations to design cars and test the aerodynamic properties of a design before the car is actually built and tested. Prior to this technological innovation, models of cars had to be built and tested in a wind tunnel, and if the model did not have the correct aerodynamic properties, it had to be redesigned, rebuilt, and retested. This testing can now occur in the laboratory before the actual expense of manufacturing. ICT is also used to eliminate paper and reduce errors in many other business processes (e.g., accounting, payroll processing).
- **Information Creation.** Information creation captures data from processes and converts them into actionable information. ICT can be used to capture large amounts of data from an organization, but if the data are not turned into actionable information, the data and the technology may have little use other than simple process automation. Frito-Lay takes sales data and places them into an executive information system so managers can determine where product sales have changed and then plan appropriate marketing activities to boost sales. In short, managers get the information they need to manage the organization more efficiently (Rothfeder, Bartimo, Therrien, & Brandt, 1990).
- **Process Resequencing.** Process resequencing enables the steps in a process to be reordered to gain efficiencies. Yan and colleagues studied the impact of manufacturing and distribution processes on the safety stock levels in a supply chain. The authors derived a model to estimate the safety stock levels and guidelines for redesigning the manufacturing and distribution process. They looked at technology and the procedure of resequencing and merging the supply chain system (Yan, Sriskandarajah, Sethi, & Xiaohang, 2002). ICT was a large component in these efforts to resequence the process.
- **Managing Processes.** Managing processes refers to tracking process data so the output can be monitored/managed. A primary function of ICT is managing business processes and tracking progress. FedEx scans packages many times as the packages travel through the company's hub-and-spoke distribution system. FedEx added extra scanning points for packages to provide additional service to customers, provide decision support capabilities for management, and provide additional error correction capabilities. To succeed in this task, the company created a technology that it called the "van scan" application where packages are scanned as they are loaded into delivery vans and electronically tied to an individual truck (Albright, 2000). This procedure allows FedEx to track packages as they travel from origin to destination, but perhaps more importantly, allows FedEx management to track how successful its logistics operations actually are.
- **Analysis.** ICT can provide the tools through which data and information created by various processes can be analyzed for better decision making. Airlines can handle many issues around scheduling flight crews through decision support tools that create effective schedules. Data used in the analysis include flight schedules, the home bases of crew members, prescheduled activities such as office and simulator duties, and requested off-duty days. Analysts use decision support technology that first construct chains of crew pairings spaced by weekly rests. Additionally, crew capacities at different domiciles and time-dependent availabilities were also considered. Then the parts of these pairing chains are rearranged into individual crew schedules with even distributions of flight time (Guo, Mellouli, Suhl, & Thiel, 2006). The result was an optimized schedule that took into account a multitude of

variables, a process that was perhaps too complex for human consideration (i.e., too many simultaneous variables to consider).

- **Aiding Geographic Scope Issues.** Systems that enhance information sharing for organizations with a broad geographic scope can be created. Organizations that have multiple locations need the capability to share information across these geographic locations. This sharing can include information generated from any business process at any location.
- **Integration.** ICT can enable integrated operating procedures (tasks) that address the activities of the organization. With offices spread across 46 states and different regulatory requirements in each state, KMG America, an employee benefit provider based in Minnetonka, Minnesota, installed technology to integrate its insurance policy production system. The company's largely manual system was replaced with a system that allows KMG to create certificates and policies on the fly. The system uses Microsoft Word to create state-specific filing documents and policy issuance templates (Woehr, 2006). Using this system, the company has been able to automate and combine its former manual operations into a single integrated policy delivery mechanism across KMG America units.
- **Digital Intellectual Asset Distribution.** In today's digital world, ICT can facilitate the capture and distribution of intellectual assets. Deloitte Touché Tohmatsu, Australia, innovated its capturing of intellectual assets—knowledge known by the firm's partners—by merging the company's Leadership & Learn, Knowledge Management (KM) department and human resource (HR) department to implement technology that facilitates knowledge sharing and changes internal remuneration of partners in the firm. "As strategic allies in the business, KM and HR are able to influence the direction of senior leadership" (Townley, 2002).
- **Disintermediation.** Reducing the number of intermediaries from a process is often the purview of process change initiatives and ICT. Intermediaries are organizations that are/were necessary for the creation and delivery of a product. For example, traditionally telephone conversations occurred . . . well . . . over the telephone. However, with the introduction of the Internet and Voice-over-IP (VoIP), the telephone and even a telephone company can be removed from the telephone conversation. It is now possible to use your computer and its microphone and speakers (or headset) to digitize your voice and have a "telephone" conversation with someone (Heresniak, 2005). The phone company has been disintermediated or removed from such a "call," resulting in a lower cost to callers and less profit for the telephone company. Disintermediation should cause an organization impacted by it to assess its competitive position and take actions to regain market share. Note: disintermediation can also occur at a departmental/process level within an organization.

In addition to opportunities for improvement/innovation, ICT also places constraints on process design initiatives. These constraints come in may forms, some of which are described here. An analyst needs to keep these constraints, or "red flags," in mind when developing recommendations for the strategic alignment of ICT. The major constraints that ICT places on process design include the following:

- **Existing IT.** Technology that is currently being used, whether appropriately or not, can constrain the ability to improve or innovate a process. If technology is already purchased, keeping the organization from taking a clean slate approach because of their existing investment, that technology can impede process change. This technology can be said to "create no return on investment, only cost." For example, a company purchases an enterprise resource planning (ERP) system for $5 million and then finds that the staff will not redesign the processes needed to use the ERP the way it was intended. The company then abandons the installation, causing a $5 million direct hit to the bottom line. Existing technology can also inhibit process change initiatives if the investment in existing technology is already large and the organization is not willing to reinvest in new technology that will bring about improved competitive position.

- **Cost of Redesigning and Availability of Commercial Applications.** Commercial software is available for many applications, some of which can be modified to meet an organization's needs. However, the costs to modify the applications are often great. The company in the previous example might invest $5 million to purchase an ERP solution and then invest an additional $5 million to redesign the solution to fit the company's needs. In order for such an ERP initiative (a process change initiative) to be successful, the company would have to commit a total of $10 million in resources, not just the $5 million that represents the original cost.
- **Cost of Technology or Process Redesign.** If the ICT solution is available to support the proposed change initiative, but the cost of the technology or the cost to redesign the business processes to use the technology is prohibitive, then ICT becomes a project constraint. Sometimes the technology is available, and it is easy to understand how the business processes can be redesigned to increase product quality, but the money is not available to complete that task. Thus, cost becomes a constraint. Again, we will use the example of installing an ERP. It is the task of the business systems analyst to determine which business processes will be affected by the ERP installation and then garner the level of commitment (e.g., financial, staff, top management, etc.) necessary for that ERP solution to be successful and thus make positive use of the resources used to buy the technology.

Summary of Major Organizational Enablers

ICT alone is rarely enough to bring about successful process change initiatives. Other organizational enablers must align to bring about positive net profit change. These enablers fall into two categories: structure and culture. The major **structural enabler** is the cross-functional team. The major categories of **culture enablers** are organizational culture, level of employee empowerment, the participatory nature of the organization, and organizational politics. ICT can be both an enabler and a constraint for process change and enhancement of competitive position. As an enabler, technology supports improvements and innovations that can bring about positive organizational changes, but as a constraint, ICT can also result in those same change initiatives being unsuccessful.

Chapter Summary

At the heart of exploiting ICT for competitive advantage is the ability to determine how ICT can be used to improve and innovate business processes. The business systems analyst must be able to take a process view of the organization and determine whether existing business processes can be supported or modified by ICT to produce an enhanced competitive position for the organization. The other task is for the business systems analyst to determine whether a clean slate approach is the correct one for process change and ICT implementation and thus the best course of action. Additionally, the business systems analyst must examine competitor technology, most often through examining competitors' products. Examination of products is often the best view that an organization can get of its competitors.

When determining which business processes are the best candidates for innovation or improvement, the business systems analyst must remain vigilant and maintain an eye on overall organizational context, which means understanding the type of organization (e.g., manufacturing, service, and information) and how the organization differs from organizations in other business sectors. Those differences require that organizational change also be handled differently from one organization to the next. The business systems analyst must monitor the processes through measurement, ownership, and levers. Measurement allows for a determination of the impact of process changes. Process owners and levers influence change and determine its success.

Business processes have objectives and attributes. Objectives are goals that the organization wants to accomplish through a business process, and attributes are properties of that process (e.g., how the process accomplishes its objectives, what resources are needed, etc.). It is essential that the business systems analyst understand the objectives of a process as well as all of its attributes before any process change initiative can be recommended or implemented.

Process change is enabled or hindered by the organizational environment. The importance of process change enablers is largely determined by the scope of the project (innovation or improvement). The major structural enablers are cross-functional teams, while the major cultural enabler is organizational politics. ICT is an enabler of change too. The characteristics of process are summarized in Figure 8-17.

Characteristic	Description
Attribute	Description of a process and how it should function
Enablers	Events and activities that must go right for a process change initiative to occur correctly
Improvement	An incremental approach to changing existing processes
Innovation	A radical clean slate approach to process change, including the creation of new processes
Lever	Forces that affect the success of a process change initiative
Measurement	Ways to determine the impact of a process change initiative
Objective	The result the organization is trying to accomplish
Ownership	Staff members who are responsible for execution of a process and ensuring that customer needs are met

This chart summarizes the key points regarding a process and can be used as reference.

FIGURE 8-17 Process Characteristics

Vignette Wrap Up

In this chapter, FedEx provides a good example of business process improvement and innovation. For example, FedEx's "logistics process" is a high-level process that involves many activities. The identification of activities and objectives within any process is the task/mission of the business systems analyst. Using a high-level view of the logistics process, FedEx redesigned its linear/grid network cargo movement logistics into a hub-and-spoke logistics system—a major innovation. FedEx had to fuse the processes of package delivery with information and delivery technologies in order to create the hub-and-spoke delivery system.

In implementing its organizational change to hub-and-spoke logistics, FedEx measured the activities of the process and produced what it perceived the customer wanted: fast, reliable, inexpensive overnight shipping with in-depth accurate package tracking information. It took years for FedEx to attain overnight package delivery services with extensive accurate tracking and easy customer access to the tracking information, but the company continued to keep clearly focused on customer preferences and developed into the successful mega-shipper that we know today.

FedEx and UPS offer two outstanding examples of new versus existing process implementation. As a start-up, FedEx was able to develop a strategy that included ICT infrastructure at its core. FedEx considered technical capability a critical success factor and built the company around it. If we look at the history of FedEx, we see a company that developed by focusing on technology and then using that technology to reach its strategic goals. FedEx management was astute enough to garner a first-mover advantage by creating the next-day shipping industry and then continued on that "technology glide path" by constantly advancing technological solutions to fulfill evolving customer needs.

It is interesting to compare the UPS experience with that of FedEx. UPS was an existing company within the shipping industry when FedEx became a new entrant in the marketplace. UPS watched as FedEx grew, but UPS was constrained by existing information and operational technologies. It was not until 1985, nearly 12 years after FedEx had created its hub-and-spoke system for package delivery logistics, that UPS had next-day delivery available to all 48 contiguous states within the United States. UPS thus remained operationally and technologically behind FedEx and had to perform considerable restructuring and new technology implementation to recapture its market share. This restructuring also required substantial business process reengineering. FedEx, however, was successful in providing solutions that solved customer problems, allowing FedEx to exploit its first-mover competitive advantage in the marketplace. While UPS was catching up operationally and technically, FedEx had already moved on to exploit another competitive advantage. UPS became a fast follower in what D'Aventi (1994) calls hypercompetition and the counterattack (see Figure 8-4).

FedEx provides a good example of value chain and supply chain overlap. FedEx's value chain includes distribution and retail outlets (parts of the supply chain) as part of its value chain while the company's supply chain includes suppliers (makers of airplanes, computers, packing materials), internal operations (operations, distribution, retail outlets), and customers. The reach of this supply chain necessitated that a supply management solution in FedEx be different from a supply chain management solution for a shipping organization dependent on external partners for all its retail activities. The supply chain and value chain models illustrate to the analyst the different ways in which one can examine how the processes in an organization are interconnected organizationally and externally.

FedEx also provides a good example of process management. FedEx tracks process data, which is a primary function of its ICT, in order to monitor and manage those data. FedEx does this tracking by scanning packages many times as the packages travel through the company's hub-and-spoke distribution system. FedEx added extra points of package scanning to provide additional services to customers, provide decision support capabilities for management, and provide additional error correction capabilities. To complete this task successfully, the company created a technology that it called the "van scan" application where packages are scanned as they are loaded onto delivery vans and electronically tied to that truck (Albright, 2000). This procedure allows FedEx to track a package's travels from origin to destination, but perhaps more importantly, it allows FedEx management to track how successful its logistics operations actually are and make process changes.

FedEx and UPS provide good examples for understanding the concepts of business processes and process innovation. FedEx is perhaps one of the most widely documented companies. You are encouraged to study FedEx more in depth to understand its business processes more fully.

End of Chapter Questions/Assurance of Learning

1. Choose a company with which you are familiar (or search the Internet for one) and examine that company's business processes. Prepare a brief report that includes the following:
   - Describes one of the company's major business processes
   - Defines the objectives and attributes of the company's business processes
   - Includes business modeling tools, such as value chain and supply chain
   - Proposes process changes to enhance the company's competitive positioning (This will require an understanding of your company's major competitors.)
2. Select one business process within a company and describe how that process extends across the various levels of management (i.e., operations, management, and strategic) Write a brief report that includes:
   - The business process and which level of management the process covers
   - A description and a graphic model of the process and the company
   - How a business systems analyst would best approach changing the process
   - An explanation of the key factors and levers involved in process change
3. Write a brief paper that describes strategies that can be used for processes to be changed by ICT implementation.
4. Describe how you would select a process for change through ICT infrastructure implementation.
5. Write a brief paper that describes the role ICT plays in product innovation.

Case Exercises

These exercises build on the case exercises from previous chapters.

1. XYZ Inc. is a hardware company that builds network hardware and wants to expand its product offerings to ensure it is a viable alternative to other network hardware manufacturers. What internal business processes should XYZ Inc. implement to ensure it is competitive? How will that impact the company and its customers?
2. Building on the process view of HealthyWay HMO, as discussed in previous chapters, select at least one business process, describe what departments/units are involved, and make recommendation for that process(es) to enhance competitive positioning through deployment of ICT.
3. Select a major business process for a company you are familiar with. Make recommendations showing how the company can improve its competitive positioning through changing that process by implementing ICT (i.e., take that process from a manual process to an automated one). Support your analysis by citing Internet and/or print articles (i.e., trade publications, journal articles).

Key Words and Concepts

convergence 215
culture
    enabler 236
enablers 209
functional view 211

hypercompetition 214
improvements 230
informational inputs 210
innovation 230
levers 224

organization culture 231
process 221
process attributes 227
process measurement 222
process objectives 227

process
    ownership 222
process view 211
structural
    enabler 236

References

Albright, B. (2000). Technology Upgrade Delivers Customer Satisfaction. *Frontline Solutions, 1*(12).

Andrew, J. P., & Sirkin, H. L. (2003). Innovating for Cash. *Harvard Business Review.*

Barua, A., C. H. Kriebel, & T. Mukhopadhyay. (1995). Information Technologies and Business Value: An Analytical and Empirical Investigation. *Information Systems Research, 6*(1), 2–23.

Boynton, A. C., Zmud, R. W., & Jacobs, G. C. (1994). The influence of IT management practice on IT use in large organizations. *MISQ, 18*(3), 299.

Chan, Y., Huff, S. L., Barclay, D. W., & Copeland, D. G. (1997). Business strategic orientation, information, systems strategic orientation and strategic alignment. *Information Systems Research, 8*(2), 125–150.

Chen, A. (2005, February 7). MasterCard cashes in on web services. *EWEEK*, 52–53.

D'Aventi, R. (1994). *Hypercompetition: Managing the dynamics of strategic maneuvering.* New York: Free Press.

Davenport, T. (1993). *Process innovation: Reengineering work through information technology.* Boston: Harvard Business School Press.

Dehning, B., Richardson, V. J., & Zmud, R. W. (2003). The value relevance of announcements of transformational information technology investments. *MIS Quarterly, 27*(4), 637–656.

Graham, J. (1972). *Systems analysis in business.* London: George Allen & Unwin.

Guo, Y., Mellouli, T., Suhl, L., & Thiel, M. P. (2006). A partially integrated airline crew scheduling approach with time-dependent crew capacities and multiple home bases. *European Journal of Operational Research, 171*(3), 1169–1181.

Hansell, A. (2000). How does CIOs' performance get assessed? Gartner Group.

Henderson, J. C., & Venkataman, N. (1991). Understanding strategic alignment. *Business Quarterly, 55*(c), 72–79.

Heresniak, E. J. (2005). From mother to MOM. *Across the Board, 42*(3), 61–62.

Krause, K. S. (1999, October 18). Not UPS with a purple tint. *Traffic World, 260*(3), 26–34.

Merriam-Webster Online Dictionary. (2006).

Oh, W., & Pinsonneault, A. (2007). On the assessment of the strategic value of information technologies: Conceptual and analytical approaches. *MIS Quarterly, 31*(2), 239–265.

Pan, G. S. C., & Flynn, D. (2003). Information systems project abandonment: A case of political influence by the stakeholders. *Technology Analysis & Strategic Management, 15*(4), 457–466.

Porter, M. E. (1990). *The competitive advantage of nations.* New York: Free Press.

Rothfeder, J., Bartimo, J., Therrien, L., & Brandt, R. (1990). How software is making food sales a piece of cake. *BusinessWeek*, 54–55.

Sauer, C., & Yetton, P. (1997). *Steps to the future. Fresh thinking on the management of IT-based organizational transformation.* San Francisco, CA: Jossey-Bass.

Smaczny, T. (2001). Is alignment between business and information technology an appropriate paradigm to manage IT in today's organization? *Management Decision, 28*(10), 797–802.

SRI. (2006). *Global Impacts of FedEx in the New Economy* Washington: SRI International.

Townley, C. (2002). People plus knowledge at Deloitte Touche Tohmatsu. *KM Review, 5*(1), 21–25.

Woehr, M. (2006). KMG taps in systems. *Insurance & Technology, 31*(3), 81.

Yan, H., Sriskandarajah, C., Sethi, S. P., & Xiaohang, Y. (2002). Supply-chain redesign to reduce safety stock levels: Sequencing and merging operations. *IEEE Transactions on Engineering Management, 49*(3), 243–258.

9 ASSESSING THE BUSINESS VALUE OF ICT RESOURCE INVESTMENTS

> **Learning Objectives**
>
> - Understand the need for measuring information technology implementation success.
> - Understand how to use economic utility to monitor soft indicators.
> - Know the difference between activity- and organizational-level measurements.
> - Be familiar with tools used to measure the payoff of ICT investments.

Organizations need to stay competitive. One way to do that is to use ICT infrastructure to maintain and garner new market share. ICT infrastructure changes can be made through process improvement or innovation. Once an organization decides on processes for improvement or innovation through ICT infrastructure implementation, it must decide how to measure the success of those process changes. Measurement included as part of the project planning allows the organization to make any mid-project adjustments that might be necessary as well as to gauge the success of the implementation. This chapter discusses methods for measurement and gives suggestions to the business systems analyst for creating measurement plans. It is essential that measurements be taken to justify ICT infrastructure investment, monitor the impact of infrastructure-mediated changes during implementation, and assess the impact of ICT infrastructure investment. These measurement methods must be defined before the change project begins.

INTRODUCTION

ICT infrastructure must be implemented to support the organization's value propositions. **Value propositions** are clear statements indicating the value delivered by an organization. ICT-driven value propositions must have a net positive affect on the organization and are implemented by incorporating technology into the organization's processes, possibly changing the process along the way. It is not enough to say that ICT implementation brings value, but that value must be shown through measurement. That measurement occurs on two levels: (1) measuring processes affected by ICT implementation, and (2) measuring the overall business value (i.e., at the organizational level) of ICT implementation. Measurement at the process level must be tailored to the actual process; for example, a process that produces insurance ID cards may be measured by the number of ID cards produced per hour. Business-level value is much harder to measure. This chapter discusses measurement opportunities and techniques that can be used by the business systems analyst to determine value provided through ICT implementation. Measurement must be planned and carried out in a systematic way. Measurement plans must be created as part of any ICT recommendations, with pro forma estimates that show value. Process-level measurements must monitor process outputs, and organizational measurements must monitor the whole enterprise so changes caused by ICT implementation can be observed early enough to catch problems, make changes, and monitor success.

As discussed in the previous chapter, ICT implementation can drive business process innovation and improvement. It is essential that when ICT is implemented, the effect of the implementation is measured, both at the process level and at the organizational level. Taken together,

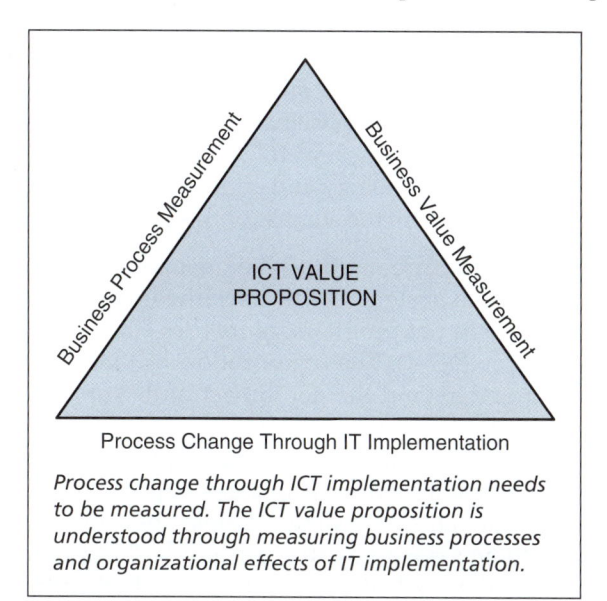

FIGURE 9-1 ICT Value Proposition

Process change through ICT implementation needs to be measured. The ICT value proposition is understood through measuring business processes and organizational effects of IT implementation.

these measurements explicate the scope of the **ICT implementation value proposition**. These relationships can be seen in Figure 9-1. The business systems analyst must implement metrics that measure the tangible and intangible value of ICT implementation. In fact, only 6 out of 10 companies measure ICT value across the organization, and 1 in 5 companies do not measure it at all (Alter, 2006). The business systems analyst is both accountable and responsible for ensuring that ICT investment provides value to the organization. That value must be estimated before a project is undertaken, measured during implementation, and again measured after the project is completed.

Measuring ICT implementation value is difficult, and that is probably why a large number of companies shy away from doing so. Showing value through measurements like *Savings Generated + Increased Revenue − Cost* is not enough to justify ICT investment. Instead of asking "What is my IT budget?" the business systems analyst should ask "What investment is the organization willing to commit in ICT, and what does the organization expect for a return on its investment?" This reframed question means that traditional tangible measures like ROI, net present value, internal rate of return, activity costing, or return on assets are no longer sufficient to justify ICT expense. They are still very important, but measurement must go further. Although it is critical that you use metrics familiar to those funding the project, it is necessary that measurement goes beyond traditional tangible measures. Intangible measures like *improved customer service* or *increased productivity* must be used alongside the tangible ones; these different types of measures require a nonfinancial methodology such as economic utility, which is discussed below. Measures used to justify a project are important when seeking its funding, monitoring its progress, as well as showing ICT value to the organization after completion. Measuring and justifying require a team approach that might include staff from the finance, accounting, and ICT departments, in conjunction with users. In this way, appropriate metrics can be developed.

Types of IT Project Measurement

The two primary ways to measure financial payoff brought about by ICT infrastructure implementation are (1) the variance approach to determining ICT payoff, and (2) the process approach to ICT payoff. Both approaches measure success in terms of net profit. In the variance approach, "necessary" and "sufficient" conditions are identified. Necessary conditions are those that are required for ICT payoff to occur, while sufficient conditions are those that explain the variance in ICT payoff. After these conditions are identified and a change in them occurs, a change in the payoff (net profit) is measured (Devaraj & Kohli, 2002).

An example of the **variance approach** might be the following:

- An organization wants to install a supply change management system with electronic data interchange among itself and with its suppliers.
- The conditions considered necessary and sufficient by the organization for this project are investment in technology and appropriate training.
- The organization will measure the success of this project in terms of net profit.

This organization plans to measure net profit before and after the implementation of the supply chain management system. It will track the investment in technology and training back to the change in net profit, using metrics such as return on investment (ROI) and net present value (NPV). The organization will measure market share and customer satisfaction to understand the net impact of its supply chain management system implementation.

In the **process approach** to ICT payoff the sequence of steps that may lead to change in net profit is examined. The process approach assumes to know the "necessary" conditions (e.g., in the preceding example, they are technology investment and training) required to achieve a payoff from any ICT infrastructure investment. In the process approach, the analyst must ascertain whether those conditions are "sufficient" to achieve the desired payoff. A process breakdown, such as decomposing the value chain into its constituent parts, is performed and each part is measured. In the preceding example, the following might occur:

- An organization wants to install a supply chain management system with electronic data interchange within itself and among its suppliers.
- The organization considers the investment in technology and appropriate training that will be necessary (required), but it also wants to make sure the individual process change is sufficient to bring about the necessary change in net profit.
- The organization is then broken down into constituent processes. For example, it uses the value chain to define major processes, then breaks—or decomposes—those major processes into smaller processes that are amenable to measurement.
- The organization measures net profit, as well as each process, before and after implementation.

The organization will still measure the success of this project in terms of net profit, but it will also measure the changes in the business processes. This type of evaluation looks at whether changes in the ICT infrastructure actually brought about the desired change within the processes as well as net profit.

DEFINING PAYOFF

Some common methods for determining ICT project payoff and for making decisions about ICT project funding include using accounting tools, tools based on economic utility, and statistical tools. One way to use these tools together to is through the Balanced Scorecard approach, which provides a total view of an infrastructure initiative. Each of these tools is summarized in the following sections. (For more complete treatment of these tools, the appropriate reference text should be consulted.) Before discussing these tools, total cost of ownership (TCO) and the technology curve theory are presented as a basis for applying all other tools.

Introductory Theories

TOTAL COST OF OWNERSHIP

Total cost of ownership (TCO) is a financial estimate that includes direct and indirect costs related to the purchase of any capital item, including ICT infrastructure. TCO goes beyond the cost of acquisition and includes other indirect costs to arrive at a total cost of ownership. Direct costs include purchase of technology, installation, and maintenance; however, many indirect costs are included in a TCO analysis as well. These costs are not

FIGURE 9-2 Total Cost of Ownership

Examples of Direct Costs	Examples of Indirect Costs
⇒ Purchase price ⇒ Maintenance ⇒ Installation ⇒ Upgrades	⇒ Training ⇒ Outage ⇒ Breach ⇒ Disaster preparedness ⇒ Disaster recovery ⇒ Floor space ⇒ Testing ⇒ Development ⇒ Decommissioning

Direct costs include those costs directly attributable to the acquisition, whereas indirect costs include the additional costs necessary for a project to meet the needs of the organization.

directly associated with the purchase of the asset but are real costs that should be included in any financial analysis of technology purchases. These indirect costs include training, cost of outage (either planned or unplanned), cost of security breach (e.g., physical breach, virus or malware breach), cost of disaster preparedness and recovery, floor space, testing, development expenses, eventual decommissioning, and others (Figure 9-2). It is easy to determine direct costs; it is much harder to determine indirect costs. It is, however, essential that any necessary and likely occurring indirect costs be included in all financial estimates.

All costs included in a TCO analysis must first be identified. Those costs, specific to the project being considered, will vary among projects. A useful TCO example is purchasing a car. At a minimum, TCO would include the purchase of the car, the cost of insurance and maintenance, the likely cost of an accident (e.g., rental of a car while yours is being repaired), and the eventual sale (or amount lost through depreciation) of the car. Together these comprise the total cost of ownership. Similar estimates can be made for the TCO of an ICT infrastructure investment.

TCO changes in different scenarios. An organization may be interested in a new system and must determine whether it is more cost-effective to build the system or buy the system. TCO differs in these two cases. When a system is built, you have extensive development costs, time lost to the development effort, internal testing, and so on. When a system is purchased, you may lose many of these indirect costs but gain the cost to modify the software and annual maintenance fees from the software developer that may be greater than the cost of in-house maintenance. The decision to build or buy may come down to the time value of having a working system now, versus having to wait for an internal development team to complete the system. This example oversimplifies the build-versus-buy decision, but it does point out the differences.

TECHNOLOGY CURVES

Technology S-Curve "The **technology S-curve** is a widely held theory that as a technology becomes more mature and reaches a natural or physical limit, the ability to improve performance takes an ever-increasing amount of effort. Companies are often overtaken by an entirely new technology that usurps their market" (Rifkin, 1994). Companies that create technology must pay attention to the needs of their existing customers and anticipate when to introduce new, possibly disruptive technologies. However, what about organizations that use technology? When do they decide to switch from one technology to another? For example, when is the appropriate time to move from gigabit Ethernet to 10 gigabit Ethernet, or when should a company scrap an old information systems platform in favor a newer, faster one? The technology S-curve, also called the technology curve, gives us some clues.

The technology S-curve charts the benefits that might accrue for technologies as a function of the maturity of the technology. Often, payback from technology depends on

FIGURE 9-3 Technology S-Curve

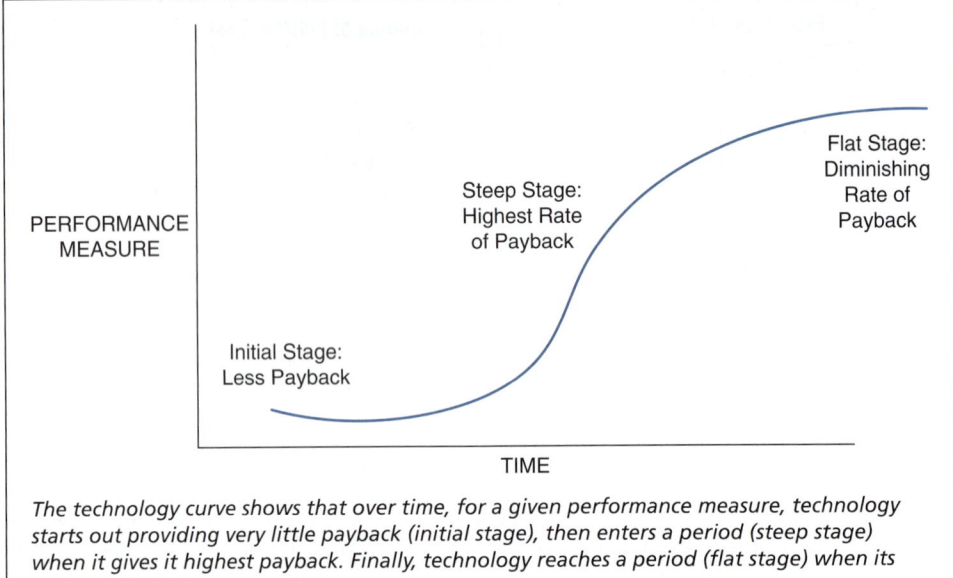

[Figure 9-3: An S-curve graph with PERFORMANCE MEASURE on the y-axis and TIME on the x-axis. Labels along the curve read: "Initial Stage: Less Payback", "Steep Stage: Highest Rate of Payback", and "Flat Stage: Diminishing Rate of Payback".]

The technology curve shows that over time, for a given performance measure, technology starts out providing very little payback (initial stage), then enters a period (steep stage) when it gives it highest payback. Finally, technology reaches a period (flat stage) when its payback diminishes.

the position along the technology S-curve (Figure 9-3). In the initial stages, a lot of experimentation results in less payback, while the highest rate of payback occurs in the steepest portion of the curve. The steep portion is a time of high-technology improvement. This steep period levels off as technology matures, and any extra investment is unlikely to produce substantial further benefits. The business that succeeds in the marketplace is the one that moves to new technology at this point (Devaraj & Kohli, 2002). Generally, it does not make sense to adopt new technology during the initial stage because the technology is not proven. It makes more sense to adopt a new technology during the start of the steep stage when the organization can gain the highest rate of payback. Finally, when a technology begins to offer diminishing payback, it is time to consider adopting a newer technology, hopefully one that is just entering its steep stage. It is all about timing.

Would a company that is using computers powered by vacuum tubes be very competitive today? Probably not. Computers were first designed to use vacuum tubes, then transistors, and finally integrated chips. The path each of these technologies took can be described by an S-curve (Figure 9-4). The ends of these S-curves overlap, and

FIGURE 9-4 Technology S-Curves for Computers

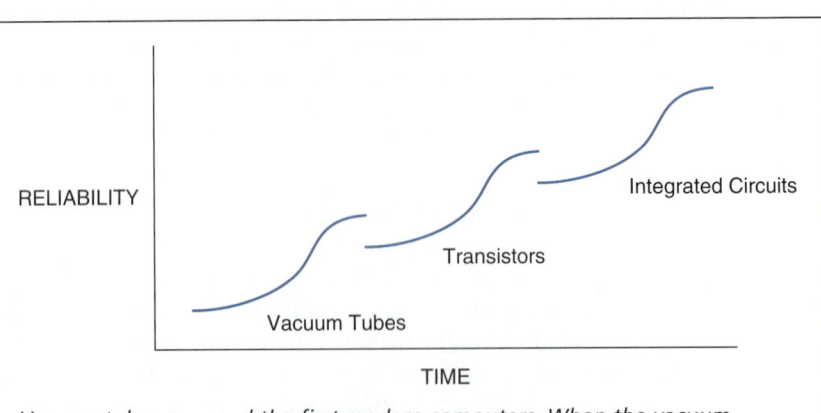

[Figure 9-4: A graph with RELIABILITY on the y-axis and TIME on the x-axis, showing three overlapping S-curves labeled "Vacuum Tubes", "Transistors", and "Integrated Circuits".]

Vacuum tubes powered the first modern computers. When the vacuum tube reached its flat stage, transistors were brought to the marketplace. As transistor-driven computers offered less payback, today's integrated circuit computers entered the marketplace. The company that stayed on top of these three technologies and timed the jump between them was able to maximize its investment in technology.

the company that could time its jump between these technologies would be most successful in maximizing its technology payback. Similar S-curves exist for other infrastructure technologies. One just needs to look at the following examples to see the growth in technology:

- The move from 10/199 megabit Ethernet to 1 gigabit Ethernet
- Processor speeds that have climbed from single hertz to gigahertz
- Older wired networks using thin-coax that supported slow network speeds to high-speed UTP, fiber optic cables, and wireless that can support multi-gigabit speeds

It's all about timing and using technology S-curves to know when to jump from existing technology to newer ones.

Using a Technology S-Curve in Decision Making Technology S-curves can be a useful tool in timing technology moves, but like any decision support tool the results are only as good as the data used to drive the tool. In addition, the tool only suggests alternatives and cannot replace the experience and knowledge of the staff using the tool. When a technology reaches the point of diminishing returns, and a new technology that accomplishes similar or related tasks is available with greater returns, it is time to consider switching to the newer technology. It is important to note that the best time to switch is when new technology has become stable enough to support the organization. Take, for example, a company that is deciding when to switch between software versions, from Version 1 to Version 2. Let us assume that Version 2 provides substantial improvements that the organization desires, but that Version 1 is adequate to meet staff and customer needs. Using the S-curve model the company would, at a minimum, consider these factors:

- The vintage of Version 1, whether its functionality meets the organization's needs, and whether sufficient technical support continues to be available for Version 1
- The maturity of Version 2, whether Version 2 has functionality required by the company to fulfill unmet need (e.g., customer-requested enhancements or products), and whether Version 2 is stable enough to be installed without exceptional technical support

In order to create technology S-curves the organization must do the following:

1. **Identify the relevant axes for the graph.** The vertical axis (y-axis) will indicate the performance criteria. It should be an element of interest that is valued by the users and management of the technology and must be something that drives the strategic use of the technology (i.e., if technology reliability is the most important factor, then that would be the metric represented on the vertical axis). The horizontal axis (x-axis) is the measure of effort. For example, it could be time.
2. **Identify technical limits on performance.** A technology has reached its technical limit regarding the performance measure at the point at which the curve flattens and the company begins to realize diminishing returns.
3. **Plot historical data.** Historical data are plotted on the performance criteria (y-axis) as well as the effort expended (x-axis). Plotting with three or four data points, along with the technical limit, may give sufficient data to approximate the S-curve and to know when to jump technologies. However, as in all graphing and analysis, more data points will give a more accurate picture. (Adapted from Foster, 1986)

An individual technology S-curve may not give much information alone, but when you plot multiple S-curves on the same graph, it is possible to time approximately when to jump to the next technology. In fact, the most successful companies will time this jump

FIGURE 9-5 Technology S-Curve Example

Considerations for Moving from Version 1 to Version 2

⇒ **Identify the relevant axes for the graph**: Index of customer satisfaction and usability

⇒ **Identify technical limits on performance**: What can Version 1 and Version 2 provide

⇒ **Plot historical data**: Plot historical data on graph

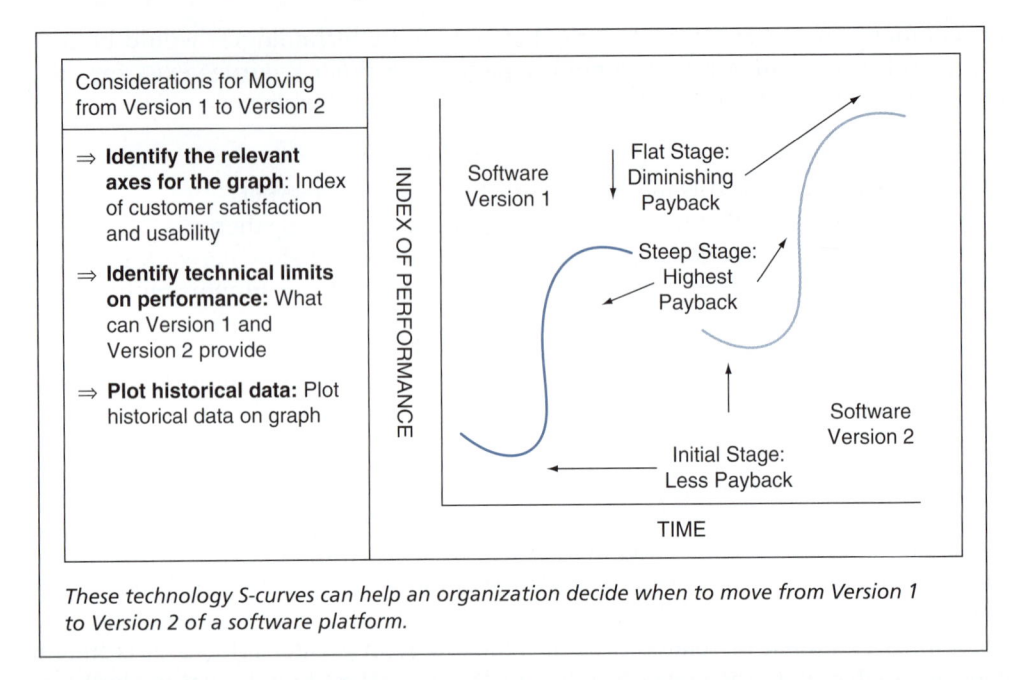

These technology S-curves can help an organization decide when to move from Version 1 to Version 2 of a software platform.

well. A graphical analysis for our example (a company attempting to time the jump from Version 1 to Version 2 of a software package) can be seen in Figure 9-5.

Technology Trend Curves A concept related to the technology S-curve is the technology trend curve. While the technology S-curve compares the resources and effort put into a technology with the way it performs, the **technology trend curve** is helpful "in providing guidance as to the nature and extent of the various technology projects that a high-technology company should invest in. In other words, it presents a simple way of examining the portfolio of technology investments to provide a quick pulse of the company" (Devaraj & Kohli, 2002). The technology trend curve shows three categories of technology (trailing-edge, leading-edge, and bleeding-edge) and looks similar to Figure 9-6. The technology tend curve can provide organizations with some guidelines regarding how to allocate their investment in technology.

The three categories—trailing-, leading-, and bleeding-edge technologies—are described as follows:

- **Trailing-edge technologies** are generally four or more years old and might include slower network technologies or desktop PCs. This technology may be suitable to meet today's needs, but may be expensive to maintain and expensive or impossible to

FIGURE 9-6 Technology Trend Curve

Trailing-Edge 10%–25%

Leading-Edge 50%–75%

Bleeding-Edge 10%–25%

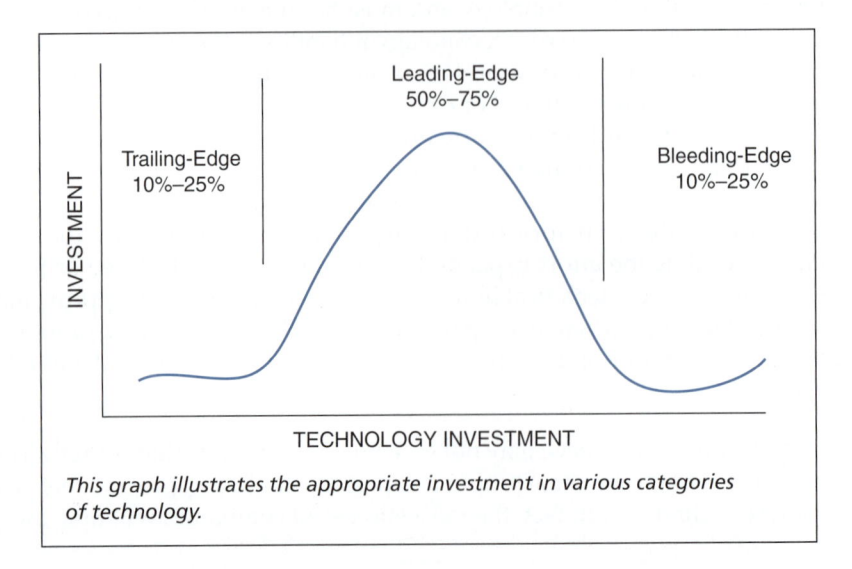

This graph illustrates the appropriate investment in various categories of technology.

Type of Technology	Percent Investment	
Trailing-Edge	10%–25%	⇒ Expensive to maintain and modify ⇒ Cost benefit and payback suboptimal
Leading-Edge	50%–75%	⇒ Fills current business needs ⇒ Supports competitive advantage cost-effectively
Bleeding-Edge	10%–25%	⇒ New technology with little or no immediate business benefit ⇒ Can be bedrock of future competitive advantage

FIGURE 9-7 Technology Investment Recommendations

modify. Therefore, the cost-benefit ratio and payback for these technologies tend to be suboptimal. Generally, no more than 10% to 25% of an organization's technology investment should be in this category.

- **Leading-edge technologies** are relatively new, usually 2–4 years old, and generally offer the best competitive advantage to businesses in fulfilling critical business functions and supporting cost-effective competition. The majority (50% to 75%) of an organization's technology investment should be in this category.
- **Bleeding-edge technologies** are new. They are often in the development or initial stages and are nascent in the marketplace. The immediate business benefit from these technologies is usually very low, owing to the immaturity and possible instability of the technology. Even though companies may not realize any immediate benefit or payoff from investment in these technologies, they may form the bedrock of future competitive advantage when implemented appropriately, especially in response to perceived or forecasted future market demands. Generally, an organization should invest between 10% and 25% in this category (Devaraj & Kohli, 2002; Fortino, 2006).

These categories are also summarized in Figure 9-7.

Technology Justification Models

Technology justification models can be broken into three types: financial approaches, economic approaches, and statistical approaches. **Financial approaches** are those measures traditionally used and understood by accounting and finance staff, and will be perhaps the most readily understood by senior management within an organization. **Economic approaches** are based on the utility or benefits that something gives; they are more abstract than financial models but allow "soft" indicators of systems value to be analyzed. Economic models are often used to represent factors such as consumer satisfaction. **Statistical approaches** take the tact that the benefit of systems value should be able to be shown using statistical analysis. Each of these approaches to showing systems value is useful, and examples of each approach are discussed here.

FINANCIAL/ACCOUNTING APPROACHES

Two common financial/accounting approaches to valuing technology investments are return on investment and cost-benefit analysis. They are indicative of how chief financial officers would view a proposed ICT investment. These approaches can be modified and expanded to cover practically any case of infrastructure implementation. The student should refer to other texts for a more thorough treatment of financial approaches to technology valuation.

Return on Investment Rate of return or **return on investment (ROI)** is an accounting valuation method. It is useful to compare the rate of return of investment options, including ICT investments. In its simplest form:

$$\text{ROI} = \text{Net Income}/\text{Book Value of Assets}$$

However, ROI can be calculated in a number of ways, including (Bragg, 2002; Walsh, 2002):

$$ROI = Net\ Income + Interest/Book\ Value\ of\ Assets$$

It is possible to modify the formula to take into account the many factors that influence cost and return. When undertaking a project, the ROI formula might be:

$$ROI = (Gain\ from\ Investment - Cost\ of\ Investment)/Cost\ of\ Investment$$

The "right" calculation includes those values that are most meaningful to the organization. Someone in marketing may compare the ROI of various products by dividing the revenue that each product generates by its expenses. Similarly, an ICT manager choosing among systems to purchase may use this formula:

$$ROI = (Gain\ from\ System - Cost\ of\ System)/Cost\ of\ the\ System$$

Let's set up a hypothetical scenario to discuss the financial models. Suppose a business systems analyst has four choices for a new user/enterprise component solution for his or her enterprise. Each choice offers different features that allow the customer service employee to handle a larger number of calls per hour. Each choice also requires different upgrades to the service/network components of the infrastructure. The cost of each option and the calculated ROI can be seen in Figure 9-8.

In the example, ROI takes into account the costs associated with the proposed solutions, and the expected gain from each solution. If you are able to quantify all the costs (i.e., total cost of ownership) and expected gains, ROI is a good tool to assist with selecting the choice that provides the highest return on investment. When using ROI this way, you would interpret ROI as follows:

- If ROI is not positive, then the investment would cost more than it generates. The organization would probably not undertake the project unless it was required to meet regulatory requirements and you were choosing among solutions that had the least impact on ROI.
- If ROI is being used to compare alternatives, the one with the highest ROI should be selected.

It is also possible to use ROI when proposing changes to infrastructure. Calculating ROI allows management to determine whether the percentage of return is acceptable before a project is undertaken. Suppose that an organization wanted to track its investment in

FIGURE 9-8 ROI Example for Comparing System Options

	Solution 1	Solution 2	Solution 3	Solution 4
Total Cost of User/Enterprise Component Solutions	$14,400	$15,300	$16,200	$15,720
Total Cost of Service/Network Component Upgrades Necessary to Support the Solution	0	1,900	1,900	2,400
Other Costs, Including Training, Support, Etc.	4,500	4,500	4,500	7,000
Total Cost of System	$18,900	$21,700	$22,600	$25,120
Expected Gain Realized from the Solution	$19,000	$27,000	$19,000	$30,000
ROI	0.01	0.24	−0.16	0.19

These data show the costs, expected gain, and ROI associated with the four solutions in the hypothetical scenario. Even though Solution 2 is not the least expensive, it provides the highest return on investment.

FIGURE 9-9 ROI Example for System Upgrade

	Expected After Upgrade
Total Cost of User/Enterprise Component Solutions	$22,500
Total Cost of Service/Network Component Upgrades Necessary to Support the Solution	4,500
Other Costs Including Training, Support, Etc.	4,500
Total Cost of System	$31,500
Expected Gain Realized from the Solution	$37,000
ROI	17%

These data show the costs, expected gain, and ROI associated with the infrastructure upgrade in the hypothetical scenario.

an infrastructure upgrade. The business systems analyst could again use the costs of the upgrades and estimate the additional gains obtained from the upgrade (see Figure 9-9). In this example, management could determine whether 17% ROI is sufficient to warrant the proposed upgrade.

The ROI accounting valuation method has several limitations and overstates return on investment for the following reasons:

- Projects that take a long time to implement will overstate ROI. In fact, the longer the project, the larger the overstatement.
- The lag between investment outlay and the realization of expected gains will cause an overstatement because timing of investment and timing of gains are not considered in the calculation.
- Organizations whose market share, income, and expenses grow faster will experience a lower ROI than slower-growing companies. (Value-Based-Management.net, 2006)

Despite these limitations, ROI provides a good rough estimate of return on investment and is a helpful tool to assist in understanding the financial differences between options.

Net Present Value **Net present value (NPV)** is used to determine the difference between the present value of cash inflows and the present value of cash outflows. For example, $10 received in one year is worth less than $10 today. In other words, receiving money now is better than later because we can take money we receive today and put it to work as an investment. That investment can be in a bank account earning interest or it can be an income-producing asset that will make money for the organization. The fact that we can invest money and realize a return on that investment is referred to as the *time value of money* (Horngren and Harrison, 1989). NPV compares the value of the dollar today to the value of the same dollar in the future. NPV is easily calculated in Microsoft Excel and it uses the cost of investment, annual payback, and discount rate in its calculations. The **cost of investment** is the amount of money spent on the technology, while **annual payback** is the amount of money that technology is expected to generate at the end of each year. The **discount rate** is management's minimum rate of return on the investment. Typically, the higher the risk, the higher the discount rate.

As an example of NPV, suppose we invest $10,000 in technology that over two years will yield a return of $11,000. Would it be better if that investment yielded $5,500 at the end of both years, or would it be better if that investment yielded $11,000 at the end of year 2? The NPV calculation (Figure 9-10) shows the answer. Annual payback

FIGURE 9-10 Example of Annual and One-Time Payback of IT

Discount Rate 10%					
	Cost of Technology	**Year 1**	**Year 2**	**TOTAL**	**NPV**
Annual Payout	$10,000	$5,500	$5,500	**$11,000**	**$7,100**
End-of-Term Payout	10,000	0	11,000	11,000	6,687

Earning $5,500 per year instead of $11,000 at the end of two payout periods provides a greater NPV.

of $5,500 is preferred to a final payback of $11,000, because the organization can put the first annual payback of $5,500 to work during year 2.

Suppose a company wants to purchase new ICT infrastructure, and the organization has identified four choices that meet the company needs, but each clearly has advantages that would yield market share differences. Those market share differences can be quantified in an expected payback by choice of technology. Management has indicated that it wants a 10% rate of return. NPV will tell us which choice gives us the best value (i.e., Figure 9-11). Choice 2, while not the highest-cost infrastructure, has the highest NPV, owing to its high payback as compared to the other choices.

Cost-Benefit Analysis It is possible to create a cost-benefit analysis (CBA) that describes the relationship between cost of a project and the associated benefits. CBA is used to quantitatively evaluate whether to follow a particular course of action or to choose between different courses of action. In its simplest form CBA is carried out using only financial costs; however, a more sophisticated approach can be used with cost-benefit measurement models that value intangible costs and benefits in terms of monetary units (i.e., dollars). Let's examine a cost-benefit example that analyzes money-based costs and benefits, with estimated expected benefit values.

Suppose an organization must decide whether it should purchase a new computer network and whether the investment will have a payback that justifies the investment. The organization can do a simple cost-benefit analysis by tallying up the cost of the equipment, training, and other costs (total cost of ownership), and the benefits of installing the equipment, and then by dividing the costs by the benefits the payback can be determined. CBA is a popular tool for deciding whether to make technology purchases. The tool requires that you calculate how much the change (i.e., installation of new computers) will cost, and the dollar-value benefit that will be achieved from the change. In the following example (Figure 9-12), expected benefits are level each year, and thus CBA expected payback can be simply calculated. When payback varies each year, however, net present value is a better indicator of the financial value derived from an investment. Including money-value estimates for intangible benefits (i.e., increased customer satisfaction and improved customer retention) in the CBA introduces an element of subjectivity. With effort, though, you should be able to arrive at a real estimate of the impact of the options being considered.

	Infrastructure Purchase Cost	**Expected Payback and Timing (with Discount Rate = 10%)**					
		Year 1	**Year 2**	**Year 3**	**Year 4**	**TOTAL**	**NPV**
Choice 1	$ 980,000	$750,000	$825,000	$ 907,500	$ 998,250	**$3,480,750**	**$1,588,429.75**
Choice 2	750,000	850,000	935,000	1,028,500	1,131,350	**3,944,850**	**2,128,099.17**
Choice 3	1,125,000	800,000	880,000	968,000	1,064,800	**3,712,800**	**1,621,900.83**
Choice 4	576,000	650,000	715,000	786,500	865,150	**3,016,650**	**1,625,123.97**

A comparison of the expected payback and timing from each of four choices for infrastructure shows that the highest-priced system (Choice 3) does not have the best payback in terms of NPV.

FIGURE 9-11 NPV Example of System Choices

FIGURE 9-12 Example of Cost-Benefit Analysis

COSTS			
Infrastructure Costs	Quantity	Cost Each	Total
PCs and Network Connections	15	$1,100	**$16,500**
Servers	3	$4,500	**13,500**
Miscellaneous Hardware			**4,500**
Training			
Hours of Training	100	$60	**6,000**
Staff Time			
Lost Staff Hours Due to Installation and Training	150	$44	**6,525**
		Total Costs (A)	**$47,025**
ANNUAL BENEFITS			
Estimated Value of Improved Customer Service/Customer Retention			$13,000
Estimated Value of Improved Data Quality			9,000
Estimated Value of Other Improvements			6,000
		Total Annual Benefits (B)	**$28,000**
Payback (A/B) = 1.55 years (rounded)			

In this example of a simple cost-benefit analysis, the payback is expressed as a number of years.

The same organization may want more specific measures of the benefits of a project. It could measure actual customer satisfaction indicators with a variety of satisfaction utility rating instruments. These utility indicators can be used alongside financial indicators to make better decisions about infrastructure investments. The next section describes the economic utility model that can be used to describe these "soft" indicators.

ECONOMIC MODELS

Economic Utility When monitoring the success of ICT infrastructure projects, it is often necessary to use "soft" indicators such as user, customer, or employee satisfaction. These indicators allow for the determination of how much "utility" something provides. In economic terms, **utility** is defined as *the amount of satisfaction that something brings to a situation* (Baumol, 1994). **Multi-attribute utility theory (MAUT)** is an economic theory and is useful when attempting to quantify "soft" indicators. Whether these soft indicators are related to system performance or to human factors, MAUT is useful because it allows the analyst to create an easy-to-rate set of attributes that can be used to measure performance, while incorporating manager's perceptions of the importance of the performance indicators.

Implementing a measurement tool using MAUT includes identifying and evaluating attributes, assigning relative weights, and aggregation. Once these things are done, the analyst can perform multiple comparisons of MAUT results (see Figure 9-13). Each of these steps is summarized here:

- **Identify Attributes to Be Monitored.** The first step in MAUT is to identify the attributes considered essential. For ICT infrastructure, these attributes might be factors such as user satisfaction, system performance metrics, or other soft system measures. The goal is to identify meaningful attributes that will allow the impact of infrastructure installation/upgrades to be evaluated.

STEPS	Attributes Identified	Attributes Evaluated	Relative Weights Assigned	Aggregation	Multiple Comparisons

Creating an MAUT instrument and analysis would include these steps.

FIGURE 9-13 Steps to Creating an MAUT Rating Instrument

FIGURE 9-14 Sample Attribute Rating Form

Questions for Customers	Scale 1 = Very Unsatisfied 50 = Neutral 100 = Very Satisfied
How satisfied are you with Company X's ...	
response time to a service request?	
efficiency of customer service representative?	
...	
This figure provides an example of attributes and the use of a rating scale to capture customer satisfaction.	

- **Evaluate Attributes.** Each attribute must be evaluated by the individuals who have the ability to rate them. For example, if customer perceptions of services offered by an organization were being evaluated, you would ask customers to rate the attributes. A convenient way to obtain ratings is to ask users to rate the attributes of interest from 1 to 100. See the sample in Figure 9-14.
- **Assign Relative Weights.** Each attribute must be assigned a relative weighting referred to as the *importance weight*. Suppose we desire to know how important each attribute is to the managers of the organization; a rating instrument that captured that information could be created (see Figure 9-15). The rating scale is similar to the one used for customers except that it asks managers to indicate how important the attribute is to their overall understanding of customer service. This step builds a consensus around what it takes to deliver good customer service.

FIGURE 9-15 Sample Attribute Rating Form

Managers, please indicate how important these attributes are to delivering good customer service.	Scale 1 = Very Unimportant 50 = Neutral 100 = Very Important
How satisfied are you with Company X's ...	
response time to a service request?	
efficiency of customer service representative?	
...	
This chart provides an example of attributes and the use of a rating scale to capture how important managers feel the individual attributes are to delivery of good customer service.	

- **Aggregation.** This step combines the data to arrive at a final score. In our example, we want a final score that will reflect customers' perceptions of the organization's customer service and the managers' perceptions of the importance of the various attributes. Of the many choices for aggregation, one of the simplest is an additive approach that averages the customer rating within each attribute, then multiplies the customer attributes average rating with the manager average importance rating, and then adds the result for each attribute to arrive at a composite score (Figure 9-16).
- **Multiple Comparisons.** Creating an MAUT score at specified times when implementing ICT infrastructure or changing a system can assist with the assessment of change brought about by the implementation. For example, let us assume you want to assess the impact of a new system. The analyst may take measurements before a new system is installed and again after the new system is implemented

FIGURE 9-16 Computation of Total Score

$$TotalScore = \sum AverageCustomerRatings * AverageManagerWeighting$$

Attribute	Average Manager Importance Rating	Before New System Average Customer Ratings	Score	After New System Average Customer Ratings	Score
Response Time	75	60	4,500	72	5,400
Efficiency	62	55	3,410	80	4,960
Overall			7,910		10,360

The manager's importance ratings of customer service attributes and the customer ratings before and after the system is implemented allow for an evaluation of the system.

FIGURE 9-17 Total Customer Satisfaction Example

(see Figure 9-17). That way, the change in customer perceptions caused by the system can be identified. For our example, the score before the new system was 7,910; and the score after the system was 10,360, or about a 30% improvement in customer satisfaction. It is important to remember that a significant lag may occur between customer and employee satisfaction increases and an ICT infrastructure project. This lag can be seen with many soft and financial metrics.

MAUT can be used to calculate the relative utility between choices or outcomes. For example, the choices can be different system purchase options, or they can be different points in time used to measure progress during a system implementation. MAUT can be used to assess many types of intangible indicators.

Utility Value Tree Sometimes it is necessary to break down complex concepts into its attributes to obtain a meaningful set of indicators. In order to simplify description and understanding of importance and utility we can describe those complex concepts using a utility value tree. A **utility value tree** provides a convenient way to describe a concept using a tiered approach. Take the example of data and information quality (DIQ) (see Figure 9-18). DIQ is believed to have four categories (intrinsic DIQ, contextual DIQ, representational DIQ, access DIQ), each with a number attributes (Wang & Strong, 1996).

Data and Information Quality (DIQ)
- Intrinsic DIQ: Believability, Objectivity, Accuracy
- Contextual DIQ: Completeness, Value Added, Relevancy, Timeliness, Reputation, Appropriate Amount
- Representational DIQ: Ease Of Understanding, Interpretability, Representational Consistency
- Access DIQ: Access-Convenience, Access-Security, Concise Representation

The utility value tree technique is sometimes useful in understanding an organization and its strategy.

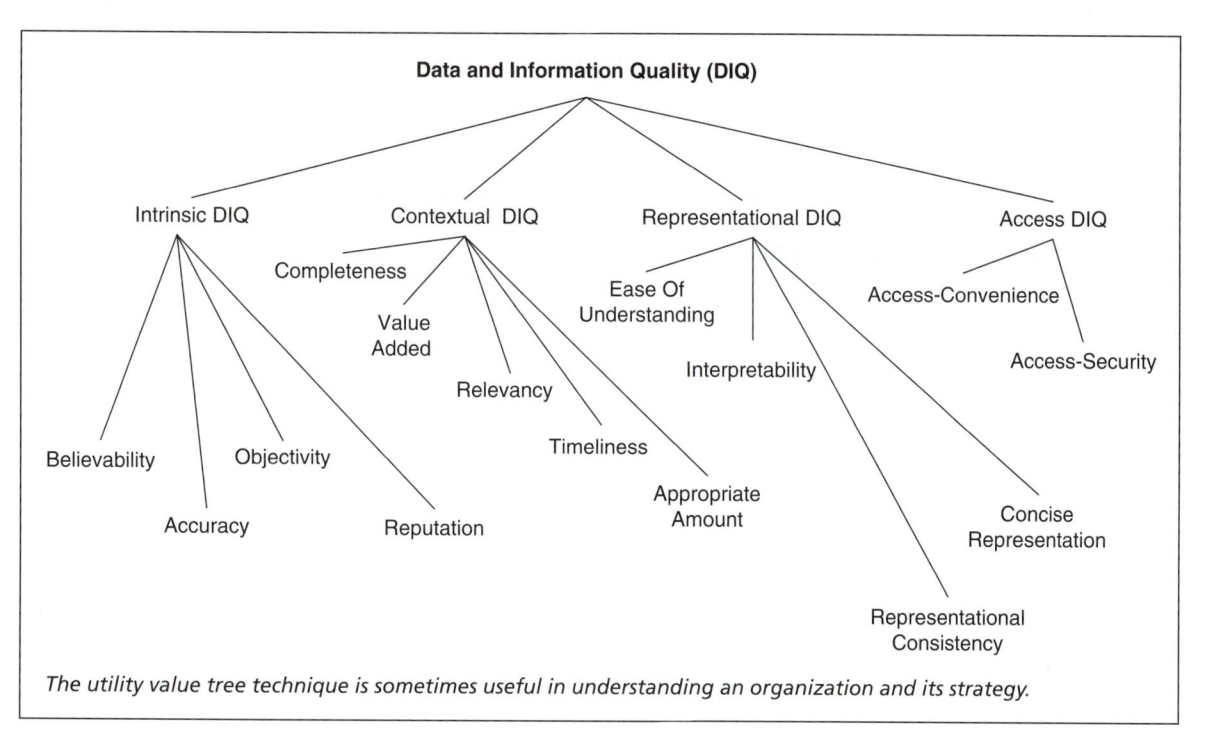

FIGURE 9-18 Utility Value Tree for DIQ

	Average Manager Importance Weight	Data and Information Quality Rating			
		Before New System		Six Months Later	
Dimensions		Average User Rating	DIQ Rating	Average User Rating	DIQ Rating
Intrinsic DIQ					
Believability	4	56	224	65	260
Accuracy	6	20	120	92	552
Objectivity	6	80	480	35	210
Reputation	6	20	120	68	408
Contextual DIQ					
Completeness	5.67	20	113.4	23	130.33
Value Added	5.67	20	113.4	32	181.33
Relevancy	5.33	40	213.2	26	138.67
Timeliness	3	20	60	94	282
Appropriate Amount	6	33	198	63	378
Completeness	5.67	20	113.4	23	130.33
Representational DIQ					
Ease of Use	5.67	30	170.1	36	204
Interpretability	5.67	50	283.5	98	555.33
Representational Consistency	4.67	60	280.2	24	112
Concise Representation	6.33	55	348.15	36	228
ACCESS DIQ					
Access-Convenience	5	40	200	56	280
Access-Security	4.67	20	93.4	54	252
Total DIQ			3,017.35		4,171.66

In this example of MAUT, managers were asked to rate the importance of various dimensions of data quality before the new system was installed, and an average manager importance rating was calculated for each dimension. Users were also asked to rate the level of quality on each dimension, which were averaged to create the average user rating. Multiplying the two ratings yields the DIQ ratings. The same exercise could be followed at a 6-month interval. By comparing the total DIQ from both points in time, the change in user perception of DIQ can be tracked.

FIGURE 9-19 Example of DIQ Ratings and Results

It is possible to create a rating instrument that takes into account user DIQ ratings and individual managers' importance weighting of the data quality items. A rating instrument can be created to rate DIQ of a system. An example of using customer ratings and relative weights for DIQ can be seen in Figure 9-19.

STATISTICAL MODELS

So far, we have discussed financial and economic approaches. In the financial approach, decisions to invest are examined in terms of capital investment options, while in the economic approach we looked at the utility changes brought about by investment in information technology. Now we will turn our attention to statistical approaches to examining technology payoff (Devaraj & Kohli, 2002). Statistical approaches provide another set of tool to examine IT payoff issues. The use of correlation and regression tools is discussed.

The Correlation Statistic Suppose an organization wants to know if a correlation exists between ICT expenditures and net profit. Using the correlation statistic, the organization would proceed as follows:

- Determine the period for which the organization desires to know whether ICT expenditures have affected net profit.
- Collect net profit and ICT expenditure data for the specified period, paying attention to how often net profit and ICT expenditures are reported. Net profit and ICT expenditure amounts need to cover the same time period (e.g., if net profit is reported by the quarter, then ICT expenditure must be as well).
- Develop a table of net profit and ICT expenditures for each period, and calculate the correlation statistic.

An example of a company that correlated quarterly ICT expenditure and net profits for the period from the first quarter of 2003 through the fourth quarter of 2005 can be seen in Figure 9-20. A perfect correlation coefficient of 1 means that as IT expenditures increase, so do net profits in perfect synchronicity. A correlation coefficient of 0 (zero) would mean that ICT expenditure is unrelated to net profit. In our example, the calculated correlation coefficient of 0.831 indicates a strong correlation between ICT expenditures and net profit.

A correlation coefficient does not tell the whole story. In fact, other variables should be considered before assuming that ICT expenditures drove the increase in net profit. The correlation coefficient is a good indicator that we should look further. Perhaps the number of orders increased, a major competitor went out of business, or a regulatory initiative required increased ICT expenditures and caused competitors to go out of business. The correlation coefficient provides a good first level of analysis; however, regression can be used to uncover deeper relationships among the various factors that affect ICT payoff.

Quarters	ICT Expenditures	Net Profit
Q1 2003	$54,236	$120,658,654
Q2 2003	62,369	135,695,456
Q3 2003	72,365	156,325,647
Q4 2004	73,569	168,356,767
Q1 2004	74,569	168,956,665
Q2 2004	56,854	135,968,456
Q4 2004	76,896	170,958,738
Q1 2005	71,568	176,359,654
Q2 2005	73,215	175,386,654
Q4 2005	72,659	176,258,767
Q4 2005	65,386	179,635,767
	Correlation	**0.831***

The company's quarterly spending on IT and its quarterly net profits show a correlation of .831 in this example.

FIGURE 9-20 Correlation Example

* This correlation can be easily calculated using the CORREL function in Excel

Regression Analysis

> Note: *This regression example may suffer from collinearity problems—that is, the variables may be so closely related that it becomes difficult to get a true indication of their independent contribution to the prediction (i.e., net profit). The sample size (i.e., number of quarters) in this example may also to be too small for the prediction to be usable or generalizable. However, the example provides an easy to understand use of regression.*

Expanding on our example of correlating ICT expenditures to net profit, let us assume that the industry is composed of a number of small companies. The introduction of government regulations required that each small company spend a substantial amount of capital on ICT to support the regulation. Two trends in the marketplace occurred because of the introduction of government regulation: (1) several of the companies went out of business because they did not have the resources to support the new regulations; and (2) as a result of the companies going out of business, our company's orders increased (as did the orders of our competitors).

The company's business systems analyst decides to do a regression analysis. To perform a regression analysis the dependent and independent variables must be defined. The dependent variable is the variable that "depends on" or "can be predicted by" the other variables. In this case, we want to see whether net profits are predicted by the number of competitors, the number of orders, or ICT expenditures. The independent variables are those variables that we believe can predict a change in net profit—in this case, ICT expenditures, number of competitors, and number of orders. The output of a regression analysis tells us how much each of the independent variables (i.e., ICT expenditures, number of competitors, number of orders) contributes to the change in the dependent variable (i.e., net profit). However, we suspect that some of the variables may contribute the same information so we must do additional statistical tests before the actual regression analysis.

The analysis would proceed as follows:

- **Define the independent variables.** In this example, the company was able to obtain the number of major competitors by financial quarter from industry reports. The company's number of orders and ICT expenditures by quarter were obtained from the company's own records (see Figure 9-21).
- **Compute the correlation matrix for the independent variables to test for multicollinearity.** A correlation matrix should be computed for the independent variables (see Figure 9-22). The correlation matrix shows that many of independent

FIGURE 9-21 Independent Variables

Quarter	Number of Major Competitors	Company's ICT Expenditures	Company's Number of Orders
Q1 2003	17	$54,236	1,043
Q2 2003	17	62,369	1,021
Q3 2003	17	72,365	1,057
Q4 2004	16	73,569	1,607
Q1 2004	16	74,569	1,535
Q2 2004	16	56,854	1,670
Q4 2004	15	76,896	1,701
Q1 2005	15	71,568	1,705
Q2 2005	14	73,215	2,105
Q4 2005	14	72,659	2,224
Q4 2005	13	65,386	2,484

These data were collected by the organization in the example to be used in its regression analysis.

	IT Expenditures	Number of Major Competitors	Number of Orders	Net Profit
IT Expenditures	1			
Number of Major Competitors	−0.347	1		
Number of Orders	0.312	**−0.974**	1	
Net Profit	0.83	−0.768	0.742	1

The correlation between the number of orders and the number of major competitors is almost perfect (r = −0.974), which indicates multicollinearity.

FIGURE 9-22 Correlation Matrix for Independent Variables

variables are strongly correlated. Especially note that the correlation between number of major competitors and number of orders is almost perfect ($r = -0.974$). These two variables appear to contribute equally to net profit and are said to be multicollinear. Multicollinearity is when two or more independent variables contribute redundant information (McClave, Benson, & Sincich, 2005). Due to multicollinearity, the independent variable—number of major competitors—will be eliminated in our regression analysis, leaving us with the two independent variables: IT expenditures and number of orders.

- Using historical data about IT expenditures and the number of orders (independent variables) and the net profit (dependent variable), it is possible to create a regression equation that explains the variance in net profit and predicts how changes in the independent variables will affect the dependent variable (see Figure 9-23). The output from regression analysis using Excel is provided in Figure 9-24. The regression analysis suggests the following:
  - The regression analysis indicates how much of the variation in net profit is explainable by changes in ICT expenditures and number of orders. The analysis reported an adjusted R-square statistic of 0.93698405, which indicates that about 94% of the variation in net profit may be explained by our chosen independent variables.
  - The F-statistic tells whether our proposed relationship between the independent and dependent variables is statistically significantly ($F = 75.34499105$). The significance (p=.000006) indicates a relationship does exist between the set of independent variables (IT expenditure, number of orders) and the dependent variable (net profit).

	Independent Variables (x range)		Dependent Variable (y range)
Quarter	IT Expenditures	Number of Orders	Net Profit
Q1 2003	$54,236	1,043	$120,658,654
Q2 2003	62,369	1,021	135,695,456
Q3 2003	72,365	1,057	156,325,647
Q4 2004	73,569	1,607	168,356,767
Q1 2004	74,569	1,535	168,956,665
Q2 2004	56,854	1,670	135,968,456
Q4 2004	76,896	1,701	170,958,738
Q1 2005	71,568	1,705	176,359,654
Q2 2005	73,215	2,105	175,386,654
Q4 2005	72,659	2,224	176,258,767
Q4 2005	65,386	2,484	179,635,767

The independent variables of IT expenditures and the number of orders and the dependent variable of net profit are used in regression analysis.

FIGURE 9-23 Final Variables for Regression Analysis

Regression Statistics	
Multiple R	0.97446767
R Square	0.94958724
Adjusted R Square	0.93698405
Standard Error	5115113.885
Observations	11

ANOVA

	df	SS	MS	F	Significance F
Regression	2	3.94271E+15	1.97136E+15	75.34499105	6.45895E-06
Residual	8	2.09315E+14	2.61644E+13		
Total	10	4.15203E+15			

	Coefficients	Standard Error	t Stat	P-value
Intercept	2017283.493	14627824.07	0.137907284	0.893721625
IT Expenditures	1772.185089	222.9428645	7.949054987	4.5722E-05
Number of Orders	22405.24545	3498.298119	6.404612956	0.000208107

FIGURE 9-24 Regression Analysis Output

- If you hold the other independent variables constant, individually the coefficients predict the following:
    - For every $1 spent on ICT we will gain $1,772.19 in net profit.
    - For every each additional order, net profit will increase by $22,405.24
- The proposed regression equation to predict changes in net profit would be:

$$\text{Net Profit} = \$2{,}017{,}283.49 + (\text{IT Expenditures} * \$1{,}772.18) + (\text{Number of Orders} * \$22{,}405.25)$$

In summary, the regression shows that that both ICT expenditures and number of orders contribute to net profit. It makes sense that number of orders significantly contributes to net profit. However, does it make sense that ICT expenditures contributes to net profit? It may, but a business systems analyst would need to interpret this analysis within the context of the company. If ICT expenditures lead to a reduction in expenses or an increase in profit per order, then yes. However, if the increase in ICT expenses does not have an identifiable role in increased net profit, then the output of the regression analysis is suspect.

Balanced Scorecard (BSC)

ICT valuation tools can be used in a unified manner to monitor ICT projects and to determine ICT payoff in a method called the **Balanced Scorecard (BSC)**. The use of the BSC and some of the tools are discussed in this section.

An Overview of the BSC Process

The Balanced Scorecard (BSC) is a way for managers to assess and monitor alignment between strategy and investment. It is useful to strategists in general and specifically useful to business systems analysts. The BSC is driven by the vision and strategy of the organization and provides a balance between financial and nonfinancial indicators. The BSC is based on the belief that managers do not need to rely on short-term financial measures as the sole indicators of the company's performance. Creation of the BSC occurs within four processes (see Figure 9-25).

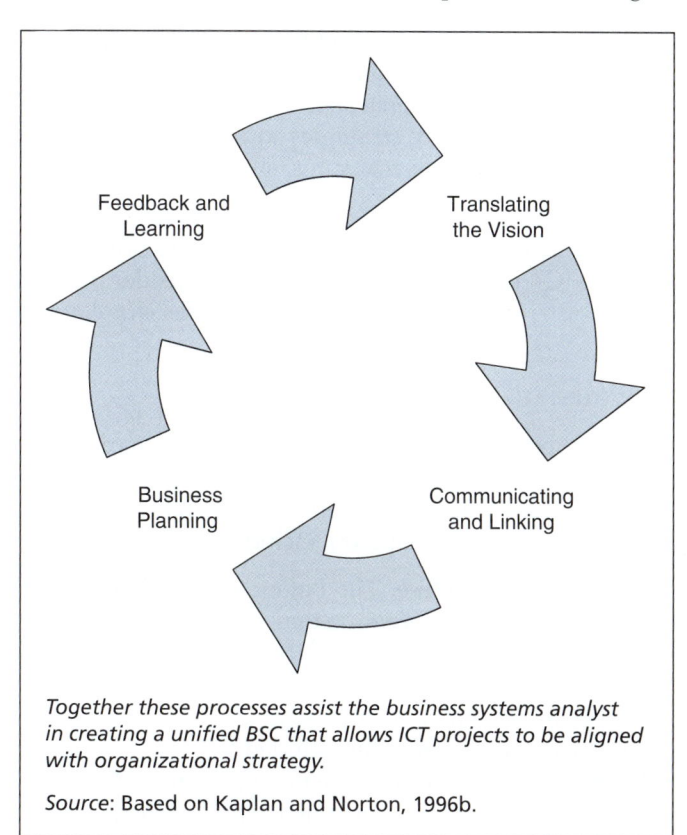

FIGURE 9-25 Balanced Scorecard Creation

Together these processes assist the business systems analyst in creating a unified BSC that allows ICT projects to be aligned with organizational strategy.

Source: Based on Kaplan and Norton, 1996b.

Cycle: Translating the Vision → Communicating and Linking → Business Planning → Feedback and Learning → (repeat)

- **Process One: Translating the Vision.** Managers build consensus around vision and strategy. For example, if the vision is "to become the premier provider of web hosting services" and the strategy is to "provide superior staff training, customer service, and technical web hosting solutions," then during this process the business systems analyst must build consensus around this vision and strategy. Lofty statements like "becoming the premier ..." or "provide superior staff ..." must be operationalized into measurable objectives. Financial measures such as gross sales or ROI provide a look back at past performance, while individual process measurements provide a "here and now" look at how the output of processes have changed as a result of ICT project implementation. Operational definitions that describe project success, in the form of objectives and measures, must be determined and agreed to by the project management team.
- **Process Two: Communicating and Linking.** Once the vision and strategy have been converted into a set of agreed-to objectives and measures, it is the responsibility of the business systems analyst and project team to communicate their strategy up and down the organization and to link it to individual department (and interdepartmental) objectives. Typically, department objectives are tied to short-term and long-term financial goals, but with the BSC, objectives should be tied to various financial and nonfinancial measures.
- **Process Three: Business Planning.** In order for an ICT initiative to be successful it must integrate business and financial planning. The business systems analyst must integrate a myriad of planning and financial skills in order for an ICT project to be successful. The analyst uses those skills to sell a project before approval, to measure the project's progress during implementation, and to show the final impact of the project after completion. The BSC measures provide goals for the business systems analyst to monitor and target, moving the organization toward its strategic objectives.
- **Process Four: Feedback and Learning.** Tracking company financial results and comparing them to short-term and long-term departmental and organization goals has traditionally been the way to measure project success. With the BSC,

feedback and review go beyond individual, departmental, and organizational financial goals to include strategic learning about customers, internal business processes, and overall organizational learning and growth. The BSC allows organizations to monitor and modify strategies to reflect real-time learning through careful articulation of objectives, measures, and targets.

These four processes of the BSC interact to create a strategic learning environment within the organization. This environment can be applied to organizational strategy, as well as to ICT projects. ICT implementations take into consideration traditional financial measures and the other perspectives that drive success (Kaplan & Norton, 1996b).

THE PERSPECTIVES WITHIN THE BSC

The BSC processes described here tell us how to create a scorecard. But what does the scorecard contain? The BSC contain four perspectives. The perspectives do not replace traditional financial measures, but complement them with measures that enable organizations to measure strategic implementation, including ICT initiatives.

- **Financial/Resource Perspective.** The Balanced Scorecard retains the financial perspective, which allows an organization to measure the economic impact of past actions. This perspective provides traditional measures relevant to past performance of the organization and recognized by the organization's management. Factors such as maximizing cost efficiency, maintaining budget targets, and return on investment (ROI) would be included.
- **Customer Perspective.** By including customers in the BSC, the business systems analyst can stay in touch with the customer-related objectives of an ICT initiative. Performance measurement and targets for customer and market segments in which the business operates must be developed. This perspective includes measurements of the value proposition that the organization will deliver to the customer, as well as factors like customer satisfaction, customer retention, new customer acquisition, customer profitability, and market share.
- **Internal Business Process Perspective.** The business systems analyst must identify critical internal business processes at which the organization must excel to provide value to its customers. Those same business processes must satisfy shareholder expectations of excellent financial returns. ICT infrastructure implementations should focus on internal processes that have the greatest impact on customer satisfaction and organizational objectives. Measures of internal business processes go beyond financial measure of performance by incorporating quality and time-based measures while at the same time focusing on the improvement of existing processes. Both short-term and long-term views of the impact of processes should be considered. Short-term objectives are concerned with operational criteria and the organization's ability to meet its financial targets, while long-term objectives should consider the innovation necessary to retain market share and to expand its offering.
- **Learning and Growth Perspective.** While the financial perspective looks at past performance and the customer and internal processes perspectives look at current performance, the learning and growth perspective looks at the future. The learning and growth perspective emphasizes what the organization must do to create long-term growth and improvement. Considering the rate at which technology changes, organizations are unlikely to be able to satisfy customer needs with existing technology. The business systems analyst must develop objectives that will propel its organization into the future and allow it to meet its financial objectives through implementing appropriate ICT initiatives.

When developing a BSC, the business systems analyst needs to create objectives, measures, and targets. An objective or goal is a clear statement of what the organization is attempting to accomplish. A measure is a metric(s) that will allow the organization to determine whether it is meeting its objective. A target is a level at which the organization will determine whether it has met its objective (Kaplan & Norton, 1996a).

AN EXAMPLE OF IMPLEMENTING A BSC

A significant challenge of an organization is to measure its human resources information system in order to justify the value-added contribution of this system to the organization's mission. The Central Intelligence Agency (CIA) of the United States used the BSC to do just that (Hagood & Freedman, 2002). The implementation of the BSC by the CIA is described next. For sake of brevity, only segments of the implementation are shown.

History of the CIA HR Information System   The HR information systems implemented at the CIA never incorporated the strategic vision of the agency. The system was grossly underused—most modules of the system were never "turned on," and many functions were programmed separately as add-on modules. "There was no strategic direction for the Agency's HR Information System, and only minimal information existed about the mission of the system or about the HRIS [HR Information System] government program organization (i.e., the government employees and contractors) that existed to maintain the new system" (Hagood & Freedman, 2002). The CIA appointed a leadership team to review the HR information system and sought the assistance of an external contractor, EDS. This group formed the HR Information System Strategic Direction Team (the Team). The Team set out to determine a strategic plan for the future direction of the HR information system, and used the BSC approach to do so.

Translating the Vision into Measures   The first part of implementing the BSC was to translate the organization's vision into goals, objectives, and measures. Initially, the Team developed a set of measures, which after alignment with the four BSC perspectives (customer, internal process, financial, and learning and growth) were found to focus mainly on the internal process perspective. The team then proceeded to develop a set of strategically aligned objectives and measures that covered all four perspectives. From the strategic vision for the CIA HRIS, they developed goals within each perspective, and then from those goals created objectives that must be met to attain the goals. For each objective, metrics necessary to monitor progress toward the objective and the source of measurement data were identified. The goals, objectives, measures, and sources for the learning and growth perspective can be seen in Figure 9-26 (Hagood & Freedman, 2002). The other perspectives would be mapped in a similar fashion.

The mapping among sources, measures, objectives, and goals for the learning and growth perspective of the BSC is illustrated here.

Source: Adapted from Hagood and Freedman, 2002.

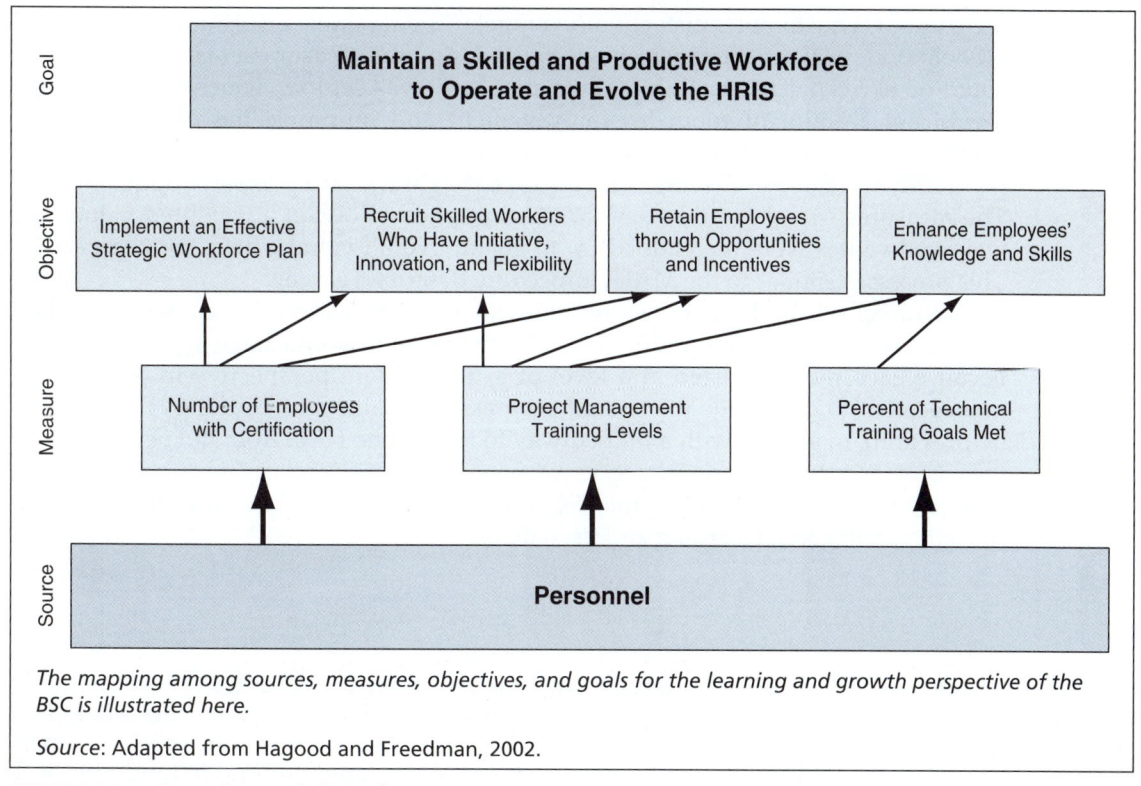

FIGURE 9-26   Learning and Growth

FIGURE 9-27 Customer's Perspective Index

Customer Satisfaction	Data Entry Errors	Help Desk Performance	Productivity Criteria
Average %	Total Errors	% Calls Resolved within Specified Time Frame	Performance
95	95	87	10
90	149	86	9
85	203	85	8
80	257	84	7

The metrics used in the customer perspective provide an overall score that shows performance of the HRIS from the customer's perspective.

Source: Based on Hagood and Freedman, 2002.

Communicating, Business Planning, and Organizational Learning. The creation of the mapping charts for all perspectives of the BSC allowed the Team to understand and communicate how the HRIS tied into the strategic goals of the CIA and its human resources department. Further, the Team was able to determine the objectives and metrics and the parties responsible for them. Individual graphs, charts, and tables were used to display the metrics and to show whether the HRIS was gaining or losing ground.

For example, to measure timeliness and accuracy of the HR help desk service, a chart tracked how quickly HR help desk calls were closed. Similarly, charts, tables, and graphs were used for the other metrics.

Single measures such as the HR help desk closure rate do not allow for the determination of how well a system is meeting higher-level objectives and strategic goals. In order to determine whether the HRIS was succeeding system-wide, the first step was to determine success within each single perspective (customer, internal process, financial, learning and growth). An index was created within each perspective. The index table in Figure 9-27 shows the score for specific levels of performance on each measure (e.g., a data entry error rate of 95 or less would yield a score of 10, while between 83% and 84% of help desk calls resolved within a specified time frame would yield a score of 6). The customer perspective index contained three objectives and associated measures: (1) customer satisfaction (average), (2) data entry error rates (errors), and (3) help desk performance (percentage calls). Using the measurements, a score of 0–10 could be derived. The starting performance level was set to 3, which was to allow a significant amount of room for improvement and minimize the risk of slipping backwards once the organization began quantifying its performance. The Team had previously weighted each score, with the total weight within a perspective equaling 100. The measures, weights, and scores were multiplied to obtain a weighted value. The weighted values were then added up to get an overall value within the perspective. This process is similar to the MAUT procedure described earlier.

To accomplish a higher-level system-wide view, the various indices were all rolled into a system perspective index. Initially, the system would have a score of 1,200, because each metric started at a level of 3. The system perspective index allowed management to determine the overall progress and value added of the HRIS system, by providing managers with a unified way to look at the HRIS from the perspective of the customer, internal business processes, financial impact, and organizational learning and growth. Implementation of the BSC in this manner affected business planning and caused organizational learning and growth.

Chapter Summary

This chapter introduces the concept of ICT payoff and ways that ICT investment should be viewed. The focus changes from "What is the budget?" to "What is the organization willing to invest in ICT, and what is the expected payback?" A number of methods to measure ICT payoff were reviewed in this chapter. These methods should be used when making decisions about new ICT investments, as well as to monitor existing ones. Organizations must be able to understand the ICT payback before investing scarce resources in ICT projects.

Measuring ICT payoff involves direct and indirect costs. Direct costs include those directly attributable to the cost of acquisition, such as the cost of hardware, software, and maintenance. In order to take a "total cost of ownership" view of an investment, however, it is necessary that indirect costs be included in any analysis of ICT payback. Indirect costs include costs necessary for a project to meet the needs of the organization, such as the cost of training, as well as the cost of decommissioning a system.

Technology curves provide a tool to examine technology investments. Technology S-curves assist with determining the best time to move from existing technology to a new one. Technology S-curve theory states that when technology is first introduced, it is expensive and does not provide optimal benefit. Once it has been installed and accepted, technology tends to give greater benefit. However, eventually all technology ages and stops providing optimal payback. It is at this point (or ideally just before) that organizations should time their move to the next new competing technology.

The other type of technology curve is the trend curve. The trend curve states that organizations should divide their investment in technology in to three types of technology: bleeding-edge technologies (early in their S-curve), leading-edge technologies (in the middle of their S-curve), and trailing-edge technologies (later in their S-curve). The organization should invest 10%–25% of its technology resources in bleeding-edge technologies, 50%–75% of its technology resources in leading-edge technologies, and 10%–25% of its technology resources in trailing-edge technologies in order to maintain its competitive edge in the marketplace.

Technology justification models are techniques used to understand ICT payback. Three categories of models were discussed in this chapter: financial/accounting models, economic models, and statistical models. Financial/accounting models include traditional calculations such as return on investment, net present value, and cost-benefit analysis. These financial indicators of performance provide recognizable estimates of the payback given by investment. They all have issues, including the tendency to misreport the payback when the payback period is extensively long. These financial models should not be used in isolation, but rather with in conjunction with other models. Economic models of payback are based on the theory of utility. Utility theory states that the impact of an investment can be measured in terms of the satisfaction (utility) that it brings. Lastly, statistical models of payback are used to examine the relationship between an investment, net profit, and other drivers of net profit. The goal of statistical analysis is to determine whether any correlation exists among variables identified as affecting net profit (or some other outcome of interest). Each of these approaches provides tools that can be applied to determining ICT payback.

The Balanced Scorecard is a tool that analyzes the question of ICT payback from the financial/resource perspective, customer perspective, internal business process perspective, and the learning and growth perspective. The BSC can be implemented by incorporating the ICT payback models presented earlier. To use the Balanced Scorecard approach to measuring ICT payback, the organization would proceed through these four processes:

- *Translating the Vision:* building consensus around the organization's vision and strategy through the use of objectives and measures
- *Communicating and Linking:* communicating the vision, strategy, and objectives through the organization and linking those objectives to short-term financial goals
- *Business Planning:* integrating a myriad of planning and financial skills to sell a project before approval and to measure goals that move the organization toward its strategic objectives
- *Feedback and Learning:* extending feedback and review beyond individual, departmental, and organizational financial goals to include strategic learning about customers, internal business processes, and overall organizational learning and growth

The perspectives and processes involve incorporating the models and tools described in this chapter. These tools are a small subset of approaches to measuring ICT payback.

Vignette Wrap Up

NOTE: The information about the FedEx balanced measures program was provided by William Artely, a former FedEx manager. This information comes from a presentation he did (2001), as well as from personal communications with the author (2006).

In this chapter, the Balanced Scorecard was introduced. The Balanced Scorecard views the organization's internal and external forces that affect organizational success. FedEx attempted what has been called a "balanced measures framework" approach to management that essentially incorporates the Balanced Scorecard approach. The FedEx approach was centered on *People-Service-Profit*. FedEx sought to "take care of our people, and they, in turn, will provide our customers with the excellent service that they deserve, and, in turn, the customer will provide us with the profitability needed to ensure our success and growth needed to take care of our people." The FedEx approach incorporated the customer, internal, learning and growth, and financial/resource perspectives of the Balanced Scorecard. The focus was employee satisfaction (people), customer satisfaction, internal processes (service), and financial achievement (profit). Each of these perspectives fed back into the organization, creating a learning organization.

An objective that FedEx measured was its ability to take care of its people. The company offered a large number of employee benefits, making employees want to work for FedEx. These benefits included health/dental benefits, job opportunities, tuition reimbursement, jumpseat privileges (employees could fly free on FedEx aircraft), cash bonuses, employee discounts, and Guaranteed Fair Treatment (an employee appeals process for resolving issues/complaints).

FedEx employed a similar strategy to keep its customers. Its objective was to retain current customers and pull potential customers from competitors. FedEx used measurable initiatives to meet this objective: the use of "hot spares," a guaranteed delivery commitment, and refunds for service failures. "Hot spares" refers to the fact that each night FedEx sends an empty plane out of the northeast and out of the northwest with the sole purpose of picking up freight from a disabled plane or an overage of freight. FedEx also keeps "hot spares" on the ground and available at a moment's notice at its hubs.

FedEx employed several measurement methods that allowed it to determine its success with these objectives. Measurement methods were put into place for employee satisfaction, customer satisfaction, and profit. FedEx implemented the Survey Feedback Action (SFA) initiative that included upward feedback and evaluation of management and the work environment. Management was required to take action within 30 days on any item within the SFA that scored less that 65%. Another employee satisfaction initiative was the Talk, Listen, and Act initiative (TLA). This informal interaction between employees and their managers provided a venue where such questions as "If you were a manager in this area, what would you change?" could be asked. Together these initiatives helped to monitor and improve employee satisfaction.

Internal process objectives and customer satisfaction were measured through the Service Quality Indicator (SQI) initiative. The SQI is a 12-component index that measures failures and looks at organizational performance through the eyes of the customer. Each component is weighted by the amount that it affects customer service. The SQI was reviewed weekly, monthly, and annually and compared against historical trends. Process measurements began at the package reception location and continued at various points throughout shipping and delivery in order to be inclusive of the entire logistics process.

The financial/resource perspective was covered using return on investment (ROI) analysis, along with other financial analyses. FedEx was very concerned with reinvesting any gains through technology back into the organization to stimulate organizational growth. In summary, FedEx used a balanced approach, covering the four perspectives.

End of Chapter Questions/Assurance of Learning

1. Why would an organization set up measurement techniques sensitive to information technology implementation/change? Give examples from your own experience.
2. Select a company with which you are familiar and analyze one of its business processes. For that process, develop measures that can be affected by information technology infrastructure. The measure must be sensitive enough to react to a change in IT.
3. Evaluate the CIA's Balanced Scorecard approach. Additionally, select one or more measures from each perspective (financial/resource, customer, internal, learning/growth) and assess how sensitive that measure(s) is to changes in information technology.
4. Explain why organizations should decide on measurement techniques before starting ICT infrastructure installation. Include specific examples.
5. Describe when a company might use economic utility–based measures to monitor soft indicators, and explain their use. Support your conclusions with examples.
6. Explain the difference between activity- and organizational-level measurements. Describe how these two types of measurements can be integrated to provide a better understanding of the effect of IT infrastructure implementation.
7. Discuss the tools used in measuring the success of an IT project. Include the benefits and shortcomings of each.

Case Exercises

These exercises build on the case exercises from previous chapters.

1. XYZ Inc. is a hardware company that builds network hardware and wants to expand its product offerings to ensure it is a viable alternative to other network hardware manufacturers. How should XYZ Inc. define the payoff to customers buying its hardware? Think about what competitive advantages XYZ Inc. offers. What technology justification models should XYZ Inc. market to its customers?
2. What is the IT payoff for HealthyWay HMO? How can it determine (a) total cost of ownership, (b) its placement on technology curves, and (c) what technology justification models make sense, and why?
3. Select a major business process for a company with which you are familiar. What is its IT payoff? How can the company determine (a) total cost of ownership, (b) its placement on technology curves, and (c) what technology justification models make sense, and why? Support your analysis by citing Internet and/or print articles (i.e., trade publications, journal articles).

Key Words and Concepts

annual payback 249
Balanced Scorecard (BSC) 258
bleeding-edge technologies 247
correlation statistic 255
cost-benefit analysis 250
cost of investment 249
discount rate 249
economic approaches 247
financial approaches 247
ICT implementation value proposition 241
leading-edge technologies 247
multi-attribute utility theory (MAUT) 251

net present value
　(NPV) *249*
net profit *241*
**process
　approach** *242*
rate of return *247*
return on investment
　(ROI) *247*
statistical approaches *247*
technology justification
　models *247*
technology S-curve *243*
technology trend
　curve *246*
total cost of ownership
　(TCO) *242*
trailing-edge
　technologies *246*
utility *251*
utility value
　tree *253*
value proposition *240*
variance
　approach *242*

References

Alter, A. E. (2006, July 16). July 2006 survey: IT value, productivity metrics still not trustworthy. *CIO Insight*.

Artely, W. (2001). Establishing an integrated performance measurement system. Retrieved from http://www.orau.gov/pbm/pbmhandbook/volume%202.pdf

Baumol, W. J. (1994). *Economics: Principles and policy*. Orlando, FL: Harcourt Brace and Company.

Bragg, S. M. (2002). *Business ratios and formulas: A comprehensive guide*. Hoboken, NJ: Wiley.

Devaraj, S., & Kohli, R. (2002). *The IT payoff*. Upper Saddle River: Prentice Hall.

Fortino, A. (2006). Personal Communication.

Foster, R. (1986). When to make your move to the latest innovation. *Across the Board*.

Hagood, W. O., & Freedman, L. (2002). Using the Balanced Scorecard to measure the performance of your HR information system. *Public Personnel Management, 31*(4), 543–557.

Horngren, C. T., & Harrison, W. T. Jr. (1989). *Accounting*. Upper Saddle River, NJ: Prentice Hall.

Kaplan, R. S., & Norton, D. P. (1996a). *The Balanced Scorecard*. Boston: Harvard Business School Press.

Kaplan, R. S., & Norton, D. P. (1996b). Using the Balanced Scorecard as a strategic management system. *Harvard Business Review,* January–February, 75–85.

McClave, J. T., Benson, P. G., & Sincich, T. (2005). *Statistics for business and economics*, 9th ed. Upper Saddle River, NJ: Prentice Hall.

Rifkin, G. (1994). Wrestling with the S-curve. *Harvard Business Review, 72*(1), 10.

Value-Based-Management.net. (2006, 10 June). *Management methods, management models, management theories*. Retrieved from http://www.valuebasedmanagement.net/index.html

Walsh, C. (2002). *Key management ratios: Master the management metrics that drive and control your business*, 3rd ed. Harlow, UK: Financial Times Prentice Hall.

Wang, R. Y., & Strong, D. M. (1996). Beyond accuracy: What data quality means to data consumers. *Journal of Management Information Systems, 14*(4), 5–34.

UNIT 3

SUMMARY

The goal for Unit 3 was to set the context for designing and recommending ICT infrastructure within the enterprise, including an overview of central ideas necessary to undertake selection, resource justification, and ongoing monitoring of ICT projects. A base of technical knowledge was built in Units 1 and 2 and a base of business knowledge was built in Unit 3. Together, these units create information stores from which the business systems analyst can draw, including business process and strategy concepts. Keep in mind that the materials in this unit are a survey and build upon coursework that the student should have had in the disciplines of accounting, finance, marketing, and management. The student is encouraged to go back and review prior coursework to fill in any gaps in these areas.

Unit 3 began by setting out to do the following:

- Discuss why management must be involved in ICT infrastructure building.
- Define competitive advantage and ways of creating it through use of an ICT infrastructure.
- Describe the role of management in ICT Infrastructure resource deployment decisions.
- Relate the concepts of business-driven infrastructure design to sustained competitive advantage.

The multilayered ICT infrastructure architecture was introduced in Units 1 and 2 and used in Unit 3, with connections made to how that architecture must be driven by organizational business strategy. The goal of building ICT infrastructure should be to gain and sustain competitive advantage. It is important to understand why management must be involved in ICT infrastructure building.

The business-driven infrastructure design methodology was introduced in Unit 3. The methodology is composed of several phases or steps:

- **Analysis Phase.** The analysis phase facilitates an understanding of the company for which the information technology infrastructure is being implemented and its industry, setting the stage for integration with the organization's business strategy. Processes are selected for innovation or improvement. Using the value propositions uncovered in the analysis phase, along with process selections, ICT recommendations are made within the layers of the technology infrastructure architecture.
- **Design.** Reconciling business analysis and ICT infrastructure recommendations, designers select hardware/software solutions to create the final design of the infrastructure. All final design documents are validated against the analysis and the recommendations.

BDID Steps and Overlap

	Project Start			Project End	
Analysis					
Design					
Implementation Planning					
Post-Implementation					

BDID flows somewhat like a waterfall, with overlap that occurs during the various steps. The BDID processes also exhibit a cyclic nature.

- **Implementation Plan.** An implementation plan describes how process change will be carried out with the selected equipment. This plan is the blueprint used to change the processes. Once engineers have built and tested the new infrastructure, it is ready to hand over to the users.
- **Post-Implementation.** Whereas implementation planning is about getting an infrastructure in place, post-implementation is about forward thinking after the initial implementation.

Understanding how to define a business process and the associated objectives and attributes of that process are part of the business systems analyst's tasks:

- Define a business process, its objectives, and its attributes.
- Understand how a business process can extend across operations, management, and strategic layers of management.
- Know the key factors involved in process change and how to use them.
- Develop strategies for ICT-mediated process change.
- Understand how to select processes for change.
- Clarify the role ICT plays in product and process innovation.

At the heart of exploiting ICT for competitive advantage is the ability to determine how ICT can be used to improve and innovate business processes. The business systems analyst must be able to take a process view of the organization and determine whether existing business processes can be supported or modified by ICT to produce an enhanced competitive position for the organization.

How an organization is structured is key to understanding which processes are the best candidates for process innovation or improvement. That means understanding the type of organization (e.g., manufacturing, service, and information). The structure, as well as its culture, will dictate measurement techniques employed, process ownership considerations, and levers that must be considered.

Describing business processes and their objectives and attributes was covered in Unit 3. Objectives are goals that the organization wants to accomplish through a business process, and attributes are properties of that process. It is essential that the business systems analyst understand the objectives of a process as well as all of its attributes before any process change initiative can be recommended or implemented.

This unit closed in Chapter 9 by covering the topic of measuring ICT value to the organization. The purpose of covering this material was so that the business systems analyst could:

- Understand the need for measuring information technology implementation success.
- Understand how to use economic utility to monitor soft indicators.
- Know the difference between activity- and organizational-level measurements.
- Be familiar with tools used to measure the payoff of IT investments

In resource-tight environments, understanding ICT payoff and ways that ICT investment should be viewed are essential to obtaining resources for ICT projects. The focus changes from "What is the budget?" to "What is the organization willing to invest in IT, and what is the expected payback?" A number of methods to measure ICT payoff were reviewed in this unit tying them to value proposition and process selection.

The topics of direct and indirect costs, as well as the total cost of ownership, were covered. These costs were linked to technology curves to provide tools to examine technology investments. Technology S-curves assist with determining the best time to move from existing technology to a new one. A technology trend curve indicates how an organization should divide its investment in technology into three types of technology: bleeding-edge technologies (early in their S-curve), leading-edge technologies (in the middle of their S-curve), and trailing-edge technologies (later in their S-curve).

Technology justification models are techniques used to understand ICT payback: financial/accounting models, economic models, and statistical models. Financial/accounting models include traditional calculations such as return on investment, net present value, and cost-benefit analysis. These financial indicators of performance provide recognizable estimates of the payback given by investment. Economic models of payback are based on the utility theory. Lastly, statistical models of payback are used to examine the relationship among an investment, net profit, and other drivers of net profit. Each of these approaches provides tools that can be applied to determining ICT payback.

The Balanced Scorecard was also discussed in this unit. It is a tool that can be used to monitor ICT payback from the financial/resource perspective, customer perspective, internal business process perspective, and the learning and growth perspective. The BSC can be implemented by incorporating the ICT payback models presented earlier.

UNIT 4

Steps to the Strategic Alignment of ICT

Unit Purpose

In Units 1 and 2, ICT concepts were introduced, and in Unit 3 the various factors that drive technology change were reviewed. Now we are ready to discuss how to (1) align ICT with an enterprise's overall strategy, (2) design and document ICT, and (3) plan for implementation and post-implementation. It is important to recognize that much ICT investment is wasted, and that the overriding goal of this unit is to show the student how to reduce that resource wastage and bring ICT into strategic alignment with the organization. Many sources have cited this waste, including a Gartner study that found that 20 percent of IT spending was wasted (Gartner Group, August 2002), an IBM survey that found that CIOs believe that 40 percent of all IT spending brought no return to the organization (IBM, 2004), and a Standish Group study that reported that 65 percent of IT projects are either challenged or fail (Cook, 2007). These statistics are frightening and should urge all IT/IS professionals to search for ways to increase the usefulness of ICT in their organizations.

The first stage in aligning ICT with an organization's strategy is analyzing the organization and its environment, and is an extended situation analysis. Analyzing the organization and its environment requires methods for understanding the organization, its industry, and its competitive environment in relation to technology. These methods are predicated on the business concepts from Unit 3, and at a minimum require the technology background of Unit 1 and Unit 2. The overriding goals of analyzing the organization and its environment are:

- Ascertain the value propositions of the organization as related to ICT.
- Determine the core competencies of the organization and the levers that drive them.
- Use environmental sensing and incorporate input from all stakeholders, both within and outside the enterprise.
- Understand the organization's goals and objectives, and determine the core ICT functionality and technologies needed to attain the goals and objectives.
- Understand the business processes and existing resources (e.g., staff, money, existing ICT) that can support the goals and objectives.
- Develop a gap analysis to understand what must be put in place to reach the goals and objectives.

Once the organization is analyzed and a gap analysis is created, we move to documenting process and technology recommendations. Methods for documenting ICT recommendations are discussed in Chapter 11, with an emphasis on using modeling tools. Designing a standard naming scheme (nomenclature) for the ICT infrastructure and creating final "user appropriate" design documents that graphically describe the infrastructure being proposed are described. With a properly designed infrastructure, we move on to summarizing the business-driven infrastructure design cycle in Chapter 12. Models for costing an infrastructure design are discussed, and implementation planning is reviewed. Implementation planning includes the use of subcontractors to complete work. Measurement of infrastructure success is again discussed and expanded on. The need for post-infrastructure implementation review is discussed along with ways for the design team to stay in touch with the user.

Unit Objectives

Be able to **develop** the value proposition(s) for an organization.

Understand how to analyze organizations within their industry context.

Know how to create and document the gap analysis for an organization, and how to relate it to ICT.

Learn how to pull together a high-level ICT design documentation useful to network engineers.

Develop an understanding of what it takes to implement ICT and its impact on the organization.

Understand ways to implement ICT.

Vignette

TSI, a Fictitious Company

This opening vignette is much longer than the vignettes in previous units because a longer vignette (more an actual business case) is necessary to demonstrate the concepts in this unit. Additionally, your instructor may want to use this case for a semester-length project. This vignette is based on previous work by the textbook author and colleague. It is reformatted and reprinted with the permission of the *Journal of Information Systems*. [Source: Gendron, M., & Jarmoszko, A. T. (2005). TSI: A teaching case for the DCN Curriculum. *Journal of Information Systems Education, 16*(3).]

Abstract This case requires strategic and business analysis, which serves the purpose of making explicit the linkages between the business needs of an organization and the ICT required to implement competitive solutions. Ticket Sales, Inc. (TSI) is a start-up business that has received venture capital seed funding. It is using the seed funding to perform a number of feasibility studies that will enable it to seek first-round venture capital. TSI is undertaking a technology feasibility study, including a five-year total cost of ownership plan. Unit 4 of this textbook uses the details of the TSI case study to show how to create the business-to-ICT linkages, or in other words bring about the strategic alignment of ICT.

Introduction Ticket Sales, Inc. (TSI) is a start-up organization that has obtained venture capital seed-funding to perform various feasibility studies. Assuming the feasibility study requested in this document demonstrates TSI's ability to attain competitive advantage through technology, TSI will seek first-round venture capital to begin operations. TSI intends to operate in the New York City area. Its mission is to:

> Employ technological solutions to provide easy access to tickets for movies, shows, and other ticketed events in large metropolitan areas.

TSI has already performed a preliminary market feasibility study, sections of which are incorporated into this document. Students, acting as a consulting company, are asked to conduct a technology feasibility and strategy study. The goals of this study include the following:

- Craft a technology strategy that would place TSI in a competitively advantageous position within the retail ticket sales industry.
- Develop a technology design and implementation plan to support the mission of TSI and enhance TSI's competitive positioning.
- Put together a five-year total cost of ownership plan for the network infrastructure and desktop technology implementation (as described elsewhere in this document).

E-Business Innovation Requirement The entertainment industry, and ticket sales in particular, is a large part of the New York City economy. TSI desires to offer tickets to its customers at kiosks and online, but needs a plan developed that will enhance its competitive positioning. Considering the number of tickets sold in this region, TSI will capture market share through convenient and accessible ticket sales. Because TSI faces many competitors, the technology solution that your consulting company proposes must allow TSI to provide better, faster, and more efficient services to ticket customers.

The Entertainment and Ticket Sales Industry in New York City TSI desires to offer tickets to its customers at kiosks and online. Considering the number of tickets sold in this region, TSI is entering a competitive market and desires to be a step ahead of its competition both in convenience and accessibility. TSI desires that your ICT proposal allow TSI to provide better, faster, and more efficient services to customers than its competitors. In short, TSI understands the role ICT plays in maintaining competitive advantage in this venture.

TSI Business Model TSI will purchase blocks of seats from each venue at a discount and resell them at the face value of the ticket without any service charge. Significant discounts are negotiable through bulk purchasing arrangements because TSI takes the risk for predicting sales levels for individual events. By purchasing blocks of seats, TSI guarantees its venue partners revenue for those seats, thus increasing their incentive to sell at substantial discounts. TSI's flexible and real-time distribution network will allow it to realize a profit on the margin for each ticket.

Staffing and Building Specs TSI will be housed in a five-story building, each floor being 7,500 square feet, for a total of 37,500 square feet. Since TSI's building is just being designed they can only give you approximate specifications. Construction will take approximately six months. Each floor of the new building will have a large closet suitable for wiring and equipment. See Table 10-1 for available details.

TABLE 10-1 Building Breakdown

Floor	Staff Members	Office	Number of Staff
First	Senior management from each major department, including CEO, CFO, and CIO	Private Office	9
	Secretary for each senior manager	Cubicle	9
	Building receptionist (also does secretarial work)	Lobby	1
Second*	IT staff	Cubicle	9
	IT manager	Private Office	1
	IT secretary	Cubicle	1
Third	Marketing staff	Cubicle	19
	Marketing manager	Private Office	1
	Marketing secretary	Cubicle	1
	Accounting staff	Cubicle	19
	Accounting manager	Private Office	1
	Accounting secretary	Cubicle	1
	Marketing/Accounting IT support staff	Cubicle	2
Fourth	Call center and operations staff	Cubicle	20
	Call center operations manager	Private Office	1
	Assistant operations manager	Cubicle	1
	Call center secretary	Cubicle	1
	Call center IT support staff	Cubicle	2
Fifth	Call center and operations staff	Cubicle	20
	Assistant operations manager	Cubicle	1
	Assistant operations manager	Cubicle	1
	Call center IT support staff	Cubicle	2

* The demarcation of all telecommunications and ICT gear will be here. The network core will be located here as well.

TSI Business Operational Objectives Based on the following summary of TSI's major business, the proposed technology solutions must support these goals and provide a five-year total cost of ownership plan. Each of the items in this summary must be provided as well as any additional technological innovations that should be considered:

- Ticket Sales and Operations
    - Connectivity for kiosks located in New York City.
    - Internet connectivity to support online (web) sale of tickets.
    - ICT hardware/software to support data storage for ticket information sales and purchases.
    - Main office desktop and remote connectivity for all authorized employees to the GenServe application.
- Infrastructure
    - Workstations and printers for all staff (see following for specifications).
    - Cost-effective, secure, and reliable Internet connectivity and wiring within TSI's new building.
    - Servers to support the organization's needs for intranet and Internet e-mail, internal databases, printing, etc.
    - A secure LAN for TSI with appropriate firewall software/hardware.
    - VPN access into the TSI network from the Internet for kiosks and employee home computers.
    - Installation and ongoing connectivity to the Internet for the main office and for all kiosks. (Note: The connectivity to the main office must have 95% uptime reliability.)
    - A backup solution for all servers and desktop PCs.
    - UPS support for all networking hardware and servers at the TSI main office.

- Service Maintenance
  - Onsite hardware service to maintain network and desktops.
  - Software maintenance for desktops, servers, etc.

Genenco (Another Fictitious Company) TSI will provide tickets exclusively through the network of kiosks and via its web site. It will purchase the web server application, client/server application, and kiosks from Genenco, Inc. Based on the marketing analysis and the outcome of the technology feasibility and strategy study, TSI will place the kiosks in various public locations throughout New York City (excerpts of the preliminary market analysis are included as follows). The projected volume of sales for web transactions and each kiosk type are discussed. The web transactions and kiosks will transmit credit card information over the Internet; therefore, end-to-end security is a major concern in the WAN design. The web and client/server (i.e., kiosk/main office) application is being custom designed and built for TSI and will be called GenServe.

The Genenco kiosk client/server and the web application will perform credit card validation/verification (as part of its software functionality) and will communicate with TSI's bank and merchant account via the Internet. TSI will use software-based credit card processing for kiosk-generated sales, and online shopping cart credit card processing for sales through TSI's web site. TSI will accept Visa, MasterCard, American Express, Discover, Diner's Club, and debit cards. The average credit card sale will be between $200 and $1,000, and the anticipated monthly volume is $250,000 to $499,999.

The kiosks will communicate directly to the TSI home office via a VPN. Hardware/software must be included in the proposed ICT design to support VPN connectivity with end-to-end security. Genenco will install and service the kiosks. The ICT infrastructure must include the form of connectivity (e.g., DSL) for each kiosk, or group of kiosks, any required interface cards (e.g., modems, network cards), and any communications hardware necessary at the kiosk location (e.g., switches/routers). The kiosks are preloaded with MS-Windows 7, a VPN client, and the GenServe client application. The GenServe client application runs as a dedicated application in the kiosk environment. Main office servers will update kiosk internal databases during normal sales transactions—those updates occur as background processing and are included in the transaction sizes given below. The updates include changes in venue, show, and seat availability.

Consumers purchasing tickets over the web will connect to the GenServe web application through the Internet via their own ISP. GenServe will employ encryption to protect credit card and personal information. The infrastructure must include all connections, hardware, and software within TSI's main office necessary for Internet connectivity.

Since this is a retail e-commerce environment, kiosk and web site response time and reliability are important factors in network design, and important to the competitive positioning. TSI conducts all of its business electronically and is financially very sensitive to interruptions in its own network and in Internet connectivity. Thus, redundancy is very important.

GenServe Hardware Requirements The GenServe application requires the following hardware be provided by TSI:

Note: Kiosks are provided by Genenco through a separate contract

- Four servers, each rack mounted; the following details are pertinent:
  - Genenco applications support multiple processors
  - Maximized Random Access Memory
  - In addition to a local hard drive, a Raid 5 TB SAN for data storage
  - Fiber optic network connection to the backbone
  - Redundant power supplies and fans
  - Current Windows server software
  - Other system management software as recommended
  - Multi-server KVM solution

Five servers of this specification are needed to support these application:

- Application Server
- MS-Commerce Server
- MS-SQL Server
- MS-Exchange Server
- MS-IIS

These servers with their associated applications are required to run the server side of the GenServe application. The ICT infrastructure design must include other servers to support the business goals of TSI (i.e., additional servers other than those required by Genenco). Virtualization solutions for the delivery of desktop applications will also be considered. Additionally, the data center must be have UPS protection to handle electrical power fluctuations, provide orderly shutdown in the case of power failure, and 20 minutes of electrical backup for all data center equipment.

Other TSI Requirements

Security. All employees will have Internet access to track theater events at venues within New York City. Therefore, management needs to be able to track Internet usage by employee. Additionally, filtering of Internet sites—which sites management considers inappropriate—is essential. Management also recognizes the need for strong protection from outside intrusion by hackers and viruses. A multilevel approach to security is expected.

Printing. Appropriate and specific types of printing will be required for different operations. Floors 1, 3, 4 and 5 will each have a Xerox Document Centre Digital Copier (leased directly from Xerox). All staff will use these as shared printers. All executives, managers, and secretaries are to have local (not shared) laser printers. The marketing department requires a shared high-speed color printer capable of 11x17 printing. A dye-sublimation printer will be considered and represents the level of quality needed by the marketing department.

Desktop PC Information. This list represents the minimum desktop configuration for ALL employees. The minimum configuration is below and should be supplemented based on an organizational need.

- Software
  - Current version of MS-Windows Desktop Operating System and MS-Office Professional Suite
  - Genenco GenServe desktop application, installed by Genenco
  - Virus and spyware protection
- Hardware (Minimum)
  - Intel or compatible processor
  - 1 TB HD (7200rpm)
  - 4GB RAM minimum
  - 24-inch flat panel monitor (Dual in the marketing department)

Preliminary Marketing Study TSI previously commissioned a preliminary marketing feasibility study to determine the feasibility of its business model, the placement of kiosks, and the expected ticket sales volume over the web and at kiosks. Selected details are discussed below.

The marketing study grouped kiosks into three categories by expected utilization: high, medium, and low. Kiosk utilization (in Table 10-2) indicates the average number of tickets expected per transaction during peak utilization.

Utilization by area (in Table 10-3) gives the number of kiosks and utilization type, the planned number of kiosks, the primary hours of operations, and the expected utilization grouping. The preliminary marketing study, conducted earlier, concluded that at this time it was not possible to estimate web sales due to a lack of data.

Proposal Requirements

Note: When this Vignette is use as a semester project, the following are the minimum requirements for the project. Your consulting company (individual or group of students) must provide the following:

- ICT needs analysis based on the business requirements, core competencies, and competitive analysis of TSI; be sure to include all ICT infrastructure requirements not provided by Genenco or Xerox—your proposal should be totally turnkey
- Recommendations for all hardware/software, including operating systems, telecommunications equipment, desktop systems, servers, equipment racks, wiring, Internet connectivity for the home office, Internet connectivity for each kiosk, network equipment and cables for each kiosk, etc.

TABLE 10-2 Kiosk Utilization

Utilization Type	Average Transaction During Primary Hours	Average Number of Tickets per Transaction
High	20	5.7
Medium	14	4.5
Low	12	2.3

TABLE 10-3 Utilization by Area

Area	Utilization	Kiosks	Primary Hours	Location
Bronx	Med	10	4:00 P.M.–11:00 P.M.	3 locations with 2 kiosks each 1 location with 4 kiosks
Brooklyn	High	5	8:00 A.M.–6:00 P.M.	all 5 in separate locations
Brooklyn	Med	5	6:00 A.M.–9:00 A.M. and 4:00 P.M.–8:00 P.M.	all 5 in separate locations
Brooklyn	Low	5	24 hours	all 5 in separate locations
Manhattan	High	30	6:00 A.M.–8:00 P.M.	5 locations with 3 kiosks each 2 locations with 2 kiosks each 11 locations with 1 kiosk
Manhattan	Med	15	5:00 A.M.–9:00 A.M. and 4:00 P.M.–8:00 P.M.	2 locations with 3 kiosks each 2 locations with 2 kiosks each 5 locations with 1 kiosk
Queens	Med	10	2:00 P.M.–10:00 P.M.	10 locations with 1 kiosk
Queens	Low	5	24 hours	5 locations with 1 kiosk
Staten Island	Med	10	24 hours	5 locations with 2 kiosks
Staten Island	Low	2	24 hours	2 locations with 1 kiosk

- A five-year total cost of ownership (TCO) plan including personnel needed to run/maintain the ICT (Note: two network technicians are included in the current staffing plan for TSI. If your proposal includes additional personnel it must be listed in the five-year TCO plan.)
- TSI requires that any proposal include a measurement plan which ensures the alignment of all recommendations with TSI's mission.

10 ANALYZING THE ORGANIZATION AND ITS ENVIRONMENT

> **Learning Objectives**
>
> - Know how to ascertain the value propositions of the organization as related to ICT.
> - Determine the core competencies of the organization and the levers that drive them.
> - Learn to use environmental sensing, incorporating input from all stakeholders, both within and outside the enterprise.
> - Develop a list of goals and objectives and align what ICT functionality and technologies are needed to attain the goals and objectives in support of the organizational ICT value proposition.
> - Understand the business processes and existing resources (e.g., staff, money, existing ICT) that can support the goals and objectives.
> - Develop a gap analysis to understand what must be put in place to reach the goals and objectives.

In this chapter, students are presented with methods for understanding the organization, its industry, and it competitive environment in relation to technology. These methods are predicated on the business concepts described earlier in this text and, at a minimum, requires the technology background of Units 1 and 2. Using the value propositions generated during the analysis described in this chapter, ICT recommendations can be made within the components of the ICT infrastructure architecture. The overarching purpose of this chapter is to have the student understand how to ascertain the ICT value proposition and how ICT can bring value to the enterprise.

STRATEGIC ALIGNMENT OF IT (SAIT)

> Note: *While academic literature refers to the strategic alignment of IT (SAIT), this textbook is referring to the alignment of both information and communication technology (ICT) when the term SAIT is used.*

SAIT: Whose Job Is It?

Today's enterprise normally has a member of the executive team (i.e., C-Suite, CEO, CIO, CFO, etc.) called the chief information officer (CIO). As stated earlier in the textbook, CIO positions, along with chief technology officers (CTOs) and chief knowledge officers (CKOs) all have in common the task of the business systems analyst, or they should have staff that performs the business systems analyst function. In other words, someone needs to be responsible for assessing the business needs of an organization and recommending the appropriate technologies to solve business problems. The job of this person is to ensure that ICT-based systems are successful and add business value. Much discussion continues about the "productivity paradox," which states that despite the dramatic increase in computer power employee productivity has grown relativity slowly (Brynjolfsson, 2009). It is the job of the business systems analyst to move past the productivity paradox and find ways for ICT-mediated solutions to bring about the strategic alignment of ICT.

ICT implementation value can come in the form of reduced costs, increased productivity, or product innovation, all of which should enhance the competitive positioning of the organization. In this chapter we will focus on ways to analyze the enterprise, within the context of its competitive industry,

---

Several of the concepts in this chapter have been previously published in the *Asia Pacific Management Review* (Gendron, Banks, & Miller, 2009).

and determine which technologies are appropriate to implement. You might say we are talking about ICT-enabled organizational change alongside the strategic alignment of ICT.

In a recent study by IBM in 2009 (The CIO Study), IBM found that 55% of the CIO's time is devoted to developing business value through IT, and the remaining 45% is devoted to more traditional stewardship of existing IT resources. Specifically, the study stated, "Today's CIOs spend an impressive 55 percent of their time on activities that spur innovation. These activities include generating buy-in for innovative plans, implementing new technologies, and managing nontechnology business issues. The remaining 45 percent is spent on essential, more traditional CIO tasks related to managing the ongoing technology environment. This includes reducing IT costs, mitigating enterprise risks, and leveraging automation to reduce costs elsewhere in the business." This necessitates that business systems analysts have skills that allow them to make recommendations that move the organization closer to the strategic alignment of ICT. Those skills are the basis of this textbook.

The person tasked with developing ICT strategy needs a number of tools that support the alignment of ICT and the enterprise strategy, commonly referred to as the strategic alignment of information technology, or **SAIT**. These tools include a number of business frameworks, an overall focus on the core competencies and mission of the enterprise, technology management frameworks and tools, and a technology focus. The interaction of these items leads to shared processes, tools, language, values, and purposes as seen in Figure 10-1.

This chapter takes the contingency perspective in aligning strategy with information technology. This perspective is based on the belief that the greatest impact on an organization's performance can be realized by utilizing ICT resources to support strategic objectives, and by understanding the organization's strategy and where ICT can support it. This chapter further builds on this perspective to incorporate the process innovation/improvement perspective discussed in Unit 3, along with a look at how organizations are strategically placed within their industries. All of these perspectives are overshadowed by a strong technology focus that keeps an eye on enhancing the organization's competitive positioning and its bottom line. All these tasks are part of the job of the CIO, CKO, CTO, and business systems analysts as they spend much of their time to spur innovation.

One may ask: Does the scale of an ICT project guarantee positive outcomes? Surely an organization that spends millions of dollars on a project must know what it is doing, right? Isn't it true that large organizations are intelligent enough to be sure of positive outcomes before committing a large amount of resources to a project? The fact is that scale

FIGURE 10-1 Building to SAIT

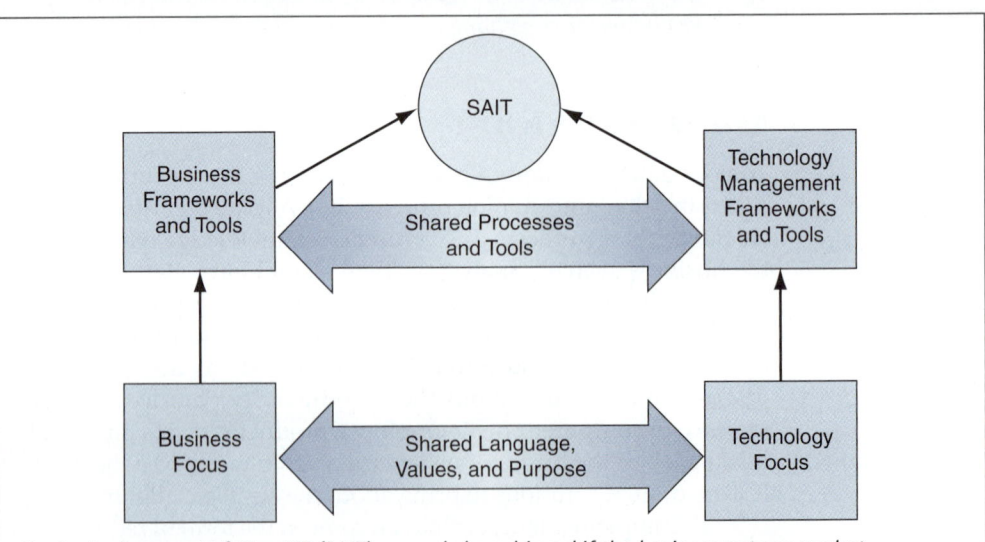

Strategic alignment of IT or ICT (SAIT) can only be achieved if the business systems analyst understands the shared processes, tools, language, values, and purposes of those with whom they work. Within the various frameworks, the business systems analyst can create the shared processes and tools that will allow everyone at the executive level to communicate effectively. The business systems analyst must possess a technology-business focus in order to create the shared language, values, and purposes that facilitate successful interaction with the members of management who approve the expenditure of organizational resources.

of a project may have little or no impact on the outcome (OECD 2001); and often the larger the project, the more apt it is to fail. For example, the textbook author is familiar with an online analytic processing (OLAP) system that was rolled out to epidemiology analysts within a U.S. health maintenance organization (HMO). This system was to allow the analysts to assess the incidence and prevalence of various diseases of the HMO members and, based on that data, set premiums. The scope of this system was large, had support of senior management and staff, and represented a substantial portion of the annual information systems budget. Still, this system was abandoned in favor of the more traditional way to perform these analyses. The analysts felt they simply did not need to use OLAP tools to do the analysis required and that existing tools did the job adequately. The scope, management and initial staff support, and economic commitment to this project did not guarantee its success. The users did not perceive that the OLAP system added value to their jobs or to the organization. The system failed because the users were not sufficiently consulted before the resources were committed for the project. This and similar situations lead to hundreds of thousands of dollars wasted, delays of other ICT projects, and a general dissatisfaction with the CIO by other executive management members and the board of directors. In the end the CIO left the organization. If users had been consulted early and the system had provided business value, the situation might have been different.

In summary, ICT needs to be implemented with careful inclusion of all stakeholders and after it has been determined that the resources will bring about closer alignment of ICT with the organization's strategy. ICT implementations must align with strategic objectives and thereby fulfill stakeholders' needs. The issue is how to attain that alignment.

SAIT: What Is It Really?

The notion of organizational "fit" has been discussed in several ways to include adaptation (personal–environmental fit), compatibility (individual–organizational fit), assimilation (organization–organization fit), and coupling (internal–external fit). All of these definitions are built around the concepts of agreement, match, or similarity between two different things. You can look at SAIT as the fit between the strategic objectives of an organization and how the organization proposes to meet its strategic objectives using ICT. The "fit" comes when the business systems analyst is able to envision the organization, align ICT implementation with the organization's strategic objectives, and cause ICT to augment the organization. Along the lines of the primary strategic orientations of firms, ICT is implemented for three competitive reasons—*cost reduction*, *quality improvement*, and *revenue growth*—each of which has been shown to have varying impacts on organizational performance:

- **Cost Reduction.** Firms can attempt to achieve market leadership by reducing cost through a number of strategies. Although all firms attempt to reduce costs, cost reduction strategies are generally aligned with Porter's strategies of cost leadership in broad markets and a low-cost focus strategy in narrow markets. These strategies can include, for example, waste reduction, lower inventories, increasing productivity, and reducing cycle times. In any cost reduction strategy, the overarching objective is to reduce costs while not sacrificing quality, with the intention of achieving or maintaining a cost leadership position within the marketplace. ICT can be leveraged in a number of ways to effectuate this strategy, including, for example, supply chain management, inventory control, or ERP systems.
- **Quality Improvement.** It is possible for a firm to gain market share by producing higher-quality goods at the same or higher costs as its competitors. Using product differentiation strategies, firms seek to distinguish their products from others in the marketplace, while at the same time increasing market share and maintaining marginal revenue. In the marketplace, the perception of value needs to be created, allowing for higher price and increased market share. ICT can be used to improve product quality through process improvement or innovation, and to enhance product perception in the marketplace through tools such as customer relationship management (CRM) methods and software.
- **Revenue Growth.** In the marketplace, revenue growth strategies focus on increased sales and profits. This approach requires using ICT to create/enhance

product offerings or to enhance sales, while at the same time maintaining market share. Perhaps an ICT-oriented revenue growth strategy is easiest to conceive in online companies like Amazon, Google, or e-Bay, but an ICT-oriented revenue growth strategy is possible in many types of companies.

Whichever strategy a firm embarks on, it is essential that it does so focused on technology and its alignment with the organization's strategic objectives. This focus will lead to the use of ICT resources to support the organization's mission, objectives, and core competencies.

It should be noted that sometimes ICT is implemented to fulfill government mandates, which may potentially be noncompetitive in nature. These mandates are normally considered "overhead" items. An example might be an adverse event reporting system a pharmaceutical company must maintain due to legislation. These types of systems need to be considered, and it may be argued that doing the "overhead" things better may make you more competitive. Still, these types of systems are generally considered *supporting services* and regarded as necessary expenses. This chapter will not focus on these supporting systems, but rather on making ICT recommendations that directly enhance the competitive positioning of the organization.

Achieving SAIT

Strategic alignment of ICT is the job of the business systems analyst. In order to bring about that alignment an analyst must understand the organization and industry in which it operates, setting the stage for a review of core strategic competencies. A successful ICT implementation must take into account the requirements of the industry (e.g., the banking industry requires a high degree of security) as well as the specific needs and characteristics of the organization. To perform this alignment, it is imperative that the business systems analyst understand the strategic direction of the organization. Various techniques can be used to achieve SAIT through an organizational search for ICT-driven value. This chapter proposes several that facilitate the achievement of this alignment, while at the same time work toward discovering the ICT value proposition within a context of tools understood by the organization's C-suite.

Value search models are used to understand how ICT can be implemented to reduce cost, improve quality, or grow revenue. When creating value search models, the business systems analyst must understand the mission and strategic objectives of the organization. The models are used to understand the operational needs of the organization, while assisting the organization in its endeavor to create value for its customers.

VALUE SEARCH MODELS: ANALYZING THE ORGANIZATION

At the core of the ICT value search is the thorough examination of the organization, through what are called **value search models**. These models are classified into three types: external, internal, and external/internal value search models. External value search models focus primarily outside the organization and yield competitive information about other similar enterprises in the same industry. Internal value search models focus primarily inside the enterprise and provide information that can be used to change the organization (e.g., process innovation or process improvement). The value search models—including corporate unbundling, value chain deconstruction, comparative SWOT analysis, and competitive forces analysis—all provide tools for the business systems analyst to discover ways to implement ICT for competitive advantage and to explain those advantages to management. Analytical work carried out using these models will provide information to aid in the understanding of where ICT can be leveraged to enhance organizational performance. Figure 10-2 summarizes the value search modeling tools.

Organizational Value Propositions

Any organization should be able to describe what it does to bring value to its customers. In other words, what does the organization offer that the customer is willing to pay money for? It may be easier to think of this in terms of something we are all familiar with—paying taxes. Suppose your local town wanted to increase taxes by

Value Search Model	Primary Strategic Focus	Primary Focus
Corporate Unbundling	Cost reduction; quality improvement	Internal
Value Chain Deconstruction	Cost reduction; quality improvement	Internal
Supply Chain	Cost reduction; revenue growth	Internal and external
Comparative SWOT Analysis	Revenue growth	Internal and external
Competitive Forces	Revenue growth	External

FIGURE 10-2 Value Search Models

1 percent to pay for a building. Will the building be perceived to have enough value (utility) to the citizens so they are willing to pay higher taxes? If yes, then the tax increase is a valid value proposition, and the citizens will likely vote for the tax increase. If not, then the tax increase will likely get voted down because of insufficient perceived value. In economic terms, this concept is referred to as "willingness to pay."

"Value" has several definitions in the dictionary (Merriam-Webster, 2009), a few of which are relevant to this discussion:

1. a fair return or equivalent in goods, services, or money for something exchanged;
2. the monetary worth of something: market price;
3. relative worth, utility, or importance <a good value at the price>

The definition for "proposition" is "something offered for consideration or acceptance" (Merriam-Webster, 2009). So, taken together, a **value proposition** is defined as *what an organization provides (proposes, offers) to its customer for which the customer considers the asking price a fair return of equivalent goods or services (value)*. The business system analyst needs to set his or her mind on understanding the organization's value proposition, and how ICT can enhance it. An organization's mission statement needs to embody its value propositions, and the value propositions must flow directly from the mission statement. The value propositions must be things that all stakeholders know about, and must become engrained into the organization. The value proposition should be evident in all corporate communications and marketing materials. All stakeholders, including customers, business partners, and employees, must know and understand the organization's value propositions. It is the value propositions that must drive the value search model quest to understand how ICT can lower cost, increase quality, grow revenue, and, to be more specific, enhance competitive positioning.

As business systems analysts apply the various value search models to their organization, they will expand their understanding of the value propositions of their organization. Internal analyses include value chain analysis and corporate unbundling, and external analyses include supply chain analysis, competitive forces analysis, and comparative SWOT analysis. During these analytical steps the business systems analyst should uncover how the organization produces value, and how the customer perceives it, yielding a well-tuned value proposition for the organization. Note that value is elusive and the mind of the consumer changes frequently—value propositions needs to be updated frequently to maintain competitive advantage. Therefore, all of the analyses introduced in the following pages take the consumer's perspective first, and then focus on the internals of the organization. Unless consumers perceive value, they will not purchase the goods and services of the organization.

Low Cost, Internal Efficiency, and Enhancing Quality Strategies

In this section we look at ways to examine the organization internally and externally to attempt to find ways to reduce cost, build internal efficiencies, or enhance product/service quality to gain market share and competitive advantage. These three ways are corporate unbundling, value chain deconstruction, and supply chain deconstruction. Each of these

> **VIGNETTE BOX 10-1**
>
> **TSI Value Proposition**
>
> TSI's mission statement:
>
> *Employ technological solutions to provide easy access to tickets for movies, Broadway shows, and other ticketed events in large metropolitan areas.*
>
> From this mission statement and other facts in the vignette, the business systems analyst can infer the value to customers is *easy access to tickets for NYC venues without added fees.* Implied in TSI's value proposition is that customers value the convenience of buying at a TSI kiosk or over the web. They are willing to trust TSI with their credit card information and value the convenience over the security of a face-to-face transaction at the theater where the credit card or cash is handled directly by another person.

options looks inward and gives the business systems analyst the opportunity to cut across organizational departmental boundaries, while supply chain deconstruction looks both inward and outward. The goal of these tools is to make it evident where ICT-mediated solutions can be implemented so the organization can excel in the marketplace through lower cost, internal efficiencies, and enhancing product quality. Because we know that consumers are likely to select products and services that have the greatest perceived value relative to the money they pay for the good or service, any ICT strategies that can lead to attainment of lower cost, internal efficiencies, or enhanced quality are likely to increase market share and enhance competitive positioning.

CORPORATE UNBUNDLING

Corporate unbundling focuses on cost reduction (e.g., lower production costs) and quality improvement strategies (i.e., enhancing an organization's product quality). It also provides opportunities to look for increased efficiencies. Reduced costs and improved value directly affect customer perception, as does increasing internal efficiencies. Because strategies that lead to internal efficiencies normally lead to cost efficiency, the reader can assume that when low-cost strategies are discussed that internal efficiency solutions are part of that discussion.

The topics of unbundling of the corporation and the impact of the Internet on organizations have been discussed by many researchers (e.g., Hagel & Singer, 1999; Porter, 2001). Hagel and Singer (1999) proposed interaction costs, shown in Figure 10-3, as an explanation for organizational reorganization and choosing whether to perform an activity internally or to outsource it. **Interaction costs** are defined as "the money and time that are expended whenever people and companies exchange goods, services, and ideas" (p. 134). Interaction costs occur in any transaction, whether it is business-to-business or consumer-to-business, and can take any number of forms, including meetings, phone calls, reports, and memos to name a few. (see Figure 10-3 for a summary of interaction costs) It is important to note that interaction costs determine, either directly or indirectly, organizational efficiency and the way organizations operate, the form they take, and which processes they keep in-house and which they outsource. This knowledge also affects where ICT is implemented and how it can best benefit the organization.

FIGURE 10-3 Interaction Costs

What Are Interaction Costs?

- Costs associated with business transactions
- Occur in business-to-business as well as consumer-to-business transactions
- Include meetings, phone calls, reports, memos, and any other hard or soft costs of running a business
- Determine how organizations operate and the form they take

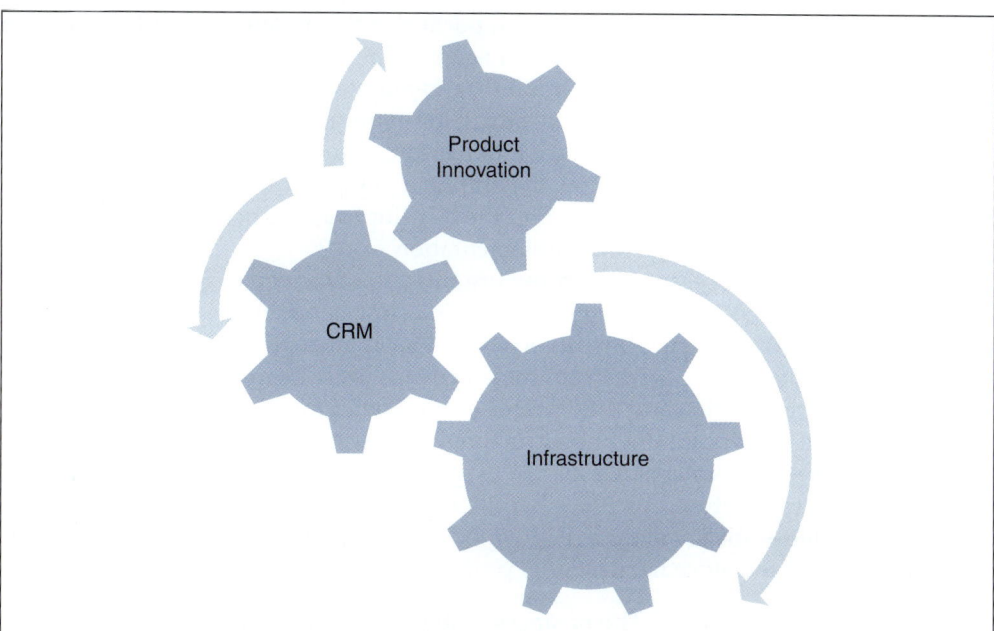

FIGURE 10-4 The Unbundled Corporation

The unbundled corporation consists of three major parts that describe how the corporation functions as a whole: (1) the customer relationship management function, (2) the product innovation function, and (3) the infrastructure function. By looking at the corporation using these functions as lenses, it is possible for the business systems analyst to devise ways to lower costs or increase the quality of organizational outputs.

Note: The size and interrelationship (i.e., which gear interlocks with another in this diagram) are not meant to suggest any relationships between the parts of the unbundled corporation. The truth is that the relationship and relative importance of each part of the corporation vary based on the product type, mission, culture, and organization of the corporation.

As shown in Figure 10-4, following interaction cost theory, it is possible to divide organizations into separate, but interacting functions, which can assist the business systems analyst in understanding the most effective places to implement ICT solutions. Corporate unbundling theory states that most organizations (corporations) are composed of three intertwined businesses (major processes): customer relationship management, product innovation, and infrastructure processes. In effect, most organizations are composed of these three businesses under one umbrella organization. Interaction costs determine how the organization will function, which parts of each major process it keeps in-house, and the form the organization will take. Understanding how this unbundling affects an organization can assist the business systems analyst in implementing ICT for competitive advantage.

Understanding the three functions of the organization will assist the business systems analyst in effectively defining the organization and identifying where ICT can provide the effective strategic support for cost reduction and product quality improvement. The customer-relationship-management portion of the organization is responsible for finding customers and building and maintaining relationships with them. The CRM function includes the sales and marketing departments and supports the organization through the marketing, sale, and service cycles. In most organizations, marketing staff attempt to attract customers and maintain relationships with them, while service staff will deal with problems and bring about resolutions that maintain a positive customer relationship. It is obvious that these staffs are in different organizational units (departments), but their interrelationship may not be so obvious. Understanding this interrelationship is key to the success of the business systems analyst's recommendations for ICT to support the CRM function of the organization. This broader approach may help reveal the networked social linkages between parts of an organizational structure that may evade a largely ICT-biased perspective.

The purpose of the product innovation portion of the organization is to "conceive of attractive new products and services" (Hagel & Singer, 1999). In all organizations, new services and products are key to attaining and maintaining competitive advantage. In an interrelationship between the product innovation and CRM processes, new products need the CRM process to make it to market, garner market share, and service and maintain customers. This interrelationship is a key point that needs to be understood by the business systems analyst, and the ICT implications need to be understood by all involved with ICT design and implementation.

Infrastructure processes within the organization manage existing operations/facilities and build new ones, including routine, low- and high-volume repetitive operations within the organization. Everything that it takes to make an organization function is included in the infrastructure processes, and it can be said that it is the "engine" of the organization and the "interface" with other functions. From the business systems analyst's standpoint, the infrastructure processes/functions represent the core business activities and perhaps the largest expenditures. In the TSI case (opening unit vignette), the infrastructure processes handle logistics for all ticket procurement and distribution, while at the same time deploying kiosks and the web site, maintaining IT, and providing all back office transactional processes.

Unbundling and Interaction Costs

The business systems analyst is challenged with how to implement technology to best support the organization. By viewing the organization unbundled along the lines just described, the business systems analyst can identify interaction costs in an attempt to decide which processes to keep in-house and which to outsource, and to understand which ICT solutions bring the greatest benefit through decreased costs or increased product quality. Quantifying interaction and transaction costs and comparing them across the options of performing a process in-house versus outsourcing is relatively simple. However, unbundling the corporation and looking for ways to decrease costs or increase quality are more complex. Suppose an analyst is looking over three enterprise resource management solutions that are believed to bring about varying cost savings to the organization, each with varying levels of support for each unbundled function, and each process contributing a varying amount to the value propositions supported by ICT implementation.

How would the business systems analyst go about selecting a solution using corporate unbundling? He or she would proceed as follows:

- Identify the organizational value proposition being supported as discussed previously in this chapter.
- Identify systems/options to support the value proposition. In other words, develop a list of available options to support the functions within the unbundled corporation and the overall value proposition. Information from earlier chapters in this textbook, will be useful in making this list.
- Determine ways to assign percentages to the various options.

It is incumbent on the business systems analyst to determine the amount each option supports the unbundled corporation and, from that point, develop a metric showing how much each option supports the organizational value proposition (e.g., Figure 10-5). Even though unbundling does not give the entire picture in selecting systems, it can be used as one tool to estimate the value of an ICT implementation.

TSI can be unbundled along the lines just described. As stated, an unbundled corporation has three major areas: CRM, product innovation, and infrastructure. Interaction costs arise within these areas as well as between them. A list of possible interaction costs and ICT solutions can be seen in Vignette Box 10-2. TSI can use ICT in a number of places to implement a cost reduction or product enhancement strategy. The list in the vignette box is meant to be representative, rather than exhaustive. You will notice that an ERP has been mentioned in this list several times, and that the opening vignette mentions that an ERP system has already been selected from Genenco, however the opening vignette does not indicate the level of ERP support given by Genenco.

Using the analysis in Vignette Box 10-2, it is possible to come up with a list of ICT recommendations. This list provides ideas that need to have costs developed, ROI

FIGURE 10-5 Unbundling the Corporation and Value Proposition Support

Option	CRM	Product Innovation	Infrastructure	Overall Value Proposition Support
1	20%	40%	15%	60%
2	15	20	25	50
3	25	65	10	70

The unbundled corporation gives the business systems analyst the opportunity to develop metrics that allow the comparison of ICT choices. The comparison can be made among options and how well they support the unbundled corporation and its value proposition, giving the business systems analyst a tool to determine which ICT options makes the most sense to implement. (Note that the options and percentages in this figure are contrived.) The business systems analyst would use the options being considered, and the percentages would be derived from the measurement tools used to ascertain the options' contribution to a particular section of the unbundled corporation or its overall support for the organization's value proposition(s). Keep in mind that any measurement tools must consider the interaction costs between each portion of the unbundled corporation.

VIGNETTE BOX 10-2

Unbundling of TSI

Area TSI Departments	Interactions That Have Costs	ICT Interaction Costs Reductions
CRM: The C-suite, Marketing, Accounting, Call Center, Operations, IT	• Meetings, phone calls, reports, memos, etc., so C-suite managers can approve any major changes that affect the customer • Development of marketing plans that attract customers based on market analysis • Process accounting and ticket transactions that result from customer interactions • Track revenues, costs, margins on an individual customer or aggregate basis • Interact with customers via phone and e-mail • Managing business relationships	• Secure e-mail systems so less paper is moved through the office • Efficient desktop workstations and appropriate software • An ERP that ties all departments together so they can share the same data • CRM software and training • Appropriate ICT security to protect customer data collected in the call center, especially if outsourced • Computer telephony integration (CTI) to support call center; integration with the local phone system or virtual call center technology
Product Innovation: The C-suite, Marketing, Operations, Accounting, Call Center, IT	• Meetings, phone calls, reports, memos, etc., so C-suite managers can approve any major product innovations • New product innovation idea generation, selection • Costing of potential new products • Assess feasibility of new products • Determining impact of introduction of new products	• Secure e-mail systems so less paper is moved through the office • Efficient desktop workstations and appropriate software • An ERP that ties all departments together so they can share the same data • Decision support systems that aid in idea generation, prioritization, and selection (e.g., Group Systems, Think Tank®)

(Continued)

Vignette Box 10-2 (Continued)

Infrastructure: The C-suite Operations IT Accounting Marketing	• Meetings, phone calls, reports, memos, etc., so C-suite managers can approve any internal operational changes • Maintenance of infrastructure • Handling transaction costs for purchasing tickets from venues • Determining which venues/events to purchase so excess (costly) purchase of tickets from venues can be avoided	• Secure e-mail systems so less paper is moved through the office • Efficient desktop workstations and appropriate software • Supply chain management solution to reduce cost of ticket procurement • Analytical tools to aid in determining customer preferences for venues/events

This chart is not meant to be exhaustive, but representative of ways ICT can be implemented to make an organization more efficient and to lower transaction costs.

The CRM area includes interaction within and between a number of departments, and can be viewed as these areas: (1) front office (direct interactions with customers, phone center), (2) back office (operations, accounting, marketing), (3) business relationships (all departments), and (4) analysis (marketing).

The product innovation area includes interaction costs within and between the C-suite, marketing, operations, accounting, and the call center. The interaction costs are mainly research and development and the costs for developing the new products. There are opportunities for the business systems analyst to bring about interaction cost savings.

The infrastructure area includes the C-suite, operations, IT, accounting, and marketing. The interaction costs are those things that keep the organization running.

---

calculated for each recommendation, and metrics established so a chart like Figure 10-5 can be developed. The list, with duplicates removed, for TSI would be:

- Secure e-mail systems so less paper is moved through the office
- Efficient desktop workstations and appropriate software
- An ERP that ties all departments together so they can share the same data
- CRM software and training
- Appropriate ICT security to protect customer data collected in the call center, especially if outsourced
- Computer telephony integration (CTI) to support call center; integration with the local phone system or virtual call center technology
- Decision support systems that aid in idea generation, prioritization, and selection (e.g., Group Systems, Think Tank)
- Supply chain management solution to reduce cost of ticket procurement
- Analytical tools to aid in determining customer preferences for venues/events

This list is only representative; interaction costs can be reduced in other places. This list focuses on interaction costs within and between areas (CRM/infrastructure/product innovation).

VALUE CHAIN DECONSTRUCTION

Value chain deconstruction is a tool to use in the search for opportunities to increase consumer value through lower cost or higher quality. Deconstruction is based on transaction cost theory and fundamentally states that "industries get unbundled and reconfigured as a result of two main developments:

1. The separation of the economics of things (physical goods) and the economics of information (digital goods) and
2. The blow-up of the trade-off between richness and reach." (Jelassi, 2005)

The first point (separation of economics of things) means that physical goods and digital goods possess different economic qualities. For example, consider the ease with which digital goods can be stored, copied, or ownership transferred versus how much more difficult the same tasks can be for physical goods. These differences affect business processes and costs. Physical goods require a different value chain that includes physical storage, shipping, handling, warehouse storage, and a very different type of service function, which means different types of business processes and costs. The business systems analyst must determine whether the organizational value proposition is physical goods/services, digital good/services, or some mixture.

As an example of the separation of economics, assume you are manufacturing office furniture. At a minimum, your organization would have to be concerned about manufacturing facilities, warehouse space, logistical support to ship products to your customers, customer service representatives who know how to repair furniture, and marketing staff that is familiar with furniture sales. Compare those requirements to a firm developing digital products like software. The firm developing software can use traditional office facilities, a staff with technical skills, probably does not need any warehouse space, logistical support may be handled through the Internet, support staff generally work at the office and use remote access to diagnose customer's software/digital problems, and marketing could happen only online. These differences in the organization change transaction costs and necessitate that the business systems analyst look at the value chain differently. In fact, understanding whether the organizational value proposition is physical goods or services, digital good or services, or some mixture is tantamount to being able to look into an organization and understand its value chain. Once you understand that value chain you can begin to make recommendations about ICT infrastructure that supports the value chain.

The "blow-up of the trade-off between richness and reach" states that in the digital environment in which we live in today, the trade-off between richness and reach have changed due to the digitalization of customer interactions and business processes, and that the associated costs and benefits have changed. *Richness* refers to how much content we are able to deliver (e.g., a hardcopy advertisement versus an online interactive advertisement), whereas *reach* refers to how many people we can cost-effectively get our advertisements to (e.g., advertising in a local newspaper versus advertising over the Internet). In the pre-digitalization era, marketing was predominantly focused on traditional media channels (e.g., TV, radio, print) while today marketing can be much more fluid through digital channels (e.g., World Wide Web, e-mail).

The concept of richness versus reach can be applied to manufacturing and selling both soft products such as computer software and services or hard products such as furniture. Start by asking these questions: Who can we reach with our products/services? and How much can we deliver? "The trade-off between richness and reach, then, not only governs the old economics of information but also is fundamental to a whole set of premises about how the business world works" (Evans & Wurster, 1997). The richness/reach discussion now centers on things like available bandwidth, server speed, and similar topics, whereas previously it centered on the distribution cost of advertisement through more traditional media such as TV or print. It can be applied to digital products/services and the value chain for companies that offer those digital products/services. The type of organization (i.e., digital goods and/or service, physical goods and/or services, or some

---

VIGNETTE BOX 10-3

Characteristics of TSI's Value Chain

TSI is a digital service that sells tickets, but what it really sells is intangible: the right to use a specific seat for a specific event at a certain time and date. Its value chain may look a bit different from an organization that sells physical goods or services. TSI collects user fees and delivers access to an event's seats.

FIGURE 10-6 Generic Value Chain

Support Activities	Firm Infrastructure and Senior (C-Suite) Management					Value
	Human Resources					
	Technology Development					
	Procurement					
Primary Activities	A1 Inbound Logistics	A2 Operations	A3 Outbound Logistics	A4 Sales and Marketing	A5 Service	

Porter's generic value chain states that two types of activities take place within an organization: primary activities and support activities. It is especially important to note that these are activities and not departments within the organization, so it is possible and even likely that these activities cut across departmental boundaries within the organization. The result of all of these activities are the creation of value.

Source: Adapted from Porter, 1980.

combination) and the understanding of the richness versus reach issues can be extended through the value chain, and the value chain can be deconstructed to locate opportunities to reduce costs or improve quality through ICT implementation.

In early work on value chain deconstruction, it was proposed that organizations would deconstruct and perhaps put some of their business functions online. Following the proposition that all organizations are digital to some level, deconstruction can be used as a way to understand the ICT needs of an organization, not just as a way to determine which functions are made available online. Value chain modeling can be thought of as an attempt to understand how an organization works—how the constituent components of a firm add value to enable product and service creation, as shown in Figure 10-6 (Porter, 1980).

The activities of the generic value chain are not organizational departments, but rather functions within the organization that add value to its products. Simply stated, the value chain model identifies the major sets of value-creating activities within an organization without regard for departmental boundaries. Because the value chain relates to and exposes value-creating activities, the technique are often used to establish the foundation for firm-level strategic planning, and can be used for ICT strategic planning as well. In order to adequately create the value chain model and to do firm-level, value chain–based strategic analysis, one must obtain a considerable amount of information about the organization. The value chain can be used to identify business processes for process improvement or innovation, and value chain deconstruction will yield information that will help align the parts and subparts of the value chain with the organizational strategic objectives and IT resources.

As a reminder of material covered in an earlier chapter: the value chain is divided into two major areas: supporting activities and primary activities. Supporting activities provide foundational aspects of the organization and support the five major primary value-creating activities. The supporting activities include:

- Firms Infrastructure (administrative structure and management)
- Human Resources (management of employees, training, hiring)
- Technology Development (ICT implementation, research and development)
- Procurement (acquiring goods at the best possible cost and quality)

The primary activities include:

- Inbound Logistics (getting raw materials into the organization)
- Operations (production)
- Outbound Logistics (getting products to the customer)
- Sales and Marketing (making potential buyers knowledgeable about the good/services offered by the organization)
- Service (ongoing product/service maintenance once the product/service is sold)

FIGURE 10-7 Deconstruction and Value Support

Option	A1	A2	A3	A4	A5	Overall Value Proposition Supported
1	20%	40%	15%	33%	75%	80%
2	15%	20%	25%	23%	42%	55%
3	25%	65%	10%	42%	11%	60%

A1–A5 refer to the value chain activities. (Refer to the example in Figure 10-6.)

The deconstructed value chain gives the business systems analyst the opportunity to develop metrics that allow the comparison of ICT choices. The comparison can be made among options and how well each supports the deconstructed value chain and its value proposition. This approach gives the business systems analyst a tool to determine which ICT option makes the most sense to implement. Although this table uses contrived options and percentages, the business systems analyst would use real and appropriate options and develop metrics as well as consider the transaction costs and added value of each ICT option.

The business systems analyst can use the organization's value chain and apply the relevant measurements in the search for value through ICT. By looking for ways to reduce cost or improve quality, the business systems analyst can add to the bottom line of the organization. The value chain can be deconstructed into disaggregated parts that can be supported by ICT. Through a deconstructed organizational value chain, the business systems analyst can parse it into smaller organizational units that provide value, and then look across those units for opportunities to implement ICT.

Deconstructing the Value Chain Value chain deconstruction means that the business systems analyst should look across the organization to find ICT-mediated value by modeling the organizational value chain and identifying places where ICT can either reduce costs or increase quality. The process would proceed as follows:

- Identify the organizational value proposition(s) being supported by the value chain.
- Obtain agreement on the current value chain among the organization's management and staff. It is necessary to get buy-in from everyone so support can be garnered for ICT recommendations.
- Develop metrics to understand how much each option contributes to the deconstructed value chain and the organizational value proposition.
- Analyze the value chain and overlay ICT options (e.g., 1, 2, and 3) on the value chain, looking for opportunities to enhance the organization.
- Develop a map of which options give greater support to which value chain activities and the overall value proposition. See Figure 10-7.

Core Competencies An organization's **core competencies** are the things essential to the way the organization works, the products and services it delivers, and what the organization does that provides value to its customers. Core competencies should give the organization competitive advantage in the marketplace. Ideally, these competencies are hard to imitate by an organization's competitors. During the value chain

---

VIGNETTE BOX 10-4

TSI's Core Competencies

TSI's Core Competencies:

- Estimating market demand for tickets at events and purchasing the right amount
- Delivering tickets to customers in a convenient and accessible fashion
- Managing ICT to make the other competencies possible

> **VIGNETTE BOX 10-5**
>
> **Deconstructed TSI Value Chain**
>
> | Support Activities | Firm Infrastructure (Operations and Senior Management) | | | | | Value: *Easy access to tickets for NYC venues without added fees* |
> |---|---|---|---|---|---|---|
> | | Human Resources (Managers from Various Departments) | | | | | |
> | | Technology Development (IT Department) | | | | | |
> | | Procurement (Marketing) | | | | | |
> | Primary Activities | A1 Inbound Logistics (Operations Department) | A2 Operations (Operations Department) | A3 Outbound Logistics (Operations Department) | A4 Sales and Marketing (Marketing) | A5 Service (Phone Center, Marketing, and Accounting) | |
>
> *For TSI's value chain, the value proposition has been stated as "easy access to tickets for NYC venues without added fees." Within Porter's value chain model here, the departments/functional areas at TSI are highlighted.*

deconstruction, a list of organizational core competencies should be developed. This list should show what the organization does well, even better than its competitors, to make the organization stand out in the marketplace. At these key points, the business systems analyst may be able to implement ICT-mediated solutions and aid the organization in attaining and maintaining competitive position. See Vignette Box 10-4 for an example of TSI's core compentencies.

Value Chain Analysis of TSI It is possible to create a value chain for TSI and deconstruct it. The organization's value proposition identified earlier in this chapter is used to show what value the chain should offer the customer (see Vignette Box 10-5).

With agreement on the value chain and the organization's value proposition, the business systems analyst can then analyze the value chain for places where ICT can reduce cost or increase quality, thus adding to the organization's bottom line or increasing customers' perceptions of the value they receive from TSI.

When analyzing TSI's value chain, we first have to consider that Genenco has already been selected as a supplier for kiosks, client/server applications, and the web server application. The TSI case also states that the person(s) doing the analysis must recommend all connectivity, other systems (in-house or outsourced), and an e-business innovation requirement. No attempt was made to specify software that holds the organizational infrastructure together (e.g., analytical software, ERP, etc.) within the vignette/case. TSI provides a list of business operational objectives that the ICT must meet. It must also produce customer value in order to gain market share, which leaves the business systems analyst with the question, "Where can we improve processes/functions or bring innovation/improvement throughout the value chain to bring value to the customer?"

Using the organizational value proposition identified earlier—easy access to tickets for NYC venues without added fees—we can look across the value chain and find recommendations that can be use to support the proposition by lowering costs, increasing perceived value by the customer, or increasing quality. However, before making such recommendations it is necessary that all appropriate people come to consensus on the value chain. Getting buy-in early in the value chain analysis project typically translates into a higher level of buy-in later when recommendations are made. The business systems analyst should gather information about the business processes in the value chain and what the process managers/owner believe needs to be done, which can be accomplished through interviews, surveys, or group meetings. Just remember that information gathering has interaction costs. Once all the required input is gathered, the value chain analysis can be done for TSI. A chart similar to the one in Vignette Box 10-6 can be constructed.

VIGNETTE BOX 10-6

Deconstruction of TSI and ICT Recommendations

<table>
<tr><th colspan="2">Value Chain Activity (TSI Department)</th><th>Recommendation</th></tr>
<tr><td rowspan="4">Support Activities</td><td>Firm Infrastructure (Operations and Senior Management)</td><td>
• Secure local instant messaging between members of staff and management/(<i>reduce cost</i>) interact on a more timely basis, and thus reduce time in meetings
• Secure for interoffice communications/make files easier to move across the network</td></tr>
<tr><td>Human Resources (Managers from Various Departments)</td><td>• Examine a number of ERP options that support HR functions/(reduce cost and increase quality) increase overall effectiveness of the HR function; perhaps create a separate HR function within the organization to manage employee training and records; decrease costs through employee training and increase quality through better trained and informed employees</td></tr>
<tr><td>Technology Development (IT Department)</td><td>• Examine the Genenco contract/(reduce cost) ensure the contract provides the necessary level of support and functionality to decrease costs while at the same time increasing and maintaining quality</td></tr>
<tr><td>Procurement (Marketing)</td><td>• Install software and analytic tools to best estimate ticket purchases from venues/(reduce cost) eliminate unnecessary purchasing of tickets from venues; (increase quality) balance customer demand with number of tickets needed so TSI does not run out of "high demand" shows and so customers get the tickets they want</td></tr>
<tr><td rowspan="5">Primary Activities</td><td>Inbound Logistics (Operations Department)</td><td rowspan="3">• Determine whether Genenco software/hardware solutions are the most cost-effective way to deliver tickets to the customer/(reduce cost)
• Develop other options and place them on the map (see Figure 10-7)</td></tr>
<tr><td>Operations (Operations Department)</td></tr>
<tr><td>Outbound Logistics (Operations Department)</td></tr>
<tr><td>Sales and Marketing (Marketing)</td><td>• Install software to aid the marketing department to create appropriate marketing materials
• Install printers of appropriate size and speed to support the creation of marketing materials</td></tr>
<tr><td>Service (Phone Center, Marketing, and Accounting)</td><td>• Determine whether Genenco is the best solution and/or possibly recommend another ERP along side of Genenco/(reduce cost/increase quality)</td></tr>
</table>

This mapping of primary and support activities to TSI's various departments provides an idea about where ICT can be used to exploit technology in order to enhance competitive advantage. This figure is not exhaustive, but rather representative of the types of ICT recommendations that could bring about competitive advantage in the marketplace.

From an overall perspective, the deconstructed value chain must look for the following:

- Seek ways to disintermediate the value chain
- Determine whether to compete or cooperate with others in the marketplace when offering complimentary, similar, or identical good/services
- Look for places to bring process improvement or innovation
- Determine possible ways to develop new/innovative products
- Examine the value chain for ways to reduce cost or improve product quality through changing the organizational structure
- Assess non-ICT ways to improve product quality or lower costs

Supply Chain Analysis Supply chain analysis gives the business systems analyst the opportunity to examine and solve potential conflicts between business partners, and examines the effect of business partner actions on the operations of the organization. Management of the entire supply chain can be a major success factor in attaining and/or maintaining competitive positioning. The supply chain is the set of activities, potentially across a number of organizations, that takes raw materials, creates final products, and moves them to the end customer. Consider this definition of a supply chain and contrast it to "logistics," which is defined as moving materials/products into and out of one individual organization (see Figure 10-8). Supply chains are composed of organizations, people, activities, and other resources that make the conversion from raw materials to final products possible. Each activity along the supply chain adds value to the raw material (or processed materials as they move through the supply chain) as it is converted by each activity to something that eventually becomes a final product. Each partner in a supply chain is vying for competitive position and attempting to maximize its profit as it sells its product to the next partner in the supply chain.

Describing the supply chain includes references to its upstream and downstream sides. Upstream refers to the less-manufactured product, while downstream refers to where the product is going to. An example will help to make this clearer. Let's assume that the plant (refinery) that manufactures gasoline is in the middle of the supply chain (i.e., the company for which we are analyzing the supply chain). In the production of gasoline, oil pumped from the ground is upstream to the company that transports the oil; the transporter of the oil (e.g., an oil tanker) delivers it to a refinery that converts the oil to gasoline and is upstream of that refinery; the refinery may use additives from other companies that are upstream to the refinery as well. Another company then transports (e.g., gas truck) the finished product (gasoline) to the filling station, where customers pump gasoline into their cars. The gas truck transport company that moves the gasoline from the plant to the filling station is downstream from the plant, and the filling station is downstream to the gas truck transport company. The customer is downstream to the filling station. Figure 10-9 may make this concept clearer.

Business analysis in a manufacturing supply chain is complex, and the business systems analyst would need to understand all the business processes and transactions that occur between the business partners (e.g., oil pumping, trucking company, refineries, etc.). In this case, it requires extensive knowledge of the petroleum industry and all partners involved in getting crude oil from the ground, through refineries, and to the

FIGURE 10-8 Difference between Supply Chain Management and Logistics

> An important point to ponder: Supply chain management and logistics are two different things. Logistics refers to how things flow into and out of your organization, while supply chain management and analysis look at the end-to-end or "raw material" to "end consumer" flow, and all the business partners that make it work. This concept is especially important because it means that the business systems analyst needs to take an internal view as well as an external "10,000-foot view" in order to envision all the partners needed to get a product to market. The key is to look for low cost, quality improvement, or other strategies that can be mediated by ICT.

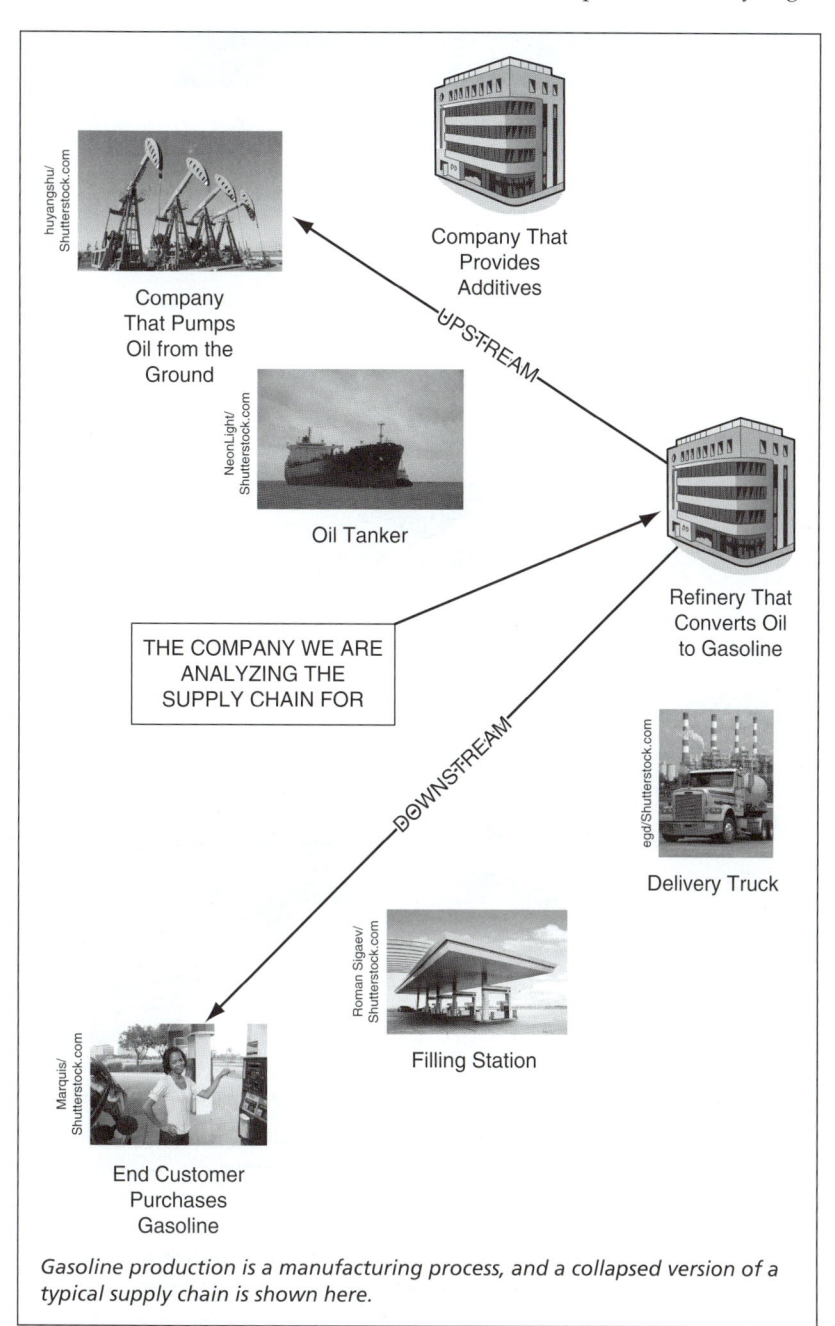

FIGURE 10-9 Gasoline Production: Upstream and Downstream in the Supply Chain

Gasoline production is a manufacturing process, and a collapsed version of a typical supply chain is shown here.

end customer. The same types of complexities exist with digital products, except you might say that the supply chain is "softer." Here, *softer* means that no physical product is produced. The supply chain could produce digital products for the service industry. In the software industry, the end product is digital. The creation of digital goods may seem to not act like a manufacturing supply chain, but in fact it shows many similarities, and the same theories do apply.

TSI gives a "softer" supply chain (see Vignette Box 10-7). It does not manufacture anything, rather it brokers *the license to the right to use a seat, in a particular venue on a particular day, for a specified period of time, and only for a particular event.* Everything TSI sells is "soft," but as an assurance that customers are getting something (e.g., value) for their payment, customers get a ticket for which they pay a "user fee." The ticket specifies the date, time, location, event, seat, and other details. The user fee (i.e., ticket price) gives the customer the ability to use a seat in a venue for a specific date/time and specific event. However, the ticket has no intrinsic value; instead, it confers the right to attend a venue, which does have value.

VIGNETTE BOX 10-7

TSI Supply Chain

UPSTREAM

Venues Providing Seats

TSI

Internet Service Provider

DOWNSTREAM

Genenco

People Purchasing Tickets over the Internet

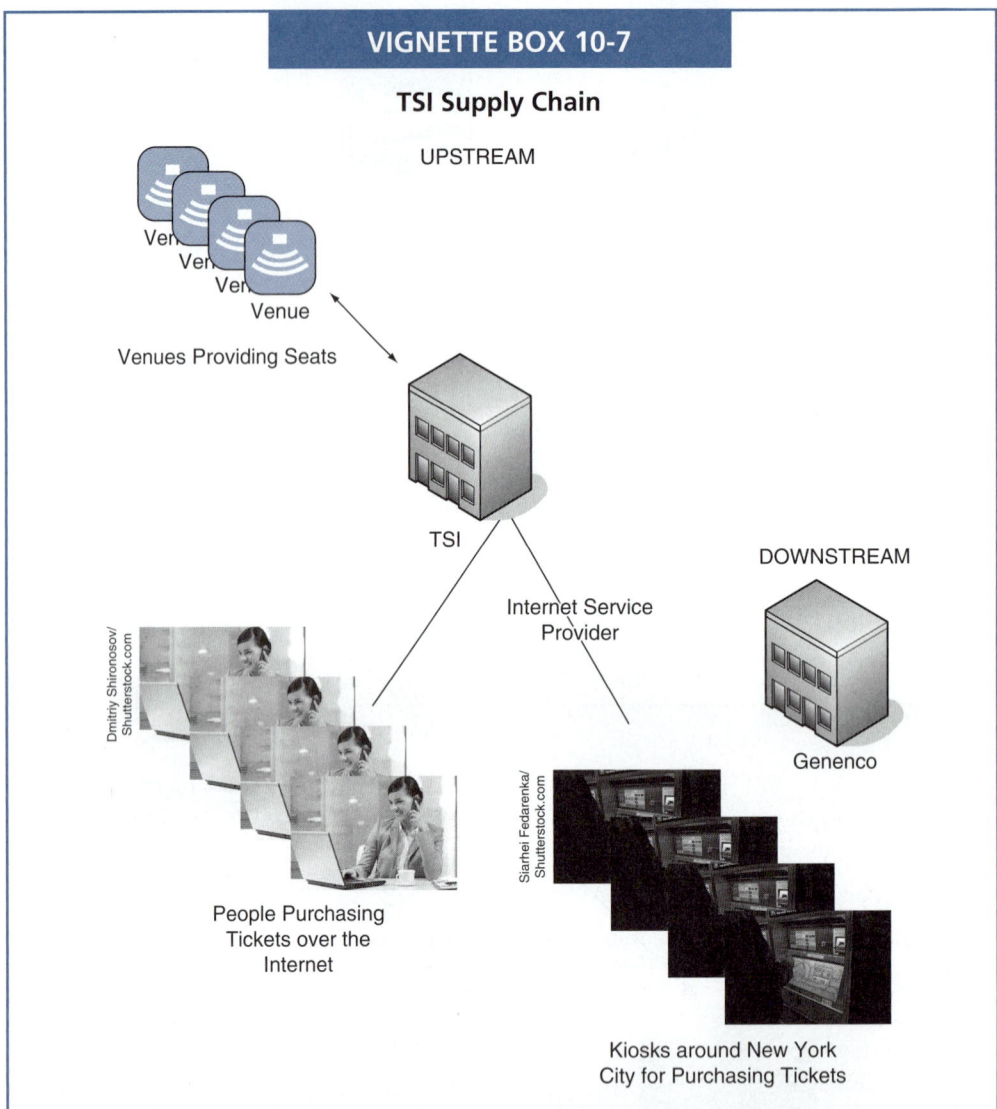

Kiosks around New York City for Purchasing Tickets

TSI's supply chain is mainly digital. TSI is an intermediary between venues and customers who want tickets to events. It could be said that the ticket sales process is reintermediated with TSI being an addition to the ticket sales process. The upstream side would include the venues that provide the theater tickets, whereas the downstream side would include the Internet service providers that give access to the Internet, Genenco that provides service/maintenance of all kiosks, and the end customers who purchase tickets over the Internet and at kiosks.

In order to analyze the supply chain, you need to know the partners and what they provide. The Global Supply Chain Forum (GSCF) provides a good way to model the supply chain and is useful when considering ICT recommendations. Figure 10-10 provides a view of information flows in the supply chain. These information flows are where the business systems analyst can make ICT recommendations, which, as stated earlier, requires that the business systems analyst understands the business processes that cut across the supply chain. This figure shows that products flow from Tier 2 suppliers (in reality, there can be any number of suppliers and customers depending on the complexity of the supply chain) through the supply chain to the customer/end-user. The manufacturer could be a physical goods manufacturer or a digital product producer. Also note that the processes within the manufacturer closely resemble the value chain discussed previously in this section.

The GSCF indicates that a number of cross-functional processes cut across all business partners. These cross-business-partner processes give ample opportunities for the business systems analyst to look at areas where ICT can be implemented to reduce cost, increase efficiency, or increase product quality. The processes the

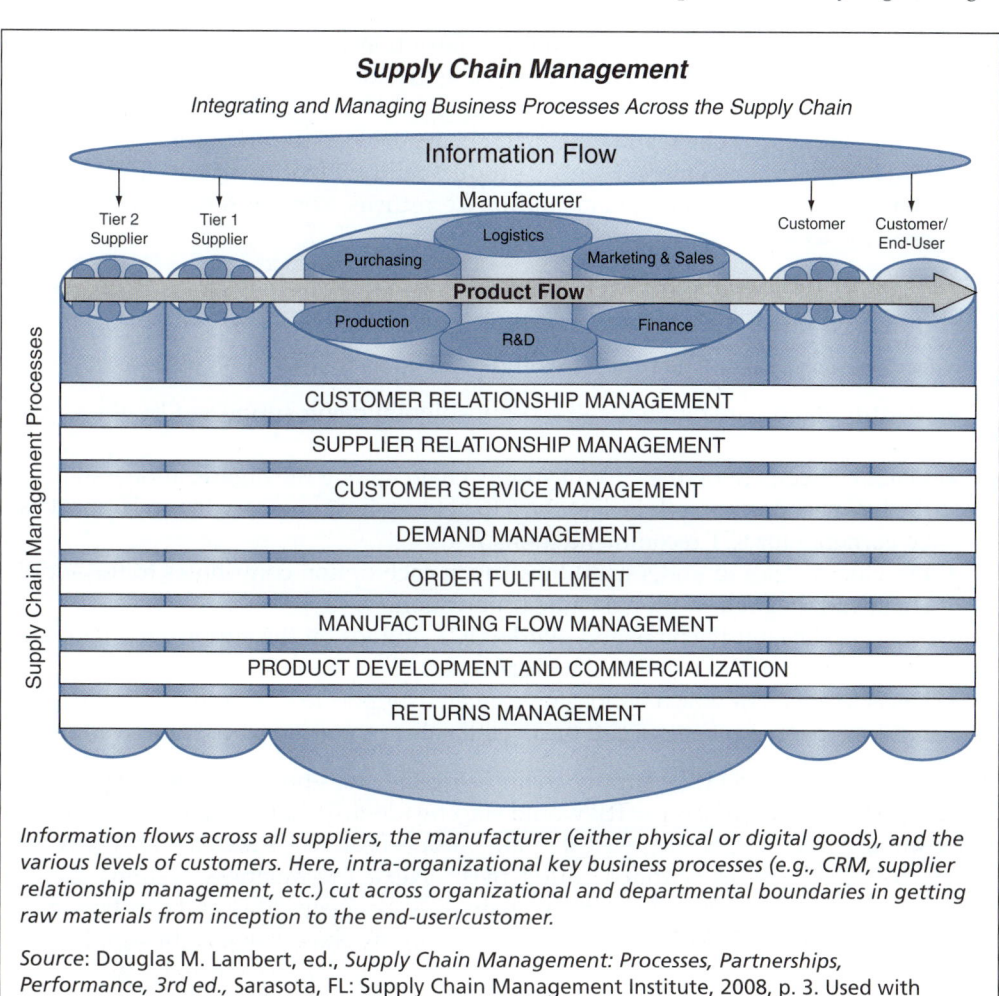

FIGURE 10-10 Information Flow–Based SCM Model

Supply Chain Management
Integrating and Managing Business Processes Across the Supply Chain

Information Flow

Tier 2 Supplier — Tier 1 Supplier — Manufacturer (Purchasing, Logistics, Marketing & Sales, Production, R&D, Finance) — Customer — Customer/End-User

Product Flow

Supply Chain Management Processes:
- CUSTOMER RELATIONSHIP MANAGEMENT
- SUPPLIER RELATIONSHIP MANAGEMENT
- CUSTOMER SERVICE MANAGEMENT
- DEMAND MANAGEMENT
- ORDER FULFILLMENT
- MANUFACTURING FLOW MANAGEMENT
- PRODUCT DEVELOPMENT AND COMMERCIALIZATION
- RETURNS MANAGEMENT

Information flows across all suppliers, the manufacturer (either physical or digital goods), and the various levels of customers. Here, intra-organizational key business processes (e.g., CRM, supplier relationship management, etc.) cut across organizational and departmental boundaries in getting raw materials from inception to the end-user/customer.

Source: Douglas M. Lambert, ed., *Supply Chain Management: Processes, Partnerships, Performance*, 3rd ed., Sarasota, FL: Supply Chain Management Institute, 2008, p. 3. Used with permission. All rights reserved. For more information, see www.scm-institute.org.

GSCF considers essential follow (note that S# stands for the supply chain cross-partner processes):

- (S1) Customer Relationship Management. Develop and provide the structure and methods by which customer relationships are created and maintained; increase customer loyalty over time. This may include negotiating the product and services agreements (PSA) for key accounts and end-users.
- (S2) Supplier Relationship Management. Develop relationships with a small number of suppliers that produce raw materials for the "manufacturing" process; negotiate PSAs between suppliers and maintain positive supplier relationships.
- (S3) Customer Service Management. Act as the key point of contact for administering the PSA to provide customers with real-time information they need (e.g., shipping dates and product availability).
- (S4) Demand Management. Balance the customer requirements, the PSA terms, and the capabilities of the supply chain; proactively assess customer needs and supplier's ability to provide goods, and synchronize both while at the same time proactively analyzing the supply chain for potential problems.
- (S5) Order Fulfillment. Define customer requirements, design a network within the supply chain that permits the organization to meets customer requirements (while minimizing total delivered cost); fulfill orders; develop a seamless process throughout the supply chain to get raw materials to the customer as finished products.
- (S6) Manufacturing Flow Management. Manage all activities necessary to move products through the suppliers, manufacturers, and distribution to the end-customer in a timely manner at the lowest possible cost.

- (S7) Product Development and Commercialization. Determine which products are in demand through environmental sensing; develop and jointly market products with partners in the supply chain; commercialize the products by creating them within the supply chain and making them available to the end-user.
- (S8) Returns Management. Manage product return, identify reasons in the supply chain for returns; manage and minimize returns; control returns as potential reusable assets.

Taken together, these cross-business-partner processes give the business systems analyst ample opportunities to find places to recommend ICT-mediated change.

Analyzing the Supply Chain The process would proceed as follows:

- Identify the organizational value proposition(s) being supported by the supply chain.
- Obtain agreement on the current supply chain among the organization's staff and the business partners. (It is necessary to get buy-in from everyone so support can be garnered for ICT recommendations.)
- Develop metrics to understand how much each option contributes to the supply chain and the organizational value proposition.
- Analyze the supply chain, and overlay ICT options on the supply chain, looking for opportunities to enhance the organization.
- Develop a map of which options give greater support to which supply chain cross-business-partner processes and the overall value proposition. See Figure 10-11.

It is possible to analyze TSI's supply chain using the cross-business-partner processes listed. Supply chain analysis for TSI would start by identifying the organization's value proposition; earlier in this chapter, TSI's value proposition was stated as "easy access to tickets for NYC venues without added fees." Next, the business systems analyst would obtain agreement on the supply chain; this has been done and can be seen in Vignette Box 10-7. The next step is to analyze the supply chain using eight supply chain cross-partner processes (for an example see, Vignette Box 10-8). Once the ICT recommendations are determined, metrics should be developed to understand how much each recommendation contributes to the supply chain, and the organization's overall value proposition (see Unit Three for examples of metrics). The final step is to develop a map of the recommendations, and their relative support of the supply chain cross-partner processes (see Figure 10-11).

The amount that each recommendation (see Vignette Box 10-8) contributes to supply chain cross-partner processes should be estimated using the appropriate metrics (note, metric were discussed in discussed earlier in this textbook). Once these percentages have been estimated, candidates can be selected for recommendation.

FIGURE 10-11 Supply Chain Analysis and Value Support

Option	S1	S2	...	S7	S8	Overall Value Proposition Supported
1	20%	40%	15%	33%	75%	80%
2	15	20	25	23	42	55
3	25	65	10	42	11	60

S1–S8 refers to the supply chain cross-functional processes.

Analyzing the supply chain gives the business systems analyst the opportunity to develop metrics for comparing ICT choices. The comparison can be made among options and how well they support the supply chain and its value proposition. With this tool, the business systems analyst could articulate real options considered appropriate, develop metrics he or she believes best for assessing the transaction costs, and evaluate the added value of each ICT option.

> ### VIGNETTE BOX 10-8
> #### TSI Supply Chain Using Cross-Partner Processes
>
> | Supply Chain Cross-Partner Processes | ICT Recommendations |
> |---|---|
> | (S1) Customer Relationship Management | • Establish secure communications between TSI and venues that cannot be repudiated for all ticket purchases. This recommendation will be useful to support all cross-partner processes. |
> | (S2) Supplier Relationship Management | |
> | (S3) Customer Service Management | • Provide secure ticket purchases via the web and kiosks. "Genenco" has already been selected but should be compared against other similar vendors' systems. |
> | (S4) Demand Management | • Contract management system (e.g., http://www.cobblestonesystems.com/, http://www.papertracer.com/). |
> | (S5) Order Fulfillment | • Consider computer-assisted telephony. |
> | (S6) Manufacturing Flow Management | • Develop/install analytical software to balance the venue contract against customer demand for particular venues/events. |
> | (S7) Product Development and Commercialization | • Make appropriate hardware available to those doing market analysis. |
> | (S8) Returns Management | • Ensure that vendor's systems (e.g., Genenco) provide sufficient supply chain management functionality. |
>
> This analysis assumes that potentially all ticket suppliers and potential customers are involved in every process (i.e., every process is an end-to-end process, both upstream and downstream). The ICT recommendations are illustrative of what can be accomplished with ICT. In reality, all of the functions can be attained using a CRM system geared toward TSI's specific industry. Perhaps one CRM platform can deliver all of the ICT functionality listed here.

Product Differentiation Strategies

Following Porter's (1980) model, corporate unbundling, value chain deconstruction, and supply chain deconstruction focus on internal/external efficiencies that enable low-cost strategies. Comparative SWOT analyses and competitive forces analysis lead to considerations of environmental scanning to determine opportunities to introduce products to markets. Comparative SWOT analyses and competitive forces analysis focus on revenue growth by differentiating the organization's product. Even though all value search models reflect a cost-reduction emphasis, the primary focus of comparative SWOT analyses and competitive forces analysis is revenue growth through unique products.

Comparative SWOT analyses emphasize environmental scanning and discovering opportunities in the environment that may require refining existing products to make those products unique, or developing new products for the markets. The main strategic goal is to identify market niches where unique, often superior, products can be sold at higher-than-average prices, leading to revenue growth. In these cases, the primary function is to discover unfulfilled market needs (opportunities) and competitive products (threats), and match them with the organization's abilities to produce that product (strengths) and the organization's deficits (weaknesses).

Competitive forces analysis (Porter, 1980) analyzes five major forces that affect industry competition. Those forces are the threat of new entrants, bargaining power of customers, bargaining power of suppliers, the threat of substitute products, and the jockeying for position among current firms in the industry. A sixth force—called co-opetition—has been added to the traditional model proposed by Porter. Co-opetition is simultaneous competition and cooperation between organization creating similar goods, and is defined more fully below. The primary function of the competitive forces analysis is to analyze the firm vis-à-vis competitors in the organization's industry.

COMPARATIVE SWOT ANALYSIS

The traditional SWOT analysis of an organization discusses strengths, weaknesses, opportunities, and threats (SWOT) and is often presented as a four-quadrant diagram (see Figure 10-12). The strengths and weaknesses are internal looking, while the opportunities and threats are external looking.

Core Competencies   The business systems analyst can think of the core competencies as the "strengths" in SWOT. The value chain analysis can provide a list of core competencies. It is helpful, prior to the SWOT analysis, to develop a list of core competencies for the organization as a springboard for the SWOT analysis. Much of the information for the core competencies can be derived from the value chain analysis.

Using the SWOT Analysis   Using the SWOT framework, it is possible to get a clear idea of where the organization sits strategically. The trick is to do this assessment from an ICT standpoint while linking the SWOT to internal and external issues. This process requires environmental scanning of both the inside of the organization (i.e., strength and weaknesses) as well as what is happening outside the organization (i.e., opportunities and threats).

"When conducting a SWOT analysis, many fall into the common mistake of confusing strengths with opportunities and weaknesses with threats. However, the difference is straightforward. Strengths and weaknesses refer to the positive and negative aspects of the organization's internal capabilities and resources, while opportunities and threats refer to external influences and factors that may affect the organization" (Evans & Wright, 2009). Business systems analysts must divert their attention from the more traditional aspects of the SWOT analysis and focus on the ICT aspects. Although this task can be a bit daunting at times, some ways that will help maintain the ICT focus include:

- Use of the value chain deconstruction and corporate unbundling models to guide the search of internal strengths and weaknesses
- Use of competitive forces analysis to understand what threats and opportunities exist in the competitive environment
- Review of internal company reports and documents (e.g., profit and loss statements or other financial analyses in which resource allocation can give clues about organizational values)
- Review of ICT budgets compared to the overall organizational budget showing how the organization values ICT and the priority it places on it
- Interaction with managers in the organization to understand internal strengths and weaknesses
- Review of publically available documents about the organization's main competitors to better understand their strategic orientation and the role ICT plays within their organizations

FIGURE 10-12 Traditional SWOT Analysis

Strengths	Opportunities
Weaknesses	Threats

In the boxes in the grid, the business systems analyst can list the strengths, weaknesses, opportunities, and threats for his or her organization. However, analysis should be expanded to the competitive SWOT analysis discussed in this section of the textbook.

FIGURE 10-13 Comparative SWOT Analysis

	Your Firm	Major Competitor One	Major Competitor Two
ICT (Internal) Strength	Fill in with appropriate information	Fill in with appropriate information	Fill in with appropriate information
ICT (Internal) Weaknesses	Fill in with appropriate information	Fill in with appropriate information	Fill in with appropriate information
ICT (External) Opportunities	Fill in with appropriate information	Fill in with appropriate information	Fill in with appropriate information
ICT (External) Threats	Fill in with appropriate information	Fill in with appropriate information	Fill in with appropriate information
Where can ICT best be used?	Look across the information in this table and list ways your firm can enhance its competitive position.		

The comparative SWOT analysis is a tool that allows the business systems analyst to compare a company's internal strengths/weaknesses and external opportunities/threats with those of its major competitors. The information about the analyst's own organization is probably readily available through corporate reports or discussions with company management, while the external information is usually much more difficult to get and usually much "softer."

A comparative SWOT analysis compares your organization to its top competitors to find where competitive advantage may be gained (see Figure 10-13). The first thing to do is to identify your organization's major competitors. This is usually not hard to do, and could be one, two, three, or more competitors. Obviously, the more competitors the business systems analyst intends to use in this comparative analysis, the more columns there will be in the analysis and the more complex it will be. Getting the information about competitors is often the hardest part of creating a comparative SWOT analysis. Corporate annual reports, governmental filings (if the competitor is a public company), and industry analysis are but a few of the resources the business systems analyst can use to complete the analysis. The Internet and its various search engines and databases also provide a wealth of information that can be used. Sometimes, the business systems analyst must make assumptions when using this "soft" information, and should indicate such in any analysis.

A model proposed to enhance the SWOT analysis is the telescopic observation (TO) framework. It was developed to provide additional structure to traditional SWOT analysis, which can be vague (Panagiotou, 2003). "Continuously transforming technologies, deregulation, ever-increasing consumer demands and expectations cause pressure and place companies under continuous risk and uncertainty when formulating strategies. ... Complex organizational internal issues, effective application, complementarily and coordination of resource requirements, paired with internal politics and the need to accomplish levels of excellence, create tension. Consequently, organizations do not exist in a vacuum but rather they exist, coexist, compete, and cooperate in a multidimensional and interrelated environment characterized by ambiguity and complexity. Understanding this environment is fundamental to formulating strategy, decision making, and strategic planning." Therefore the traditional SWOT analysis that originated in the Harvard Business School to analyze cases has been extended into the telescopic observation (TO) strategic framework:

- (T)echnology advancements
- (E)conomic considerations
- (L)egal and regulatory requirements
- (E)cological and environmental issues
- (S)ociological trends
- (C)ompetition
- (O)rg anizational culture

FIGURE 10-14 Firm-Level Telescopic Observation

	T	E	L	E	S	C	O	P	I	C
(Internal) Strengths										
(Internal) Weaknesses										
(External) Opportunities										
(External) Threats										

The letters in the "telescopic" observation are defined as (T)echnology advancements; (E)conomic considerations; (L)egal and regulatory requirements; (E)cological and environmental issues; (S)ociological trends; (C)ompetition; (O)rganizational culture; (P)ortfolio analysis; (I)nternational issues; (C)ost efficiencies and cost structures.

- (P)ortfolio analysis
- (I)nternational issues
- (C)ost efficiencies and cost structures

This TO strategic framework list provides a convenient way for the business systems analyst to look into an organization and ask questions about that organization. Analysis could start with taking your organization and each of its competitors, and completing a TO analysis for each. (See Figure 10-14.)

This individual firm-level analysis can then be used to create a comparative SWOT analysis. The goal of the comparative SWOT analysis is to learn ways your organization can differentiate its products or introduce new products to the marketplace. It means that significant thought must be put into data collection about your organization and about its competitor(s). The comparative SWOT analysis, when combined with other tools, should give the business systems analyst data and information, enabling him or her to make ICT recommendations.

The comparative SWOT analysis will yield information the business system analyst could use as one more piece of the puzzle when asking "How can ICT add value to the organization?" An example of a comparative SWOT analysis for TSI is provided in Vignette Box 10-9.

COMPETITIVE FORCES ANALYSIS

Even though the five forces model is mature (Porter, 1980), it still has merit for looking at what external forces affect an organization. The Porter **five forces model** is useful for industry analysis and strategy development. This textbook would be remiss if it did not take the business systems analyst into the strategy realm via Porter's five forces analysis in order to look at the organization from an external strategic standpoint. Explicating the competitive forces is about examining what an organization is doing by way of product creation and differentiating those products from that of the competitor. ICT can aid in product differentiation and act as a revenue enhancer through increased market share, which is the foundation of looking at the forces that put pressure on an organization.

According to Porter, the five forces create a micro-environment around the organization that brings pressure on the organization to create products that are differentiated from others. The forces consist of aspects close to the company that affect its ability to provide products/services at a profit to the organization's customer. Examining the five forces is useful in making a qualitative assessment of an organization's place within the market. Because the forces are always changing, competitive forces analysis should be done frequently as a normal part of competitive environmental sensing and scanning that organizations do. The goal of applying the five forces model is to assist your organization, through ICT recommendations, in differentiating its products and aiding the organization in returning greater than its industry's average profitability (i.e., revenue growth). Competitive forces analysis is industry-level analysis and aids the business systems analyst in fulfilling the value proposition within a specific industry. Note that an industry is defined as a market where similar or closely related products/services are sold to buyers.

VIGNETTE BOX 10-9

TSI Comparative SWOT Analysis

	TSI	Competitor 1	Competitor 2
Strengths	• No service charges • Tickets sold at face value • Kiosks all across NYC • Convenient kiosk locations in areas frequented by thousands of people daily	• Multilingual 24/7 call center for ordering • Broadway's official ticket source • Gift certificates over the phone • Seating charts available online	• 25% to 50% discounted tickets • Small service charge compared to some competitors • Gift certificates by phone or physical booth
Weakness	• Credit/Debit card payment only • New to the market • Pressure to sell all tickets on hand • Limited market—NYC events only	• Not international • Focused only on plays, musicals, and comedies • Service charges • Lack of physical sales locations • Offers few event types • 3-min window to fill out online orders	• Ticket sales at booths only • Accepts only cash or travelers check for payment at their booths • Tickets available only the day of an event • Offers few event types • Long lines for tickets • Only two booths in NYC to choose from
Opportunities	• Become a well-known brand through advertising • Expand beyond NYC • Become better than competitors through innovative technology	• Expand overseas • Start selling tickets for other events such as concerts and special events	• Expand outside NYC • More venues becoming aware of their services • Eventually offer tickets for a wide range of events
Threats	• Well-established competitors • Vendors with exclusive rights to venues • Easily accessible substitute goods	• New technologies and television • Other ticket vendors with more selection	• Venues offering discounts at their own box office • Online ticket vendors and resellers with similar discounts
ICT Recommendations	• Considering that TSI will own the tickets, analytical software and techniques to determine ticket volume to purchase is essential. • TSI may want to consider reducing ticket prices within last few hours before an event occurs; this will require a software change by Genenco. • TSI may want to consider branching out to a larger market than NYC as dependence on one market is dangerous; this would require that the ICT infrastructure be robust enough to handle this expansion. • TSI needs to enter the NYC market strongly in order to develop brand recognition and market share quickly; TSI's dependence on technology (it only sells tickets) is a weakness; this will require a robust network with a high degree of fault tolerance.		

Using telescopic observation, a SWOT analysis for TSI and its two major competitors can be performed. This SWOT analysis looks at the business models and major issues faced by TSI and its top two competitors. A number of ICT recommendations are made as part of this analysis. Like TSI, the competitors are fictitious.

Source: Based on Tri State Consulting, 2006.

The five forces are defined here, along with a description of how the business systems analyst can use them:

- **Threat of Substitute Products.** Buyers have a propensity to use substitute products, which means that your firm's current or new products must stand out from the competition. The perceived value of your organization's product must be greater than the substitute. Your organization must also offer a better price/performance trade-off than substitutes. Another issue to consider is buyer switching costs—that is, how much does it cost the buyer to switch from using your organization's products to that of your competitors, or conversely how much does it cost the customer to switch from the competitor to your company's product. Costs can be in real dollars, or they can be intangible factors such as time or distance traveled to purchase a product. Consumers' perceived level of product differentiation also needs to be factored into any ICT recommendations. The business systems analyst can make a difference in all of these areas.
- **Threat of New Competitors.** New companies entering a market may face existing barriers to entry (e.g., government licensure, patents, etc.). If these barriers are high, then the likelihood that a new competitor will enter the marketplace is low. However, if the barriers to entry are low, then the likelihood of new competition is high. This factor is a large consideration when selecting products to produce and markets to compete in. When a business systems analyst recommends entering a market, the analyst must consider the effects of product branding. An organization that has created brand loyalty or recognition is likely to maintain market share, making entry into the market difficult for new competitors. Potential barriers for new entrants into a market also include the start-up and ongoing capital requirements. Low capital requirements will make it easier for new entrants, while high capital requirements will make entry harder. It's fairly easy to understand that market incumbents have the "home court advantage"; they have knowledge of the industry and experience that gives them that advantage. The amount of industry knowledge necessary to be successful in a market is yet another factor that affects how big the threat of new entrants will be. A final consideration for new entrants to a market is reaction and potential retaliation by organizations already in the market. Will they run negative advertisement campaigns or attempt to hire the skilled employees in your geographic area (probably at higher pay than your organization can), or will "co-opetition" result? When a business systems analyst is looking at the impact of new competitors, the analyst should consider all of these things and temper any recommendations by understanding these issues.
- **Competitive Rivalry.** The size of an industry and the number of competitors affects how an organization acts. A large number of competitors and the diversity of those competitors (i.e., similar or substitute goods/services) affects how difficult it is to maintain competitive advantage. Conversely, if an organization faces few competitors, or limited substitute products, then maintaining competitive advantage may be easier. The rate of industry growth and the size of the market also need to be considered. A rapidly growing industry or an expanding market may signal that it's time to make a resource investment into technology. These considerations, along with the current global implications of competition, should give the business systems analyst information to make informed recommendation about ICT investments. Often the goal is sustainable competitive advantage through product improvisation/differentiation.
- **Bargaining Power of Customers.** Customers have bargaining power. The number of customers and their percentage of an organization's income are directly proportional to how much effort the organization is going to put into things like CRM or other customer-facing ICT solutions. The size of a customer base and how much any one customer contributes to an organization's bottom line influences decisions. A fair amount of customer leverage exists in a market with a large number of suppliers. Fewer suppliers for given products means that the customer has fewer choices, and thus less leverage with suppliers. Buying volume, buyer's

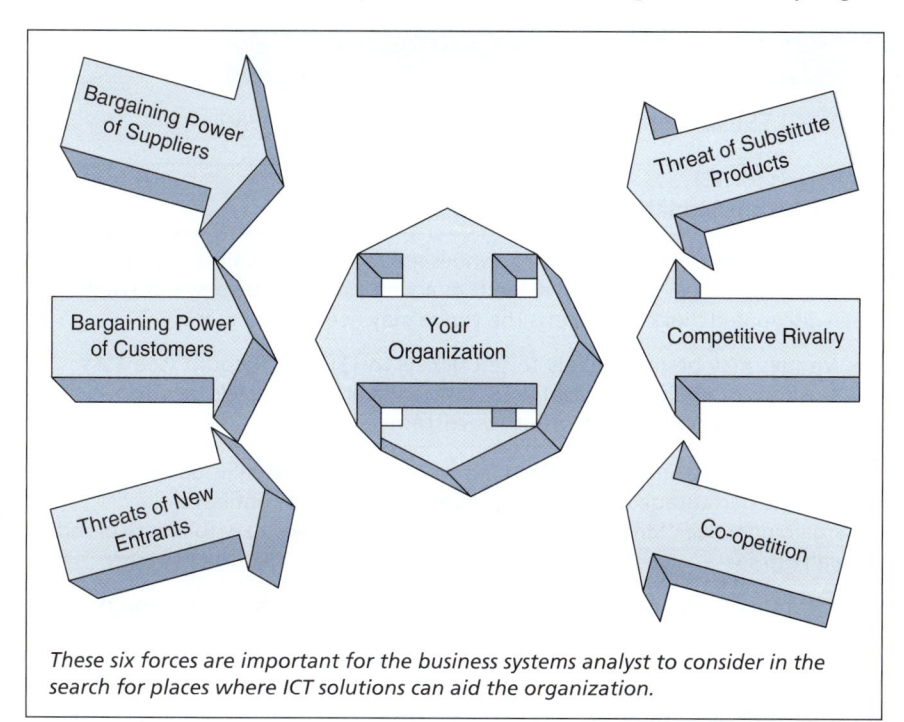

FIGURE 10-15 The Six Forces Model

These six forces are important for the business systems analyst to consider in the search for places where ICT solutions can aid the organization.

switching costs, availability and acceptability of substitute products, buyer price sensitivity, and importance of product differentiation are all things to consider.

- **Bargaining Power of Suppliers.** Suppliers have bargaining power. If the cost of switching to a new supplier is high, then the supplier has power. A greater number of suppliers for the same goods/services means the power of suppliers is low. Power can come in the form of product price, availability, or lead time. If a number of suppliers are available and their products will fulfill your needs, then their bargaining power is fairly low. However, switching suppliers can have a dramatic impact on the final products your organization can produce. If the products that are input to your organization vary greatly, they may affect your organization's ability to create products of sufficient quality to retain your customer base. All of these things need to be considered by the business systems analyst in making ICT recommendations that assist with product creation.

The five forces model has been extended by Brandenburger and Nalebuff (1996), where they added the concept of a sixth force to explain the reasons behind strategic alliances or complementors in an industry. The sixth force is defined as the complementary products that bring about strategic alliances among competitors and has been called **co-opetition**—a combination of the terms *collaboration* and *competitors* (Gnyawali & Park, 2009). Considering that about 50% of strategic relationships occur between firms within the same industry or among competitors, and that the "power of co-opetition will only grow as products become more complex and competition widens globally," firm- and industry-level co-opetition is important to examine when looking for ICT recommendations to enhance competitive positioning (see Figure 10-15).

Using the six forces model, you can analyze the external forces that impact TSI's competitive positioning. An example of that analysis can be seen in Vignette Box 10-10.

GAP ANALYSIS

In the search for value through ICT, it is helpful to do a gap analysis. The **gap analysis** asks "Where is my organization today?" and "Where do we want to get to?" It is a tool to summarize all of the other analyses and formalize the ICT recommendations. The business systems analyst first needs to start by "taking stock" in where the organization is and determine where it wants to be. It is critical that a project champion be identified and be indicated on the gap analysis. This tool is used for project planning.

VIGNETTE BOX 10-10

TSI Six Forces Analysis

Competitive Force	Analysis for TSI • ICT Recommendations/Consideration
Bargaining Power of Supplier	Although New York City has many venues, each event normally is only held at one specific venue. This could mean that an individual venue may not want to sell discounted blocks of tickets. The venue may need inducements. • Venues may be more likely to sell tickets to TSI at a discount (see TSI's business model in the case) if TSI puts a kiosk at a venue's location to make ticket purchasing easier for customers.
Bargaining Power of Customer	Because TSI's customers are individuals who, taken individually, do not contribute to a large percentage of ticket sales, each customer does not have much bargaining power. Still, excellent customer service is necessary to create brand loyalty to TSI. • CRM should be installed to ensure brand loyalty through building positive customer relationships.
Threat of New Entrants	The barriers to new entrants into the online ticket sales industry are not very high. However, using kiosks makes the barriers much higher. The major barriers are (1) the capital needed to start a business based on kiosks and ICT, and (2) securing locations for kiosk placement. TSI is in the processes of seeking venture capital to address barrier #1, and has already addressed barrier #2, putting TSI in a competitive position relative to new entrants. • Although not specifically an ICT recommendation or consideration, TSI should move quickly into the market to capitalize on its business model. This rapid movement could affect which technologies are selected for the ICT infrastructure.
Threat of Substitute Products	Many substitute products are available, including traveling outside of New York City for events, and even watching television. • TSI needs to ensure its marketing is comprehensive and that its network of kiosks provides excellent support to the customer for event, seat, and date selection. The Genenco software should be reviewed for thoroughness in meeting these customer-centric objectives, as well as ensuring that the network has the necessary redundancy to provide the maximal uptime.
Competitive Rivalry	A large number of competitors to TSI include the two largest that were analyzed in the SWOT analysis. • TSI may want to consider branching out to a larger market than New York City as dependence on one market is dangerous; this would require that the ICT infrastructure be robust enough to handle expansion, possibly opening a branch office or even relocating the office from the New York City area.
Co-opetition	• TSI may want to consider entering into co-opetition agreements with its competitors to expand its supply chain. • TSI's business model includes a co-opetition arrangement with all venues from which it buys tickets because virtually all venues sell tickets at their own box office. This factor necessitates that TSI manage the supply chain very well.

This six forces analysis looks at externalities that impact TSI's business. This list (bullet points) of ICT-related recommendations should be considered in the gap analysis discussed in the next section.

Where is the organization today?	Where do we want to be in "X" years (target)?	What will it take to get to our target?	Who is responsible for the project (i.e., project champion)?

Note: "X" refers to the number of years that the organization sees for the fulfillment of its strategic vision—often 3, 5, or 10 years—and is usually decided by senior management.

FIGURE 10-16 ICT-Based Gap Analysis

In Figure 10-16, completing the column "Where is the organization today?" is fairly straightforward. An inventory of those things that already exist in the organization is a good place to begin, as are interviews with managers and other people in the organization who can provide insight into the current state of the organization. It may also include making an inventory of things enumerated in documents (e.g., the TSI case). Completing the column "Where do we want to be in "X" years?" takes more work—this question could just as easily be "what objectives do we want to meet and when (X)?" Obviously, defining "X" is the first step, which is often the purview of senior management. Once "X" is defined, the business systems analyst knows the amount of time available to complete the project/objective. It could be that "X" is zero—the organization wants to upgrade its ICT infrastructure now—in which case the column heading perhaps should be changed to "Where do we want to be today?" The gap analysis is a flexible tool, and the column headings can change based on the time horizon or other factors, but the concepts are always the same: "The organization is here" but "the organization wants to be there (target)," so "What will it take to get to our target?" The column "Who is responsible for the project?" will take negotiating with the organization's management, project leaders, and staff. Buy-in from the project champions is essential, and they should be brought into the process early during the analysis with the value search tools. The value search tools described earlier in this chapter allow for the analysis and understanding of where the organization wants to be and gives a comprehensive competitive overview. The value search tools each play a role in completing the gap analysis and provide the following information:

- Corporate unbundling and value chain deconstruction are internally focused tools and their primary focus is to assist the organization in fulfilling a cost-leadership strategy. Both of these tools are useful in making ICT recommendations that reduce cost or improve quality.
- Supply chain analysis focuses both internally and externally to help the organization attain cost leadership, which can be accomplished through ICT recommendations that reduce cost or grow revenue.
- Comparative SWOT analysis and competitive forces analysis are externally focused since they compare the organization to its top competitors and external stakeholders. The primary focus of these tools is to assist the organization in attaining a product differentiation advantage in the marketplace. ICT recommendations should focus on product differentiation and growth in revenue.

A summary of the tools and their uses can be seen in Figure 10-17. As part of the gap analysis, the column "What will it take to get to our target?" needs to be completed with the resources necessary to get there. These resources include time, money, buy-in from potential champions of projects, technology resources, skills, and human resources to name but a few. It is no easy task and takes thoughtful analysis of the current situation and the target, and then a realistic look at the resources necessary. Falling short at this point almost ensures failure, and realistic expectations for what can be achieved given available time and resources must be set. Without realistic

FIGURE 10-17 Value Search Tools and Their Use in Gap Analysis

Value Search Tools	Primary Strategic Purpose	Gap Analysis Use Type of Recommendations
Corporate Unbundling *Internally Focused*	Cost Leadership	Enhance organization through ICT that will reduce cost or improve quality
Value Chain Deconstruction *Internally Focused*	Cost Leadership	Enhance organization through ICT that will reduce cost or improve quality
Supply Chain Analysis *Internally and Externally Focused*	Cost Leadership	Enhance organization through ICT that will reduce cost or grow revenue
Comparative SWOT Analysis *Externally Focused*	Product Differentiation	Enhance organization through ICT that will grow revenue
Competitive Forces Analysis *Externally Focused*	Product Differentiation	Enhance organization through ICT that will grow revenue

expectations, the proposed projects will probably not succeed. As was discussed earlier, just because a project is of large scope or scale, success is not guaranteed. Many factors (recall the various concepts from Unit 3) must be aligned to make an ICT project successful.

Reflecting back on TCO, technology curves, technology justification models, the Balanced Scorecard, and the value search tools, the business systems analyst must decide which models make the most sense for analyzing the organization and creating recommendations. As part of the overall analysis of options, economic and resource-based analyses must be done. It is up to the business systems analyst, in consultation with organizational management, to decide on which types of economic and resource-based analyses are appropriate.

For TSI, the gap analysis may take the form of "Where do we want to be when we open our doors?" and "Where do we want to be five years from now?" Separating all of the ICT recommendations from the value search models into those two timeframes would take coordination with management. The TSI gap analysis (see Vignette Box 10-11) assumes that the basic infrastructure has been built as specified in the vignette; this analysis shows where the organization wants to be in five years.

VAL IT FRAMEWORK

Before leaving the subject of analyzing an organization to create ICT value, the Val IT framework is introduced. This framework posits six typical challenges organizations face in creating ICT value (IT Governance Institute, 2009), all of which should be considered by the business systems analyst in the search for adding ICT value:

- **Problems in delivering technical capabilities.** Often an enterprise's delivery processes and competencies within its ICT function that are not mature enough to effectively and efficiently deliver the technology capabilities needed to support business operations and enable business change. This challenge highlights the need to improve ICT governance and management processes either before or in conjunction with the introduction of value management practices.
- **Limited or no understanding of ICT expenditures.** Rarely do executives enjoy a sufficiently transparent view of ICT expenditures and ICT-enabled investments across all ICT services, assets, and other resources. Often, decision makers can only estimate how much they are investing. What benefits they are gaining for the expense and what the full business rationale for the commitment might be can be elusive. Expenditures are frequently sourced from many different uncoordinated budgets, resulting in significant duplication and conflict in demand for resources.

VIGNETTE BOX 10-11

TSI Selected Recommendations from Value Search Models

ICT Recommendation	Where is the organization today?	Where do we want to be in 5 years (target)?	What will it take to get to our target? Project Champion/Team
Install an ERP that ties all departments together so they can share the same data	The basic infrastructure should be robust enough. Genenco has some ERP functionality.	A full ERP geared toward TSI's business	Additional servers; perhaps a virtual infra-structure; more ICT staff; a more robust ERP than the current Genenco software -**All department managers**
Computer telephony integration (CTI) to support call center; integration with the local phone system or virtual call center technology	This is not part of the ICT infrastructure. The initial infrastructure (ICT and phone) should be built keeping this in mind.	A CTI system that fully integrates Genenco's application with the telephone system	A new telephone system, additional ICT resources -**Managers from the call center, operations, and IT along with appropriate staff**
Decision support systems that aid in idea generation, prioritization, and selection (e.g., Group Systems, Think Tank®)	ICT should be robust enough if a hosted solution is chosen. Assume a hosted solution is chosen.	A hosted DSS that aids in idea generation	Contract with an application solutions provider (e.g., Think Tank) -**Marketing managers/staff**
TSI may want to consider branching out to a larger market than New York City as dependence on one market is dangerous; ICT infrastructure must be robust enough to handle this expansion	From current location, TSI's infrastructure will support additional satellite offices.	Three satellite offices located in major markets in the United States	Lease remote location, hire staff, obtain leased circuits to support data and voice communication between the satellite office and the main offices; build infrastructure and deploy kiosks in satellite locations - **All senior management**
CRM installed to ensure brand loyalty through building positive customer relationships	Genenco has some CRM functionality.	Full CRM solution	Either pay to have Genenco modified or purchase a CRM that interfaces with Genenco's application - **Managers from each department**
Annual review of Genenco performance and its impact on customer service, brand loyalty, and CRM	Metrics to measure Genenco's performance on various dimensions need to be developed.	Based on several years of data, determine whether Genenco is the most appropriate provider for kiosks; this should be monitored annually during the five years with periodic feedback to TSI management and Genenco	Staff time to develop metrics and to measure performance -**All senior managers and all department managers**

This gap analysis looks at a select set of recommendations from the value search models. The recommendations assume that the basic infrastructure is built and TSI has "opened its doors." Many other recommendations in addition to the ones selected for this example can be made.

- **Business abdication of decision making to the ICT function.** When the roles, responsibilities, and accountabilities of the ICT function and other business functions are unclear, then the ICT function tends to usurp the driver's seat, determining which ICT-enabled business investments should be pursued, prioritizing these business investments based on the ICT function's limited insights, and inappropriately relieving the business of its responsibility in defining and defending the business rationale used to justify every single ICT-enabled investment decision.
- **Communication gaps between the ICT function and the business.** Close collaboration between the IT function and other business functions is crucial to value creation. When such a partnership is absent, communication suffers, inefficiencies mount, synergies fail to emerge, and the work environment tends to devolve into a culture of blame. In some cases, the ICT function is relegated to the role of follower, instead of innovator, and is engaged in investment proposals too late in the decision-making process to contribute significant value. In other cases, the ICT function is blamed for not delivering value from ICT-enabled investments—value that only other business functions, in partnership with the ICT function, can deliver.
- **Questioning of the value of ICT.** Ironically, while most enterprises continue to invest more and more in technology, many of their key executive decision makers continue to question whether value is actually realized from these investments. Frequently, the dominant focus is merely on managing ICT costs rather than understanding, managing, and leveraging ICT's role in the process of creating concrete business value. As ICT-enabled investments increasingly involve significant organizational change, the failure to shift focus from cost to value will continue to be a major constraint to realizing value from these investments.
- **Major investment failure.** When ICT projects stumble, the business costs can be enormous—and highly visible. Project cancellations can trigger unexpected ripples of impact across the business. Delays can cost millions, and budget overruns can starve other projects of crucial resources. Amongst the most common examples of ICT investment failures are poorly planned enterprise resource planning (ERP) and customer relationship management (CRM) initiatives. In fact, Gartner estimates that these large-scale IT debacles represent the largest major cause of value leakage (Huber, 2002). Exacerbating this issue is the fact that, in many cases, problems are ignored until it is far too late to take any corrective action.

The same report by the IT Governance Institute goes on to list six optimal or desired states for value creation involving ICT. They are not meant to be an exhaustive list of best practices for value management, but illustrative:

- **Awareness and communications.** The ICT function is trusted because it generally delivers what it promises. Value management is well understood and adopted as the prevailing culture of investment decision making at the C-suite level (executive management). Decision makers understand and accept that value management practices, when in place, enhance competitive positioning and, when absent, erode it.
- **Responsibility and accountability.** Key staff (e.g., the business systems analyst) identifies attractive opportunities, investment decision makers pick and actively support the winners, and project managers detect and deal with losers early. Business functions drive investment decision making and benefit/resource balancing processes. Executive management becomes involved in these processes based not on internal politics or executive whim but on objective data. The business case for each investment has a fully committed business sponsor from a specified business function. Well-defined accountabilities exist for the business sponsor and project manager for each investment. Collaboration—supported by clear roles, responsibilities, and processes—helps avoid organizational gaps and overlaps by defining what the business requires and how ICT will provide it. Key

issues such as investment criteria, payback periods, and the selection of the individual investments to be funded are decided on at the executive and/or board level, supported by input from the heads of business functions and the CIO.
- **Goal setting and measurement.** The alignment of investments with corporate strategy is continuously monitored. Returns from investments are more stable and increasingly predictable. All ICT expenditures contribute to the enterprise's strategy in a demonstrable and internally auditable manner. ICT's role in the creation of value and ICT costs are not sources of executive concern because they are transparent and predictable and, therefore, manageable. There is significant increase in the percentage of successful investments as measured in terms of benefits realization and contribution to value. Regular review of investment in projects measure benefit realization, strategic alignment, costs, and risks. They also monitor progress toward value creation. Management information and forecasts are consistent, relevant, accurate, and timely and made available on a regular basis. Enterprise-wide ICT maintenance costs are included among operating costs. Key indicators have been established to assess the level of maturity of value management processes and practices.
- **Policies, standards, and procedures.** The process of investment planning begins with consideration of business benefits targeted, rather than existing resource constraints. Value management is considered "business-as-usual"—a part of day-to-day operations. The interrelationship between business benefits sought and the resources needed to achieve them is known and actively managed. All business case rationales are required to include cost-benefit justification based on the total cost of all changes required to realize the benefits, including changes to areas such as business models and processes, people skills and competencies, organizational structure, and technology. A clear distinction is made between one-time investment expenditures and ongoing operational costs; both are considered over the full economic life cycle of the investment. Investments are categorized to distinguish between mandatory and discretionary investments. Investment decisions are made using objective criteria that are measurable, verifiable and repeatable. The portfolio of all business change investment projects is continuously reviewed and updated, based on the needs of the enterprise as a whole, rather than on those of individual business functions in order to exploit synergies and avoid duplication of effort and double counting of business benefits. There is a formal process for retiring investment programs when expected benefits have been realized, or when it is determined that no further benefits are achievable.
- **Skills and expertise.** Effective program and project management processes are in place and are recognized as essential management practices for value creation. Portfolio management practices and structures are applied across different investment types, including those that are and are not based on technology.
- **Tools and automation.** Standard tools are engaged across the enterprise to evaluate investments, detect exceptions, and identify positive trends, as well as to evaluate and communicate the performance of individual investments and the overall portfolio.

This list is overwhelming, but it sets targets for creating an organization that objectively creates and understands ICT value creation. Creating an organization that adopts this list will require a culture shift. Most organizations do not manage the ICT resource as one that produces value, but rather as a required part of the infrastructure within the value or supply chain. The business systems analyst should search to create value through ICT and assist the organization in the quest to become one that adopts a culture that recognizes that value. One way proposed by the IT Governance Institute to assess where an organization is in relation to a culture that recognizes ICT-mediated value is the Value Management Quick Assessment (see Figure 10-18). This tool allows an organization to understand where it is today and where it needs improvement.

Value Management Quick Assessment	Management is unaware of the need for the practice.	Management is aware and committed to adopt the practice.	Implementation of the practice has begun.	Implementation of the practice is well underway.	The practice is adopted and achievement monitored.	The practice is embedded in the enterprise's way of working.
	0	1	2	3	4	5
ICT-enabled investments are managed as a portfolio of investments.						
ICT-enabled investments include the full scope of activities required to achieve business value.						
ICT-enabled investments are managed through their full economic life cycle.						
Value delivery practices recognize that there are different categories of investments that are evaluated and managed differently.						
Value delivery practices define and monitor key metrics and respond quickly to any changes or deviations.						
Value delivery practices engage all stakeholders and assign appropriate accountability for the delivery of capabilities and the realization of business benefits.						
Value delivery practices are continually monitored, evaluated, and improved.						

Source: Enterprise Value: Governance of IT Investments, Getting Started with Value Management 2.0 © 2008 ITGI®. All rights reserved. Used by permission.

FIGURE 10-18 Value Management Quick Assessment

Once the business systems analyst knows how the organization views ICT as a value creation investment, the analyst can assist in the process of moving from level 0, "Management is unaware of the need for the practice," to level 5, "This practice is embedded in the enterprise's way of working." The best approaches for making this move have been summarized by the IT Governance Institute as follows.

- **Approach 1: Build Awareness and Understanding of Value Management**
  - **The Challenge**—The need to create value is not adequately appreciated by key decision makers and stakeholders in the enterprise. Value does not just naturally "emerge" from normal business plans or activities; it has to be actively created. The problem is that, while the concepts of value management have been around for decades, the notion of value creation and preservation through business change [and ICT implementation] in modern enterprises is usually treated as an implied principle and not a conscious and pervasive tenet to guide behavior.
  - **The Symptoms**—There is no shared understanding of what constitutes value for the enterprise, what level of effort is required to realize it, or how to measure value. As a result, opportunities to realize value are missed or fail in execution, and value is often eroded or destroyed.
  - **The Solution**—Establish broad-based awareness of the need for value management; nurture understanding of what is involved in developing this capability; and build a strong internal executive and management commitment to improving and sustaining value creation over time.
  - **What Should Change**—Organizational and individual behavior should change to take a broader enterprise-wide view and a more disciplined, value-driven approach to decision making.
  - **The Benefits**—The benefits include increased understanding and acceptance of the need for IT and the other business functions to work together in partnership, supported by clear roles, responsibilities, and accountabilities related to value management, leading to increased value realization from IT-enabled investments.

- **Approach 2: Implement or Improve Governance**
  - **The Challenge**—Processes, roles and responsibilities, and accountabilities related to realizing value from ICT-enabled investments need to be clearly defined and accepted.
  - **The Symptoms**—The roles, responsibilities, and accountabilities of ICT and other business functions are unclear. Business decisions are made by the ICT function; ICT decisions are made by the business. A "culture of blame" predominates, with persisting confusion relating to accountability, responsibility, and sponsorship.
  - **The Solution**—Establish a governance framework with clearly defined roles, responsibilities, and accountabilities. Ensure that it is supported by strong and committed leadership, appropriate processes, organizational structures and information, and a well-aligned reward system.
  - **What Should Change**—Organizational and individual attitudes and behaviors should evolve toward a broader, more strategic enterprise perspective. Executives and managers should take a more disciplined, value-driven approach to decision making and accountability.
  - **The Benefits**—More effective and efficient decision making leads to increased trust between the IT function and the rest of the business, and results in increased value realization from IT-enabled investments.

- **Approach 3: Undertake an Inventory of Investments**
  - **The Challenge**—Little, if any, visibility exists into the number, scope, and cost of current and planned ICT-enabled investments or the resources either allocated or needed to support these investments.
  - **The Symptoms**—Overall expenditures on IT across the enterprise are not known, and often come from many different and uncoordinated budgets, with significant duplication. There is extensive conflict in demand for resources.

- **The Solution**—Establish portfolios of proposed and active investments, IT services, assets, and other resources, and apply portfolio management disciplines to their management.
- **What Should Change**—Organizational and individual attitudes and behaviors should change to take a broader enterprise view and embrace greater transparency. The appropriate processes and practices must be in place to support this.
- **The Benefits**—There is an increased understanding of exactly what sums of money are being spent on which investments, in which areas of the business, and by whom. There is also better identification of opportunities to increase value through improved allocation of funds, reductions in overall enterprise cost by eliminating redundancies, more effective use of resources, and reduction in risk from better understanding of the "health" of portfolios.

- **Approach 4: Clarify the Value of Individual Investments**
  - **The Challenge**—There is no consistently applied process for determining the value of potential or current investments (where value is total life-cycle benefits net of total life-cycle costs adjusted for risk and, in the case of financial value, the time value of money).
  - **The Symptoms**—There is persistent questioning of whether ICT investments have generated value. Business cases (i.e., actual business uses as found through value search models) for ICT-enabled investments are nonexistent or poorly prepared and are usually considered merely an administrative checklist required to secure funding. Little, if any, pre-investment information on costs or analytical rigor in defining benefits or value exists. There are few or no metrics to enable monitoring of what, if any, value is to be or has been created. It is assumed that technology, or the ICT function, will "magically" deliver value.
  - **The Solution**—Establish a process to develop and update comprehensive and consistently prepared business cases (e.g., use the value search models) for ICT-enabled investments, including all of the activities required to create value. The business case should be developed through a top-down approach, starting with a clear articulation of the desired business outcomes and progressing to a description of what actions need to be accomplished by whom (e.g., the gap analysis). These business cases should be updated and used as an operational tool throughout the complete economic life cycle of the investment.
  - **What Should Change**—Organizational and individual attitudes and behaviors should change to put more effort into the planning of investments and the development and regular updating of business cases.
  - **The Benefits**—A more objective assessment of business cases enables "apples to apples" comparisons across different types of investments. There are better opportunities to weigh individual investments based on their relative value against other investments available and a stronger track record in selecting the best. There is less uncertainty and risk that the value projected will not be realized.

- **Approach 5: Conduct Investment Evaluation, Prioritization, and Selection**
  - **The Challenge**—There is no consistently applied process for objectively evaluating the relative value of all proposed and current ICT-enabled investments—especially with respect to prioritization and selecting those investments with the highest potential value and enabling their ongoing evaluation.
  - **The Symptoms**—Most investment decisions are subjective. Many are often highly political. Once a decision is made to proceed with an investment, it is rarely revisited (usually only when a crisis has occurred). Poorly performing investments are rarely remediated or cancelled early enough to mitigate losses and, if cancelled, are regarded as failures for which someone should be held accountable.

- **The Solution**—Implement portfolio management disciplines to categorize ICT-enabled business investments. Establish and rigorously apply criteria to support consistent and comparable evaluation of the investments throughout their full economic life cycle.
- **What Should Change**—Organizational and individual attitudes and behaviors should change to take a broader enterprise view and embrace greater transparency.
- **The Benefits**—There is increased opportunity to create value through selecting investments with the greatest potential to deliver value. This is followed by active management of those investments and early cancellation of investments when it is apparent value cannot be realized.

The Val IT framework contains recommendations for ICT governance practices that can be embedded within the organization to realize the value-driven implementation of ICT. The Val IT framework exposits a number of processes that should be used in addressing shortcomings in the organization. These shortcomings include (1) problems in delivering technical capabilities, (2) limited or no understanding of IT expenditures, (3) business abdication of decision making to the ICT function of the organization, (4) communication gaps between the ICT function and the business, (5) questioning of the value of ICT, (6) major investment failure, (7) change in funding, and (8) shifts in the market or the economy. The Val IT framework contains a long list of processes that can be used to address these shortcomings. Fuller treatment of these processes can be found in *Enterprise Value: Governance of IT Investments, The Val IT Framework 2.0* (IT Governance Institute, 2008).

Chapter Summary

Today's business systems analyst, CIO, CKO, CTO, and anyone else in the enterprise responsible for ICT infrastructure building must do so by making recommendations that generate value for the organization. It is essential that they are able to analyze the organization, make value-generating recommendations, and communicate those recommendations to others. The best way to communicate those ideas is through shared understanding and language, such as is used in the value search models described in this chapter—including corporate unbundling, value chain deconstruction, comparative SWOT analysis, and competitive forces analysis. These models force the business systems analyst to look both internally in the organization and externally at the competitive landscape for places to bring improvement to an organization's current business processes, as well as places to bring new innovative products and processes online. When improvement and/or innovation are recommended, they must be done so as to bring value to the customer, not just for the sake of building ICT infrastructure. This chapter closed with a summary of the Val IT framework by the IT Governance Institute. The framework offers tools for the business systems analyst to understand where the organization is in relation to ICT's role in bringing value. That framework both posits challenges that organizations face in their quest for ICT value, as well as posits approaches to those challenges.

Vignette Wrap Up

TSI was presented in the opening vignette in great detail. Through this chapter, pieces of that detail were used to illustrate how to use the value search models. However, only pieces of the vignette were used, leaving the student with many unanswered questions and needing to complete the search for value for TSI. After presenting each of the value search models, an illustrative gap analysis was presented. Many of the facts relayed in the opening vignette will be used in the next chapter where documenting a network design is discussed. It is important that the student understands the use of the value search models and the gap analysis before moving on to the next chapter.

End of Chapter Questions/Assurance of Learning

1. Select a company with which you are familiar and work through the value search models and create a gap analysis for that company. A large amount of business research and a substantial amount of analytical work are expected.
2. Define what a value proposition is, and how it is created. Describe the value proposition for several companies you are familiar with.
3. Develop a list of core competencies and the levers that drive them for a large organization you are familiar with.
4. Develop a list of goals and objectives and align what ICT functionality and technologies are needed to attain the goals and objectives in support of the organizational ICT value proposition.

Case Exercises

These exercises build on the case exercises from previous chapters.

1. XYZ Inc. is a hardware company that builds network hardware and wants to expand its product offerings to ensure it is a viable alternative to other network hardware manufacturers. Write a brief paper and presentation showing how XYZ Inc. can assist its customers in the strategic alignment of IT.
2. Create the value search models for HealthyWay and perform a gap analysis. Make recommendations based on your analysis. Present the models, analysis, and recommendations to the class.
3. Select a company you are familiar with and document the company using the Val IT Value Management Quick Assessment. Based on your analysis of this assessment make recommendations to help that company enhance its competitive advantage. Present your analysis to the class.

Key Words and Concepts

analyzing the organization 278
analyzing the supply chain 290
comparative SWOT analysis 296
contingency perspective 276
co-opetition 301
core competencies 287
corporate unbundling 280
cost reduction 277
cross-functional processes 292
C-suite 275
five forces model 298
gap analysis 301
Global Supply Chain Forum (GSCF) 292
infrastructure processes 282
interaction costs 280
product differentiation strategies 295
product innovation 281
productivity paradox 275
quality improvement 277
revenue growth 277
SAIT 276
sixth force 296
strategic alignment of ICT 275
supply chain analysis 290
telescopic observation (TO) 297
Val IT framework 304
value chain deconstruction 284
value chain modeling 286
Value Management Quick Assessment 309
value proposition 279
value search models 278

References

Barua, A. K. (1995). Information technologies and business value: An analytical and empirical investigation. *Information Systems Research*, 2–23.

Brandenburger, A. M., & Nalebuff, B. J. (1996). *Co-opetition*. New York: Doubleday.

Brynjolfsson, E. (2009). The productivity paradox of information technology. *Communications of the ACM*, 36 (12), 67–77.

Cook, R. (2007, July 17). How to spot a failing IT project. *CIO Magazine*.

Dehning, B., Richardson, V. J., & Zmud, R. W. (2003). The value relevance of announcements of transformational information technology investments. *MIS Quarterly*, 637–656.

Evans, C., & Wright, W. (2009, Winter). The "How to ..." series 12. How to conduct a SWOT analysis. *British Journal of Administrative Management*, 10–11.

Evans, P. B., & Wurster, T. S. (1997). Strategy and the new economics of information. *Harvard Business Review*, 71–82.

Gartner Group. (2002, August). *The elusive business value of IT*. Gartner Group.

Gendron, M., Banks, D., & Miller, D. (2009). Effective strategic alignment of IT: Implications for the CIO as a member of the C-suite. *Asia Pacific Management Review*, 395–405.

Gnyawali, D. R., & Park, B.-J. (2009). Co-opetition and technology innovations in small and medium-sized enterprises: A multilevel conceptual model. *Journal of Small Business Management*, 47 (3), 308–330.

Hagel, J., & Singer, M. (1999, March–April). Unbundling the corporation. *Harvard Business Review*, 133–141.

Huber, N. (2002, March 21). Gartner: Firms waste £351bn each year on ill-conceived IT projects. *ComputerWeekly.com (UK)*.

IBM. (2004, August 17). *IBM strategy and change survey of Fortune 1000 CIOs*, as presented to SHARE in New York by Doug Watters.

IT Governance Institute. (2008). *Enterprise value: Governance of IT investments, the Val IT Framework 2.0*. Rolling Meadows, IL: IT Governance Institute.

IT Governance Institute. (2009). *Enterprise value: Governance of IT investments; getting started with value management*. Rolling Meadows, IL: IT Governance Institute.

Jelassi, T. (2005). *Strategies for e-business: Creating value through electronic and mobile commerce*. Harlow, UK: Prentice Hall.

Krause, K. S. (1999, October 18). Not UPS with a purple tint. *Traffic World*, 260(3), 26–34.

Merriam-Webster. (2009). *Value*. Retrieved October 7, 2009, from http://www.merriam-webster.com/dictionary/value

Mirrian-Webster. (2009). *Proposition*. Retrieved October 17, 2009, from http://www.merriam-webster.com/dictionary/proposition

OECD. (2001). *The hidden threat to e-government: Avoiding large government IT failures; PUMA policy brief (8)*. Retrieved October 17, 2009, from http://www.OECD.org

Panagiotou, G. (2003). Bringing SWOT into focus. *Business Strategy Review*, 14(2), 8–10.

Porter, M. E. (1980). *Competitive advantage.* New York: Free Press.

Porter, M. (2001, March). Strategy and the Internet. *Harvard Business Review*, 52–78.

Supply Chain Management Institute. (2009). *Our relationship-based business model.* Retrieved October 21, 2009, from http://scm-institute.org/Our-Relationship-Based-Business-Model.htm

Symons, C. (2006). Measuring the business value of IT. Retrieved May 7, 2008, from http://www.forrester.com/rb/Research/measuring_business_value_of_it/q/id/40267/t/2

Tri State Consulting. (2006). *Technology proposal for Ticket Sales, Inc.* Part of a student project at CCSU.

Additional Readings

Li, W., & Ye, L. (1999). Information technology and firm performance: Linking with environmental, strategic and managerial contexts. *Information and Management*, 35(1), 43–51.

Symons, C. (2006). *Measuring the business value of IT.* Retrieved May 7, 2008, from http://www.forrester.com/rb/Research/measuring_business_value_of_it/q/id/40267/t/2

11 DESIGNING ICT: DOCUMENTING PROCESS AND TECHNOLOGY RECOMMENDATIONS

> **Learning Objectives**
>
> - Understand business process modeling and how it can assist the business systems analyst in conveying ideas and recommendations.
> - Know how to use business process modeling notation and how to convey business process concepts using this notation.
> - Understand the necessity to model business processes before making ICT technology recommendations, and then be able to document both the business processes and the necessary ICT infrastructure.
> - Develop good process modeling skills, and good ICT infrastructure documentation skills.

Designing ICT solutions must be approached on two levels: first, business processes must be understood, optimized, and documented, and only then can technology solutions be designed to support the optimized business processes. In this chapter, methods for documenting business processes and ICT recommendations are discussed. Documents are produced at two levels: (1) the process level, showing how ICT will be implemented to improve/innovate business tasks; and (2) the design and recommendation level, so ICT engineers can build infrastructure. Documentation may seem to be one of the most boring and thankless jobs, but it is one of the most critical. The documents produced must be appropriate for management to understand the business processes and associated ICT recommendations, so engineers can build the recommended infrastructure, and for users to comprehend the purpose of the ICT being built. This chapter will use the TSI vignette introduced at the start of this unit and one of the recommendations from the gap analysis from the previous chapter as the basis for documentation. First, business process modeling (BPM) will be introduced using TSI as an example. Then a process improvement recommendation from the previous chapter's gap analysis will be used to extend basic BPM concepts as well as introduce concepts necessary for business processes to be understood and optimized. Next, the TSI vignette will be used to introduce infrastructure design concepts. Along the way, best practices will be introduced in "Best Practice" boxes. Two modeling tools will be used in this chapter, Business Process Visual ARCHITECT Animacian by Visual Paradigm (Visual Paradigm, 2009), and Microsoft Visio (Microsoft, 2007). Visual ARCHITECT is available to academic institutions for free. Visio is a software package available from Microsoft. Academic versions of Visio for institutions and students are available.

THE TOTAL DIAGRAM SET

In order to document a complete set of ICT recommendations the following are needed:

- Process Innovation/Improvement Documents
    - The organization's mission, vision, and objective for process innovation or improvement
    - A list of all recommendations for process improvement/innovation, including:
        - How the change fulfills the organization's mission, vision, and objectives, along with a gap analysis linked to objectives and measurements, and showing the project champions/teams necessary for improvement/innovation success
    - The process map showing a high-level view of the organization's business processes, indicating which processes are to be improved/innovated
    - Business processes "as-is" and "to-be" diagrams (BPD) for all processes that are to be innovated or improved

- ICT Design Working Documents
  - A thorough functionality list based on the agreed to process change documents
  - ICT hierarchy
  - Bandwidth estimations
- ICT Design Documents
  - Document list
  - Context diagram
  - ICT diagrams for all objects in the core and workgroups
  - Diagram notes for all objects numbered and lettered in the context diagram and the other ICT diagrams

This is a daunting list of documentation and diagrams that need to be created by business analysts so they can hand off the design recommendations to an ICT engineer for implementation. The process of creating these documents is an integrative one in which users, managers, ICT engineers, and other stakeholders must be in constant communication to ensure that these documents reflect the best alignment between organizational strategy and ICT resources. The following sections will review techniques to create many of these documents, while others have been reviewed elsewhere in this textbook.

BUSINESS PROCESS MODELING

Process Modeling is started by creating a Business Process Map. The business analyst needs to identify some key things before embarking on the creation of a process map and/or a business process diagram.

- **Identify the objective/mission of a modeling project.** The business analyst should meet with the appropriate stakeholders (e.g., users, managers, customers) and understand the business processes and if/why business process changes are needed. If changes are needed they should be specifically documented and agreed to by all parties, and a project team should be identified. As an example, the TSI gap analysis in the previous chapter is the outcome of these activities.
- **Measurable goals must be set.** As was discussed earlier in this textbook, ICT projects can be measured in a number of ways. The business analyst should create measurement instruments and set measurable goals for any new processes or change projects. The analyst collects baseline data on these goals before any change initiative is undertaken in order to later ascertain the impact of any implemented change.
- **Identify strategies to meet goals.** Among the many ways to achieve goals, the business analyst should identify various strategies that make sense for the organization. Such strategies might include process automation, outsourcing, or process improvement/innovation, to name a few possibilities.
- **Identify related business processes.** Business processes hardly ever stand alone. They have inputs and outputs that affect other processes, especially considering that most work is decomposed into tasks carried out by different individuals/systems. If any one task is "held up" for some reason, it affects other tasks in the process flow.
- **Identify the necessary project champions.** An inability to identify essential project champions consigns most projects to failure. Every organization, process, and set of information has essential people who make it happen. These people need to be identified and brought into any change (i.e., improvement or innovation) initiative early so they buy in to any potential changes. Project champions are the "heartbeat" of project change management.

PROCESS MAP

The main elements of a process map are (1) process, (2) receive event, (3) send event, and (4) process link. Each is described in Figure 11-1.

FIGURE 11-1 Process Map Symbols

Elements	Symbol
Process: represents business activity at high level (multiple pools, lanes, and processes can be enveloped in one process symbol at this level)	Process
Receive Event: something arriving at an organization is represented by a receive event (e.g., an order arrives)	Receive
Send Event: an organization sends a message or document to another organization, indicated by this symbol	Send
Process Link: the connector between all other element in the process map	⟶

Using the process map symbols, TSI's business model, value proposition from Vignette Box 11-1, and core competencies from Vignette Box 11-2, an overall business processes map can be defined. This map will define the high-level processes that represent the core competencies for TSI and how they interconnect. Information for creating this high-level process map comes from the value search models discussed in the previous chapters. The high-level process map can be seen in Vignette Box 11-3. Note, this is just one example of a process map for TSI—the student may see other ways the value propositions, core competencies, and overall business map can be created.

PROCESS MODELING

Business process modeling (BPM) is taking the processes of an organization and representing them graphically so a given process can be designed, improved, or innovated. Making these models is typically the job of the business systems analyst; however, others

---

VIGNETTE BOX 11-1

TSI Business Model and Value Proposition

Business Model: TSI will purchase blocks of seats from each venue at a discount and resell them at the face value of the ticket without any service charge. Significant discounts from venues will be negotiable through bulk purchasing arrangements because TSI takes the risk for predicting sale levels for individual events. By committing to purchase blocks of seats, TSI guarantees its venue partners revenue for blocks of seats, thus increasing the venue's incentive to sell at substantial discounts. TSI's flexible and real-time distribution network will allow it to realize a marginal profit for each ticket sold.

Value Proposition: From TSI's mission statement and other facts in the vignette, the business systems analyst can infer the value to the customer is *easy access to tickets for New York City venues without added fees*. Normally, it is necessary for the analyst to understand his or her organization and to extrapolate the value proposition from knowledge about the organization—for illustrative purposes the organizational value proposition is given here.

VIGNETTE BOX 11-2

TSI's Core Competencies

- Estimating market demand for tickets at events and purchasing the right amount
- Delivering tickets to customers in a convenient and accessible fashion
- Managing ICT to make the other competencies possible

It is normally necessary for the business systems analyst to infer the core competencies about their organization from their knowledge of the organization—however, for illustrative purposes these core competencies are given here.

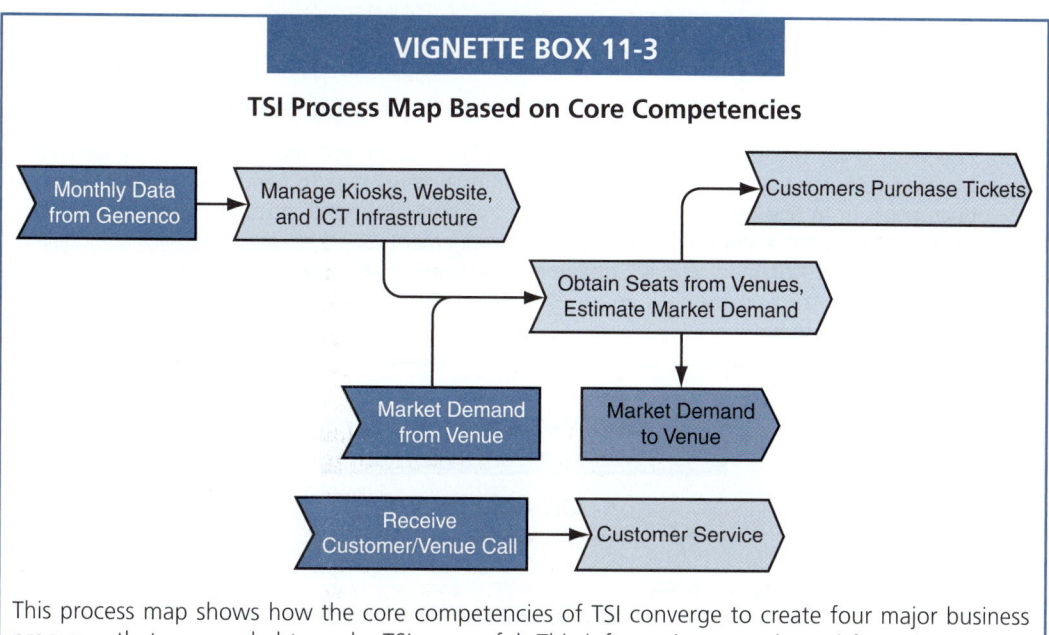

> **VIGNETTE BOX 11-3**
>
> **TSI Process Map Based on Core Competencies**
>
> [Process map diagram showing: Monthly Data from Genenco → Manage Kiosks, Website, and ICT Infrastructure → Obtain Seats from Venues, Estimate Market Demand → Customers Purchase Tickets; Market Demand from Venue → Market Demand to Venue; Receive Customer/Venue Call → Customer Service]
>
> This process map shows how the core competencies of TSI converge to create four major business processes that are needed to make TSI successful. This information was gleaned from the opening vignette and the analysis of the value search models.

in the organization who desire to implement/innovate/improve business processes will find BPM useful. For the purposes of this textbook, BPM is used because it provides appropriate tools for the analyst to "pitch" ideas to management for their consideration. Although BPM can be used to describe process implementation/improvement/innovation that does not require ICT, we will focus on BPM that uses ICT. Our main goal is the search for alignment between organizational strategy and the use of organizational ICT resources committed to process implementation/improvement/innovation projects. The two modeling languages commonly used to represent business processes to stakeholders are **business process modeling notation (BPMN)** and Unified Modeling Language (UML). BPMN will be used throughout this textbook because it is easily understood by nontechnical individuals. It offers sufficient expressivenesses to model complex business processes, while at the same time it can be naturally mapped to - business execution languages. UML is a language that helps developers specify, visualize, and document models of software systems, and is targeted at system architects and software engineers. BPMN is targeted at business systems analysts, system architects, and software engineers (Owen & Raj, 2003). These facts make BPMN an appropriate choice for the business systems analyst.

Techniques for capturing user/system requirements are the purview of a system analysis and design course, whereas techniques for making recommendations based on an organization's ICT strategy are the purview of the business systems analyst. In small organizations these tasks may be the responsibility of the same person; however in larger organizations the business analyst and the systems analyst are apt to be two different people who need to work to together to create appropriate ICT. Even though numerous techniques and competing modeling notation specifications are available, BPMN is used in this textbook because it is easily understood and explained. It has its roots in flowcharting, which is something many individuals in business are already familiar with. BPMN is introduced as a way to document business processes recommendations.

Using business process modeling (BPM) has several advantages (Havey, 2005). These include the following:

- **Formalize existing processes.** Sometimes organizations evolve organically—in other words, they build over time without the benefit of analysis to create efficient processes. BPM can be used to document existing processes so they can be easily understood.
- **Improve existing processes.** Improving existing processes is the "bread and butter" of BPM. As we look at business process modeling notation (BPMN), we

> ## BEST PRACTICE 11-1
>
> ### Workflow versus Business Process Modeling
>
> The term *workflow* emerged around the time that document management emerged as a technology. Some analysts believe that the term *workflow* refers to handling the flow of paper documents from one person to the next, within a manual process, possibly assisted by a document management system. *Business process management (BPM)* refers to graphically modeling the convergence of manual (i.e., document and human-based) processes with automated processes, and tracking the task and message flow between multiple participants within and between organizations.

> ## BEST PRACTICE 11-2
>
> ### Uses of BPMN
>
> - Formalize existing processes
> - Improve existing processes
> - Facilitate the automation of manual processes
> - Keep human talent to solve hard problems
> - Create efficient process flows
> - Increase productivity in existing processes
> - Simplify government and regulatory compliance

will examine taking an existing process (called the "as-is" process) and analyzing it so it can be optimized in some way (called the "to-be" process).

- **Facilitate the automation of manual processes.** When manual processes are modeled, often the model will shows areas that can be automated. This automation can then free the human participants in the process to handle the more difficult problems rather than being saddled with repetitive tasks.
- **Keep human talent to solve hard problems.** During process modeling, when manual processes are automated or the processes are made more efficient in some other way, human talent can focus on managing problems that cannot be easily handled by business rules implemented in software.
- **Create efficient process flows.** BPM allows the analyst to spot places within a process where tasks, information, and/or messages do not flow efficiently. In these places the analyst can make changes to organizational processes and bring about efficiencies that positively improve the organization's bottom line.
- **Increase productivity in existing processes.** When a process is modeled, often the business analyst will determine places where human productivity can be increased and automated processes can be optimized.
- **Simplify government and regulatory compliance.** When processes are modeled, and government regulations are overlaid on the modeled processes, places where compliance may best be implemented can often be seen. "Seeing" processes graphically should simplify regulatory compliance.

Business Process Modeling Notation and Diagrams

It may sound confusing, but business process modeling notation (BPMN) is not process oriented. In other words, it does not tell you the steps to model processes, nor does it tell you how to do any business task. BPMN is not a set of steps for modeling business processes, but rather it is a set of specifications that standardize graphical symbols and rules used to diagram business processes. BPMN is based on flowcharting techniques and is similar to activity diagrams in UML. Because BPMN does not provide the business analyst with a "cookbook method to process design," it allows the analyst to apply his or her critical thinking skills using a set of easily understood graphical symbols to create diagrams useful to a variety of stakeholders. This capability is helpful because it allows designers from different domains and organizations to understand each other's business process diagrams. BPMN creates a bridge between stakeholders, including the business analyst and the systems analyst, and the technical user and the business user. This bridge is created through shared language and understanding of **business process diagrams (BPDs)**. BPMN is constrained to support modeling of business processes; other types of organizational modeling are not included (e.g., organizational structure, data modeling, etc.). Note that even though BPMN will show the flow of data and messages within an organization, it is not data flow diagramming. Data and message flows are different from the highly technical IT-centric data flows described in a data flow diagram. BPMN is meant for the user to understand how information moves through an organization without regard to specific technical constraints of ICT infrastructure.

BPDs are created for various reasons. When the business analyst wants to understand current business processes, identify bottlenecks, or introduce operational efficiencies, creating business process diagrams is a good place to start. The BPD gives the analyst a good way to document an understanding of a business process, convey that understanding to the user and technical staff, and validate business processes through a shared language like BPMN. These same BPDs give managers a way to understand how teams under their supervision operate, as well as create documentation so those teams and their processes can be analyzed for value-producing opportunities.

BPMN standards are maintained by the Object Management Group (OMG). OMG was started in 1989 as an international, open membership, not-for-profit computer industry consortium. OMG's modeling standards—BPMN, UML, and Model Driven Architecture (MDA)—are designed to enable visual design, execution, and maintenance of software and other processes. This includes IT systems modeling and BPM. OMG's standard-setting activities involve a request-for-proposal process, e-mail discussions, meetings, and member-only voting on standards ratification. As an open membership group, OMG invites prospective members to attend meetings as guest observers (Object Management Group, 2009).

As of January 2009, BMPN 1.2 is the current version ratified by OMG.[*] Businesspeople are comfortable with visualizing business processes using BPMN because it is similar to the familiar flowcharting format. When business analysts study the way companies work, they often define business processes with simple flow charts. This approach can create a technical gap between the format of the initial design of business processes and the format of the languages and technologies used to implement them. This gap needs to be bridged with a formal mechanism that maps the appropriate visualization of the business processes (a notation) to the appropriate execution format for these business processes. BPMN is a tool that can fill that gap. Interoperation of business processes at the human level rather than the software level can be solved with standardization provided by BPMN. BPMN provides a business process diagram (BPD) that is designed for use by the people who design and manage business processes (Object Management Group, 2009). The diagrams created using BPMN are also suitable for the engineers who select technologies and implement them. Finally, they can be used by systems analysts so they understand an organization's business processes and can develop software specifications to support an organization in its quest for aligning strategy and business processes with ICT resource commitments.

The BPMN specification defines the notation and semantics of a business process diagram (BPD) and represents the amalgamation of best practices within the business modeling community. The intent of BPMN is to standardize a business process modeling notation in the face of many different modeling notations and viewpoints. In doing so, BPMN provides a simple means of communicating process information to other business users, process implementers, customers, and suppliers.

---

[*] BPMN version 2.0 was published by PMG in January 2011. The changes do not impact any of the information presented in this textbook.

> **BEST PRACTICE 11-3**
>
> **BPMN Graphical Representations and Markers**
>
> - Visual shapes and icons used for graphical representation are identified in the specification. They are determined within the standard and are defined to create a standard visual language that all process modelers will recognize and understand.
> - There is flexibility in the size, color, line type, and text positions of the graphical elements defined in the BPMN standard except where specified in the standard (i.e., any deviation from the basic standards must not conflict with existing standards).
> - BPMN may be extended as follows:
>   - New markers or indicators may be added to graphical elements.
>   - New shapes (graphical elements) may be added to diagrams but the new shape may not conflict with any other element of the BPMN standard.
>   - Graphic elements in the standard can be colorized to indicate specific meanings and used to extend the information contained by the element as specified in the standard (e.g., red could be used to indicate a high-level process whereas green could be used to indicate a lower-level process).
> - Any extensions to BPMN shall not change any existing specifications or definitions for graphical elements or markers (e.g., changing a square into a triangle, or changing rounded corners into squared corners, etc.).
> - Some business process modeling software tools use naming conventions that are different from the standard. For example, *WebSphere* uses the term *business item* for *data*, and the term *repository* for *facility*.

A key element of BPMN is the choice of shapes and icons used for the graphical elements identified in this specification. The intent is to create a standard visual language that all process modelers will recognize and understand (Object Management Group, 2009). The notation also provides a common set of graphical objects, connectors, and process flows readily understood by users, managers, and those making resource allocation decisions.

DIFFERENCES IN TERMINOLOGY

Even though the nomenclature used by BPMN has been standardized, any given organization that does modeling may use different terms to mean the same thing. BPNM uses the term *resource* to mean people or equipment to be used; *activity* is a task to be performed with assigned resources; and *facilities* refers to a collection of resources. However, IBM, a leader in the business process modeling movement, uses a different set of terms in its product WebSphere Business Modeler. WebSphere uses *activities* and *resources*, but uses the term *business item* for "data," and *repository* for "facility." All of the concepts from the BPMN standard are represented in IBM's implementation of BPMN, but the terms are different. It is important that the analyst recognize these differences as they use different tools. The high-level rules for using BPMN can be found in Best Practice 11-3.

STAFF VERSUS MANAGERS

It is important to note that both managers and staff should be consulted when creating BPDs (see Best Practice 11-4). Staff will usually tell you how a process actually operates, while managers will tell you how a process should operate—that disconnect is often a place to start the search for opportunities to enhance processes, bring about efficiencies, and restructure workflows within existing processes.

BUSINESS PROCESS MODELING NOTATION AND PROCESS TYPE

BPMN is used to communicate how business processes work or how they should be changed. The purpose of BPMN is to create shared understanding and language so that a large number of audiences can communicate about business processes. Three basic types of submodels are found within a BPMN model:

Chapter 11 • Designing ICT: Documenting Process and Technology Recommendations   321

FIGURE 11-2 Private Business Process

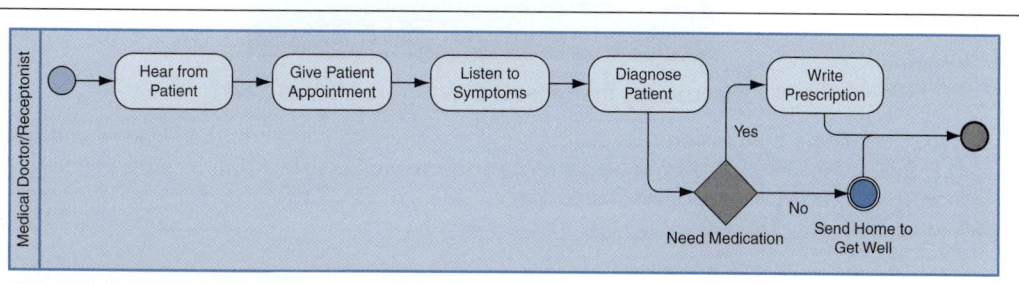

This BPD shows the business processes of the doctor's office without showing any of the details of the other participants (e.g., the patient or the pharmacist) or the message flows between them.

- **Private (Internal) Business Processes.** These processes are internal to a specific organization and are the types of processes normally referred to as **workflow** or BPM processes. They are contained within one pool, and message flows are used to deliver messages between pools. (Pools are discussed in the following text.) See Figure 11-2 for an example.
- **Abstract (Public) Processes.** These processes provide a higher-level view of private business processes, which shows those activities that communicate outside private business processes. See Figure 11-3 for an example.
- **Collaboration (Global) Processes.** These processes show interactions between business processes of different organizations. Activity represents the sequence of tasks within a process, and message flows are used to represent the exchanges between organizations. Each organization should have a pool, and the participants should be within lanes in their organization's pool. See Figure 11-4 for an example.

In BPNM processes are represented with graphical elements, markers, and connections. Semantic elements are associated with graphical elements, markers, and connections and allow further definition of the graphical objects. BPNM specifies public, private, and collaboration processes. This textbook will focus on high-level and detailed private processes, as well as activities and messages that create public processes.

BPM TERMS

Several terms will help with understanding business process models:

- **Process definition** is also referred to as the problem statement. This statement gives the details of the process in text. For example, from TSI the business model gives a high-level process definition and can be seen in Vignette Box 11-1 (on p. 316, but referenced here as a good example).

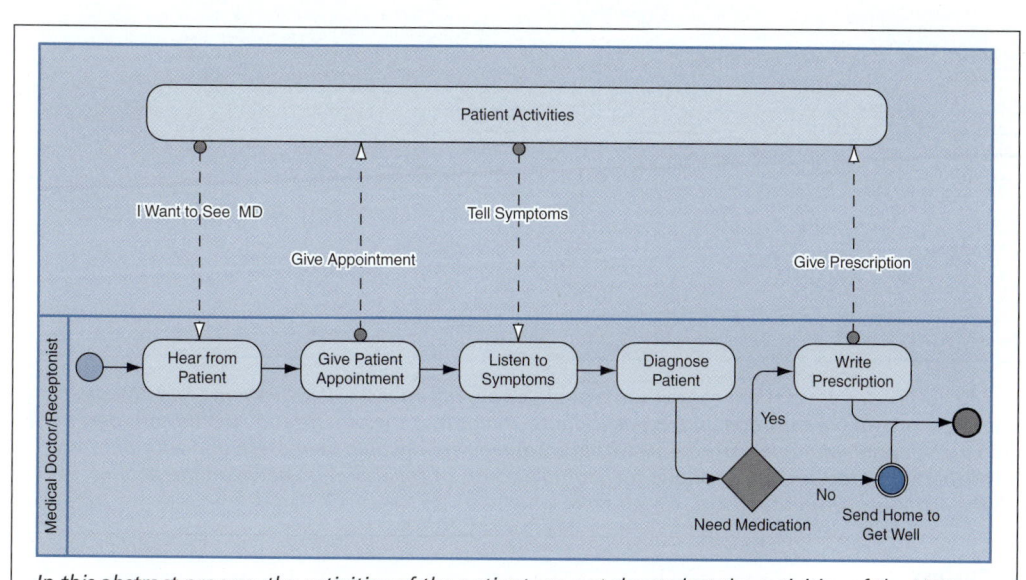

FIGURE 11-3 Abstract (Public) Business Process

In this abstract process, the activities of the patient are not shown but the activities of the MD's office are. The patient activities have been added to Figure 11-3 and are abstract.

BEST PRACTICE 11-4

Discussing Processes: Managers Versus Staff

When creating a business process diagram, it is important to consult both managers and staff members. Managers will tell you how a process should work, while a staff member will tell you how the process is actually being carried out.

BEST PRACTICE 11-5

Use of Pools and Lanes

The BPMN standard is a bit confusing in describing pools and lanes. The standard refers to both of these under the category swim lanes. The confusion comes in when you call the category swim lanes and one of the subcategories a lane. The difference is straightforward, but the way they are categorized is confusing. Pools are used to contain processes within organizations, and lanes are used to subdivide organizations into participants like the example given in Figure 11-5. Note: Sequence flows (solid lines with arrows) are used between tasks within pools (even across lanes within a pool), whereas message flows (dotted lines with arrows) are used between pools.

- **Process instance** is one occurrence of the process. For example, if 10 customers are purchasing tickets at TSI kiosks simultaneously, then there would be 10 instances of the *Purchase Tickets* process.
- **Task/Activity** is one step in the process. For example, the process *Contact MD* would be one task/activity in the sequence of processes in Figure 11-4.
- **Automated task** is a specific activity automated by some type of system or technology.
- **Manual task** is performed by human participants.

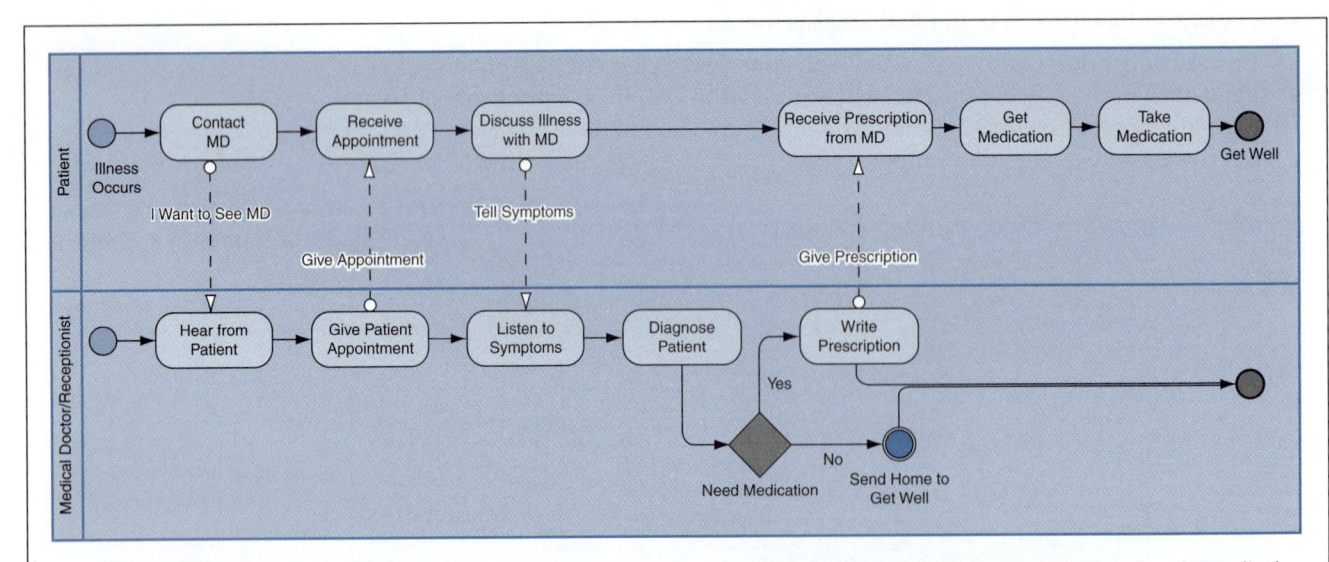

The collaboration between the MD's office and the patient contains two pools (or organizations) called "Patient" and "Medical Doctor/Receptionist." Each pool represents an organization and its participants. Things that the organization would consider internal to them are represented in their pool. Multiple participants within an organization would be represented with different swim lanes within a pool. This collaborative process diagram shows the multiple points of collaboration between the patient and medical doctor, along with the actual processes that occur in each swim lane.

FIGURE 11-4 A Collaborative Process

PARTICIPANTS

Diagrams made using BPNM must take the point of view of the participant into account. Each person viewing a process will see it from their vantage point, meaning that processes over which they have direct control will be seen as internal, and processes under someone else's control will be seen as external. This consideration is important when debugging processes because you need to know who the process owners are (i.e., those who see the process as internal). The interaction between a medical doctor and a patient exemplifies this issue (see Figure 11-4). Each knows what they must do to get the patient well, and each sees that as their responsibility or process.

POOLS AND LANES

Before we get into describing the full set of BPMN symbols and connectors it will be helpful to differentiate between pools and lanes. The OMG BPMN Standard V1.2 is confusing on this topic because it uses a grouping called *swim lanes* to include two types of objects called **pools** and **lanes**. It causes confusion when you have two parts of the standard called something so similar—a category called *swim lanes* and an object called *lanes*. Differentiating between the objects is fairly straightforward; *pools* normally represent different organizations, and *lanes* are the different participants within the organization. Figure 11-5 should make this distinction clearer. The notation in the rest of this textbook will use *pools* to represent organizations, and *lanes* to represent participants within the organization. Where processes are organization-wide or being diagrammed at the organization level, it is not necessary to indicate the *lanes* (participants), only *pools* will be used. When a diagram includes participants, *lanes* will be used inside of *pools*.

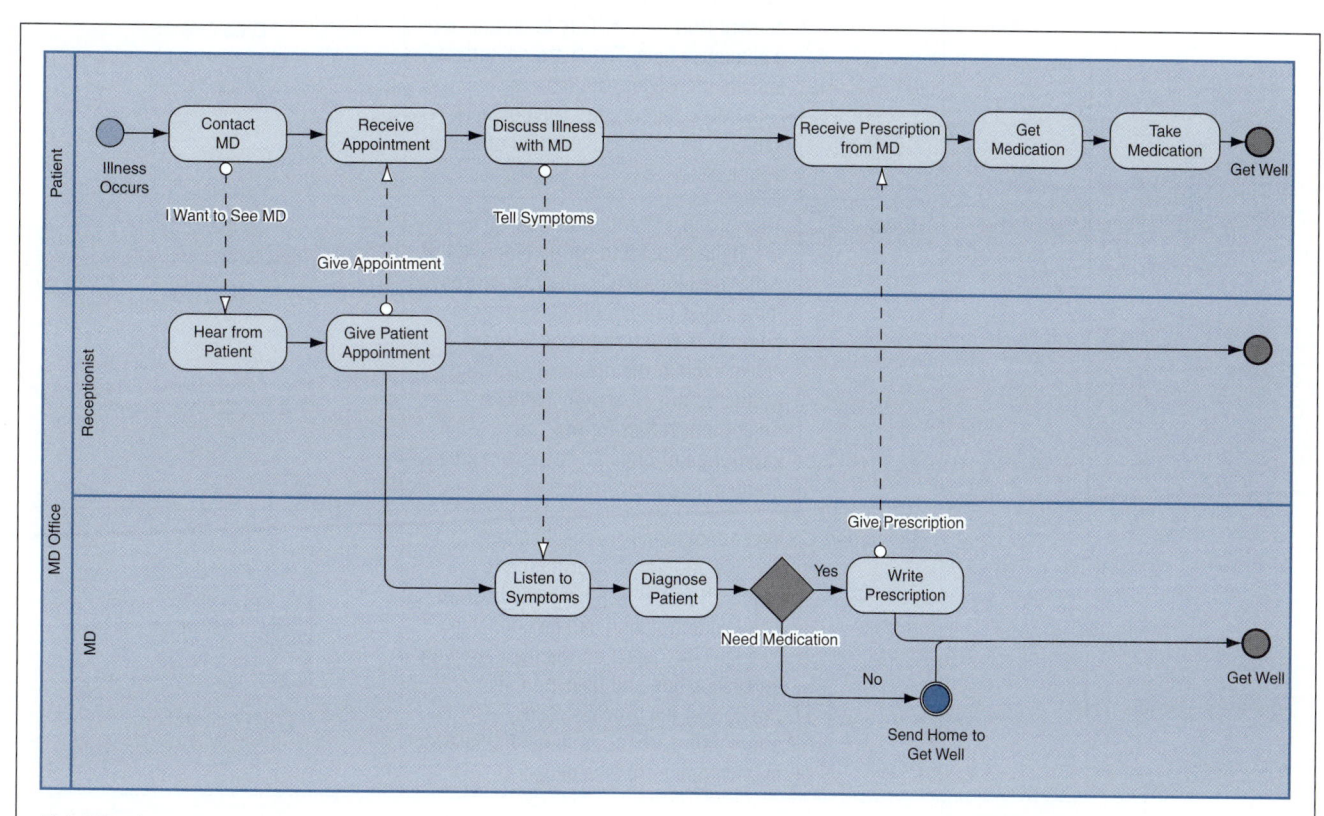

This BPD shows two pools: the "Patient" (organization) and the "MD Office" (organization). The "MD Office" (organization) is divided into two lanes, the "MD" (participant) and the "Receptionist" (participant).

FIGURE 11-5 Medical Encounter with Multiple Pools and Multiple Swim Lanes

GRAPHICAL ELEMENTS

Business process diagrams (BPD) use a core group of graphical elements. These core elements are designed to be simple, while at the same time able to describe the complexity of business processes. Four types of core elements include the following:

- **Swim lanes:** groupings of primary elements into pools and lanes
- **Flow objects:** the main graphical elements that define the behavior of the business process; include events, activities, and gateways
- **Connecting objects:** includes sequence flow, message flow, and association
- **Artifacts:** symbols that provide additional information about other objects; include data objects, group, and annotation in BPMN specifications (Some modeling tools add other artifacts to aid in documentation of BPDs.)

The core elements contain objects that are described in Figure 11-6.

FIGURE 11-6 Core BPD Elements

Elements	Object	Description	Notation
Artifacts	Data Objects	Data objects generally associate with flow objects (events, activities, and gateways). An association will be used to make the connection between flow objects and data objects. This allows the behavior of the process to be modeled without the data objects to reduce clutter. Data objects can show as sent from one activity to another via a sequence flow. These are not inter-activity messages, but data (or "payload") that is sent. Data objects can also be used as input and output of a process.	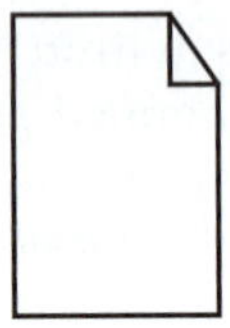 Data Object
	Group	This group artifact is a visual mechanism used to group elements of a diagram informally. In other words, the analyst can create a category of items that group together to more easily explain the model. The group artifact is not an activity or flow object, but rather represents categories of objects. Groups can be created across swim lanes.	 Group
	Annotation	Text annotations are mechanisms to provide additional information to the reader of a business process diagram. The text annotation can be connected to a specific object on the diagram with an association and have no effect on the flow of the process. Text annotations are for documentation and clarification purposes only.	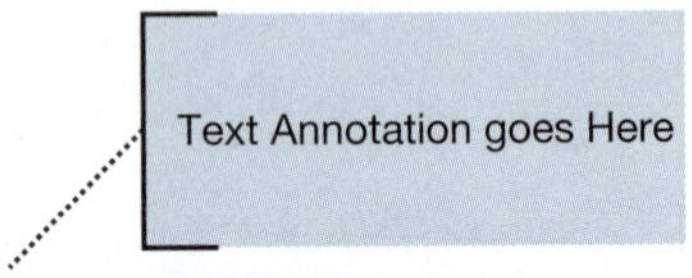 Text Annotation goes Here / Text Annotation

FIGURE 11-6 Continued

Elements	Object	Description	Notation
Flow Objects	Events	The three types of events include the *start event*, which indicates where a particular process will start. The start event will have a trigger (i.e., something that makes the process begin), and the trigger event is indicated in the open circle. The *end event* indicates where a process ends. The *intermediate event* indicates where something happens within a process that affects that process (i.e., it will not stop or start the process but changes it somehow). Intermediate events include places where messages are expected or sent, delays are expected, or exception handling or compensatory activity occurs.	Start Event Intermediate Event End Event
	Activities	An activity is work that a company performs. The three types of activities include *process, subprocess,* and *task*. The process is a higher-level (i.e., rolled up) version of subprocesses, or it is a stand-alone process. A subprocess can be used to give the detail of a process. Tasks are single units of work and are not used when work is not broken down into finer levels of process modeling detail.	Process Without Subprocess Process with Subprocess Task
	Gateways	Gateways are used to control sequence flows. They indicate branching based on specified conditions. Gateways are not considered business activities (processes) but rather something that controls sequence flows between activities.	Gateway
Connecting Objects	Sequence Flow	Sequence flows show the order in which activities, events, and gateways will be performed. Sequence flows can cross swim lanes in a pool but not pools.	Sequence Flow
	Message Flow	Message flows show the flow of a message between two entities (pools). Message flows are NOT used within a pool.	Message Flow
	Association	Associations are used to associate information and artifacts with flow objects. An association is also used to show activities that compensate for other activities.	Association

(Continued)

FIGURE 11-6
Continued

Elements	Object	Description	Notation
Swim Lanes	Pool	A container that represents participants in a process (e.g., a specific business entity for company). This object can also be used to represent more general roles such as buyer, seller, or manufacturer. A pool is a container of the sequence flow (see Connecting Objects), and is typically used to separate different organizations (i.e., each organization is represented by a different pool).	*Name*
	Lane	A lane is a subpartition in a pool. Lanes are used to organize and categorize activities within a pool. The analyst can define the meaning of lanes; however, they are often used for to define staff (e.g., managers), systems (e.g., CRM), or departments (e.g., accounting). Lanes can be used for any subgrouping in a pool.	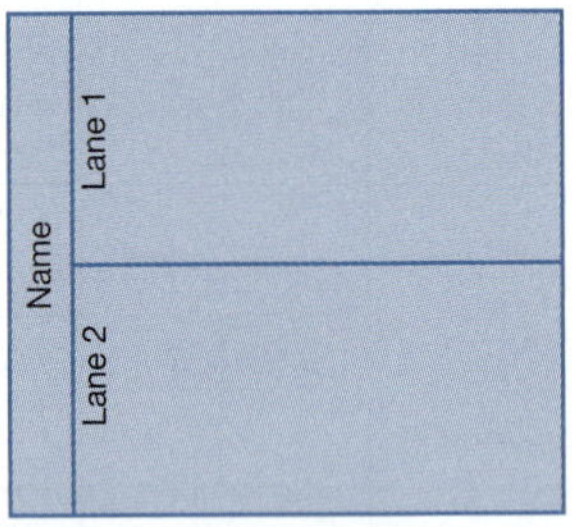 *Name* / Lane 1 / Lane 2

BASIC BUILDING BLOCKS

Four basic building blocks are used when creating business process diagrams (BPDs): (1) sequence of steps, (2) conditions, (3) loops, and (4) parallel activities. They are described in Figure 11-7.

COMPENSATION ACTIVITIES

Compensation activities are processes that "compensate" for another process. For example, suppose you attempt to purchase a shirt at the store with your credit card. However, your credit card is declined. The credit card company will want to keep a record of your attempt to make a purchase and the declination, rather than just undo the purchase transaction. During that transaction, the compensation activity would be to not charge your credit card but to record the transaction as declined. An example can be seen in Figure 11-8. This BPD contains three pools called *Buyer, Store, and Credit Card Company*. The buyer process has three tasks: select a shirt to buy, bring shirt and credit card to the cashier, and leave store. The store process starts by attempting to charge the credit card, and then has a gateway indicating that the card was either successfully charged or not; if the card was charged successfully then the buyer gets the shirt, the credit card, and a receipt; if the card was not charged successfully then the buyer

FIGURE 11-7 Basic Building Blocks of BPD

Types or Activities	Sample
Sequence of Steps: tasks that are done in the order indicated by the BPD	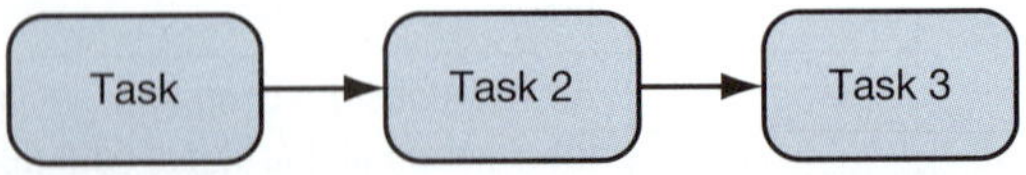 Task → Task 2 → Task 3
Conditions: tasks that are done based on a particular condition (gateway) being passed	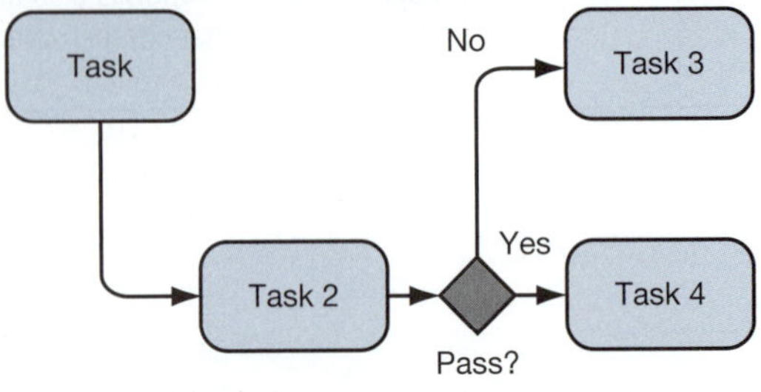 Task → Task 2 → Pass? — No → Task 3; Yes → Task 4

Chapter 11 • Designing ICT: Documenting Process and Technology Recommendations 327

FIGURE 11-7 Continued

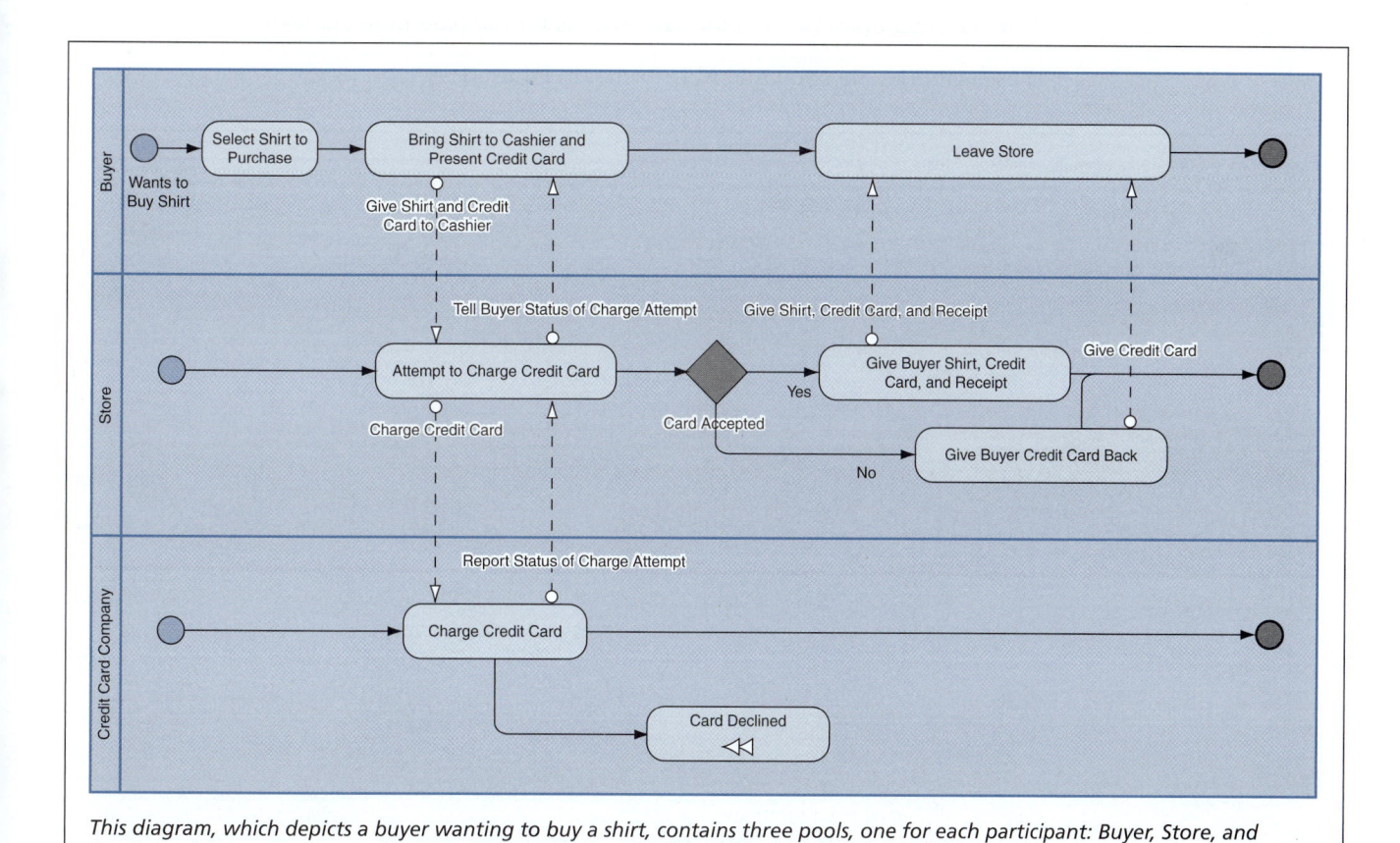

Types or Activities	Sample
Loops: tasks that are redone based on the outcome of a condition (gateway)	*(diagram: Task loops back from "No" branch of Pass? gateway; Yes branch leads to Task 4, via Task 2)*
Parallel Activities: tasks that are done at the same time and extend from a parallel gateway	*(diagram: Task → Task 2 → parallel gateway → Task 3 and Task 4)*

The four basic building blocks in building business process diagrams are (1) a sequence of steps, (2) conditions, (3) loops, and (4) parallel activities.

(Diagram: Three swimlane pools — Buyer, Store, Credit Card Company — depicting a credit card transaction flow.)

Buyer: Wants to Buy Shirt → Select Shirt to Purchase → Bring Shirt to Cashier and Present Credit Card → Leave Store

Store: Attempt to Charge Credit Card → Card Accepted? — Yes: Give Buyer Shirt, Credit Card, and Receipt; No: Give Buyer Credit Card Back → Give Credit Card

Credit Card Company: Charge Credit Card → Card Declined (compensation)

Messages: Give Shirt and Credit Card to Cashier; Tell Buyer Status of Charge Attempt; Give Shirt, Credit Card, and Receipt; Charge Credit Card; Report Status of Charge Attempt

This diagram, which depicts a buyer wanting to buy a shirt, contains three pools, one for each participant: Buyer, Store, and Credit Card Company. The credit card company has a compensatory task in case the credit card is declined. The compensatory task is noted by the symbol *(Card Declined icon)* where the double arrow on the bottom of the task indicates that the task is compensating for an event in the main process.

FIGURE 11-8 Credit Card Declination and Compensation Activities

just gets the credit card back. The credit card company has two tasks: the first to charge the credit card, and then a compensatory activity if the card cannot be charged. Message flows occur between many of the tasks. The credit card processes are at a very high level, mainly because the store's business analyst probably does not know what actually happens in the credit card company, but is most familiar with the interactions between the store and the customer.

COLLABORATIVE DIAGRAMS

The patient and MD example given previously will be used to show how business process modeling notation (BPMN) can be used to build a simple collaborative business process diagram. The activities of the pharmacist will be added to the BPD used earlier. First, let's start by describing the activities:

- The three participants in this BPD are the patient, the MD, and the pharmacist.
- The patient initiates this process by contracting an illness, and then contacts the MD's office for an appointment.
- The MD's office gives an appointment, and the patient arrives at the appointed time.
- The patient meets with the MD and discusses any symptoms.
- The MD diagnoses the patient and determines whether medication is needed.
- If medication is needed, the MD gives the patient a prescription; if medication is not needed the patient is sent home to get better.
- If the patient receives a prescription, the patient goes to the pharmacy and gets medicine. The patient then takes the medication in order to get better.
- The end point in all of the processes is for the patient to get well.

These activities are shown in BPD format in Figure 11-9.

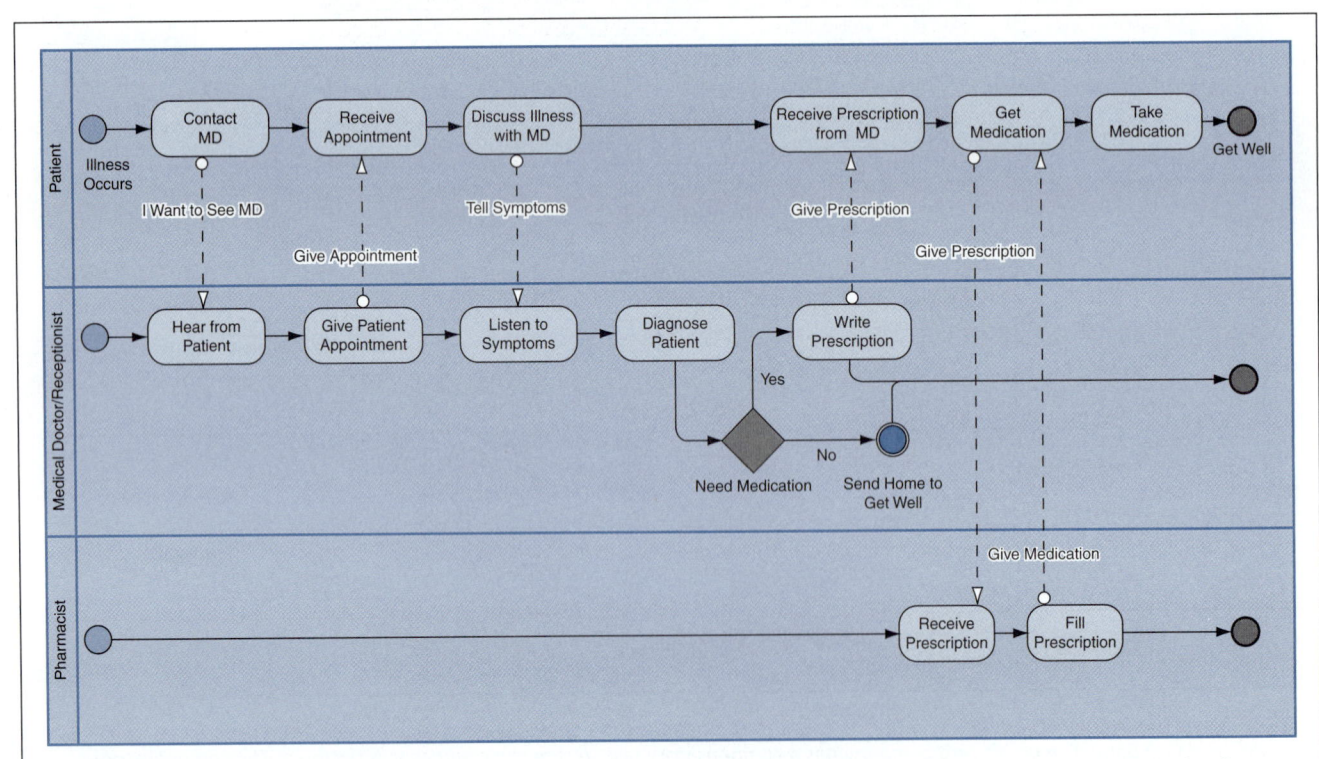

This BPD uses BPMN to graphically show the three participants' tasks in the overall process of getting a patient well. The diagram uses a common start event (patient illness), a common end event (patient well), and a number of tasks, message flows, and sequence flows to get from start to end.

FIGURE 11-9 Patient, MD, and Pharmacist BPD

Using BPMN notation, the BPD in Figure 11-9 would be constructed as follows:

- Three pools [Pool] would be created: Patient, Medical Doctor, Pharmacist
- Within each a start event ○ is created, then the tasks [Task] that the participant would do are placed. If there are gateways ◆ Gateway, they are included.
- Message flows are created across pools for information passed during each task.
- Each flow is then ended with an end event ●.

Using TSI to Introduce Modeling

With basic business process notation and modeling described, we will now turn to usage of business process modeling notation, within business process diagrams. Several refinements of BPMN will also be introduced. We will use the TSI vignette from the start of this unit for this purpose. The process map was shown earlier in this chapter, and we will now turn attention to the process diagrams.

INITIAL EXAMPLE OF CREATING A BUSINESS PROCESS DIAGRAM

Below, we will take one of TSI's core competencies processes (Customers Purchase Tickets) and create a business process diagram for it. This process will take the customer-centric view (i.e., the customer will initiate the transaction and drive what happens) with the customer selecting a show, venue, and date/time. Once the customer provides his or her credit card information, TSI takes that information and attempts to charge the credit card. TSI passes the credit card information to a credit card company that attempts to charge the card. If the card is valid and has available credit, the card is charged and TSI prints the tickets. The tickets can be printed either at a kiosk or on a customer's PC printer if it is a web sale. The credit card company has a compensatory activity—card declined—for which it records the transaction attempt but does not charge the credit card. In this diagram several new graphical symbols are introduced:

- The end event with a message ✉ allows a message flow between pools (across organizations) at the end of a process. It is used in the TSI pool as the end of TSI's processing of the transaction.
- The text annotation [ ] with an association [ ] to a task [Task] allows for additional documentation for tasks on the BPD. It used in the Customer pool to provide additional documentation for the *Capture Credit Card Demographics* and *Print Ticket and/or Receipt* tasks.

The "Customer Purchase Ticket" BPM described here can be seen in Vignette Box 11-4.

MODELING ICT RECOMMENDATIONS FOR TSI

We will use one element of TSI's business recommendations—*Handling a Customer Service Call: Computer telephony integration (CTI) to support call center; integration with the local phone system or virtual call center technology*—as an example. Details of that selected recommendation for TSI can be seen in Vignette Box 11-5, which identifies mission/objectives, goals, strategies, related business processes, and project champions so the business analyst can embark on the steps necessary to effectively create business process diagrams. Analysts can collect data from participants, design the process, and verify the design of the process by sharing their BPMs with staff and managers asking them to review the diagrams and run through the actual processes (i.e., follow the process flow by actually watching participants perform their work) to ensure BPM

VIGNETTE BOX 11-4

Customer Purchase Ticket BPD

Customer swimlane: Purchase Ticket → Select Event → Select Venue → Select Date/Time → Capture Credit Card and Demograhics → Print Ticket and/or Receipt

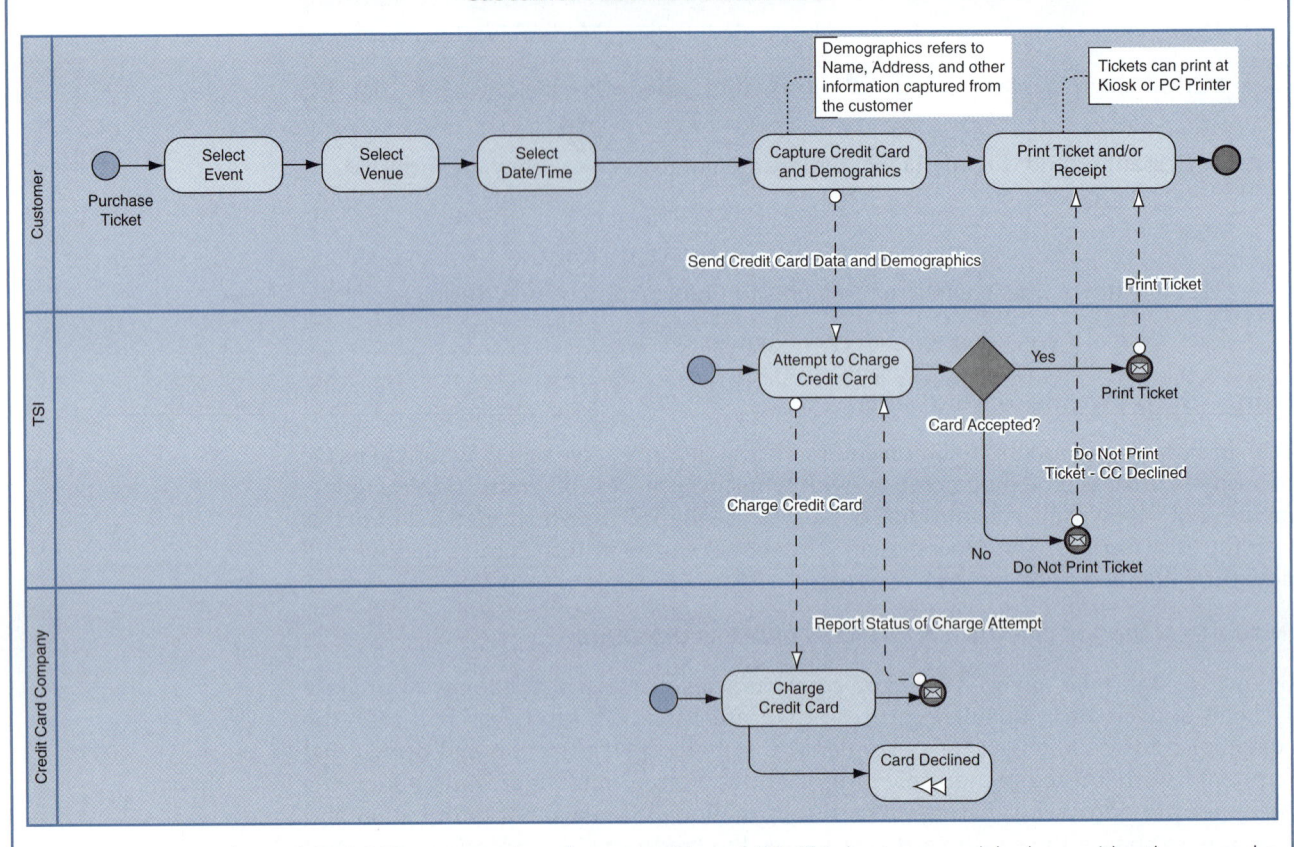

Note: Demographics refers to Name, Address, and other information captured from the customer

Note: Tickets can print at Kiosk or PC Printer

TSI swimlane: Attempt to Charge Credit Card → Card Accepted? — Yes → Print Ticket; No → Do Not Print Ticket (Do Not Print Ticket - CC Declined)

Credit Card Company swimlane: Charge Credit Card → Card Declined

Messages: Send Credit Card Data and Demographics; Charge Credit Card; Report Status of Charge Attempt; Print Ticket

The "Customer Purchase Ticket" BPD captures the value proposition of TSI. This business model, along with others, can be used to expand on TSI recommendations generated in the previous chapter.

VIGNETTE BOX 11-5

TSI Selected Recommendation

ICT Recommendation (ICT Strategy)	Where is my organization today? (Related Processes)	Where do we want to be in 5 years? (Target/Goal/Objective and Measurement)	What will it take to get to our target? -Project Champion/Team
Handling a Customer Service Call: Computer telephony integration (CTI) to support call center; integration with the local phone system or virtual call center technology	This is not part of the ICT infrastructure. The initial infrastructure (IT and phone) should be built keeping this in mind.	A CTI system that fully integrates Genenco's application with the telephone system and will (1) reduce the average amount of time spent on each call, (2) reduce the average time customers spend on hold, and (3) increase customer satisfaction survey results.	A new telephone system, additional ICT resources -Managers from the call center, operations, and IT along with appropriate staff

This recommendation from the previous chapter's analysis assumes that the basic infrastructure is built at TSI, and TSI has "opened its doors." Many other recommendations can be made other than the one selected for this example.

correctness. An analyst who has completed these steps should be fairly certain that the BPMs are correct, and perhaps even have found places to redesign the process to bring about efficiencies.

We will assume that TSI is up and running. As-is versus to-be modeling will now be introduced. Put simply, **as-is process** modeling visualizes existing workflows, while **to-be process** modeling develops target business workflows to achieve the (optimal) stated goals of the process redesign. When creating as-is processes, do not fall into the trap of trying to solve workflow problems; instead, focus on how things are currently done. When you create the to-be process you can focus on process change. It is important that all stakeholders are consulted when creating both the as-is and to-be processes. Staff will tell the analyst how things currently work in the as-is process, and what will work in the new to-be process. Managers are apt to tell the analyst how things should work versus how they actually work. Care must be taken to ensure that both staff and managers do not create artificial roadblocks to process change or spend too much time on process exceptions that occur infrequently (e.g., the exception that happens once every five years, but just occurred last week so it is fresh in their minds).

Creating the to-be process is based on analyzing the as-is process. The business analyst will start with the as-is process and discuss recommendations based on careful analysis, gathering stakeholder input and developing project goals and objectives with management. Recommendations may include (1) processes left as-is, (2) processes changed to improve operational efficiency through automation or process redesign, (3) processes that are introduced (innovation), or scrapped and redesigned, or perhaps (4) outsourcing tasks to reduce costs/improve efficiencies. For TSI, a recommendation has been selected to show how to document as-is and to-be processes. The ICT strategy, goals, objectives, measurement, project team, and a gap analysis for those that recommendation are described in Vignette Box 11-5.

TSI's Process: Handling a Customer Service Call   Current "as-is" processes for handling a customer service call at TSI is diagrammed in Vignette Box 11-6 and consists of the following steps:

- **Incoming Call.** An incoming call is placed to TSI. The customer calls the toll-free phone number at TSI and gets a call tree asking the caller to select the correct option. The current call tree has the following options: 1 = resolve a credit card issue, 2 = resolve a ticketing issue, 3 = report a technical issue (i.e., down kiosk or website), and 0 = talk to the next available agent because none of the other options apply. A venue-only option "987" is not announced in the message. This option is shared with venue staff so they can be directed to someone who specifically deals with venue-related issues. A caller who knows the 5-digit extension of the person he or she is trying to reach can also dial that extension.

BEST PRACTICE 11-6

As-Is and To-Be Processes

An analyst who is reviewing existing processes should start by creating an "as-is" business process model. The as-is model should describe how the existing process works. It is best to talk to staff who actually perform the process being studied rather than just their managers. Managers will tell you how the process should work, while staff will tell you how the process actually works. Often the difference between staff and a manager's perceptions can give clues leading to process improvement. Once the as-is process is created, the analyst can analyze it, and create the "to-be" process. The to-be process should show the more efficient idealized process. This to-be process should be reviewed by staff and managers to ensure that all stakeholders have input into the new process.

- **Caller Selection.** Based on the caller's selection:
  - 0 = the caller is transferred to the operator who ascertains who the person wants to talk to and routes them to the right person.
  - 1 = the caller is transferred to a customer service representative who handles credit card issues by
    - Requesting customer phone number in order to pull up the customer history and obtain records
    - Contacting the credit card company as necessary
    - Finalizing the call
  - 2 = the caller is transferred to a customer service representative who handles ticketing issues (e.g., kiosk or website printed the wrong ticket/venue/date/time, ticket did not print, etc.), by
    - Requesting customer phone number in order to pull up the customer history and obtain records
    - Processing the ticket issue
    - Finalizing the call
  - 3 = the caller is transferred to Genenco, an external company, who then determines the call type and then either
    - Resolves the issue with the TSI website maintained by Genenco
    - Handles the issue with a kiosk maintained by Genenco
  - 987 = the caller is transferred to a special Venue Team at TSI that handles calls from venues. This extension is not announced to callers, but is given to venues so they can get priority service. The Venue Team will ascertain the transaction type (e.g., issue with seats listed in TSI's database, additional seats available for inclusion in TSI's database, an accounting/billing error, etc.). The Venue Team will process the call accordingly.
  - A caller who enters an extension (5 digits) will be transferred to that person.
- **Call Finalized.** A call is finalized when the incoming call is transferred to TSI customer service or the Venue Team. In the process the customer/venue is asked to complete a short survey about his or her experience during this call. Results from the survey allow customer service and the Venue Team at TSI to improve their call efficiency. Any call transferred outside of TSI (i.e., to Genenco) will not utilize the Call Finalized process because those calls are under the control of the outside vendor.
- **Genenco Calls.** When a call is transferred to Genenco, the call type is determined by asking the customer to press "1" to report an issue with TSI's website, or press "2" to report an issue with a kiosk. The call is then transferred to the right staff member at Genenco to handle the issue through the internal processes at Genenco.
- **Credit Card Company Calls.** When a customer service representative feels it is necessary, he or she will call a credit card company while the customer is on the phone in order to facilitate resolving credit card issues. The credit card company will receive the credit card info and, through its internal processes, it will correct the credit card issue.

A few notable differences are found in the BPM in Vignette Box 11-6. Three new symbols have been introduced:

(1) the event driven gateway ⬧, (2) the task with subprocesses, [Process +], and (3) the intermediate event ●. The event driven gateway indicates that an external event (i.e., a customer presses a specific phone key) causes the process to branch. The plus sign at the bottom of the task/process indicates that a complex subprocess exists beneath the process in the diagram—there may be subsidiary BPMs that describe the complex subprocess. These symbols are not new, but rather extensions of the gateway and task symbols previously introduced. These extensions are called **types**. The intermediate event symbol (an extension of the start/stop events) indicates something occurs in the process that is not a specific task but rather an event, like a call transferring. This diagram is from TSI's perspective. The internal processes to TSI are extensively diagrammed, while the external processes of Genenco and the credit card company are shown at a high level and are on this BPM for clarity from the perspective of TSI. Analysts will probably not know as much

Chapter 11 • Designing ICT: Documenting Process and Technology Recommendations 333

VIGNETTE BOX 11-6

TSI As-Is Customer Service Process BPM

[Business process model diagram showing swim lanes for Incoming Call, TSI (Customer Service and Venue Team), Genenco, and Credit Card Company. The Incoming Call lane shows: Initiate Call to TSI Customer Service → Phone Menu Tree - Select Option → Give Requested Information, with Customer Data flowing to Request Customer Details. The Customer Service lane shows: Operator Selects Option, Capture Select Option in Telephone System, Operator Requests Where to Transfer, Phone Option? gateway branching to "1" (Request Customer Details → Obtain Records → Credit Card Issue → Contact Credit Card Company → Call Finalized) and "2" (Request Customer Details → Obtain Records → Ticket Issue → Call Finalized), with "3" Transfer Call to Genenco and "987" Transfer to Venue Team, Extension Transfer. The Venue Team lane shows: Receive Venue Call → Call Type? gateway branching to Seat (Process Seat Transaction) and Accounting (Process Accounting Transaction) → Call Finalized. The Genenco lane shows: Determine Call Type → Technical Call Type? gateway branching to "1" (Web Issue) and "2" (Kiosk Issue). The Credit Card Company lane shows: Receive Credit Card Info → Correct Credit Card Issue.]

This business process model (BPM) shows the as-is customer service process at TSI.

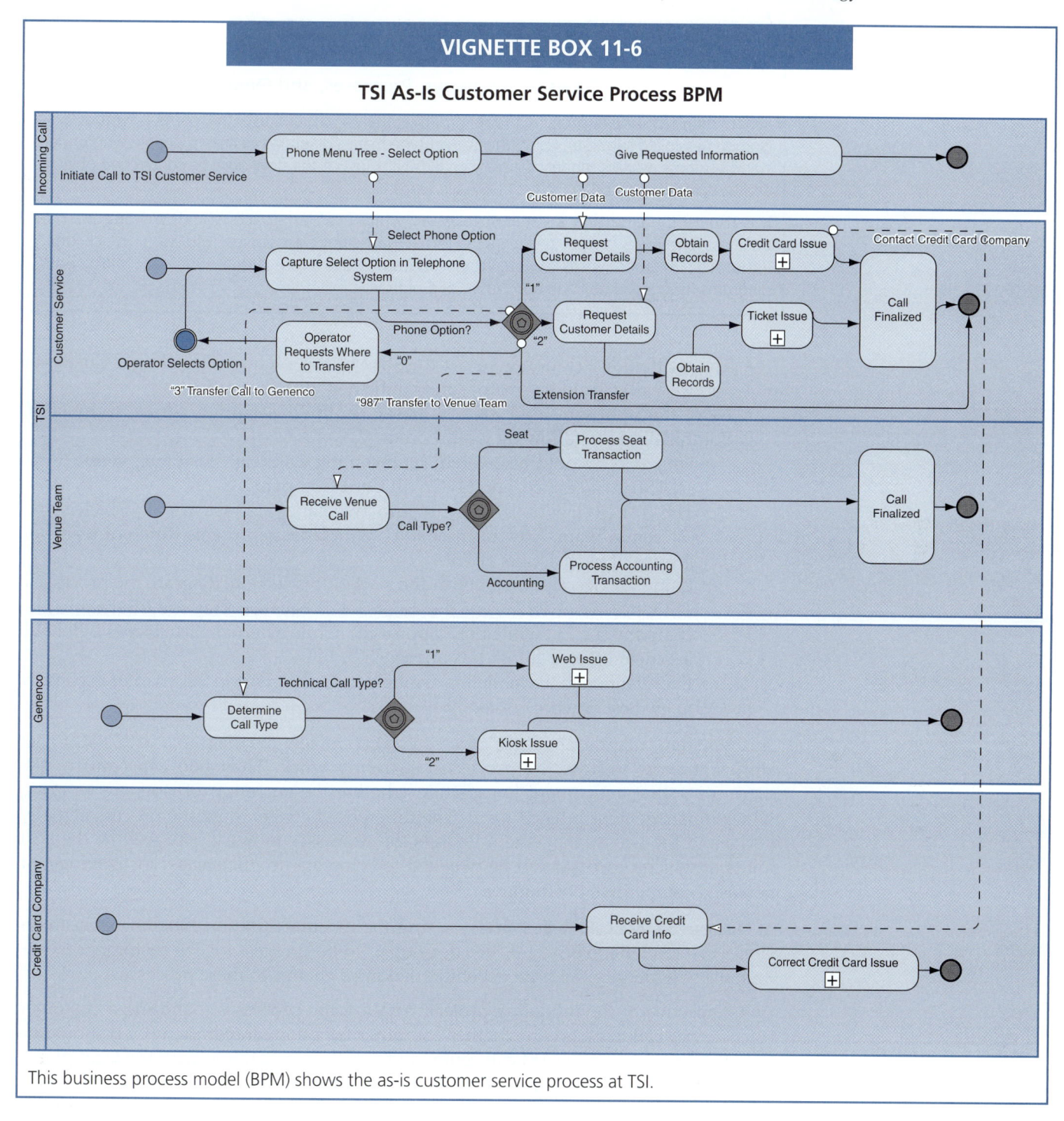

about the external participants as they do about their own company. This "white box" approach to TSI means greater detail, while the "black box" approach to external participants means less detail for their processes. Note, TSI has a pool with two lanes—(1) customer service, and (2) venue team—the other participants are in their own pools.

TSI Customer Service Call: As-Is Process Creating the customer service BPM for TSI can be broken down to the following steps:

- The analyst interviews the staff at TSI, Genenco, and perhaps the credit card company. Interviews at TSI would yield the greatest detail because it is the company that employs the analyst. Genenco would yield the next greatest detail as a subcontractor to TSI. Credit card companies would probably yield the least amount of detail because they are most external to TSI.

> **BEST PRACTICE 11-7**
>
> **Types of Gateways, Processes, and Events**
>
> When doing business process modeling, the analyst should use the correct symbol type (sometimes called subtype). Using the correct type makes diagrams clearer to people who understand business process modeling notation (BPMN). Most of the flow objects, connecting objects, and artifacts introduced in Figure 11-6 have types.
>
> It is usually the case that an analyst takes a "white box" approach when modeling internal business processes, while modeling external participant processes follows a "black box" approach. In other words "white box" diagrams have more detail, whereas "black box" diagrams have less detail and are shown at a high level.

- The written description given at the start of this section (Handling a Customer Service Call) would be created, and confirmed with the staff.
- Next, the BPM would be created based on the description agreed to by staff. For this BPM the following would occur:
    - Four pools would be created: (1) Incoming Call (e.g., customer. venue, etc.), (2) TSI, (3) Genenco, and (4) Credit Card Company.
    - The TSI pool would be split into two lanes: (1) Customer Service and (2) Venue Team. Each of these two swim lanes represents different teams or groups of participants at TSI.
    - Using the description given at the start of this section, diagram the processes. TSI's processes will have the most detail because they are internal to the company (i.e., a "white box" approach), while external participants will have less detail (i.e., a "black box approach").
    - Pay attention to the modeling symbols and rules given in this chapter, especially to the Best Practice boxes.

Once you have diagrammed this process you can review the diagrams with staff to get confirmation as to how the processes currently work. Then you can confirm the diagrams with management to ascertain whether the current processes are working the way management intends them. The difference between how the process actually works and the way management intends the processes to work may well be the best points at which processes can be tweaked to bring about efficiencies, cost savings, or increased competitive positioning.

TSI Customer Service Call: To-Be Process Using the recommendation *Handling a Customer Service Call* in Vignette Box 11-5, let's develop a "to-be" process for TSI customer service. First, we will identify the drivers behind making a change to these processes:

- Objective of the modeling project. Analyze the process of handling a customer service call to ascertain whether computer telephony integration (CTI) should be used to support the TSI call center and whether integration with the local phone system or virtual call center technology is appropriate.
- Measurable objectives and goals must be set. The objectives might be to use a CTI system that fully integrates Genenco's application with the TSI telephone system in order to (1) reduce the average amount of time spent on each call, (2) reduce the average time customers spend on hold, and (3) increase customer satisfaction survey results. Measurement tools need to be created, baseline data need to be collected and goals need to be set for these objectives before any change initiative is undertaken in order to evaluate the impact of any implemented change.
- Strategies to meet goals. Two candidates are to move TSI from where it is today to (1) an integrated solution using CTI on site at TSI, or (2) to a virtual call center technology.
- Related business processes. The participants in the processes are (1) the customer, (2) TSI staff (venue team and customer service), (3) Genenco staff, and

> ### BEST PRACTICE 11-8
>
> **As-Is BPM Best Practices**
>
> - Separate pools are used for all organizations.
> - Where specific participants within the organization need to be indicated, the pools are broken into separate swim lanes.
> - Process diagrams can occur with a pool or within a swim lane, but sequence flows cannot cross pools or swim lanes.
> - Sequence flows should be used within pools/swim lanes to indicate how a process flows, whereas message flows should be used between pools/swim lanes.
> - Pools should be separated by space in the diagram for clarity (see separation between Incoming Call, TSI, Genenco, and Credit Card Company in Vignette Box 11-6).
> - Each pool/swim lane should have its own start and stop event.
> - Use just one start and one stop event per pool/swim lane where possible, unless using multiple events makes the process clearer.
> - Symbols should use the correct type.
> - Subprocesses should be used to indicate and document complex tasks.
> - Align symbols and text for maximum clarity.
> - Gateway symbols should have a brief question indicating the purpose of the gateway (e.g., *Phone Option?* or *Call Type?*).
> - Do not allow sequence flows and message flows to cross unrelated symbols unless it's impossible to prevent or in some way makes the process flow clearer.

(4) credit card company staff. Each of these participants has its own business processes that must be articulated in some way in relation to TSI's business processes.
- Needed project champions. Managers and staff from the call center, operations, and IT must be identified as they are essential to the success of any change process.

The analyst needs to identify places where the as-is process can be improved while keeping in mind the goals of the process change initiative and associated strategies articulated above. After thorough analysis, TSI may decide to change its customer service processes. Changing those processes and implementing the CTI solution are the substance of the to-be business process diagrams discussed next.

During the analysis of the as-is process, the business analyst must meet with staff and managers to determine where changes might be made. Using the mission and objectives already articulated and knowledge of the domain (in this example it is customer service at TSI) as well as his or her analytical skills, the analyst must come up with a number of recommendations. They must also keep in mind the strategies agreed to by stakeholders. Once recommendations are prepared, they must be vetted with the staff and managers. At this point it is a good idea to have identified champions who will work with the analyst to ensure that the recommendations are given a proper airing with managers and staff. Many projects fail because these champions are not identified early enough or the changes are not thoroughly vetted. This part of creating the to-be process is perhaps the most time-consuming part, but once done, recommendations can be made.

After thorough analysis and verification with all stakeholders for TSI, the following recommendations might be made:

- All customer service and Venue Team members should be cross-trained to handle any call type that comes in to TSI.
- As recommended in Vignette Box 11-5, a CTI solution should be implemented. This system should allow customers and venues to register phone numbers that will automatically be transferred to the appropriate team (customer service or venue team). The system should automatically pull up customer and venue records based on the incoming phone number.

- The TSI ICT infrastructure should allow customers and venues to register their phone number. A call coming from a registered phone number should automatically be transferred to the appropriate team rather than routing through the initial menu when customers call TSI. The initial call menu will also recognize the "hidden 987" number to transfer to the Venue Team.
- Genenco processes will not be changed because they are external to TSI, and Genenco has opted to keep its existing processes.
- The credit card company will no longer appear as part of the business process model because TSI's customer service representatives will no longer call credit card companies on behalf of customers. Rather, customers will be told to call their credit card company directly when credit card issues are identified.

Implementing these changes will result in the simplified process model that can be seen in Vignette Box 11-7. The to-be process can be described as:

- **Incoming Call.** An incoming call is placed to TSI. The customer calls the toll-free phone number at TSI and gets either (1) transferred automatically because their phone number is registered or (2) a call tree asking the caller to select the correct option. The recommended modified call tree has the following options: 1 = speak to a customer service representative, 2 = report a technical issue (i.e., down kiosk or website), and 0 = talk to the next available person because neither other option applies. A venue-only option "987" is not announced in the message. This option is shared with venue staff so they can be directed to someone who specializes in venue-related issues. A caller who knows the 5-digit extension of the person he or she is trying to reach can also dial that extension.
- **Caller Selection.** Based on the caller's selection:
  - 0 = the caller is transferred to the operator, who ascertains who the person wants to talk to and routes them to the right person.
  - 1 or a "registered customer phone number" = the caller is transferred to a customer service representative who is trained to handle all types of calls:
    - The customer phone number is used to pull up the customer records. If the phone number is not in TSI records, the customer service representative pulls up the customer records by name or credit card number.
    - Call is finalized.
    - If a credit card issue is identified during the call, the customer service representative requests that the customer contact the credit card company directly.
  - 2 = the caller is transferred to Genenco, an external company, who then determines the call type and then either
    - Resolves the issue with the TSI website maintained by Genenco
    - Handles the issue with a kiosk maintained by Genenco
  - **Venue Call.** A venue-registered phone number or entering "987" causes the call to be transferred to a customer service team member who specializes in venue issues. The "987" extension is not announced to callers, but is given to the venues so they can get priority service. The customer service team member will ascertain the transaction type (e.g., issue with seats listed in TSI's database, additional seats available for inclusion in TSI's database, an accounting/billing error, etc.). The call will be processed accordingly.
  - A caller who enters an extension (5 digits) will be transferred to that person.
- **Call Finalized.** A call is finalized when the TSI customer service team member has completed an incoming call. In the process the customer/venue is asked to complete a short survey about his or her experience during the call. Results from the survey allow customer service team at TSI to improve their call efficiency. Any call transferred outside of TSI (i.e., to Genenco) will not utilize the Call Finalized process because those calls are under the control of the outside vendor.
- **Genenco Calls.** When a call is transferred to Genenco, the call type is determined by Genenco by asking the customer to press "1" to report an issue with TSI's website, or "2" to report an issue with a kiosk. The call is then transferred to the correct staff member at Genenco to handle the issue through the internal processes at Genenco.

Chapter 11 • Designing ICT: Documenting Process and Technology Recommendations   337

VIGNETTE BOX 11-7
TSI Customer Service To-Be BPM

[BPM diagram showing swim lanes for Incoming Call, TSI (Customer Service and Customer Service Venue Process), and Genenco, with tasks including Phone Menu Tree - Select Option, Give Requested Information, Capture Select Option in Telephone System, Operator Requests Where to Transfer, Pull Up Customer Data, Process CS Issue, Call Finalized, Pull Up Venue Records, Handle Venue Issue, Determine Call Type, Web Issue, Kiosk Issue.]

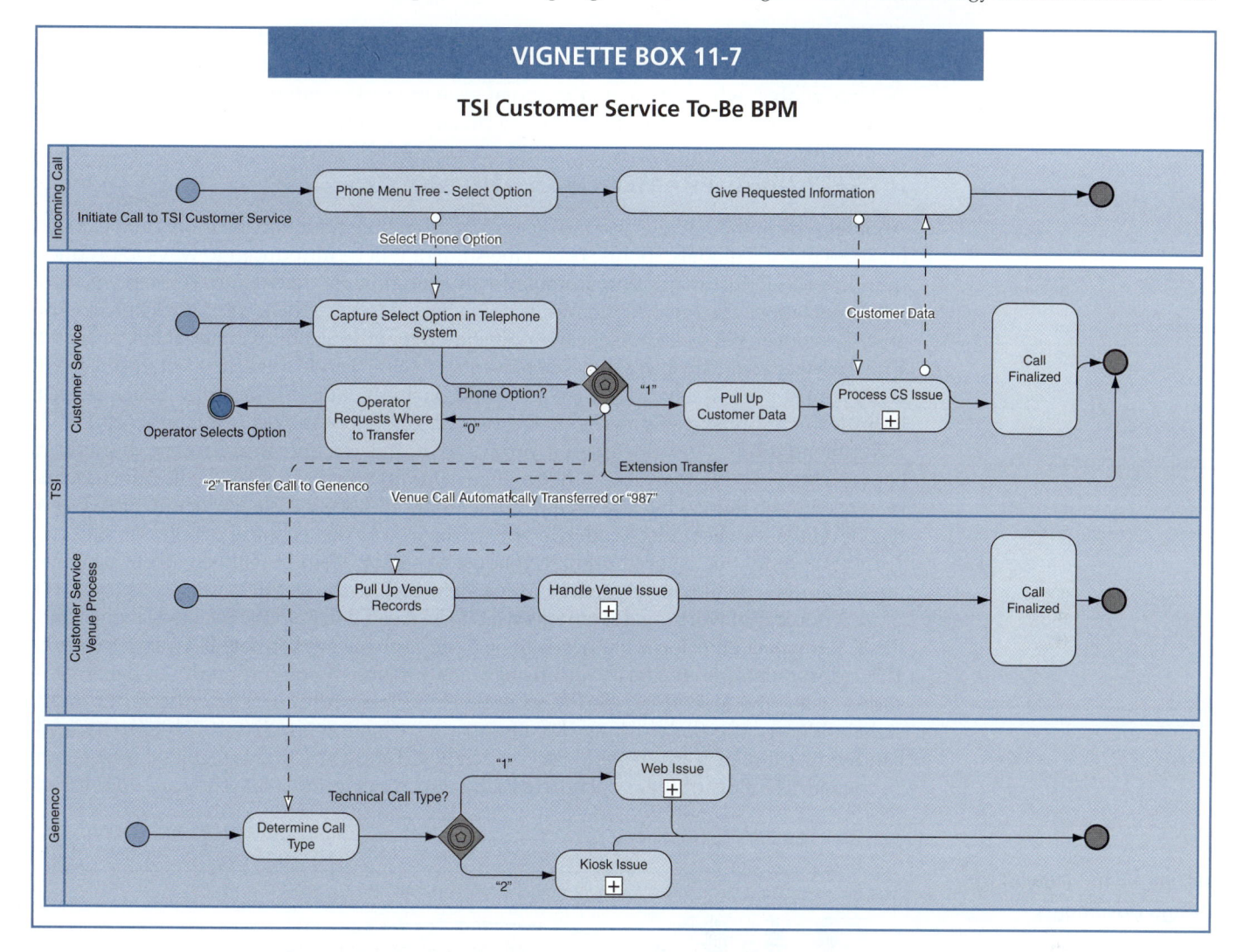

SUBPROCESSES

The BPM in Vignette Box 11-7 has several processes that include extensive and sometimes complicated subprocesses, which are indicated by the task symbol with a plus sign at the bottom [Process +]. A separate process diagram for each task with subprocesses should be created. These subprocesses are documented in their own BPM using the same notation as higher-level processes, but "exploded" out into their more atomic parts. If you were creating models for the customer service processes at TSI, you would create subprocess models for all tasks that have subprocesses.

Systems Analysis and the Use of Data Flow Diagrams

When creating BPMs the business system analyst has the specific task of creating high-level diagrams that can be handed over to all stakeholders, including the systems analyst. Business process models are meant to be "human friendly" graphical representations of business processes that also take into account the manual and automated processes. They are not meant to exactly represent how these processes are turned into information systems, but instead provide sufficient documentation to enable the systems analyst to use the BPMs, gather additional input from users, and create information systems, perhaps using UML. BPMs are not meant to replace or supplant the work of the system analyst, but rather to complement the work of the system analyst with a commonly understood set of notation (i.e., business process modeling notation). Data flow diagrams, use case diagrams, and UML are the purview of the system analyst, whereas business process modeling is the purview of the business analyst. Once the business analyst confers with staff and managers, creates process models, and thoroughly documents those models, the business analyst is then ready to hand off that documentation to the systems analyst who can create the actual system implementation models. The system analyst will prepare the documentation necessary for software creation/implementation.

ICT TECHNICAL FRAMEWORKS AND MODELS

Another type of modeling is used to create is ICT documentation that support and explain business process models. In this section the student will be introduced to ways to produce high level-ICT documentation suitable for ICT engineers' discussion, refinement, and implementation. The business analyst is not expected to have the technical background of an ICT engineer, but must possess an understanding of the technical material in Unit 1 and Unit 2, as well as the business material presented in Unit 3 and Unit 4. In short the business analyst must possess a hybrid of technical and business skills. This chapter which started by introducing business process modeling concepts now moves to documenting ICT recommendations. The documents produced in this section must foster discussion between the business analyst and the engineer. During that discussion, the ICT documents may need to be refined but the final documents should be suitable to document ICT at a high level that can be understood by engineers as well as nontechnical people. We will use TSI to exemplify this diagramming technique. Microsoft Visio ™ will be used to produce these diagrams. Again, Best Practice boxes will be included.

A number of **working documents** need to be created to help the business analyst and the ICT engineer envision what needs to be done to create appropriate ICT infrastructure. These documents are created by the business analyst who thoroughly analyzed the organization using the tools described in previous chapters and must have the input of all stakeholders. Once the working documents (i.e., functionality list, ICT hierarchy, and bandwidth estimates) are created, then the actual ICT infrastructure design documents can be created. The flow of these documents can be seen in Figure 11-10. They are interlinked

FIGURE 11-10 Flow of ICT Design Documents

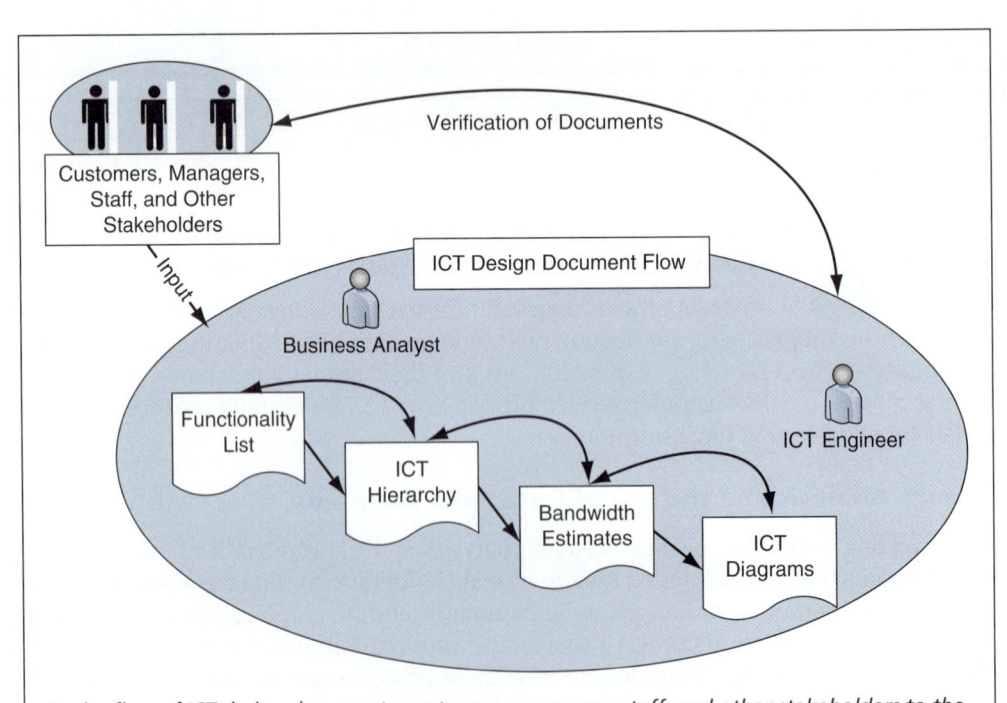

In the flow of ICT design documents, customers, managers, staff, and other stakeholders to the ICT design must have input to the design process. Once all input is gathered, the business analyst and ICT engineer work together to create the functionality list, ICT hierarchy, bandwidth estimates, and the final ICT diagrams. The content and substantial interaction between these documents will be used by the analyst to create these documents and the engineer to create the actual infrastructure.

Component	Functionality	ICT List
Network Components	Network Infrastructure Hardware (think Layers 1 and 2 from Unit 1)	
	Network Operating Platform(s)	
	Internet Connectivity	
Service Components		
User Components	Desktop Hardware	
	Desktop Software	
Enterprise-Wide Components		

Enter required information in shaded areas

FIGURE 11-11 ICT Recommendations by Component

with a good bit of "back and forth" between them occurring before the business analyst is ready to create the final ICT diagrams. All of the working documents and the final ICT diagram, when taken together, should make a complete set of documents the ICT engineer can use to create the technical specifications necessary to deploy the ICT infrastructure. The business analyst and the engineer both need to ensure the documents are correct.

Functionality List

The first step in creating high-level network diagrams is to create a list of functionalities that are required to support the organization's mission and objectives, and any process change recommendations and objectives. This list is often compiled by interviewing users and managers, as well as incorporating the recommendations made by the business analyst. Such a list must reflect the business needs of the organization, consider how the infrastructure will affect the competitive position of the organization, and incorporate the business analyst's recommendations. A **functionality list** will also provide the basis for creating all design documents. The list can be broken down into the various components discussed throughout this textbook: network components, service components, user components, and enterprise-wide components, shown in Figure 11-11. This figure already contains some of the standard components used in building an initial ICT infrastructure. It should be modified to include what is currently in place in the organization, and how the ICT infrastructure would be changed/updated. The column *ICT List* would be completed with recommendations to support ICT functionality. Think of Figure 11-11 as a list of notes to be used during the creation of high-level network documentation. These notes should be expanded to include the entire infrastructure necessary to support the recommendations.

In Figure 11-11 several components already show functionality items. These functionalities are included because they are fairly common, but should be removed or edited as required by the infrastructure. Other functionalities must be added to accomplish the goals for building the ICT infrastructure. The functionalities already listed include:

- **Network Components**
  - **Network Infrastructure.** Decisions must be made about the hardware (Layer 1 and Layer 2 from the hybrid TCP-IP/OSI model) infrastructure. As indicated earlier in this text, we will focus on Ethernet and TCP-IP. However, the business analyst must know about other technologies (e.g., Token Ring) and modify the functionality list as needed to reflect the other technologies already in place or to be installed in the organization.
  - **Network Operating Platform(s).** A number of platforms may be appropriate, including Microsoft, open source, Unix, and Sun, among others. The operating platform can be from a single vendor, or a combination, largely based on the scope, scale, and goals of the ICT implementation.
  - **Internet Connectivity.** Internet connectivity will ordinarily be purchased from an Internet service provider (ISP). Necessary bandwidth, redundancy, and Service Level Agreements are but a few considerations when selecting an ISP.
- **Service Components.** No functionalities are listed for this component; however, most ICT infrastructure will normally have at least one server and/or service component.
- **User Components.** At least two functionalities are normally seen in user components:
  - Desktop Hardware
  - Desktop Software
- **Enterprise-Wide Components.** Again, no functionalities are listed for this component. Small organizations may not have any enterprise-wide components, but larger organizations will probably have them. It depends on the size/scope and type of organization, its process flow, and how the organization operates.

Using the opening vignette for this unit we will complete a sample list of ICT recommendations for TSI and incorporate the recommendation for a CTI solution from Vignette Box 11-5. This list can be seen in Vignette Box 11-8. Note, the functionality and ICT lists will be dramatically different based on the recommendations included—for example, if a cloud-based solution is used for the marketing department the list will change greatly.

The information in the ICT recommendation list will be used for two purposes. First, it will be used in discussions with the ICT engineer. These discussions should happen early so the engineer can have input into the high-level design documents that will be created. Having the engineer give input early in the process can prevent costly ICT infrastructure changes later during the implementation phase. In fact, consultation with the engineer should occur throughout the creation of the ICT recommendation list, ICT hierarchy, bandwidth estimates, and the final high-level design documents. For example, this consultation might be important if an engineer recommends that TSI look at virtualization solutions to reduce the number of physical servers in TSI's data center, rather than use typical desktop workstations.

ICT Hierarchy

When implementing ICT infrastructure, it is helpful to visualize the network as a hierarchy. In doing so, the business analyst (and later the engineer) can spot places where additional hardware/software or other components will be needed. The **ICT hierarchy** shows the network core, the backbone (vertical runs), as well as the cabling to the desktop (horizontal runs). It may look similar to an organization chart, but it lays out cable runs and interconnectivity rather than an organizational hierarchy. The ICT hierarchy is composed of one symbol type and its interconnections, as shown in Figure 11-12. This symbol set is simple and meant to diagram ICT at a high level. The ICT hierarchy should help the analyst and engineer identify the areas of greatest bandwidth need. An example of an ICT hierarchy can be seen in Vignette Box 11-9.

Description	Symbol
Major ICT elements are represented by a rectangle. These symbols are used to show major groupings of ICT. The color of the symbol indicates the different types of ICT. The description should be short and explain the ICT grouping.	Description
Interconnections are lines of various thicknesses and colors used to represent ICT connections between groupings of major ICT elements. Their color indicates type and speed of interconnection (i.e., each different type like fiber optic or UTP, and each different speed like 10 Mbps or 1 Gbps should be a different color).	

FIGURE 11-12 ICT Hierarchy Symbols

VIGNETTE BOX 11-8

TSI ICT Recommendation List

Component	Functionality	ICT and Notes
Network Components	Network Infrastructure Hardware (Layers 1 and 2 from Unit 1)	1) 10-gigabit Ethernet will be used for the backbone (all vertical runs) using fiber optics 2) Gigabit Ethernet will be used to Desktop (all horizontal runs), using UTP
	Network Operating Platform(s)	1) Microsoft Windows-based server and desktop solutions will be used (because it is supported by Genenco)
	Internet Connectivity	1) A T1 or T3 ISP must be selected (probably a T3 line to give maximum speed to all kiosks) 2) Redundant Internet connectivity should be considered 3) Connectivity for all kiosks must be determined
	Web Servers	1) Will run Genenco Web services. 2) Must support MS-IIS and .net
	Firewall	1) Robust enough to protect the TSI network 2) Allow for managers to obtain individual and department-level usage tracking data for all network users 3) Must also track and provide utilization reporting for all kiosks
	Required Genenco Servers Configured as: 1. Application 2. MS-Commerce 3. MS-SQL 4. MS-Exchange	1) Four servers, each rack mounted, and with the following specifications as required by Genenco. (See unit opening vignette for details)
	SAN	1) A highly redundant 5 TB SAN for data storage
	Uninterruptable Power Supply (UPS)	1) UPS for all network hardware and servers

(Continued)

Vignette Box 11-8 (Continued)

Component	Functionality	ICT and Notes
Service Components	VPN access	1) Needs to be able to handle all kiosks connecting through VPN as well as other users connecting to access office network (e.g., when at home or on the road)

	Backup	1) A backup device is needed that will provide nightly backup for:
		  a. SAN
		  b. All servers
		  c. All executives' PCs
		  d. All managers' PCs
		  e. All secretaries' PCs

	E-Mail	1) Support for about 200 concurrent e-mail addresses, offsite web-based e-mail portal 2) Microsoft Exchange Server and Outlook recommendation requires an additional server for support
	Print Services	1) A print server robust enough to handle 100-plus users and print queues for all Document Centers needed
	File Services	1) Transaction-based data will be stored in the Genenco application and associated database 2) File services must provide file-shares so staff and managers can store/copies files remotely
User Components	Desktop Hardware	1) As specified by Genenco.

	Desktop Software	1) As recommended by Genenco:
		  a. Current version of MS-Windows Desktop Operating System and MS-Office Professional Suite
		  b. Genenco GenServe desktop application, installed by Genenco
		  c. Virus and spyware protection
		2) *Genenco Desktop Software must be updated to include CTI integration—need to see that this is completed*

	Printing	1) Floors 2, 3, 4, and 5 will each have a Document Center Digital Copier (leased directly from vendor), with *network connectivity provided for each*; all staff will use these as shared printers 2) Executives on the first floor, every manager, and secretary are to have their own local laser printer 3) The marketing department requires a shared high-speed color printer capable of printing on 11x17 paper

Component	Functionality	ICT and Notes
Enterprise-Wide Components	Ticket Sales—via Kiosk	1) VPN—see page 342
	Ticket Sales—via Web	1) Genenco will provide—see page 342 for hardware
	Desktop Components—to support ticket sales and the organization overall	1) Genenco will provide—see page 342 for hardware
	Server Software—to support ticket sales and the organization's core business	1) Genenco will provide—see page 342 for hardware

BEST PRACTICE 11-9

ICT Functionality List

When creating an ICT functionality list, there are some general rules to follow:

1) Customers, users, staff, managers, and other stakeholders should be involved in the process of creating the ICT functionality list.
2) The engineer (in a small organization this person might be the business analyst) must be involved in creating the ICT functionality list so hardware, software, and implementation are considered.
3) The ICT functionality list given in Figure 11-11 contains a number of things normally found in the ICT infrastructure. The business analyst must add other functionalities needed by his or her organization.
4) The ICT framework introduced in this textbook provides a convenient way to segregate ICT recommendations. In some cases, like TSI's enterprise-wide software in Vignette Box 11-8, components will overlap. When that happens, the functionality list should cross-reference itself.
5) When completing the ICT and Notes column, indicate the functionality as specifically as possible so the ICT engineer can provide the best solution. Where certain hardware/software is predetermined, list it exactly as required.

BEST PRACTICE 11-10

ICT Hierarchy Best Practices

Network hierarchies are useful to envision the network in a simple block diagram. The diagram provides a good starting point for the business analyst and the engineer to envision all of the network/ICT-connected components, infrastructure needs, bandwidth bottlenecks, and other infrastructure issues. This diagram is far from actual implementation but is useful in the process of designing ICT infrastructure. Some best practices for creating this diagram include the following:

1) All ICT and network-connected components should be shown in this diagram.
2) The goal is not to get too detailed, but rather to show the infrastructure on a one-page (if possible) graphic so designers can get a high-level view.
3) A title, symbol key, and interconnect key should be provided.
4) A date and signature block are needed to allow multiple hierarchies to be put in date order, making it easy to identify the most recent. Also, if the analyst who provided this hierarchy is identified, that person can be queried with any questions.
5) Any hierarchy provided by an external company should include the company's name and phone number.
6) Different speeds or types of interconnects that are used should be color coded.

VIGNETTE BOX 11-9

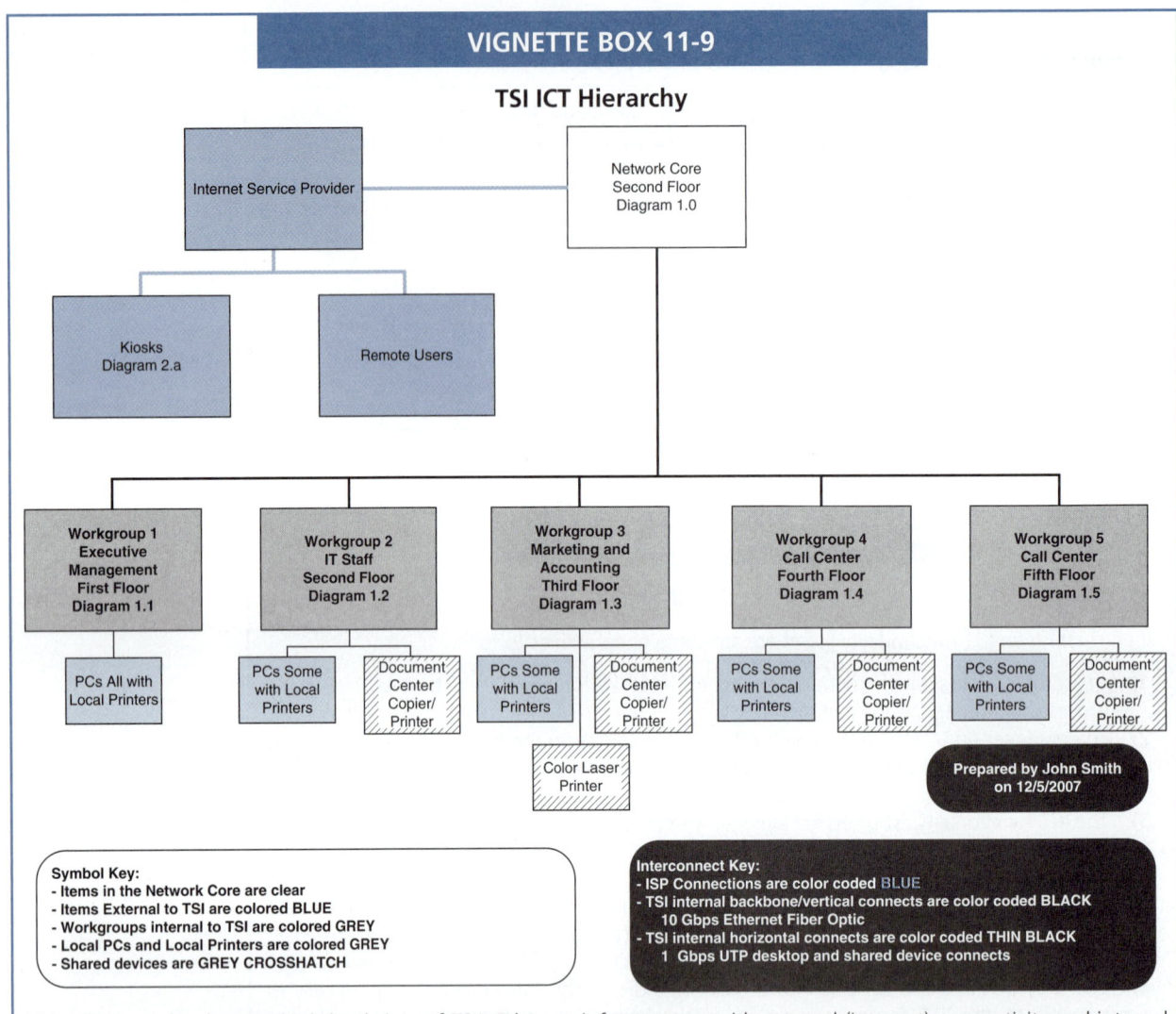

TSI ICT Hierarchy

```
                    Internet Service Provider ─── Network Core
                              │                   Second Floor
                              │                   Diagram 1.0
                    ┌─────────┴─────────┐
                  Kiosks            Remote Users
                Diagram 2.a
```

Workgroup 1 — Executive Management, First Floor, Diagram 1.1
  – PCs All with Local Printers

Workgroup 2 — IT Staff, Second Floor, Diagram 1.2
  – PCs Some with Local Printers
  – Document Center Copier/Printer

Workgroup 3 — Marketing and Accounting, Third Floor, Diagram 1.3
  – PCs Some with Local Printers
  – Document Center Copier/Printer
  – Color Laser Printer

Workgroup 4 — Call Center, Fourth Floor, Diagram 1.4
  – PCs Some with Local Printers
  – Document Center Copier/Printer

Workgroup 5 — Call Center, Fifth Floor, Diagram 1.5
  – PCs Some with Local Printers
  – Document Center Copier/Printer

Prepared by John Smith on 12/5/2007

Symbol Key:
- Items in the Network Core are clear
- Items External to TSI are colored BLUE
- Workgroups internal to TSI are colored GREY
- Local PCs and Local Printers are colored GREY
- Shared devices are GREY CROSSHATCH

Interconnect Key:
- ISP Connections are color coded BLUE
- TSI internal backbone/vertical connects are color coded BLACK
   10 Gbps Ethernet Fiber Optic
- TSI internal horizontal connects are color coded THIN BLACK
   1 Gbps UTP desktop and shared device connects

This ICT hierarchy shows a high-level view of TSI's Ethernet infrastructure with external (Internet) connectivity and internal devices. Such a diagram provides the business analyst and the ICT engineer a quick way to survey the infrastructure and understand its scale and scope.

Estimating Bandwidth Needs

Doing bandwidth calculations are probably out of the purview of most business analysts, but the subject is introduced here so the business analyst is familiar with how engineers might go about calculating "the need for speed." It is important to estimate bandwidth because overhead alone can potentially push utilization beyond capacity and lead to degradation in ICT infrastructure performance. This method for estimating bandwidth is given by Microsoft (Microsoft, 2009). The following assumptions are made for these estimations:

- The infrastructure is IP over Ethernet, which means packet switching.
- Each packet includes about 20 bytes of header and other protocol information (overhead).
- Packet size is not fixed, thus the ratio of data to overhead can vary.
- The protocol we will examine is HTTP, and a typical request (e.g., GET http://www.microsoft.com/default.asp) including TCP/IP headers consists of no more than a few hundred bytes.
- The server being requested displays HTML and the average page size is 5 KB (5,000 bytes or 40,000 bits), which is nearly equivalent to a full page of printed text.
- The server is connected to the Internet through a T1 line (1.54 Mbps).
- Because the file size being transmitted is so small (5 KB), the overhead is substantial (about 30%); for a large file, the overhead would be a smaller portion.

Chapter 11 • Designing ICT: Documenting Process and Technology Recommendations   **345**

Connection Type*	5 KB Pages per Second with Overhead
56 Kbps frame relay	About 1 page
128 Kbps ISDN	Just over 2 pages
640 Kbps DSL	About 11 pages
T1 (1.544 Mbps)	Just under 28 pages
T3 (44.736 Mbps)	About 808 pages
100 Mbps Ethernet (best case transmission 80 Mbps)	Approximately 1,440 pages
1 Gbps Ethernet (best case transmission 800 Mbps)	Approximately 14,400 pages

*Several transmission rates are used in this table: KB = kilobytes, Kb = kilobits, Mbps = megabits per second, and Gbps = gigabits per second. The pages per second have been updated from the Microsoft example to reflect corrections in the calculations. Also, the rate limiting factor (pages per second) is the slowest connection: if the sending side is the slowest side then it will limit the transmission rate, while if the receiving side is the slowest it will limit the reception rate.

FIGURE 11-13 5 KB Pages/Second over Various Connection Types

For a single http request from this server, the following ICT traffic would be generated:

- Initial TCP connection—approximately 180 bytes or 1,440 bits
- Client get request—approximately 256 bytes or 2,048 bits
- 5 KB file sent plus overhead—5,120 bytes or 40,960 bits
- Additional Protocol overhead—approximately 1,364 bytes or 10,912 bits

Approximately 6,920 bytes are sent for one page from the server in this example. To calculate the number of bits, multiply the number of bytes by 8 (remember there are 8 bits per byte) and you would get 55,360 bits. As stated previously, this server is connected to the Internet via a T1 line, giving a maximum throughput of 1.544 Mbps. If you divide the 1.544 Mbps available bandwidth by the 55.36 Kbps per page (1,544,000/55,360) you would find that the maximum transmission rate is just under 28 pages per second. Using this information, it is possible to estimate the number of 5 KB pages per second that can be sent over various types of transmission facilities. A sample of some of these transmission rates can be seen in Figure 11-13.

Several caveats apply to these bandwidth calculations. Specifically, the following should be considered:

- Adding a small graphic to a web page will change the page/second results. A small JPG file can easily be bigger than the 5 KB page, greatly increasing page size (think doubling or tripling the page size at a minimum) and reducing the per-page throughput by half or more.
- Most web pages are not static text, and include multimedia content. Therefore pages are likely to be much greater in size than our example 5 KB page.
- When estimating bandwidth, the overhead of ICT technologies like VPN, frame relay, and ATM must be taken into account. The bottom line is that there is no "free ride"—ICT technologies have overhead, and overhead must be estimated and considered in all calculations.
- In today's age of fast processors and large amounts of memory on servers, "A site that serves primarily static HTML pages, especially pages with a simple structure, is likely to run out of network bandwidth before it runs out of processing power. In contrast, a site that performs a lot of dynamic page generation, or that acts as a transaction or database server, uses more processor cycles and can create bottlenecks in its processor, memory, disk, or network." (Microsoft, 2007)
- It is the slowest connection that creates bottlenecks. Imagine a link from Client A to Server B that must traverse a T1 connection, a 1 Gbps Ethernet connection, and a 56 Kb connection. The 56 Kb connection will create the bottleneck and determine the fastest transmission rate available overall. A faster connection to a server may improve server performance, but a slow link to a client will degrade overall performance. This is an important consideration in customer satisfaction.
- In the absence of an SLA or using some form of packet shaping, the most common way to avoid data collisions with Ethernet is overprovisioning. In other words, because Ethernet is fairly inexpensive, substantially more bandwidth than is

> ### VIGNETTE BOX 11-10
>
> **Assumptions and Calculations for TSI Kiosk Traffic**
>
> | Line | Kiosk Expected Utilization Type → | LOW | MEDIUM | HIGH |
> |---|---|---|---|---|
> | 1 | Average Number of Tickets Per Transaction | 2.3 | 4.5 | 5.7 |
> | 2 | Base Transaction Octets | 150000 | 150000 | 150000 |
> | 3 | Octets per Ticket | 180000 | 180000 | 180000 |
> | 4 | Average Transactions per Primary Hour per Kiosk | 12 | 14 | 20 |
> | 5 | Average Estimated Transaction Size in Octets | 564000 | 960000 | 1176000 |
> | 6 | Average Bits/Hour | 54,144,000 | 107,520,000 | 188,160,000 |
> | 7 | Average bps | 15040.00 | 29866.67 | 52266.67 |
>
> Based on information from the opening vignette TSI's kiosks are categorized into three types (Low, Medium, and High utilization). In addition to assumptions from the opening vignette, these calculations are subject to a number of additional assumptions.

believed to be necessary should be provided. That way optimal performance is more likely to be achieved.
- Bandwidth estimates should be for peak load periods, in other words, during the time when the maximum amount of capacity is needed.

Using this technique to estimate bandwidth needs, it is possible to estimate TSI's need for bandwidth at the main office. The structure of the example given has been modified and supplemented to estimate bandwidth for TSI. The following assumptions are used in these calculations:

- These calculations only estimate kiosk traffic. Other traffic (e.g., website traffic) would have to be estimated based on marketing research not included in the opening vignette.
- The infrastructure is IP over Ethernet, which means packet switching.
- Each packet includes about 20 byes of header and other protocol information (overhead).
- Packet size is not fixed, thus the ratio of data to overhead can vary.
- The protocol used by the Genenco application is HTTP, and a typical request (e.g., GET http://www.aaa.com/default.asp) including TCP/IP headers consists of no more than a few hundred bytes.
- The goal is to calculate the maximum bandwidth necessary at the main office, which is expressed as maximum bandwidth during primary hours of kiosk operation. The data for these calculations come from the opening vignette. Additional assumptions for kiosk traffic are given.

The steps to calculating peak bandwidth by kiosk are as follows:

- Calculate the amount of traffic generated at a kiosk. The kiosks are grouped into three types: low, medium, and high utilization. These utilization types represent the maximum utilization during peak hours.
- Calculate the average bits per second (bps) during peak hours.
- Group the kiosks by location and type, then by primary utilization hours (see the unit opening vignette for details).
- Add network traffic within hours and determine maximum (highest) point of utilization.
- Add appropriate overhead factors.
- Determine the type of connection necessary to support the maximum point of utilization.

Let's examine each step in the spreadsheet in Vignette Box 11-10, the following is shown:

- **Line 1:** The average number of tickets per customer transaction during peak hours
- **Line 2:** The base number of octets per transaction, including all overhead—gets, puts, and other data
- **Line 3:** The number of octets per ticket purchased, or actual data transmitted between kiosk and the home office for each ticket purchased
- **Line 4:** The average number of transactions expected per primary hour
- **Line 5:** Average estimated transaction size in octets, computed as follows:

    (Base octets Line 2 + (# tickets Line 1 * Octets per ticket Line 3))

- **Line 6:** Average Number of bits per hour, computed as follows:

    Estimated Transaction Size in Octets (Line 5) × Average Transactions per Hour (Line 4) × Number of Bits/Octet (8)

- **Line 7:** Average bits per second (bps), computed by dividing average number of bits per hour (Line 6) by 3,600 (seconds/hour)

At this point the peak average bps for each type of kiosk is known. This information can then be used to calculate the overall bandwidth needs for TSI's data center. For our example, only the Manhattan kiosks will be used to keep this spreadsheet simple. To calculate total bandwidth requirements, the kiosks need to be broken down by time period of highest utilization, which can be accomplished by using more columns in the spreadsheet, or adding values together. The point is to make the hour time slots as accurate as possible. This spreadsheet can be expanded to include all types of kiosks in all locations. Vignette Box 11-11 shows the results of these calculations and includes the location in the heading of the column, the kiosk type in Line 1, and the time period of peak utilization in Lines 4 through 27. The data for this table come from the opening vignette and the calculations in Vignette Box 11-10. The columns shaded in blue are filled in as follows:

- **Line 1:** The kiosk utilization type (Low, Medium, High)
- **Line 2:** The number of kiosks for that location
- **Line 3:** The bps for that kiosk utilization type as calculated in Vignette Box 11-10, multiplied by Line 2.
- **Lines 4 through 27:** The time period for the location specified in the header and the utilization type. This number is copied or referenced from Line 3.

The column titled MO TOTAL refer to the TSI main office bandwidth needs and are calculated as follows:

- **Line 1:** Not used for the main office
- **Line 2:** Add together the shaded blue column Line 2 data
- **Line 3:** Not used for the main office
- **Lines 4 through 27:** Add together the line data for the two Manhattan kiosks (blue columns)
- **Line 28:** The highest point of utilization of all hourly (Lines 4 through 47) totals, divided by 1,000 to turn into Kbps
- **Line 29:** The estimated factor used to account for VPN overhead, which depends on the VPN type
- **Line 30:** The estimated overprovisioning factor to be used in the absence of an SLA
- **Line 31:** The maximum traffic, calculated by multiplying Line 28 by Line 29, then multiplying that result by Line 30

It is possible to break down these calculations by location, kiosk type, and number of kiosks at the location, which allows the analyst and engineer to estimate the bandwidth necessary at each location. (See Vignette Box 11-12.)

PERFORMANCE AND COST CONSIDERATIONS

The performance goals of ICT infrastructure must be considered when estimating bandwidth. In the preceding Microsoft example it was easy to estimate the number of 5 KB pages per minute that were acceptable. The calculations are approached

VIGNETTE BOX 11-11

Calculating Total Bandwidth Needs of TSI (an excerpt using Manhattan)

Line	MO = Main Office →	MO TOTAL	Manhattan High	Manhattan Medium
1	Utilization			
2	# of Kiosks	45	30	15
3	bps for all kiosks		1568000.00	448000.00
4	Midnight			
5	1:00 a.m.			
6	2:00 a.m.			
7	3:00 a.m.			
8	4:00 a.m.			
9	5:00 a.m.	448000		448000.00
10	6:00 a.m.	2016000	1568000.00	448000.00
11	7:00 a.m.	2016000	1568000.00	448000.00
12	8:00 a.m.	2016000	1568000.00	448000.00
13	9:00 a.m.	2016000	1568000.00	448000.00
14	10:00 a.m.	1568000	1568000.00	
15	11:00 a.m.	1568000	1568000.00	
16	Noon	1568000	1568000.00	
17	1:00 p.m.	1568000	1568000.00	
18	2:00 p.m.	1568000	1568000.00	
19	3:00 p.m.	1568000	1568000.00	
20	4:00 p.m.	2016000	1568000.00	448000.00
21	5:00 p.m.	2016000	1568000.00	448000.00
22	6:00 p.m.	2016000	1568000.00	448000.00
23	7:00 p.m.	2016000	1568000.00	448000.00
24	8:00 p.m.	2016000	1568000.00	448000.00
25	9:00 p.m.			
26	10:00 p.m.			
27	11:00 p.m.			
28	Highest point of utilization (Represented in Kbps)	2016		
29	ICT Overhead Factor (i.e., VPN)	1.2		
30	Over provisioning factor (estimate)	1.5		
31	Maximum Traffic Generated (Represented as Kbps)	3628.8		

This chart shows the bandwidth necessary for TSI to support the Manhattan kiosks. Adding all locations, kiosk types, and peak time periods would determine the total bandwidth needs.

somewhat differently in the TSI example. We do not ask just "how many customer ticket purchase transactions are acceptable" but rather must "estimate the number of transactions per hour and then determine how much bandwidth is needed to support those transactions with acceptable response time." The Microsoft example takes a production-centric view—how many pages per second. The TSI view takes a customer-centric view—how much bandwidth is necessary to support the transaction load. Both of these views represent performance goals, albeit from different vantage points.

When estimating bandwidth, you need to consider the cost of that bandwidth. A few major ways to measure those costs include:

- **Customer Opportunity Costs.** Customers' time is a commodity they probably cherish. In the TSI example, customers are probably using the kiosk to buy tickets to save time. If the kiosks are not fast enough, customers are less likely to use the TSI kiosk again, or even worse they may abandon their current transaction in favor of another way to purchase the desired tickets.
- **Employee Opportunity Costs.** All businesses are only as good as their employees, and an excessively slow network access can frustrate employees. It can also cause employees to spend too much time on one given task, while ignoring or delaying another. The ignored or delayed task is the lost opportunity cost of a slow network.

VIGNETTE BOX 11-12

TSI Bandwidth Calculations for Staten Island by Location

Line		MO TOTAL	Staten Island	Staten Island	Staten Island	Staten Island	Staten Island	Staten Island	Staten Island
1	Utilization		Medium	Medium	Medium	Medium	Medium	Low	Low
1L	Location Number		1	2	3	4	5	6	7
2	# of Kiosks	12	2	2	2	2	2	1	1
3	bps	23840	4266.67	4266.67	4266.67	4266.67	4266.67	1253.33	1253.33
4	**Midnight**	23840.00	4266.67	4266.67	4266.67	4266.67	4266.67	1253.33	1253.33
5	1:00 A.M.	23840.00	4266.67	4266.67	4266.67	4266.67	4266.67	1253.33	1253.33
6	2:00 A.M.	23840.00	4266.67	4266.67	4266.67	4266.67	4266.67	1253.33	1253.33
7	3:00 A.M.	23840.00	4266.67	4266.67	4266.67	4266.67	4266.67	1253.33	1253.33
8	4:00 A.M.	23840.00	4266.67	4266.67	4266.67	4266.67	4266.67	1253.33	1253.33
9	5:00 A.M.	23840.00	4266.67	4266.67	4266.67	4266.67	4266.67	1253.33	1253.33
10	6:00 A.M.	23840.00	4266.67	4266.67	4266.67	4266.67	4266.67	1253.33	1253.33
11	7:00 A.M.	23840.00	4266.67	4266.67	4266.67	4266.67	4266.67	1253.33	1253.33
12	8:00 A.M.	23840.00	4266.67	4266.67	4266.67	4266.67	4266.67	1253.33	1253.33
13	9:00 A.M.	23840.00	4266.67	4266.67	4266.67	4266.67	4266.67	1253.33	1253.33
14	10:00 A.M.	23840.00	4266.67	4266.67	4266.67	4266.67	4266.67	1253.33	1253.33
15	11:00 A.M.	23840.00	4266.67	4266.67	4266.67	4266.67	4266.67	1253.33	1253.33
16	**Noon**	23840.00	4266.67	4266.67	4266.67	4266.67	4266.67	1253.33	1253.33
17	1:00 P.M.	23840.00	4266.67	4266.67	4266.67	4266.67	4266.67	1253.33	1253.33
18	2:00 P.M.	23840.00	4266.67	4266.67	4266.67	4266.67	4266.67	1253.33	1253.33
19	3:00 P.M.	23840.00	4266.67	4266.67	4266.67	4266.67	4266.67	1253.33	1253.33
20	4:00 P.M.	23840.00	4266.67	4266.67	4266.67	4266.67	4266.67	1253.33	1253.33
21	5:00 P.M.	23840.00	4266.67	4266.67	4266.67	4266.67	4266.67	1253.33	1253.33
22	6:00 P.M.	23840.00	4266.67	4266.67	4266.67	4266.67	4266.67	1253.33	1253.33
23	7:00 P.M.	23840.00	4266.67	4266.67	4266.67	4266.67	4266.67	1253.33	1253.33
24	8:00 P.M.	23840.00	4266.67	4266.67	4266.67	4266.67	4266.67	1253.33	1253.33
25	9:00 P.M.	23840.00	4266.67	4266.67	4266.67	4266.67	4266.67	1253.33	1253.33
26	10:00 P.M.	23840.00	4266.67	4266.67	4266.67	4266.67	4266.67	1253.33	1253.33
27	11:00 P.M.	23840.00	4266.67	4266.67	4266.67	4266.67	4266.67	1253.33	1253.33
28	**Highest Point of Utilization (represented in Kbps)**	23.840	4.267	4.267	4.267	4.267	4.267	1.253	1.253

(Continued)

Vignette Box 11-12 (Continued)

29	ICT Overhead Factor (i.e., VPN)	1.200	1.200	1.200	1.200	1.200	1.200	1.200	1.200
30	Overprovisioning Factor	1.500	1.500	1.500	1.500	1.500	1.500	1.500	1.500
31	Maximum Traffic Generated (represented as Kbps)	42.912	7.680	7.680	7.680	7.680	7.680	2.256	2.256

This spreadsheet adds Line 1L to specify each kiosk's location. Only Staten Island is shown here for brevity and clarity. The spreadsheet can be extended to include all locations, but would be very large at that point. By calculating the bandwidth needed at each location, the engineer can determine total connectivity requirements. Note: The numbers used in this table do not reflect the utilization numbers given in Vignette Box 11-10. They are given here as representative examples of that might be done to compute bandwidth.

- **Time Savings and Cost Savings.** To put it simply, time is money. Slower network access will probably mean that employees will get network- and Internet-intensive tasks done at a slower pace. Again, look at the TSI opening vignette: a customer service employee who needs to look up data on the Internet or intranet will be able to service fewer customers per hour if the ICT infrastructure is slow; and fewer customers per hour may mean that TSI has to hire more customer service representatives to reach the same customer/hour goal.
- **Choosing the Right ISP.** Sometimes the faster connection works out to be cheaper than the slower connection. It may be better to get a WiMAX, cable, or DSL connection rather than a dial-up connection, even when you do not need the speed of these faster connections. The "always on" nature of these faster connections is probably worth the extra cost in customer/employee satisfaction, as compared to dial-up, which may have call setup time that slows things down. Just think about the experience of being at a bank cash machine and waiting a long time. That machine may be dialing out; the connection would be much faster with an "always on" connection.

These performance and cost considerations listed are the core ones that should get the analyst thinking about ways to save money, increase productivity, retain customers, and ultimately increase the organization's bottom line.

Creating High-Level ICT Design Documents

Using the working documents discussed in the previous section, the business analyst can now generate high-level diagrams suitable for the users, staff, managers, and the ICT engineer to understand the ICT infrastructure. It is important that the analyst is in constant consultation with all stakeholders to ensure that the diagrams depict what stakeholders envision. It may be possible that once stakeholders see the ICT infrastructure in a high-level diagram, they may notice things that were not apparent in the earlier design documents. Refer back to Figure 11-10 to better understand the relationship between the analyst, engineer, and other stakeholders. Making corrections and redoing documents now is better than expending resources on ICT infrastructure only to find out that that the infrastructure does not deliver what was envisioned by everyone.

Currently no generally adopted or recognized standards are available for drawing high-level ICT infrastructure diagrams, so this section provides a number of diagramming recommendations for creating "user-friendly" and consistent documents.

Chapter 11 • Designing ICT: Documenting Process and Technology Recommendations 351

> **BEST PRACTICE 11-11**
>
> **The Importance of Document Review with All Stakeholders**
>
> When creating ICT documents it is important that an analyst consult with users, staff, and managers throughout the design process to ensure the accuracy of business process diagrams, functionality lists, bandwidth estimations, and high-level ICT infrastructure designs. It is also necessary to refer back to any written ICT infrastructure specifications (e.g., the TSI opening vignette).

The documents used in this section have been generated with Microsoft Visio, and all symbols used are available in that software product. Some global considerations for diagrams include:

- Diagrams must be clear, uncluttered, and concise.
- Each diagram must contain a title identifying it, a key identifying un-labeled elements on the diagram, and the name of the creator(s) of the diagram.
- Outside of the standard symbols (e.g., the cloud to represent packet-switched networks), most symbols can be representative of what the users/stakeholders and engineers understand.
- The typologies should be clear. For example, our diagrams will be using an Ethernet star typology whose backbone can be shown as ⎯⎯⎯, whereas a TCP/IP mesh typology will be shown as a cloud.
- Number all elements of the diagram that will be used to create lower-level diagrams.
- Letter all elements of the diagram that will NOT have lower-level diagrams, but will appear in the diagram notes described below.
- Use an ICT infrastructure context diagram to show the entire organization, its partners, and the related ICT infrastructure. Based on the complexity of the infrastructure and the number of partners that share data, the ICT infrastructure context diagram may be complex and take a good bit of work to create. Infrastructure diagrams must tie directly to the infrastructure being created, and to the subsequent diagrams.

In the following sections examples of creating high-level design diagrams will be shown based on the opening vignette. The **diagram list** (Vignette Box 11-13) shows which high-level diagrams will be included in this example. The list would be expanded to include all interconnections if it were a real diagram list.

> **VIGNETTE BOX 11-13**
>
> **TSI Diagram List**
>
> - TSI Context Diagram
>   - TSI Main Office Core Diagram 1.0
>   - TSI First Floor Workgroup Diagram 1.1—note a number is used at the end to signify that there will be subsequent diagrams
>   - ....
>   - TSI Fourth Floor Workgroup Diagram 1.4
>   - TSI Kiosk Diagram 2.0
>   - Diagram 2.0(A)—note a letter is used at the end of show that there will be no subsequent diagrams
>   - Diagram 2.0(B)
>
> The abbreviated diagrams listed in this figure are arranged in a hierarchy that coincides with the interconnections shown in the TSI context diagram. This diagram list supplements the documentation by showing which diagrams are included, how they interconnect, and whether there are subsequent diagrams (by ending with a number).

BEST PRACTICE 11-12

Diagramming Conventions

- Diagrams must be clear, uncluttered, and concise.
- Each diagram should have a title.
- Use identifying keys.
- Be sure to include the creator(s) of the diagram.
- Number each page in the title, except the ICT infrastructure context diagram—it should indicate that it is the context diagram for the infrastructure.
- If there are a number of diagrams, include a diagram list.
- Include a diagram note page for every diagram explaining the content of each diagram.
- Most ICT high-level diagram symbols can be representative of what the users/stakeholders and engineers understand.
- A common symbol for the Ethernet star backbone is .
- A common symbol for a TCP/IP network is .
- Number all elements of the diagram that will be used to create lower-level diagrams.
- Letter all elements of the diagram that will NOT have lower-level diagrams, but will appear in the diagram notes.
- Use a context diagram to show the entire organization, its partners, and the related ICT infrastructure.

TSI'S CONTEXT DIAGRAM

For the context diagram in Vignette Box 11-14, the elements are documented in the diagram notes in (see Vignette Box 11-15).

When **diagram notes** are included in a real diagram set (i.e., not in this textbook), they contain real facts and not instructions for creating them. The diagram notes are

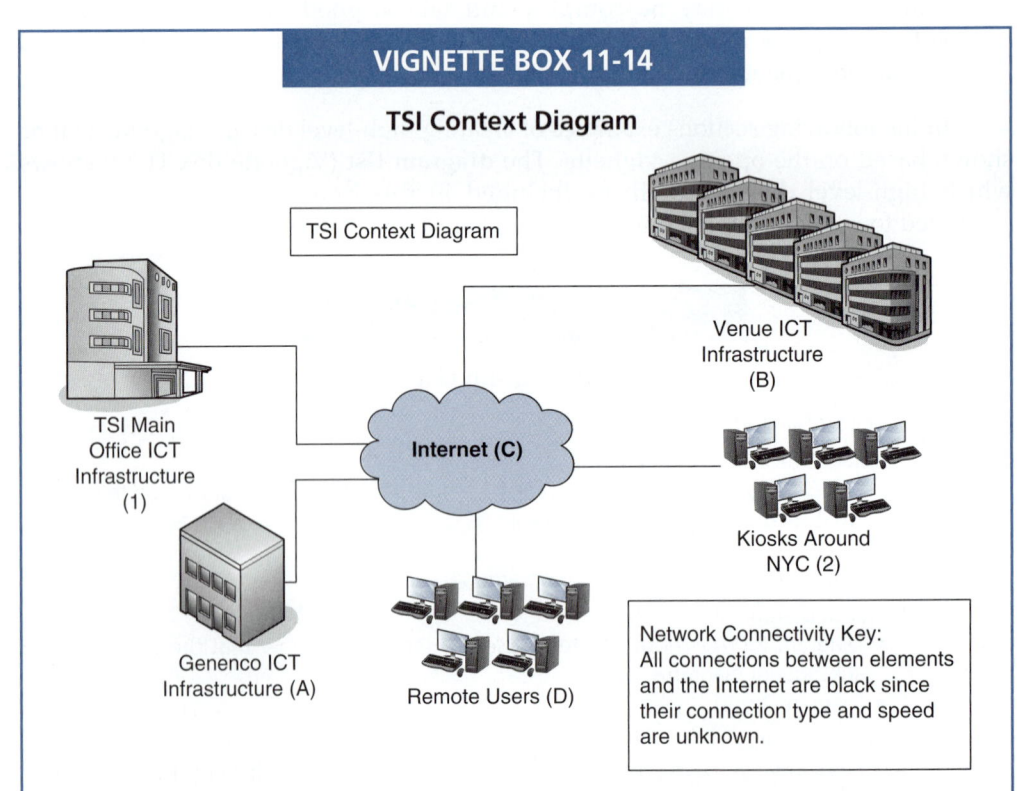

VIGNETTE BOX 11-14

TSI Context Diagram

- TSI Main Office ICT Infrastructure (1)
- Venue ICT Infrastructure (B)
- Internet (C)
- Genenco ICT Infrastructure (A)
- Remote Users (D)
- Kiosks Around NYC (2)

Network Connectivity Key: All connections between elements and the Internet are black since their connection type and speed are unknown.

This diagram provides a high-level depiction of TSI's ICT infrastructure content with its major internal and external ICT technologies. It should also show the major stakeholders. Letters are used for items without subsequent diagrams, and numbers are used for items with separate diagrams. A diagram note is attached explaining the lettered and numbered items.

> **VIGNETTE BOX 11-15**
>
> **TSI Context Diagram Notes**
>
> - **(1) TSI Main Office Infrastructure**—This element represents the TSI infrastructure. Its number is used to explain the element and is used in subsequent page numbering.
> - **(2) Kiosks Around NYC**—These are under the direct control of Genenco, and the number will be used for subsequent diagrams. Note the multiple kiosks layered in this element and the number to be shown in a subsequent diagram.
> - **(A) Genenco ICT Infrastructure, (B) Venue ICT Infrastructure, (C) Internet, and (D) Remote Users**—These elements represent external partners/users of TSI's main office ICT infrastructure. Because TSI has no control over the technology used at these locations, they will not require further diagrams. They were "lettered" so they could be referenced in these diagram notes. (Note that the building for "venues" and the PCs for "remote users" were layered multiple times in the diagram to show that there were a number of these elements that would be interconnected. However, no indication was given as to how many. If the number were known, it would be shown in these diagram notes.)
> - One format (thin black line) was used for all interconnectivity between elements and the Internet. The reasons are that much of the Internet connectivity is not under TSI's control, and there may be multiple types of (2) Kiosk Internet connectivity. If the TSI Main Office (1) Internet connectivity is known it could be shown.

> **BEST PRACTICE 11-13**
>
> **Diagram Notes**
>
> - Diagram notes must indicate the letters and numbers of elements used in diagrams.
> - Each letter/number should have a name.
> - Each number/letter should have a thorough description of its function and other pertinent information.
> - The page number for diagram notes should be the same as the diagram for which it gives detail, except with a letter appended (e.g., "A" or more letters if needed).

> **BEST PRACTICE 11-14**
>
> **Connecting Diagrams**
>
> Best Practices for Diagramming Workgroups:
>
> - Unless the ICT diagram is very small, each workgroup should be shown on its own page.
> - When using multiple pages use the same symbol and name on the main diagram and on the connected diagram. See Vignette Box 11-16 and Vignette Box 11-18. Each of these diagrams uses the same symbol and name for the First Floor Workgroup, 1.1.
> - Number subsequent diagrams using dotted decimal notation like in the example given in the preceding bullet point When there is no subsequent diagram end the numbering with a letter. Both "numbered" and "lettered" items must have corresponding diagram notes.

created on a separate page and attached to the actual diagrams. All pages of the diagram notes should be numbered the same as the diagram to which they pertain.

TSI'S MAIN OFFICE CORE DIAGRAM 1.0

The diagram notes for Vignette Box 11-16 can be seen in Vignette Box 11-17.

WORKGROUP DIAGRAMS

With the Network Core Diagram 1.0 completed, we will now move to workgroup diagrams. We will diagram two of the workgroups for illustrative purposes, then we will

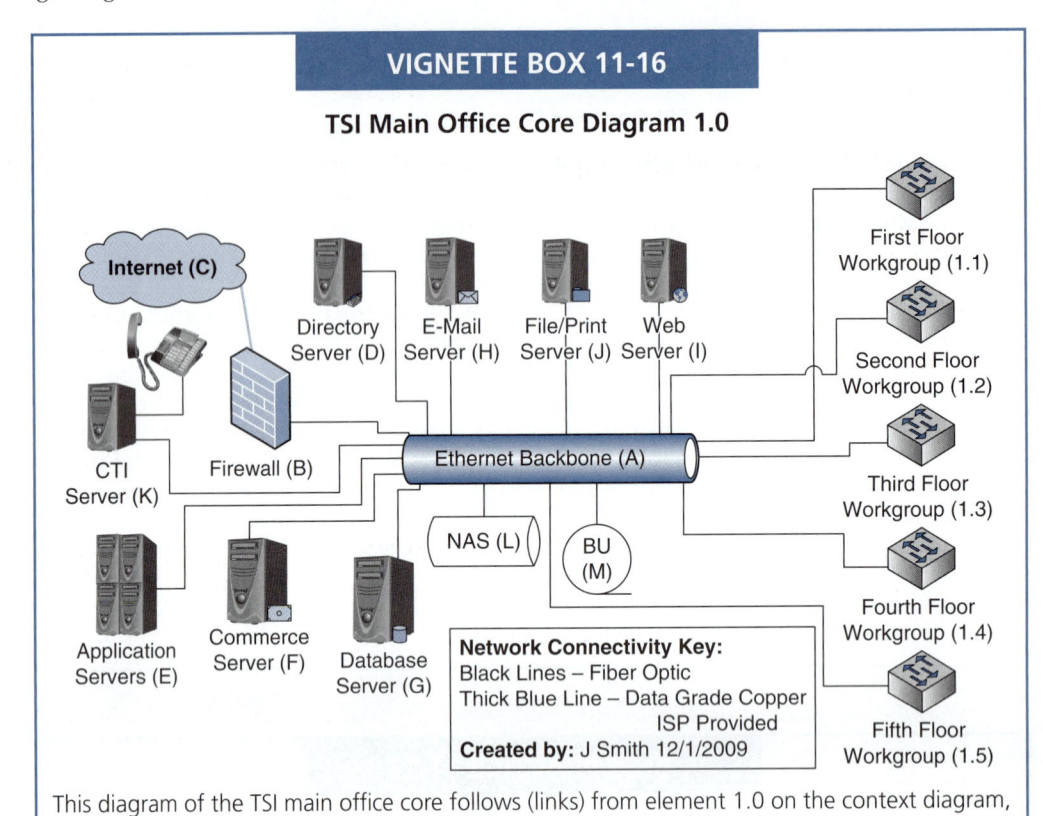

VIGNETTE BOX 11-16

TSI Main Office Core Diagram 1.0

Network Connectivity Key:
Black Lines – Fiber Optic
Thick Blue Line – Data Grade Copper
ISP Provided
Created by: J Smith 12/1/2009

This diagram of the TSI main office core follows (links) from element 1.0 on the context diagram, and has five workgroups that link to other diagrams (1.1, 1.2,…).

VIGNETTE BOX 11-17

TSI Main Office Core Diagram 1.0 Notes

- **(A) Ethernet Backbone**—This backbone runs from the network core through TSI's main building. It will be fiber optic. This backbone consists of network connections in the core and the vertical runs through riser space in TSI's building.
- **(B) Router/Firewall**—This is shown separately because it provides such important connectivity. This unit will also have a CSU/DSU that allows for interconnection between TSI's and the ISP's networks. This firewall will also handle all VPN traffic.
- **(C) Internet**—The TCP/IP packet-switched network connection is provided by the ISP.

Servers (D, E, F, G, H, I, J, K)—Several servers are required. The five servers (E) through (I) have been specified by Genenco in the opening TSI vignette. Servers (D), (J), and (K) have been added by the systems analyst to support ICT functionality. The list of servers are as follows:

- **(D) Directory Server**—This server will provide management of identities and resources in the ICT environment and manage access permissions through a single login. This server will run MS-Active Directory®.
- **(E) Application Servers**—This server will provide application services for Genenco applications as specified in the TSI opening vignette.
- **(F) Commerce Server**—As specified in the TSI opening vignette, this server will run MS-Commerce Server® and provide e-commerce services to the other servers.
- **(G) Database Server**—This server will run Microsoft SQL Server® and provide database services.
- **(H) E-Mail Server**—This server, specified by Genenco as Microsoft Exchange®, will handle all e-mail for TSI.
- **(I) Web Server**—This server will handle all web traffic for ticket sales and for an intranet for TSI. It will run Microsoft Internet Information Server®.
- **(J) File/Print Server**—MS-Windows Server.
- **(K) CTI Server**—This server will handle the computer telephony integration and is connected to the network as well as to the phone system.

> - **(L) NAS**—This ICT device is network attached storage and will allow for multi-terabyte storage attached to the network and provide file-based storage services to other devices on the network.
> - **(M) Backup**—This device will provide nightly backup services to other devices on the network and network users.
>
> Workgroup Diagrams
> - Workgroup diagrams (1.1, 1.2, ...) indicate that they will have subsequent diagrams.

move to the kiosk diagrams. As examples, the first floor workgroup will be diagrammed first, and then the fourth floor workgroup will be diagrammed.

First Floor Workgroup Diagram The first floor contains separate offices for each major department and other senior managers including the CEO, CFO, CIO, vice president of marketing, and vice president of operations (call center). Each senior manager has a secretary, and there is a receptionist for the building. A total of 13 people are located on the first floor, each with his or her own PC and local printer. C-suite executives also have a laptop with a docking station. The diagram is shown in Vignette Box 11-18.

The diagram notes for Vignette Box 11-18 can be seen in Vignette Box 11-19.

Fourth Floor Workgroup Diagram Now we will move on to diagramming the fourth floor workgroup. This workgroup has two different desktop configurations and two shared printers. Otherwise it is similar to Vignette Box 11-18. The major differences are in the shared printers and the diagram notes that include information for the network engineers.

TSI KIOSK DIAGRAM 2.0

Now, for a final example of creating diagrams we will look at kiosk configurations for TSI and introduce best practices for breaking complex diagrams across multiple pages. This breaking-down involves sub-numbering as shown in Best Practice 11-17. As a rule, do not break individual configurations across pages, but rather include an entire configuration on

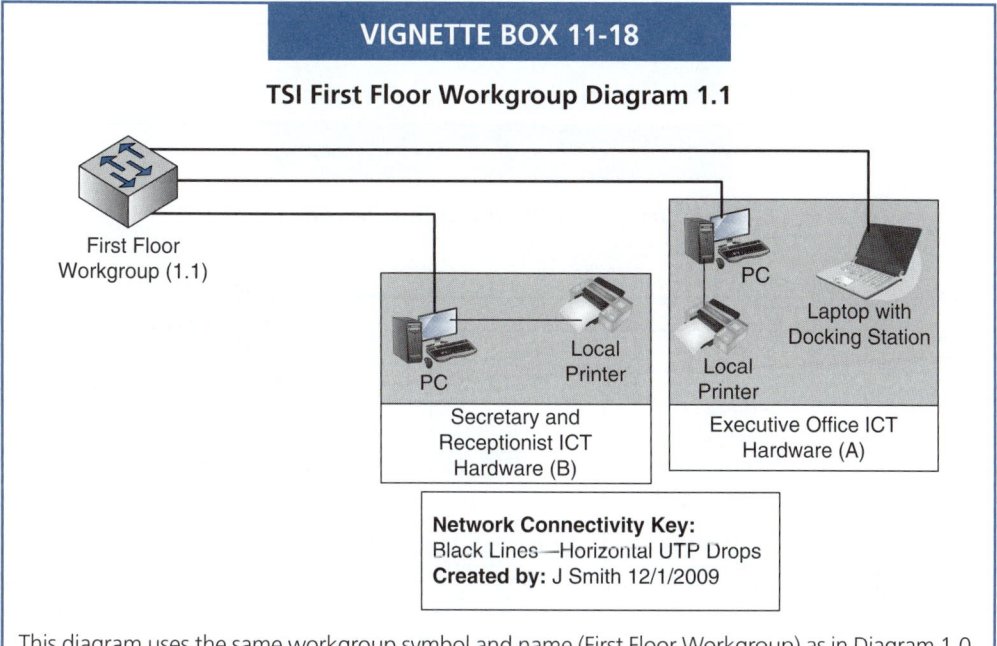

VIGNETTE BOX 11-18

TSI First Floor Workgroup Diagram 1.1

First Floor Workgroup (1.1)

Secretary and Receptionist ICT Hardware (B): PC, Local Printer

Executive Office ICT Hardware (A): PC, Local Printer, Laptop with Docking Station

Network Connectivity Key:
Black Lines—Horizontal UTP Drops
Created by: J Smith 12/1/2009

This diagram uses the same workgroup symbol and name (First Floor Workgroup) as in Diagram 1.0. It shows the two types of ICT configurations in the first floor workgroup. Additional types of ICT configurations would be shown separately (e.g., if the receptionist had different hardware than the secretaries, it would be shown separately). The number of each configuration is shown in the diagram notes. (When all diagrams are completed, the analyst will go back and correct the page numbers (i.e., page Y of X).)

VIGNETTE BOX 11-19

TSI First Floor Workgroup Diagram 1.1 Notes

- **(A) C-suite Executive Office ICT Hardware**—Each of the six executive offices has the same hardware configuration, including a desktop PC with a local printer and a laptop for use when away from the office. The laptop will have a docking station. The PC and docking station will be connected to the Ethernet backbone with a UTP drop. The printer will be connected to the local PC via a USB cable. Multiple network drops or wireless will be needed to support this connectivity.
- **(B) Secretary and Receptionist ICT Hardware**—Each of the locations for the six secretaries and one receptionist within this workgroup has the same hardware configuration that includes a desktop PC with a local printer. The printer will be connected to the local PC via a USB cable.

BEST PRACTICE 11-15

Showing Different Configurations

A few rules help make the diagram clearer:

- Each different configuration should be shown in a box.
- Details about the number of items with that configuration should be shown in the diagram notes.

BEST PRACTICE 11-16

Diagram Notes for Network Engineer

Diagram notes should contain detailed information for the network engineer. For example, the shared printer in Vignette Box 11-20 needs extra documentation—the printer should only be shared with the marketing management and staff.

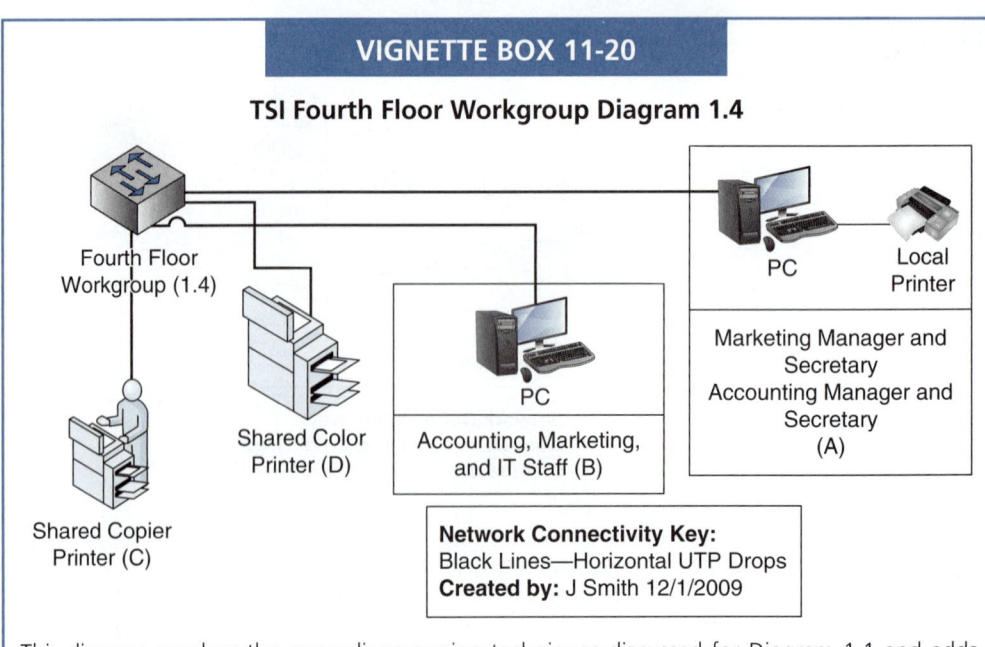

VIGNETTE BOX 11-20

TSI Fourth Floor Workgroup Diagram 1.4

Fourth Floor Workgroup (1.4)

Shared Copier Printer (C)

Shared Color Printer (D)

PC

Accounting, Marketing, and IT Staff (B)

PC

Local Printer

Marketing Manager and Secretary
Accounting Manager and Secretary
(A)

Network Connectivity Key:
Black Lines—Horizontal UTP Drops
Created by: J Smith 12/1/2009

This diagram employs the same diagramming techniques discussed for Diagram 1.1 and adds shared printers. Note that the Shared Color Printer (D) is only used by the marketing staff, which will be indicated in the diagram notes.

Chapter 11 • Designing ICT: Documenting Process and Technology Recommendations 357

> ### VIGNETTE BOX 11-21
>
> **TSI Fourth Floor Workgroup Diagram 1.4 Notes**
>
> - **(A) Marketing Manager and Secretary, Accounting Manager and Secretary**—These staff will have a desktop PC and a local printer. They will also have access to the Shared Copier Printer (C). The marketing staff will also have access to the Shared Color Printer (D).
> - **(B) Accounting and Marketing Staff**—These staff will have a desktop PC. They will also have access to the Shared Copier Printer (C). Only the marketing staff will have access to the Shared Color Printer (D).
> - **(C) Shared Copier Printer**—This will be a copier attached to the network via a UTP drop that will be shared by all staff on this floor.
> - **(D) Shared Color Printer**—This will be a color printer attached to the network via a UTP drop that will be shared by the marketing staff on this floor, as well as the VP of marketing and the VP's secretary on the first floor.

an individual diagram, then show the next configuration on the next diagram. TSI Kiosk Diagram 2.0 will be broken into Diagrams 2.0(A) and 2.0(B) to show how this is done. Note that only the kiosks in Manhattan will be shown in these diagrams.

It is also possible to combine the high and medium kiosks, assuming the configurations are the same (i.e., use the same ISP connectivity to connect to the Internet and the same network infrastructure at each location). The design of these documents is largely up to the analyst, but must show maximum detail so the ICT engineer can implement the configurations. The combined diagram can be seen in Vignette Box 11-25 and Vignette Box 11-26.

> ### BEST PRACTICE 11-17
>
> **Breaking Down Complex Diagrams**
>
> - When creating complex diagrams, it is often best to break diagrams onto multiple pages, which is best accomplished by creating diagrams with sublettering. For example, Diagram 2.0 could be broken into 2.0(a), 2.0(b), 2.0(c), and so on.
> - Do not break individual configurations across pages. However, it is okay to show different configurations on different pages.

> ### VIGNETTE BOX 11-22
>
> **TSI Kiosk Diagram 2.0(A)**
>
> [Diagram showing Internet (A) connected via DSL to three separate DSL Modem Router Switch configurations with Kiosks]
>
> - Location: Manhattan (D)
>   Utilization: High
>   11 Locations, 1 Kiosk Per
>   ISP Connection: DSL
>
> - Location: Manhattan (C)
>   Utilization: High
>   2 Locations, 2 Kiosks Per
>   ISP Connection: DSL
>
> - Location: Manhattan (B)
>   Utilization: High
>   5 Locations, 3 Kiosks Per
>   ISP Connection: DSL
>
> **Network Connectivity Key:**
> Black Lines are UTP Drops
> Blue Lines are DSL
> Created by: J Smith 12/1/2009
>
> This diagram contains the first part of the Manhattan kiosks. Diagram 2.0(B) contains the balance of the Manhattan kiosks.

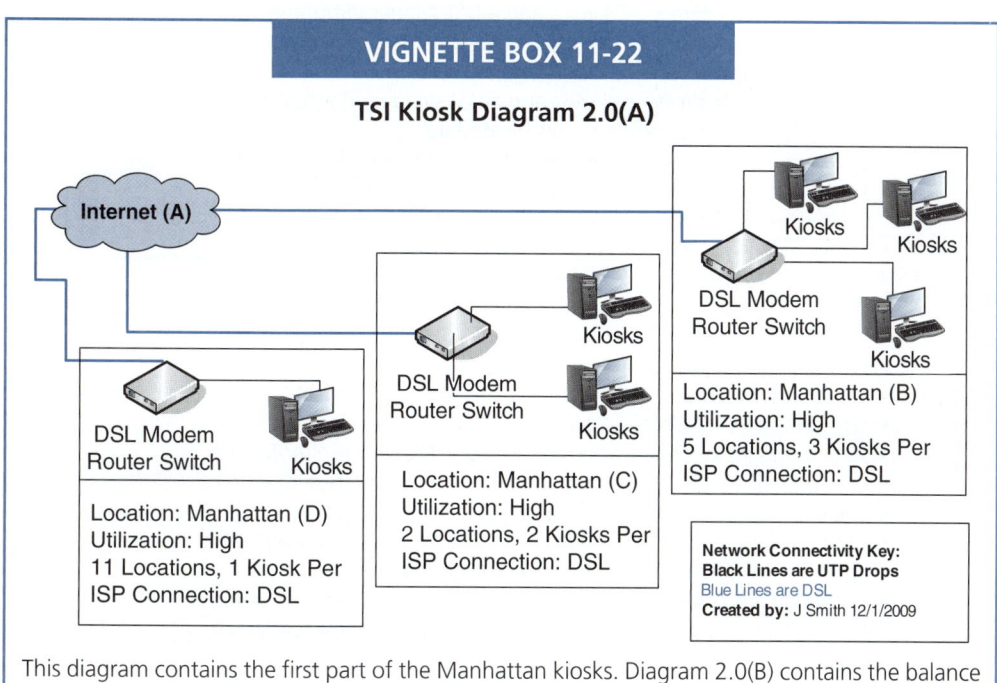

358 Unit 4 • Steps to the Strategic Alignment of ICT

VIGNETTE BOX 11-23

TSI Kiosk Diagram 2.0(B)

Location: Manhattan (B)
Utilization: Medium
2 Locations, 3 Kiosks Per
ISP Connection: DSL

Location: Manhattan (C)
Utilization: Medium
2 Locations, 2 Kiosks Per
ISP Connection: DSL

Location: Manhattan (D)
Utilization: Medium
5 Locations, 1 Kiosk Per
ISP Connection: DSL

Network Connectivity Key:
Black Lines are UTP Drops
Blue Lines are DSL
Created by: J Smith 12/1/2009

This diagram contains the balance of the Manhattan kiosks. Note that the diagram has the same number (2.0) as the other kiosk diagram, but has a letter appended (B) to show that the diagrams are part of object 2 from the context diagram.

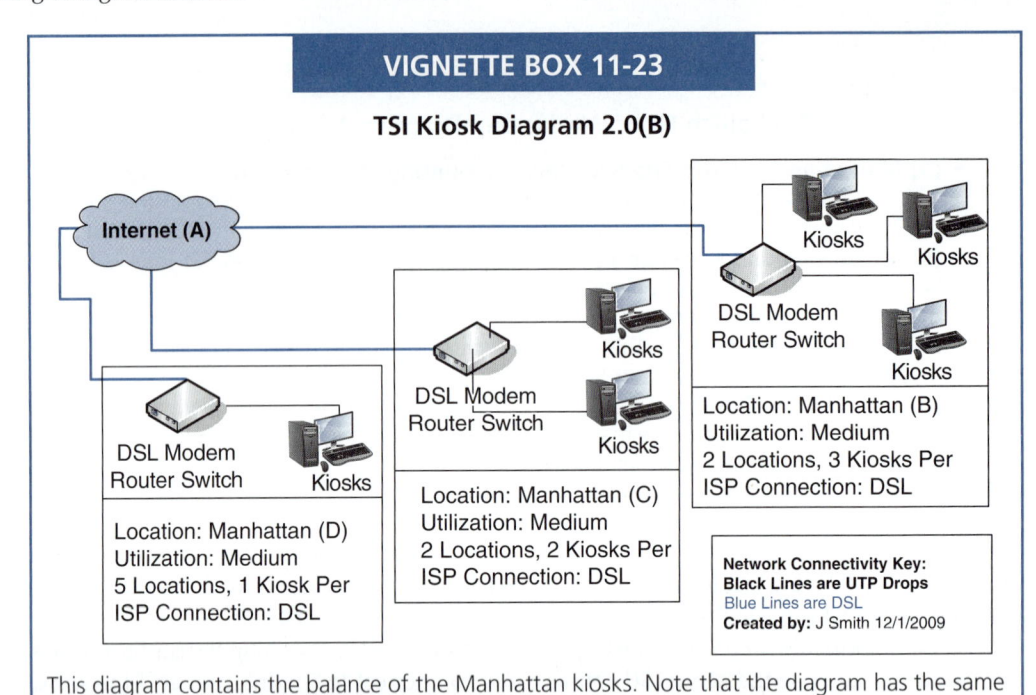

VIGNETTE BOX 11-24

TSI Kiosk Diagram 2.0 (A and B) Diagram Notes

These diagrams show Kiosks A and B in Manhattan. These kiosks were split by kiosk utilization type. Both diagrams are included in these notes.

- (A) in both diagrams represents Internet Connections provided by an ISP. All connections are DSL.
- Diagram A (B)—High Utilization kiosks located at:
    - Location One Address—3 kiosks and a DSL Modem/Router/Switch
    - Location Two Address—3 kiosks and a DSL Modem/Router/Switch
    - Location Three Address—3 kiosks and a DSL Modem/Router/Switch
    - Location Four Address—3 kiosks and a DSL Modem/Router/Switch
    - Location Five Address—3 kiosks and a DSL Modem/Router/Switch
- Diagram A (C)—High Utilization Kiosks located at:
    - Location One Address—2 kiosks and a DSL Modem/Router/Switch
    - Location Two Address—2 kiosks and a DSL Modem/Router/Switch
- Diagram A (D)—High Utilization kiosks located at:
    - Location One Address—1 kiosk and a DSL Modem/Router/Switch
    - Location Two Address—1 kiosk and a DSL Modem/Router/Switch
    - Location Three Address—1 kiosk and a DSL Modem/Router/Switch
    - Location Four Address—1 kiosk and a DSL Modem/Router/Switch
    - Location Five Address—1 kiosk and a DSL Modem/Router/Switch
    - Location Six Address—1 kiosk and a DSL Modem/Router/Switch
    - Location Seven Address—1 kiosk and a DSL Modem/Router/Switch
    - Location Eight Address—1 kiosk and a DSL Modem/Router/Switch
    - Location Nine Address—1 kiosk and a DSL Modem/Router/Switch
    - Location Ten Address—1 kiosk and a DSL Modem/Router/Switch
    - Location Eleven Address—1 kiosk and a DSL Modem/Router/Switch
- Diagram B (B)—Medium Utilization kiosks located at:
    - Location One Address—3 kiosks and a DSL Modem/Router/Switch
    - Location Two Address—3 kiosks and a DSL Modem/Router/Switch

- Diagram B (C)—Medium Utilization kiosks located at:
  - Location One Address—2 kiosks and a DSL Modem/Router/Switch
  - Location Two Address—2 kiosks and a DSL Modem/Router/Switch
- Diagram B (D)—Medium Utilization kiosks located at:
  - Location One Address—1 kiosk and a DSL Modem/Router/Switch
  - Location Two Address—1 kiosk and a DSL Modem/Router/Switch
  - Location Three Address—1 kiosk and a DSL Modem/Router/Switch
  - Location Four Address—1 kiosk and a DSL Modem/Router/Switch
  - Location Five Address—1 kiosk and a DSL Modem/Router/Switch

In these diagram notes, each "Location # Address" is replaced with the actual address of the location.

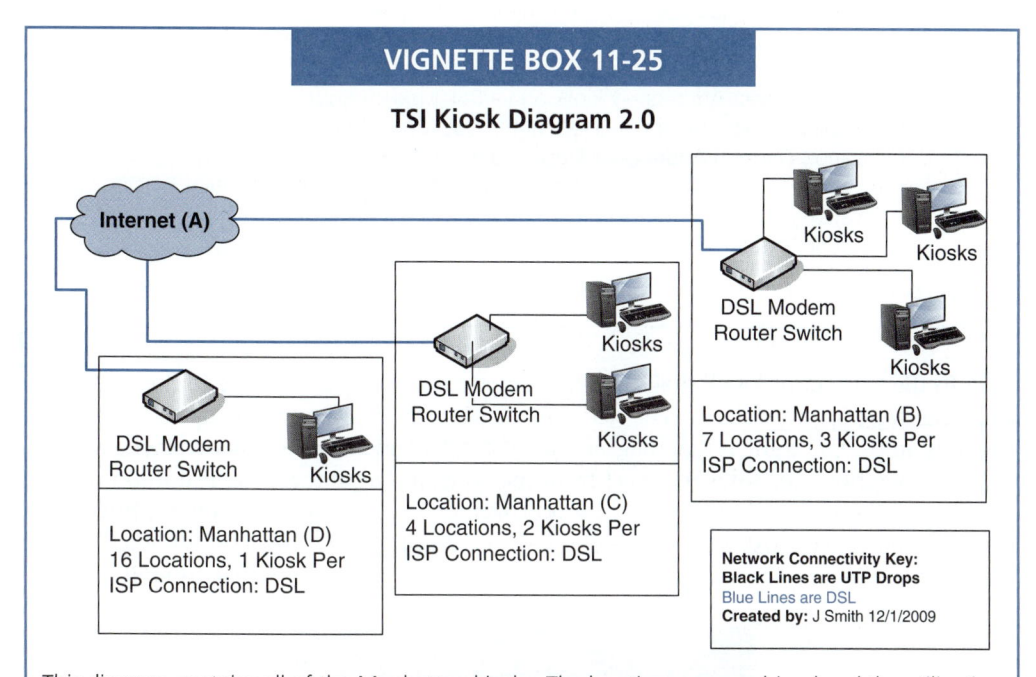

VIGNETTE BOX 11-25

TSI Kiosk Diagram 2.0

Internet (A)

DSL Modem Router Switch — Kiosks
Location: Manhattan (D)
16 Locations, 1 Kiosk Per
ISP Connection: DSL

DSL Modem Router Switch — Kiosks
Location: Manhattan (C)
4 Locations, 2 Kiosks Per
ISP Connection: DSL

DSL Modem Router Switch — Kiosks
Location: Manhattan (B)
7 Locations, 3 Kiosks Per
ISP Connection: DSL

Network Connectivity Key:
Black Lines are UTP Drops
Blue Lines are DSL
Created by: J Smith 12/1/2009

This diagram contains all of the Manhattan kiosks. The locations are combined and the utilization is left off. This diagram is shows the same configurations as TSI Kiosk Diagram 2.0(A) and TSI Kiosk Diagram 2.0(B), but combined into one diagram.

VIGNETTE BOX 11-26

TSI Kiosk Diagram 2.0 Diagram Notes

These diagrams show Kiosks A and B in Manhattan. These kiosks were broken up by utilization type. Both diagrams are included in these notes.

- (A) represents Internet Connections provided by an ISP. All connections are DSL.
- (B)—Three kiosks located at:
  - Location One Address—3 kiosks and a DSL Modem/Router/Switch
  - Location Two Address—3 kiosks and a DSL Modem/Router/Switch
  - Location Three Address—3 kiosks and a DSL Modem/Router/Switch
  - Location Four Address—3 kiosks and a DSL Modem/Router/Switch
  - Location Five Address—3 kiosks and a DSL Modem/Router/Switch
  - Location Six Address—3 kiosks and a DSL Modem/Router/Switch
  - Location Seven Address—3 kiosks and a DSL Modem/Router/Switch
- Diagram A (C)—Two kiosks located at:
  - Location One Address—2 kiosks and a DSL Modem/Router/Switch
  - Location Two Address—2 kiosks and a DSL Modem/Router/Switch

(Continued)

> **Vignette Box 11-26 (Continued)**
>
> - Location Three Address—2 kiosks and a DSL Modem/Router/Switch
> - Location Four Address—2 kiosks and a DSL Modem/Router/Switch
> - Diagram A (D)—One kiosk located at:
>   - Location One Address—1 kiosk and a DSL Modem/Router/Switch
>   - Location Two Address—1 kiosk and a DSL Modem/Router/Switch
>   - Location Three Address—1 kiosk and a DSL Modem/Router/Switch
>   - Location Four Address—1 kiosk and a DSL Modem/Router/Switch
>   - Location Five Address—1 kiosk and a DSL Modem/Router/Switch
>   - Location Six Address—1 kiosk and a DSL Modem/Router/Switch
>   - Location Seven Address—1 kiosk and a DSL Modem/Router/Switch
>   - Location Eight Address—1 kiosk and a DSL Modem/Router/Switch
>   - Location Nine Address—1 kiosk and a DSL Modem/Router/Switch
>   - Location Ten Address—1 kiosk and a DSL Modem/Router/Switch
>   - Location Eleven Address—1 kiosk and a DSL Modem/Router/Switch
>   - Location Twelve Address—1 kiosk and a DSL Modem/Router/Switch
>   - Location Thirteen Address—1 kiosk and a DSL Modem/Router/Switch
>   - Location Fourteen Address—1 kiosk and a DSL Modem/Router/Switch
>   - Location Fifteen Address—1 kiosk and a DSL Modem/Router/Switch
>   - Location Sixteen Address—1 kiosk and a DSL Modem/Router/Switch
>
> In these diagram notes, each "Location # Address" is replaced with the actual address of the location.

In the first set of kiosk diagrams in Vignette Box 11-22 and Vignette Box 11-23, the diagrams were split for clarity. The decision of splitting diagrams is left up to the analyst. The most important thing is that diagrams are consistent and clear. The analyst who decides to split a diagram (i.e., take an object from the context diagram and split it into multiple subsidiary diagrams) should do so by modifying the diagram list shown above, and append a letter to the diagram number to indicate the splitting. The diagram notes should indicate that the diagrams are split and what diagram numbers comprise the split sections.

> **BEST PRACTICE 11-18**
>
> **Splitting Diagrams**
>
> - When splitting diagrams, append a letter to the diagram number to show the diagrams are combined but for clarity's sake are shown on separate pages.
> - For all diagrams, including split diagrams, use the diagram notes to give the ICT engineer the maximum amount of information to facilitate implementation of the configurations (e.g., the location information shown in the kiosk diagram notes).

Chapter Summary

This chapter is geared toward delineating the job of the business analyst and differentiating it from the systems analyst and the ICT engineer. The business analyst must possess a myriad of skills including:

- Understanding organizations and how they create strategy
- Aligning strategy with organizational change efforts
- Being able to assist members of the organization in identifying business processes that are candidates for improvement/innovation
- Documenting current processes ("as-is") as well as how they should be modified ("to-be")
- Translating to-be processes into ICT recommendations
- Documenting ICT recommendations so the systems analyst and ICT engineer can implement them

The business analyst who can effectively employ these skills should be able to help the organization attain the alignment between organizational strategic objectives and ICT resources.

This chapter covered a number of skills necessary for the business analyst including how to document business processes, build business process diagrams (BPDs), and translate business process improvement/innovation into ICT design documents. Methods for documenting ICT design were also covered.

Vignette Wrap Up

In this chapter the TSI Vignette was used to show how to document business processes. This chapter directly builds on the previous chapter discussion of making strategic change in organizations and uses recommendations from earlier chapters to describe business process modeling. The TSI vignette is replete with many recommendations and other opportunities where the business systems analyst can make recommended change. Next, the TSI vignette was used to teach ICT documentation techniques, and included one recommendation from the business process changes suggested in previous chapters. Together, the business process modeling and the ICT diagramming create a complete set of documents that can be understood by all stakeholders, including the systems analyst and the ICT engineer.

End of Chapter Questions/Assurance of Learning

1. What are the differences between workflow and business process modeling, and how might business process modeling assist the systems analyst and ICT engineer in building software systems and ICT infrastructure?
2. Describe how business process modeling can assist the business analyst in conveying ideas and recommendations for process improvements/innovations.
3. Write out a description of the business process modeling graphical language and describe the use of each symbol.
4. Write a short paper describing how it is necessary for the business analyst to model processes before making ICT recommendations.
5. Prepare a presentation teaching nontechnical staff how to interpret business process diagrams.
6. Prepare a presentation covering the major components of ICT technology diagramming and why it is important to prepare these diagrams for use by the systems analyst and ICT engineer.
7. Discuss why users, managers, the system analyst and ICT engineers should be involved in all process modeling and ICT diagramming exercises. What benefit results from their involvement?

Case Exercises

These exercises build on the case exercises from previous chapters.

1. XYZ Inc. is a hardware company that builds network hardware and wants to expand its product offerings to ensure it is a viable alternative to other network hardware manufacturers. Write a brief paper and presentation describing how XYZ Inc. can assist its customers in documenting ICT process and technology recommendations by the way XYZ Inc. builds, designs, and markets its hardware.
2. Select a business process for HealthyWay HMO and, using BPMN, model its "as-is" process. Then make recommendations and create a "to-be" process through the implementation of ICT.
3. Select a company you are familiar with and document its ICT infrastructure using the high-level ICT design documents techniques discussed in this chapter. Present these documents to the class.

Key Words and Concepts

abstract (public) processes *321*
artifacts *324*
as-is process *331*
automated task *322*
bandwidth, performance and cost considerations *347*
business process diagrams (BPDs) *319*
business process modeling (BPM) *316*
business process modeling notation (BPMN) *317*
collaboration (global) processes *321*
compensation activities *326*
connecting objects *324*
context diagram *352*
diagram list *351*
diagram notes *352*
diagram set *314*
flow objects *324*
functionality list *339*
ICT hierarchy *340*
ICT technical frameworks and models *338*
lanes *323*
manual task *322*
Object Management Group *319*
pools *323*
private (internal) business processes *321*
process definition *321*
process instance *322*
process map *315*
subprocesses *337*
swim lanes *324*
task/activity *322*
to-be process *331*
types *332*
Unified Modeling Language *317*
WebSphere Business Modeler *320*
workflow *321*
workgroup diagrams *353*
working documents *338*

References

Havey, M. (2005). *Essential business process modeling.* Cambridge: O'Reilly.

Microsoft. (2009, December 17). *Estimating Bandwidth.* Retrieved December 17, 2009, from http://technet.microsoft.com/en-us/library/cc785130(WS.10).aspx

Microsoft. (2007). *Visio.* Redmond, WA: Microsoft.

Object Management Group. (2009). *About the Object Management Group.* Retrieved November 14, 2009, from http://www.omg.org/gettingstarted/gettingstartedindex.htm

Object Management Group. (2009). *Business Process Model and Notation (BPMN) Version 1.2.* Needham, MA: Object Management Group.

Object Management Group. (2009). *Catalog of business strategy, business rules and business process management specifications.* Retrieved November 15, 2009, from http://www.omg.org/technology/documents/br_pm_spec_catalog.htm

Owen, M., & Raj, J. (2003). *BPMN and business process management: Introduction to the new business process modeling standard.* Popkin Software.

Visual Paradigm. (2009, November 16). *Business Process Visual Architect.* Cheung Sha Wan, Kln, Hong Kong.

12 SUMMARIZING THE BUSINESS-DRIVEN INFRASTRUCTURE DESIGN CYCLE: ANALYSIS, DESIGN, IMPLEMENTATION, AND POST-IMPLEMENTATION

> **Learning Objectives**
>
> - Describe the complete infrastructure planning and implementation cycle.
> - Gain a better understanding of why cost-benefit and other types of analysis of infrastructure options, as well as why post-implementation analyses are important.
> - Better understand how bandwidth planning is important to competitive positioning.
> - Understand the importance of all phases of the business-driven infrastructure design cycle.

This chapter pulls together the information from all previous chapters and emphasizes the interaction that is necessary between the business analysts, ICT engineers, systems analysts, users, managers, customers, and all other stakeholders. Methods for coming to consensus on which business recommendations are appropriate, and how they are to be implemented, have been discussed in previous chapters. As was indicated, consensus should have been accomplished through extensive discussion, business analysis, appropriate use of business process modeling, and the creation of a set of agreed-to ICT working and design documents. Once these things are completed, the business analyst is ready to work with team members to begin implementation of the ICT infrastructure.

THE BUSINESS-DRIVEN INFRASTRUCTURE DESIGN CYCLE

In previous chapters, a number of tools, skills, and techniques were described in depth:

- The introduction of the information and communication technology (ICT) infrastructure architecture with its various components and how technologies fit into those components
- An understanding of business infrastructure design, the functional view of organizations, conceptual frameworks that underpin business-driven infrastructure design, business processes, and assessing the business value of ICT
- Steps to attain the strategic alignment of ICT, including how to analyze an organization and its environment to design ICT infrastructure while getting stakeholder buy-in, culminating in a set of business process and ICT design documents, and finally the actual implementation of ICT infrastructure

This chapter shows students how all the skills and knowledge previously presented in this textbook are integrated so they can plan the ICT infrastructure, its implementation, and the necessary post-implementation review.

The precursor to infrastructure design is understanding which technologies are available and suitable for building ICT infrastructure. Unit 1 provided an introduction to ICT infrastructure by introducing the information and communication technology (ICT) infrastructure architecture with all of its components and constituent technologies. This is a "framework," and additional technologies not covered in this textbook can easily be placed into this it. Once the framework is understood, and the business analyst knows how to place other technologies into framework, the analyst is ready to create ICT infrastructure. In fact, it's a good idea for students to review this framework to ensure their understanding, because understanding it is essential to good ICT recommendation creation. The ICT infrastructure must be created using the analytical techniques discussed in earlier chapters, including pre-implementation cost-benefit (or other metrics-based) planning, along with good business process planning, and systematic measurement of ICT implementation outcomes. All of these activities must focus on stakeholders of the ICT implementation, especially the customer and users.

With the foundational concepts from earlier chapters understood, the business analyst is ready to plan infrastructure. The flow of the business-driven infrastructure design process, which was introduced in earlier chapters, can be seen in Figure 12-1.

As we have discussed previously in this textbook, the four phases of the business-driven infrastructure design process include (1) analysis, (2) design, (3) implementation, and (4) post-implementation. Some overlap occurs among the phases, and it is reasonable to expect that, as the business analyst progresses through the phases, new information will become available. New information will cause the business analyst to go back and update previous documents to reflect that new information. Even though the phases are presented as a cycle it is important to return to earlier phases to correctly update the documentation so that the final design will be correct.

FIGURE 12-1 Flow of Business-Driven Infrastructure Design Process

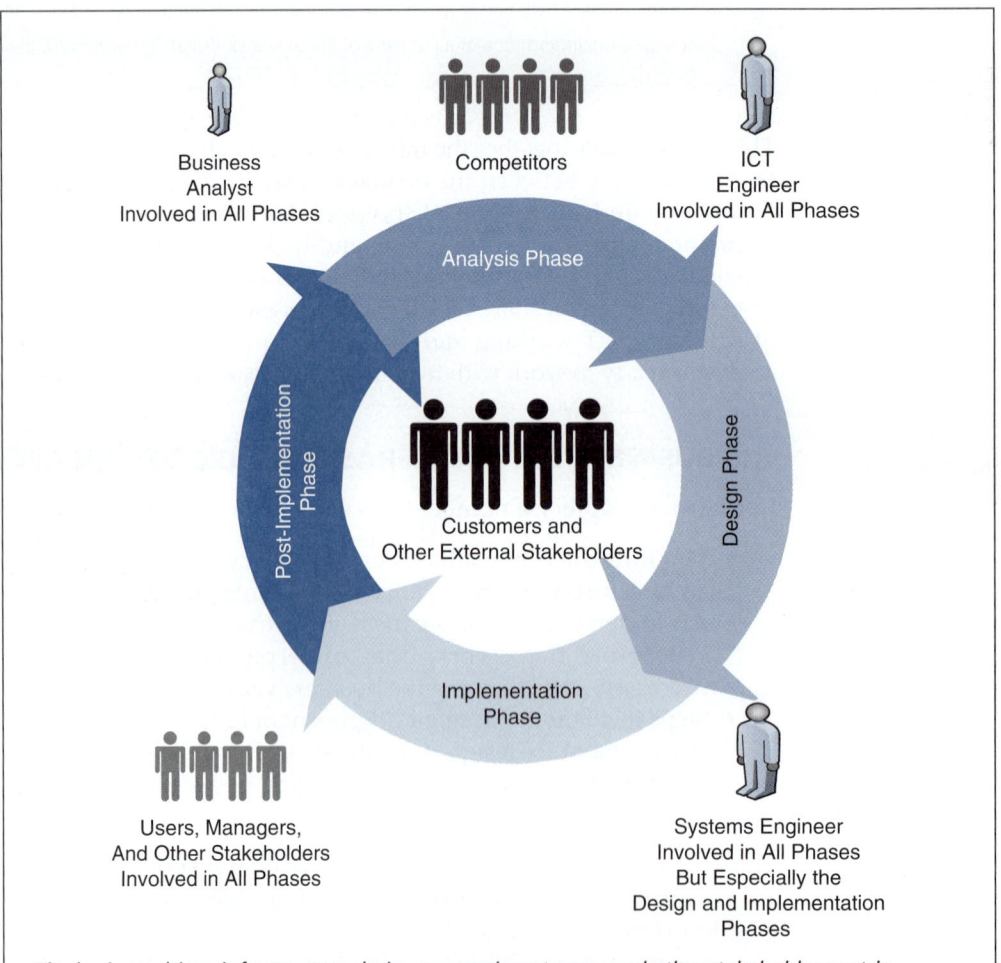

The business-driven infrastructure design process is customer- and other stakeholder-centric. The four phases (analysis, design, implementation, and post-implementation) are both overlapping and cyclic. The phases are overlapping because sometimes information that becomes evident in one phase affects a previous one, which means going back and updating previous documentation. The phases are cyclic in the sense that once ICT infrastructure is implemented, post-implementation review is undertaken, leading back into the analysis phase because the competitive environment is always in a state of flux. The various participants who surround the cyclic process shown in this figure are discussed in the textbook.

> ### VIGNETTE BOX 12-1
> #### TSI and Customer Perceptions of Ticket Sales
>
> As an example, is competitive advantage created for TSI if it builds ICT infrastructure that supports ticket sales and customers do not use it because they do not like something about kiosk design, the speed of purchase, the way customer service complaints are handled, or some other aspect of the ticket purchasing experience? Without customers, there would be no profit for TSI.

The Business-Driven Infrastructure Design Team

Keep in mind that business-driven infrastructure design, by its very nature, is team-oriented and customer-centric. By that, we mean that the customer and other stakeholders are central to designing ICT infrastructure and therefore must be in the center of the process. All assumptions, design decisions, and business process flows must be examined from the customer's perspective. In Figure 12-1, the customer is shown in the middle diagram—customers must be the driving force behind all decisions that are made. An example of the need for a customer-centered approach can be seen in Vignette Box 12-1.

A number of people are involved in all business-driven infrastructure design phases. This team approach to problem solving does not involve just the business analyst as a decision maker. The business analyst is responsible for moving the various phases forward by acting as a coordinator, recommender, designer, and documentation expert. The business analyst may possess the skills and knowledge covered earlier in this textbook and may even be the primary person who drives the phases, but the business analyst is not a "lone ranger." The business analyst needs to understand what technologies are available, but that person is not expected to be an expert on all technologies. Other members of the team, such as customers, external stakeholders, ICT engineers, and systems analysts bring background and specialized knowledge. A good example might involve using the technology WiMAX to provide connectivity for TSI's kiosks around New York City and can be seen in Vignette Box 12-2. This example typifies why the business analyst needs to keep current on technologies. The analyst does not need to be a technical expert, but rather an expert on the business application of technologies, as well as able to discern which technologies are worth pursuing.

The ICT engineer and the systems analyst need to be members of the infrastructure design team as well as a part of all business-driven infrastructure design phases. Their participation on the team, from the initial analysis through the final phase of post-implementation, is essential. Many of the activities of the ICT engineer, systems analyst, or server administrator may occur in parallel during the business-driven infrastructure design phases, so it is important to have all appropriate technical staff involved early in the design process as experts who can speak to the viability of ICT infrastructure options. Even though technically oriented staff may be more involved in the design and implementation stages, their presence is beneficial at all phases.

The users, managers, and other internal and external stakeholders also need to be part of the team responsible for all phases of business-driven infrastructure design. They provide valuable input, and even though this point was made earlier in the

> ### VIGNETTE BOX 12-2
> #### TSI and WiMAX
>
> A business analyst who recommends WiMAX for TSI needs to know what WiMAX is and how it can bring business value, but no business analyst is expected to know all of the technical details of WiMAX or how to implement it. That said, the business analyst does need to understand any technology to be recommended, along with its business implications, and how to cost justify its use.

textbook, it's worth making again—*managers will tell you how a business process is supposed to work, while customers, users, and staff are more apt to tell you what actually occurs.* Customers and users bring unique perspectives that make it essential that they are part of the team.

Next, we will turn to describing each phase of the business-driven infrastructure design. Keep in mind that even though these phases are listed in a defined order, and that the diagram shows a cyclic set of phases (Figure 12-1), the process will almost always encounter new information that causes the business analyst, in conjunction with the business-driven infrastructure design team, to revisit earlier phases as they attend to process improvements and innovation when building and maintaining a customer-centric ICT infrastructure.

Analysis Phase

The **analysis phase** facilitates an understanding of the company and the industry for which the ICT infrastructure is being implemented. In effect, it sets the stage for ICT infrastructure alignment with the organization's business strategy. The major outputs of the analysis phase include *(1) extensive research about the organization and its competitors*, as well as a *(2) list of ICT-mediated objectives* and a *(3) gap analysis*. Standard business modeling tools are used to analyze company needs and develop a background on the industry from the ICT perspective. The goal is to create value propositions on which to base process creation and change initiatives supported by ICT infrastructure recommendations. These propositions and the resultant recommendations must tie directly back to the organization's business strategy. Getting to ICT value propositions of an organization can be tricky, but certain steps can help the analyst in this process. Understanding the ICT value proposition takes a team effort on the part of the business analyst, users, staff, managers, identified project champions, and others. This team will eventually feed directly into the team needed for the design phase of the business-driven infrastructure design process.

THE ORGANIZATION AND ITS COMPETITIVE ENVIRONMENT

All organizations must understand and define the marketplace in which they do business. It is essential that the business analyst conducts research to learn about its competitors. Gaining competitive advantage requires that your organization know about its competitors' good/services. Part of that knowledge includes the awareness of what the competitors provide to their customers, and how your organization can respond to provide better products/services. Often it is a competitors' uniqueness that helps that company garner market share. Therefore, your organization needs to know what a competitor's uniqueness is and what competitive threat it poses. It is also essential that your organization know what customer expectations are and how to provide products/services that the customer perceives as superior. The analyst can only get to this information through solid business research. Some information will be "hard data" from sources such as annual reports of your competitors. Other information will be "soft data" that comes from white papers, industry analyst reports, or trade journals. Studying hard and soft data will assist your organization in selecting the specific strategic approaches to take. Strategic approaches (e.g., focused, industry-wide, price, product quality) must be a central part of the organization's infrastructure design team conversation. This information will drive many of the ICT infrastructure decisions.

ORGANIZATIONAL OVERALL STRATEGY

Your company can decide on an industry-wide strategic approach that affects an entire industry. TSI is a prime example, as described in Vignette Box 12-3.

TSI could also pare back its efforts and take a less risky approach. TSI could change its business model with a strategic approach that focuses on a specific area of

> ## VIGNETTE BOX 12-3
>
> ### TSI's Industry-Wide Approach
>
> TSI's Mission Statement
>
> > Employ technological solutions to provide easy access to tickets for movies, Broadway shows, and other ticketed events in large metropolitan areas.
>
> This approach will affect the way the ticket sales industry in New York City operates. As part of its unique business model, TSI will purchase blocks of seats from each venue at a discount and resell them at the face value of the ticket without any service charge. TSI believes that significant discounts are negotiable through bulk purchasing arrangements because TSI takes the risk for predicting sale levels for individual events. By committing to purchase blocks of seats, TSI guarantees its venue partners revenue for those seats, thus increasing the venues' incentive to sell at substantial discounts. TSI's flexible and real-time distribution network allows it to realize a profit on the margin for each ticket. Also, the fact that TSI will **sell tickets at face value with no service charge or markup** makes them unique in the industry. Taken together, these strengths will greatly affect theater sales in the NYC area. In other words, if successful, TSI could change the industry and would be taking an industry-wide strategic approach.

its business. For example, TSI could focus on ticket delivery as opposed to a more ubiquitous approach that includes delivery and pricing (see Vignette Box 12-4).

Organizations also need to decide on either a cost-leadership strategy in which the organization aims to be a low-cost producer of goods/services, or a product differentiation strategy in which the organization produces products that are distinct in the marketplace. The organization can also use a combination of these strategies. Some possibilities for TSI can be seen in Vignette Box 12-5.

Use of Business Models The best way for the business analyst to determine which strategic approach to recommend is to analyze the industry and the organization, and then work with management and users to determine which strategy is best. Business modeling tools, such as those introduced earlier in this textbook, should also be used to determine the ICT value proposition as well as which strategies are most likely to succeed. These business models must be selected for their usefulness to the organization and in making ICT infrastructure recommendations. These business models and tools include:

- Information technology planning process
- Functional vs. process organizational view
- Value chain analysis
- Competitive forces analysis
- Supply chain analysis
- Strength, weaknesses, opportunity, and threat analysis
- ICT infrastructure, business strategy, and process change models

> ## VIGNETTE BOX 12-4
>
> ### TSI Focused Approach
>
> TSI could use the same mission statement:
>
> > Employ technological solutions to provide easy access to tickets for movies, Broadway shows, and other ticketed events in large metropolitan areas.
>
> In a more traditional model, TSI would purchase tickets at face value and then charge a service fee or markup on tickets. TSI's product differentiation would be sales through kiosks. This strategic approach focuses on a new delivery mechanism but works within the existing financing framework of the industry. This approach would be a focused approach.

VIGNETTE BOX 12-5

TSI Strategic Focus Example

	Cost Leadership	Product Differentiation
Industry-Wide	TSI could select a strategy to sell tickets using a new business model for the industry (e.g., purchasing tickets at a discount and selling at face value without service charges), and delivering tickets through a unique arrangement of kiosks and the web. That strategy should produce an industry-wide low-cost solution (i.e., no service charges) while still providing tickets at face value (i.e., maintaining quality). **This strategy is industry-wide because of the change in delivery model for tickets; it is cost leadership because of the purchasing arrangements from venues and the sales to customers without service charges.**	TSI could choose a strategy in which it provides a unique delivery mechanism though kiosks and the web. It could maintain the traditional ticket markup structure used by its competitors. This strategy could produce products (i.e., ticket sales) unique to an industry-wide marketplace at a price that is fair to the customer. But TSI only differentiates itself on product delivery, not on cost leadership. **This strategy is industry-wide because of the change in delivery systems for tickets; if you consider ticket delivery part of the product, then this new delivery method strategy is also product differentiation. The traditional costing model (i.e., ticket cost plus service charge) is not done in this strategy, which would not lead to a cost leadership position.**
Focused	TSI could adopt a strategy in which it sells tickets to the consumer at a discounted price, based in its bulk buying, but does not focus on a unique technology-based delivery system. Sales would occur through "traditional" box office locations. This strategy is largely non-ICT related. It should be noted that this strategy should provide a low-cost solution while still maintaining quality (i.e., the same tickets at a lower price—look at www.tkts.com for an example). **This strategy would be focused on cost leadership, with no ICT infrastructure to support sales, but the purchasing arrangement and the way ticket sales prices are derived should create the cost leadership strategy necessary to gain competitive advantage.**	TSI could sell tickets through an ICT Infrastructure of kiosks, and use a discounted pricing structure (i.e., discounted ticket price plus service charge). It could provide product differentiation through a strategy that creates a "ticket buying club" where the customer pays an annual fee to become a member of the club. **This strategy is focused on produce differentiation through a unique delivery system and ticket discounts based on membership in a "theater ticket buying club."**

This figure gives examples of how TSI might develop strategies which can potentially be translated into competitive advantage through ICT implementation.

- Hypercompetition model
- ICT initiative economic outcome model
- Organizational approaches to product innovation
- ICT initiative objective setting and attributes
- Strategic alignment of IT
- ICT-based gap analysis

These tools give the business analyst methods for modeling and planning. They can all be used to plan and make ICT infrastructure recommendations based on the competitive environment and the objectives of the organization.

It is essential that your organization knows and understands its competitive marketplace. Unless the organization knows what the competition is doing, it will not know whether it can provide a product/service better, cheaper, faster, or in a more innovative way. The only way to understand those factors is to study and analyze the competitive marketplace. It is also necessary to thoroughly understand what the customer needs and wants. Without understanding the customer, it is not possible to determine an effective strategic direction.

STRATEGY IN ALIGNMENT WITH ICT

Once the competitive marketplace and the customer's needs, desires, and perceptions are understood, then the organization can clarify its mission and vision statements. It is from those statements that strategic plans can be developed to outline what the company wants to become. Additionally, those strategic plans provide the basis from which ICT infrastructure annual operating plans can be set. These ICT operating plans indicate the specific objectives that can be filled by ICT infrastructure, the resources that are necessary to obtain the objectives, and identification of the project champions. Based on this objective-driven gap analysis, the ICT department of an organization can establish plans for specific ICT projects.

As the gap analysis is developed, a list of business processes that are candidates for creation/innovation/improvement will emerge, which sets the stage for business process modeling as discussed in the previous chapter. The business analyst creates process maps, "as-is" business process models, and "to-be" business process models. The gap analysis helps determine what is needed to move from "as-is' processes to "to-be" processes. Some reasons we create business process models are to show how we can reduce cost, improve product/service quality, grow revenue, and show regulatory compliance. No process should be created or changed unless the process is thoroughly understood and the reasons for changing it can be justified and explained through setting objectives.

Business processes should also be created or changed only if they have a role in creating value for the organization (i.e., supporting the organization's value proposition). Often that value creation comes in the form of cost reduction, improvement of product quality, revenue growth, or regulatory compliance, but whatever the reason is, it must be known. Sometimes it is not apparent how processes contribute to value creation. For example, processes that strengthen external partner ties or create co-opetition may have a direct impact on an organization's ability to create value, or they may not. It is important to understand the effect of competitive forces when creating externally facing business processes.

Business processes that support existing organizational strengths are often the best candidates for process improvements or innovation. The same is true of processes that are weak and do not contribute sufficiently to the organization's value proposition. Often they can be improved so they provide greater support to the organization. Finally, business processes that exploit opportunities in the marketplace or deal with competitive threats are prime candidates.

All processes that are selected as candidates for creation/improvement/innovation must have objectives and measurement plans to determine the success of the new process. Plans discussed earlier in this textbook include:

- Variance approach (e.g., improved customer service, increased productivity, increase in net profits)
- Process approach

- Total cost of ownership
- Financial/accounting approaches
  - Return on investment
  - New present value
  - Cost-benefit
- Economic models
  - Economic utility
  - Multi-attribute utility theory
- Statistical models
  - Correlation statistics
  - Regression models
- Balanced Scorecard (with its four quadrants)
  - Translating the vision
  - Communicating and linking
  - Business planning
  - Feedback and learning

It is essential that appropriate measurement tools are selected and plans created that measure business processes *before* and *after* process change in order to assess the impact of the change.

Once objectives are set and measurement plans are in place, it is a good time to make preliminary decisions about the actual ICT infrastructure. (Note that strategic alignment occurs through setting objectives and creating measurement plans before any ICT recommendations are made—it is essential that the business analyst understand the goals and how success is defined before any recommendations are made so that we know if, when implemented, the recommendations have the desired effect.) At this point the team should have an initial understanding of what hardware will be needed to support the various components of the ICT infrastructure architecture. An initial list of those components should be documented as a starting place for ICT infrastructure design.

All the documentation gathered during the analysis phase must be reviewed, and all business processes must be considered as candidates in an expanded gap analysis. This expanded gap analysis will allow the business analyst and ICT engineer to make recommendations that can be designed and implemented. As part of the analysis phase all of the documentation created (e.g., business models/tools) should be closely studied to ensure that strategic objectives align with the mission and vision statements. All of these tasks must be done in concert and alignment with the business models already discussed. The ICT infrastructure components in the preliminary list should be reviewed to ensure that they will support the objectives identified in the gap analysis. This should ensure that you are aligning ICT with organizational strategy. The analysis phase is summarized in Figure 12-2.

Design Phase

The first step of the **design phase** is to review the information, recommendations, and gap analysis from the analysis phase of the business-driven infrastructure design process. These recommendations and the gap analysis were reconciled with the mission, vision, and strategic objectives of the organization during the analysis phase, and now the job of the business analyst is to build on the recommendation the team created as part of the analysis phase. The team will continue into the design phase and most likely be a continuation of the analysis team with potentially more staff added. At a minimum, the team must consist of the business analysts, project champions, users, staff, managers, network engineers, and systems analysts to design an ICT infrastructure that will support the strategic objectives solidified in the gap analysis. The gap analysis will provide guidance showing the business

> - Analysis of the Organization and Its Competitive Environment
>   - Define the marketplace and do research to understand who the competitors are, what they provide to customers, what makes the competitors unique and a competitive threat, what customer expectations are, and how to provide superior products/service.
>   - Decide on an industry-wide strategic approach or a strategic approach that focuses on a specific area of its business.
>   - Decide on a cost-leadership strategy where the organization aims to be a low-cost producer of goods/services or a product differentiation strategy where the organization produces products that make the organization appear different in the marketplace.
>   - Develop whichever models make sense from a functional and/or departmental perspective (e.g., value chain, supply chain, competitive forces, value web, etc.).
> - Based on the analysis, develop/understand the organization's mission and vision and ensure strategic alignment of ICT recommendations.
>   - Understand customers' needs and desires.
>   - Clarify the organization's mission and vision statements.
>   - Develop a set of objectives that can be fulfilled by ICT infrastructure.
>   - Ensure strategic alignment of ICT recommendations with the organization's mission, vision, and strategic objectives by selecting those recommendations that fit the organization's vision and strategic objectives.
> - Develop a list of business processes that are candidates for creation/innovation/improvement.
>   - Understand which business processes should be improved and which should be innovated; obviously, existing organizations are candidates for process innovation (e.g., moving from as-is processes to to-be processes), while new organizations are candidates for initial process design.
>   - Determine why each business process is being implemented (e.g., cost reduction, quality improvement, revenue growth, regulatory compliance, etc.).
>   - Understand each business process role in value-creating activities; external partner relationships; competitive forces; support of organizational strengths and strengthening of an organization's weaknesses, exploitation of opportunities, and dealing with competitive threats.
> - Make initial infrastructure recommendations.
> - Update the gap analysis.
>   - Know where the organization is now, where it wants to be, what it will take to get there, and who the project champions are.
>   - Develop a measurement plan to gauge the success of business process improvement/innovation (e.g., Balanced Scorecard, technology justification models, etc.).
>
> This summary of the analysis phase of the business-driven infrastructure design model is based on material found in throughout the textbook. Please consult those earlier chapters for specific details.

FIGURE 12-2 Analysis Phase Summary

processes that must be created/improved/innovated to achieve competitive positioning. The three streams in the design phase can be seen in Figure 12-3. This figure is not meant to indicate a division of labor, but rather to show which members of the team will principally drive each section of the ICT infrastructure architecture design. It is important to note that each component of the architecture and each project within those components must have project champions. The same is true of those projects that cut across components, such as enterprise-wide components. A project champion(s) finds resources and drives projects to completion. Other team members provide the business analyst and project champion the input and skills necessary for the project to be successful. Several steps will most likely be going on simultaneously during the design phase:

- Since business processes has been identified, process modeling can occur.
- The initial ICT infrastructure list can be verified and the ICT infrastructure design begun.
- Systems analysis and design can be started once processes are modeled and everyone knows how the business will function.

FIGURE 12-3 Team Involvement in the ICT Architecture Design Phase

ENTERPRISE-WIDE SOFTWARE COMPONENTS Enterprise-wide software, including ERP, e-commerce/e-business, document management, knowledge management, and other specialized applications.	**User Components**	Items that directly interface with the user, including workstations, printers, scanners, associated software (especially desktop applications), and specialized applications
	Service Components	Those network parts that facilitate network operations with direct user interface, including printing services, inter/intra office communications (i.e., telephone or fax), network attached storage, database/application servers, security servers and appliances, and VPN technology.
	Network Components	Those items/concepts traditionally thought of as networking and telecommunications equipment, including network switching and routing hardware, media, outside vendor interconnects (i.e., T1, T3, DSL), and cabinetry, patch panels, and associated items.

Within the ICT Architecture, the light grey shows those components traditionally implemented under the direction of the ICT infrastructure engineer (network engineer), and the light blue components will most likely involve the ICT engineer and the systems analyst. Enterprise components (white background) will most likely involve all members of the ICT infrastructure team, because enterprise-wide components cut across all the other components. These guidelines provide the business analyst with a starting place in the process of creating ICT infrastructure.

BUSINESS PROCESS DESIGN

Once the business analyst knows which processes are candidates for creation/improvement/innovation, process design can continue. The analyst should use the list of candidate processes and the associated gap analysis to develop a process map, and then compare that map to the gap analysis to determine whether any components are missing. Once the process map is developed and agreed to by the team, the work of creating individual process models can be started.

Chapter 11 discussed process mapping and modeling in depth. A set of business process documents should be developed in conjunction with user, staff, manager, and other stakeholder input. This set of business process diagrams can be used in discussions with the ICT engineers and systems analysts to determine what ICT infrastructure must be put in place in order for proper implementation of the business processes. It is also a good time to develop cost estimates for implementation of the business processes. Several costing models (e.g., total cost of ownership) have been discussed in previous chapters. As part of the costing process, the team must decide which, if any, processes (or parts of processes) should be contracted to an external vendor, and which processes should be kept in-house. Cloud-based services could be considered at this point. Costing for implementation and running of the business processes (e.g., interaction costs) can be determined. The true total cost of ownership will not be known until the ICT infrastructure has been designed and ICT cost estimates created, but business processes have interaction costs that can be used to determine which processes are the best candidates for implementation. These choices will determine the most appropriate ICT infrastructure and perhaps change the list of recommended business processes selected for implementation, improvements, or innovations.

BUILDING PHYSICAL ICT INFRASTRUCTURE

With the analysis phase completed, the business process diagrams done, the business process costs estimated, and the final set of processes to implement selected, the business analyst can now work with the ICT engineers to create ICT infrastructure design documentation. In order to create this documentation package and update the total cost of ownership estimates, many choices need to be made, including the following:

- Determine bandwidth needs of the organization by analyzing the business processes and associated software to determine peak bandwidth loads.
- Select ICT typologies and components/services required to support the business processes.

- Analyze each component within the ICT infrastructure architecture and select ICT hardware needed to support the business processes uncovered during the analysis phase.
- Determine whether building the infrastructure with in-house staff or contracting out the project makes the most sense.
- Perform site surveys to determine physical locations for all ICT components and ensure the feasibility of their placement.
- Determine ICT staffing needs to support the business processes.
- Update total cost of ownership estimates to include all decisions made thus far.

Organization Size Most of the material and techniques taught in this textbook apply to medium and large organizations. The analyst must scale the materials and techniques to the size of the organization and the scope of the projects under consideration. All of the techniques should be followed; it is just a matter of extent and scope. A smaller organization is not likely to require the same amount of analysis or planning as a larger organization. With a set of preliminary specifications, like in the opening vignette for TSI, the business-driven infrastructure design planning cycle will need to be adapted because much of the analysis is already done. The key is for the business analyst to be flexible and adapt to the situation.

Site Surveys Site surveys are an important part of the design phase and must be done for all locations, including data centers, wireless access points, cable pathways, network switches, routers, and desktops as these can dramatically impact cost, and thus the total cost of ownership. The site survey may also impact which technologies are chosen—for example, an organization may choose a wireless solution because its facilities are too difficult to wire. It is essential that appropriate locations for all ICT infrastructure are known. It does not matter whether the networking portion of the infrastructure is wired, wireless, or both; it is essential that thorough site surveys are done. Part of the survey will include a complete review of all documentation (i.e., process maps and models, initial ICT infrastructure documentation) so everyone understands the physical, electrical, and other needs to successfully implement the ICT infrastructure. An example for TSI is found in Vignette Box 12-6.

A thorough site survey will assess the necessary physical space, appropriate electrical supply, appropriate environmental conditions (e.g., air conditioning, humidity control), the ability to provide the desired number of cable drops, and the ability to provide the pathways to get to the desired locations. For wireless networks, placement of wireless access points must be assessed so optimal placement can be determined.

Desktop Configuration Considerations Important considerations include the business process and software requirements for staff desktops. Such things as processor speed, amount of memory, factor form (e.g., slim desktop, minitower), type/size/resolution of monitors, printing needs, and whether a scanner is needed are a few of the considerations. It is also important to consider the number of network drops (for a wired network) or number of network devices connected

---

VIGNETTE BOX 12-6

TSI's Need for Site Surveys

It would be essential that TSI review its plans for a new building to ensure that it provides adequate physical locations for ICT components. Any review would look at electrical power, network drops, and locations for desktop computers. In addition to TSI's main office, each location where kiosks will be placed needs its own site survey to ensure that each has the appropriate space, electrical power, and facilities for Internet connectivity.

wirelessly. With the proliferation of technology, staff often need more than one connection to the network. They may also possibly need other options such as Bluetooth.

Final Design Documents Having made many of the ICT infrastructure design decisions, final design documents can be created and validated against the analysis documentation. Throughout the design phase, the analyst must keep an eye on the total cost of ownership of solutions being recommended. A number of economic, accounting, and financial analysis tools should be employed to determine whether ICT and business process implementation are cost effective as this may affect which recommendations are funded.

A final reminder on deciding which ICT infrastructure projects to undertake: Prior to undertaking any ICT infrastructure project, a business analyst must measure the value of that project and determine whether the project is cost justified. The models covered in an earlier chapter provide the tools necessary to evaluate the scope of the ICT implementation value proposition.

A design phase summary is included in Figure 12-4.

Implementation Phase

The ICT **implementation phase** involves making sure that all sites are ready for installation of the recommended hardware and software. This phase of the business-driven infrastructure design cycle is largely under the purview of the ICT engineer and systems analyst; however, it is most likely the business analyst who coordinates the functions and ensures that the ICT infrastructure fulfills the strategic initiative identified during the analysis phase.

ICT HARDWARE INFRASTRUCTURE INSTALLATION

During the initial stages of the design phase, all issues identified during the site surveys must be addressed and corrected, including installation and testing of the following:

- Environmental and power conditioning
- Network drops
- Wireless access points
- All hardware and software necessary to support the business processes of the organization

FIGURE 12-4 Design Phase Summary

- Develop an agreed-to set of business process map/models and ICT document set, including estimates of bandwidth needs.
- Perform a site survey and inspection; determine physical requirements for ICT infrastructure (i.e., electrical, wired networking, wireless networking) and adapt as necessary; prepare requirements documentation; recommend necessary building changes.
- Cost ICT infrastructure implementation.
- Determine whether using external services (e.g., cloud- or web-based services) is appropriate or if it is better to build internal infrastructure to support necessary services.
- Select and cost ICT components for each process improvement/innovation (i.e., components for each layer of the ICT infrastructure architecture framework).
  - If building internal ICT infrastructure, determine whether the infrastructure is best built with in-house staff or outsourced.
  - Develop the total cost of ownership for the implementation.
  - Use appropriate accounting, financial, economic, statistical, or other tools to determine payback of ICT implementation.

The business-driven *infrastructure design model includes the design phase activities as summarized in this figure.*

In addition to the physical ICT considerations, appropriate personnel must be hired and trained in the hardware and software.

The business analyst must have an understanding of the ICT infrastructure tasks for building the data center (network core) and implementing the desktop configurations (workgroups). This list introduces what must be completed to build out the network core and workgroups, a summary of which can be seen in Figure 12-5. While the business analyst will probably not be directly involved in these activities, they are included for completeness as they may add to the total cost of ownership.

Confirm ESD Procedures   The ICT engineer must provide details of any local electrostatic discharge (ESD) procedures and precautions that must be followed at the customer site—different customers will have different requirements (e.g., a pharmaceutical company will have different requirements than an oil company). These requirements might include testing personal ESD wrist straps and connecting them to common bonding points, the wearing of additional specialist equipment such as coats and heel straps, and so on. Where additional equipment is required to avoid ESD, it must be included as part of the costs.

Prepare Installation Area   Details of any actions required to prepare the installation area and the responsibilities for carrying this out must be determined. Examples could be providing lifting equipment, fitting of rack stabilizers, and so on. These items should have been identified in the site survey.

Build Cabinets   Details of any cabinet supply and build requirements must be provided. Include the installation of any cabinet fittings, such as DC distribution rails, cable management, and so on. Cabinets and associate fittings can be costly.

Install Cabinet Power Feeds, Rails, and Protective Grounding   Any special requirements for the equipment power supply and grounding must be determined. It is essential that the correct power supply and grounding are provided. For AC supplies, appropriate sockets should be provided in appropriate locations. For DC supplies, cabling should be provided to the equipment position with an appropriate connector. The ICT engineer must connect to the equipment to verify that the power is isolated. All power leads are to be labeled, including details of grounding requirements.

Unpack Equipment   The implementation team is to check that packaging has not been damaged in transit (e.g., check tip and shock indicators.) They are to check that equipment is in good condition when removed from packaging and assemble it. All packaging should be retained until implementation is complete. When equipment needs to be shipped in the original packing material, such as for RMA purposes, the equipment and packing must be matched accurately. The organization must arrange for the removal of packaging from site when all implementation activities have been completed.

Physically Install Equipment, Including Cables between New Network Devices   The ICT engineer should provide details of how the equipment should be positioned physically within the cabinet. Information from the design documents must be included detailing rack/equipment positioning and specific implementation instructions. Referring to the installation documentation that is supplied with each piece of equipment, highlight any points that relate to the specific implementation, and include details where the standard installation document does not provide sufficient information.

Record Equipment Serial Numbers; Check against Delivery Documentation   Provide serial numbers for field-replaceable items. It is important that equipment serial numbers are tracked throughout the implementation. The ICT engineer or project manager should ensure that the serial numbers recorded in this document are compared to those recorded during staging, which will ensure that the records used for support purposes are updated as required and that sufficient spares are held.

FIGURE 12-5 ICT Infrastructure and Core Buildout Overview

- Confirm electrostatic discharge procedures.
- Prepare installation area.
- Build cabinets.
- Install cabinet power feeds, rails, and protective grounding.
- Unpack equipment.
- Physically install equipment, including cables between new network devices.
- Record equipment serial numbers; check against delivery documentation.
- Install intracabinet power cabling and protective grounding cabling.
- Install intra- and intercabinet communications cables.
- Verify circuit termination in network core patch panel.
- Install and test Internet connectivity.
- Power up equipment.
- Verify/load system software/firmware.
- Configure equipment.
- Load server-based software.
- Add equipment to network.
- Complete installation tests.
- Complete commissioning tests.
- Go live!

Source: Adapted from Pearson Education, Peachpit Press, 2010.

Install Intracabinet Power Cabling and Protective Grounding Cabling The ICT engineer must provide details of any intra-cabinet power cabling to be installed, considering possible effects of electromagnetic interference as well as any limitations on cable length.

Install Intra- and Intercabinet Communications Cables The ICT engineer must provide details of the intra- and intercabinet communications cabling to be installed, considering possible effects of electromagnetic interference as well as any limitations on cable length.

Verify Circuit Termination in Network Core Patch Panel Details of the patching requirements that are necessary to connect carrier circuits must be given by the ICT engineer, and the engineer must document how this should be verified.

Install and Test Internet Connectivity Working with representatives from the ISP, the ICT engineers must install and verify the operation of all Internet connectivity.

Power Up Equipment Once all data center equipment and cabling are installed, the ICT engineer-specified power-up procedure must be followed. The installation should refer to the site survey to identify any restrictions as to how the equipment should be powered up.

Verify/Load System Software/Firmware The ICT engineers and the system administrators will install operating system software and firmware or they will come preinstalled from the manufacturer. They must also carry out any necessary upgrades.

Configure Equipment All ICT hardware must be configured to meet the recommendation and components/services specified during the analysis phase.

Load Server-Based Software The ICT engineers and the server administrators must install the server-based applications and test their functionality before adding other equipment to the network.

Add Equipment to Network ICT engineer-directed connections to add workgroups to the network must be followed. That includes materials uncovered during the site surveys performed earlier. For complete testing of the network, all desktop equipment must be installed, software applications installed, and tested.

Complete Installation Tests The business analyst, ICT engineer, and others must perform high-level installation tests to ensure that the ICT infrastructure network core is operating as specified. Product documentation material provides the low-level (hardware) test details. The aim of installation tests should primarily be to prove that each piece of equipment is operational.

Complete Commissioning Tests All members of the business-driven infrastructure design team should be involved in high-level set of commissioning tests. ICT engineers should perform low-level operational tests, while users and other team members should perform high-level operational tests. The aim of commissioning tests should primarily be to prove that each site, network core, and workgroup is operational. The results of these tests should be documented.

Go Live! With all tests successfully completed, the ICT infrastructure is ready to go live. There is much planning and coordination needed between business strategy, ICT engineers, and other stakeholders before an actual build out can occur. Although it is true that the business analyst may not have much hands-on participation in the build out, it is important that he or she knows what the ICT engineer and systems analyst need to do to bring the business-driven infrastructure design recommendations from paper to reality. It is equally important that the indirect cost (e.g., time, salaries, etc.) of the build out be included in all value-based calculations.

The preceding sections summarize the implementation of ICT infrastructure. This list is not meant to be complete, but rather give the business analyst an idea of what must be done to bring the ICT infrastructure design online. This list of tasks should be expanded/contracted as necessary, based on the size of the organization and the ICT infrastructure being brought online. However, no matter the size of the ICT infrastructure, this list represents things that must be considered—again the scope and scale of these activities is largely dependent on the scope and scale of the ICT infrastructure and the organization. Keep in mind that all implementation activities affect the total cost of ownership. Figure 12-6 gives a summary of the implementation phase.

Post-Implementation Phase

The **post-implementation phase** is about following the infrastructure after going live. Measurement systems put into place to monitor the success of the ICT infrastructure allow the organization to be forward thinking after the initial implementation. Constant monitoring of ICT infrastructure utilization and measurement against objectives uncovered during the analysis phase will aid in ensuring that the ICT infrastructure performs as planned and aids the organization in maintaining competitive advantage.

It is reasonable to expect that information will be gathered during the previous phases of the business-driven infrastructure design process regarding expected growth, but even so, the "Go Live" point is the first time real customer-based data about

---

The implementation phase is largely the purview of the ICT engineer, systems analyst, server administrators, and their teams, therefore these items are briefly covered here so the business analyst is familiar with these activities. It is broken into two parts: (1) ICT infrastructure, and (2) software infrastructure.

- ICT Infrastructure
  - Implement electrical for desktop and data center configurations.
  - Implement environmental controls for data center.
  - Implement appropriate wired network drops and wireless ICT hardware.
  - Implement Internet connectivity.
  - Deploy data center hardware and operating systems.
  - Deploy desktop hardware (e.g., workstations, printers, etc.) and operating systems.
  - Test all Internet, data center, and desktop connectivity.

- Software Infrastructure
  - Deploy data center applications.
  - Deploy desktop applications.
  - Test software infrastructure.

- Go Live!

This figure summarizes the business-driven infrastructure design model implementation phase activities.

FIGURE 12-6 Implementation Phase Summary

FIGURE 12-7 Post-Implementation Phase Summary

- Implement and monitor the measurement plan to gauge the success of the ICT and software infrastructure that has been implemented.
- Monitor the marketplace and competitor actions to ensure that your organization maintains its competitive stature.
- Recommend changes and as necessary return to the analysis phase. Work through the design stage and implementation stage as necessary.

This figure summarizes the business-driven infrastructure design model post-implementation phase activities.

user/customer satisfaction and ICT infrastructure performance can be gathered. These data should be used to create a plan for infrastructure upgrades. It is at this point that the business-driven infrastructure design cycle returns to the analysis phase. It is continually necessary to revisit business strategy, update business models, update value propositions and infrastructure recommendations, and better understand your competitor's impact upon your ICT infrastructure and business planning. Alignment of ICT infrastructure with strategic planning is an ongoing function that will keep infrastructure abreast of changes in the organization and competitive business environment. Post-implementation feeds back directly to the earlier BDID phases. A summary of the post-implementation phase and its activities can be seen in Figure 12-7.

SPECIAL CONSIDERATIONS IN THE POST-IMPLEMENTATION PHASE

Measuring ICT Infrastructure Success By this point in the ICT infrastructure analysis, design, and implementation process, a number of objectives have been identified. It is essential that the business analyst and other members of the team keep on top of taking measurements and aligning those measurements with the objectives set earlier. It is easy to assume that once the ICT infrastructure is running, everyone can go back to business as usual. That assumption is dangerous! Once the ICT infrastructure is online, it is essential that it is diligently monitored to assure strategic alignment.

Monitoring Bandwidth An important consideration in building ICT infrastructure is the maintenance of necessary bandwidth, especially in applications where the customer is sensitive to bandwidth needs. The case of AT&T (a major U.S. telecommunications provider) and deployment of the iPhone teaches a valuable lesson. Upon initial release of the iPhone, AT&T had the exclusive right to sell and provide network services for the iPhone (an Apple Inc. product). AT&T never understood that the iPhone was going to be a data guzzler. The *New York Times* explains the problem:

> It's a data guzzler. Owners use them like minicomputers, which they are, and use them a lot. Not only do iPhone owners download applications, stream music and videos and browse the Web at higher rates than the average smartphone user, but the average iPhone owner can also use 10 times the network capacity used by the average smartphone user. . . . The result is dropped calls, spotty service, delayed text and voice messages and glacial download speeds as AT&T's cellular network strains to meet the demand. Another result is outraged customers. (Wortham, 2009)

The problems will only get worse as new versions of the iPhone that are faster and require more bandwidth are introduced. As the concentration of iPhones increases in metropolitan areas, AT&T's infrastructure must keep pace with user demands, otherwise its networks will degrade further, resulting in greater customer dissatisfaction. Here are several potential solutions that might solve the problem, each of which would have to be analyzed and compared against the services offered by AT&T's competitors:

- Other telecommunication carriers could be allowed to deploy the iPhone (which has happened), potentially decreasing the reliance on the AT&T network. However, this option means that AT&T would lose its exclusive right to sell and provide telecommunications support for the iPhone, which could mean a loss of market share.

> **VIGNETTE BOX 12-7**
>
> **TSI's Need to Monitor Bandwidth**
>
> TSI is composed of a network of kiosks. A preliminary marketing study estimated the number of kiosks established per location and the estimated number of tickets sold during prime hours of sales at those locations. Those estimates drove the bandwidth estimates for the home office and for each kiosk location. If those estimates are wrong, or if customer demand surpasses the estimates, TSI could potentially lose market share because customers find TSI's ticket delivery system too slow or unwieldy. It is essential that TSI monitor its sales by location and the amount of time it takes customers to complete sales. Otherwise TSI could lose market share to more traditional methods of ticket sales.

- AT&T could upgrade its network in areas where the iPhone is heavily deployed. This solution would be expensive for AT&T and would need a thorough cost-benefit analysis.
- AT&T could charge more, or differently (e.g., based on usage), for iPhone data services. This option would need careful study because of its potential impact on the market.

Any potential solutions that AT&T might consider for the iPhone would need careful analysis before a choice is made; however, the lack of bandwidth caught AT&T by surprise. Being caught by surprise is not a situation any company wants to find itself in. An example of TSI's need to watch bandwidth can be seen in Vignette Box 12-7. Bandwidth, latency, and length of transactions are a good proxy for ICT infrastructure activity and should be watched closely.

Reviewing and Updating the Gap Analysis The gap analysis, with its associated objectives and measurements, is one of the main tools that can be used to keep ICT infrastructure in alignment with strategy. The gap analysis should be constantly monitored and kept up to date. It will require that "gaps" are identified through keeping the other modeling tools up to date (e.g., supply chain, value chain, etc.). This essential post-implementation activity needs to be a priority for the organization. If keeping the gap analysis up to date is not a priority, the organization may quickly fall behind its competitors; lose touch with customer perceptions, needs, and desires; and thus lose market share.

Staying in Touch with Users and Customers Organizations can easily lose market share after initial infrastructure implementation by not constantly monitoring customer desires and perceptions. Although it has been mentioned several times in this textbook, it is important enough to mention again here: *Customer perceptions, likes, and dislikes change constantly.* The successful organization constantly monitors its customers, whether through focus groups, customer surveys, reporting from the organization's CRM system, or in many other ways. What is important is that customers are the center of all ICT and strategy planning and that they are a primary consideration when making ICT infrastructure recommendations and changes. Too many organizations are driven by internal policies, politics, or bureaucratic procedures, whereas the successful customer-driven organization focuses on the customer's perceptions.

Figure 12-8 shows how customers can create innovations: "as companies increasingly involve customers in the process of product design, the results tell the tale. Innovation driven by users is not only more organic—it enables the community to pre-declare its approval" (*CRM Magazine*, 2010). This figure contains some ideas that are ICT-related and some that are not, but gives the analyst the flavor of what a customer-driven approach can bring to the marketplace.

Types of Measurement Many types of measurements and tools have been introduced in this textbook. The business analyst and the team must choose which types of analysis are appropriate to measure the impact of ICT infrastructure on business objectives. Because no "one size fits all" list works for this task, the team must create/select the right tools that measure the right things.

Company	How Idea Was Obtained	Customer Idea	Result
Dell	Dell IdeaStorm Community Form	Put Ubuntu on the list of operating systems when building a PC.	In May 2007, Dell started selling three computer systems with Ubuntu preinstalled.
Starbucks Coffee	www.mystarbucksidea.com	Distribute plugs to prevent coffee spillage through lids.	In early 2008, Starbucks shops began carrying little green "Splash Sticks"—part swizzle stick, part splash guard.
Netflix	A contest to improve (by at least 10%) the algorithm used to predict "movies you may like"	The first to break the threshold was "BellKor's Pragmatic Chaos"—a merger of a few original teams.	Awarded the $1 million Grand Prize to BellKor in September 2009—and immediately announced a second competition to involve demographic data in the prediction algorithm.
Flying Dog	Open Source Beer Project	Invited customers and home brewers to create (and recommend changes and modifications to) a new beer recipe.	The frothy beverage—appropriately named "Collaborator Doppelbock"—hit stores in October 2008.
LEGO	www.LegoFactory.com	The toy company set up a consumer-friendly digital design program and invited LEGO fans of all ages to create their own brick sets.	The designs were put to a vote on the web site, and the top 10 were incorporated into three packaged sets sold through the company's direct retail channels, Lego.com, and its catalog service.

FIGURE 12-8 Five Great Customer-Driven Innovations

Chapter Summary

This chapter summarizes the business-driven infrastructure design (BDID) process. The infrastructure planning and implementation cycle (also called the BDID) was reviewed. Each phase—analysis, design, implementation, and post—implementation was discussed. This chapter was meant to pull together the massive amounts of information covered throughout this textbook and provide a framework in which the student can place this information.

Vignette Wrap Up

In this closing chapter, the opening vignette about TSI was used to discuss various issues about how the business-driven infrastructure design process should be implemented. Specifically, these issues were discussed:

- **The customer's likes/dislikes/perceptions about TSI's use of kiosks to deliver tickets.** What good is ICT infrastructure that supports ticket sales if the customers do not use it because they do not like something about the kiosk design, speed of purchase, the way customer service complaints are handled, or some other aspect of the ticket purchasing experience?
- **Use of WiMAX for TSI kiosk deployment.** In order to recommend WiMAX for TSI, a business analyst needs to know what WiMAX is and how it can bring business value, but the business analyst is not expected to know all of the technical details of WiMAX or how to implement it. The business analyst does need to understand a technology before recommending it as well as its business implications, and know how to cost-justify the use of any specific technology.
- **TSI's use of an industry-wide approach.** TSI could impact the way the ticket sales industry in New York City operates through an industry-wide approach. TSI's business model is unique. TSI believes significant discounts are negotiable through bulk purchasing arrangements because TSI takes the risk for predicting sale levels for individual events. By committing to purchase blocks of seats, TSI guarantees its venue partners revenue for those seats, thus increasing their incentive to sell to TSI at substantial discounts. TSI's flexible and real-time distribution network will allow it to realize a profit on the margin for each ticket. Also, the fact that TSI will "sell tickets at face value with no service charge or markup" makes it unique in the industry. If successful, TSI could change the industry and is taking an industry-wide strategic approach.
- **TSI's use of a focused approach.** TSI could use the same mission statement but could use a more traditional model in which it purchases tickets at face value and charges a service fee or markup on tickets. TSI's product differentiation would

be sales through kiosks. This strategic approach focuses on a new delivery mechanism, but works within the existing financing framework of the industry. This would be a more focused approach.
- **TSI's overall strategy.** TSI could employ a number of strategies, which could be industry-wide or focused on a specific area of the ticket industry. Within an industry-wide approach or focused approach, TSI could employ a cost leadership or a product differentiation approach. A description of these strategies and approaches was described in Vignette Box 12-5.
- **Site surveys.** The need for organizations to perform site surveys to ensure the availability of physical locations for ICT components, including electrical power, network drops, and locations for desktop computers, was discussed. In the case of TSI, in addition to TSI's main office, each location where kiosks will be placed will require a site survey to ensure that these external locations have the appropriate space, electrical power, and facilities for Internet connectivity.
- **TSI's need to monitor bandwidth.** TSI is composed of a network of kiosks. A preliminary marketing study estimated the number of kiosks per location and the estimated number of tickets sold during prime hours of sales. Those estimates drove the bandwidth estimates for the home office and for each kiosk location. TSI could lose market share to more traditional methods of ticket sales if they do not monitor bandwidth.

In this chapter TSI was used to discuss the business infrastructure design process. The student should use the TSI examples, and incorporate that information with the rest of the textbook to better understand the business infrastructure design process.

End of Chapter Questions/Assurance of Learning

1. Select a company that you are familiar with (it could be your current employer). Write an essay describing each phase of the business infrastructure design process, and give examples of how you would use this process to aid the company in its search for customer-mediated ICT infrastructure value.
2. For the same company in question #1, make strategy recommendations (hint: use Vignette Box 12-5 as a format) that will aid the company in using ICT to increase market share.
3. Using the business models, develop a technology gap analysis and objectives for TSI, the company in the opening vignette.
4. Develop a plan for a company you are familiar with (or TSI) for all phases of the business infrastructure design process. Then develop a document that describes the implementation of the plan.
5. Create an ICT objective-based measurement plan for any company you select.

Case Exercises

These exercises build on the case exercises from previous chapters.
1. XYZ Inc. is a hardware company that builds network hardware and wants to expand its product offerings to ensure it is a viable alternative to other network hardware manufacturers. Write a brief paper and presentation expanding on the XYZ case exercise from Chapter 11 showing specific ways in which XYZ Inc. can benefit its customers during the analysis, design, implementation, and post-implementation phases of business-driven infrastructure design.
2. Prepare a paper and presentation documenting all phases of the business-driven infrastructure design process for HealthyWay HMO. Use this exercise to pull together the case exercises for HealthyWay from all previous chapters.
3. Select a company you are familiar with and document all phases of its business-driven infrastructure design process. Prepare a paper and presentation. Present your analysis to the class.

Key Words and Concepts

analysis phase 366
bandwidth 381
Building Physical ICT Infrastructure 372
business-driven infrastructure design cycle 363
business-driven infrastructure design team 365
business models 367
business process design 372
customers 365
design phase 370
gap analysis 366
implementation phase 374
measuring ICT infrastructure success 378
overall strategy 366
post-implementation phase 377
site surveys 373
strategy in alignment with ICT 369
users 363

References

CRM Magazine. (2010, February 23). 5 great customer-driven innovations. CRM Magazine, 14(1), 28.
Pearson Education, Peachpit Press. (2010, February 22). Implementation plan template. Retrieved Feb 22, 2010, from http://ptgmedia.pearsoncmg.com/images/1587200880/appendix/Appendix4-B.doc.
Wortham, J. (2009, September 2). Customers angered as iPhones overload AT&T. New York Times.

UNIT 4

SUMMARY

Unit 4 summarized the steps in the strategic alignment of ICT—how businesses align their IT resource expenditures with their strategic focus. Previous to Unit 4, a number of technical and general organizational and strategic topics were introduced in Units 1, 2, and 3. Unit 4 used TSI extensively. That case was used to pull together business-driven infrastructure design concepts, including ways to analyze an organization and its environment.

Analyzing an organization and its environment requires methods for understanding the organization and its industry, as well as its competitive environment. Remember, the purpose of this textbook is to keep a focus on the technology aspects of competition, which, in the twenty-first century, can be a large driver for gaining market share. The goal of this analysis is to use standard business tools (e.g., value chain analysis, supply chain analysis, gap analysis, etc.) to understand how ICT can enhance an organization's competitive positioning in the marketplace. Earlier in the text, the ICT infrastructure architecture was introduced, as was the purpose of organizational, industry, and competitive analysis—to develop objectives and a gap analysis that allows the organization to determine how it is going to fulfill the ICT value proposition.

Among the learning objectives of Unit 4 were learning how to create the ICT value proposition and relating it to the need for ICT infrastructure. In order to do so, the core competencies of the organization needed to be defined as well as what drives them. In order to create the ICT value proposition, the business analyst must sense the environment, incorporating input from all stakeholders within and outside the organization. The alignment of ICT infrastructure with organizational strategy can only be done by determining what ICT resources the organization currently has, what goals and objectives it desires to fulfill, how ICT infrastructure can assist in fulfilling those goals and objectives, and what ICT resources it will take to fulfill them.

A major part of meeting goals and objectives is in understanding the business processes of an organization. Whether it is "as-is" or "to-be" processes in an existing organization, or it is creating new processes for a new organization, the business analyst must be able to tie these processes back to the organization's goals and objectives to ensure strategic alignment. Business processes must be linked closely to the goals and objectives stated in the gap analysis. It is important that the business analyst understand how to draw the linkage from organizational strategy, goals, and objective to the creation of sustainable ICT infrastructure, buttressed by the organization's business processes.

It is important to know how to align ICT infrastructure recommendations with strategy, but it is equally important to know how to document those processes and technology recommendations. Earlier chapters discussed some tools to document business processes and the associated technology recommendations. It is important that the business analyst understand business process modeling and how it can assist in conveying ides and recommendations about business processes to those not familiar with modeling techniques. Business process modeling notation was introduced as a way to describe and document business processes, concepts, and recommendations. It is essential that business processes are understood and modeled before ICT recommendations are made. The business analyst needs to be able to document the business process as well as work with the ICT engineer in the modeling of the actual infrastructure. A strong linkage between the business process models and the ICT infrastructure models is critical.

In this unit, the entire business-driven infrastructure design cycle was reviewed in an attempt to bring together all the topics from previous chapters. The goal was for the student to gain better understanding of how all the chapters fit together, and a better understanding of why business analysis was emphasized in earlier chapters. It is the analysis phase that provides the bedrock for the design, implementation, and post-implementation phases of the business-driven infrastructure design cycle. Some time was spent giving the business analyst insight into what the ICT engineer and systems analyst need to get done to bring ICT infrastructure and its associated systems online. As the process moves into the post-implementation phase, the business analyst is encouraged to keep a close eye on the customers and their desires, as well as bandwidth consumption and planning.

GLOSSARY

Note: The numbers in parenthesis following the definition denote the pages the term can be found on.

access control. Protection of confidential, important, or secure information by implementing credentials that identify the user in order to control access to ICT network and other specific resources. (170)

access control list (ACL). A list of users on a network and their permitted access to network resources. (118, 171)

Address Resolution Protocol (ARP). Responsible for converting a Layer 3 address (i.e., an IP address) to a hardware address (i.e., a MAC address). (32)

adware. Any software that automatically displays advertisements to a computer with the purpose of generating revenue for a software author. (166)

analog. Continuous data that exist along a continuum and includes thing like sound, temperature, time, and weight. (6)

analysis phase. The phase of business-driven infrastructure design that facilitates an understanding—through research, objective development, and modeling tools—of the company and the industry for which the ICT infrastructure is being implemented. (366)

annual payback. The amount of money that technology is expected to generate at the end of each year in an NPV calculation. (249)

application layer. Layer 5 of the TCP/IP–OSI architecture, consisting of a number of protocols (e.g., FTP, HTTP, HTTPS, SMTP, POP). (30)

application servers. Hardware (e.g., a PC server) that has software which standardize business logic within an organization and makes that logic available through application program interfaces. (114)

application-as-a-service. Any cloud-based application delivered through a browser to an end user's PC. (147)

artifacts. Symbols that provide additional information about other objects, and include data objects, group, and annotation in BPMN specifications. (321)

Asynchronous Transfer Mode (ATM). A packet-switching protocol that operates at the data link layer of the five-layer hybrid TCP/IP-OSI model and originally designed to provide faster video and voice services over ISDN. (88)

asynchronous transmission. The encoding of a data stream that is preceded by a bit, octet, or larger more complicated synch word that allows the receiver to synchronize itself to the incoming data stream. (13)

attenuation. A signal becoming weaker as it propagates. (10)

automated task. In business process models, a specific activity automated by some type of system or technology. (320)

Balanced Scorecard (BSC). A method of using valuation tools and other hard/soft measures in a unified manner to monitor organizations and their projects. The BSC is especially useful to determine ICT payoff. (258)

bleeding-edge technologies. Technologies that are new, often in the development or initial stages and nascent in the marketplace, with typically very low immediate benefit or payoff from investment but that may form the bedrock of future competitive advantage when implemented appropriately; part of the technology trend curve that should consist of between 10% and 25% of an organization's technology investment. (247)

bus typology. Network in which all hosts attach to one common bus (media) that allows communication among the hosts. (25)

business process diagrams (BPDs). A graphical representation of business process workflows and designs that communicate a variety of information to various stakeholders. (319)

business process modeling (BPM). Representing the processes of an organization graphically so a given process can be designed, improved, or innovated. The two major types are *as-is BPM* and *to-be BPM*. (316)

business process modeling notation (BPMN). A modeling language commonly used to represent business processes to stakeholders. (317)

business systems analyst. The person who understands the technologies and their capabilities in order to ensure that all the technologies fit together to support the business processes, products, and strategy of the organization. (1, 188)

business-driven infrastructure design (BDID). A series of phases—analysis, design, implementation planning, and post-implementation—that assume the iterative approach characterized by a fair amount of "going back-and-forth" in the process of developing an ICT infrastructure. (202)

carrier sense multiple access with collision avoidance + acknowledgment (CSMA/CA+ACK). The way in which 802.11 devices control traffic between WAPs and clients. (61)

carrier sense multiple access with collision detection (CSMA/CD). A scheme to determine whether a bus is busy or whether a computer can use it and send a message; used in wired Ethernet. (50)

channels. Portions of bands within the frequency spectrum that are dedicated to specific types of signals. (55)

ciphertext. Information that has been through an encryption process. (171)

client-server computing. The request-response cycle through which most interactions occur across the Internet, where one computer requests information (the client) and one computer responds with the information (server). (16)

cloud computing. The evolutionary product of the Internet and its protocols and standards, defined by layers of abstraction in which developers or users may not know the specific technologies that are employed in the cloud, but they know the service they want performed. (135)

committed information rate (CIR). A data rate that is guaranteed for Frame Relay connections. (85)

compensation activities. Processes that "compensate" for another process (e.g., when a credit card is declined the card processor may have a compensation activity that records the declination and performs other related business logic). Compensation activities are described in BPMN. (326)

Glossary

connecting objects. Graphical elements in business process diagrams (BPDs) that include sequence flow, message flow, and association. (324)

convergence. The merging of distinct technologies, industries, or devices into a unified whole that characterizes wireless communications providers today. (215)

co-opetition. A sixth force in an industry analysis in which complementary products bring about strategic alliances among competitors. (301)

core competencies. The things essential to the way the organization works, the products and services it delivers, or what the organization does that provide value to its customers and give the organization competitive advantage in the marketplace. (287)

corporate unbundling. A value search model that focuses on cost reduction (lower production costs) and quality improvement strategies (enhancing an organization's product quality), as well as increased efficiencies. (280)

cost of investment. The amount of money spent on the technology in an NPV calculation. (249)

cost reduction. A firm's attempt to achieve market leadership by reducing cost through a number of strategies that reduce cost and thus the final price to the consumer. (277)

cross talk. A special case of EMI in which conductors in a cable interfere with each other. (10)

cultural enablers. Forces or influences, such as organizational culture, level of employee empowerment, the participatory nature of the organization, and organizational politics, that bring about successful process change. (236)

cybercrime. Illegal or malicious activities that use personal computers, corporate or personal networks, or the Internet to perpetrate illegal activities, including illegal physical and digital access or alteration. (161)

data link layer. Layer 2 of the hybrid TCP/IP–OSI architecture. (32)

database servers. A centralized place for organizations to store their data and give access to users and applications on the network; a back-end function that does the actual data manipulation and storage. (115)

database-as-a-service. A cloud-based database management system (DBMS) that allows an application to utilize the database that best fits the application. (147)

denial-of-service (DoS). Cyber attacks that originate from a single source with the objective of overwhelming the target system, thereby preventing it from exchanging data with other systems or using the Internet. (168)

design phase. The phase of business-driven infrastructure design that reviews the information, recommendations, and gap analysis from the analysis phase and includes steps such as process modeling, verifying the initial ICT infrastructure list, and designing ICT infrastructure. (370)

desktop productivity software. Software that enables users to make their workstation useful on the job, such as word-processor, electronic spreadsheet, and presentation software. (125)

diagram list. A listing of the high-level diagrams included in the design documentation. (351)

diagram notes. Attached to actual diagrams to convey facts needed in the creation/change of the infrastructure. (352)

digital data. Data that represent real-world information, such as weight, sound, temperature, or pictures, and are coded as a number of bits (octets). (6)

directory server. Normally one centralized server that maintains the list of credentials and associated ACLs, along with a mapping of logical names of resources to actual physical locations as part of a network's operating system. (118)

discount rate. Management's minimum rate of return on an investment; typically, the higher the risk, the higher the discount rate. (249)

disruptive technologies. Technologies that provide a new way of doing things that do not initially meet the needs of the market, or is a product for which a market may not currently exist, often overturning the dominant technology in the marketplace. (186)

distributed denial-of-service attack (DDoS). A variant of the DoS attack that originates from a number of coordinated sources, rather than from a single source. (168)

economic approaches. Technology justification models that are based on the utility or benefit that something gives and allow "soft" indicators of value to be analyzed. (247)

electrical magnetic interference (EMI). Radio interference that results from the operations of the components in a device or piece of equipment. (9)

e-mail server. A server that handles the e-mail in an organization. It handles protocols such as POP, SMTP, and IMAP. This is a common application often hosted by the organization's ISP. (113)

enablers. Forces or influences, such as information and communication technology (ICT), structural organizational change, and cultural/organizational change, that facilitate process innovation and improvement. (209)

encapsulation. The process of putting a message inside another message so it can be transmitted; the reverse of decapsulation. (34)

encryption. Changing information for transmission over a network, using some type of algorithm, into a form that is unintelligible to anyone who does not possess the algorithm and the cipher used with the algorithm. (171)

end-to-end layer. The transport layer (Layer 4) of the hybrid TCP/IP-OSI model responsible for detecting and correcting any errors found in the message from the layers below it. (36)

enterprise applications. Same as enterprise-wide components. (1)

enterprise resource planning (ERP) system. A complicated set of ubiquitous software that supports business processes and cuts across the enterprise, including front-end and back office services, and operates as one system or application. (125)

enterprise-wide components. From the information and computer technology infrastructure architecture, enterprise-wide software, including ERP, e-commerce/ebusiness, document management, knowledge management, and other specialized applications. (125)

ephemeral ports. Type of transport ports, sometimes called dynamic or private ports, in the range of 49152–65535 and randomly chosen by a host as source ports associated with instances of an application. (35)

Ethernet. Computer networking technologies for LANs, standardized in IEEE 802.3. (13, 41)

exploit tools. Publicly available software tools that allow would-be intruders to determine the vulnerabilities of a computer system or network. (169)

fast follower. A company that duplicates the technologies/products created and implemented by its competitor; the competitor would be a first mover. (190)

financial approaches. Technology justification models based on traditional accounting and finance measures used and understood by accounting and finance staff, and perhaps most readily understood by senior management within an organization. (247)

first-mover advantage. A company's innovative use of technology or some other business process that allows it to gain substantial market share by creating consumer value before its competition. (190)

five forces model. A framework developed by Michael Porter that is useful for industry analysis and strategy development in which five forces that affect an organization's ability to provide products/services at a profit to its customers are examined when making a qualitative assessment of its place within the market. (298)

flow objects. The main graphical elements in business process diagrams (BPDs) that define the behavior of the business process; include events, activities, and gateways. (324)

focused approach. A strategy for achieving long-term and above-average performance that impacts a specific area of a business but may not necessarily impact an entire industry. (191)

frequency spectrum. Signals that range from zero to infinity measured in hertz; all wireless devices operate at channels within the frequency spectrum. (54)

full-duplex. Communication in which both parties can transmit simultaneously. (12)

functional view. The view that defines the departmental and management levels of the organization by breaking it into functional areas—namely finance, sales and marketing, manufacturing, accounting, and finance—that are further divided into levels of management to include strategic, management, knowledge, and operational levels. (211)

functionality list. A list that reflects the business needs of the organization, considers how the network will affect the competitive position of the organization, and incorporates the business analyst's recommendations that will be used in the organization's ICT infrastructure, including network components, service components, user components, and enterprise-wide components. (339)

gap analysis. A tool used to summarize analyses of "Where is my organization today?" and "Where do we want to get to?" and to formalize the ICT recommendations. (301)

General Packet Radio Service (GPRS). A mobile data standard that allows data transmission through a GSM cellular network to provide data services virtually anywhere GSM cellular exists. (92)

hacking. Circumventing computer security to break into a computer via a network or the Internet in order to gain access or do damage to the target computer. (169)

half-duplex. Communication in which only one party can be transmitting at a time. (12)

handoff. Occurs when a mobile client, such as a wireless laptop, travels too far from an access point and then switches to an access point with the same SSID closer to the client. (61)

horizontal runs. Cables that normally are limited to one floor of an office building and run horizontally between a workgroup switch and a device. (43)

hosted applications. Client-server computing in which a client (e.g., a web browser, e-mail client, etc.) is used to access the hosted application, giving users access to remote servers. (137)

ICT hierarchy. The network core, the backbone (vertical runs), as well as the cabling to the desktop (horizontal runs) laid out in a chart that indicates interconnectivity; composed of one symbol type and its interconnections. (340)

ICT value proposition. A business systems analyst's estimation of the ICT's investment value to the organization confirmed by measurements taken before a project is undertaken, during implementation, and again after the project is completed. (241)

identity theft. Occurs when a cyber attacker collects enough personal information about the identity of another person and uses it. (169)

IEEE 802.11. The most prevalent WLAN technology, which can be used to extend the hardwired Ethernet LAN in an enterprise situation or to provide wireless access in the home or small office. (56)

implementation phase. The phase of business-driven infrastructure design that involves making sure that all sites are ready for installation of the recommended hardware and software; this phase is largely under the purview of the ICT engineer and systems analyst but regularly coordinated by the business analyst to ensure that the ICT infrastructure fulfills the strategic initiative identified during the analysis phase. (374)

improvements (process). Small incremental changes that look to modify existing processes, may be one-time or incremental/continuous, and are generally conceived or implemented in a "bottom-up" approach throughout the organization. (230)

industry-wide approach. Implementation of strategic initiatives that produce an industry-wide, low-cost solution while maintaining quality. (191)

information and communication technology (ICT) infrastructure. A multilayered architecture, driven by the business imperatives of the enterprise and the technology that must support them. (1)

information-as-a-service. Any cloud-based service that provides an application programming interface (API) or other similar method through which an application uses/consumes information. (147)

infrastructure processes. Everything that it takes to make an organization function and typically represent the core business activities and perhaps the largest expenditures. (282)

infrastructure-as-a-service. Placement of servers in someone else's data center. (148)

innovation (process). A large one-time initiative that uses a clean-slate approach and creates a new process or examines an existing process for opportunities to enhance its output in a dramatic way. (230)

integration-as-a-service. Applications that include the features traditionally found in enterprise application integration but delivered as a service. (147)

interaction costs. Costs—both money and time—that occur in any transaction, whether it is business-to-business or consumer-to-business, and determine, either directly or indirectly, organizational efficiency and the way organizations operate. (280)

internet. A "network of networks," the largest of which is the Internet. (23)

Internet layer. Layer 3 of the hybrid TCP/IP–OSI architecture, with its common protocols of Internet Protocol (IP), IP Security (IPSEC), and Address Resolution Protocol (ARP), used for communicating between networks. (32)

Internet Message Access Protocol (IMAP). Used to transfer e-mail. (114)

IPsec. VPN-provided security to layers above Layer 3 to protect everything within the IP packet (e.g., transport and application layer parameters and payloads). (100)

keys. Bits of a specific length that provide the parameters needed by an encryption algorithm to transform plain text into ciphertext, and conversely from ciphertext into plain text; also used in digital signatures. (171)

lanes. A part of the BPMN standard, an object that normally represents the different participants within the organization. (323)

latency. A delay in propagated data getting from its source to its destination. (16)

leading-edge technologies. Technologies that are relatively new, usually 2–4 years old, and generally offer the best competitive advantage to businesses in fulfilling critical business functions and supporting cost-effective competition; part of the technology trend curve that should consist of the majority (50% to 75%) of an organization's technology investment. (247)

levers (process). Those forces that influence the success of a process change initiative. (224)

local area network (LAN). A computer network that covers a relatively small geographic area that is physically connected and normally built using cabling in a building or on a campus, or is wireless. (18)

logic bomb. Software code inserted into software that is triggered when certain criteria are met. (168)

malware. Short for "malicious software," which includes viruses, Trojan horses, worms, and any other software designed to attack an organization's or person's technology. (165)

management-as-a-service. Any on-demand service that provides the ability to manage one or more cloud services, including typology, resource utilization, virtualization, and uptime management. (148)

manual task. In business process models, an activity performed by human participants. (322)

mesh typology. Network that consists of a number of devices interconnected with trunk lines creating a redundancy in the network with multiple paths between hosts in the mesh. (27, 103)

metro ethernet. A technology provided by telecommunications carriers and harmonized around the Ethernet (IEEE 802 workgroup) standards to be highly scalable, provide a higher level of reliability and quality of service through extensive service management components, is normally shared by a number of organizations on a "pay-as-you-go" basis, and is regularly designed to cover an large metropolitan area. (97)

metropolitan area network (MAN). A computer network similar to a WAN in that it uses carrier circuits to interconnect networks within a city or metropolitan area. (19)

modulation. Taking a digital data stream (e.g., 01011101) and turning it into a sound that represents the data. (13)

Multi-attribute utility theory (MAUT). An economic theory that is useful when attempting to quantify "soft" indicators related to system performance or to human factors and allows the analyst to create an easy-to-rate set of attributes that can be used to measure performance, while incorporating manager's perceptions of the importance of the performance indicators. (251)

multifunction devices. Devices that support printing, scanning, copying, and/or faxing simultaneously. (125)

multiplexing. Combining several data streams into one signal so they can be transmitted over a carrier circuit. (13)

Multiprotocol Label Switching (MPLS). A packet-switched networking technology that exists at "Layer 2.5" of the hybrid OSI-TCP/IP model and can carry virtually any kind of traffic, including IP packets, ATM cells and Ethernet frames. (22, 96)

MUX. Device that performs multiplexing through modulation/demodulation. (13)

name resolution. The process of converting human-friendly names into numeric addresses, such as converting www.microsoft.com to 60.55.12.249. (30)

net present value (NPV). An accounting valuation method used to determine the difference between the present value of cash inflows and cash outflows. (249)

network attached storage (NAS). Storage technologies based on file-oriented protocols. (111)

networking and telecommunications. Technical concepts concerning the protocols, standards, hardware, and software involved in implementing a technology infrastructure. (1)

permanent virtual circuits (PVC). Virtual channels providing a dedicated circuit link between two facilities, which are normally preconfigured by the ISP for packet mode communication and established for a long period, meaning they are seldom broken or disconnected. (81)

personal area network (PAN). Technologies that are a good solution for replacing cables for wireless access in your personal area, such as Bluetooth. (63)

phishing. A form of social engineering in which the user receives an e-mail that appears to come from a legitimate business requesting verification of some confidential information and warns of some undesirable consequences if the request is not followed. (168)

platform-as-a-service. A subscriber-based service that typically includes application, interface, and database development, along with storage, testing, and other technologies, that delivers those services to users from cloud-based hosted data centers. (147)

point of presence (POP) connection. The place where a subscriber connects to the services of a network provider (e.g., an ATM cloud). (25)

policy server. Often the same as a directory server; may be an additional server in the network core that administer's network policies. (118)

pools. A part of the BPMN standard, an object that normally represents different organizations. (323)

Post Office Protocol v3 (POP3). Common e-mail transfer protocol; used to receive incoming e-mail over the Internet. (113)

post-implementation phase. The phase of business-driven infrastructure design that follows the infrastructure after going live and involves measurement systems and constant monitoring of ICT infrastructure utilization against objectives set during the analysis phase. (377)

private clouds. Networks (usually with some type of routing) that provide services or connectivity available to users (either internal or external) either directly connected to the cloud or through secure VPN tunnels over the Internet. (145)

private (internal) business processes. Processes internal to a specific organization, or workflow. (321)

process. A defined set of work activities with known inputs and known outputs. (221)

process approach to ICT payoff. An approach to measuring ICT payoff that examines change in net profit based on known "necessary" conditions and the determination of whether those conditions are "sufficient" to achieve the desired payoff. (242)

process definition. In business process models, a statement of the problem that gives the details of the process in text. (321)

process instance. In business process models, one occurrence (instantiation) of the process. (322)

process owners. Those individuals who manage the activities within processes and are in the best position to champion process changes and bring about positive effects for the organization from those changes. (222)

process view. The view, which is essential to implementing improvement and innovation, that allows for organizational processes to be identified and cross-departmental processes to be defined. (211)

process-as-a-service. Application delivery through the cloud that supports business processes through combining other services to create metaapplications. (147)

propagation effects. Factors that affect a signal as it travels across media, such as electrical magnetic interference (EMI), cross talk, and attenuation. (9)

protocol data unit (PDU). A message that has a specific format governed by protocols, using a *message trailer–message body–message header* format. (34)

public cloud. Internet connectivity that is provided at a low cost per bit transmitted for a large number of users. (145)

public switched data networks (PSDN). ISP-provided public packet-switched (i.e., routed) facilities that allow the customer to connect via a POP. (80)

radio frequency modulation. Techniques to propagate signals between WAPs and the host's wireless access device. (58)

registered ports. Type of transport port (layer 4 of the hybrid TCP/IP-OSI Model) in the range of 1024–49151 that can be registered with the Internet Corporation of Assigned Numbers and Names and are assigned to specific applications. (34)

remote access VPN. A network-provided service component through which users interact and obtain access to network resources via software on their PCs that allows them to create secure connections. (98)

return on investment (ROI). An accounting valuation method that is useful to compare the rate of return of investment options, including ICT investments: ROI = Net Income/Book Value of Assets. (247)

revenue growth. A firm's attempt to gain market share by strategies that focus on increased sales and profits and may use ICT to create/enhance product offerings or to enhance sales, while at the same time maintaining market share. (277)

ring typology. A network in which the circuit is fashioned in a ring and devices hang off that ring, which allows communication among the devices. (27)

script kiddies. A subculture within the hacking community that includes people who practice hacking by using scripts or software written by other people but who do not precisely know how the script or software works. (169)

Secure Sockets Layer (SSL). A cryptographic protocol that preceded Transport Layer Security (TLS) and provided secure communications over the Internet through its encryption for the layers above the transport layer. (172)

security-as-a-service. Virus defense, firewall management, and e-mail filtering as well as sophisticated services like identity management offered through directory services, which provide cyber security via cloud offerings. (147)

service components. Those parts of the network that facilitate network operations and with which the user may directly interface, including printing services, inter/intra office communications (i.e., telephone or fax), and network accessible storage. (71, 107)

Service Set Identifier (SSID). A string of up to 32 alphanumeric characters that all wireless access devices and WAPs that wish to communicate with each other must have in common; a WAP name. (59)

service-oriented architecture (SOA). Object-oriented programming at the heart of cloud computing that focuses on system design principles and reuses objects within or between applications across the network. (137)

Simple Mail Transfer Protocol (SMPT). Common e-mail transfer protocol; used to transfer outgoing e-mail over the Internet. (113)

site surveys. Part of the design phase of the *business-driven infrastructure design* process in which all locations of the ICT infrastructure, including data centers, wireless access points, cable pathways, network switches, routers, and desktops, are documented; include a complete review of all documentation (i.e., process maps and models, initial ICT infrastructure documentation) that enables everyone to understand the physical, electrical, and other needs to successfully implement the ICT infrastructure. (373)

site-to-site VPN. A typical VPN that transmits data using the Internet in which each location/building has a VPN gateway that secures communication between gateways, but not within the buildings. (98)

sniffer. A program that intercepts data in IP packets and examines each packet in search of the desired information; also known as a packer sniffer. (168)

social engineering. A cyber attack that manipulates people into divulging confidential information rather than using techniques such as worms, viruses, or scanning to gain access to that information. (168)

socket. The IP address and the transport layer port number written together in the form of IP_ADDRESS:PORT_NUMBER. (35)

software as a service (SaaS). Object-oriented programming defined as software on demand and designed to be delivered over the Internet or some other network. (137)

spam. Unsolicited commercial e-mail that floods users' e-mail inboxes and probably represents the most annoying type of cyber attack or malware. (169)

spyware. Software that collects information about the user and transmits it to a third party without the user's knowledge or consent. (166)

star typology. The most common type of LAN implemented today through which hosts are connected to switches through a drop cable and switches are interconnected through a series of trunk lines, most often implemented as an Ethernet network. (25)

statistical approaches to determining ICT value. Technology justification models that use statistical analysis to show the benefit and value of a system. (247)

storage area networks (SAN). Technology that provides storage to network users using block mode (rather than file system mode). (111)

storage-as-a-service. The ability to leverage storage that physically exists at remote locations in the cloud but logically appears as local storage to any application. (147)

structural enabler. Forces or influences, such as the cross-functional team, that bring about successful process change. (236)

structured cabling. A number of well-defined subsystems that together form the infrastructure necessary to create a unified phone or data network, and based on standards that outline the use of various media. (64)

sustaining technologies. Technologies that offer newer, better, or cheaper ways to do the same task and refer to those successive incremental improvements to performance that market incumbents incorporate into their existing products. (187)

swim lanes. Used in business process diagrams (BPDs) for graphical groupings of primary elements into pools and lanes. (324)

switched virtual circuits (SVC). Virtual channels that provide a dedicated circuit link between two facilities for packet mode communication and are disconnected at the end of each connection. (81)

synchronous transmission. The encoding of data into signals that the media can propagate with some type of pulse signal being included (either on the same wire or an adjacent one) to indicate the start and end of one bit/octet. (13)

System-Fault-Risk (SFR) framework. A framework for analyzing ICT infrastructure for security risk, which looks at the threat of cyber attacks, their cause and effect, and assesses the following characteristics: objective, propagation, attack origin, action, vulnerability, asset, state effects, and performance effects. (162)

task/activity. In business process models, one step in the process. (322)

technology S-curve. A widely held theory that as a technology becomes more mature and reaches a natural or physical limit, the ability to improve performance takes an ever-increasing amount of effort. (243)

technology trend curve. Three categories of technology (trailing-edge, leading-edge, and bleeding-edge) that provide guidance in assessing the nature and extent of various technology projects that a company should invest in. (246)

testing-as-a-service. A provider-offered ability to test applications through cloud-delivered algorithms that can test web sites, applications, and other software. (148)

thin clients. Part of a larger infrastructure deployment in which the client device consists of a small component with monitor, keyboard, mouse, network, and USB connections and used in a virtualized server-centric environment. (107)

to-be process. Modeling that develops target business workflows to achieve the (optimal) stated goals of the process change. (332)

total cost of ownership (TCO). A financial estimate that includes direct costs (e.g., purchase of technology, installation, and maintenance) and indirect costs (e.g., training, cost of planned or unplanned outage, cost of security breach, disaster preparedness and recovery, floor space, testing, development expenses, eventual decommissioning, etc.) related to the purchase of any capital item, including ICT infrastructure. (242)

trailing-edge technologies. Technologies that are generally 4 or more years old, suitable in meeting today's needs, but potentially expensive to maintain and expensive or impossible to modify, resulting in a suboptimal cost-benefit ratio and payback; part of the technology trend curve that should consist of no more than 10%–20% of an organization's technology investment. (246)

Transmission Control Protocol/Internet Protocol (TCP/IP). Standard promulgated by the Internet Society; the top three layers (i.e., 5, 4, 3) of the hybrid TCP/IP–OSI architecture, which describe the application (5), transport (4) and internet layers (3). (19)

transport layer. Layer 4 of the hybrid TCP/IP–OSI architecture, which consists of Transmission Control Protocol (TCP), User Datagram Protocol (UDP), and Internet Control Message Protocol (ICMP), that performs error checking and error correction and is responsible for the end-to-end communications. (31)

Transport Layer Security (TLS). A cryptographic protocol that provides secure communications over the Internet through its encryption for the layers above the transport layer. (172)

transport mode. An IPsec mode of operation that provides secure host-to-host communication and requires special software on the hosts involved in the VPN connection. (100)

transport port. A number added to the transport PDU that indicates the application on the sending host that should receive the response, and the application on the receiving host that should receive the request. (34)

Trojan horse. Software that appears to perform a desirable function but in reality allows unauthorized access to a user's computer by the creator of the software. (166)

tunnel mode. An IPsec mode of operation that provides secure site-to-site communication and requires specialized VPN gateway servers at each location. (100)

Types (process). Extensions, or subprocesses, of gateway and task symbols. (332)

Universal Serial Bus (USB) connections. A standard for cables and protocols that connect computer peripherals to a computer and may provide a power source. (106)

user components. Those things that expose all other services of the network to the user, enabling user interaction through a desktop device. (119)

utility. In economic terms, the amount of satisfaction that something brings to a situation. (251)

utility value tree. A tiered approach to describing and understanding the indicators that specify the value of a complex scenario/system. (253)

value chain deconstruction. A tool to use in the search for opportunities to increase consumer value through lower cost or higher quality. (284)

value proposition. A clear statement of what an organization can provide to its customers, which might include decreased cycle times, increased market share, and improved operational efficiency. (202, 279)

value search models. Models—including corporate unbundling, value chain deconstruction, comparative SWOT analysis, and competitive forces analysis—that provide tools for the business systems analyst so they can make a thorough examination of the organization, to discover ways to implement ICT for competitive advantage, and to explain those advantages to management. (278)

variance approach to ICT payoff. An approach to measuring ICT payoff in terms of net profit in which "necessary" conditions that are required for ICT payoff to occur and "sufficient" conditions that explain the variance in ICT payoff are identified. (242)

vertical runs. Between-switch cables in a LAN that often run between floors, interconnecting switches. (43)

virtualization. The decoupling of a user's desktop and application from the actual hardware, allowing for centralization of software management and lesser expensive devices (e.g., thin client) on the user desktop. (116)

virus. Malicious software that can replicate itself and often attaches itself to existing legitimate software on a computer system, thus modifying the files on the system. (166)

vishing. A method of phishing that specifically uses voice-over-Internet protocols (VoIP) and exploits call center software. (168)

Voice over IP (VoIP). Telephony technology that uses packet-switched networks to facilitate communications within and between offices, and to non-VoIP locations via the Public Switched Telephone Network (PSTN). (109)

wardriving. A method that involves patrolling locations to gain access to wireless computer networks using a remote device such as a PDA or a laptop. (169)

Web servers. Client-server computing devices that accept HTTP requests from user clients and respond to those requests with an HTTP response message. (112)

well-known ports. Type of transport layer ports in the range of 0–1023. (34)

wide area network (WAN). A network that interconnects individual computers, buildings, or locations using carrier circuits and is larger in geographic scope. (18)

wireless access point (WAP). A device that connects a host to a wireless network using the host's wireless access device. (57)

wireless technologies. Information and communication technology infrastructure that allows an organization to deploy devices (e.g., computers and printers) as part of its network without running wires to each location. (54)

workflow. Processes internal to a specific organization, or BPM processes. (321)

working documents. The recorded input of all stakeholders, as well as the business analyst who thoroughly analyzed the organization using various tools, in the process of creating an appropriate ICT infrastructure. (338)

Worldwide Interoperability for Microwave Access (WiMAX). A Layer 1/Layer 2 standard that has been codified by the IEEE 802.16 subcommittee and used to deliver point-to-point circuits from an ISP to an organization or end user. (93)

worm. A self-replicating stand-alone program that depends on security shortcomings of the target computer, often consuming network bandwidth or deleting files on the host system. (167)

INDEX

A

Abstract (public) processes, 321
Access control, 170–171
Access control lists (ACLs), 118, 171
ActiveHealth Management, 142
ActivePHR, 142
Activities, 325
Adaptor card, 43
Addressing, 30
Address Resolution Protocol (ARP), 32
Adobe Portable Document Format (PDF), 124
Advanced Encryption Standard (AES), 59
Adware, 166
Alliance for Enterprise Security Risk Management (AESRM), 160
Allway Sync, 147
Amazon Web Services (AWS), 138–139
AMD processors, 105
American College of Cardiology, 142
American National Standards Institute (ANSI), 22
Analog data, 6–7
Analysis phase, 366–370
    organizational overall strategy, 366–369
    organization and competitive environment, 366
    strategy in alignment with ICT, 369–370
    summary of, 369–370
Annual payback, 249
Anti-spam filters, 175
Anti-virus tools, 175
Apple, 105
Application-as-a-service, 147
Application delivery infrastructure (ADI), 116–117, 120
Application layer (layer 5), 30–31, 37
Application programming interface (API), 147
Application servers, 73, 114–115
Application virtualization, 116–117, 120
Artifacts, 324
As-is process, 331–333, 335
Association, 325
Asymmetric digital subscriber line (ADSL), 33
Asymmetric key algorithms, 172
Asynchronous Transfer Mode (ATM), 88–92
    ATM cells (PDU), 88–89
    ATM traffic, 89–90
    components and pricing, 90–91
    enterprise use of, 91–92
    multiprotocol environments, 90
    QOS guarantees, 89–91
    technical description, 88–90
    virtual circuits, 89
Asynchronous Transfer Model (ATM), 22
Asynchronous transmission, 13
ATM Forum, 22
Attacks and threats, 163
    delivery methods, 169
    exploits, 169
    human-focused cyber attacks, 168–169
    physical-focused attacks, 165
    technology-focused cyber attacks, 165–168
    See also individual types of attacks and threats
Attacks and threats, stopping, 170–180
    access control, 170–171
    client host solutions, 174–175
    educating the user, 179–180
    encryption, 171
    keys, 171–172
    network solutions, 175–179
    planning and policies, 170
    SSL/TLS, 172–174
Attenuation, 10–11
ATX motherboard factor form, 105
Automated task, 322
Azure. *See* Microsoft Azure
Azure Platform AppFabric, 149–150

B

Balanced Scorecard (BSC), 258–262
    implementing, example of, 261–262
    overview of, 258–260
    perspectives in, 260
Bandwidth
    data compression and, 13–14
    determining, 372
    hubs and, 43
    Hz and, 55
    link aggregation and, 47
    multiplexing and, 13
    needs, estimating, 344–350
    performance and cost considerations, 347–350
    phone system and, 28, 29
    post-implementation phase and, 378–379
    speed measurements and, 15–16
    symmetric *vs.* asymmetric compression and, 15
BDID. *See* Business-driven infrastructure design (BDID)
Between network layers, 35–36
Bleeding-edge technology, 247
Bluetooth, 63
Boomi, 147
BPD. *See* Business process diagrams (BPD)
BPM. *See* Business process modeling (BPM)
BPMN. *See* Business process modeling notation (BPMN)
Bridges, 44
Building physical ICT infrastructure, 372–374
    design phase in, 372–374
    desktop configuration considerations, 373–374
    final design documents, 374
    organization size, 373
    site surveys, 373
Built-in adaptors, 106
Business and technology paradigm, 189–190
Business-driven infrastructure design (BDID), 202–205
Business-driven infrastructure design (BDID) cycle
    analysis phase, 203, 366–370
    design phase, 203, 370–374

Business-driven infrastructure design (BDID) cycle (*Continued*)
　implementation phase, 203, 374–377
　post-implementation phase, 204, 205, 377–379
　steps and overlap, 202–203
Business-driven infrastructure design (BDID) team, 365–366
Business models, 367
Business process design, 372
Business process diagrams (BPD), 318–320
　building blocks, 326
　collaborative, 328
　compensation activities, 326–328
　initial example of, 329
　modeling recommendations, 329–337
　staff *vs.* managers, 320, 322
　subprocesses, 337
　symbol types, 334
Business process diagrams (BPD), elements in, 324, 326–328
　artifacts, 324
　connecting objects, 324, 325
　flow objects, 324, 325
　swim lanes, 324, 326
Business processes, 208–239
　changes in, 209–211, 230–236
　defined, 221, 224–225
　economic outcomes in, ICT impact on, 212–213
　existing infrastructure *vs.* new infrastructure, 214–215
　ICT implementation, 209
　ICT used in, 213–214
　information providers and, 218–221
　introduction, 208–209
　levers of, 224
　measurement of, 222–223
　objectives and attributes in, 227–228
　in the organization, 221
　organizational reach in, 224
　organizational types and, 215–221
　overarching, 224–225
　ownership of, 222, 223
　product innovation, vision for, 225–227
　service providers and, 215–218
　value chain in, 224, 228–229
　view of the organization, 197–199, 211–212
Business process modeling (BPM), 315–338
　advantages of, 318–320
　data flow diagrams, 337–338
　defined, 317
　key concepts, 315
　modeling languages in, 317 (*See also* Business process modeling notation (BPMN))
　process map, 315–318
　terms, 321–322
　workflow *vs.*, 318
Business process modeling notation (BPMN), 318–328
　graphical representations and markers, 320
　intent of, 319
　OMG standards, 319
　participants, 323
　pools and lanes, 323
　process type, 320–321
　terminology, 319
　uses of, 317–318
　See also Business process diagrams (BPD)
Business systems analyst, 1
　comparative SWOT analysis and, 296, 297–298
　competitive forces analysis and, 298, 300–301
　corporate unbundling and, 281–282
　defined, 188
　gap analysis and, 301, 303, 304
　SAIT and, 275–278
　supply chain analysis and, 290–291
　Val IT framework and, 304–307
　value chain analysis and, 288–290
　value chain deconstruction and, 285, 287
　value proposition and, 279–280
Bus typology, 25, 26

C

Cable, 24, 33
Cabling (vertical and horizontal runs), 69–70
CardioSmart, 142
Caremark, 142
Carrier circuits, 17
Carrier sense multiple access
　with collision avoidance + acknowledgment (CSMA/CA+ ACK), 61–62
　with collision detection (CSMA/CD), 50, 53, 61
Cascading Style Sheets, 21
Cast Iron Systems, 147
CD, 121
CD/DVD, 121
CD-ROM, 121
CD-RW, 121
Certified Information Systems Security Professional (CISSP) framework, 170
Channels, 55, 58–59
Chatter, 147
Chief information officer (CIO), 275
Chief knowledge officer (CKO), 275
Chief technology officer (CTO), 275
Ciphertex, 171
Circuit switching, 27–28
Citrix, 105
Client host solutions, 174–175
Client security, 175
Client-server computing, 16, 137–138
Client-side software firewall, 175
Client-to-service layers, 36
Cloud-based applications, 144, 148, 150
Cloud computing, 135–159
　abstraction, 137
　business case for, 157
　capital *vs.* operational expenditures and, 154–155
　corporate LAN-based applications *vs.*, 138–139
　defined, 136
　hosted applications *vs.*, 137–138
　integration of on-premises and cloud-based resources, 156
　introduction, 136
　organizational impact of, 155–156
Cloud computing, attributes of, 139–141
　fault tolerance, 141
　geo-replication, 141

metered by use, 141
scalable and elastic, 140
security, 141
service-based, 139–140
shared resources, 140–141
uses Internet technologies, 141
Cloud computing, developing in, 144–152
considerations for, 152–153
Microsoft Azure, 148–150
on premises *vs.*, 153–154
private *vs.* public cloud, 144–145
service types in the cloud, 146–148
Sopima, 150–152
summary, 152
Cloud-computing abstraction, 137
Cloud computing vendors, 141–144
Google Apps, 143–144
HealthVault, 142–143
Coax cable, 24
Collaboration (global) processes, 321, 322
Collaborative diagrams, 328
Commissioning tests, 377
Committed information rate (CIR), 85
Communications interoperability, 19
Comparative SWOT analysis, 296–298, 299
core competencies, 296
telescopic observation framework, 297
using, 296–298
Compensation activities, 326–327
Competitive advantage, 189–190
Competitive forces
affecting infrastructure, 200
analysis, 298, 300–301
Porter's five forces model, 298, 300–301
Components
enterprise-wide, 125–127
PC hardware, 105–107
service, 107–119
user, 119–125
Computer network and carrier concepts, 17–19
carrier circuits, 17
communications interoperability, 19
geographic scope, 18–19
Connecting objects, 324, 325
Context diagram, 352, 353
Contingency perspective, 276
Convergence, 215–216
Cooperating organizations affecting infrastructure, 201
Co-opetition, 296, 301
Copper cable, 24
Core competencies
in comparative SWOT analysis, 296
in value chain deconstruction, 287–288
Corel WordPerfect Office, 125
Corporate LAN wiring, 65–74
Corporate unbundling, 280–284
CRM function, 281
defined, 280
infrastructure processes, 282
interaction costs, 282–284
product innovation, 282

Correlation statistic, 255
Cosmos Tong, 138–139
Cost-benefit analysis, 250–251
Cost-leadership strategy, 192–193, 367–368
Cost of investment, 249
Cost reduction, 277
CPU, 105, 106–107
Cross-functional processes, 292–294
Cross talk, 10
CSMA/CD, 50–51
C-suite, 278, 283–284, 286, 306
Cultural enablers, 236
Customer, 365–366
in analysis phase, 366, 371
cost-benefit analysis and, 250–251
CRM in value chain and, 228–229
economic utility and, 251–253
in implementation phase, 375
information processes and, 220
perspectives in BSC, 259–262
in post-implementation phase, 379
preferences, 222, 225
service providers and, 217
technology S-curve and, 243, 245–246
Customer-driven innovations, examples of, 380
Customer relationship management (CRM)
in corporate unbundling, 281
in enterprise-wide components, 126
in value chain, 228–229
CVS Caremark, 142
Cybercrime, 161

D

Data and information quality (DIQ), 253–254
Database-as-a-service, 147
Database management system (DBMS), 147
Database servers, 73, 115–116
Data center, 69
Datacenter-as-a-service, 148
Data circuit-terminating equipment (DCE), 86
Data communication techniques, 11–16
client-server computing, 16
data compression, 13–15
full *vs.* half duplex, 12
message synchronization, 13
modulation and multiplexing, 13
serial *vs.* parallel, 11–12
speed measurements and bandwidth, 15–16
symmetric *vs.* asymmetric communications, 15
Data compression, 13–15
Data flow diagrams, 337–338
Data link layer (layer 2), 32, 37
frames and, 52–53
standards, 42
Data networks, 28–29
Data objects, 324
Data representation, 6–7
Data terminal equipment (DTE), 86–87
Dead spots, 63
Decapsulation, 97
Dedicated hosting, 148
Demilitarized zone (DMZ), 177–178

Denial-of-service (DoS), 168
Design documents
    connecting, 353
    context diagram, 352, 353
    diagram list, 351
    diagramming conventions, 352
    diagramming recommendations, 351
    diagram notes, 352–353, 356
    document review, 351
    flow of, 338–339
    high-level, creating, 350–360
    kiosk diagram, 355, 357–360
    workgroup diagrams, 353–357
    working documents, 338–339
Designing ICT solutions, 314–361
    business process modeling, 315–338
    diagram set, 314–315
    ICT technical frameworks and models, 338–360
Design phase, 203, 370–374
    building physical ICT infrastructure, 372–374
    business process design, 372
    summary of, 374
Desktop, 119
Desktop factor form, 105, 106
Desktop optical devices, 121
Desktop productivity software, 125
Desktop virtualization, 116–117, 120
Diagram list, 351
Diagram notes, 352–353, 356
Diagram set, 314–315
Differentiation, 192–193
Digital data, 6–7
Digital signatures, 175, 176
Digital subscriber line (DSL)
    connections, 17
    limit to data transmitted by, 15
    physical layer standards, 33
    vs. WiMAX, 95
Directory server, 74, 118
Discount rate, 249
Disk on demand, 147
Disruptive technologies, 186–187
Distributed denial-of service attack (DDoS), 168
DVD, 121
Dye-sublimation printer, 122

E

Economic approaches, 251–253
    economic utility, 251–253
    utility value tree, 253
802.2 LCC, 42
802.3, 44, 53–54, 61
802.11, 56–63
    Ethernet and, 57
    frequency spectrum and channels, 58–59
    handoff and, 61
    multiple users and, 61–62
    personal area network and, 63
    Service Set Identifier and, 59
    technical details, 58
    wireless propagation problems in, 62–63
    wireless security in, 59–60
    WLAN technologies in, 57
Elastic Block Store (EBS), Amazon, 138–139
Elastic Compute Cloud (EC2), Amazon, 138–139, 151
Elasticity, 140
Elastic Load Balancing, Amazon, 138–139
Electromagnetic interference (EMI), 9–10, 63
Electrostatic discharge (ESD) procedures, 375
Ellison, Larry, 136
E-mail
    filtering, 148
    server, 74, 113–114
    spam and, 169, 175
Enablers, 230–236
    cultural, 236
    defined, 209
    ICT as, 233–236
    innovation *vs.* improvement, 230–231
    organizational, 231–233
    structural, 236
Encapsulation, 34
Encryption, 171, 175
End-to-end layers, 36
Enterprise applications, 1–2
Enterprise resource planning (ERP) system, 125–127
    best practices built in, 126
    organization types that use, 126–127
    services in, 126
Enterprise use
    of ATM, 91–92
    of GPRS, 92–93
Enterprise-wide components, 125–127
    benefits of, 127
    best practices, 126
    ERP system, 125–127
    SAP, 126
    vendors, 126
Entrance facility, 67
Ephemeral ports, 35
Equipment
    installation of, 375–377
    racks, 68–69
    rooms, 67–68
Ethernet, 13, 41–77
    adaptor cards in, 43
    bridges in, 44
    CSMA/CD and, 50–51
    data link layer and frames, 52–53
    802.11 LANS, 57–63
    evolution of, technical details of, 48–49
    frames and, 51
    frequency spectrum and, 54–55
    hubs in, 43
    introduction, 41–42
    LAN-based, 56–63 (*See also* 802.11)
    layers (*See* Layers in TCP/IP-OSI architecture)
    MAC addresses and, 51
    media in, 43
    microwave, 55
    personal area network and, 63
    repeaters in, 43–44
    satellite, 55

summary, 53–54
switch characteristics, 44–48
WiMAX, 55–56
See also Wireless technologies
Ethernet II, 42
Ethernet layer 1. *See* Physical layer (layer 1)
Ethernet layer 2. *See* Data link layer (layer 2)
Ethernet layer 3. *See* Internet layer (layer 3)
Ethernet layer 4. *See* Transport layer (layer 4)
Ethernet layer 5. *See* Application layer (layer 5)
Ethernet layers. *See* Layers in TCP/IP-OSI architecture
Ethernet Raw, 42
Ethernet Snap, 42
Events, 325
Experimentation, cloud computing and, 156
Exploits, 169
Exploit tools, 169
Extensible Markup Language (XML), 21
External forces affecting infrastructure, 200–201
competing forces, 200
cooperating organizations, supply chain, 201

F

Facebook, 149
Factor form, 105
Fast follower, 190
Fault tolerance in cloud computing, 141
Federal Communication Commission (FCC), 20
Fiber Distributed Data Interface (FDDI), 32, 54
Fiber optic (FO), 24
File services, 71–72
Financial approaches, 247–251
cost-benefit analysis, 250–251
net present value, 249–250
return on investment, 247–249
Firestorm, 169
Firewall
client-side software firewall, 175
management, 148
multi-tiered, 177–178, 179
in wired LAN, 177–178
in wireless LAN, 178–179
First-mover advantage, 190
Five forces model, 298, 300–301
Flow objects, 324, 325
Focused approach, 191–192, 368
Form Factor, switches and, 44–45
Frame Relay, 84–88
committed information rate, 85
components and pricing, 86–87
future of, 88
multiprotocol environments, 86
networks, public *vs.* private, 88
PDU, 86
purpose of, 32
technical description, 85
virtual circuits, 85
Frame Relay Access Device (FRAD), 87
Frame Relay Alliance, 22
Frame Relay PDU, 86
Frames, 51
Frequency effect on propagation problems, 63
Frequency spectrum, 54–55, 58–59
Full-duplex communication, 12
Functionality list, 339–340, 341–343
Functional view of the organization, 195–197, 199, 211

G

Gap analysis, 301–305, 379
Gartner Group, 139–141
Gateways, 325
General accepted accounting practice (GAAP), 126, 154
General Packet Radio Service (GPRS), 92–93
connectivity, 92
enterprise use of, 92–93
vs. WiMAX, 94
Generic value chain, 286
Geo-replication in cloud computing, 141
Geostationary orbit (GEO), 33, 55–56
Gigahertz (GHz), 107
Global Supply Chain Forum (GSCF), 292–294
Go Daddy, 148
Google, 149
Google Apps, 143–144, 147, 151, 156
Governance systems, 148
Graphical user interface (GUI), 119
Green, Jeff, 161
Group artifact, 324

H

Hacking, 169
Half-duplex communication, 12
Handoff, 61
Hardware, PC, 105–107
address, 30
factor form, 105
PC options, 105–106
PC selection, summary of, 107
processor speed, 106–107
regulations and standards, 22–23
thin clients, 107
HealthVault, 142–143
High data rate digital subscriber line (HDSL), 33
High earth orbit (HEO), 33
Home LAN wiring, 74–75
Horizontal runs, 69–70
Hosted applications, 137–138
HTTP, 30–31
HTTPS, 30–31
Hubs, 43
Human break-ins (hacking), 169
Human-focused cyber attacks, 168–169
human break-ins (hacking), 169
identity theft, 169
phishing, 168
social engineering, 168
spam, 169
vishing, 168
Human resources (HR), 126, 198
Hybrid architecture, 19, 20
See also TCP/IP-OSI architecture
Hypercompetition, 214, 215
Hypertext Markup Language (HTML), 21

396 Index

I

ICANN (the Internet Corporation for Assigned Numbers and Names), 161
ICT hierarchy, 340–341, 343–344
ICT implementation value proposition, 240–241
ICT infrastructure
 building physical, 372–374
 computer network and carrier concepts, 17–19
 data communication techniques, 11–16
 data representation and signal propagation, 6–11
 decisions, strategic management and, 189
 defined, 1
 designing, 314–361
 external forces affecting, 200–201
 gap analysis, 301–305
 implementing, 275–276
 introductory concepts, 5–40
 network components in, 2
 processes, 282
 project planning in, 201–202
 regulations and standards, 19–23
 service components in, 2
 strategic alignment, 275–278
 success, measuring, 378
 switching hierarchies, 27–30
 TCP/IP-OSI architecture, 19–37
 user components in, 2
 value search models, 278–301
 wired media, 24–27
ICT payoff, 241–263
 Balanced Scorecard, 258–262
 process approach to, 242
 technology justification models, 247–258
 technology S-curve, 243–246
 technology trend curve, 246–247
 total cost of ownership, 242–243
 variance approach to, 242
ICT technical frameworks and models, 338–360
 bandwidth needs, estimating, 344–350
 functionality list, 339–340, 341–343
 ICT hierarchy, 340–341, 343–344
 See also Design documents
Identity theft, 169
IEEE Standards Association (IEEE-SA), 21
IETF protocol, 172–173
Image scanners, 124–125
 image quality, 124
 software, 124
Implementation phase, 374–377
 ICT hardware infrastructure installation, 374–377
 planning, 203
 summary of, 377
Improvements, 230–231
Inbound logistics, 198
Industry-wide approach, 191, 192, 368
Informational inputs, 210–211
Information and communication technology (ICT) infrastructure. *See* ICT infrastructure
Information-as-a-service, 147
Infrastructure-as-a-service, 148
Inkjet printer, 121
Innovation, 230–231

Installation area, preparing, 375
Institute of Electrical and Electronics Engineers (IEEE), 21
Integrated services digital network (ISDN), 33, 81
Integration-as-a-service, 147
Integration of on-premises and cloud-based resources, 156
Intel-based desktops and servers, 105
Interaction costs, 282–284
Inter/intra-office communications, 109–111
 See also Voice over IP (VoIP)
International Organization for Standardization (ISO), 21–22, 126
 ERP system and, 126
Internet
 vs. internet, 23
 resources in cloud computing, leveraging, 156
 technologies in cloud computing, 141
Internet Architecture Board (IAB), 21
Internet Control Message Protocol, 31
Internet Engineering Task Force (IETF), 21
Internet layer (layer 3), 32, 37
Internet Message Access Protocol (IMAP), 114
Internet Protocol (IP), 30, 32
Internet Society, The (ISOC), 21
Introduction, 41–42
IP addresses, 30, 32, 36
IPsec, 100
IPsec transport mode, 100
IPsec tunnel mode, 100
IP Security (IPSEC), 32
IP v4/v6, 21
IT Asset Management (ITAM), 148
IT infrastructure-enabled change, 233–236

J

JCT1, 22

K

Keys, 171–173
 asymmetric key algorithms, 172
 symmetric key algorithms, 172–173

L

Label printers, 123
Labels, MPLS, 96–97
Label switch routers (LSRs), 96–97
LAN
 building, 64–75 (*See also* Ethernet; LAN wiring)
 corporate LAN-based applications *vs.* cloud computing, 138–139
 defined, 18
 equipment found in, 23
 LAN pricing *vs.* WAN pricing, 78
 security in wired LANs, 176–178
 security in wireless LANs, 178–179
 WAN connections used to extend, 78–103
LAN-based wireless (WLAN), 56–63
 See also 802.11
Lanes, 323, 326
LAN wiring, 64–75
 application servers, 73
 assumptions, 65–66

cabling (vertical and horizontal runs), 69–70
corporate, 65–74
database servers, 73
data center, 69
directory server, 74
e-mail server, 74
entrance facility, 67
equipment racks, 68–69
equipment rooms, 67–68
file services, 71–72
home, 74–75
network attached storage, 73
nomenclature, 70–71
print services, 72
service components, 71
storage area networks, 73–74
structured cabling, 64–65
structured portion of LAN, 66–67
work area components, 70
Laptops, 105
Laser printers, 121–122
Latency, 16
Layer 2 Tunneling Protocol (L2TP), 32
Layers in TCP/IP-OSI architecture
application layer (layer 5), 30–31, 37
data link layer (layer 2), 32, 37
Internet layer (layer 3), 32, 37
introduction to, 19
physical layer (layer 1), 32–34, 37
regulations and standards, 22–23
transport layer (layer 4), 31–32, 37
Leading edge routers (LERs), 96–97
Leading-edge technologies, 247
Levers, 224
Link aggregation, 47
Local area network (LAN). *See* LAN
Logical Link Control (LLC), 53
Logic bombs, 168
Low earth orbit (LEO), 33, 56
Lunarpages, 148

M

MAC addresses, 51
  filtering, 47
Malware, 165–166
Managed switches, 46–48
  change speed or duplex setting of ports, 46
  enabling/disabling ports, 46
  link aggregation, 47
  MAC filtering, 47
  port authority, setting, 46
  SNMP monitoring, 47
  spanning tree protocol, 47
  vendor specific option, 48
  VLAN parameters, setting, 47–48
Management-as-a-service, 148
Management role in technology decisions, 193–195
Manual task, 322
Marketing/sales, 198
McAfee, 148, 161
Measuring ICT infrastructure success, 378

Media
  in Ethernet, 43
  switch characteristics and, 45–46
  wired, 24–27
Media Access Control (MAC), 30, 36
Medium earth orbit (MEO), 33, 56
Mesh typology, 27, 28
  ATM pricing and, 89, 90
  Frame Relay pricing and, 87
  WAN pricing and, 82–83
Message flow, 325
Message format, 34
Message synchronization, 13
Metro Ethernet, 97–98
Metropolitan area networks (MAN), 19
  MPLS, 97, 98
  pure Ethernet, 97–98
MFA Forum, 22
Microsoft Active Directory, 149
Microsoft Azure, 148–152
  Azure Platform AppFabric, 149–150
  SQL Azure, 149, 151–152
  Windows Azure, 149
Microsoft Exchange Server, 156
Microsoft Office, 125
Microsoft operating systems, 119
Microsoft Outlook, 156
Microwave, 55
Mikola, Markus, 151
Model Driven Architecture (MDA), 319
Modeling recommendations, 329–337
  as-is process, 331–333, 335
  to-be process, 331, 334–337
Modem, 33
Modulation, 13
Modulator, 13
Monitor, 106
MPLS MAN, 97, 98
MS-SQL, 147
Multi-attribute utility theory (MAUT), 251–253
Multicore processors, 107
Multifunction devices, 125
Multipath interference, 63
Multiple users
  CSMA/CA + ACK and, 61–62
  frames and, 51
  MAC addresses and, 51
  network and, 50–51
Multiplexing, 13
Multiprotocol environments
  ATM, 90
  Frame Relay, 86
Multiprotocol Label Switching (MPLS), 22, 96–97
  benefits, 97
  and Frame Relay Alliance, 22
  labels, 96–97
  LERs and LSRs, 96–97
  PDU, 96–97
  QOS quarantees, 96, 97
  technical description, 96–97
MUX, 13
MYSQL, 147

N

Name resolution, 30
Net present value (NPV), 249–250
Net profit, 210–211, 222–223, 241–242, 253–258
Network, multiple users and
    CSMA/CD, 50–51
    frames, 51
    MAC addresses, 51
Network adaptor, 106
Network attached storage (NAS), 73, 111–112
Network components in ICT infrastructure, 2
Networking and telecommunications, 1
Network services, 1, 2
Network solutions, 175–179
    wired, 176–178
    wireless security, 178–179
Network technology, 3
NMAP, 169
Nomenclature, 70–71

O

Object Management Group (OMG), 319
Office document management centers, 122
Office printers, traditional, 121–122
On-demand service, 148
OpenOffice, 125
Open source software, 125
Open System Interconnection (OSI), 19
    See also TCP/IP-OSI architecture
Operating systems, 119
    access control and, 171
Operations, 198
Oracle, 126, 136, 147
Oracle PeopleSoft, 126
Organizational enablers, 231–233
Organizational overall strategy, 366–369
Organizational value propositions, 278–279
Organizational views of the infrastructure, 195–199
    business processes view, 197–199, 211–212
    comparison of, 199
    functional, 195–197, 199, 211
    of technology infrastructure, 195–199
Organization culture, 231, 232
Outbound logistics, 198
Out of phase, 63
Overall strategy, 366–369

P

Packet-switched networks, 27–29
Parallel data communication techniques, 11–12
PC. *See* Personal computer (PC)
PCI slots, 105
Permanent virtual circuits (PVC), 81–82
Personal area network (PAN), 63
Personal computer (PC), 120
    hardware, 105–107
    options, 105–106
    selection, summary of, 107
Phishing, 168
Phone system, 27–28
Physical-focused attacks, 165

Physical layer (layer 1), 32–34, 37
    propagation and, 51–52
    standards, 51–52
Pixels per inch (PPI), 124
Plain old telephone system (POTS), 135
Platform-as-a-service, 147
Plotters, 123
Points of presence, 79–80
Point-to-point (PPP), 25, 32
    connections, 79
    over ATM (PPPoA), 32
    over Ethernet (PPPoE), 32
Policy servers, 118
Pools, 323, 326
Popping, label, 97
Portable Document Format (PDF), 124
Porter, Michael, 190
Ports used by Ethernet switches
    change speed or duplex setting, 46
    number/type of, 44
    port authority, setting, 46
Post-implementation phase, 204, 205, 377–379
    gap analysis, reviewing and updating, 379
    measurement types, 379
    measuring ICT infrastructure success, 378
    monitoring bandwidth, 378–379
    staying in touch with users and customers, 379
    summary of, 378
Post Office Protocol v3 (POP3), 113–114
Power supply, 106
PPTP, 32
Pricing
    ATM, 90–91
    Frame Relay, 86–87
    LAN *vs.* WAN, 78
    PSDN, 82–84
Pricing, mesh typology
    ATM and, 89, 90
    Frame Relay and, 87
    WAN and, 82–83
Printers, 121–123
    office printers, traditional, 121–122
    specialty printers, 122–123
Printing services, 72, 108–109
Private (internal) business processes, 321
Private cloud, 144–145
Process approach, 242
Process-as-a-service, 147
Process attributes, 227–228
Process change, 209–211
    enablers of, 230–236
Process definition, 321
Process instance, 322
Process levers, 224
Process map, 315–318
    business model, 316
    core competencies, 316, 317
    elements of, 315–316
    value proposition, 316
Process measurement, 222–223
Process Modeling, 316–318

Process objectives, 227–228
Processor speed, 106–107
Process ownership, 222, 223
Process view of the organization, 197–199, 211–212
Procurement, 198
Product differentiation strategies, 295–301
    competitive forces analysis, 298, 300–301, 367, 368
    SWOT analysis, 296–298, 299
Product innovation, 282
    integration, 225
    licensing, 226–227
    orchestration, 225–226
    vision for, 225–227
Productivity paradox, 275
Project planning in the infrastructure, 201–202
Propagation, 9, 62–63
Protocol data unit (PDU)
    ATM (cells), 88–89
    defined, 34
    Frame Relay, 86
    MPLS, 96–97
Protocol Organizations, 20
Protocols
    ATM in multiprotocol environments, 90
    IETF, 172–173
    regulations and standards, 22
    reliable, 31
    SMTP, 113–114
    SNMP, 47
    spanning tree, 47
    TCP, 31
    TCP/IP, 19
    UDP, 31
    See also Multiprotocol environments; Protocol data unit (PDU); TCP/IP-OSI architecture
Public cloud, 144–145
Public switched data network (PSDN), 80–81
    vs. ISDN, 81
    pricing, 82–84
Public switched telephone network (PSTN), 80–81
Pure Ethernet MAN, 97–98
Pushing, label, 97

Q

Quality improvement, 277
Quality of service (QOS) guarantees
    ATM, 89–91
    MPLS, 96, 97
    WiMAX, 94–95
Quicken, 147

R

Rack-mount, 105, 106
Radio frequency modulation, 58–59
RADIUS server, 60
Random access memory (RAM), 105, 106, 120
Rapid attenuation, 63
Rate of return, 241, 247–249
RC4, 59
Red Hat, 147
Registered ports, 34–35

Regression analysis, 256–258
Regulations and standards, 19–23
    FCC, 20
    global, 21–22
    layers and hardware, 22–23
    protocols, 22
    vendor compliance with, 20–21
Reliable protocol, 31
Remote access VPN, 98–99
Repeaters, 43–44
Request-to-send/clear-to-send (RTS/CTS), 62
Return on investment (ROI), 247–249
Revenue growth, 277
Ring typology, 27
Routers
    in indirect communication, 35–36
    in layer 3, 23
    in MPLS, LERs and LSRs, 96–97
    in switching hierarchies, 27–29
Routing *vs.* switching, 42

S

Sales Cloud, 147
Salesforce, 147
SAP, 126
Sarbanes-Oxley legislation, 126
Satellite, 33, 55, 56
Scaling, 140
Scanners, 124–125
Script kiddies, 169
Secure Socket Layer (SSL), 172–174
    VPN, 100–101
Security, 160–182
    in cloud computing, 141
    cybercrime, 161
    cyclic flow in, 161–162
    introduction, 161
    servers, 118
    SFR Framework, 162–163, 164
    wireless, 802.11 and, 59–60
    See also Attacks and threats
Security-as-a-service, 147–148
Separation of economies, 284–285
Sequence flow, 325
Serial data communication techniques, 11–12
Service, 198
Service Cloud, 147
Service components, 2, 71, 107–119
    application servers, 114–115
    database servers, 115–116
    e-mail server, 113–114
    inter/intra-office communications, 109–111
        (*See also* Voice over IP (VoIP))
    printing services, 108–109
    SANs and NAS, 111–112
    security and policy servers, 118
    summary of, 119
    virtualization, 116–117
    web servers, 112–113
Service-oriented architecture (SOA), 137
Service Set Identifier (SSID), 59

Shadow zones, 63
Signal propagation, 7–11
Signal-to-noise ratio (SNR), 10–11
Simple Mail Transfer Protocol (SMTP), 113–114
Simple Network Management Protocol (SNMP), 47
Simple Storage Service (S3), Amazon, 138–139, 147
Site surveys, 373
Site-to-site VPN, 98–99
Sixth force, 296, 301
Six Wave (6waves) Inc., 138–139
SnapLogic, 147
Sniffer, 168
Social engineering, 168
Socket, 35
Softchoice, 148
Software as a service (SaaS), 137, 156
Sonet/SDH, 27
Sopima, 150–152
Spam, 169, 175
Spanning tree protocol (STP), 47
Specialized applications, 125
Specialty printers, 122–123
Speed measurements, 15–16
Spyware, 166
SQL Azure, 149, 151–152
Stackable switches, 45
Star typology, 25, 26
Statistical approaches, 253–258
    correlation statistic, 255–256
    regression analysis, 256–258
Storage area networks (SANs), 73–74, 111–112
Storage-as-a-service, 147
Strategic alignment of information technology (SAIT), 275–278
    achieving, 278
    business systems analyst, 275–277
    productivity paradox, 275
    reasons for implementing, 277–278
Strategic management and infrastructure decisions, 189
Strategy in alignment with ICT infrastructure, 369–370
Strategy in ICT infrastructure, 188–195
    business and technology paradigm, 189–190
    cost leadership and differentiation, 192–193
    focused approach, 191–192
    industry-wide approach, 191, 192
    management role in technology decisions, 193–195
    organizations and technology, 193, 194
    strategic management and infrastructure decisions, 189
Structural enablers, 236
Structured cabling, 64–65
Structured portion of LAN, 66–67
Subprocesses, 337
Subscribers, 88
Subscriber stations/units, WiMAX and, 94
SunGard Banner, 126
SUN platform, 105
Supplier relationship management (SRM), 126
Supply chain analysis, 290–295
    affecting infrastructure, 201
    business system analyst in, 290–291
    GSCF, 292–294
    vs. management and logistics, 290
    softer, 291
    upstream and downstream sides of, 290
    value chain and, 228–229
    value support and, 294
Support activities, 198
Sustaining technologies, 187
Swapping, label, 97
Swim lanes, 324, 326
Switch characteristics, 44–48
    Ethernet standards, speeds, and media, 45–46
    Form Factor, 44–45
    number/type of ports, 44
    Power over Ethernet (PoE), 46
    stackable, 45
    switching matrix, 46
    switch method, 46
    See also Managed switches
Switched virtual circuits (SVC), 81–82
Switches, 44
Switching, routing *vs.*, 42
Switching hierarchies, 27–30
    addressing, 30
    data networks and packet switching, 28–29
    phone system and circuit switching, 27–28
Switching matrix, 46
Switch method, 46
SWOT. *See* Comparative SWOT analysis
Symmetric digital subscriber line (SDSL), 33
Symmetric key algorithms, 172–173
Symmetric *vs.* asymmetric communications, 15
Synchronous Optical Network (Sonet/SDH), 33
Synchronous transmission, 13
System-Fault-Risk (SFR) framework, 162–163, 164

T

Task/activity, 322
TCP/IP-OSI architecture, 19–37
    concepts related to, 34–35
    indirect communication, 35–37
    regulations and standards, 19–23
    See also Layers in TCP/IP-OSI architecture
Technology decisions, management role in, 193–195
Technology-focused cyber attacks, 165–168
    adware, 166
    denial-of-service, 168
    logic bombs, 168
    malware, 165–166
    sniffer, 168
    spyware, 166
    Trojan horse, 166
    viruses, 166–167
    worm, 167
Technology infrastructure, 186–207
    business-driven infrastructure design, 202–205
    business systems analyst in, 188
    defined, 1–3, 186–188
    disruptive technologies in, 186–187
    external forces affecting, 200–201
    organizational views, 195–199
    project planning, 201–202
    strategy and, 188–195
    sustaining technologies in, 187
    value-driven business modeling, 202

Technology justification models, 247–258
  economic approaches, 251–253
  financial/accounting approaches, 247–251
  statistical approaches, 253–258
Technology S-curve, 243–246
Technology trend curve, 246–247
Telecommunication Standardization Sector (ITU-T), 22
Telescopic observation (TO), 297–299
Testing-as-a-service, 148
Text annotation, 324
Thermal printers, 123
Thin clients, 107, 120
TLS/SSL VPN, 100–101
To-be process, 331, 334–337
Token Ring, 27, 32, 50, 53, 54, 86
T1, 33
Total cost of ownership (TCO), 242–243
Tower PC, 105, 106
Traffic contracts, 89–90
Trailing-edge technologies, 246–247
Transmission Control Protocol (TCP), 31
Transmission Control Protocol/Internet Protocol (TCP/IP), 19
  See also TCP/IP-OSI architecture
Transport layer (layer 4), 31–32, 37
Transport Layer Security (TLS), 172–174
  VPN, 100–101
Transport mode, 100
Transport port, 34, 35
Trojan horse, 166
T3, 33
Tunneling, 98
Tunnel mode, 100
Twisted-pair cable, 10, 11, 24
Types, 332

U

Unicode, 7, 8
Unicode Consortium, 7
Unicode Transformation Format (UTF), 7
Unified Modeling Language (UML), 317
Uniform Resource Locators (URL), 30
Universal serial bus (USB) connection, 106
User components, 2, 119–125
  desktop, 119
  desktop optical devices, 121
  desktop productivity software, 125
  image scanners, 124–125
  multifunction devices, 125
  PC, 120
  printers, 121–123
  specialized applications, 125
  thin clients, 120
User Datagram Protocol (UDP), 31
User Interface, 6
Users, 365–366
  in analysis phase, 366, 367
  in design phase, 370
  in implementation phase, 377
  in post-implementation phase, 379
Utility, 251–253
Utility value tree, 253

V

Val IT, 304–311
Value, defined, 279
Value chain, 224, 228–229
  characteristics of a process in, 229
  CRM in, 228–229
  customer and customer satisfaction, 229
  defined, 224
  infrastructure implementation and, 228–229
  modeling, 286
  supply chain and, 228–229
Value chain deconstruction, 284–295
  analysis of value chain, 288–290
  blow-up of the trade-off between richness and reach, 285–286
  core competencies, 287–288
  defined, 284
  generic value chain, 286
  primary activities, 286
  process of, 287
  separation of economies, 284–285
  supply chain analysis, 290–295
  supporting activities, 286
Value-driven business modeling, 202
Value Management Quick Assessment, 307, 308
Value proposition, 202, 240, 279–280
Value search models, 278–301
  corporate unbundling, 280–284
  defined, 278
  organizational value propositions, 278–279
  product differentiation strategies, 295–301
  value chain deconstruction, 284–295
Variance approach, 242
Vectors and infection strategies, 167
Vertical runs, 69–70
Video adaptor, 106
Virtual circuits, Frame Relay and, 85
Virtual desktop infrastructure (VDI), 116–117, 120
Virtualization, 116–117, 120
Virtual private network (VPN)
  security in, 177
  WAN VPNs, 98–101
Viruses, 166–167
  anti-virus tools, 175
  defense against, 148
  vectors and infection strategies, 167
Vishing, 168
Visionary role, 193–194
Voice over IP (VoIP), 21, 109–111
  business benefits of, 110
  calls, types of, 109–110
  shortcomings, 111

W

W3C, 21
WAN, 18–19, 98–101
  IPsec, 100
  LAN extended by, 78–103
  TLS/SSL, 100–101
  types, 98–99
WAN connection types, 79–82
  PCV and SVC, 81–82

WAN connection types (*Continued*)
  points of presence, 79–80
  PSDN, 80–81
WAN pricing, 82–84
  LAN *vs.* WAN, 78
  mesh typology and, 82–83
  PSDN and, 82–84
WAN technologies, 84–98
  ATM, 88–92
  Frame Relay, 84–88
  GPRS, 92–93
  Metro Ethernet, 97–98
  MPLS, 96–97
  WiMAX, 93–95
WAN VPNs, 98–101
  IPsec, 100
  TLS/SSL, 100–101
  types, 98–99
WAP, 57
Wardriving, 169
Web servers, 112–113
WebSphere Business Modeler, 320
Web 2.0, 156
Well-known ports, 34
WEP, 59
Wide area network (WAN). *See* WAN
Wi-Fi Protected Access (WPA), 59–60
WiFi *vs.* WiMAX, 94–95
"Willingness to pay" concept, 279
WiMAX, 55–56, 93–95
  vs. DSL, 95
  vs. GPRS, 94
  at layer 1 and layer 2, 94
  purpose of, 32
  QOS quarantees, 94–95
  subscriber stations/units, 94
  vs. WiFi, 94–95
Windows 7, 119
Windows Azure, 149
Windows LifeID, 149

Wired Equivalent Privacy (WEP), 59
Wireless
  described, 33
  Ethernet (*See* 802.11)
  LAN-based, 56–63
  signal propagation, 62–63
  standards, 43, 58
  See also Wireless technologies
Wireless access point (WAP), 57
WirelessMan. *See* WiMAX
Wireless metropolitan area network. *See* WiMAX
Wireless technologies, 54–63
  802.11, 56–63
  frequency spectrum and, 54–55
  LAN-based, 56–63 (*See also* 802.11)
  microwave, 55
  personal area network (PAN), 63
  satellite, 55
  WAP, 57
  WiMAX, 55–56
  WiMax, 55–56
  WLAN, 56–57
  WPA, 59–60
  WPA2, 59–60
Within network layers, 35
Work area components, 70
Workflow, 321
Workgroup diagrams, 353–357
Working documents, 338–339
Worldwide Interoperability for Microwave Access. *See* WiMAX
World Wide Web Consortium (W3C), 21
Worm, 167
WPA, 59–60

X

X.25, 82, 84
  See also Frame Relay

Y

Yahoo, 149